ANDROID™ BOOT CAMP FOR DEVELOPERS USING JAVA™

A GUIDE TO CREATING YOUR FIRST ANDROID APPS

THIRD EDITION

ANDROID™ BOOT CAMP FOR DEVELOPERS USING JAVA™

A GUIDE TO CREATING YOUR FIRST ANDROID APPS

CORINNE HOISINGTON

CENGAGE Learning®

Australia • Brazil • Mexico • Singapore • United Kingdom • United States

CENGAGE Learning

Android Boot Camp for Developers Using Java: A Guide to Creating Your First Android Apps, Third Edition
Corinne Hoisington

Product Director: Kathleen McMahon

Product Team Manager: Kristin McNary

Senior Product Manager: Jim Gish

Senior Content Developer: Alyssa Pratt

Development Editor: Lisa Ruffolo, The Software Resources

Product Assistant: Abigail Pufpaff

Marketing Manager: Eric LaScola

Senior Production Director: Wendy Troeger

Production Director: Patty Stephan

Senior Content Project Manager: Jennifer K. Feltri-George

Managing Art Director: Jack Pendleton

Cover image(s): ©traffic_analyzer/iStock, ©pictafolio/iStock, ©marty8801/iStock, ©MakaronProduktion/iStock, ©Artos/Shutterstock

Library of Congress Control Number: 2015942358
ISBN: 978-1-305-85799-5

Cengage Learning
20 Channel Center Street
Boston, MA 02210
USA

Cengage Learning is a leading provider of customized learning solutions with employees residing in nearly 40 different countries and sales in more than 125 countries around the world. Find your local representative at **www.cengage.com**

Cengage Learning products are represented in Canada by Nelson Education, Ltd.

For your course and learning solutions, visit **www.cengage.com**

Purchase any of our products at your local college store or at our preferred online store **www.cengagebrain.com**

Printed in the United States of America
Print Number: 01 Print Year: 2016

Brief Contents

Contents

CHAPTER 2 Simplify! The Android User Interface **33**

CHAPTER 4 Explore! Icons and Decision-Making Controls 129

CHAPTER 11 Discover! Persistent Data 417

CHAPTER 12 Finale! Publishing Your Android App 455

Preface

Welcome to *Android Boot Camp for Developers Using Java: A Guide to Creating Your First Android Apps, Third Edition*. This book is designed for people who have some programming experience or are new to Java programming and want to move into the exciting world of developing apps for Android mobile devices on a Windows or Mac computer. Google Android is quickly becoming the operating system of choice for mobile devices, including smartphones and tablets, with nearly three-quarters of the world's mobile devices running on the Android platform. To help you participate in the growing Android market, this book focuses on developing apps for Android devices.

Approach

The approach used in *Android Boot Camp for Developers Using Java, Third Edition*, is straightforward. You review a completed Android app and identify why people use the app, and then analyze the tasks it performs and the problems it solves. You also learn about the programming logic, Java tools, and code syntax you can use to create the app. Next, you work through a hands-on tutorial that guides you through the steps of creating the Android app, including designing the user interface and writing the code. After each step, you can compare your work to an illustration that shows exactly how the interface should look or what the code should contain. Using the illustrations, you can avoid mistakes in creating the app and finish the chapter with an appealing, real-world Android app.

The main tool used in *Android Boot Camp for Developers Using Java, Third Edition*, is the standard one developers use to create Android apps: Android Studio, a free, open-source integrated development environment (IDE). Android Studio includes an emulator for testing your apps, so you don't need a smartphone or tablet to run any of the apps covered in this book. Instructions for downloading and setting up Android Studio are provided later in this preface.

What This Book Is

This book introduces you to writing apps for Android mobile devices. It familiarizes you with the development software for creating Android apps, programming logic used in the apps, and Java code that puts the software design and logic into practice. You don't need an Android device because you can run the apps you create in this book by using an Android emulator.

What This Book Is Not

Because this book is targeted to those new to developing Android apps, it doesn't cover advanced topics, such as application programming interfaces (APIs) for each platform. Instead, this book provides a launch pad to begin your journey into creating Android apps for fun and for profit.

In addition, this book is not an exhaustive information resource. You can find a wealth of information, tutorials, examples, and other resources for the Android platform online. You should learn enough from this book that you can modify and make use of code you find to fit your needs. The best way to learn how to create Android apps is to write code, make mistakes, and learn how to fix them.

Organization and Coverage

Chapter 1 introduces the Android platform and describes the current market for Android apps. You create your first Android project using Android Studio and become familiar with the Android Studio interface and its tools. As programming tradition mandates, your first project is called Hello Android World, which you complete and then run in an emulator.

Chapter 2 focuses on the Android user interface. While developing an app for selecting and displaying healthy recipes, you follow a series of steps that you repeat every time you create an Android app. You learn how to develop a user interface using certain types of controls, select a screen layout, and write code that responds to a button event (such as a tap or click). While creating the chapter project, you develop an app that includes more than one screen and can switch from one screen to another. Finally, you learn how to correct errors in Java code.

Chapter 3 covers user input, variables, and operations. You develop an Android app that allows users to enter the number of concert tickets they want to purchase, and then tap or click a button to calculate the total cost of the tickets. To do so, you create a user interface using an Android theme and add controls to the interface, including text fields, buttons, and spinner controls. You also declare variables and use arithmetic operations to perform calculations, and then convert and format numeric data.

Chapter 4 discusses icons and decision-making controls. The sample app provides healthcare professionals with a mobile way to convert the weight of a patient from pounds to kilograms and from kilograms to pounds. You create this project using a custom application icon, learn how to fine-tune the layout of the user interface, and include radio buttons for user selections. You also learn how to program decisions using If statements, If Else statements, and logical operators.

Chapter 5 describes how to use lists, arrays, and web browsers in an Android app. You design and create an Android app that people can use as a traveler's guide to popular attractions in Chicago, Illinois. To do so, you work with lists, images, and the Switch decision structure. You also learn how to let users access a web browser while using an Android app.

Chapter 6 explains how to include audio such as music in Android apps. The sample app opens with a splash screen and then displays a second screen where users can select a song to play. To develop this app, you create and set up a splash screen, learn about the Activity life cycle, pause an Activity, and start, play, stop, and resume music playback.

Chapter 7 demonstrates how to use an Android layout tool called a GridView, which shows thumbnail images in a scrolling grid. When the user taps or clicks a thumbnail, the app displays a larger image below the grid. You also learn how to use an array to manage the images.

In **Chapter 8**, you design a calendar program that includes a DatePicker control for selecting a date to book a reservation. Because this app is designed for a larger tablet interface, you also learn how to design an app for a tablet device and add an Android Virtual Device specifically designed for tablets.

Chapter 9 continues to explore Android apps designed for tablet devices. In this chapter, you create a multipane interface, with a list of options in the left pane, and details about the selected option in the right pane. Each pane displays a different layout and Activity. To create the multipane interface, you work with the Master/Detail Flow template.

Chapter 10 explains how to create two types of animation. Using a frame-by-frame animation, you animate a series of images so that they play in sequence. Using a motion tween animation, you apply an animated effect to a single image.

Chapter 11 shows you how to create an Android app that requests data, stores it, and then modifies that data to produce a result throughout multiple activities. You learn about the ways Android apps can save persistent application data, and then use one—the SharedPreferences class—to store data for an airline's customer rewards app.

In **Chapter 12**, you learn how to publish an Android app to the Google Play Store. Before publishing the app, you test it, prepare it for publication, create a package and digitally sign the app, and then prepare promotional materials.

Features of the Book

Android Boot Camp for Developers Using Java, Third Edition, includes the following features:

- *Objectives*—Each chapter begins with a list of objectives as an overview of the topics discussed in the chapter and as a useful study aid.
- *GTKs, In the Trenches, and Critical Thinking*—GTK stands for Good to Know. These notes offer tips about Android devices, Android apps, and the Android development tools. The In the Trenches features provide programming advice and practical solutions to typical programming problems. The Critical Thinking features pose thought-provoking questions and provide answers related to programming and Java.
- *Figures and tables*—The chapters contain a wealth of screen shots to guide you as you create Android apps and learn about the Android marketplace. In addition, many tables are included to give you an at-a-glance summary of useful information.
- *Step-by-step tutorials*—Starting in Chapter 1, you create complete, working Android apps by performing the steps in a series of hands-on tutorials that lead you through the development process.

- *Code syntax features*—Each new programming concept or technique is introduced with a code syntax feature that highlights a type of statement or programming structure. The code is analyzed and explained thoroughly before you use it in the chapter project.
- *Summaries*—At the end of each chapter is a summary list that recaps the Android terms, programming concepts, and Java coding techniques covered in the chapter so that you have a way to check your understanding of the chapter's main points.
- *Key terms*—Each chapter includes definitions of new terms, alphabetized for ease of reference. This feature is another useful way to review the chapter's major concepts.
- *Developer FAQs*—Each chapter contains many short-answer questions that help you review the key concepts in the chapter.
- *Beyond the Book*—In addition to review questions, each chapter provides research topics and questions. You can search the web to find the answers to these questions and further your Android knowledge.
- *Case programming projects*—Except for Chapter 12, each chapter outlines realistic programming projects, including their purpose, algorithms, and conditions. For each project, you use the same steps and techniques you learned in the chapter to create a running Android app on your own.
- *Quality*—Every chapter project and case programming project was tested using Windows 8 and Mac OS X computers.

Student Resources

Source code and project files for the chapter projects and case programming projects in this text are available at www.CengageBrain.com.

For complete instructions on downloading, installing, and setting up the tools you need to perform the steps in this book, see the section titled "Prelude! Installing the Android SDK with Android Studio" later in this preface.

For the Instructor

Android Boot Camp for Developers Using Java, Third Edition, is intended to be taught as a complete course dedicated to the mobile programming of the Android device or as an exploratory topic in a programming class or literacy course. Students can develop Android applications on a Windows or Mac computer using the Android Studio emulator in a traditional or online class. Offering such a stimulating topic that is relative to today's huge growth in the mobile environment brings excitement to the programming classroom. The Android platform is fully free and open-source, which means all students can access these tools on their home computers.

Instructor Resources

The following teaching tools are available on the Instructor Companion Site (sso.cengage.com) to instructors who have adopted this book:

Instructor's Manual. The Instructor's Manual follows the book chapter by chapter to assist in planning and organizing an effective, engaging course. The manual includes learning objectives, chapter overviews, ideas for classroom activities, and abundant additional resources. A sample course syllabus is also available.

Test Bank. Cengage Learning Testing Powered by Cognero is a flexible, online system that allows you to:

- author, edit, and manage test bank content from multiple Cengage Learning solutions
- create multiple test versions in an instant
- deliver tests from your LMS, your classroom or wherever you want

PowerPoint presentations. PowerPoint slides are available for each chapter. They're offered as a teaching aid for classroom presentations, to make available to students on the network for chapter review, or to be printed for classroom distribution. Instructors can add their own slides for additional topics or customize the slides with access to all the figure files from the book.

Solution files. Solution files for all chapter projects and the end-of-chapter exercises are provided.

Prelude! Installing the Android SDK with Android Studio

Setting Up the Android Environment

To begin developing Android applications, you must first set up the Android programming environment on your computer. To establish a development environment, this preface walks you through the installation and setup for a Windows or Mac computer. The Android Software Development Kit (SDK) allows developers to create applications for the Android platform. The Android SDK includes Android Studio along with sample projects including source code, development tools, an emulator, and required libraries to build Android applications, which are written using the Java programming language.

Although installing the Android SDK with Android Studio is easy, you must follow the instructions in this preface to correctly prepare for creating an Android application. Before writing your first application in Chapter 1, complete the following general steps to successfully install the Android SDK with Android Studio on your computer:

1. Prepare your computer for the installation.
2. Download and install the Android Studio Integrated Development Environment (IDE).
3. Add an Android SDK.
4. Set up the Android emulator.

Preparing Your Computer

The Android Software Development Kit is compatible with Windows Vista (32- or 64-bit), Windows 7 (32- or 64-bit), Windows 8.x (32- or 64- or 128-bit), Windows 10 (32- or 64- or 128-bit), Mac OS X (Intel only), and Linux with 2 GB of RAM minimum for all platforms. Java Development Kit (JDK) 7 must already be installed on the PC. To install the basic files needed to write an Android application, your hard drive needs at least 1 GB of available space. Android Studio is the officially recommended IDE of Android app development, replacing Eclipse.

Unless otherwise noted in the chapter, all screenshots are provided courtesy of Android Studio.

Before getting started, confirm that the latest free Java updates for your computer have been installed. If necessary, go to the site java.com to install the latest Java updates to prepare for the Android installation. You cannot install Android Studio unless the Java updates are installed.

Downloading the Android SDK with Android Studio

The preferred Java program development software for mobile applications is called the Android SDK, which includes Android Studio plus additional tools. The Android SDK provides you with the API libraries and developer tools necessary to build, test, and debug apps for Android. The Android SDK with Android Studio is a free and open-source integrated development environment (IDE). The AVD Manager provides a graphical user interface in which you can create and manage Android Virtual Devices (AVDs) that run in the Android emulator.

To download the Android SDK with Android Studio and then start Android Studio, complete the following steps. Note that the images shown in the figures may look different on your computer.

STEP 1

- Use a browser to open the webpage **http://developer.android.com/sdk/**.

The Download page opens in the browser (Figure 1).

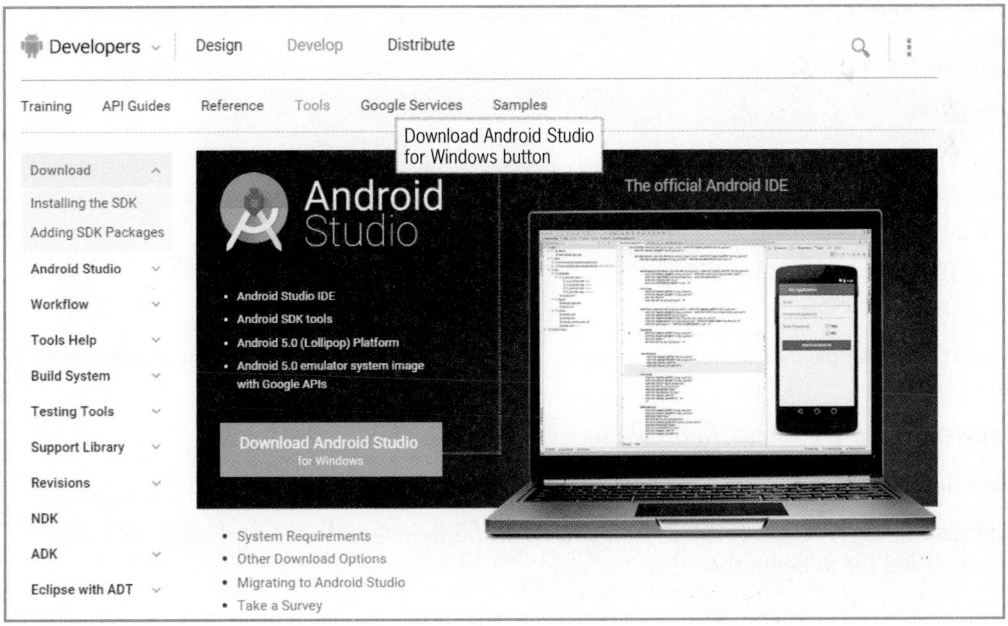

Figure 1 Android Studio download site

STEP 2

- Tap or click the Download Android Studio button to download the most recent version of the Android Studio. If you are using a Mac, the button is named Download Android Studio for Mac.

The website detects whether you are installing the Android SDK on a computer running Windows or Mac OS X. The latest Android system image for the emulator is included with this installation.

The Terms and Conditions webpage opens (Figure 2).

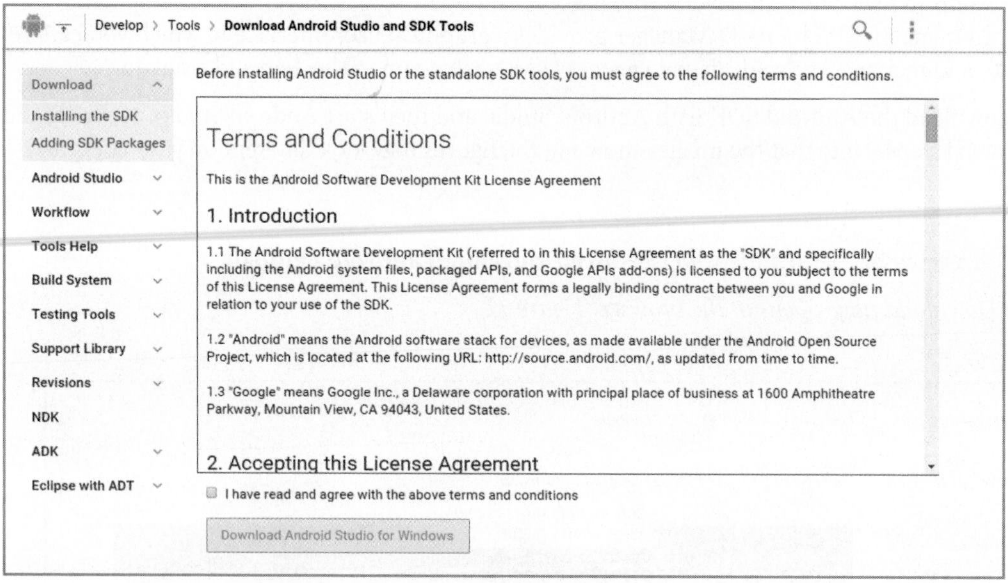

Figure 2 Terms and Conditions of Android Studio

STEP 3

- Scroll down the page and then tap or click the 'I have read and agree with the above terms and conditions' check box.
- Tap or click the Download Android Studio for Windows or for Mac button.
- Save the file on your computer.
- Navigate to the location of the downloaded file, and then double-tap or double-click the downloaded file to begin the setup.

The Android Studio Setup dialog box opens (Figure 3).

Figure 3 Android Studio Setup dialog box

STEP 4

- Tap or click the Next button to continue the download and installation process. If you are using a Mac, drag the Android Studio icon to the Applications folder.
- Accept the default settings throughout the rest of the download and installation of Android Studio.
- By default, Android Studio opens after the installation of the program.

Android Studio starts. You may want to create a shortcut on the desktop to make it easier to start Android Studio. After successfully downloading the Android Studio, you are ready to begin coding with various pre-installed emulators, ready to test your newly built apps. This textbook uses the Nexus 5 built-in emulator for testing purposes of smartphone apps.

Mac System Requirements

Before you install the software, be sure that your Mac meets the following system requirements by completing the following step:

STEP 1

- Tap or click the Apple icon on the Mac toolbar, and then tap or click About This Mac to open the About This Mac dialog box and view your current operating system version. Your operating system should be Mac OS X 10.5.8 or later (x86 only).
- In the About This Mac dialog box, verify that your Mac has an Intel processor. If the processor is displayed as Unknown, tap or click the More Info button, if possible, to display the processor type.

Acknowledgments

Android Boot Camp for Developers Using Java, A Guide to Creating Your First Android Apps, Third Edition, is the product of a wonderful team of professionals working toward a single goal: providing students with pertinent, engaging material to further their knowledge and careers. Thank you to the folks at Cengage—specifically Senior Product Manager Jim Gish; Senior Content Developer Alyssa Pratt; Senior Content Project Manager Jennifer Feltri-George; Developmental Editor Lisa Ruffolo, and Danielle Shaw, the MQA tester.

Writing a book is similar to entering a long-term relationship with an obsessive partner. Throughout the journey, life continues around you: teaching classes full time, presenting around the world, and celebrating family births and birthdays. As the world continues, those closest to you allow you to focus on your reclusive writing by assisting with every other task. My husband, Timothy, is credited with taking part in my nomadic life and most of all for his love, sous chef capabilities, and patience. Special thanks to my six children, Tim, Brittany, Ryan, Daniel, Breanne, and Eric, for providing much needed breaks filled with pride and laughter. To the newest members of my family, my grandsons Liam and Lochlan, who make me smile like no others, and yes we will go outside in just a minute. And a special thanks to Lisa Ruffolo as my developmental editor and master wordsmith who truly went above and beyond the call of duty with this fast-turnaround new project.

CHAPTER 1

Voilà! Meet the Android

In this chapter, you learn to:

- Understand the market for Android applications
- Identify the role of the Android device in the mobile market
- Describe the features of the Android phone
- Identify which languages are used in Android development
- Describe the role of Google Play in the mobile marketplace
- Create an Android project using Android Studio
- Explain the role of the Android project view
- Specify the use of layout and widget controls in the user interface
- Execute an Android application on an emulator
- Open a saved Android project in Android Studio

Welcome to the beginning of your journey in creating Android phone applications and developing for the mobile device market. Mobile computing has become the most popular way to make a personal connection to the Internet. Mobile phones and tablets comprise the fastest growing category of any technology in the world. Mobile phone usage has quickly outgrown the simple expectation of voice calls and text messaging. An average data plan for a mobile device, often called a smartphone, typically includes browsing the web, playing popular games such as Candy Crush or Words with Friends, using business applications, checking email, listening to music, recording live video, and mapping locations with GPS (global positioning system).

When purchasing a smartphone, you can choose from many mobile operating systems (OSs), including the iOS for the iPhone, Google Android, and Microsoft Phone. Recently, the Android phone has become the sales leader, outselling its competitors. The Android market is exploding with more than a million new activations of Android phones per day and over one billion total activations of Android devices now being used worldwide. Android users download more than 1.5 billion apps and games from Google Play each month. Nearly 73 percent of the world's mobile devices run on the Android platform. About 12.7 percent of the world's mobile devices run on the iOS platform.

IN THE TRENCHES

More than one-third of all U.S. households have canceled their landlines for the convenience of handling only one bill from a mobile carrier.

Creating mobile applications, called **apps**, for the Android phone market is an exciting new job opportunity. Whether you become a developer for a technology firm that creates professional apps for corporations or a hobbyist developer who creates games, niche programs, or savvy new applications, the Android marketplace provides a new means to earn income.

GTK

According to *U.S. News & World Report*, an App Developer is considered the top job in the technology field, earning a median salary of $90,060.

Meet the Android

The Android phone platform is built on a free operating system primarily created by a company called Android, Inc. In 2005, Google obtained Android, Inc., to start a venture in the mobile phone market. Because Google intended the Android platform to be open source, the Android code was released under the Apache license, which permits anyone to download the full open-source Android code for free. Two years later, Google unveiled its first open-standards mobile device called the Android (Figure 1-1). In less than a decade, the Android phone market has grown into the world's best-selling phone platform.

Figure 1-1 Android phone

Android is the first open-source technology platform for mobile devices. Being an **open-source operating system** effectively means that no company or individual defines the features or direction of the development. Organizations and developers can extract, modify, and use the code for creating any app. The rapid success of the Android phone can be attributed to the collaboration of the **Open Handset Alliance** (*openhandsetalliance.com*), an open-source business alliance of 80 firms that develop standards for mobile devices. The Open Handset Alliance is led by Google. Other members include companies such as Samsung, Sony, HTC, Texas Instruments, Kyocera, and LG. Google has produced their own phone, a modular device, under the name Project Ara. Competitors such as Apple, which produces the iPhone, do not have an open-source coding environment, but instead work with proprietary operating systems. The strength of the open-source community lies in the developers' ability to share their source code. Even though the open-source Android software is free, many developers are paid to build and improve the platform. For example, proprietary software such as the Apple operating system is limited to company employees licensed to build a program within the organization. The Android open-source platform allows more freedom so people can collaborate and improve the source code.

Many phone manufacturers install the Android operating system on their brand-name mobile phones due to its open-source environment. The open-source structure means that manufacturers do not pay license fees or royalties. With a small amount of customization, each manufacturer can place the Android OS on their latest devices. This minimal overhead allows manufacturers to sell their phones in the retail market for relatively low prices, often less than $100. Low prices on Android mobile devices have increased the sales and popularity of these devices.

The open-source community also makes Android phones attractive for consumers. Android has a large community of developers writing apps that extend the functionality of the devices. Users, for example, can benefit from over 1.3 million apps available in the Android marketplace, many of which are free. Because the Android phone platform has become the leader in sales in the mobile market, the Android application market is expected to keep pace.

GTK

On average, each smartphone worldwide runs 41 apps.

Android Phone Device

The Android phone is sold by a variety of companies under names you may recognize, such as Moto X, Galaxy, Droid, Xperia, OnePlus, Nexus, and HTC One (Figure 1-2).

Figure 1-2 Android models

IN THE TRENCHES
Android has ventured into the television market as well. Chromecast is a thumb drive that enables web streaming to television.

GTK
Chinese mobile phone manufacturers Huawei, Xiaomi, and Lenovo have a combined market share of four percentage points, according to technology research firm Gartner.

Android devices come in many shapes and sizes, as shown in Figure 1-2. The Android OS powers all types of mobile devices, including smartphones, tablets, netbooks, watches, MP4 players, automobiles, and Internet TVs. Android devices are available with a variety of screen dimensions. Many devices support a landscape mode where the width and height are spontaneously reversed depending on the orientation of the device. As you design Android apps, the screen size affects the layout of the user interface. To take full advantage of the capabilities of a particular device, you need to design user interfaces specifically for that device. For example, a smartphone and a tablet not only have a different physical screen size, but also different screen resolutions and pixel densities, which change the development process. As you develop an Android app, you can test the results on an **emulator**, which duplicates how the app looks and feels on a particular device. The Android emulator mimics all of the hardware and software features of a typical mobile device, except that it cannot place actual phone calls. You can change the Android emulators to simulate the layout of a smartphone with a 4.5-inch screen or a tablet with a larger screen, both with high-density graphics. Android automatically scales content to the screen size of the device you choose, but if you use low-quality graphics in an app, the result is often a poorly pixelated display. As a developer, you need to continue to update your app as the market shifts to different platforms and screen resolutions.

The Android phone market has many more hardware case and size options than the 4-inch to 5.5-inch screen options of an iPhone. Several Android phones such as the Galaxy, Droid, and Nexus offer screens 4 inches or larger. This extra space is excellent for phone users who like to watch movies, play games, or view full web pages on their phone. In addition, many types of tablets, also called slates, run on the Android platform. Popular models of Android tablets include the Google Nexus, Samsung Galaxy, Amazon Kindle, and LG Pad. The Android tablets are in direct competition with other tablets and slate computers such as the iPad (various generations) and Windows tablets.

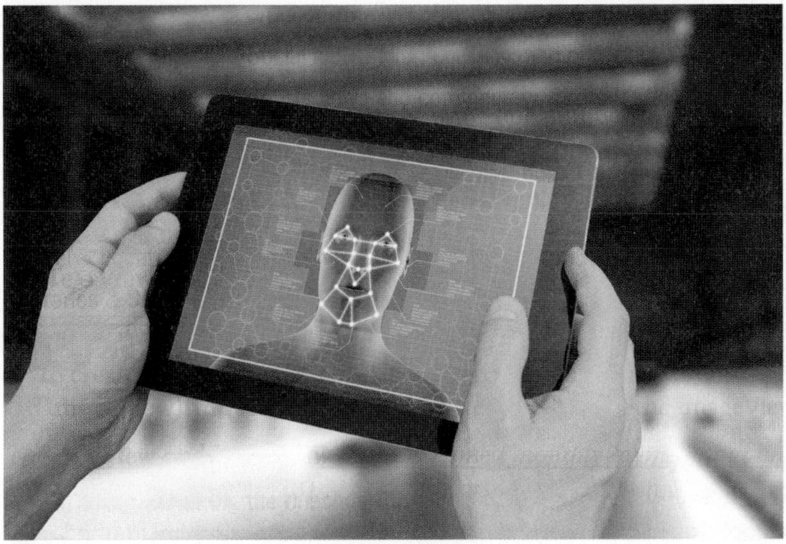

© iStock.com/Maxiphoto

Figure 1-3 Android tablet

Features of the Android

As a developer, you must understand a phone's capabilities. The Android platform offers a wide variety of features that apps can use. Some features vary by model. Most Android phones provide the features listed in Table 1-1.

Feature	Description
3-D graphics	The interface can support 3-D graphics for a 3-D interactive game experience or 3-D image rendering.
Facial recognition	Android provides this high-level feature for automatically identifying or verifying a person's face from a digital image or a video frame.
Front- and rear-facing camera	Android phones can use either a front- or rear-facing camera, allowing developers to create applications involving video calling.
Multiple language support	Android supports multiple human languages.
On-screen keyboard	The on-screen keyboard offers suggestions for spelling corrections as well as options for completing words you start typing. The on-screen keyboard also supports voice input.
Power management	Android identifies programs running in the background using memory and processor resources. You can close those apps to free up the phone's processor memory, extending the battery power. For optimized gaming, Android supports the use of a gyroscope, gravity and barometric sensors, linear acceleration, and rotation vector, which provide game developers highly sensitive and responsive controls.
Voice-based recognition	Android recognizes voice actions for calling, texting, and navigating with the phone.
Wi-Fi Internet tethering	Android supports tethering, which allows a phone to be used as a wireless or wired hot spot that other devices can use to connect to the Internet.

Table 1-1 Android platform features

Writing Android Apps

Android apps are written using the Java programming language. **Java** is a language and a platform originated by Sun Microsystems. Java is an **object-oriented programming language** patterned after the C++ language. Object-oriented programming encourages good software engineering practices such as code reuse. The official tool for Android application development, released in December 2014, is called **Android Studio**, an integrated development environment (IDE) for building and integrating application development tools and open-source projects. Android Studio IDE is exclusively dedicated to the purpose of creating Android applications. Prior to Android Studio, Eclipse ADT was the primary Android development environment. Eclipse developed applications in many programming languages, including Java, C, C++, COBOL, Ada, and Python.

As shown in the preface of this book, the first step in setting up your Android programming environment to install the free Android Studio IDE on your PC or Mac computer. The installation includes the Android **Software Development Kit (SDK)**, which runs in Android Studio. The Android SDK includes a set of development tools that help you design the interface of the program, write the code, and test the program using a built-in Android handset emulator. Another language called **XML** (Extensible Markup Language) is used to assist in the layout of the Android emulator.

Android Emulator

The Android emulator lets you design, develop, prototype, and test Android applications without using a physical device. When you run an Android program in Android Studio, the emulator starts so you can test the program. You can then use the mouse to simulate touching the screen of the device. The emulator mimics almost every feature of a real Android handset except for the ability to place a voice phone call. A running emulator can play video and audio, render gaming animation, and store information. Multiple emulators are available within the Android SDK to target various devices and versions from early Android phones onward. Developers should test their apps on several versions to confirm the stability of a particular platform. Android Studio includes a live layout editing mode that previews an app's user interface across a range of devices (Figure 1-4).

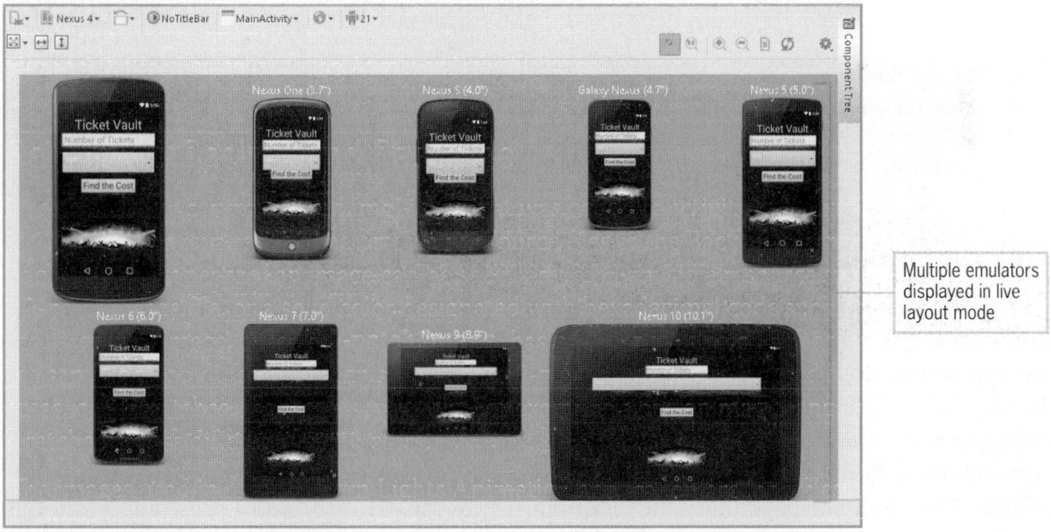

Figure 1-4 Android Studio live layout mode

The first Android version, release 1.0, was introduced in September 2008. Each subsequent version adds new features and fixes any known bugs in the platform. Android has adopted a naming system for each version based on sugary treats and dessert items, as shown in Table 1-2. After the first version, dessert names have been assigned in alphabetical order.

Version Name	Release Date
1.0 First version	September 2008
1.5 Cupcake	April 2009
1.6 Donut	September 2009
2.0 Éclair	October 2009
2.2 Froyo (Frozen Yogurt)	May 2010
2.3 Gingerbread	December 2010
3.0 Honeycomb	February 2011
4.0 Ice Cream Sandwich	May 2011
4.1 Jelly Bean	July 2012
4.4 Kit Kat	October 2013
5.0 Lollipop	November 2014

Table 1-2 Android version history

Critical Thinking

When creating an app, should I target the most current Android version only?

To support as many Android devices as possible, you should set the minimum development version to the lowest available that allows your app to provide its core feature set.

Getting Oriented with Market Deployment

The Android platform consists of the Android OS, the Android application development tools, and a marketplace for Android applications. After you write and test a program, you compile the app into an Android package file with the filename extension .apk. Programs written for the Android platform are sold and deployed through an online store called **Google Play** (*play.google.com*), which provides registration services and certifies that the program meets minimum standards of reliability, efficiency, and performance. Google Play requires that you sign an agreement and pay a one-time registration fee (currently $25). After registration, you can publish your app on Google Play, provided the app meets the minimum standards. You can also release updates as needed for your app. If your app is free, Google Play publishes your app at no cost. If you want to charge for your app, the standard split is 70 percent of sales for the developer and 30 percent for the wireless carriers. For example, if you created an app for your city that featured all the top restaurants, hotels, attractions, and festivals and sold the app for $1.99, you would net $1.39 for each app sold. If you sell 5,000 copies of your app, you would earn almost $7,000. You can use Google Play to sell a wide range of content, including downloadable content, such as media files or photos, and virtual content such as game levels or potions (Figure 1-5). As an Android developer, you have the opportunity to develop apps for a fairly new market and easily distribute the app to the millions of Android mobile device owners. Google Play has nearly 300,000 more apps than the iTunes App Store—a difference of about 17 percent more.

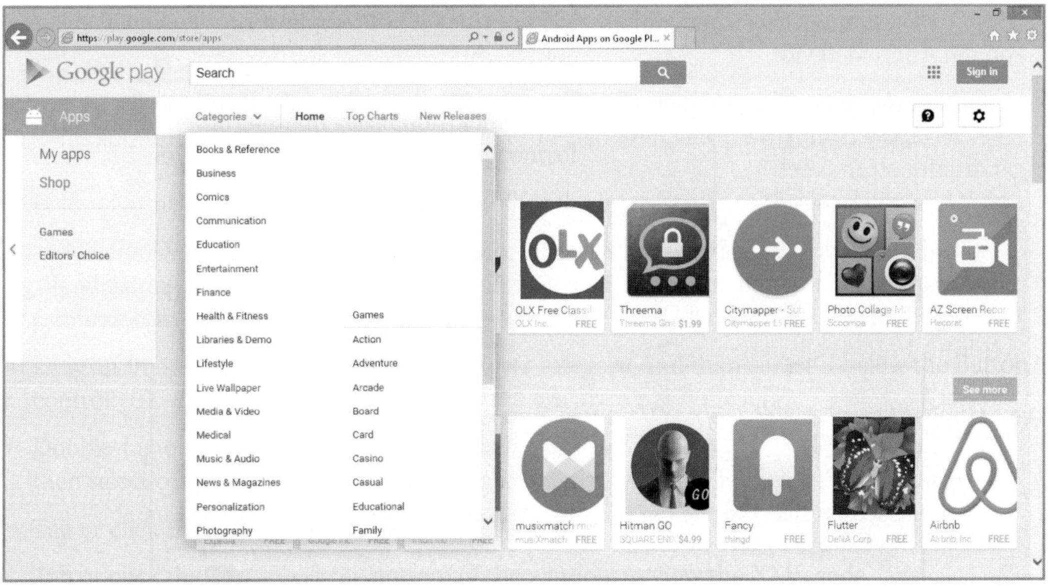

Google Inc.

Figure 1-5 Google Play

IN THE TRENCHES
The Apple iTunes App Store charges a $99 yearly registration fee to publish an app through the iPhone Dev Center. The iTunes App Store has a much more rigorous standards approval process than Google Play.

The online company Amazon also has a separate Appstore (*amazon.com/appstore*) where Android apps can be deployed and sold. The Amazon Appstore for Android is a category listed on Amazon.com. Customers can shop for apps from their PCs and mobile devices. The Amazon Appstore has an established marketing environment and search engine that displays a trusted storefront and creates app recommendations based on customers' past purchases. The Amazon Appstore charges a $99 annual developer program fee, which covers application processing and account management for the Amazon Appstore Developer Program. Amazon also pays developers 70 percent of the sale price of the app; in addition, you can post free apps.

First Venture into the Android World

After installing Android Studio (*developer.android.com/sdk*) as instructed in the preface of this book, the next step is to create your first Android application. As programming tradition mandates, your first program is called Hello Android World. The following sections introduce you to the elements of Android Studio and provide a detailed description of each step to create your first app.

Opening Android Studio to Create a New Project

To create a new Android project, you first open Android Studio. A message may appear that updates are available for Android Studio. Install the updates to confirm that you have the latest version of Android Studio. As you create your first project, you provide the following information:

- *Application name*—This is the human-readable title for your application, which will appear on the Android device.
- *Company domain*—This uniquely identifies your app in Google Play. Developers typically use a company's domain name. For example, the domain name of this book is androidbootcamp.net.
- *Package name*—This Java package namespace is where your source code will reside. Android Studio creates the package name by reversing the entered company domain, inserting a period, and then adding the application name. The package name must be unique when posted in Google Play. The package name would be net.androidbootcamp. HelloAndroidWorld in this example.
- *Project location*—This location indicates the directory on your hard drive or USB drive where you store the files related to this Android Studio project.
- *Form factor*—This value reflects the form factor used to display the app. Form factors include the screen size and the types of devices such as a phone, tablet, TV, wearable (watch), and Google Glass.
- *Minimum SDK*—This value specifies the minimum application programming interface (API) level required by your application
- *Add an activity to mobile*—This selection determines the activity that the Android device will use. An activity is similar to a window or screen event that opens when you launch an app. Creating an activity is optional, but an activity is almost always used as the basis for an application.
- *Activity name*—Use the name for the class that is generated by the plug-in. This will be a subclass of Android's Activity class. An activity is a class that can run and do work, such as creating a user interface.

Creating the Hello Android World Project

A project is equivalent to a single program or app using Java in Android Studio. Be sure you have a blank USB (Universal Serial Bus) drive plugged into your computer so you can store the Android project on this USB drive. To create a new Android project, follow these steps:

STEP 1

- Open the Android Studio program.

The Android Studio dialog box opens displaying the Welcome to Android Studio page (Figure 1-6). If you already have a project open, tap or click File on the menu bar and then tap or click New Project.

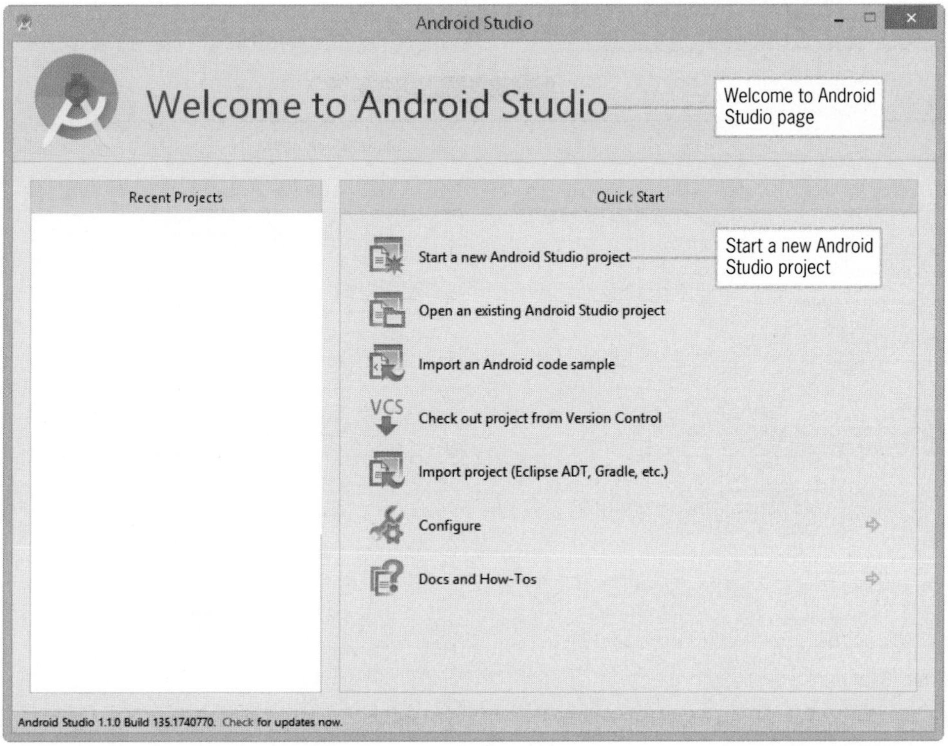

Figure 1-6 Android Studio dialog box

STEP 2

- In the Quick Start list, tap or click Start a new Android Studio project to open the Create New Project dialog box.
- On the Configure your new project page, enter the Application name **Hello Android World**.
- In the Company Domain text box, type **androidbootcamp.net**. The Package name text box displays the Company Domain entry backwards, a period, and the text that you entered in the Application name text box without spaces.
- Type **D:\Workspace** in the Project location text box.

A new application named Hello Android World is configured to be saved on the D:\Workspace USB drive (Figure 1-7). A workspace is a directory where Android Studio stores the projects that you define. When you specify the Workspace directory name, Android Studio creates files within this directory to manage the project.

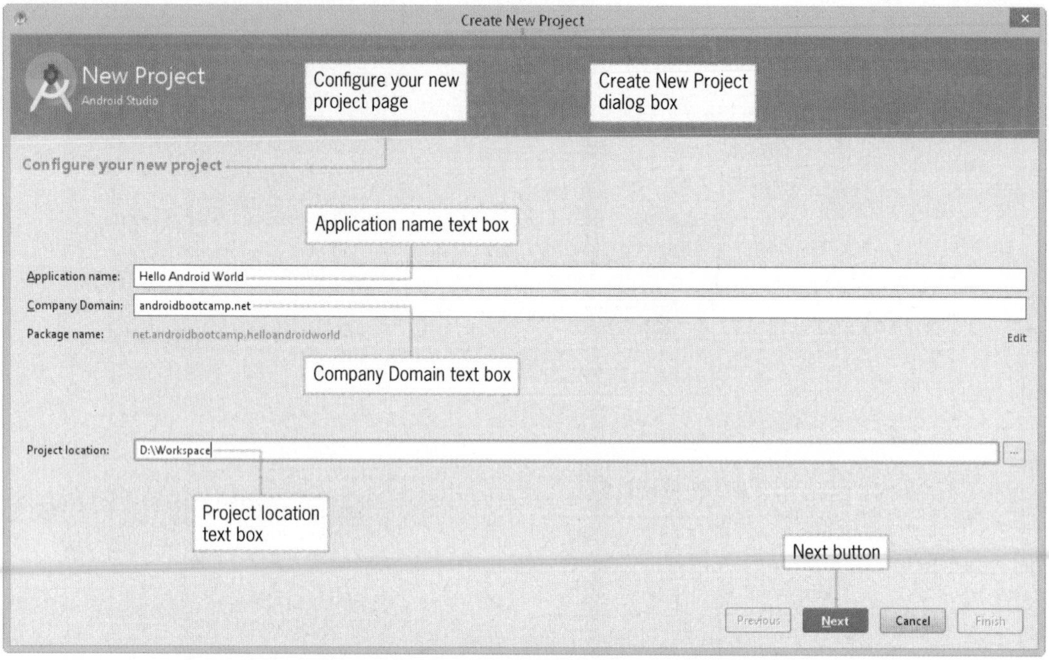

Figure 1-7 Configure your new project

GTK

Throughout the rest of this book, the USB drive is called the D: drive, though you should select the drive on your computer that represents your USB device. If you are using a Mac, enter **\Volumes\USB_DRIVE_NAME** instead of D:\Workspace.

STEP 3

- Tap or click the Next button on the Configure your new project page.
- If necessary, tap or click the Phone and Tablet check box to select the form factor for running your app.
- If necessary, select API 15: Android 4.0.3 (IceCreamSandwich) for the Minimum SDK.

The form factors and minimum SDK are selected (Figure 1-8).

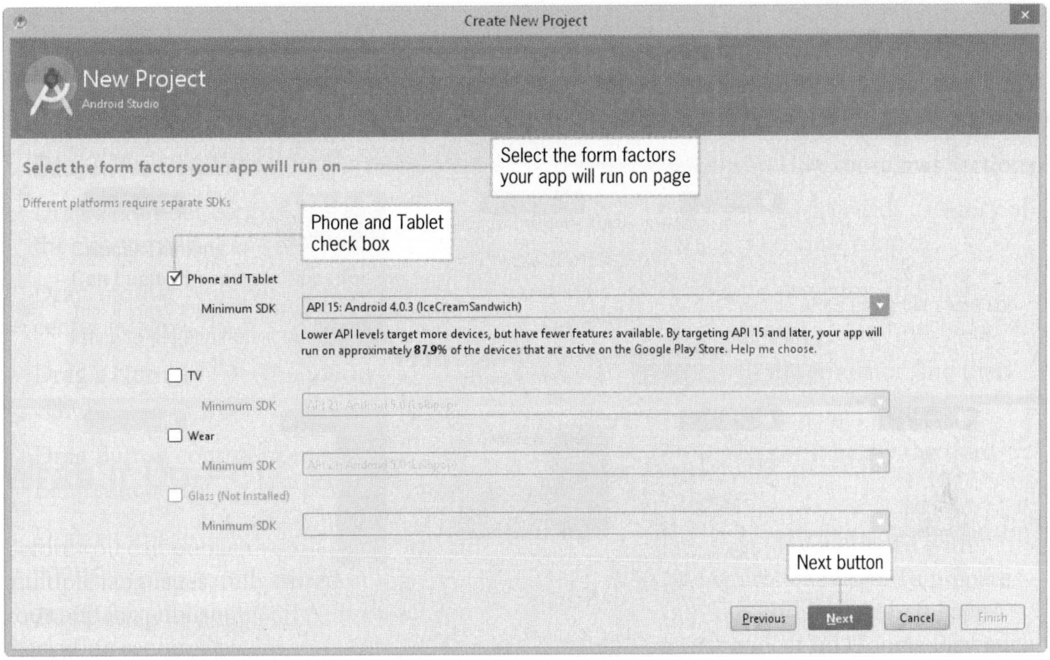

Figure 1-8 Form factors

STEP 4

- Tap or click the Next button on the Select the form factors your app will run on page.
- If necessary, tap or click Blank Activity to add an Activity to the new project.

The Blank Activity is added to the Android application project (Figure 1-9).

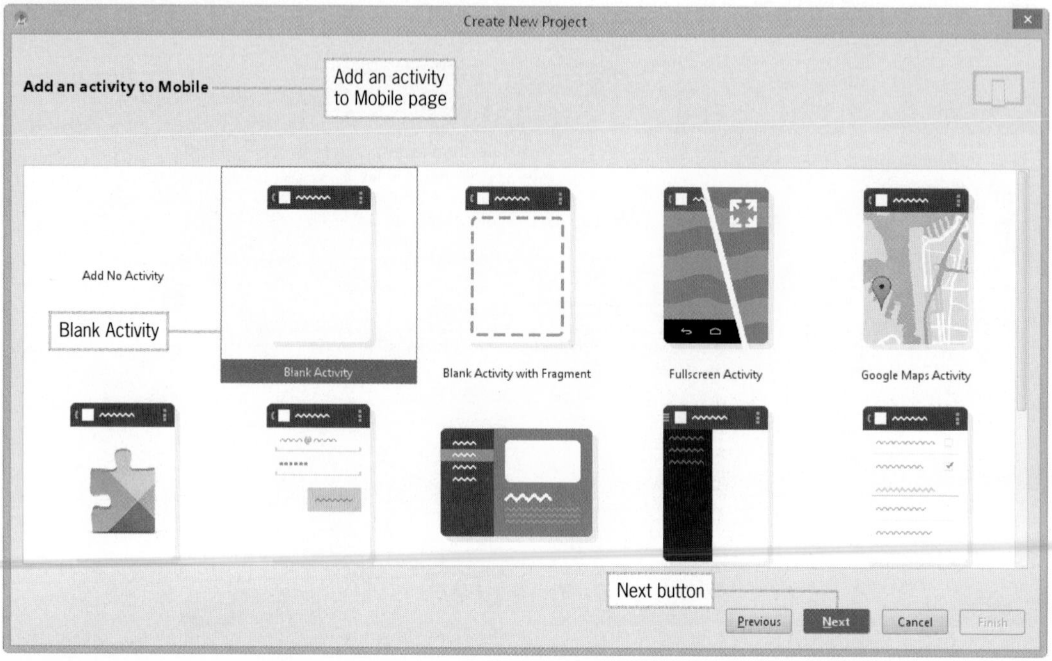

Figure 1-9 Add a blank Activity

STEP 5

- Tap or click the Next button on the Add an activity to Mobile page.

By default, a new blank Activity is created named MainActivity with the layout activity_main (Figure 1-10).

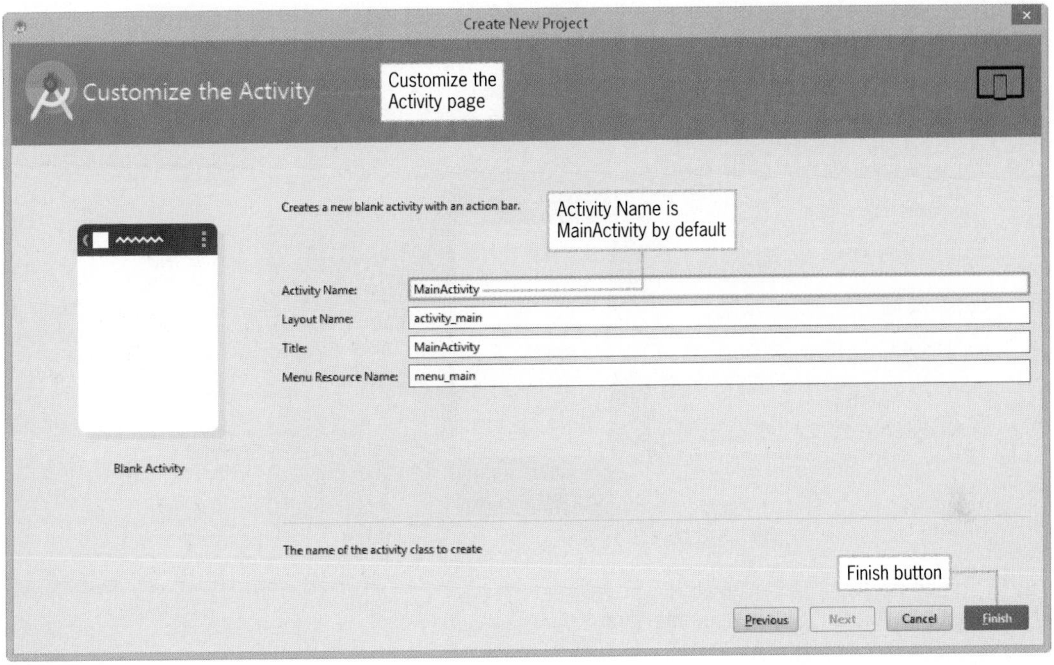

Figure 1-10 Creating MainActivity

STEP 6

- On the Customize the Activity page, tap or click the Finish button.

The Android project files are created on the USB drive. The project Hello Android World appears in the left pane of Android Studio (Figure 1-11).

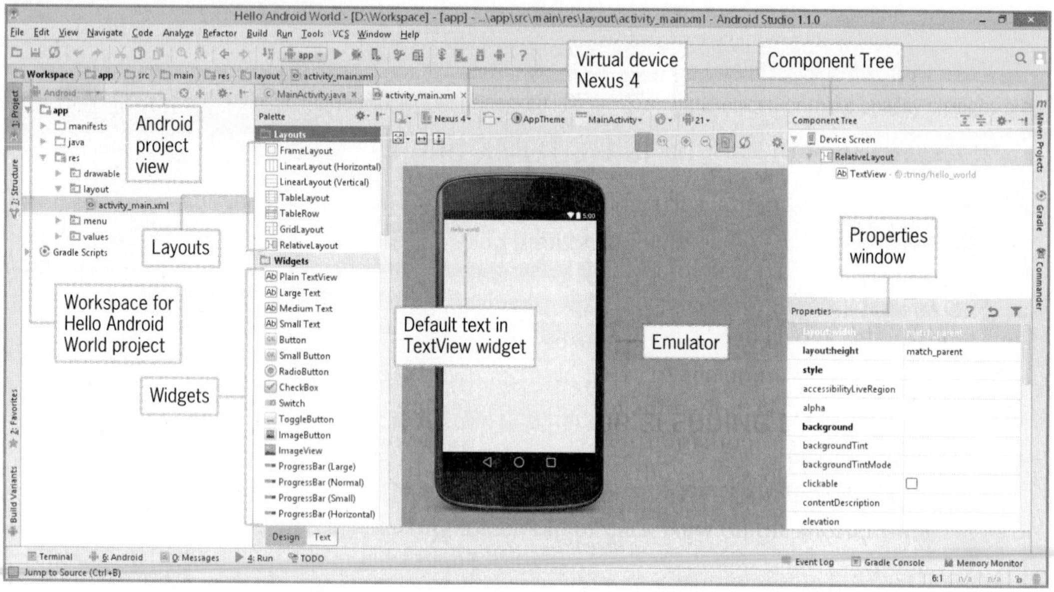

Figure 1-11 Android Studio user interface

Building the User Interface

This first Android app will display the simple message, "Hello World – My First Android App." Beyond the tools and gadgets of the Android environment, what will stand out most is the user experience—how a user feels while using a particular device. Ensuring an intuitive user interface that does not detract from functionality is the key to successful usage. Android supports two ways of building the user interface of an application: through Java code and through XML layout files. The XML method is preferred as it allows you to design the user interface of an application without needing to write large amounts of code. Both methods and more details about building the user interface are covered in later chapters.

Taking a Tour of the Android Project View

The **Android project view** on the left side of the Android Studio program window contains the key source application folders for the project. As shown in Figure 1-11, the Android project view includes files in the following folders:

- The **manifests folder** includes the **AndroidManifest.xml** file, which contains all the information about the application that Android needs to run.
- The **java folder** includes the Java code source files for the project.
- The **res folder** contains all the resources, such as images, music, and video files that your application may need. The user interface named activity_main.xml is in a subfolder of the res folder named layout.

Designing the User Interface Layout within the Virtual Device

To assist in designing the Android user interface, the Android SDK includes layout files. You can create a layout and then add widgets to the layout. A **layout** is a container that can hold as many widgets as needed. A **widget** is a single element, also called an object, such as a TextView, Button, or CheckBox control. By default, a TextView widget displays the text Hello World within the emulator. The **Properties pane** to the right of the emulator contains the properties and settings of the currently active Android app project or object. A **property** describes what an object can do; for example, if you change the text property of a TextView object, the updated text is displayed in the emulator. Upcoming chapters demonstrate many layouts, each with unique properties and characteristics.

Instead of displaying the output of your app during testing stages of development only on a smartphone, Android Studio displays an emulator configuration for design and layout purposes called the **Android Virtual Device (AVD)**. Typically a developer tests her app on various virtual devices to provide a useful and accurate environment. To change the virtual device and view the properties, follow these steps:

STEP 1

- Tap or click 'the virtual device to render the layout with' button (the emulator button) directly to the right of the Palette on the activity_main.xml tab, and then tap or click Nexus 5 (5.0", 1080 x 1920, xxhdpi). You can test your app using any of the smartphone and tablet emulators as long as the virtual device has been installed, but throughout this text, select the Nexus 5 emulator.

The Nexus 5 emulator is displayed on the activity_main.xml tab. Note that Android placed a default TextView control in the emulator (Figure 1-12).

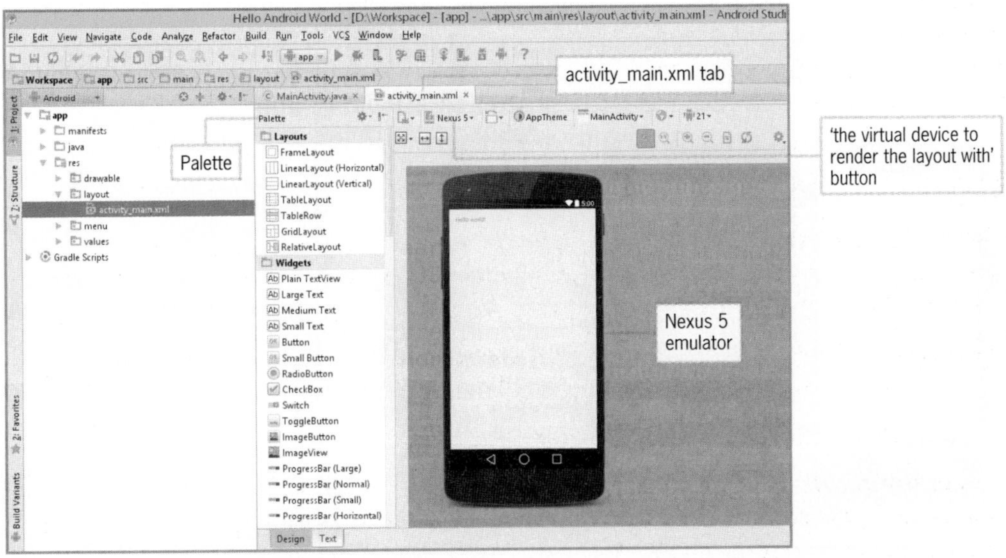

Figure 1-12 Nexus 5 Android Virtual Device

STEP 2

- In the emulator, select the default TextView control, which reads Hello World!

The default TextView control is selected and displayed in a blue selection box (Figure 1-13).

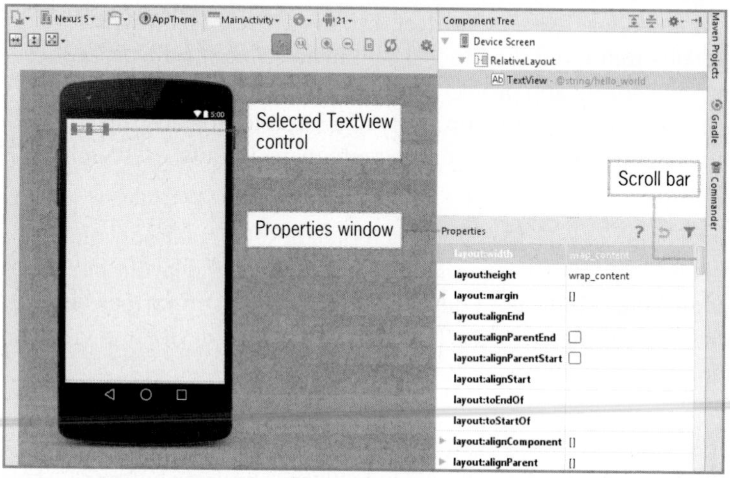

Figure 1-13 Selected TextView control

STEP 3

- Scroll down the Properties pane to display the text property.

The text property of the default TextView control is displayed (Figure 1-14). The Component Tree indicates that the TextView control is selected. The **Component Tree** *shows you the structure of your emulator layout.*

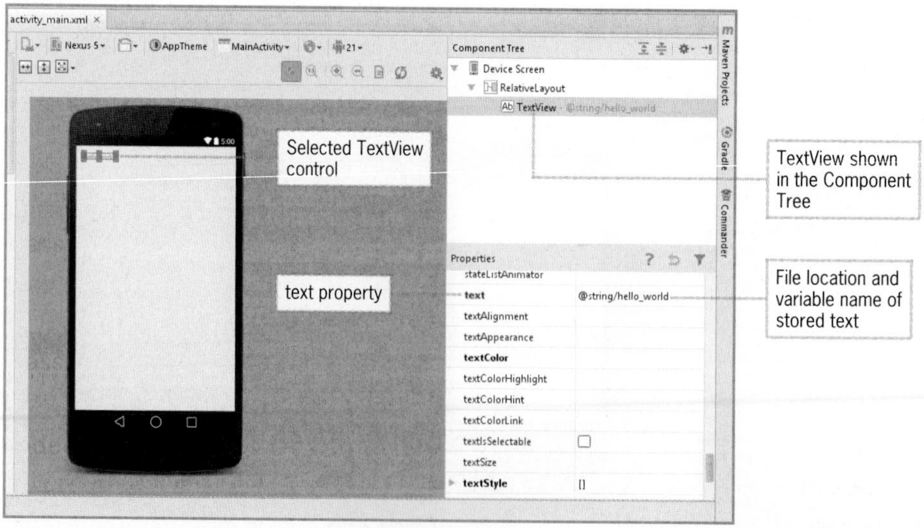

Figure 1-14 text property of the TextView control

Modifying the Text in the TextView Control

By default a TextView control displaying the text Hello World! is placed on the emulator. Instead of placing text directly in the text property or hardcoding the text, Android Studio recommends that values such as text strings be stored in the form of resources within the res folder. The simplest way to update text is by modifying resource files instead of changing the application XML source code. If the Hello Android World app was developed for multiple spoken languages such as Spanish and Chinese, the resource file could contain the translated text.

To change the text property in the TextView widget on the emulator to display the appropriate message, the resource file shown in Figure 1-14 links to @string/hello_world. The @string portion refers to the strings.xml file location within the res folder and values subfolder in the Android project view. The hello_world portion is a default variable within the strings.xml file assigned to the value Hello World. When the app is executed, Android Studio loads text and media resources from the project's res folder including the text stored in the strings.xml file in the values subfolder. To modify the text within the strings.xml file, follow these steps:

STEP 1

- In the Android project view, tap or click the expand arrow for the values subfolder in the res folder to expand the folder's contents.
- Double-tap or double-click the strings.xml file to display the strings.xml tab in the Project window.

Three default string text values are displayed in strings.xml tab in the Project window (Figure 1-15).

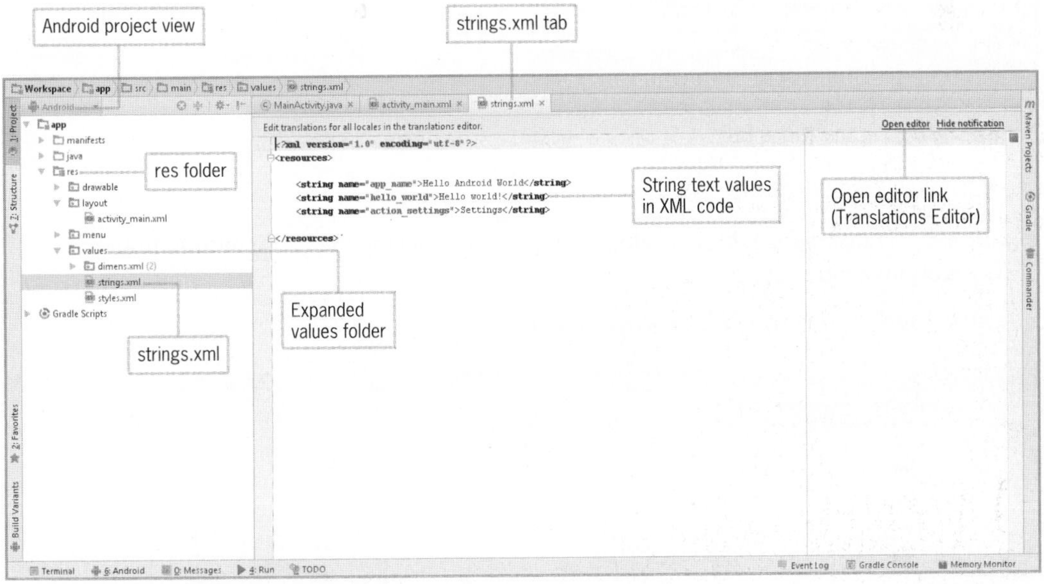

Figure 1-15 strings.xml default values

STEP 2

- Tap or click the Open editor link on the right side of the Project window to display the Translations Editor tab.
- Tap or click the Default Value (Hello world!) to the right of the hello_world Key column in the Translations Editor.
- At the bottom of the Translations Editor tab, type **Hello World – My First Android App** in the Default Value text box.

The hello_world default value is changed to Hello World – My First Android App in the Translations Editor (Figure 1-16).

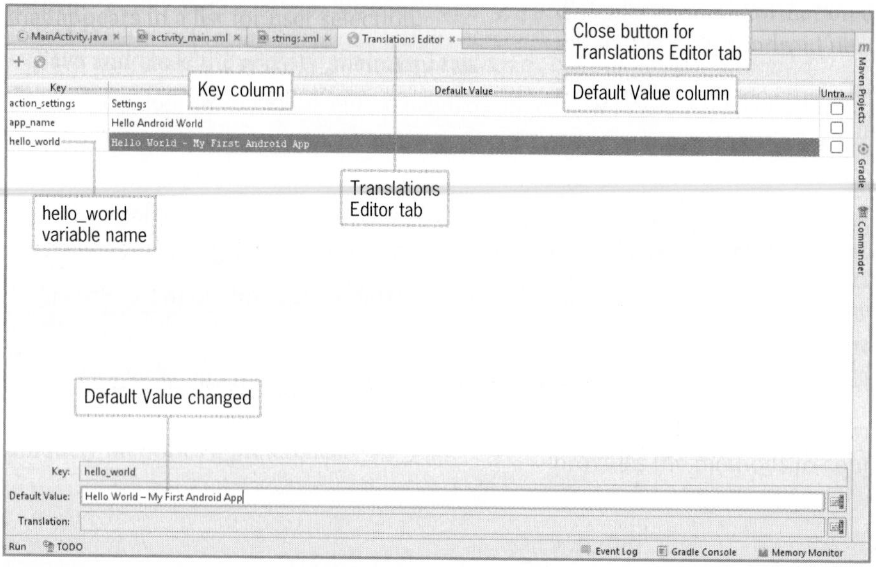

Figure 1-16 Translations Editor

STEP 3

- Close the Translations Editor window by tapping or clicking the Close button on the Translations Editor tab.

The hello_world text is modified in strings.xml (Figure 1-17).

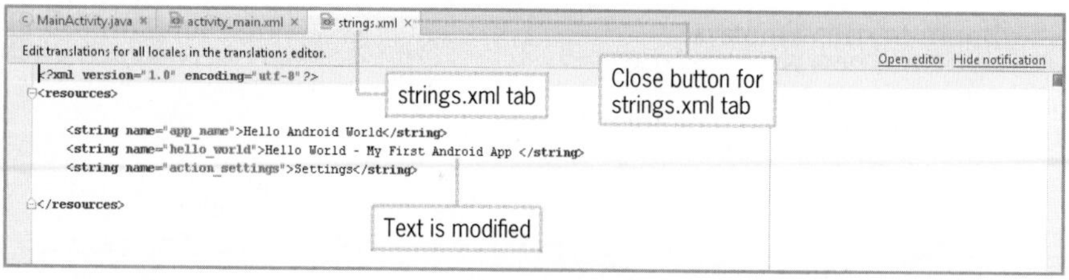

Figure 1-17 Modified strings.xml

STEP 4

- Close the strings.xml tab by tapping or clicking its Close button.

The TextView control displays the modified text in the emulator (Figure 1-18).

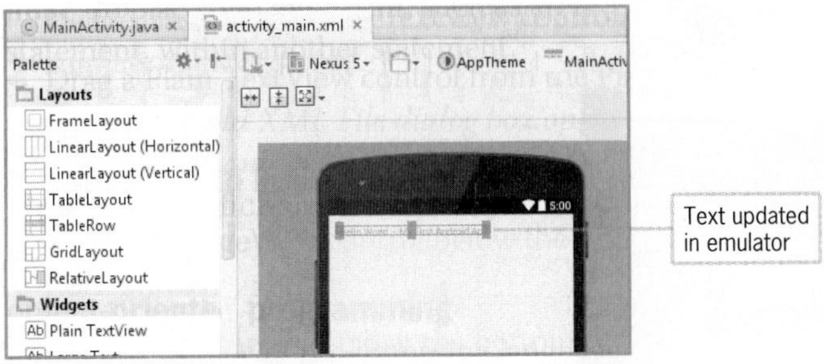

Figure 1-18 Emulator with TextView control

Critical Thinking

Can I change the text by directly typing in the strings.xml file?

Yes, you can modify the XML code, but as a beginner in Android development, the Translations Editor is simpler to use.

GTK

To deploy your app to an actual Android device instead of the emulator, plug in your device to your development machine with a USB cable. You may need to install the appropriate OEM USB driver for your device if you are using a Windows operating system. In Android Studio, tap or click Run on the toolbar and select Run.

Testing the Application in the Emulator

Time to see the finished result! Keep in mind that the Android emulator (virtual device) runs slowly. It can take over a minute to display your finished results in the emulator. The first time you run the app, the emulator opens. Run the app a second time to send it to the open emulator and test the app. Even when the emulator is idling, it consumes a significant amount of CPU time, so you should close the emulator when you complete your testing. To run the application, follow these steps:

STEP 1

- Tap or click the Run 'app' button on the toolbar.

The Choose Device dialog box slowly opens (Figure 1-19).

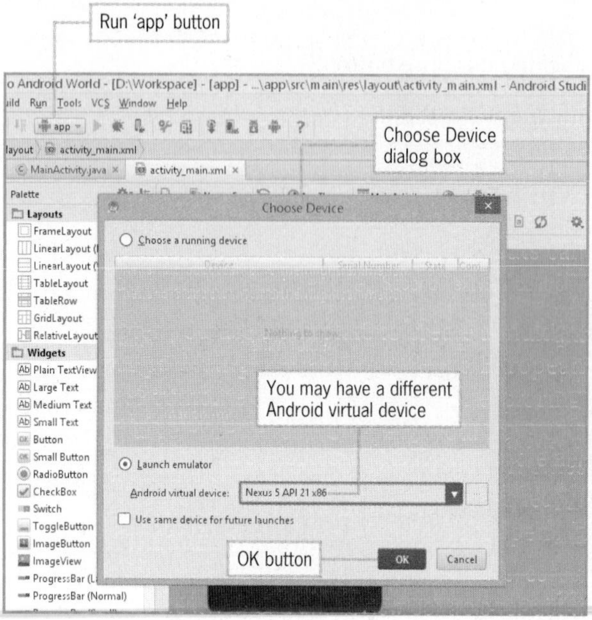

Figure 1-19 Choose Device dialog box

STEP 2

- If necessary, select Nexus 5 API 21 x86 (or a recent version emulator) in the Android virtual device list.
- Tap or click the OK button in the Choose Device dialog box.

The emulator slowly begins to open displaying the time in the center and a lock at the bottom. This may take over one full minute (Figure 1-20).

STEP 3

- Tap or click the lock icon and slide it upward toward the time in the vertical center of the screen to unlock the virtual device. If you are using a Mac, drag the lock icon until it changes to an unlock icon.

After the Android device is unlocked, the emulator displays an analog clock and the App button (six small squares within a circle) (Figure 1-21).

Figure 1-20 Android emulator

Figure 1-21 Emulator unlocked

STEP 4

- Tap or click the Run 'app' button on the toolbar again to launch the code into the opened emulator.

The Choose Device dialog opens again displaying the running emulator option (Figure 1-22).

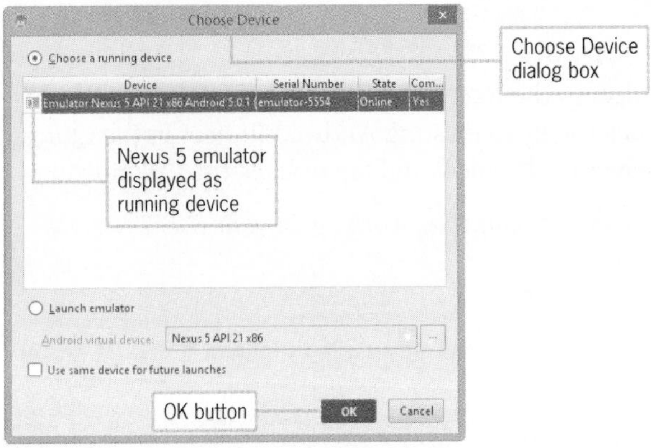

Figure 1-22 Choose Device dialog box displays the running emulator

STEP 5

- Tap or click the OK button in the Choose Device dialog box.

The Hello Android World app opens in the emulator with the modified message (Figure 1-23).

STEP 6

- Close the emulator by tapping or clicking the Close button.
- Tap or click File on the menu bar and then tap or click Close Project.
- If necessary, tap or click the Disconnect button.

The emulated application window closes. The program is saved each time the program is run. Tap or click Quit Android Studio if you are working on a Mac.

GTK
Shift+F10 is the Windows shortcut key combination for running your Android application in Android Studio. On a Mac, the shortcut keys are Command+Shift+F11.

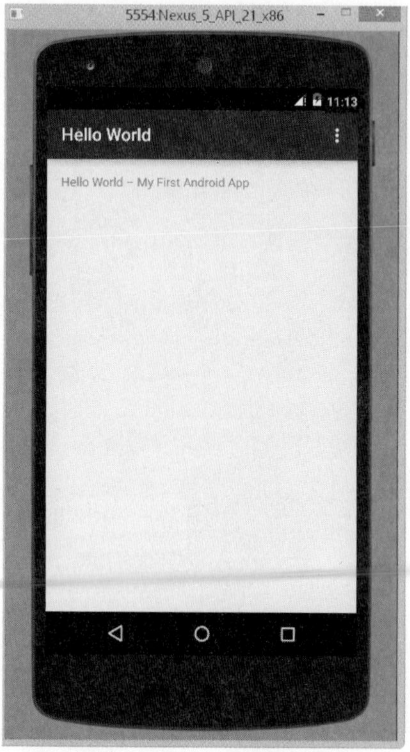

Figure 1-23 Hello Android World app displayed in emulator

Opening a Saved App in Android Studio

After you save a project and close Android Studio, you might need to open the project and work on it again. To open a saved project, you can follow these steps:

STEP 1

- Open Android Studio.
- Tap or click the Hello Android World project in the Recent Projects column. If the project is not listed in the Recent Projects, tap or click Open an existing Android Project in the Quick Start column and navigate to the path of the saved project and tap or click the OK button.

The program loads into Android Studio. You can now continue working on your user interface and code.

Wrap It Up—Chapter Summary

This chapter has provided an overview of the Android open-source platform, which is positioned for fast innovation without the restraints of a proprietary system. With its rich feature set, the Android Studio environment allows you to develop useful, inventive Android apps for the platform with the largest market share. In the first chapter project, Hello Android World, you completed steps that start your journey to create more interesting applications in future chapters.

- The Android operating system is released under a full open-source license for free.
- The Android OS powers all types of mobile devices, including smartphones, tablets, Internet TVs, Android wearable devices like watches, and Google Glass.
- To write Android apps, you can use Android Studio, a dedicated development environment for building Android applications, using Java, an object-oriented programming language.
- The Android emulator lets you design, develop, prototype, and test Android applications without using a physical device. When you run an Android program in Android Studio, the emulator starts so you can test the program as if it were running on a specified Android mobile device.
- The Android platform consists of the Android OS, the Android application development platform, and Google Play, a marketplace for Android applications.
- Android supports two ways of building the user interface of an application: through Java code and through XML layout files. The XML method is preferred as it allows you to design the user interface of an application without needing to write large amounts of code.
- The Android project view on the left side of the Android Studio program window contains the folders for an Android project.
- To design a user interface for an Android app, you can create a layout, which is a container that displays widgets such as TextView, Button, and CheckBox controls, also called objects.
- The text property can be updated using the Translations Editor opened from the strings.xml file in the values folder.
- After you create an application, you can run it in the Android emulator to test the application and make sure it runs correctly.

Key Terms

Android project view—A pane on the left side of the Android Studio program window that contains the folders for the current project.

Android Studio—The recommended IDE for writing Java programs and for building and integrating application development tools and open-source projects for Android.

Android Virtual Device (AVD)—The AVD displays an emulator configuration for design and layout purposes.

AndroidManifest.xml—A file containing all the information Android needs to run an application.

app—A mobile application.

Component Tree—A pane in the Android Studio project window that displays the structure of the emulator layout.

emulator—Software that duplicates how an app looks and feels on a particular device.

Google Play—An online store that sells programs written for the Android platform.

Java—An object-oriented programming language and a platform originated by Sun Microsystems.

java folder—The folder that includes the Java code source files for the project.

layout—A container that can hold widgets and other graphical elements to help you design an interface for an application.

manifests folder—The folder that includes the AndroidManifest.xml file, which contains all the information about the application that Android needs to run.

object-oriented programming language—A type of programming language that allows good software engineering practices such as code reuse.

Open Handset Alliance—An open-source business alliance of 80 firms that develop open standards for mobile devices.

open-source operating system—Organizations and developers can extract, modify, and use the source code free of charge and copyright restrictions.

Properties pane—The window that contains the properties and settings of the currently active project or object.

property—A characteristic of a project or object that describes what it can do.

res folder—A project folder that contains all the resources, such as images, music, and video files, that an application may need.

Software Development Kit (SDK)—A package containing development tools for creating applications.

widget—A single element such as a TextView, Button, or CheckBox control, and is also called an object.

XML—An acronym for Extensible Markup Language, a widely used system for defining data formats. XML assists in the layout of the Android emulator.

Developer FAQs

1. What is the dessert name that starts with an "L" to describe an Android version?
2. What is the one-time cost for a developer's account at Google Play?
3. When you post an Android app at Google Play, what percentage of the app price does the developer keep?
4. How much is Amazon's annual fee for a developer's account?
5. What is the web address of Google Play?
6. Which two languages are used in creating an Android app in Android Studio?
7. In which subfolder is the activity_main.xml file stored?
8. Name three widgets mentioned in this chapter.
9. What is the name of the widget that was used in the Hello Android World app?
10. Which two key combinations can you press to run an Android app in Android Studio?
11. Which Android version is Kit Kat?
12. Using the alphabetical theme for Android version names, name three possible future names for the next versions of Android device operating systems.
13. What does XML stand for?
14. What does SDK stand for?
15. Where are music and image files saved within the Android project view?

Beyond the Book

Search the web for answers to the following questions to further your Android knowledge.

1. Research a particular model of a popular Android smartphone or tablet device and write a paragraph on this device's features, specifications, price, and manufacturer.
2. Name five Android mobile device features not mentioned in the "Meet the Android" section of Chapter 1.

3. What is the current annual cost for a developer's account at the Windows Store? Even though the mobile side of the Windows Store is marginal, why are many app developers learning to create Windows Store apps?
4. Go to the Google Play website and take a screen shot of each of the following app categories: education, gaming, mapping, travel, and personal hobby. Place screen shots in a word processor document and label each one to identify it.

Case Programming Projects

Complete one or more of the following case programming projects. Use the same steps and techniques taught within the chapter. Submit the program you create to your instructor. The level of difficulty is indicated for each case programming project.

Easiest: ★

Intermediate: ★★

Challenging: ★★★

Case Project 1–1: Famous Technology Quotes App ★

Requirements Document

Application title:	Tech Quotes
Purpose:	In the Tech Quotes app, a technology quote of your choice is displayed.
Algorithms:	The opening screen displays the famous technology quote of the day. Find a quote online.
Conditions:	You may change the quote to one of your own (Figure 1-24).

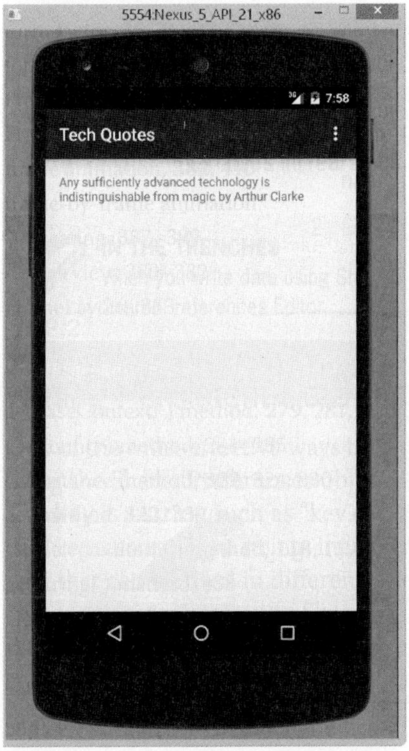

Figure 1-24 Tech Quotes app

Case Project 1–2: Android Dessert Names App ★★

Requirements Document

Application title:	Dessert Names
Purpose:	In the Dessert Names app, the Android version names (desserts) introduced in Chapter 1 are displayed.
Algorithms:	The opening screen displays the dessert names of Android versions listed in this chapter.
Conditions:	Replace the strings.xml text (Figure 1-25).

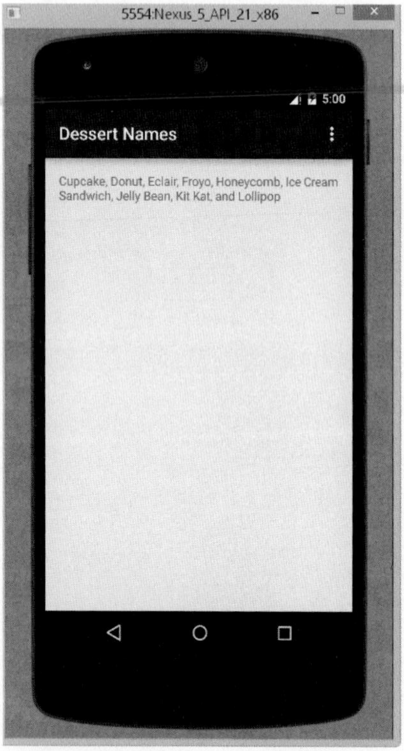

Figure 1-25 Dessert Names app

Case Project 1–3: Large Tech Companies ★★★

Requirements Document

Application title:	Large Tech Companies
Purpose:	In the Large Tech Companies app, the present top five technology companies in the world are displayed.
Algorithms:	The opening screen displays the present top five world technology companies separated by a comma. Please research this topic and order them based on revenue. The current companies may not be in the same order as displayed in Figure 1-26.

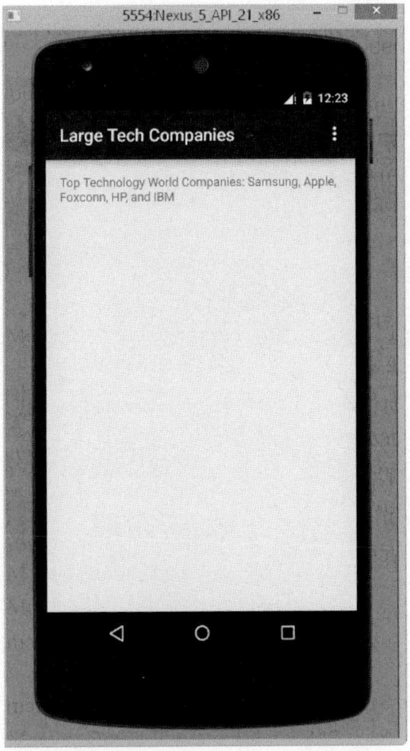

Figure 1-26 Large Tech Companies app

Case Project 1-3: Large Tech Companies

CHAPTER 2

Simplify! The Android User Interface

In this chapter, you learn to:

- Develop a user interface using the TextView, ImageView, and Button controls
- Add text in strings.xml using the Translations Editor
- Create an Android project that includes a Button event
- Describe Relative and Linear layouts for the user interface
- Create multiple Android Activities
- View activities in the Android Manifest file
- Add a Java class file
- Add line numbers to a code window
- Write code using the onCreate method
- Display content using the setContentView command
- Open a second screen using a Button event handler
- Use an OnClickListener to detect user interaction
- Launch a second screen using a startActivity method
- Correct errors in Java code
- Run the completed app in the emulator

Before a mobile app can be coded using Java, it must be designed. Designing a program can be compared with constructing a building. Before cement slabs are poured, steel beams are put in place, and walls are erected, architects and engineers must design the building to ensure it will perform as required and be safe and reliable. The same holds true for a computer app developer. Once the program is designed within the user interface, it can be implemented through the use of Extensible Markup Language (XML) and Java code to perform the functions for which it was designed.

Designing an Android App

To illustrate the process of designing and implementing an Android app, in this chapter you will design and code the Healthy Recipes app shown in Figure 2-1 and Figure 2-2.

Figure 2-1 Healthy Recipes Android app
© iStock.com/ovcharova

Figure 2-2 Second screen with recipe

The Android app in Figures 2-1 and 2-2 could be part of a larger app that is used to display Healthy Recipes. The Healthy Recipes app begins by displaying the recipe name, which is Bruschetta Recipe, and an image illustrating the ingredients. If the user taps the VIEW RECIPE button, a second window opens displaying the full recipe, including the ingredients and preparation for making bruschetta.

IN THE TRENCHES

If you own a data plan phone, tablet, or slate device, download the free app called Epicurious to get an idea of how this Healthy Recipes app would be used in a much larger application.

The Big Picture

To create the Healthy Recipes application, you follow a set of steps that you repeat every time you create an Android application.

1. Create the user interface, also called an XML layout, for every screen in the application.
2. Create a Java class, also called an Activity, for every screen in the application.
3. Code each Java class with the appropriate objects and actions as needed.
4. Test the application in the Android emulator.

Using the Android User Interface

Before any code can be written for an Android application, you design the user interface to control the user experience. An Android application can run on various form factors such as a smartphone, smartwatch, tablet, wearable glasses, televisions, robotics, car, and many other devices. **Form factor** refers to the screen size, configuration, or physical layout of a device. For an Android application, the user interface is a window on the screen of any mobile device in which the user interacts with the program. The user interface is stored in the res/layout folder in the Android project view. The layout for the user interface is stored as XML code. Special Android-formatted XML code is extremely compact, which means the application uses less space and runs faster on the device. Using XML for layout also saves you time in developing your code; for example, if you develop this recipe app for use in eight human languages, you could use the same Java code with eight unique XML layout files, one for each language. To open the layout of the user interface of the Healthy Recipes app and begin the application, follow these steps:

STEP 1

- Open the Android Studio program.
- On the Welcome to Android Studio page of the Android Studio dialog box, tap or click the Start a new Android Studio project selection in the Quick Start category.
- In the Create New Project dialog box, enter the Application name **Healthy Recipes**.
- In the Company Domain text box, type **androidbootcamp.net**. The Package name displays the Company Domain in reverse order, a period, and the text that you entered for the Application Name without spaces.
- In the Project location text box, type **D:\Workspace** (\Volumes\USB_DRIVE_NAME on a Mac).

A new application named Healthy Recipes is configured to save on the USB drive (Figure 2-3).

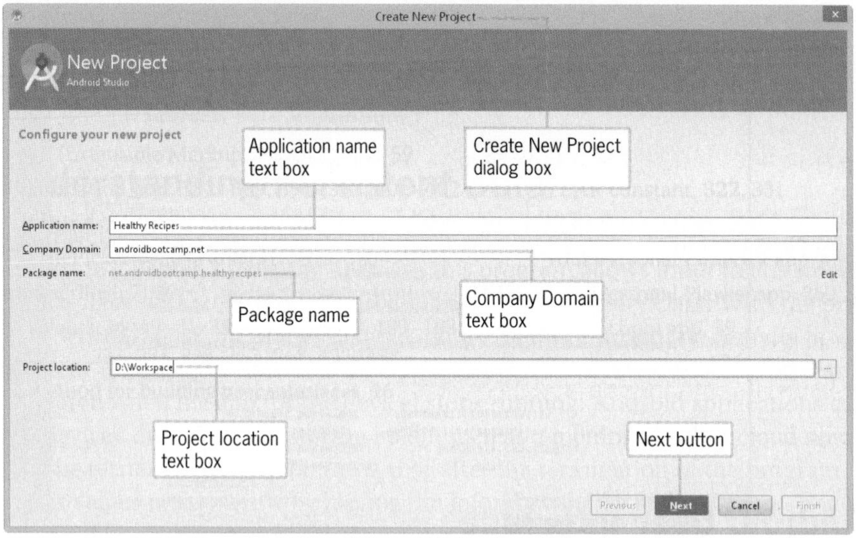

Figure 2-3 Configure your new project

STEP 2

- Tap or click the Next button on the Configure your new project page of the Create New Project dialog box.
- If necessary, tap or click the Phone and Tablet check box to select the form factor for your app.
- If necessary, select API 15: Android 4.0.3 (IceCreamSandwich) for the Minimum SDK.

The form factors and minimum SDK are selected (Figure 2-4).

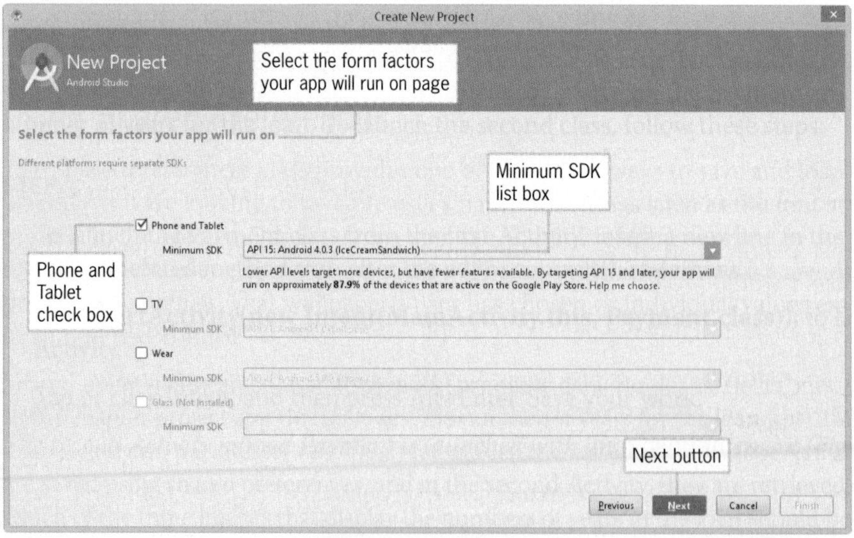

Figure 2-4 Form factors for the Healthy Recipes app

STEP 4

- Tap or click the Next button on the Select the form factors your app will run on page.
- If necessary, tap or click Blank Activity to add an Activity to the new project.
- Tap or click the Next button on the Add an activity to Mobile page.

A new blank activity is created named MainActivity with the layout activity_main (Figure 2-5).

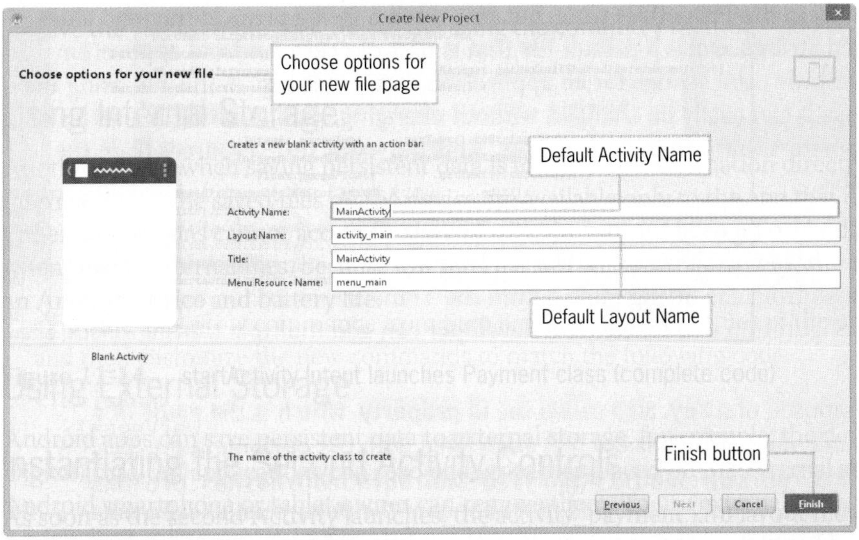

Figure 2-5 Creating a blank Activity

STEP 6

- Tap or click the Finish button on the Choose options for your new file page.
- Tap or click the Hello world! TextView widget (displayed by default) in the emulator and press the Delete key.
- Tap or click 'the virtual device to render the layout with' button (the emulator button) directly to the right of the Palette on the activity_main.xml tab, and then tap or click Nexus 5 (5.0", 1080 x 1920, xxhdpi).

The Android Healthy Recipes project files are created on the USB drive. The Android project view for Healthy Recipes appears in the left pane, the Hello world TextView widget is deleted, and the Nexus 5 virtual device is selected.

Using the String Table in the Translations Editor

In Chapter 1, you used the Translations Editor to add text to the TextView control by changing the text in the strings.xml file. Instead of adding text directly in a TextView control's text property, you add it to the strings.xml file. Entering text in a single file offers significant advantages. For example, suppose you are hired to write an app and you enter text in the text property of each control. After testing the app, your customer decides to change all the text within the app. Now you have to check for the original text control by control, file by file, including .xml and .java files, for all the text you have inserted, and then replace it. As a time-saving alternative, Android provides the strings.xml file inside the Resources folder. If your customer wants to change all the text within the app, you can go to a single file location to make the changes.

The string items that are displayed in the TextView control in the Healthy Recipes app will not be typed directly in the Properties pane, but instead in a string array in the res/values folder. A file named **strings.xml** is a default file that is part of every Android application and contains commonly used strings for an application. You enter text in this file using the String table because it can easily be changed without changing code. A **string** is a series of alphanumeric characters that can include spaces. Android loads text resources from the project's String table.

The String table can also be used for localization. **Localization** is the use of the String table to change text based on the user's preferred language. For example, Android can select text in Spanish from the String table within the Translations Editor, based on the current device configuration and locale. The developer can add multiple translations in the Translations Editor.

Every string is composed of a **key**, also called the **id property**, which is the name of a control, and a default value, which is the text associated with the control. In the Healthy Recipes app, the first TextView control displays the text Bruschetta Recipe. The name of the control is txtTitle, which is specified in its key, and the default value is Bruschetta Recipe. The second control on the opening screen is an ImageView control that displays an image of the finished recipe. To create an application that is accessible to those with visual disabilities, add descriptions to the user interface controls that can be read out loud to your user by a speech-based accessibility service such as a screen reader. To display an on-screen description of the recipe image for accessibility purposes, add the description text to the String table using a key and default value pair. The Button control that displays the text VIEW RECIPE specifies btnRecipe as its key and VIEW RECIPE as its default value. To add the text for TextView, ImageView, and Button controls to the strings.xml file for the opening screen, follow these steps.

STEP 1

- In the Android project view, expand the values folder within the res folder.
- Double-tap or double-click the strings.xml file to display its default string resources.

The strings.xml tab is displayed, showing the string resources. Notice that the strings.xml file already contains three default strings (Figure 2-6).

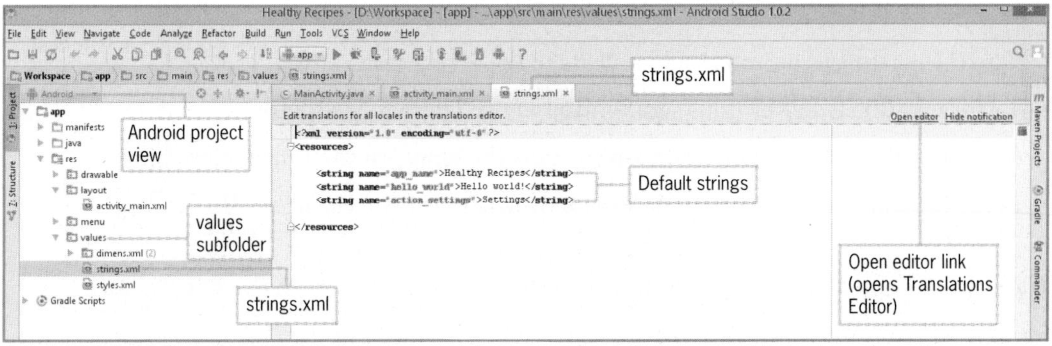

Figure 2-6 Default string resources

STEP 2

- Tap or click the Open editor link.
- Tap or click the Add Key (plus sign) button in the Translations Editor.
- In the Key text box, type **txtTitle** to name the string for the TextView control.
- In the Default Value text box, type **Bruschetta Recipe** to define the text to display.

The key and default value of the TextView control are entered using a Translations Editor dialog box (Figure 2-7).

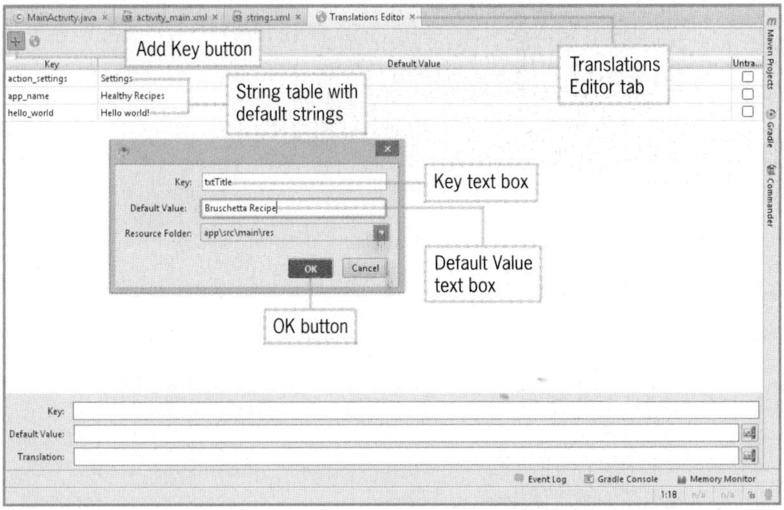

Figure 2-7 Adding a string for a TextView control

STEP 3

- Tap or click the OK button to add txtTitle to the String table.
- Tap or click the Add Key (plus sign) button in the Translations Editor.
- In the Key text box, type **description** to name the string for the ImageView control.
- In the Default Value text box, type **Recipe Image** to explain the image that will be displayed.

The key and default value of the ImageView control are entered in the dialog box (Figure 2-8).

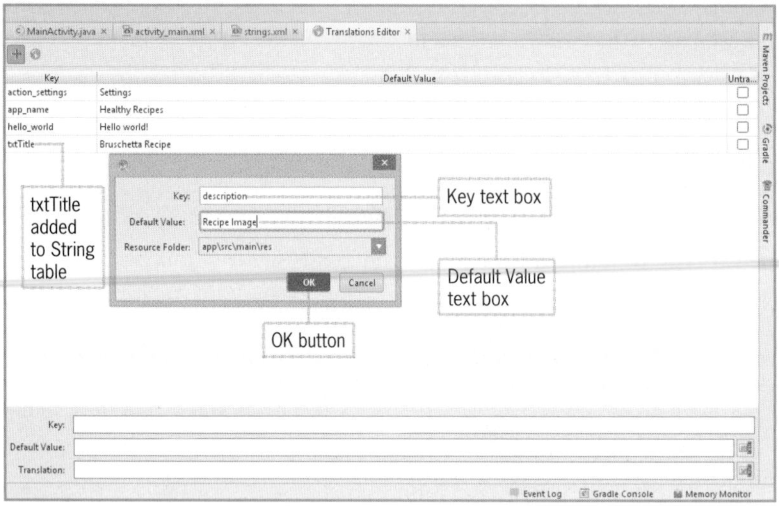

Figure 2-8 Entering an ImageView key and default value for accessibility

STEP 4

- Tap or click the OK button.
- Tap or click the Add Key (plus sign) button in the Translations Editor.
- In the Key text box, type **btnRecipe** to name the string for the Button control.
- In the Default Value text box, type **View Recipe** to define the text.

The key and default value of the Button control is entered in the dialog box (Figure 2-9).

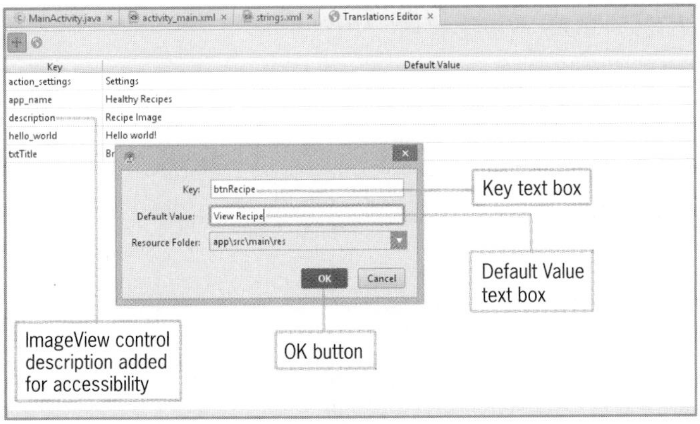

Figure 2-9 Adding a string for a Button control

The second screen of the Healthy Recipes app displays the ingredients and directions for preparing the bruschetta recipe. Notice in Figure 2-1 and 2-2 that both screens display the same opening Bruschetta Recipe title using the txtTitle string twice. To add the rest of the text displayed on the second user interface, follow these steps:

STEP 1

- Tap the OK button to add the string for the Button control to the String table, and then tap or click the Add Key (plus sign) button in the Translations Editor.
- In the Key text box, type **txtIngredients** to name the string for a TextView control to display on the second app screen.
- In the Default Value text box, type **Ingredients** to define the text, and then tap or click the OK button to add the string to the String table.
- Using the techniques taught in this step, add the strings in Table 2-1 to the String table in the Translations Editor.

Key	Default Value
txtItem1	4 plum tomatoes
txtItem2	6 basil leaves
txtItem3	3 garlic cloves, chopped
txtItem4	3 TB olive oil
txtDirections	Directions
txtMix	Combine the ingredients and add salt to taste. Top French bread slices with mixture.

Table 2-1 Strings for the second screen in the Healthy Recipes app

The text for the first and second user interfaces are added to the Translations Editor (Figure 2-10).

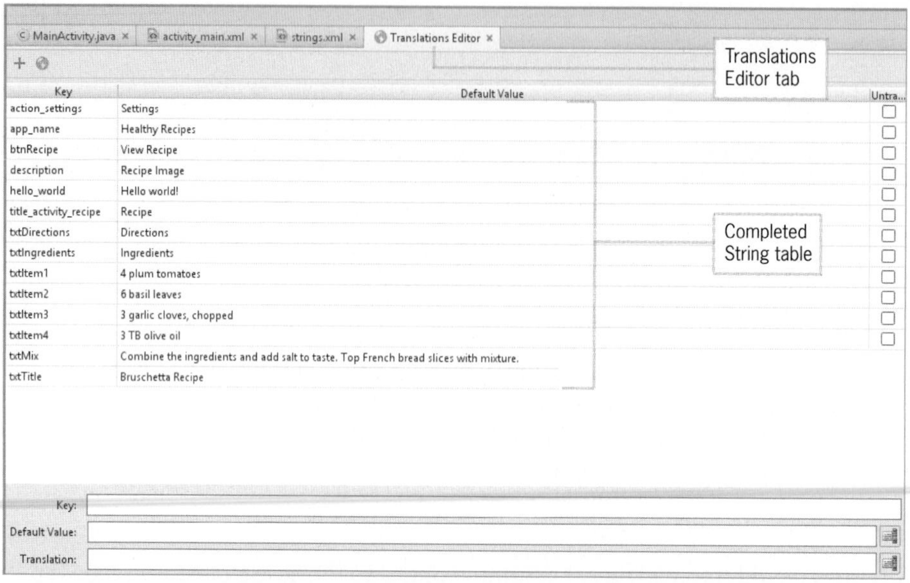

Figure 2-10 Completed String table on the Translations Editor tab

STEP 2

- Close the Translations Editor tab.
- Close the strings.xml tab.
- Tap or click the Save All button to save the Android project.

Relative Layouts and Linear Layouts

The Android user interface includes a layout resource designer that organizes how controls appear on the app's various screens. The Design tab at the bottom of activity_main.xml displays the default user interface, which uses a resource file defined as a Relative layout by default. A **Relative layout** organizes layout components in relation to each other as shown in Figure 2-11. This provides more flexibility in positioning controls than other layouts. Each layout can be placed on the emulator by dragging and dropping the control on the screen. As shown in Figure 2-11, four ImageView controls are placed anywhere the developer desires. Using a Relative layout, you can place an ImageView, TextView, RadioButton, or Button control to the left of, to the right of, above, or below another control. Layout resources are stored as XML code in the res/layout resource directory for the Android application corresponding to the user interface template displayed by tapping or clicking the Text tab in activity_main.xml.

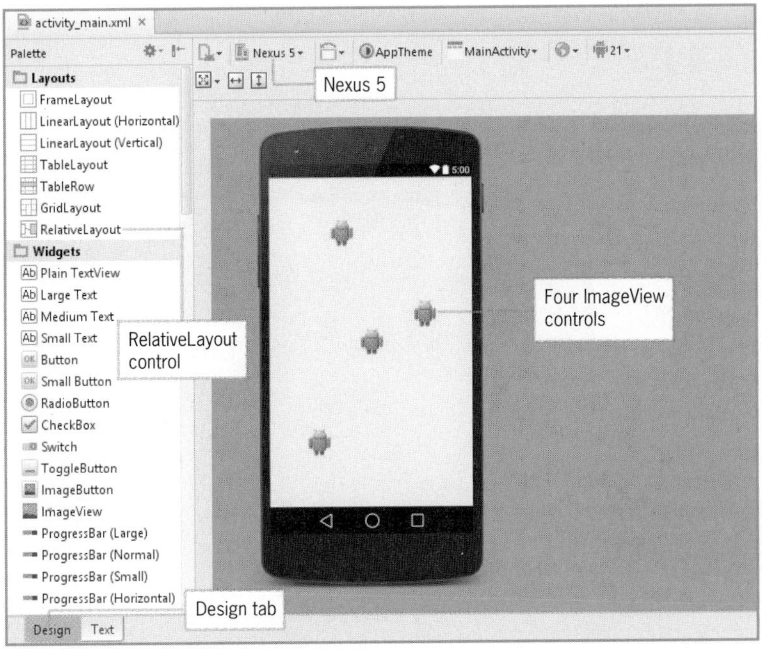

Figure 2-11 Relative layout

Another layout called a **Linear layout** organizes layout components in a vertical column or horizontal row. In Figure 2-12, multiple ImageView controls (Android icons) were dragged onto the emulator window. A Linear layout (vertical) places each control directly below the previous control to form a vertical column. To change the default Relative layout to a Linear layout, drag the LinearLayout (Vertical) layout from the Layouts category in the Palette to the emulator. If you select a vertical Linear layout and drag the images onto the emulator, the images are arranged vertically in multiple rows, as shown in Figure 2-12. Linear layouts are common for forms that display controls in a single row or column.

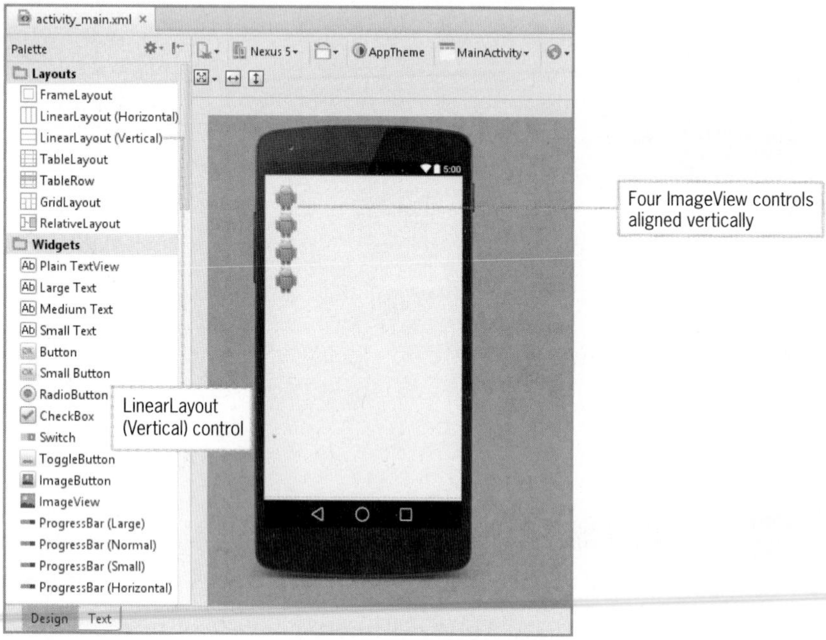

Figure 2-12 Linear layout with vertical orientation

GTK

Other layouts you can use include a Frame layout, Table layout, Table Row layout, and Grid layout. You also can use a combination of layouts, which means you can nest controls within one another.

Designing the Healthy Recipes Opening User Interface

When the Healthy Recipes app opens, the initial screen as shown in Figure 2-1 displays a TextView control with the text Bruschetta Recipe, an ImageView control with a picture of the ingredients for bruschetta, and a Button control with the text VIEW RECIPE. Notice that the controls are not in a Linear layout, but use a Relative layout so they are placed freely on the screen. You can modify a control's properties using the Properties pane. To change the property of a control, select the control first, and then change the appropriate property, such as the text or size, in the Properties pane.

Android Text Properties

The most popular text properties change the displayed text, modify the size of the text, and change the alignment of the text. The **text property** uses text from a string resource to display within the control. The **textSize property** can use various units of measurement, as shown in Table 2-2. The preferred unit of measurement is often **sp**, which stands for scaled-independent pixels. The reason for using this unit of measurement is that if a user has set up an Android phone to display a large font size for more clarity and easier visibility, the font in the app will be scaled to meet the user's size preference.

Unit of Measure	Abbreviation	Example
Inches	in	"0.5in"
Millimeters	mm	"20mm"
Pixels	px	"100px"
Density-independent pixels	dp or dip	"100dp" or "100dip"
Scaled-independent pixels	sp	"10sp"

Table 2-2 Measurements used for the textSize property

On the opening screen of the Healthy Recipes app, the TextView control for the title, ImageView control for the bruschetta picture, and Button controls can all be centered on the screen using a guide, a green dashed vertical line that appears when a control is dragged to the emulator. The Relative layout allows controls to be placed anywhere, but the green dashed line centers each control perfectly.

GTK

All Palette controls such as TextView and ImageView can use a property called layout:margin top. For example, if you type 50dp to the right of the layout:margin top property, the control is placed 50 pixels from the top of the screen to help you design an exact layout.

The TextView control that is used to represent the title is named txtTitle. To name the TextView control, you use the id property. The prefix txt indicates that this is a TextView control. The prefix of the object conveys information about the meaning of the control. To place a centered TextView control on the emulator using the default Relative layout, follow these steps:

STEP 1

- In the Widgets category in the Palette, select the widget named Plain TextView. Drag the Plain TextView control near the top of the emulator.
- To center the Plain TextView control, drag it to the center of the emulator until a green dashed vertical line identifying the window's center is displayed.

The Plain TextView control is placed in the emulator (Figure 2-13).

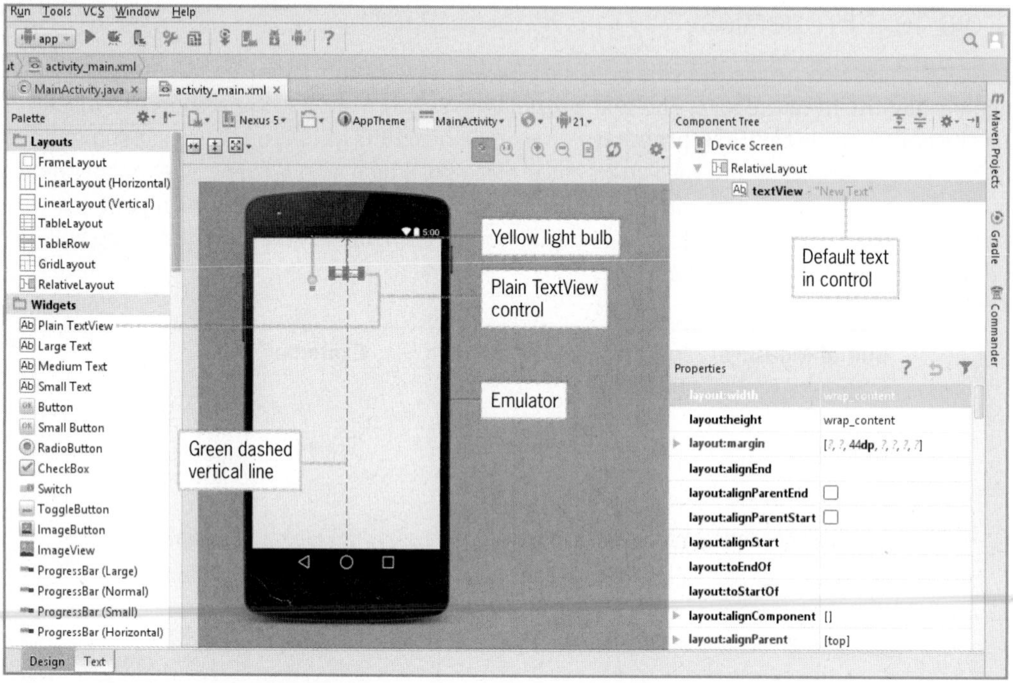

Figure 2-13 Plain TextView control

GTK

The yellow light bulb to the left of the TextView control in Figure 2-13 means that the control is presently hard-coded with default text 'New Text' in the text property. This warning symbol disappears after the text in the String table is associated with the TextView control.

STEP 2

- Double-tap or double-click the TextView control on the emulator to display the text and id editing panel.
- Type **txtTitle** in the id text box to name the TextView control.

The text and id editing panel opens to identify the text and id properties of the TextView control. The id property specifies the name of the TextView control as txtTitle (Figure 2-14).

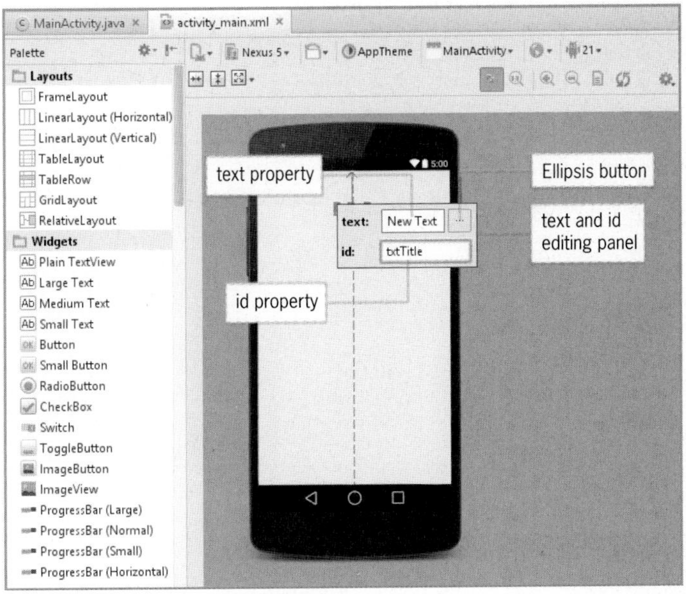

Figure 2-14 text and id editing panel

STEP 3

- Tap or click the ellipsis button (three dots) in the text and id editing panel.
- Scroll down the Resources listing on the Projects tab to locate txtTitle and then tap or click txtTitle.

The text resource txtTitle from the strings.xml file is selected and the text Bruschetta Recipe is displayed (Figure 2-15).

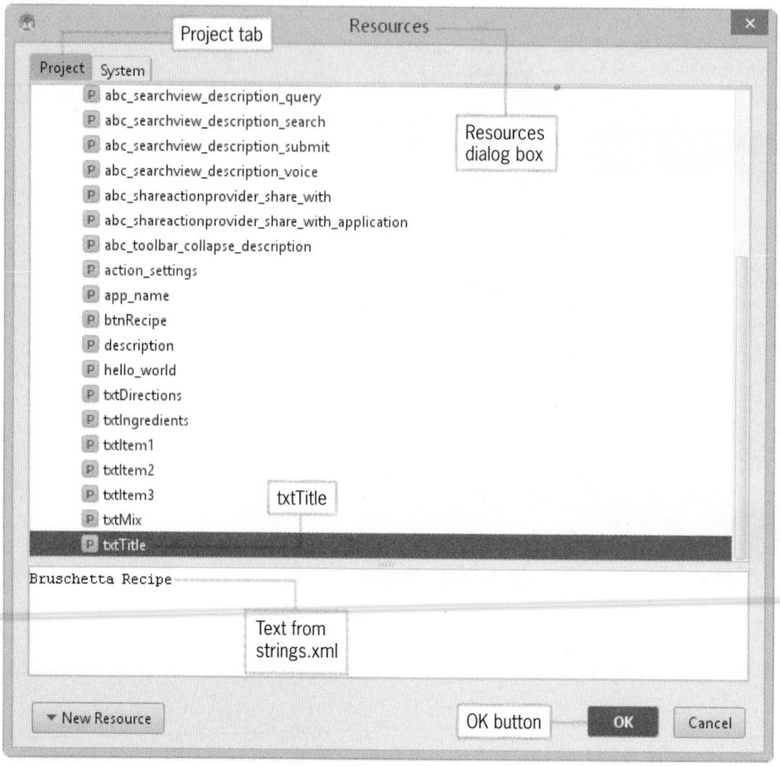

Figure 2-15 Resources dialog box

STEP 4

- Tap or click the OK button to close the Resources dialog box and add the txtTitle string to the txtTitle TextView control.
- Scroll down the Properties pane on the right side of the window to the textSize property.
- Tap or click to the right of the textSize property, type **40sp** to represent the scaled-independent pixel size, and then press Enter.

The TextView control displays the text Bruschetta Recipe using a text size of 40sp (Figure 2-16).

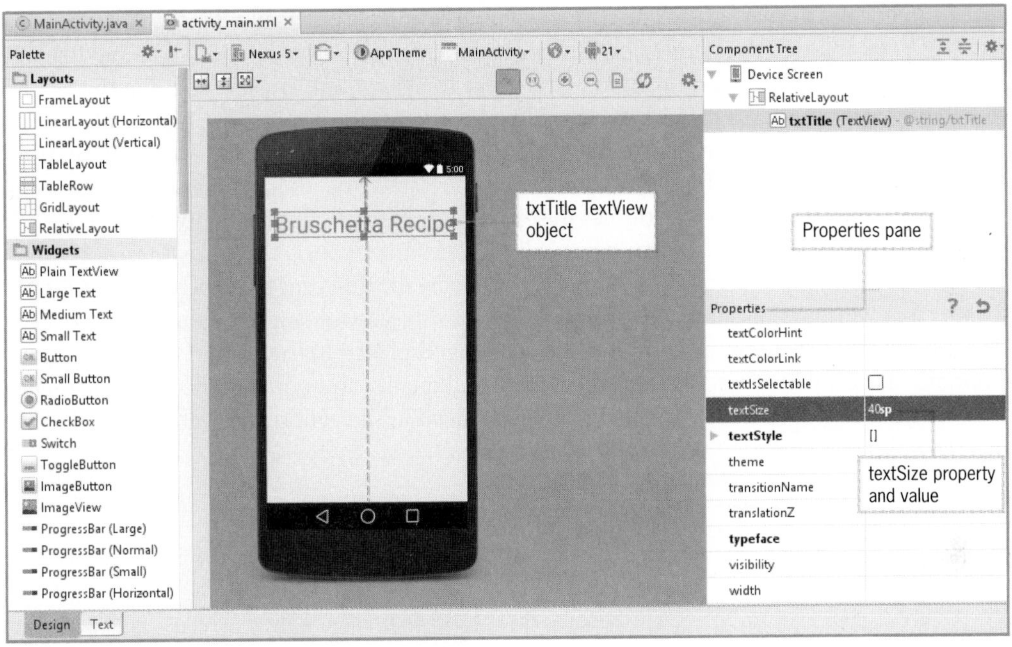

Figure 2-16 Title displayed on the emulator

GTK
Throughout the book, note that Windows computers have an Enter key, but Mac computers use the Return key.

GTK
The top free Android apps are Gmail, Chrome browser, Angry Birds, Facebook, Skype, and Twitter, in that order.

Adding a File to the Resources Folder

In the Healthy Recipes application, an image of bruschetta is displayed in an ImageView control. Images provide a visually appealing way to convey information to your users without explicitly stating it. Before you can insert the ImageView control in the emulator, you must place the appropriate picture file in the resources folder. In the Android project view, the res (resource) folder contains a folder named *drawable.* The graphics used by the application can be stored in this folder. Android supports three types of graphic formats: .png (preferred), .jpg (acceptable), and .gif (discouraged).

Critical Thinking
How can I convert an Android camera .jpg photo to the preferred .png file type?
On a PC, Windows Paint can convert picture file types. On a Mac, Paintbrush is a similar program for image file type conversion.

Android categorizes device screens using two general properties: size and density. You should expect that your app will be installed on devices with screens that vary in both size and density. Android creates a Drawable resource for any of these images when you save them in the res/drawable folder. Android projects have multiple drawable folders that are named after the resolution of the device. The five drawable folders are identified with the dpi (dots per inch) densities shown in Table 2-3. To declare different layouts and images for different sized screens, you must place these alternative resources in separate directories, similar to how you do for different language strings. Android automatically scales your layout to properly fit the screen. An app developer can create images designed specifically for different sized screens that look crisp and clear without any scaling or blurring. For example, a wide high-resolution image can be designed specifically for a horizontal tablet screen and placed in the xxhdpi folder. By using appropriate images, you can achieve the best graphical quality and performance on all screen densities. In this text for brevity, one image will be placed in the generic drawable folder for testing purposes.

Name	Description
drawable	Generic resources for any screen
xxhdpi	Resources for extra, extra high-density screens
xhdpi	Resources for extra high-density screens
hdpi	Resources for high-density screens
mdpi	Resources for medium-density screens
ldpi	Resources for low-density screens

Table 2-3 Drawable folders

Place the Bruschetta image in the res/drawable folder to be used by the ImageView control, which links to the resource image. You should already have the student files for this text that your instructor gave you or that you downloaded from the webpage for this book *(www.cengagebrain.com)*. To place a copy of the bruschetta.png image from the USB drive into the res/drawable folder, follow these steps:

STEP 1

- If necessary, copy the student files to your USB drive. Open the USB folder containing the student files.
- To copy the bruschetta.png file, tap or click bruschetta.png file on the USB drive, then press Ctrl+C.
- To paste the image file into the drawable folder, press and hold or right-click the drawable folder in the Android project view.

A shortcut menu opens (Figure 2-17).

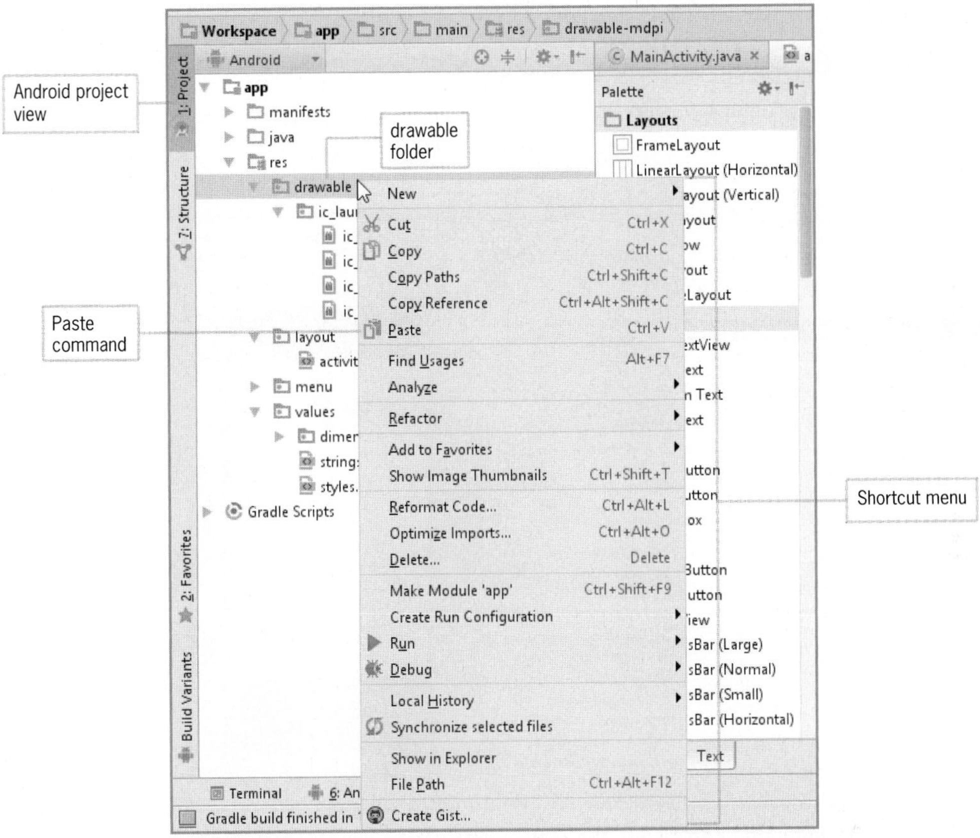

Figure 2-17 Shortcut menu for pasting a copied file

STEP 2

- Tap or click Paste on the shortcut menu.

The Copy dialog box confirms the name and directory to which the image is being copied (Figure 2-18).

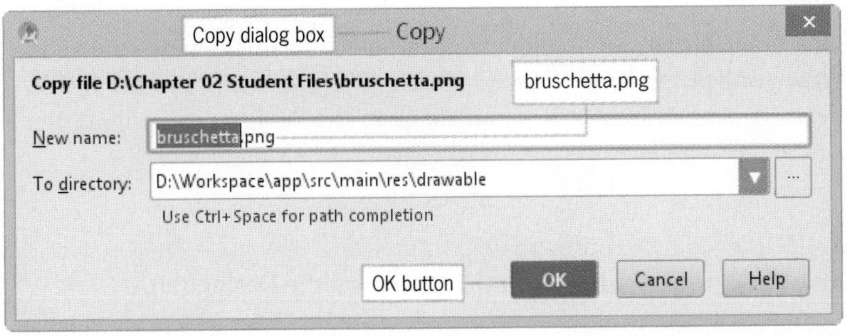

Figure 2-18 Copy dialog box

STEP 3

- Tap or click the OK button in the Copy dialog box.

A copy of the bruschetta.png file appears in the drawable folder (Figure 2-19).

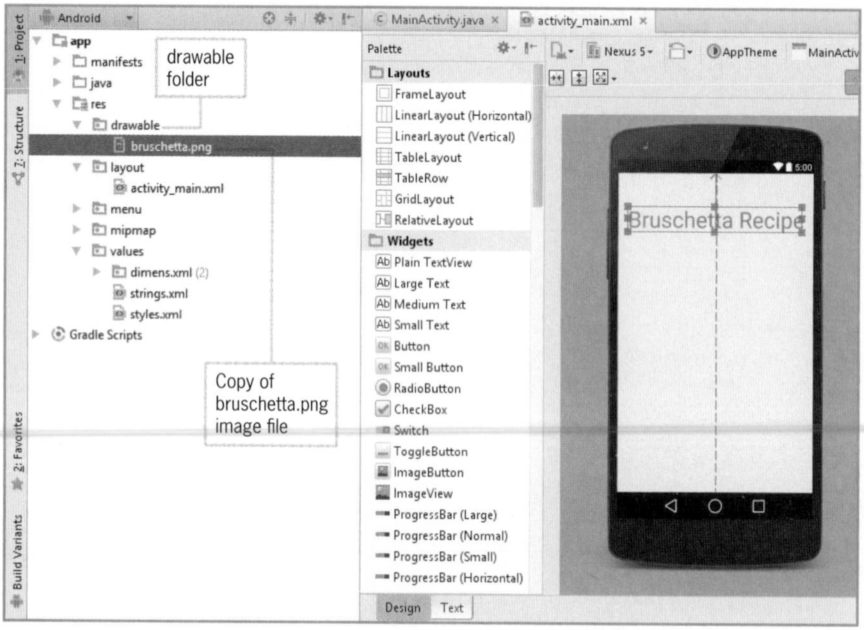

Figure 2-19 bruschetta.png copied into the drawable folder

GTK

Extra, extra high-density graphics have 480 dots per inch (typically a tablet). Extra high-density graphics have 320 dots per inch, high-density graphics have 240 dots per inch, medium-density graphics have 160 dots per inch, and low-density graphics have 120 dots per inch.

Adding an ImageView Control

After an image is placed in a drawable resource folder, you can place an ImageView control in the emulator. An **ImageView control** can display an icon or a graphic such as a picture file or shape on the Android screen. To add an ImageView control from the Widgets category of the Palette, follow these steps:

STEP 1

- Tap or click ImageView in the Widgets category in the Palette on the Design tab.
- Drag an ImageView control to the center of the emulator until a green dashed vertical line appears, indicating the control is centered. Release the mouse button.

The ImageView control (small blue square placeholder) is centered in the emulator (Figure 2-20).

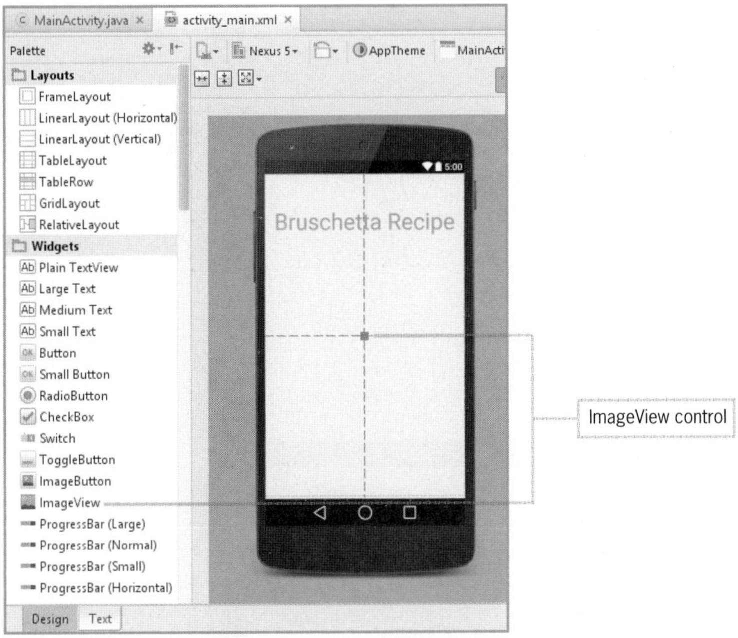

Figure 2-20 ImageView control placeholder centered in the emulator

STEP 2

- Double-tap or double-click the ImageView placeholder to open the src and id editing panel.
- Type **imgRecipe** in the id text box to name the ImageView control.
- Tap or click the ellipsis button (three dots) in the src and id editing panel.
- Scroll down the Resources listing and then tap or click bruschetta in the Drawable category to select the image from the drawable folder.

The bruschetta image is selected in the Resources dialog box (Figure 2-21).

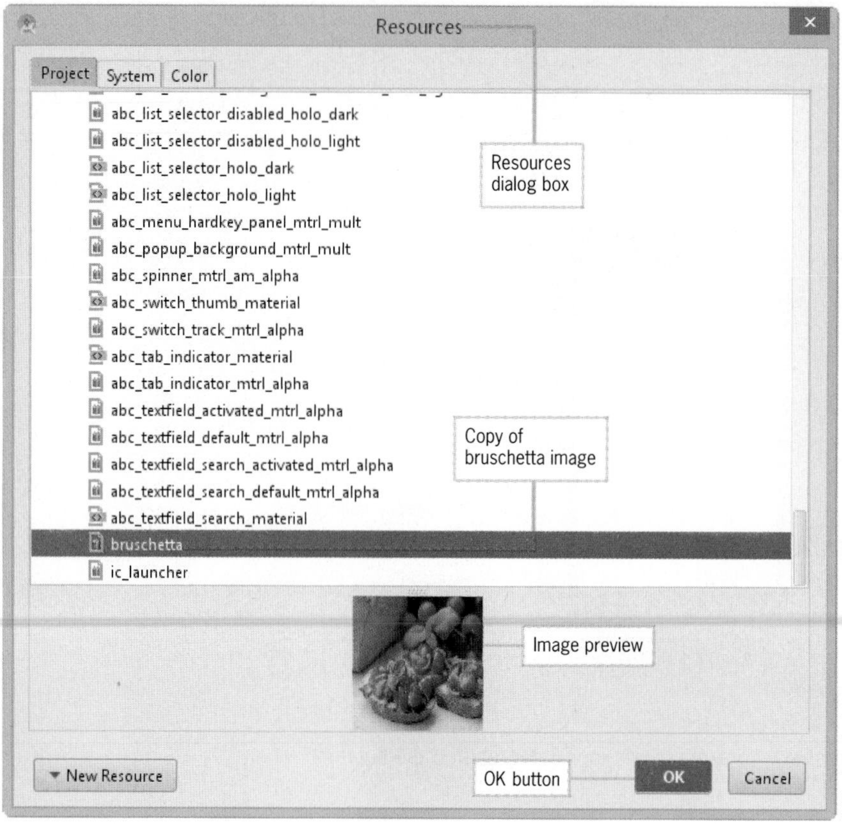

Figure 2-21 Assigning the bruschetta image to the ImageView control

STEP 3

- Tap or click the OK button to close the Resources dialog box.
- Scroll down the Properties pane to display the contentDescription property.
- Tap or click the ellipsis button to the right of the contentDescription property.
- Scroll down the Resources listing in the Resources dialog box and tap or click description.

The description string resource from strings.xml is assigned to the contentDescription property, which will display a description of the imgRecipe ImageView control for accessibility purposes (Figure 2-22).

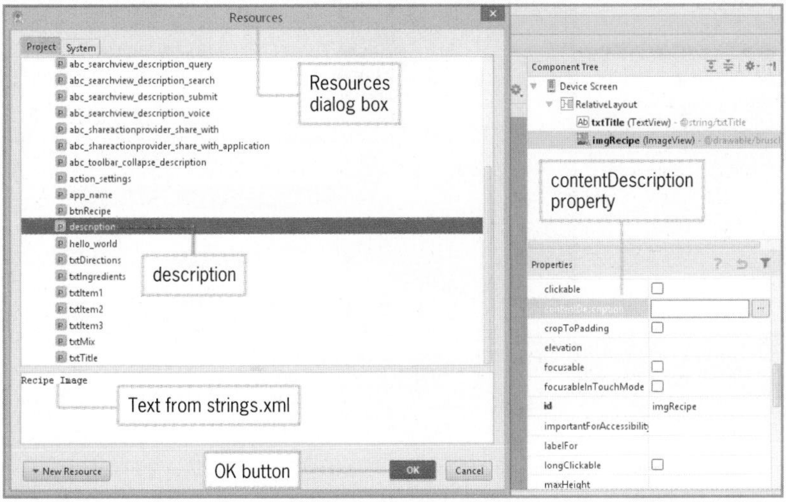

Figure 2-22 Assigning the description strings resource to the ImageView control

STEP 4

- Tap or click the OK button to close the Resources dialog box.

The bruschetta image is displayed in the emulator (Figure 2-23).

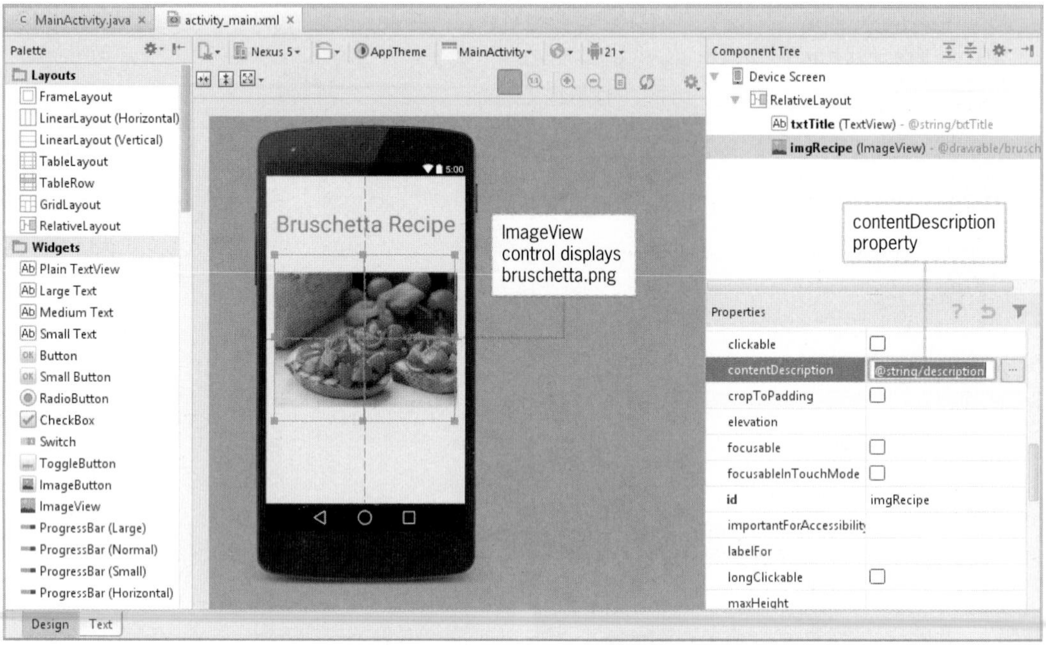

Figure 2-23 ImageView control with image and contentDescription property

IN THE TRENCHES
When you are selecting images for your app, consider using the advanced search features of Google or Bing to locate an open-source license graphic. An open-source license is a type of license for images that allows the picture to be used, modified and/or shared under defined terms and conditions.

Adding a Button Control

A Button control is a commonly used control in a graphical user interface. For example, you probably are familiar with the OK button used in many applications. Generally, when the program is running, buttons are used to cause an event to occur. The Android SDK includes four types of button controls: Button, Small Button, ToggleButton, and ImageButton. The Button control is provided in the Widgets category in the Palette. In the Healthy Recipes app, the user taps a Button control to display the bruschetta recipe on a second screen. To name the Button control, you use its id property. For example, use btnRecipe as the id property for the Button control in the Healthy Recipes app. The prefix btn represents a button in the code. The id btnRecipe is used to code the Button control in the Java code. To add a Button control from the Widgets category of the Palette, follow these steps:

STEP 1

- Drag the Button control to the emulator below the ImageView control until a green dashed vertical line appears, indicating the control is centered. Release the mouse button.

- Double-tap or double-click the Button control and type **btnRecipe** in the id text box within the text and id editing panel.
- Tap or click the ellipsis button and scroll down the Resources listing.
- Tap or click btnRecipe and then tap or click the OK button to close the Resources dialog box.
- In the Properties pane, change the textSize property to **36sp** and press Enter.

The Button control is named btnRecipe and displays the text VIEW RECIPE, which has the text size of 36sp (Figure 2-24).

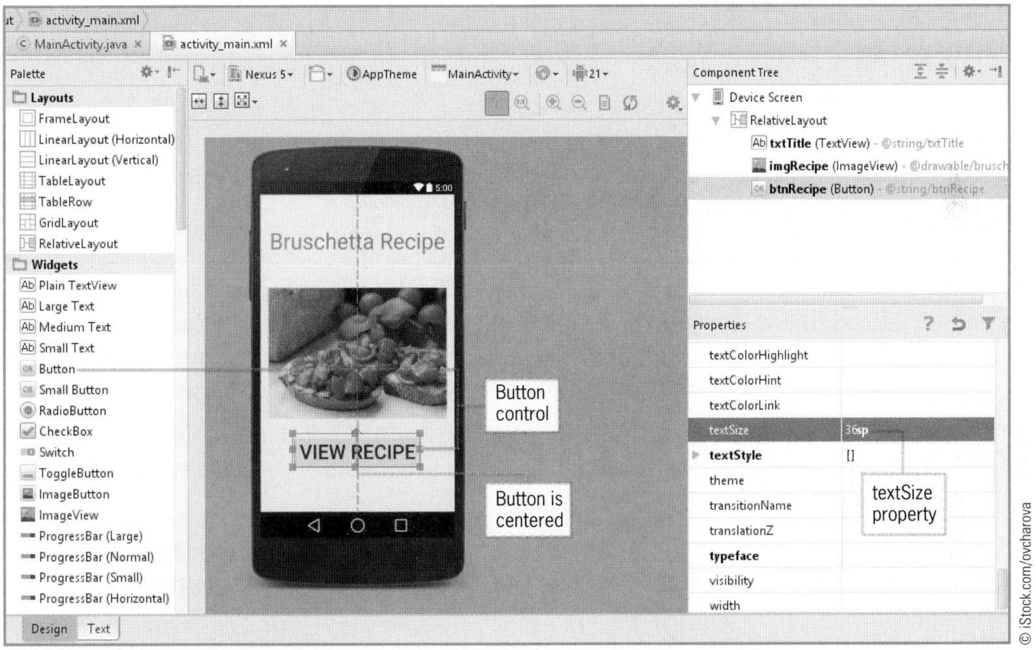

Figure 2-24 Button control

Creating Activities

The Healthy Recipes app displays two screens, as shown in Figures 2-1 and 2-2. The system requirement for this app is for the user to select a recipe name and then tap a button to display the recipe details. Screens in the Android environment are defined in layout files. Figure 2-24 shows the completed design for the first screen, which is defined in activity_main.xml.
A second screen must be created and designed in a layout file named activity_recipe.xml. Each of the two screens is considered an Activity. An **Activity**, one of the core components of an Android application, is the point at which the application makes contact with your users. For example, an Activity might create a menu of websites, request a street address to display a map,

or even show an exhibit of photographs from an art museum. An Activity is an important component of the life cycle of an Android app. You can construct activities by using XML layout files and a Java class.

Planning a Program

As you acquire the skills necessary to design an Android user interface, you are ready to learn about the program development life cycle. The program development life cycle is a set of phases and steps that developers follow to design, create, and maintain an Android program. Following are the phases of the program development life cycle:

1. *Gather and analyze the program requirements*—The developer must obtain the information that identifies the program requirements and then document these requirements.
2. *Design the user interface*—After the developer understands the program requirements, the next step is to design the user interface. The user interface provides the framework for the processing that occurs within the program.
3. *Design the program processing objects*—An Android app consists of one or more processing objects that perform the tasks required in the program. The developer must determine what processing objects are required, and then determine the requirements of each object. Your design of the user interface plays an important part in keeping the overall Android experience consistent and enjoyable to use.
4. *Code the program*—After the processing object has been designed, the object must be implemented in program code. Program code consists of the instructions written using XML and Java code that ultimately can be executed.
5. *Test the program*—As the program is being coded, and after the coding is completed, the developer should test the program code to ensure it is executing properly.

GTK

You can use comments to document your code. Comments are ignored by the Java compiler. When you want to make a one-line comment, type two forward slashes (//), and then enter your comment. For example:

```
// This is a single-line comment
```

Another way to comment is to use block comments. For example:

```
/* This is a
block comment
*/
```

Adding a Class File

The src folder in the Android project view includes the MainActivity.java file. This file contains the MainActivity class that opens the activity_main.xml screen, which you designed for the app's user interface. In object-oriented terminology, a class describes a group of objects that establishes an introduction to each object's properties. A **class** is simply a blueprint or a template for creating objects by defining its properties. Classes are the fundamental building blocks of a Java program. Classes are categories, and objects are items within each category. An **object** is a specific, concrete instance of a class. When you create an object, you instantiate it. When you **instantiate**, you create an instance of the object by defining one particular variation of the object within a class, giving it a name, and locating it in the memory of the computer. Each class needs its own copy of an object. A class determines what data an object can hold and the way it can behave when using the data. For instance, imagine a set of design plans for a Mini Cooper car detailing how this vehicle will be manufactured as the class. Next, imagine you are ordering your own Mini Cooper car (instantiating your own copy) using the design plans (class), selecting one that is candy apple red with a racing stripe. A class can be instantiated countless times, but each instantiation creates a new and unique object, just like BMW can create thousands of Mini Cooper cars.

Later in this chapter, Java code is added to the MainActivity class to recognize the action of tapping the Button control to open the recipe screen. Recall that each screen represents an Activity. In addition, each Activity must have a matching Java class file within the java folder. A second Activity named Recipe.java creates a corresponding XML file named activity_recipe.xml that displays the layout for the second screen. The activity_recipe.xml layout file can then be designed as shown in Figure 2-2. It is a Java standard to begin a class name with an uppercase letter, include no spaces, and emphasize each new word with an initial uppercase letter. An XML layout filename typically starts with a lowercase letter using the same name as the class name.

GTK

Using an uppercase letter to begin a Java class name and starting each new word with an uppercase letter is known as **Pascal case**.

GTK

If you are running API version 22 or later, the ActionBarActivity class name in any Java Activity may appear as strikethrough text. The app will run perfectly, but for any app in this book, you can replace ActionBarActivity with AppCompatActivity.

To add a second Java class with a second XML layout page to the application, follow these steps:

STEP 1

- Close the activity_main.xml tab.
- In the Android project view, expand the java folder and the first net.androidbootcamp.healthyrecipes package to view the MainActivity Java class.
- To create a second class, press and hold or right-click the first net.androidbootcamp.healthyrecipes folder (package name), tap or click New on the shortcut menu, and then tap or click Activity.

The Activity shortcut menu is displayed to add a second activity (Figure 2-25).

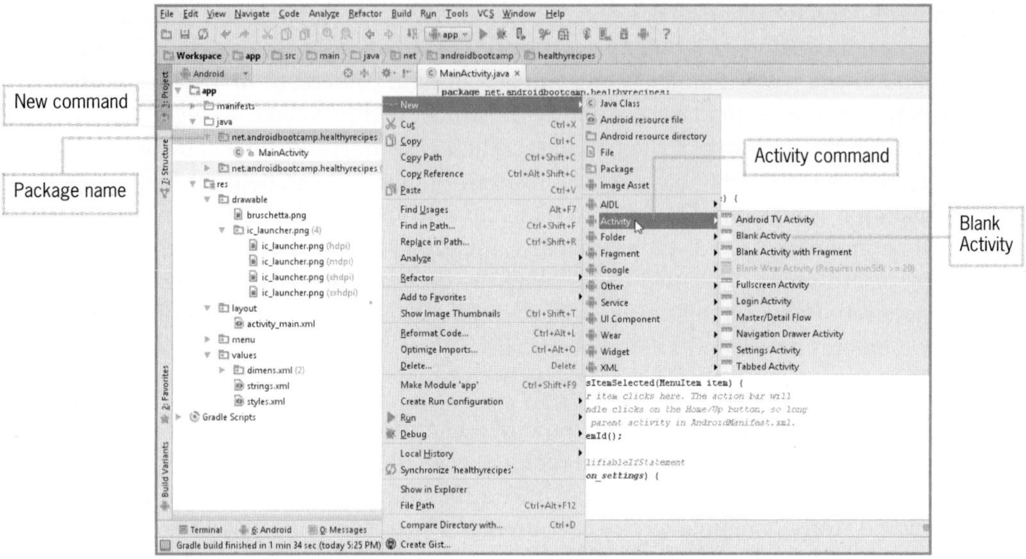

Figure 2-25 Activity shortcut menu

STEP 2

- Tap or click Blank Activity to create a second Activity class.
- In the Activity Name text box, type **Recipe** to create a second class.

A new class named Recipe is named with the second layout, activity_recipe (Figure 2-26).

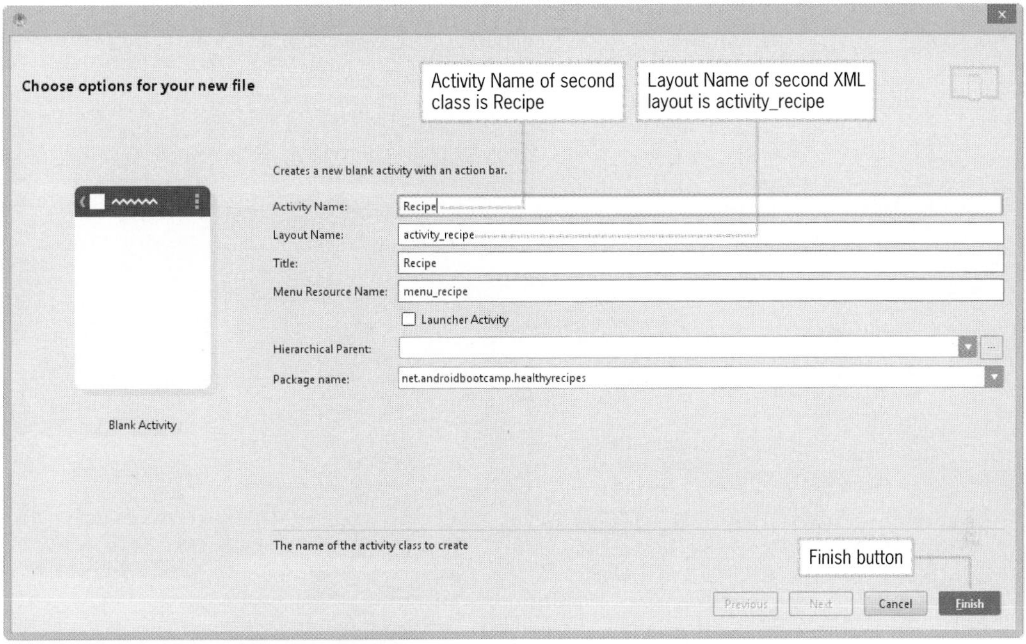

Figure 2-26 Creating the Recipe class

STEP 3

- Tap or click the Finish button to finish creating the Recipe class and XML layout for the second screen.
- Delete the default Hello World! TextView object from the activity_recipe.xml emulator.
- Using the techniques taught earlier in the chapter, create the second user interface, activity_recipe.xml, as shown in Figure 2-27 with multiple TextView controls.

The second user interface, activity_recipe.xml, is designed (Figure 2-27).

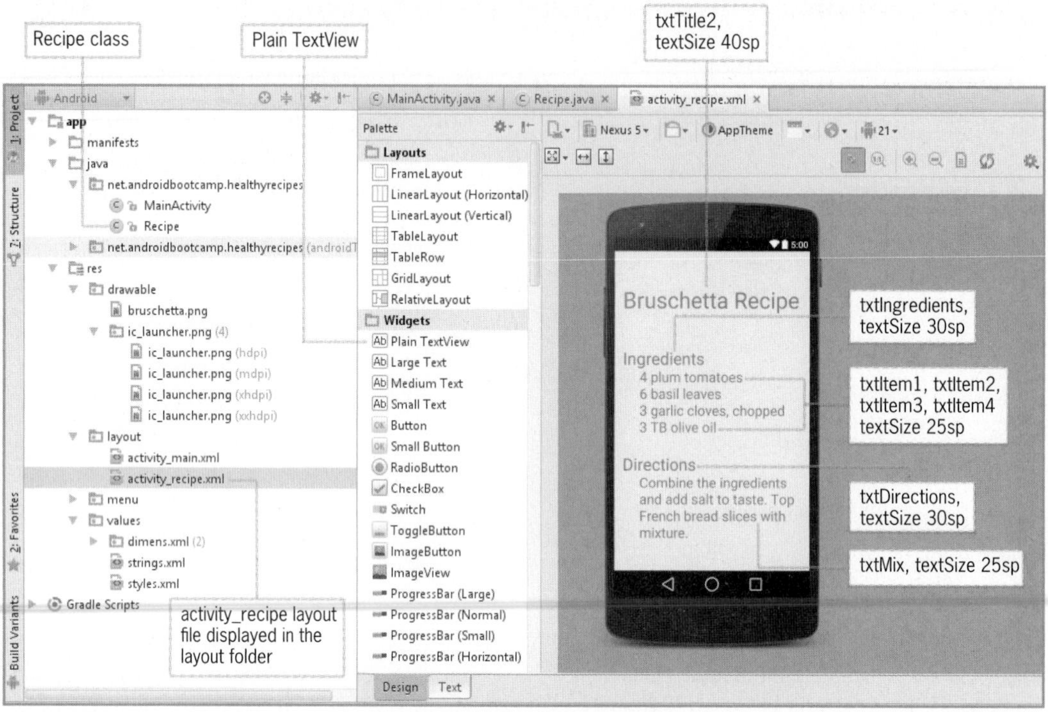

Figure 2-27 User interface for activity_recipe.xml

STEP 4

- Close the activity_recipe.xml tab.
- Tap or click in the Recipe.java code window.
- Display line numbers in the code window by tapping or clicking View on the menu bar and then tapping or clicking Active Editor.
- Tap or click Show Line Numbers.

The Recipe.java class is created and line numbers are displayed (Figure 2-28).

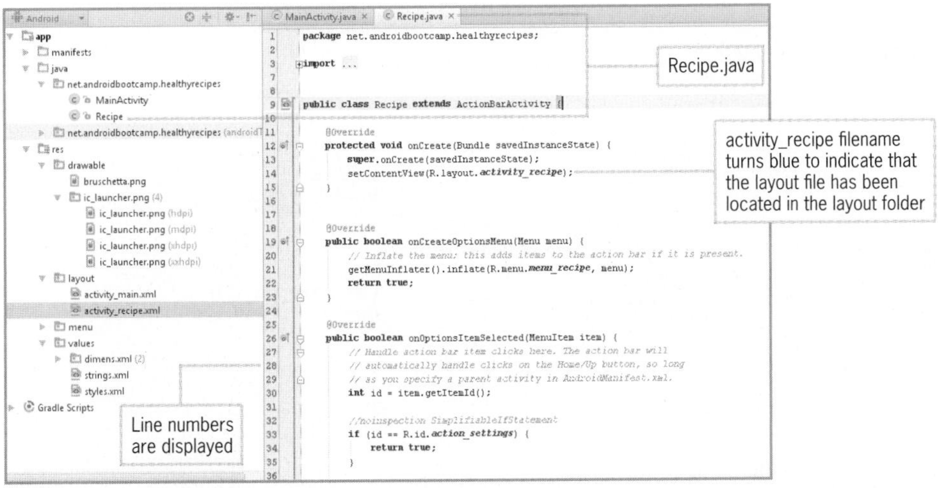

Figure 2-28 New Recipe class in the Healthy Recipes project

The Android Manifest File

An Android project is made up of far more than the XML layout files that create the user interface. The other important components of any Android project are the Android Manifest file and the Java code in the Java classes. The **Android Manifest** file is necessary in every Android application and must be named AndroidManifest.xml exactly. The Android Manifest file provides all the essential information to the Android device, such as the name of your Java application, a listing of each activity, any permissions needed to access other Android functions such as the use of the Internet, services, broadcast receivers, and the minimum level of the Android API. This file lets the Android system know what the components are and under what conditions they can be launched. AndroidManifest.xml is like a project manager of a business process that determines which activities are scheduled, the permissions that are necessary, and the device versions needed to get the job done.

Android Studio automatically adds each activity you create to the Android Manifest file. In the Healthy Recipes app, the Android Manifest is only aware of the initial activity named MainActivity. To see which Activities an application contains, if necessary expand the manifests folder, and then double-tap or double-click the AndroidManifest.xml file in the Android project view as shown in Figure 2-29. Notice that Line 11 calls an activity named MainActivity. The intent in Lines 13-17 is to launch the opening screen. Line 20 calls the second activity named Recipe. The AndroidManifest.xml file must contain an entry for each activity.

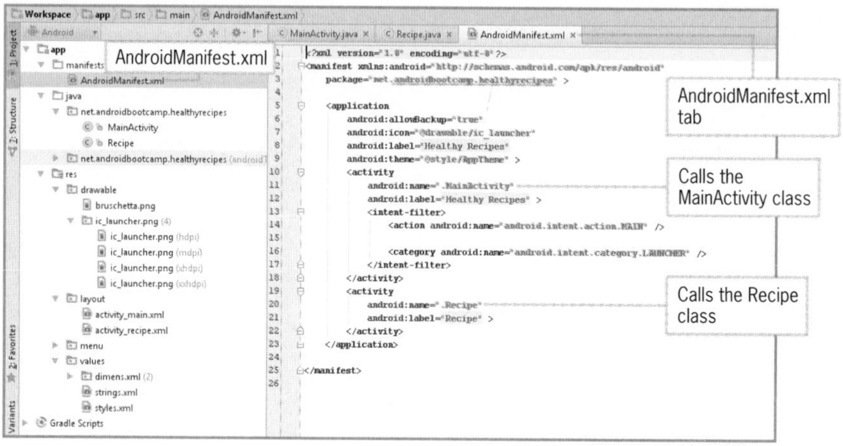

Figure 2-29 AndroidManifest.xml

Coding the Java Activity

When the user taps an application icon on his or her Android phone or tablet, the MainActivity.java code is read by the device processor. The entry point of the Activity class is the onCreate( ) event handler, which is called a method. A **method** is a set of Java statements that can be included inside a Java class. The **method body** contains a collection of statements that defines what the method does. The onCreate method is where you initialize the Activity. Imagine a large stack of papers on your desk. The paper on top of the stack is what you are reading right now. Android also has a stack of activities. The onCreate method places this new activity on top of the stack.

Coding an onCreate Method

In the chapter project, the first activity displayed in the opening screen layout designed in activity_main.xml is the currently running activity. When the user taps or clicks the VIEW RECIPE button, the activity_main.xml screen closes and a new Activity that displays the actual recipe (activity_recipe.xml) is placed on top of the stack and becomes the running activity. The syntax for the onCreate method is:

Code Syntax

```
public void onCreate(Bundle savedInstanceState) {
    super.onCreate(savedInstanceState);
}
```

The method begins with *public void*, which are special keywords that Java uses to determine the type of method. They must always be in all lowercase letters. Void is called the **return type** of the method. A void return type means that the method does not return anything. At the end of the public void statement is an opening curly brace. The closing curly brace appears at the end of the method. Inside the braces is the onCreate method, where the first user interface must be opened. Activities have no clue which user interface should be displayed on the screen. For a particular user interface to open, code must be added inside the onCreate method to place that specific activity on top of the stack. The Java code necessary to display the content of a specific screen is called **setContentView**, which has the following syntax:

Code Syntax

```
setContentView(R.layout.activity_main);
```

In the code syntax, R.layout.*activity_main* represents the user interface of the activity_main. xml layout (the opening screen), which displays the opening title, bruschetta image, and VIEW RECIPE button. The R represents the term Resource, as the layout folder resides in the res folder.

Displaying the User Interface

The MainActivity.java file was created automatically by Android Studio and already contains the onCreate method and setContentView(R.layout.activity_main) code, as shown in Lines 12 and 14 in Figure 2-30. Line 12 starts the method and Line 14 displays the activity_main.xml layout when the application begins. Android Studio automatically codes the onCreate method for opening the activity_recipe.xml layout when the Recipe.Java class is launched.

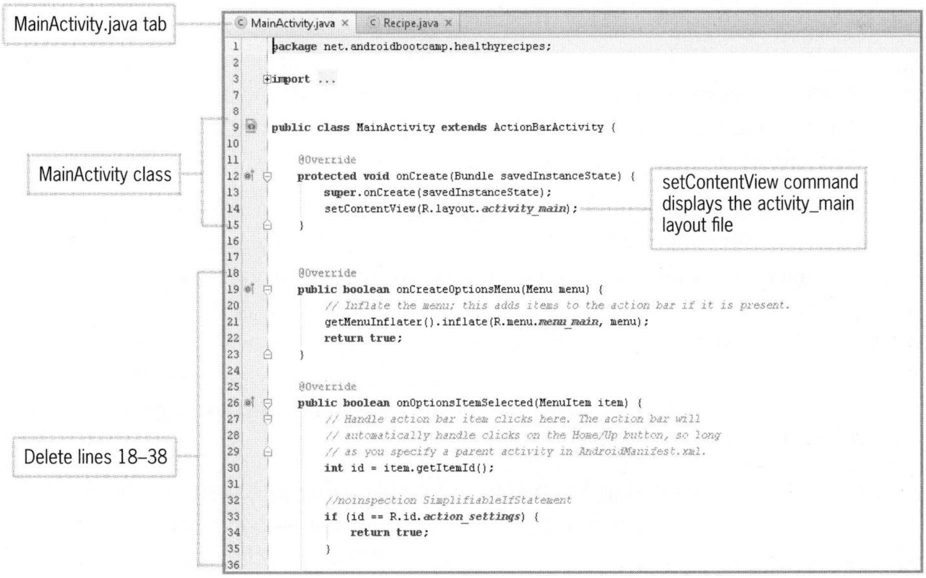

Figure 2-30 MainActivity.java code for OnCreate method

Creating a Button Event Handler

Android phones and tablets have touchscreens that create endless possibilities for user interaction, allowing the user to tap, swipe, and pinch in or out to change the size of the screen. As you program with this event-driven language, users typically see an interface containing controls, buttons, menus, and other graphical elements. After displaying the interface, the program waits until the user touches the device. When the user reacts, the app initiates an event, which executes code in an **event handler**, which is a part of the program coded to respond to the specific event. In the Healthy Recipes app, users have only one interaction—they can tap the Button control to start an event that displays the bruschetta recipe. When the user taps the Button control, code for an event listener is necessary to begin the event that displays the activity_recipe.xml file on the Android screen. This tap event is actually known as a click event in Java code. In the Healthy Recipes application, the MainActivity.java code must first contain the following sections:

- Class property to hold a reference to the Button object
- OnClickListener( ) method to await the button click action
- onClick( ) method to respond to the click event

The Healthy Recipes application opens with a Button control on the screen. To use that button, a reference is required in the MainActivity.java file. To reference a Button control, use the following syntax to create a Button property:

Code Syntax

```
Button button = (Button)findViewById(R.id.btnRecipe);
```

The syntax for the Button property includes the findViewById( ) method, which is used by any Android Activity. This method finds a layout view in the XML files that you created when designing the user interface. The variable button in the code contains the reference to the Button control.

After the code is entered to reference the Button control, you can press Alt+Enter to import the Button type as an Android widget (Option+Return on Mac). When you **import** the Button type as an Android widget, you make the classes from the Android Button package available throughout the application. An import statement is automatically placed at the top of the Java code. An **import statement** is a way of making more Java functions available to your specific program. Java can perform almost endless actions, and not every program needs to do everything. So, to limit the size of the code, Java has its classes divided into packages that can be imported at the top of your code.

After the Button property is referenced in MainActivity.java, an OnClickListener( ) method is necessary to detect when the user taps an on-screen button. Event listeners wait for user interaction, which is when the user taps the button to view the recipe in the case of the chapter project. When an OnClickListener is placed in the code window, Java creates an onClick auto-generated stub. A **stub** is a piece of code that actually serves as a placeholder to declare itself, and it has just enough code to link to the rest of the program. The following syntax is needed for an OnClickListener method that listens for the Button control:

Code Syntax

```
    button.setOnClickListener(new OnClickListener() {
    public void onClick(View v) {
    // TODO Auto-generated method stub
    }
});
```

The last step to code is to call the startActivity( ) method, which opens the second Activity displaying the activity_recipe.xml user interface. The startActivity( ) method creates an intent to start another Activity such as to start the recipe Activity class. The intent needs two parts known as parameters: a context and the name of the Activity that is being opened. A context in Android coding means that any time you request that program to launch another Activity, a context is sent to the Android system to show which initiating Activity class is making the request. The context of the chapter project is MainActivity.this, which references the MainActivity.java class. The following syntax line launches the Recipe Java class:

Code Syntax

```
startActivity(new Intent(MainActivity.this, Recipe.class));
```

Coding a Button Event Handler

When the activity_main.xml layout is initially launched by the MainActivity.java class, it is necessary to code how the Button control interacts with the user. When this View Recipe button is tapped, the MainActivity.java class must contain code to launch the activity_recipe.xml layout (activity) and to begin the second Java class called Recipe.java. To initialize the Button control and code the Button handler to launch the second Activity class, follow these steps:

STEP 1

- Tap or click the MainActivity.java tab to open its code window.
- Tap or click in the code window and show line numbers.
- Delete Lines 18–38 to simplify the code.
- Tap or click to the right of setContentView(R.layout.activity_main); in Line 14, and then press Enter.

- To initialize and reference the Button control with the id name of btnRecipe, type **Button button = (Button) findViewById(R.id.btnRecipe);**
- After the code is entered to reference the Button control, point to the red text of the first Button command.

The Button control named btnRecipe is referenced in MainActivity.java. By pointing to the Button command, an error message is displayed (Figure 2-31). Notice the red curly line under the MainActivity.java tab name indicating an existing error within the code.

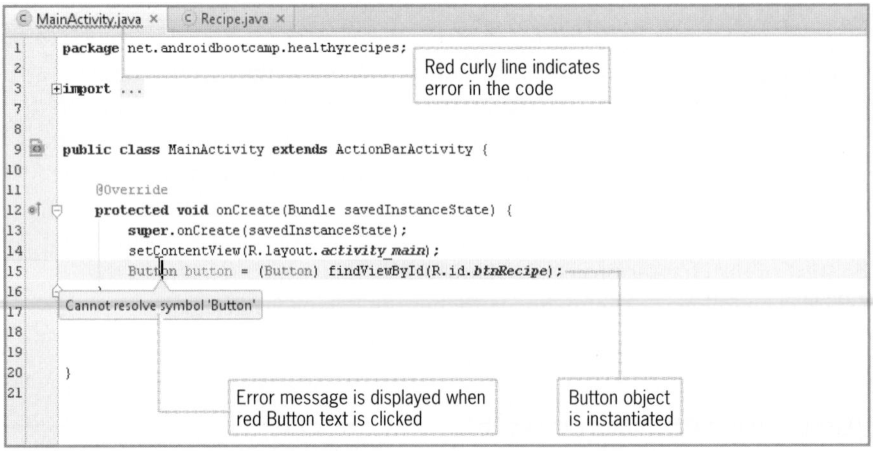

Figure 2-31 Button instantiated

STEP 2

- Press Alt+Enter simultaneously (Option+Return on Mac) to resolve the syntax error and import the Button class.
- Tap or click the expand icon (plus sign) in Line 3 to display the import statements.
- Tap or click the Save All button on the Standard toolbar to save your work.

The Button library is imported into this project (Figure 2-32).

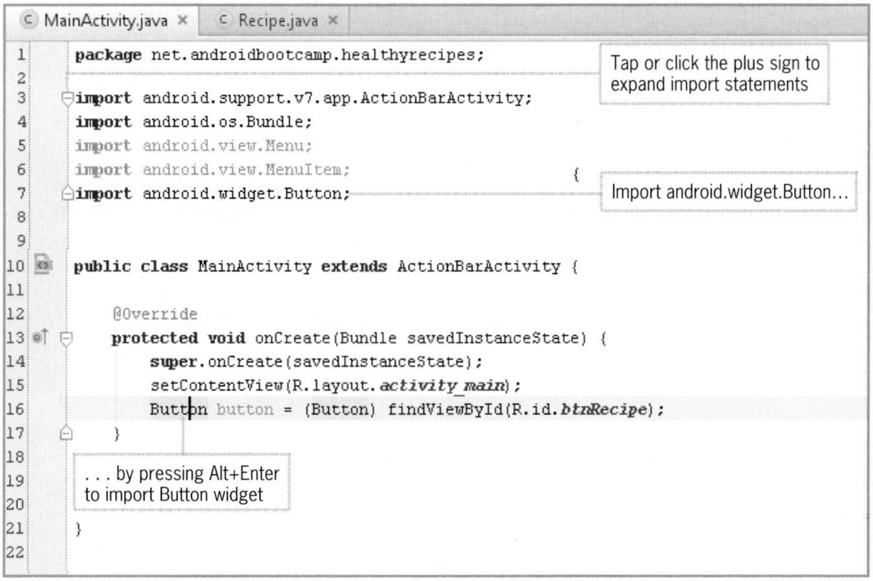

Figure 2-32 Button instantiated

STEP 3

- Tap or click at the end of Line 16 and press Enter.
- To code the button listener that awaits user interaction, type **button.seton** to display an auto-complete listing with all the possible entries that are valid at that point in the code.
- Double-tap or double-click the first setOnClickListener to select it from the auto-complete listing.
- In the parentheses, type **new On** (must have an uppercase 'O') to view possible auto-complete options.

The auto-complete listing for the OnClickListener is displayed (Figure 2-33).

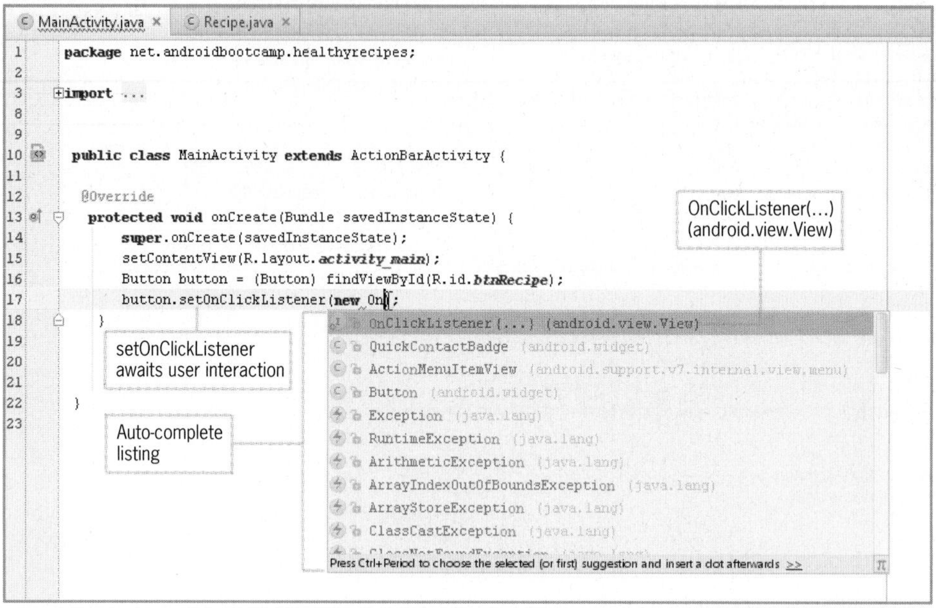

Figure 2-33 Auto-complete listing

STEP 4

- Double-tap or double-click the first choice, which lists an OnClickListener (...) (android.view.View). Auto-generated code adds an onClick method.
- If necessary, tap or click View if the text is red and then press Alt+Enter to Import View.
- Tap or click to place the insertion point on Line 21 inside the public void onClick (View v) braces.

An OnClickListener auto-generated stub appears in the code (Figure 2-34).

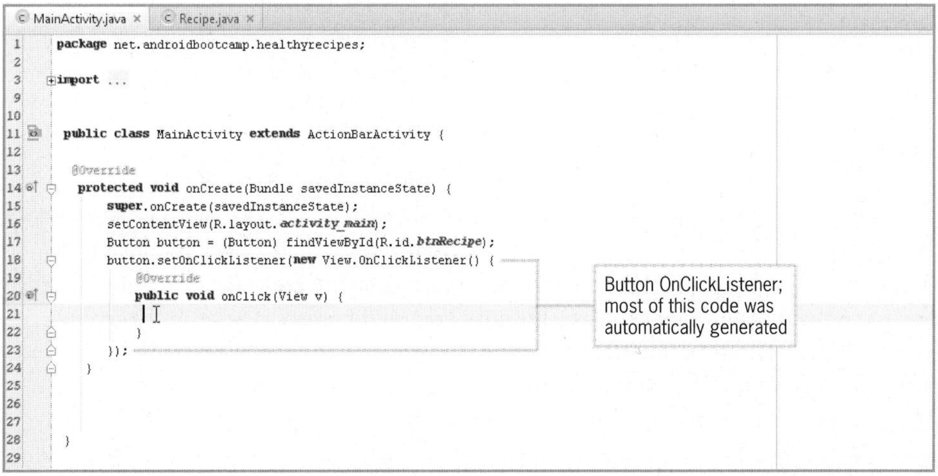

Figure 2-34 Inserting the Button OnClickListener stub

STEP 5

- Type **startA** and select startActivity(Intent intent) from the auto-complete listing.
- In the parentheses, change the intent text by typing **new Int** and then double-tap or double-click Intent (android.content) in the auto-complete listing.
- In the next set of parentheses, type **MainActivity.this, Recipe.class**.
- Tap or click the Save All button on the toolbar.

The startActivity code launches the intent to open Recipe.class (Figure 2-35).

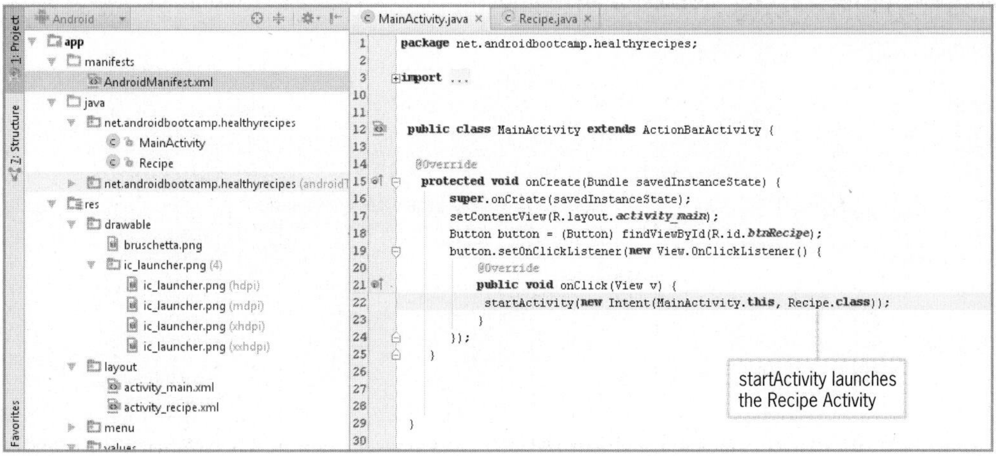

Figure 2-35 Complete code for MainActivity.java

IN THE TRENCHES

In years past, a software developer would have to wait many months for his or her software to be published and placed in stores for sale. In today's mobile market, app stores have become the de facto app delivery channel by reducing time-to-shelf and time-to-payment and by providing developers with unprecedented reach to consumers. If your app passes the quality Google Play tests, your app can be available in the store in a matter of days.

Correcting Errors in Code

Using the built-in auto-complete listing to assist you when entering code considerably reduces the likelihood of coding errors. Nevertheless, because you could create one or more errors when entering code, you should understand what to do when a coding error occurs. One possible error you could commit would be to forget a semicolon at the end of a statement. In Figure 2-36, when the application is run, a dialog box opens stating your project contains error(s), please fix them before running your application. A red wavy underline identifies the error location. When you point to the error icon, Java suggests the possible correction to the syntax error in the code. When you run an app that contains an error, an error listing appears at the bottom of the screen with possible suggestions of how to fix the error. After a semicolon is placed at the end of the line, the application is run again and the program functions properly.

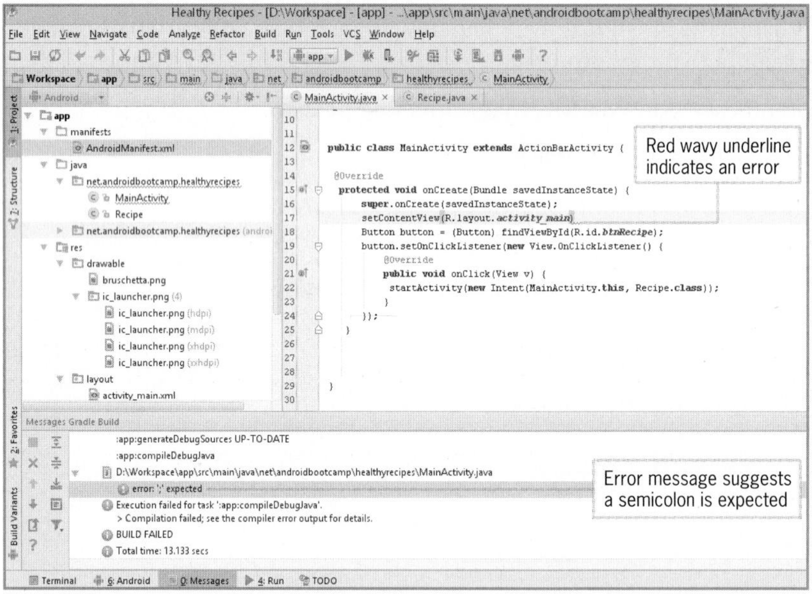

Figure 2-36 Syntax error

Saving and Running the Application

Each time an Android application is tested in the emulator, the programming design and code are automatically saved. If you start your project and need to save it before completion, tap or click the Save All button on the toolbar. As shown in Chapter 1, tap or click the Run 'app' button on the toolbar to test the application in the emulator. A dialog box opens the first time the application is executed requesting which emulator you would like to launch. Tap or click Launch emulator and select Nexus 5 API 21x86 or a similar emulator and tap or click the OK button. When the emulated Android main screen appears, unlock the emulator. Run the application again to send the code to the emulator. The application opens in the emulator window, where you can click the VIEW RECIPE button to view the bruschetta recipe.

Wrap It Up—Chapter Summary

This chapter described the steps to create the graphical user interface for the Healthy Recipes program. As you can see, many of the steps required are somewhat repetitive in the design; that is, the same technique is used repeatedly to accomplish similar tasks. When you master these techniques, together with the principles of user interface design, you will be able to design user interfaces for a variety of programs.

- Instead of adding text directly to a control's text property, you add it to the strings.xml file by working with the String table in the Translations Editor.
- Relative layouts arrange screen components freely on the screen. Linear layouts arrange screen components in a vertical column or horizontal row.
- Popular text properties for controls include the text property, which specifies the string resource to use for displaying text in the control, and the textSize property, which specifies the size of the text.
- To display graphics such as pictures and icons in an Android app, you use an ImageView control. Before you can place an ImageView control in the emulator, you must place a graphics file in the resources folder (drawable).
- An Activity is the point at which the application makes contact with your users and is one of the core components of the Android application. The chapter project has two Activities, one for each screen.
- Each screen represents an Activity and each Activity must have a matching Java class file.
- Every Android application has an Android Manifest file (named AndroidManifest.xml), which provides essential information to the Android device, such as the name of your Java application and a listing of each Activity. Android Studio automatically adds each Activity to the file.
- A method is a set of Java statements that can be included inside a Java class. The onCreate method is where you initialize an Activity. You use the setContentView command to display the content of a specific screen.

- When the user taps a Button control in an Android app, the code for an event listener, or click event, begins the event associated with the Button control. Event listeners such as the OnClickListener method wait for user interaction before executing the remaining code.
- In an Android app that contains more than one Activity, or screen, you use the startActivity( ) method to create an intent to start another Activity. The intent should contain two parameters: a context and the name of the Activity being opened. A context shows which initiating Activity class is making the request.
- When you run an Android application, a dialog box opens if your project contains any errors. Look for red error icons and red curly lines, which identify the location of the errors. Point to a red curly line to have Java suggest a correction to a syntax error in the code.

Key Terms

Activity—An Android component that represents a single screen with a user interface.

Android Manifest—A file with the filename AndroidManifest.xml that is required in every Android application. This file provides essential information to the Android device, such as the name of your Java application and a listing of each Activity.

class—A group of objects that establishes an introduction to each object's properties.

event handler—A part of a program coded to respond to the specific event.

ImageView control—A control that displays an icon or a graphic from a picture file.

import—To make the classes from a particular Android package available throughout the application.

import statement—A statement that makes more Java functions available to a program.

instantiate—To create an object of a specific class.

intent—Code in the Android Manifest file that allows an Android application with more than one Activity to navigate among Activities.

Linear layout—A layout that arranges components in a vertical column or horizontal row.

method—A set of Java statements that can be included inside a Java class.

method body—The part of a method containing a collection of statements that defines what the method does.

object—A specific, concrete instance of a class.

Pascal case—Text that begins with an uppercase letter and uses an uppercase letter to start each new word.

Relative layout—A layout that arranges components in relation to each other. Relative layout is the default layout of the emulator.

setContentView—The Java code necessary to display the content of a specific screen.

sp—A unit of measurement that stands for scaled-independent pixels.

stub—A piece of code that serves as a placeholder to declare itself, containing just enough code to link to the rest of the program.

text property—A property that references a string resource to display text within a control.

textSize property—A property that sets the size of text in a control.

Developer FAQs

1. How many drawable folders are available in the res folder?
2. If you were creating an app in many different languages, would you have to write the entire program from scratch for each language? What part of the program would stay the same? What part of the program would be different?
3. In which subfolder in the Android project view are the XML files stored?
4. Which three controls were used in the chapter project?
5. What is the difference between a Linear layout and a Relative layout?
6. Is the default layout for an Android screen Linear or Relative?
7. Which measurement is most preferred for text size? Why?
8. What does px stand for?
9. What does sp stand for?
10. What does dpi stand for?
11. Which picture file types are accepted for an ImageView control?
12. Which picture file type is preferred?
13. In which property can you describe an ImageView control for screen readers (accessibility)?
14. Which three properties were changed in the chapter project for the Button control?
15. What is the property that defines the name of a Button control?
16. Write one line of code that would launch a second class named Wireless from the present MainActivity class.
17. Write one line of code that declares a Button control with the variable named button that references a button in the XML layout with the Id property of btnStarWars.
18. Write one line of code that opens the XML layout named lemon.
19. Which two keys are pressed to auto-complete a line of Java code?
20. What character is placed at the end of most lines of Java code?

Beyond the Book

Search the web for answers to the following questions to further your Android knowledge.

1. Linear and Relative layouts are not the only types of Android layouts. Name three other types of layouts and write a paragraph describing each type.
2. Why are .png files the preferred type of image resource for the Android device? Write a paragraph that gives at least three reasons.
3. How much does an average Android app developer profit from his or her apps? Research this topic and write 150–200 words on your findings.
4. Research the most expensive Android apps currently available at Google Play. Name three expensive apps, their price, and the purpose of each.

Case Programming Projects

Complete one or more of the following case programming projects. Use the same steps and techniques taught within the chapter. Submit the program you create to your instructor. The level of difficulty is indicated for each case programming project.

Easiest: ★

Intermediate: ★★

Challenging: ★★★

Case Project 2–1: Youth Hostel App ★

Requirements Document

Application title:	Youth Hostel App
Purpose:	In a youth hostel reservations app, a hostel is selected and an address and other information are displayed.
Algorithms:	1. The opening screen displays the name of a hostel, an image, and a Button control (Figure 2-37). Research a real name of a hostel and address and cost range to display in your own customized app. 2. When the user selects a hostel, an address and a cost range are displayed in a second screen (Figure 2-38).
Note:	The hostel image is provided with your student files.

© iStock.com/LanceB

Figure 2-37 Youth Hostel app—first screen

Figure 2-38 Youth Hostel app—second screen

Case Project 2–2: Segway Rental App ★

Requirements Document

Application title:	Segway Rental App
Purpose:	In a Segway rental app, a Segway tour is selected and the Segway image is displayed with rental information.
Algorithms:	1. The opening screen displays the title of the app, a description, and a Button control (Figure 2-39). 2. When the user chooses to rent a Segway, an image displaying the Segway and tour price is shown (Figure 2-40).
Note:	The Segway image is provided with your student files.

Figure 2-39 Segway Rental app—first screen

Figure 2-40 Segway Rental app—second screen

Case Project 2–3: Your School App ★★

Requirements Document

Application title: Your School App

Purpose: This large app provides information on every school in your country. Create two screens for the app. You use the app to select the name of a school, and then display information about the selected school.

Algorithms:

1. The opening screen displays the name of your school, a picture of your school, and a Button control. Create your own layout.
2. The second screen displays the name of your school, a picture of your logo, the school address, and the phone number. Create your own layout.

Case Project 2–4: Business Card App ★★

Requirements Document

Application title: Business Card App

Purpose: This app provides your business card information with your own picture. Create two screens for the business card app. You use the app to select the name of a business contact, and then display detailed business card information.

Algorithms:

1. The opening screen displays the name of the contact, your picture converted to a .png file, and a Button control. Create your own layout.
2. The second screen displays your business card information. Create your own layout.

Case Project 2–5: Your Contacts App—Address Book ★★★

Requirements Document

Application title:	Your Contacts App—Address Book
Purpose:	This large app provides business contact information in an address book. Create two screens for contacts for the app. You use the app to select a particular contact, and then display that person's information.
Algorithms:	1. The opening screen displays two names of contacts with the last name starting with the letter J. Each contact has a separate Button control below the name. Create your own layout. 2. The second screen displays the name, address, phone number, and picture of the contact. Create your own layout.
Conditions:	Three Java classes and three XML layouts are needed.

Case Project 2–6: Latest Music Scene App ★★★

Requirements Document

Application title:	The Latest Music Scene
Purpose:	This large app called The Latest Music Scene contains the latest music news. Create two screens for two music news stories. You use the app to select a particular music news story title, and then display an image and a paragraph about the music news story.
Algorithms:	1. The opening screen displays two music news story titles that you can create based on the music stories in the news. Each music news story has a separate Button control below the name and displays a small image. Create your own layout. 2. The second screen displays the name of the music story and a paragraph detailing the news. Create your own layout.
Conditions:	Three Java classes and three XML layouts are needed.

CHAPTER 3

Engage! Android User Input, Variables, and Operations

In this chapter, you learn to:

- Use an Android theme
- Add a theme to the Android Manifest file
- Add text to the String table
- Add an XML array string to strings.xml
- Develop a user interface using Text Fields
- Describe the role of different Text Fields
- Display a hint using the hint property
- Develop a user interface using a Spinner control
- Add a prompt to a Spinner control
- Declare variables to hold data
- Code the GetText( ) method
- Understand arithmetic operations
- Convert numeric data
- Format numeric data
- Code the SetText( ) method
- Run the completed app in an emulator

In the Healthy Recipes app developed in Chapter 2, the user tapped or clicked a button in the user interface to trigger events, but not to enter data. In many applications, users enter data and the program uses the data in its processing. Engaging the user by requesting input customizes the user experience each time the application runs. When processing data entered by a user, a common requirement is to perform arithmetic operations on the data to generate useful output information. Arithmetic operations include adding, subtracting, multiplying, and dividing numeric data.

To illustrate the use of user data input and arithmetic operations, the Android app in this chapter allows the user to enter the number of concert tickets to purchase. The application then calculates the total cost of the concert tickets. Figure 3-1 shows the user interface for the app named Concert Tickets with the company name Ticket Vault displayed at the top of the screen.

Figure 3-1 Concert Tickets Android app

In Figure 3-2, the user entered 4 as the number of tickets to purchase. When the user clicked the FIND THE COST button, the program multiplied 4 times the concert ticket cost ($79.99) and then displayed the result as the total cost of the concert tickets, as shown in Figure 3-2. To create this application, the developer must understand how to perform the following processes, among others:

1. Apply a theme to the design of the Android screen.
2. Update the theme in the styles.xml file.

3. Define all text displayed in a String table using the Translations Editor.
4. Define the text displayed in the array using XML in the strings.xml file.
5. Define a Text Field control for data entry. For this app, the quantity of tickets entered should be a number. Using a specific Text Field for positive integers prevents users from entering an incorrect value.
6. Define a Spinner control to allow users to select the performance group.
7. Convert data to use it for arithmetic operations.
8. Perform arithmetic operations with the data the user enters.
9. Display formatted results.

Figure 3-2 Four tickets purchased for a concert

Android Themes

To prevent each Android app from looking too similar, the Android SDK includes multiple themes that provide individual flair to each application. A **theme** is a style applied to an Activity or an entire application. Themes are Android's mechanism for applying a consistent style to an app or Activity. The style specifies the visual properties of the elements that make up a user interface, such as color, height, padding, and font size. Some themes change the background wallpaper of the Activity, while others hide the title bar or display an action bar. Some themes display a background depending on the size of the mobile device. You can preview themes in the emulator in activity_main.xml. The default theme for Nexus 5 shows the title bar displaying the app name with a white background when running the app. Figure 3-3 displays the Holo. Light theme with a light translucent background and a title bar on the emulator. The light and transparent themes are sheer and allow you to see the starting home screen through the background. Figure 3-4 displays a Material theme (Material.Dialog.NoActionBar) for dialog boxes and Activities, with no action bar at the top. The Black theme shown in Figure 3-5 displays a black background with a gray title bar.

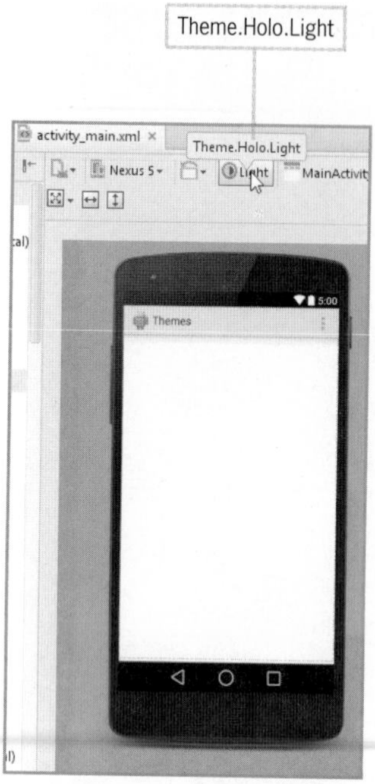

Figure 3-3 Holographic theme

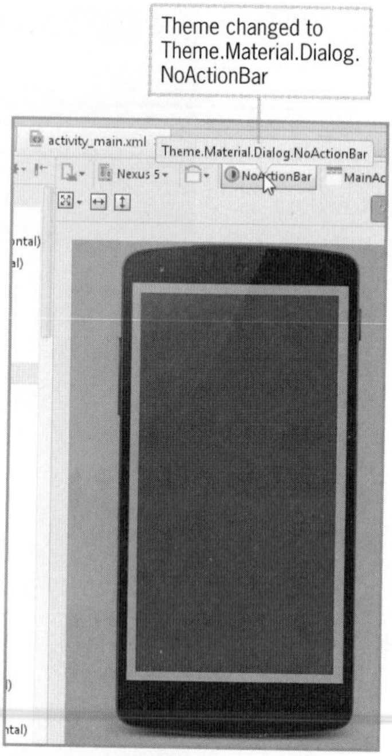

Figure 3-4 Material theme with no action bar

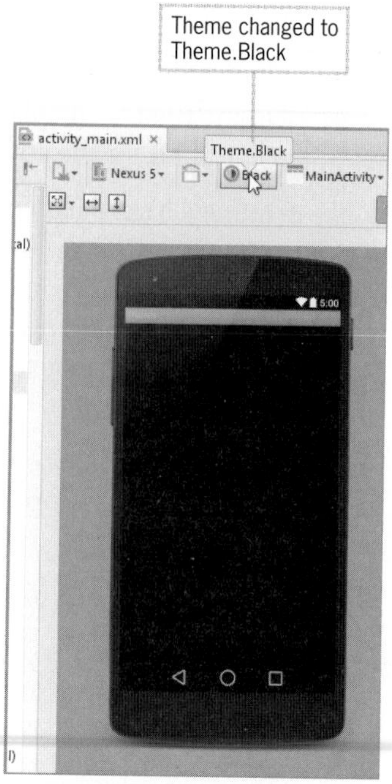

Figure 3-5 Black theme

Previewing a Theme

By changing the theme in the emulator in the activity_main.xml file, you can preview what the new theme looks like, but to change it permanently in the application, you must define the themes in the styles.xml file within the values subfolder for the Activity. After placing the theme in the styles.xml file, Android Studio updates the AndroidManifest.xml file to include the new theme. You can add a predefined system theme or a customized theme of your own design. The Concert Tickets chapter project uses the predefined system theme named Theme.Black.NoTitleBar. To create the Concert Tickets application and preview the Theme.Black.NoTitleBar theme, follow these steps:

STEP 1

- Open the Android Studio program.
- Tap or click Start a new Android Studio project in the Quick Start list.
- On the Configure your new project page of the Create New Project dialog box, enter **Concert Tickets** in the Application name text box.
- In the Company Domain text box, type **androidbootcamp.net**, if necessary.
- In the Project location text box, type **D:\Workspace\ConcertTickets**, if necessary.

A new application named Concert Tickets is configured to be saved on the D:\Workspace USB drive (Figure 3-6).

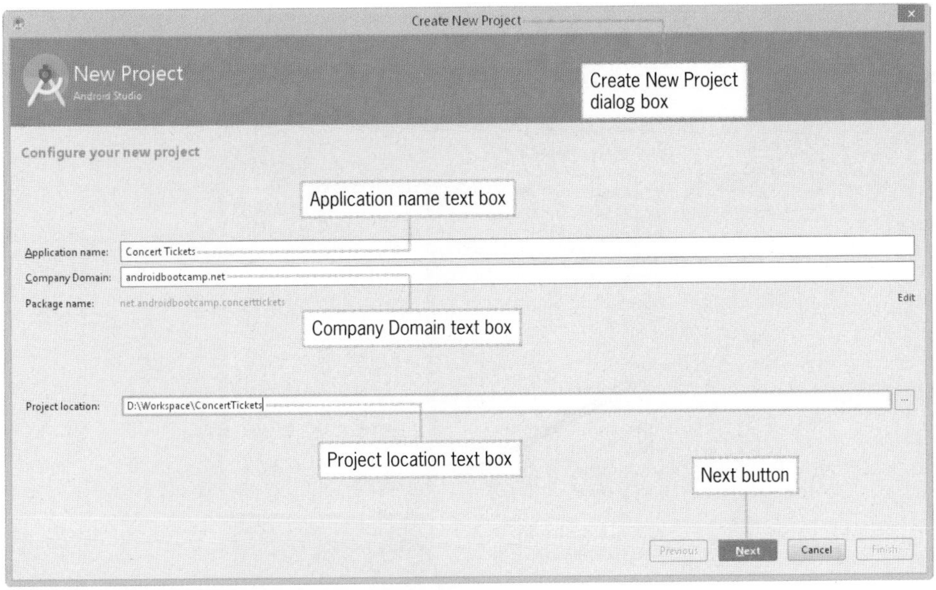

Figure 3-6 Configuring the Concert Tickets project

STEP 2

- Tap or click the Next button on the Configure your new project page.
- If necessary, tap or click the Phone and Tablet check box to select the form factor for running your app.
- Tap or click the Next button on the Select the form factors your app will run on page.
- If necessary, tap or click Blank Activity to add an Activity to the new project.
- Tap or click the Next button on the Add an activity to Mobile page.
- On the Choose options for your new file page, tap or click the Finish button.
- Tap or click the Hello world! TextView (displayed by default) in the emulator and press the Delete key.
- Tap or click 'the virtual device to render the layout with' button (emulator button) directly to the right of the Palette on the activity_main.xml tab, and then tap or click Nexus 5 (5.0", 1080 x 1920, xxhdpi).

The activity_main.xml file is displayed on the Design tab and the Hello world TextView widget is deleted (Figure 3-7). The emulator displays the default AppTheme.

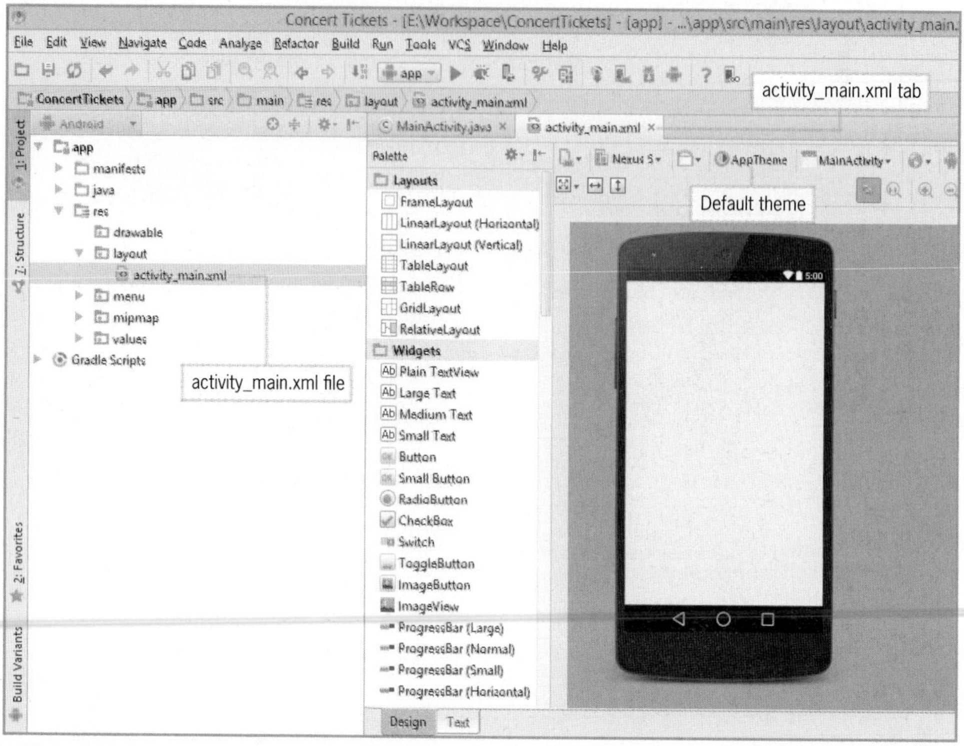

Figure 3-7 activity_main.xml for the Concert Tickets project

STEP 3

- Tap or click the AppTheme button to display a list of built-in themes in the Select Theme dialog box.
- In the search box in the upper-left section of the Select Theme dialog box, type **black**.

A list of themes with the text "black" in the name is displayed in the Select Theme dialog box (Figure 3-8).

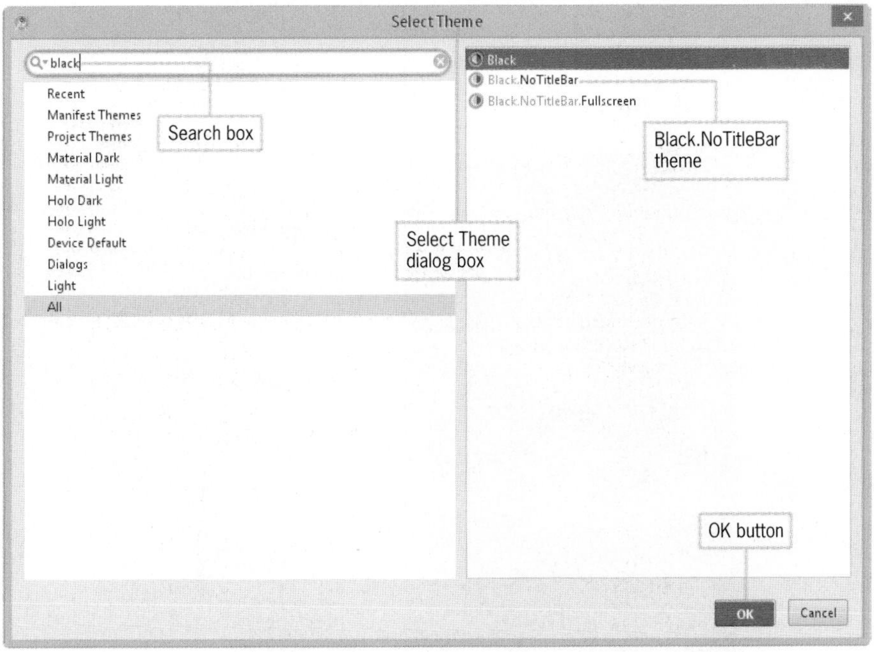

Figure 3-8 Select Theme dialog box

STEP 4

- Select Black.NoTitleBar and then tap or click the OK button.

The theme changes to Black.NoTitleBar. Android Studio removes the title bar in the emulator and displays the background as black (Figure 3-9).

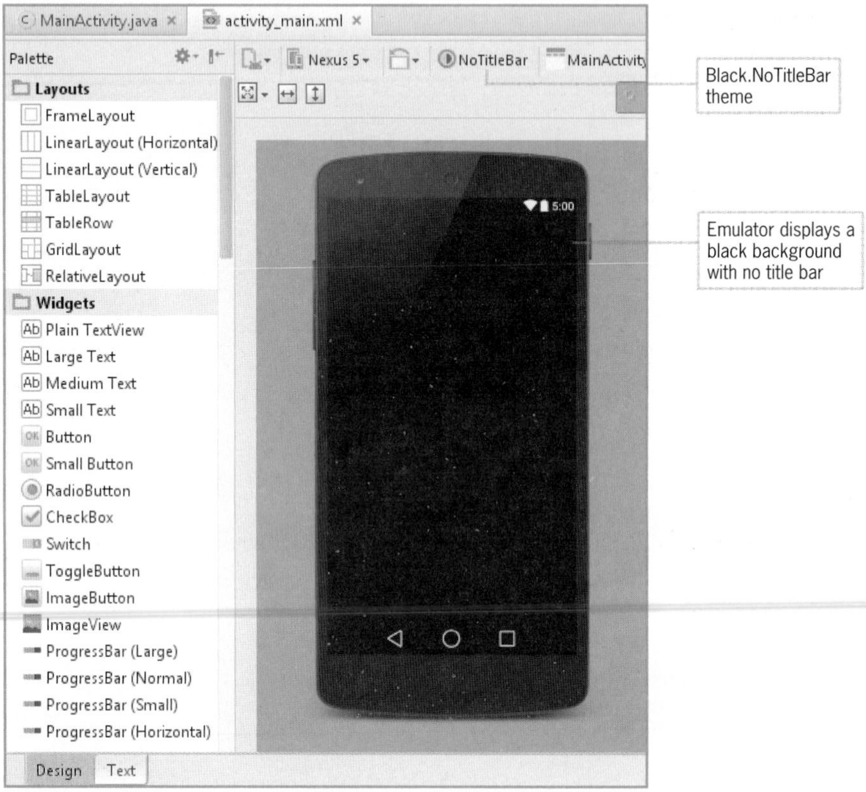

Figure 3-9 New theme applied

Updating the Theme in the styles.xml File

At this point, the theme appears only in the activity_main.xml graphical layout as a preview for design purposes, but to display the theme in the finished application, you must update the styles.xml file in the res/values folders to include the change in the theme layout. A theme is a style applied to an entire app, rather than an individual layout file. Table 3-1 displays a few samples of XML code for common themes.

Theme Code in styles.xml	Description
<style name="AppTheme" parent="Base.Theme.AppCompat">	Black background, grey title bar
<style name="AppTheme" parent=" Base.Theme.AppCompat.Light ">	White background, grey title bar
<style name="AppTheme" parent="Theme.AppCompat.Light.NoActionBar">	White background, no title bar

Table 3-1 XML code for common themes

After you add the new theme name to the XML code in the styles.xml file, Android Studio updates the AndroidManifest.xml file to include the new base application theme throughout all the Activities. To update the theme for the app within the styles.xml file, follow these steps:

STEP 1

- In the Android project view, expand the values subfolder and then double-tap or double-click the styles.xml file.
- Tap or click after the first quotation mark following parent= " and delete the current theme within the quotes.
- After the first quote, type **Base.Theme.AppCompat** allowing auto-complete to assist in spelling the theme name correctly.

The Android theme is updated within the Activity in the styles.xml file (Figure 3-10).

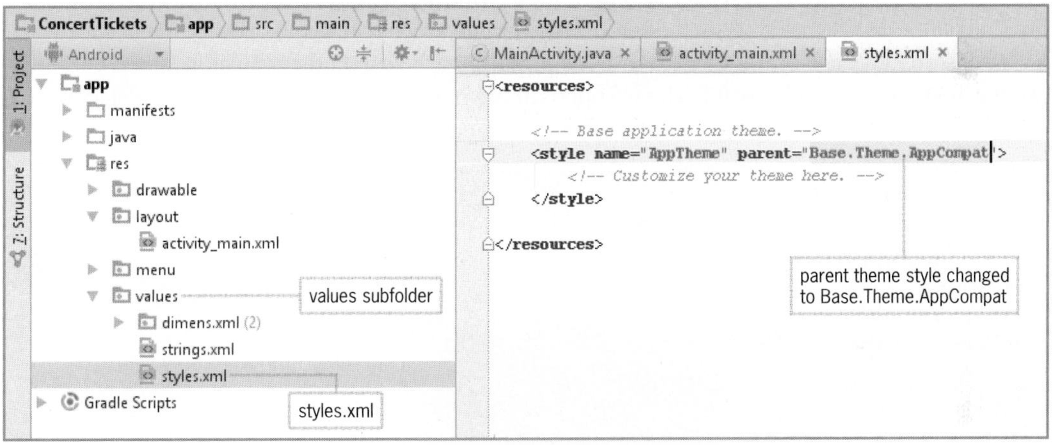

Figure 3-10 Updated theme coded in the styles.xml file

STEP 2

- Close the styles.xml tab and tap or click the Save All button on the Standard toolbar.

The AndroidManifest.xml file is updated by styles.xml to include the black theme when the app runs.

Simplifying User Input

On the Android phone, users can enter text in multiple ways that include entering input through an on-screen soft keyboard, an attached flip button hard keyboard, and even voice-to-text capabilities on most phone models. The on-screen keyboard is called a **soft keyboard**, which is positioned at the bottom of the screen over the application window. Touch input can vary from tapping the screen to using gestures. Gestures are multitouch interactions such as pressing two fingers to pan, rotate, or zoom. The primary design challenge for mobile web applications is how to simplify the user experience for an application that appears on screens measuring from a few inches square to much larger tablets. To meet the challenge and maximize the user experience, you need to use legible fonts, simplify input, and optimize each device's capabilities. Certain Android widgets such as those in the Text Fields category allow specific data types for user input, which simplifies data entry. For example, a numeric Text Field only accepts numbers from the on-screen keyboard, limiting accidental user input, such as by touching the wrong location on a small touchscreen.

IN THE TRENCHES

A decade ago, nearly every mobile phone offered an alphanumeric keypad as part of the device. Today a touchscreen full QWERTY keyboard is available to allow users to enter information, engage in social networking, surf the Internet, and view multimedia.

Using Android Text Fields

In the Concert Tickets application shown in Figure 3-1, the user enters the quantity of tickets that he or she intends to purchase to attend the concert event. The most common type of mobile input is text entered by touch input from the soft (on-screen) keyboard or the attached keyboard used by a tablet. An app can request user keyboard input with the Text Field controls in the Android Studio Palette (Figure 3-11). With Text Fields, the input can be received on the mobile device with an on-screen keyboard or the user can use the physical keyboard on the emulator. When you tap the Text Field control, a soft keyboard opens at the bottom of the Android device. Select the characters/numbers from the keyboard and tap the check mark to enter the selected values.

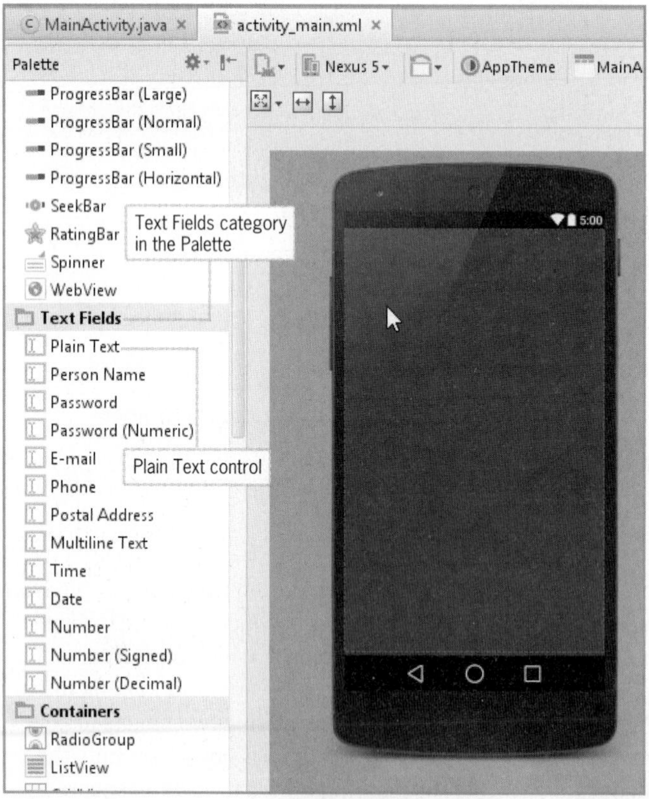

Figure 3-11 Text Fields category

A mobile application's Text Field controls can request different input types, such as plain text (a person's name, password, email address, phone number; postal code, multiline text, a time, a date) and numbers. You need to select the correct Text Field for the specific type of data you are requesting. As shown in Figure 3-11, each Text Field control allows you to enter a specific data type from the keyboard. For example, if you select the Phone Number Text Field, Android deactivates the letters on the keyboard because letters are not part of a phone number.

GTK

The AutoComplete TextView control can suggest the completion of a word after the user begins typing the first few letters. For example, if the input control is requesting the name of a city where the user wants to book a hotel, you could suggest the completed name from a coded listing of city names that match the prefix entered by the user.

In the chapter project, the Concert Tickets application requests the number of concert tickets. This quantity is an integer value because you cannot purchase part of a ticket. By selecting the Number Text Field, users can enter only positive integers from the keyboard. The app does not accept letters and symbols from the keyboard, which saves you time as the developer because you do not have to write lengthy data validation code.

IN THE TRENCHES

An application with an appealing graphical design is preferred over applications that are mostly text. Good graphic design communicates simplicity and engages the user.

Adding a Text Field

In the Concert Tickets application, a single screen opens when the application runs, with a Number Text Field requesting the number of concert tickets desired. One way to name a Text Field is to use the id property in the Properties pane to enter a name that begins with the prefix txt, which represents a text field in the code. The Java code uses the id property to refer to the widget. A descriptive variable name such as txtTickets can turn an unreadable piece of code into one that is well documented and easy to debug.

Using the String Table

The string items that are displayed in the controls in this app will not be typed directly in the Properties pane, but instead in a string array in the res/values folder. In the Concert Tickets app, the first TextView control displays the text Ticket Vault, and the Button control displays the text FIND THE COST. You also need text to prompt users to enter text and to display a description of the concert image shown on the screen. You add the names of groups performing at the concert in later steps using XML code. To add the Key and Default Value text for Text Field, Button, and ImageView controls to the strings.xml file, follow these steps.

STEP 1

- Double-tap or double-click the strings.xml file in the values subfolder to display its contents.
- Tap or click the Open editor link.

- Tap or click the Add Key (plus sign) button in the Translations Editor.
- In the Key text box, type **txtTitle** to name the string.
- In the Default Value text box, type **Ticket Vault** to define the text.

The Key and Default Value of the TextView control are entered into the strings.xml Translations Editor within a dialog box (Figure 3-12).

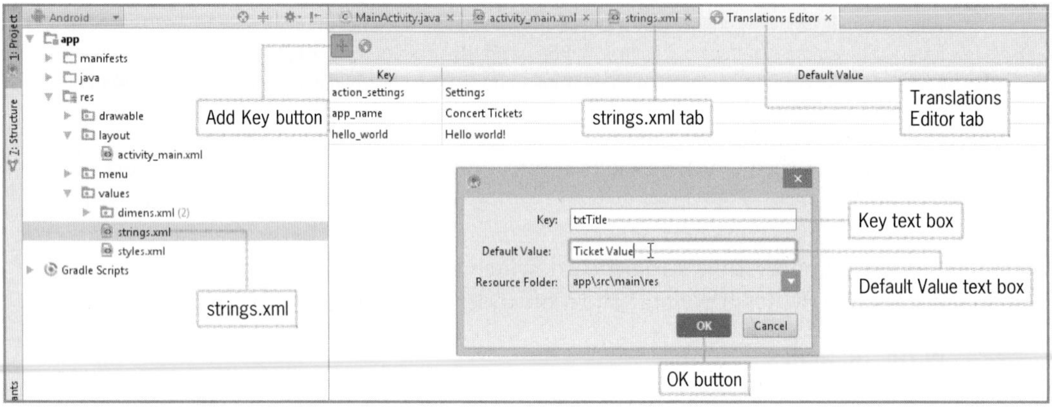

Figure 3-12 Adding strings

STEP 3

- Tap or click the OK button to add txtTitle to the String table.
- Tap or click the Add Key button and then add the strings in Table 3-2 to the Translations Editor using the techniques learned in earlier chapters.

Key	Default Value
txtTickets	Number of Tickets
prompt	Select Group
description	Concert Image
btnCost	FIND THE COST

Table 3-2 String table text

The Keys and Default Values of the Text Field, Button, and ImageView controls are entered into the strings.xml file (Figure 3-13).

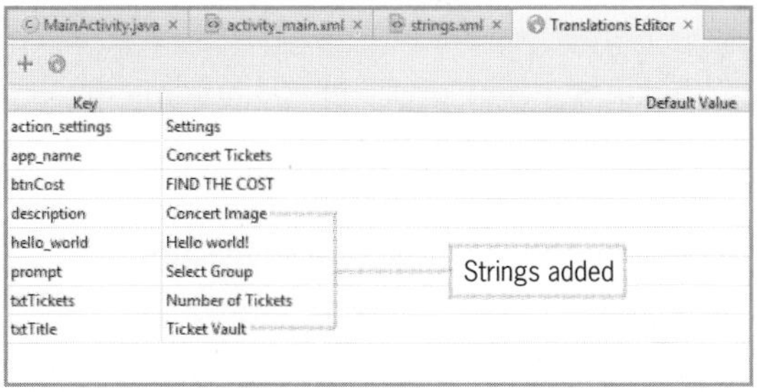

Figure 3-13 Multiple strings added to the Translations Editor

STEP 3

- Close the Translations Editor tab.

Adding a String Array

The TextView, Spinner, Button, and ImageView controls each reference an individual string of text assigned in the strings.xml file, but if a control holds multiple text strings, it is best to use a **string array** that can be referenced from the String Resources in the application. A string array defines a string resource of related items in a central location within strings.xml. In the Concert Tickets app, the user can select one of three performance groups: Life Revealed, Spatial Sense, and Zig Zag. Each of the three concert groups is an **item** within the string array. An item defines an individual entry within a string array. You place the text items representing the performance groups in strings.xml as a string array resource tied together within one array name. You can populate a control such as a Spinner with a string array resource by adding XML code in strings.xml.

Android Studio has a considerable amount of built-in knowledge of XML syntax and Java programming methods that you can use to complete your code. As you type the String array XML code, the Android Studio editor offers suggestions in a panel that can complete the statement. Figure 3-14 shows the editor suggesting possibilities for the string-array statement in the strings.xml window. By selecting the second suggestion in Figure 3-14 and then pressing Ctrl+period, you add the correct syntax to the statement. As you type an XML or Java line of code, Android Studio refines and add suggestions where appropriate. If a suggestion is not displayed automatically, you can manually press Ctrl+space to invoke possible code completion suggestions. All XML code begins with a less than (<) symbol and ends with a greater than (>) symbol. To add a string array to the strings.xml file to represent the three concert groups using code completion, follow these steps.

STEP 1

- Tap or click in the strings.xml window and add line numbers by pressing and holding or right-clicking the gray margin to the left of the code and then tapping or clicking Show Line Numbers.

- Tap or click Line 10, press Enter, and type **<s** to view the auto-completion suggestions.

Auto-completion suggestions are displayed in the strings.xml code window (Figure 3-14).

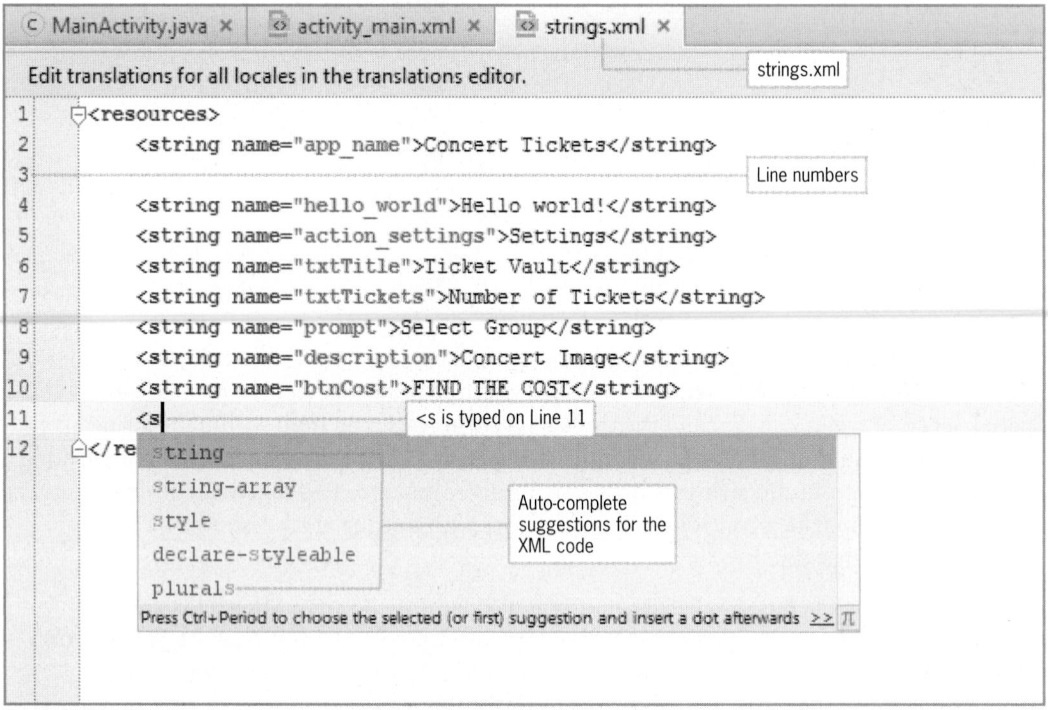

Figure 3-14 XML code auto-completion suggestions

STEP 2

- Tap or click string-array and press Ctrl+period to add the suggested XML code for a string array.
- Tap or click between the quotation marks in Line 11 and replace the period between the quotation marks by typing **txtGroup** to name the text array that holds the three concert group names.
- Tap or click after the closing quote, type **>** to end the string-array name statement, and then press Enter.

The string-array XML code named txtGroup is added. The closing statement </string-array> is added automatically by the editor in Android Studio (Figure 3-15).

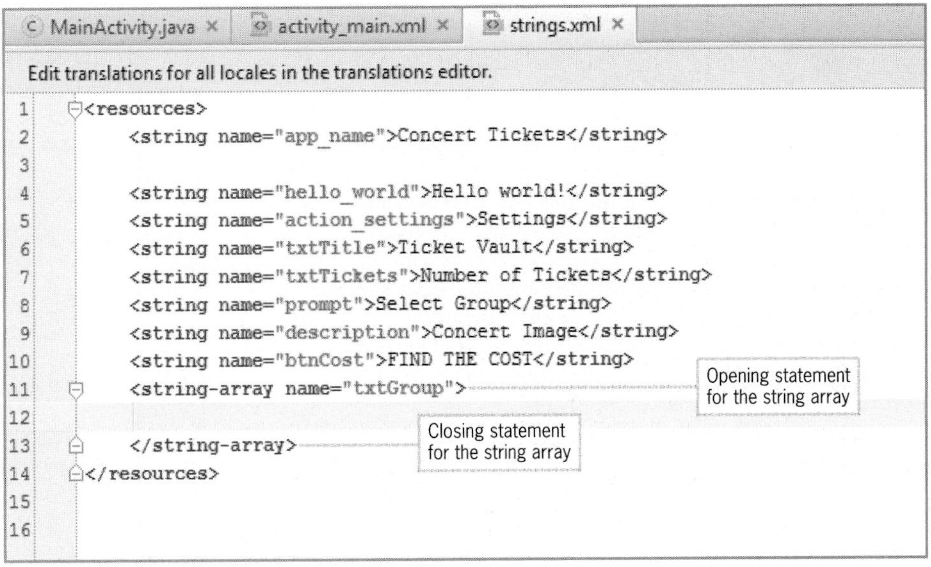

Figure 3-15 Opening and closing XML statements of the string array

STEP 3

- Type **<item>** and let the editor automatically add the closing statement, </item>.
- If necessary, tap or click between the opening and closing XML item statements and type **Life Revealed** as the name of the first item in the txtGroup array.
- Add a new line, type **<item>Spatial Sense**, and let the editor automatically add the closing item XML code.
- On the next line, type **<item>Zig Zag** and let the editor automatically add the closing item XML code.

Three items are added to the txtGroup String array (Figure 3-16).

MainActivity.java × activity_main.xml × strings.xml ×

Edit translations for all locales in the translations editor.

```
<resources>
    <string name="app_name">Concert Tickets</string>

    <string name="hello_world">Hello world!</string>
    <string name="action_settings">Settings</string>
    <string name="txtTitle">Ticket Vault</string>
    <string name="txtTickets">Number of Tickets</string>
    <string name="prompt">Select Group</string>
    <string name="description">Concert Image</string>
    <string name="btnCost">FIND THE COST</string>
    <string-array name="txtGroup">
        <item>Life Revealed</item>
        <item>Spatial Sense</item>
        <item>Zig Zag</item>
    </string-array>
</resources>
```

Three groups added to the txtGroup string-array XML code

Figure 3-16 string-array with three items added

GTK

Another use of auto completion is statement completion. Press Shift+Ctrl+Enter (Shift-Cmd-Enter on Mac OS X) to automatically fill the closing code portions when possible.

After the strings and string arrays are set, you can add controls to the emulator. To begin the design of the emulator screen and to add a TextView and Text Field controls, follow these steps:

STEP 1

- Tap or click the Save All button on the Standard toolbar and close the strings.xml tab.
- With activity_main.xml open and displaying the emulator screen, drag and drop the Plain TextView widget onto the top part of the emulator.
- To center the TextView control, drag the control to the center of the screen until a green dashed vertical line identifying the screen's center is displayed.
- Double-tap or double-click the TextView object on the emulator to display the text and id editing panel.
- In the id text box, type **txtTitle** to name the TextView object.

- Tap or click the ellipsis button (three dots) to the right of the text property text box in the editing panel.
- Scroll down the Resources listing below the Projects tab to locate txtTitle, tap or click txtTitle, and then tap or click the OK button.
- In the textSize property, type **48sp** and then press Enter.

The text resource txtTitle from the strings.xml file is selected and the text Ticket Vault is displayed in the size of 48 scalable pixels (Figure 3-17).

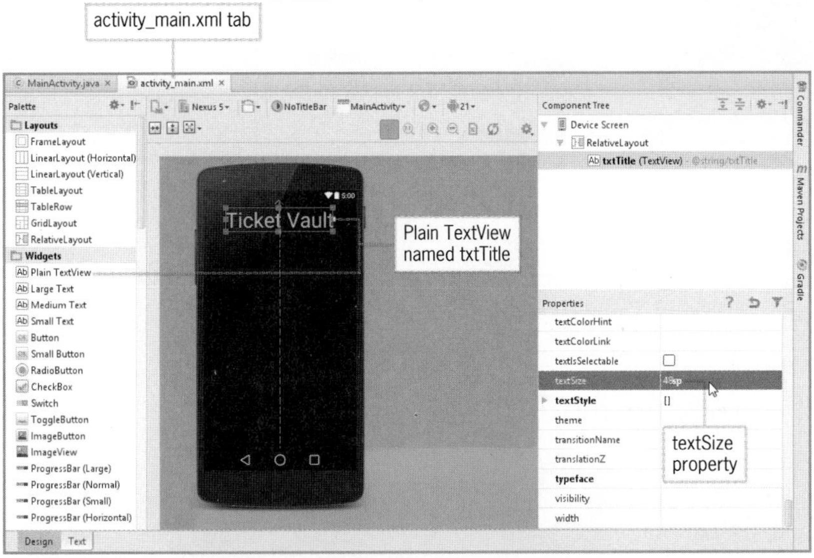

Figure 3-17 Title added to emulator

STEP 2

- Scroll down to the Text Fields category in the Palette.
- Drag and drop the Number Text Field control onto the emulator below the Ticket Vault text.
- Drag the control to the center of the screen until a green dashed vertical line identifying the screen's center is displayed.
- Double-tap or double-click the Text Field object and type **txtTickets** in the id text box to reference this control later in the Java code.
- Set the textSize property to **36sp** and press Enter.

A Number Text Field control named txtTickets with the size of 36sp is added to the emulator to allow the user to enter the number of tickets (Figure 3-18).

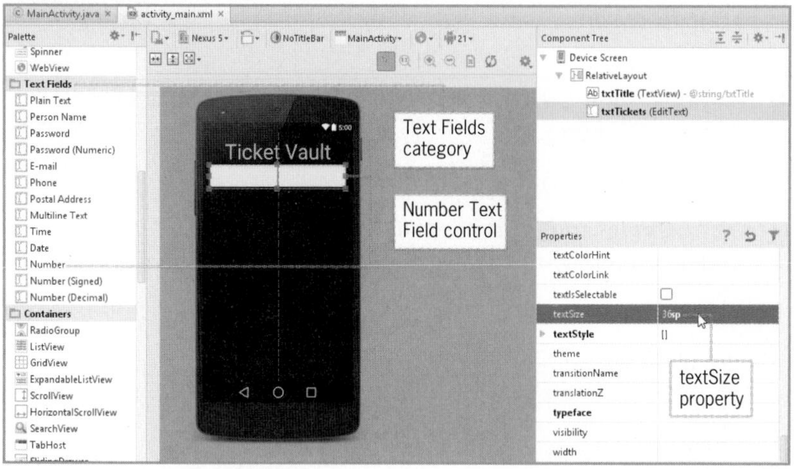

Figure 3-18 String Array

IN THE TRENCHES

Chromecast, a popular Google online entertainment system, provides HDTV movies, television shows, and music from Google Play apps.

Setting the Hint Property for the Text Field

When the Concert Tickets program runs, the user needs guidelines about the input expected in the Text Field control. These guidelines can be included in the hint property of the Text Field control. A **hint** is a short description of a field that is visible as light-colored text (also called a watermark) inside a Text Field control. Instead of typing the hint directly into the hint property, the preferred way is to enter the value in the String table. When the user taps or clicks the control, the hint is removed and the user is free to type the requested input. The purpose of the hint in Figure 3-19 is to request expected values in this field, without the user having to select and delete default text.

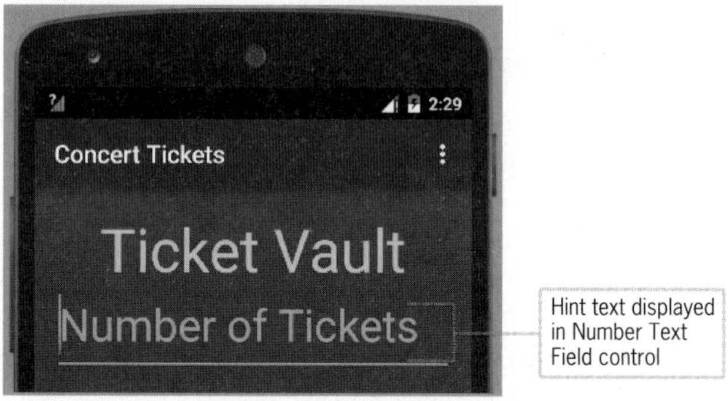

Figure 3-19 Hint in Text Field control

To set the hint property for the Text Field control, follow these steps:

STEP 1

- With the txtTickets Text Field control selected on the emulator, scroll the Properties pane and then tap or click to the right of the hint property.
- Tap or click the ellipsis button of the hint property.
- Scroll down the Resources dialog box and tap or click txtTickets to select the assigned string.

The hint text txtTickets is selected in the Resources dialog box (Figure 3-20).

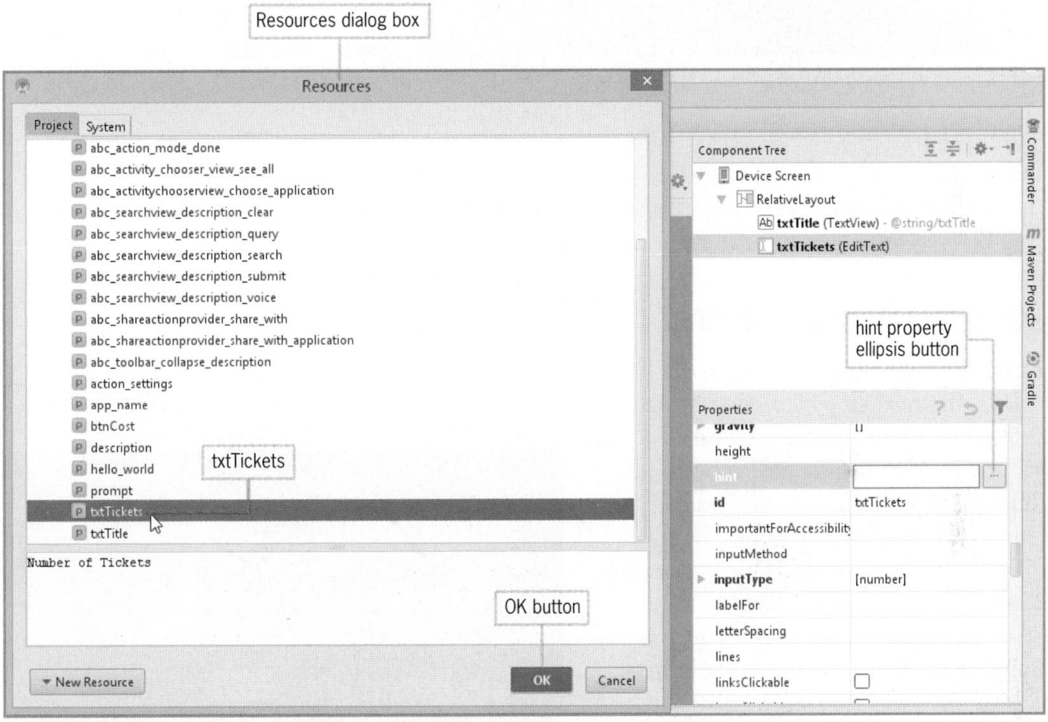

Figure 3-20 Resources dialog box for hint property of the Text Field control

STEP 2

- Tap or click the OK button.

A watermark hint requests the number of tickets as input in the Text Field control (Figure 3-21).

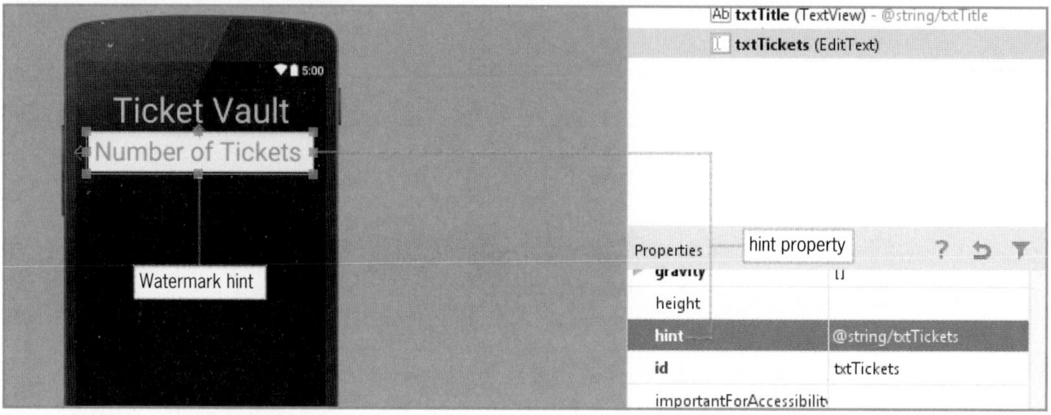

Figure 3-21 Hint added to Text Field control

GTK
If your activity_main.xml emulator fails to update, try saving your project to update the emulator. You can also refresh your Android Studio project by tapping or clicking Build on the menu bar, and then tapping or clicking Clean Project.

Using the Android Spinner Control

After the user enters the number of tickets, the next step is to select which concert to attend. Three musical groups are performing next month: Life Revealed, Spatial Sense, and Zig Zag. Due to possible user error on a small on-screen keyboard, it is much easier for a user to use a Spinner control instead of actually typing the group names. A **Spinner control** is a widget similar to a drop-down list for selecting a single item using touch from a fixed listing, as shown in Figure 3-22. The Spinner control displays a prompt with a list of strings called items assigned in strings.xml in a pop-up window without taking up multiple lines on the initial display.

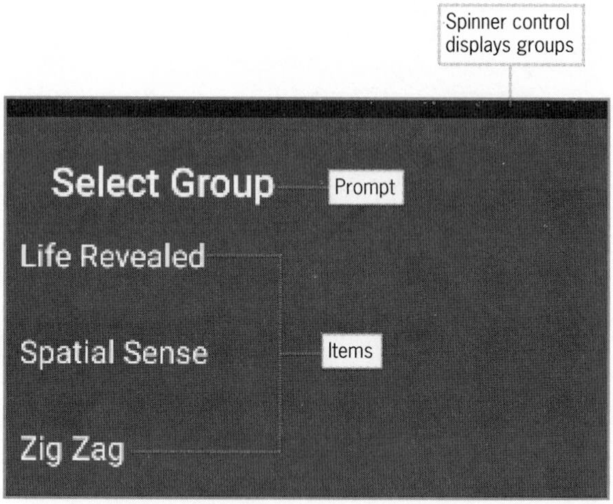

Figure 3-22 Spinner control

In the Concert Tickets app, a String array for the Spinner control named txtGroup is necessary to hold the three concert group names as individual string resources in strings.xml. The strings.xml resources file provides an easy way to update commonly used strings throughout your project, instead of searching through code and properties to alter a string array within the application. For example, each month the concert planners can simply change the text in the strings.xml file to reflect their new concert events. A **prompt**, which can be used to display instructions at the top of the Spinner control using the prompt property, also is stored in strings.xml and is named prompt.

The Spinner property called **entries** connects the string array in strings.xml to the Spinner control so it can be displayed in the application. The Spinner control is located in the Widgets category of the Palette. As you define the Spinner control, the spinnerMode property sets the Spinner control to either the dialog mode or dropdown mode. The dialog mode use a pop-up dialog box for selecting the Spinner items. The dropdown mode displays the items in a list box. The following steps add the Spinner control to the Android application using the dialog mode:

STEP 1

- With the activity_main.xml tab open, scroll to view the Widgets category in the Palette.
- Drag and drop the Spinner control below the Text Field and center it horizontally.
- Double-tap or double-click the Spinner object and type **txtGroup** in the id text box.
- Tap or click the spinnerMode arrow.

The spinnerMode property displays the options for the Spinner control named txtGroup (Figure 3-23).

Figure 3-23 spinnerMode property options

STEP 2

- Tap or click the dialog mode.
- In the Properties pane, tap or click to the right of the prompt property.
- Tap or click the ellipsis button to display the Resources dialog box.
- Scroll down and tap or click prompt to display instructions when the user touches the Spinner control.
- Tap or click the OK button.
- In the Properties pane, tap or click to the right of the entries property.
- Type **@array/txtGroup** and press Enter to reference the three items added to the strings.xml file to display the String array in the Spinner control when the app runs.

The prompt property connects to the resource named @string/prompt. The entries property connects to the resources of the String Array @array/txtGroup. The actual groups are displayed in the Spinner when the app is executed in the emulator (Figure 3-24).

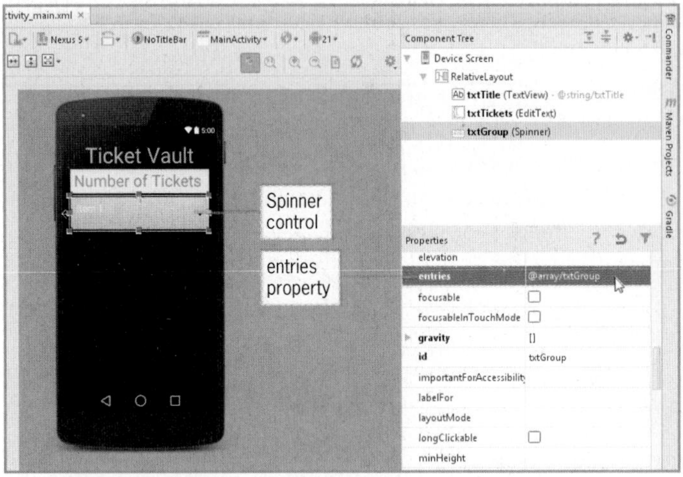

Figure 3-24 Spinner control prompt and entries properties

Adding the Button, TextView, and ImageView Controls

After the user enters the number of tickets and the concert group name, the user taps the FIND THE COST button to calculate the cost with a Button event. The app calculates the total cost by multiplying the number of tickets by the cost of each ticket ($79.99), and then displays the name of the group and total cost of the tickets in a TextView control.

An ImageView control displayed on an Android device should be accessible to everyone. Accessibility should be addressed for people with limited or no vision, who might be using a built-in screen reader to assist them in using the app. An ImageView control should have a content description for those who cannot see the image. For example, the Concert Tickets app displays a picture of a concert. By setting the contentDescription property for the ImageView control to the String text "Concert Image," the viewer can imagine what the image looks like based on your description.

An image file named concert.png, provided with your student files, is displayed in an ImageView control for the Concert Tickets app. You should already have the student files for this text that your instructor gave you or that you downloaded from the webpage for this book (www.cengagebrain.com). To add the Button, TextView, and ImageView controls to the emulator, follow these steps:

STEP 1

- In the activity_main.xml tab, drag the Button control from the Widgets category in the Palette to the emulator and center it below the Spinner control.

- Double-tap or double-click the Button object and type **btnCost** in the id text box to reference this control later in the Java code.
- Tap or click the ellipsis button to the right of the text property.
- Scroll down and tap or click btnCost and then tap or click the OK button.
- Change the textSize property to **34sp**. Save your work.

The Button control named btnCost displays the text FIND THE COST from the btnCost String and the size is changed to 34sp (Figure 3-25).

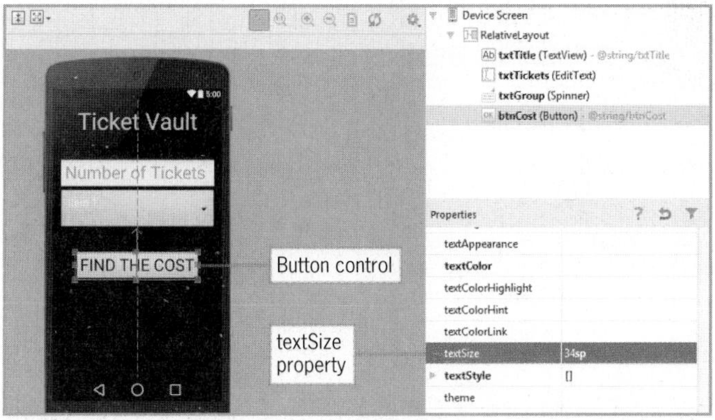

Figure 3-25 Adding a Button control

STEP 2

- From the Widgets category in the Palette, drag the Plain TextView control to the emulator and center it below the Button control.
- Double-tap or double-click the Plain TextView object and type **txtResult** to the right of the id property.
- Delete the text New Text shown in the text property.
- In the Properties pane, tap or click to the right of the textSize property, type **22sp**, and then press Enter.

The txtResult TextView control is added to the emulator with the Text property blank (Figure 3-26).

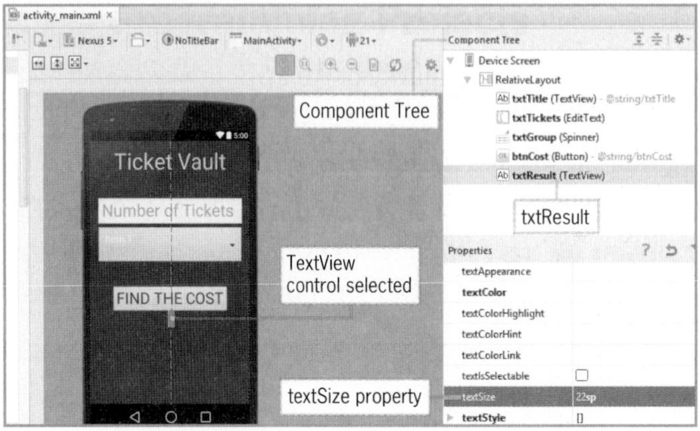

Figure 3-26 Adding a TextView control to display results

Critical Thinking
The Plain TextField object is difficult to locate because it does not have text in the text property. Is there an easier way to locate it?
Yes. Tap or click the txtResult object in the Component Tree.

STEP 3

- To add the ImageView control, first copy the student files to your USB drive (if necessary).
- Open the USB folder containing the student files.
- Copy the concert.png file from the USB folder and press and hold or right-click the drawable folder in the Android project view pane. Tap or click Paste.
- Tap or click the OK button in the Copy dialog box.
- In the activity_main.xml tab, drag the ImageView control to the emulator and center it below the TextView control at the bottom of the emulator.
- In the id property of the Properties pane, type **imgConcert** to name the ImageView object.
- Tap or click the ellipsis button (three dots) to the right of the src property in the Properties pane, scroll down the Resources listing, tap or click concert in the Drawable category to select the image from the drawable folder, and then tap or click the OK button.
- With the image selected, tap or click the ellipsis button to the right of the contentDescription property in the Properties pane. Select description, and then tap or click the OK button.

The concert image is displayed at the bottom of the emulator with a content description for accessibility purposes (Figure 3-27).

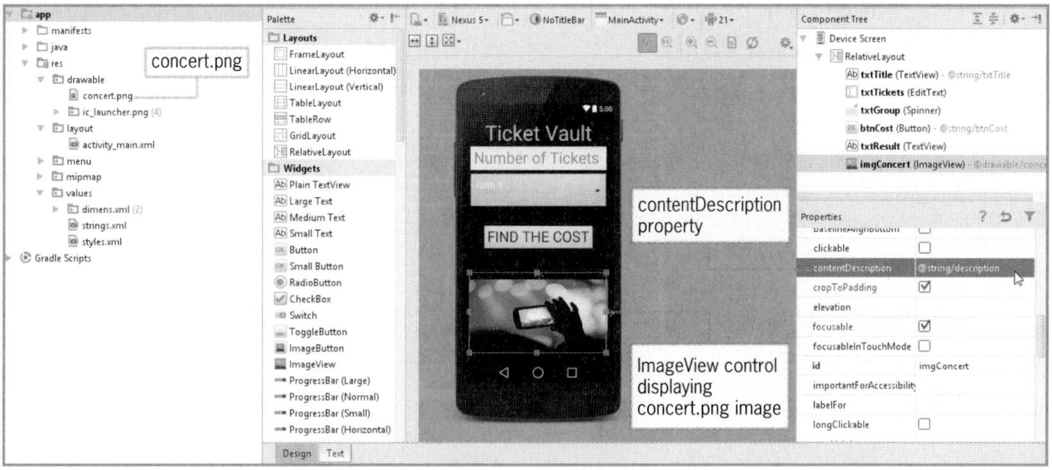

Figure 3-27 Adding an ImageView control

Coding the EditText Class for the Text Field

To handle the input that the user enters into the numeric Text Field control in the chapter project, you use the EditText class, which extracts the text and converts it for use in the Java code. The code must assign the extracted text to a variable. A Java program uses a **variable** to contain data that changes during the execution of the program. In the chapter project, a variable named tickets holds the text entered in the Text Field for the number of tickets. The following code syntax declares (or initializes) the tickets variable, which contains the extracted EditText class text from the user's input. Notice the code syntax begins with the word **final**, indicating that tickets is a final variable. A final variable can be initialized only once; any attempt to reassign the value results in a compile error when the application runs.

Code Syntax

```
final EditText tickets = (EditText)findViewById(R.id.txtTickets);
```

GTK

You can include spaces before and after the equal sign or you can omit them. Java considers either format correct.

Recall that if you want to refer to a control in the Java code, you can use the id property to name the control when you add it to the interface. For example, the Text Field control has the id txtTickets. Now you can access the control in the code using the findViewById( ) method. In the parentheses, the R refers to resources available to the app, such as a layout control, the Id indicates that the resource is identified by the id property, and txtTickets is the assigned id.

Next, assign the txtTickets Text Field control to the variable named tickets. To collect the ticket input from the user, code the EditText class for the Text Field by following this step:

STEP 1

- In the Android project view, expand the java folder and the first net.androidbootcampconcerttickets, and then double-tap or double-click MainActivity to open the code window.
- If necessary, display the line numbers.
- Delete Lines 18-38 to simplify the code window.
- Tap or click to the right of the line setContentView(R.layout.*activity_main*);.
- Press Enter to insert a blank line.
- To initialize and reference the EditText class with the Id name of txtTickets, type **final EditText tickets = (EditText)findViewById(R.id.txtTickets);**.
- Tap or click the first EditText displayed in red text, press Alt+Enter, and then select Import Class to import the Java library for the EditText control.

The EditText class extracts the value from the user's input for the number of tickets and assigns the value to the variable named tickets. Variables that the program has not used appear in gray text. This color is removed when a value is assigned later in the program (Figure 3-28).

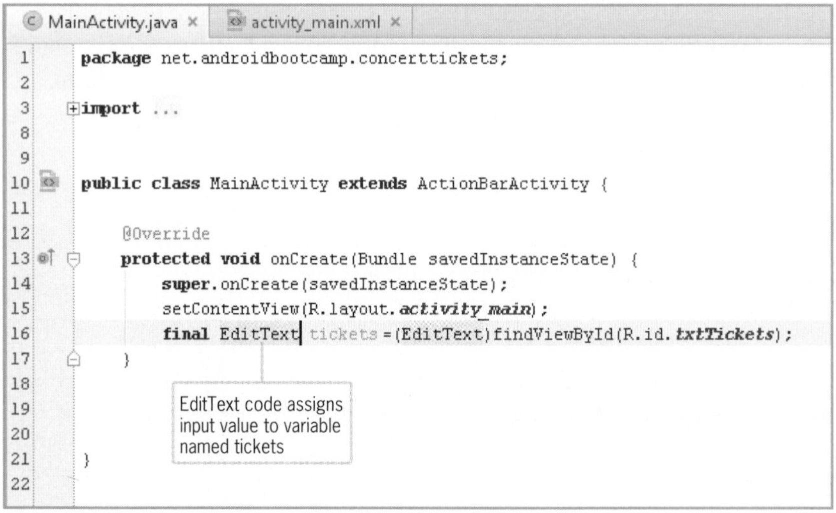

Figure 3-28 Coding the EditText class for the Text Field

Coding the Spinner Control

The user's selection of the concert group must also be assigned to a text variable and stored in the computer's memory. For this application, assign the selection made from the Spinner control (txtGroup) to a variable named group using the following code:

Code Syntax

```
final Spinner group = (Spinner)findViewById(R.id.txtGroup);
```

To collect the input from the user's group selection, code the Spinner control by following this step:

STEP 1

- After the EditText line, press Enter to create a new line.
- To initialize and reference the Spinner control with the Id name of txtGroup, type **final Spinner group = (Spinner)findViewById(R.id.txtGroup);**.
- Tap or click the red text Spinner, press Alt+Enter, and then select Import Class to import the Spinner control.

The Spinner control assigns the value from the user's input to the variable named group (Figure 3-29).

Figure 3-29 Coding the Spinner control

Instantiating the Button Control

After the user inputs the number of tickets and the concert group name, the onClickListener waits patiently in the background and listens for the user to tap or click the FIND THE COST button to calculate the cost in a Button event. The Button event OnClick handler executes the portion of code that calculates the cost of the tickets when the button is touched. After the app calculates the total cost by multiplying the number of tickets by the cost of each ticket ($79.99), the name of the group and total cost of the tickets are displayed in a TextView control. The TextView control is instantiated to the variable named result using the following code:

Code Syntax

```
final TextView result = ((TextView)findViewById(R.id.txtResult));
```

To instantiate the Button control, set up the Button listener, and initiate the TextView control. To display the results, follow these steps:

STEP 1

- If necessary, tap or click to the right of the code line that assigned the Spinner control to the variable named group, and then press Enter.
- To initialize the Button control with the id of btnCost, type **Button cost = (Button)findViewById(R.id.btnCost);**.
- Tap or click Button (red text), press Alt+Enter, and then select Import Class to import the Button control as an Android widget. Press Enter at the end of the statement.

The Button control is initialized and the Button type is imported (Figure 3-30).

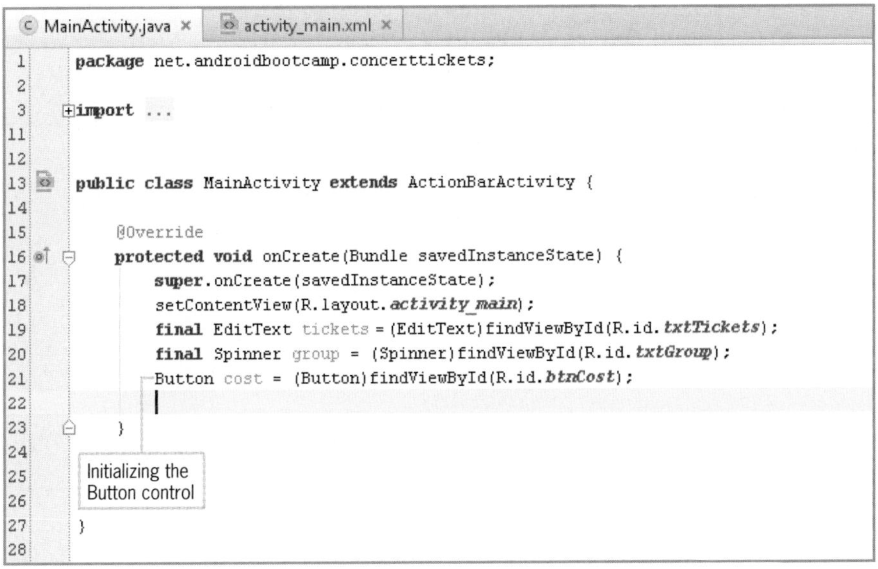

Figure 3-30 Instantiated Button class

STEP 2

- To code the button listener that awaits user interaction, type **cost.seton** to display an auto-complete listing with all the possible entries that are valid at that point in the code.
- Double-tap or double-click the first setOnClickListener to select it from the auto-complete listing.
- In the parentheses, type **new On** (must have an uppercase 'O') to view possible auto complete options, and then double-tap or double-click the OnClickListener option.

The Button control is initialized and an OnClickListener auto-generated stub appears in the code window (Figure 3-31).

MainActivity.java × activity_main.xml ×

```
1   package net.androidbootcamp.concerttickets;
2
3   import ...
12
13
14  public class MainActivity extends ActionBarActivity {
15
16      @Override
17      protected void onCreate(Bundle savedInstanceState) {
18          super.onCreate(savedInstanceState);
19          setContentView(R.layout.activity_main);
20          final EditText tickets = (EditText)findViewById(R.id.txtTickets);
21          final Spinner group = (Spinner)findViewById(R.id.txtGroup);
22          Button cost = (Button)findViewById(R.id.btnCost);
23          cost.setOnClickListener(new View.OnClickListener() {
24              @Override
25              public void onClick(View v) {
26
27              }
28          });
29      }
30
31
32
33  }
34
```

Button OnClickListener

Figure 3-31 Initializing the OnClickListener

STEP 3

- After the line of code beginning with cost.setOnClickListener in Line 23, press Enter, and then type **final TextView result = ((TextView)findViewById(R.id.txtResult));**.
- Tap or click TextView and import the TextView widget.

The TextView control txtResult is assigned to the variable named result (Figure 3-32).

MainActivity.java × activity_main.xml ×

```java
package net.androidbootcamp.concerttickets;

import ...


public class MainActivity extends ActionBarActivity {

    @Override
    protected void onCreate(Bundle savedInstanceState) {
        super.onCreate(savedInstanceState);
        setContentView(R.layout.activity_main);
        final EditText tickets = (EditText)findViewById(R.id.txtTickets);
        final Spinner group = (Spinner)findViewById(R.id.txtGroup);
        Button cost = (Button)findViewById(R.id.btnCost);
        cost.setOnClickListener(new View.OnClickListener() {
            final TextView result = ((TextView)findViewById(R.id.txtResult));
            @Override
            public void onClick(View v) {

            }
        });
    }



}
```

txtResult TextView control assigned to result variable

Figure 3-32 TextView control code

Critical Thinking

How can I combine the Button control with the ImageView control to create a button with an image overlay?

The ImageButton control displays a button with an image instead of text that the user can tap or click. Place the image in the drawable folder and then reference the picture as the source of your ImageButton.

GTK

Variable names are case sensitive and should be mixed case (camel case) when they include more than one word, as in costPerItem. Java variables cannot start with a number or special symbol. Subsequent characters in the variable name may be letters, digits, dollar signs, or underscore characters.

Declaring Variables

As you have seen, the user can enter data in the program using a Text Field control. In the Concert Tickets app, a mathematical equation multiplies the number of tickets by the cost of the tickets to calculate the total cost. When writing programs, it is convenient to use variables instead of the actual data such as the cost of a ticket ($79.99). As you learned in the previous section, two steps are necessary in order to use a variable:

1. Declare the variable.
2. Assign a value to the variable.

The declared type of a value determines which operations are allowed. At the core of Java code are eight built-in primitive (simple) types of data.

Primitive Data Types

Java requires all variables to have a data type. Table 3-3 lists the primitive data types that all computer platforms support, including the Android SDK.

Type	Meaning	Range	Default Value
byte	Often used with arrays	–128 to 127	0
short	Often used with arrays	–32,768 to 32,767	0
int	Most commonly used number value	–2,147,483,648 to 2,147,483,647	0
long	Used for numbers that exceed int	–9,223,372,036,854,775,808 to 9,223,372,036,854,775,807	0
float	A single precision 32-bit floating-point number	+/–3.40282347 ^38	0
double	Most common for decimal values	+/–1.79769313486231570 ^308	0
char	Single character	Characters	0
boolean	Used for conditional statement	True or false	False

Table 3-3 Primitive data types in Java

In the Concert Tickets program, the tickets cost $79.99 each. To declare this cost, use a double data type, which is appropriate for decimal values. A statement should both declare the variable and assign a value for costPerTicket, as shown in the following code syntax. The requested quantity of tickets is assigned to a variable named numberOfTickets, which represents an integer. To multiply two values, the values must be stored in one of the numeric data types. When the program computes the total cost of the tickets, it assigns the value to a variable named totalCost, also a double data type, as shown in the following code:

Code Syntax

```
double costPerTicket = 79.99;
int numberOfTickets;
double totalCost;
```

String Data Type

In addition to the primitive data types, Java has another data type for working with text. The String type is a class and not a primitive data type. Most strings that you use in the Java language are an object of type String. A string can be a character, word, or phrase. If you assign a phrase to a String variable, place the phrase between double quotation marks. In the Concert Tickets app, after the user selects a musical group from the Spinner control, the program assigns that group to a String type variable named groupChoice, as shown in the following code:

Code Syntax

```
String groupChoice;
```

GTK

When defining variables, good programming practice dictates that the variable names you use should reflect the actual values to place in the variable. That way, anyone reading the program code can easily understand the use of the variable.

Critical Thinking

Should I assign a postal code to a number variable or a String variable?

Assign a postal code to a String variable. Assign numbers to a String variable when you do not plan to use those values mathematically.

Declaring the Variables

You typically declare variables in an Android application at the beginning of an Activity. The code must declare a variable before it can be used in the application. To initialize, or declare, the variables, follow this step:

STEP 1

- In MainActivity.java on Line 15 within the class, press the Tab key to indent the text, and then insert the following four lines of code to initialize the variables in this activity:

  double costPerTicket = 79.99;

  int numberOfTickets;

  double totalCost;

  String groupChoice;

The variables are declared at the beginning of the activity (Figure 3-33).

```
package net.androidbootcamp.concerttickets;

import ...


public class MainActivity extends ActionBarActivity {
    double costPerTicket=79.99;
    int numberOfTickets;
    double totalCost;
    String groupChoice;
    @Override
    protected void onCreate(Bundle savedInstanceState) {
        super.onCreate(savedInstanceState);
        setContentView(R.layout.activity_main);
        final EditText tickets = (EditText)findViewById(R.id.txtTickets);
        final Spinner group = (Spinner)findViewById(R.id.txtGroup);
        Button cost = (Button)findViewById(R.id.btnCost);
        cost.setOnClickListener(new View.OnClickListener() {
            final TextView result = ((TextView)findViewById(R.id.txtResult));
            @Override
            public void onClick(View v) {

            }
        });
    }




}
```

variables declared

Figure 3-33 Declaring variables for the activity

GetText( ) Method

At this point in the application development, all the controls have been assigned variables to hold their values. The next step is to convert the values in the assigned variables to the correct data type for calculation purposes. After the user enters the number of tickets and the concert group name, the user taps or clicks the FIND THE COST button. Inside the OnClickListener code for the button control, the text stored in the tickets EditText control can be read with the **GetText( )** method. By default, Java reads the text in the EditText control as a String type. However, you cannot use a String type in a mathematical function. To convert a string into a numerical data type, you use a **Parse** class. Table 3-4 displays the Parse types that convert a string to a common numerical data type.

Numerical Data Type	Parse Types
Integer	Integer.parseInt( )
Float	Float.parseFloat( )
Double	Double.parseDouble( )
Long	Long.parseLong( )

Table 3-4 Parse type conversions

To extract the string of text entered in the EditText control and convert it to an integer data type for the number of tickets, the following syntax is necessary:

Code Syntax

```
numberOfTickets = Integer.parseInt(tickets.getText( ).toString( ));
```

To code the GetText( ) method, convert the value in the tickets variable into an integer data type, assign it to a variable named numberOfTickets, and follow this step:

STEP 1

- In MainActivity.java, inside the OnClickListener onClick method stub on Line 30, press the Tab key, and then type **numberOfTickets = Integer.parseInt(tickets.getText( ).toString( ));**.

The GetText( ) method extracts the text from tickets, converts the string to an integer, and assigns the value to numberOfTickets (Figure 3-34).

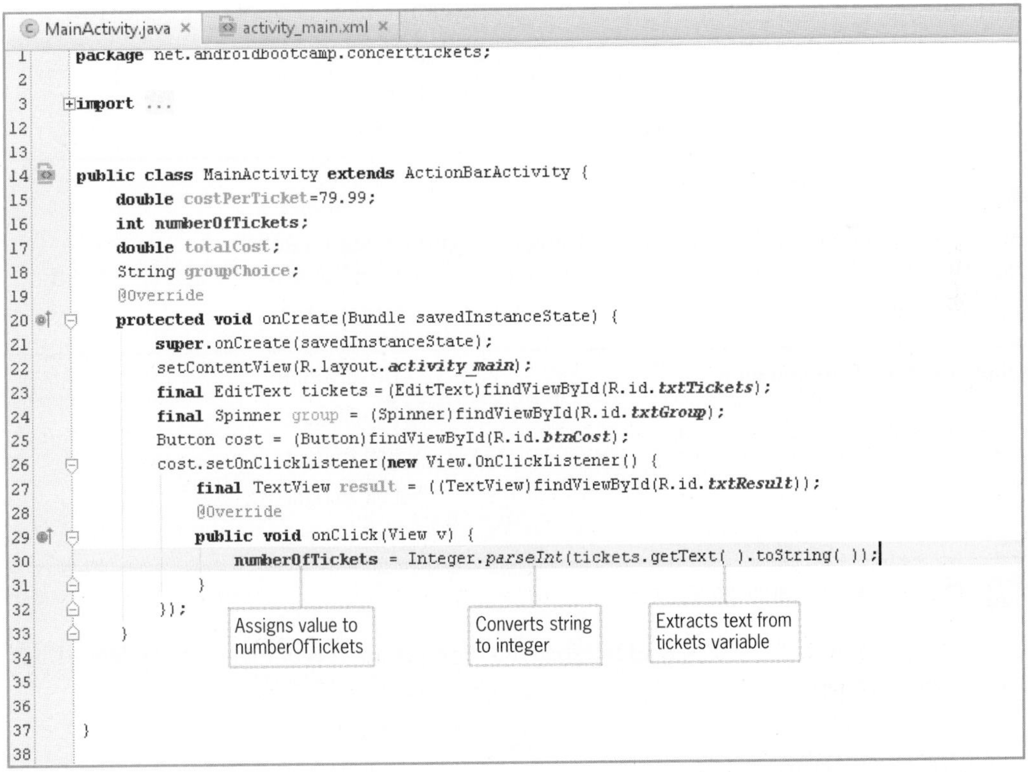

Figure 3-34 Converting a string to an integer

Working with Mathematical Operations

The ability to perform arithmetic operations on numeric data is fundamental to many applications. Many programs require arithmetic operations to add, subtract, multiply, and divide numeric data. For example, the Concert Tickets app must multiply the cost of each ticket by the number of tickets in order to calculate the total cost of the concert tickets.

Arithmetic Operators

Table 3-5 shows a listing of the Java arithmetic operators, along with their use and an example of an arithmetic expression showing their use.

Arithmetic Operator	Use	Assignment Statement
+	Addition	value = itemPrice + itemTax;
–	Subtraction	score = previousScore – 2;
*	Multiplication	totalCost = costPerTicket * numberOfTickets;
/	Division	average = totalGrade / 5.0;
%	Remainder	leftover = widgetAmount % 3;
		If widgetAmount = 11 the remainder = 2
++	Increment (adds 1)	golfScore ++
– –	Decrement (subtracts 1)	points – –

Table 3-5 Java arithmetic operators

When multiple operations are included in a single assignment statement, the sequence of performing the calculations is determined by the rules shown in Table 3-6, which is called the order of operations.

Highest to Lowest Precedence	Description
( )	Parentheses
++ – –	Left to right
* / %	Left to right
+ –	Left to right

Table 3-6 Order of operations

For example, the result of 2 + 3 * 4 is 14 because the multiplication is of higher precedence than the addition operation.

Formatting Numbers

After computing the total ticket cost, the program should display the result in currency format, which includes a dollar sign and commas if needed in larger values, and rounds off to two places past the decimal point. Java includes a class called **DecimalFormat** that provides patterns for formatting numbers for output on the Android device. For example, the pattern "$###,###.##" establishes that a number begins with a dollar sign character, displays a comma if the number has more than three digits, and rounds off to the nearest penny. If the pattern "###.#%" is used, the number is multiplied by 100 and rounded to the first digit past the decimal point. To establish a currency decimal format for the result of the ticket cost, use the following code syntax to assign the decimal format to a variable named currency and later apply it to the totalCost variable to display a currency value:

Code Syntax

```
DecimalFormat currency = new DecimalFormat("$###,###.##");
```

To code the calculation computing the cost of the tickets and to create a currency decimal format, follow this step:

STEP 1

- In MainActivity.java, after the last line entered, insert a new line, type **totalCost = costPerTicket * numberOfTickets;** and then press Enter.
- To establish a currency format, type **DecimalFormat currency = new DecimalFormat("$###,###.##");**.
- Import the DecimalFormat class, if necessary.

The equation computes the total cost of the tickets and DecimalFormat creates a currency format to use when the total cost is displayed (Figure 3-35).

```
        Button cost = (Button)findViewById(R.id.btnCost);
        cost.setOnClickListener(new View.OnClickListener() {
            final TextView result = ((TextView)findViewById(R.id.txtResult));
            @Override
            public void onClick(View v) {
                numberOfTickets = Integer.parseInt(tickets.getText( ).toString( ));
                totalCost = costPerTicket * numberOfTickets;
                DecimalFormat currency = new DecimalFormat("$###,###.##");
            }
        });
```

Equation calculates ticket cost

Pattern formats results as currency

Figure 3-35 Calculating and formatting the ticket cost

Displaying Android Output

In Java, computing the results does not mean displaying the results. To display the results that include the name of the group and the final cost of the tickets, first assign the name of the group to a String variable.

GetSelectedItem( ) Method

To obtain the text name of the concert group that the user selected in the Spinner control, you use a method named GetSelectedItem( ). The **GetSelectedItem( )** method returns the text label of the currently selected Spinner item. For example, if the user selects Zig Zag, the GetSelectedItem( ) method assigns this group to a String variable named groupChoice that was declared at the beginning of the activity, as shown in the following code:

Code Syntax

```
groupChoice = group.getSelectedItem( ).toString( );
```

GTK

A method named GetSelectedIndex( ) can be used with a Spinner control to determine if the user selected the first, second, or subsequent choice. For example, if GetSelectedIndex( ) is equal to the integer 0, the user selected the first choice.

SetText( ) Method

Earlier in the Android project, the method GetText( ) extracted the text from the Text Field control. In an opposite manner, the method SetText( ) displays text in a TextView control. SetText( ) accepts a string of data for display. To join variable names and text, you can concatenate the text with a plus sign (+). In the following example, the variable completeSentence is assigned *Android is the best phone platform.* This sentence is displayed in a TextView object named result.

Example:

```
String mobile = "Android";
String completeSentence = mobile + " is the best phone platform";
result.setText(completeSentence);
```

The syntax for the SetText( ) method is shown in the following code. In this example, the result is displayed in the TextView control named result, and includes the string that uses the concatenation operator, the plus sign connecting variables to the string text.

Code Syntax

```
result.setText("Cost for " + groupChoice + " is " +
currency.format(totalCost));
```

The currency.format portion of the code displays the variable totalCost with a dollar sign and rounds off to the nearest penny. The output for result is displayed in Figure 3-2: Total Cost for Spatial Sense is $319.96. To code the GetSelectedItem( ) method and the SetText( ) method, follow these steps to complete the application:

STEP 1

- In MainActivity.java after the last line of code entered, insert a new line and type **groupChoice = group.getSelectedItem( ).toString( );** to assign the concert group to the String variable groupChoice.
- Insert a new line, and then type **result.setText("Cost for " + groupChoice + " is " + currency.format(totalCost));** to display the output.

The getSelectedItem( ) method identifies the selected group and setText( ) displays the selected group with the total cost of the tickets (Figure 3-36).

MainActivity.java × activity_main.xml ×

```
package net.androidbootcamp.concerttickets;

+import ...


public class MainActivity extends ActionBarActivity {
    double costPerTicket=79.99;
    int numberOfTickets;
    double totalCost;
    String groupChoice;
    @Override
    protected void onCreate(Bundle savedInstanceState) {
        super.onCreate(savedInstanceState);
        setContentView(R.layout.activity_main);
        final EditText tickets = (EditText)findViewById(R.id.txtTickets);
        final Spinner group = (Spinner)findViewById(R.id.txtGroup);
        Button cost = (Button)findViewById(R.id.btnCost);
        cost.setOnClickListener(new View.OnClickListener() {
            final TextView result = ((TextView)findViewById(R.id.txtResult));
            @Override
            public void onClick(View v) {
                numberOfTickets = Integer.parseInt(tickets.getText( ).toString( ));
                totalCost = costPerTicket * numberOfTickets;
                DecimalFormat currency = new DecimalFormat("$###,###.##");
                groupChoice = group.getSelectedItem( ).toString( );
                result.setText("Cost for " + groupChoice + " is " + currency.format(totalCost));
            }
        });
    }




}
```

Figure 3-36 Completed code

STEP 2

- To view the finished application, tap or click the Run 'app' button on the Standard toolbar to test the application in the emulator.
- If necessary, select the Nexus 5 or similar emulator and then tap or click the OK button.

- Unlock the emulator.
- Run the app a second time to send the code to the emulator.
- When the application opens in the emulator, enter the number of tickets using the on-screen keyboard to enter the number of tickets and select a group from the Spinner control. To view the results, tap or click the FIND THE COST button.

The Concert Tickets Android app is executed (Figures 3-1 and 3-2).

Wrap It Up—Chapter Summary

In this chapter, you have learned to declare variables and write arithmetic operations. In the chapter project, you used new controls such as the Text Field to enter text and the Spinner control to select from multiple items. You used the GetText( ) and SetText( ) methods to extract and display data, respectively. An Android theme was also applied to the application.

- You can assign a theme to an activity or entire application to define its appearance and style and to prevent each Android app you develop from looking too similar.
- Preview a theme by tapping or clicking the AppTheme button in the emulator, and then selecting a theme. To change the theme permanently in the application, define the theme in the styles.xml file for each Activity.
- Use Text Fields to request input from users, who can enter characters using an on-screen keyboard or a physical keyboard. You need to select the correct type of Text Field control for the type of data you are requesting.
- The strings.xml file is part of every Android application by default and contains strings used in the application, such as text displayed in a TextView, Spinner, or Button control. You can edit a string in strings.xml to update the text wherever it is used in the application. In strings.xml, you can also include prompt text that provides instructions in a Spinner control. In the Java code, use the GetSelectedItem( ) method to return the text of the selected Spinner item.
- To provide guidelines so users enter the correct data in a Text Field control, use the control's hint property to display light-colored text, also called a watermark, describing what to enter. The user clicks the control to remove the hint and type the requested input.
- To handle the input that users enter into a Text Field control, you use the EditText class, which extracts the text and converts it for use in the Java code. The extracted text must be assigned to a variable, which holds data that changes during the execution of the program. To extract the string of text entered in an EditText control, use the GetText( ) method. To display the extracted text in a TextView control, use the SetText( ) method.

- To use a variable, you must first declare the variable and then assign a value to it. The declared type of a value determines which mathematical operations are allowed. Variables in an Android application are typically declared at the beginning of an Activity.
- After assigning variables to hold the values entered in controls, you often need to convert the values in the assigned variables to the correct data type so the values can be used in calculations. To use string data in a mathematical function, you use the Parse class to convert the string into a numerical data type.

Key Terms

DecimalFormat—A class that provides patterns for formatting numbers in program output.

entries—A Spinner property that connects a string array to the Spinner control for display.

final—A type of variable that can only be initialized once; any attempt to reassign the value results in a compile error when the application is executed.

GetSelectedItem( )—A method that returns the text of the selected Spinner item.

GetText( )—A method that reads text stored in an EditText control.

hint—A short description of a field that appears as light text in a Text Field control.

item—In a Spinner control, a string of text that appears in a list for user selection.

localization—The use of the String table to change text based on the user's preferred language.

Parse—A class that converts a string into a number data type.

prompt—Text that displays instructions at the top of the Spinner control.

soft keyboard—An on-screen keyboard positioned over the lower part of an application's window.

Spinner control—A widget similar to a drop-down list for selecting a single item from a fixed listing.

string—A series of alphanumeric characters that can include spaces.

string array—Two or more text strings.

strings.xml—A default file that is part of every Android application and holds commonly used strings in an application.

theme—A style applied to an Activity or an entire application.

variable—A name used in a Java program to contain data that changes during the execution of the program.

Developer FAQs

1. What is an Android theme?
2. Which is the name of the default theme?
3. In an app, suppose you want to use the theme with a grey title bar and a white background. What entire line of code is needed in the styles.xml file to support this theme?
4. What is a soft keyboard? Be sure to include its location in your answer.
5. Which five controls were used in the chapter project?
6. Which Text Field control is best for entering an amount that contains an overdrawn checking account amount?
7. Which property of the Spinner control adds text at the top of the control such as instructions?
8. What is the name of the file that holds commonly used phrases (arrays) of text in an application?
9. What is a single string of information called in a string array?
10. Which property do you assign to the string array that you create for a Spinner?
11. Write the following variable in camel case: NUMBEROFDELAYS.
12. Write a declaration statement for each of the following variables using the variable type and variable name that would be best for each value. Assign values if directed.
    a. The smallest data type you can use for your age
    b. The population of the state of Maine
    c. Your weekly pay using the most common type for this type number
    d. Assign the first initial of your first name
    e. Assign the present minimum wage using the most common type for this type of number
    f. Assign the name of the city in which you live
    g. Assign the answer to a true/false question for whether your age is over 16.
13. Name two numeric data types that can contain a decimal point.
14. What is the solution to each of the following arithmetic expressions?
    a. 3 + 4 * 2 + 9
    b. 16 / 2 * 4 + 4
    c. 40 – (6 + 2) / 8
    d. 3 + 68 % 9

15. Write a GetText( ) statement that converts a variable named deficit to a double data type and assigns the value to the variable named financeDeficit.

16. Assign the text of the user's choice of a Spinner control named careerName to the variable named topCareers.

17. If a variable named amount is assigned to the value 57,199.266, what would these statements display in the variable called price?

```
DecimalFormat money = new DecimalFormat("$###,###.##");
price.setText("Salary = " + money.format(amount));
```

18. Write a line of Java code that assigns the variable jellyBeans to a decimal format with six digits and a comma if needed, but no dollar sign or decimal places.

19. Write a line of Java code to use concatenation to join the phrase "Welcome to the ", versionNumber (an int variable), and the phrase "th version" to the variable combineStatement.

20. Write a line of Java code that assigns a number to the variable numberChoice, which indicates the user's selection. If the user selects the first group, the number 0 is assigned; if the user selects the second group, the number 1 is assigned; and if the user selects the third group, the number 2 is assigned with the same variables used in the chapter project.

Beyond the Book

Search the web for the answers to the following questions to further your Android knowledge.

1. Name 10 themes used in your Android SDK not mentioned in this chapter.

2. Search for three real Android apps that sell any type of tickets. Name five features of each of the three apps.

3. A good Android developer always keeps up with the present market. Open the page https://play.google.com. Find this week's featured tablet apps and write about the top five. Write a paragraph on the purpose and cost of each for a total of five paragraphs.

4. Open the search engine Bing.com and then tap or click the News tab. Search for an article about Android devices with this week's date. Insert the URL link at the top of a new document. Write a summary of the article containing 150–200 of your own words.

Case Programming Projects

Complete one or more of the following case programming projects. Use the same steps and techniques taught within the chapter. Submit the program you create to your instructor. The level of difficulty is indicated for each case programming project.

Easiest: ★

Intermediate: ★★

Challenging: ★★★

Case Project 3–1: Catalina Island Boat Express App ★

Requirements Document

Application title:	Catalina Island Boat Express App
Purpose:	Catalina Express has 30 daily departures between Long Beach and Catalina Island. Create a simple app that determines how many boat tickets the user needs and whether the ticket is for going to Catalina Island or heading back to Long Beach. The app displays the total price for the fare in one direction.
Algorithms:	1. The app displays a title; an image; and a Text Field, Spinner, and Button control (Figure 3-37). The two options in the Spinner control include To Catalina Island and To Long Beach. Each single passenger ticket is $34 for one way. 2. When the user taps or clicks the Button control, the number of tickets and the total cost of the fare is displayed (Figure 3-38).
Conditions:	Use a black theme, Spinner prompt, string array, and hint property.

Figure 3-37 Catalina Island Boat Express App

Figure 3-38 Ticket and fare confirmation

Case Project 3–2: Triathlon Registration App ★

Requirements Document

Application title:	Triathlon Registration App
Purpose:	A triathlon registration app allows an athlete to register for one of three national triathlons to qualify for the Ironman World Championship.
Algorithms:	1. The triathlon registration app has two Text Fields: One requests the number of athletes on the user's team ($725), and the other requests the location. A Spinner control allows the athlete to select one of the three possible locations: Lake Placid, Big Island Hawaii, and Miami. The app also displays a title, an image, and a Button control (Figure 3-39). 2. After the user taps or clicks the Button control, the selected location and the total team cost are displayed in a TextView control (Figure 3-40).
Conditions:	Use a theme, a title, an image, a Spinner prompt, a string array, and a hint property.

Figure 3-39 Triathlon Registration App

Figure 3-40 Location and total cost confirmation

Case Project 3–3: Paint Calculator App ★★

Requirements Document

Application title: Paint Calculator App

Purpose: The paint section of a large home store wants to provide a paint calculator app to calculate the number of gallons needed to paint a room. The amount of paint in gallons is displayed.

Algorithms:

1. The app displays a title; an image; two Text Fields; and Spinner, Button, and TextView controls. The Spinner control shows five colors of paint for selection. The user enters the room's height in feet and the distance in feet around the room.
2. The color and the exact number of gallons in decimal form are displayed.

Conditions: A gallon is needed for every 250 square feet for a single coat of paint. Display the result rounded to two decimal places. Select five names for paint for the Spinner control. Use a theme, Spinner prompt, string array, and hint property.

Case Project 3–4: Chicago Cab Fare App ★★

Requirements Document

Application title: Chicago Cab Fare App

Purpose: Create an app that estimates the cost for cab fare in Chicago. The app calculates the cost of the trip and requests a reservation for a smart car, traditional sedan, or minivan.

Algorithms:

1. The app requests the distance in miles for the cab ride and your preference for the requested cab: a smart car, traditional sedan, or minivan. The cab fare has an initial fee of $3.00. The mileage rate of $3.25 per mile is also charged.
2. The app displays the name of a cab company, a picture of a logo, and the results of the requested type of cab with the cost of the fare. Create your own layout.

Conditions: Use a theme, Spinner prompt, string array, and hint property. Decimal mileage is possible.

Case Project 3–5: Split the Bill App ★★★

Requirements Document

Application title: Split the Bill App

Purpose: You are out with friends at a nice restaurant. This app splits the bill, including the tip, among the members of your party.

Algorithms:

1. A welcome screen displays the title, image, and button that displays a second screen. The input/output screen requests the restaurant bill and the number of people in your group. The Spinner control asks about the quality of service: Excellent, Average, or Poor.
2. Calculate an 18 percent tip and divide the restaurant bill with the tip included among the members of your party. Display the tip amount and the individual share of the bill.

Conditions: Use a theme, Spinner prompt, string array, and hint property.

Case Project 3–6: Piggy Bank Children's App ★★★

Requirements Document

Application title:	Piggy Bank Children's App
Purpose:	A piggy bank app allows children to enter the number of quarters, dimes, nickels, and pennies that they have. The child can select whether to save the money or spend it. Calculate the amount of money and display the amount that the child is saving or spending. Create two screens: a welcome screen and an input/output screen.
Algorithms:	1. A welcome screen displays the title, image, and button that takes the user to a second screen. The input/output screen requests the number of quarters, dimes, nickels, and pennies. A Spinner control should indicate whether the children are saving or spending their coins. Create your own layout. 2. The results display how much the child is saving or spending.
Conditions:	Use a theme, Spinner prompt, string array, and hint property.

CHAPTER 4

Explore! Icons and Decision-Making Controls

In this chapter, you learn to:

- Create an Android project with a custom icon
- Change the text color in controls using hexadecimal colors
- Align controls using the gravity properties
- Determine layout with the layout:margin properties
- Place a RadioGroup and RadioButtons in Android applications
- Write code for a RadioGroup control
- Make decisions using an If statement
- Make decisions using an If Else statement
- Make decisions using logical operators
- Display an Android toast notification
- Test the isChecked property
- Make decisions using nested If statements

Developers can code Android applications to make decisions based on the input of users or other conditions that occur. Decision making is one of the fundamental activities of a computer application. In this chapter, you learn to write decision-making statements in Java, which allows you to test conditions and perform different operations depending on the results of that test. You can test for a condition being true or false and change the flow of what happens in a program based on the user's input.

The sample program in this chapter is designed to run on an Android phone or tablet device at a hospital. The Medical Calculator application provides nurses a mobile way to convert the weight of a patient from pounds to kilograms and kilograms to pounds. Most medication amounts are prescribed based on the weight of the patient. Most hospital scales display weight in pounds, but the prescribed medication is often based on the weight of a patient in kilograms. For safety reasons, the exact weight of the patient must be correctly converted between pounds and kilograms. The nurse enters the weight of the patient and selects a radio button, as shown in Figure 4-1, to determine whether pounds are being converted to kilograms or kilograms are being converted to pounds. The mobile application then computes the converted weight based on the conversion formulas: The conversion formulas are: kilograms = pounds * 2.2 and pounds = kilograms / 2.2. To validate that correct weights are entered, if the value is greater than 500 for the conversion from pounds to kilograms or greater than 225 for the conversion from kilograms to pounds, the user is asked for a valid entry. If the user enters a number out of the acceptable range, a warning called a toast message appears on the screen. When the app is running, a nurse enters 225 for the value of the weight of the patient and selects the Convert Pounds to Kilograms radio button shown in Figure 4-1. After tapping the Convert Weight button, the application displays 102.3 kilograms (rounded off to the nearest tenth place) in a red font, as shown in Figure 4-2. By using a mobile device, the nurse can capture patient information such as weight directly at the point of care anywhere and anytime and reduce errors made by delaying entry on a traditional computer in another location.

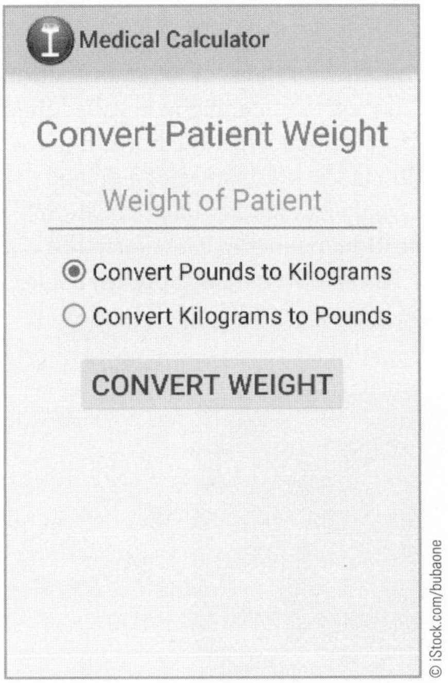

Figure 4-1 Opening screen of the Medical Calculator

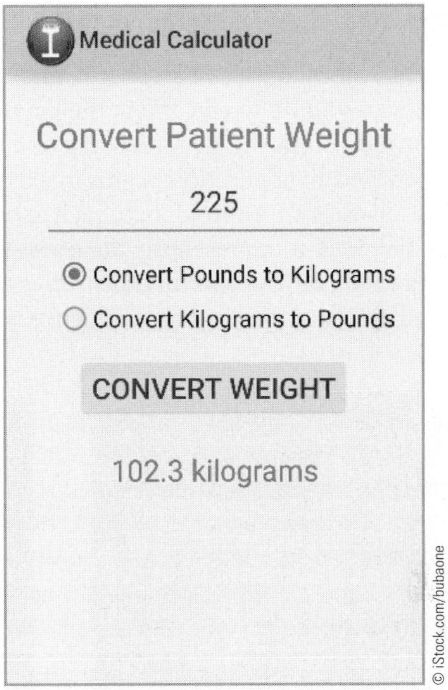

Figure 4-2 Results screen of the Medical Calculator

To create this application, the developer must understand how to perform the following processes:

1. Create a customized launcher icon.
2. Add the icon using code to display in the ActionBar
3. Define a TextField for the data entry of the weight of the patient.
4. Define a RadioGroup to select pounds to kilograms or kilograms to pounds.
5. Display a Toast message for data validation.
6. Convert data so it can be used for arithmetic operations.
7. Perform arithmetic operations on data the user enters.
8. Display formatted results.

IN THE TRENCHES

Medical device apps are changing the entire patient point-of-care system. Apps now used in hospitals include mobile patient records, drug prescription references, medical journals, surgical checklists, dosage calculators, radiology imagery, and disease pathology.

Using the Launcher Icon

By default, Android places a standard Android icon as the graphic to represent your application on the device's home screen and in the Launcher window. To view the opening icon called the **launcher icon** on the home screen, tap or click the application listing icon at the bottom of the emulator when an application begins to execute, as shown in Figure 4-3. Instead of a default icon that displays an Android logo, each app published to Google Play should have a custom graphic (Figure 4-3) representing the contents of your application. Launcher icons form the first impression of your app on prospective users in Google Play. With so many apps available, a high-quality launcher icon can influence users to purchase your Android app.

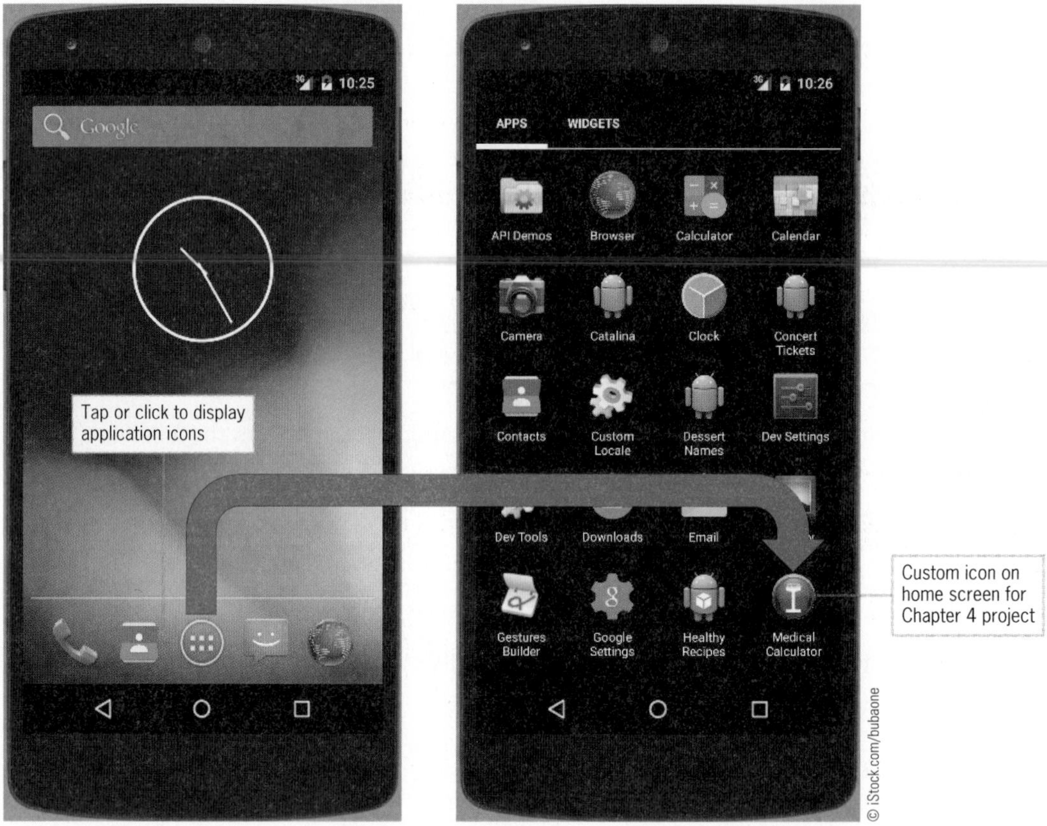

Figure 4-3 Android home screen and launcher icons

GTK

Tap the circle with six small squares at the bottom of the emulator to view the Android home screen and the icons.

An icon is a graphic that takes up a small portion of screen space and provides a quick, intuitive representation of an app. As you design a launcher icon, consider that an icon can establish brand identity. A unique image logo and program name can communicate your brand to potential customers. In the Medical Calculator app, the scale icon shown in Figure 4-4 clearly communicates that this icon launches a program about weight. A simple image with a clear visual cue like the scale has a memorable impact. It also helps users find the app on the Google Play site. Google Play suggests icons should be simple and bold in design. For example, for a paint graphics program, an icon shaped like a thin art paintbrush may be hard to distinguish from a pencil image, but a large cartoonlike paintbrush can convey its purpose easily.

Figure 4-4 Launcher icon for the Medical Calculator app

Google Play also specifies the size and format of all launcher icons for uniformity. Launcher icons should be saved in the .png file format. Based on your target device, Table 4-1 specifies the size of a finished launcher icon. You can use programs such as Microsoft Paint, Mac Paintbrush, and Adobe Photoshop to resize the icon to the correct number of pixels. In the chapter project, the icon dimension is 48 × 48 pixels for the high-density screen used by the application, but the Asset Studio within Android Studio can automatically resize icons to the appropriate size necessary for different device platforms.

Resolution	Dots per Inch (dpi)	Size (px)
ldpi (low-density screen)	120	36 × 36
mdpi (medium-density screen)	160	48 × 48
hdpi (high-density screen)	240	72 × 72
xhdpi (extra high-density screen)*	320	96 × 96
xxhdpi (extra extra high-density screen)*	440	144 × 144

Table 4-1 Launcher icon sizes

* Used by some tablets

GTK

When you publish an app to Google Play, you must provide a 512 × 512 pixel, high-resolution application icon in the developer console as you upload your program. This icon is displayed on the Google Play site to provide a description of the app and does not replace your launcher icon.

Google Play recommends a naming convention for launcher icons. Typically, the prefix ic_launcher is used to name launcher icons for Android apps. In the case of the Medical Calculator app, the launcher icon is named ic_launcher_weight.png. After a custom icon is placed within the project, Android renames the icon to the name ic_launcher.png.

GTK

Vector-based graphics are best to use for icon design because the images can be scaled without the loss of detail and are easily resized.

Customizing a Launcher Icon

Instead of using the built-in generic Android logo icon, you can display a custom launcher icon on the home screen. The custom icon image can be automatically placed in the res\mipmap folder by adding an image asset using a built-in wizard in Android Studio. The Image Asset wizard creates multiple icons for different screen resolutions and provides a live preview of the resized icons. The Image Asset wizard uploads and replaces the current launcher icon named ic_launcher.png with a custom icon of your choice. To perform the following steps, you need an image file named ic_launcher_weight.png, provided with your student files, to use as the custom launcher icon for the Medical Calculator app. You should already have the student files for this text that your instructor gave you or that you downloaded from the webpage for this book (*www.cengagebrain.com*). To begin the chapter project, add a customized launcher icon and select a theme, by following these steps:

STEP 1

- Open the Android Studio program.
- In the Create New Project dialog box, enter **Medical Calculator** in the Application name text box.
- In the Company Domain text box, type **androidbootcamp.net**, if necessary.
- In the Project location text box, type **D:\Workspace\MedicalCalculator** (if necessary, enter a different drive letter that identifies the USB drive) to select a workspace and then tap or click the OK button.
- Tap or click the Next button on the Configure your new project page of the Create New Project dialog box.
- If necessary, tap or click the Phone and Tablet check box to select the form factor for your app.
- Tap or click the Next button on the Select the form factors your app will run on page.
- If necessary, tap or click Blank Activity to add an Activity to the new project.
- Tap or click the Next button on the Add an activity to Mobile page.
- Tap or click the Finish button on the Choose options for your new file page.
- Tap or click the Hello world! TextView widget (displayed by default) in the emulator and press the Delete key.
- Tap or click 'the virtual device to render the layout with' button (emulator) directly to the right of the Palette on the activity_main.xml tab, and then click Nexus 5 (5.0", 1080 × 1920, xxhdpi).

The new Android Medical Calculator project has an application name with a MainActivity and an activity_main.xml file (Figure 4-5).

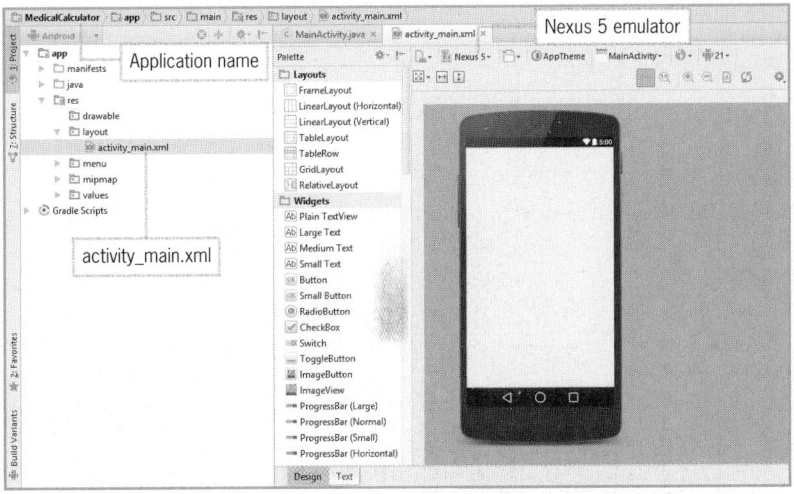

Figure 4-5 New Android application named Medical Calculator

STEP 2

- In the Android Project view, tap or click the activity_main.xml file.
- Tap or click File on the menu bar and then tap or click New.

The New menu opens in Android Studio (Figure 4-6).

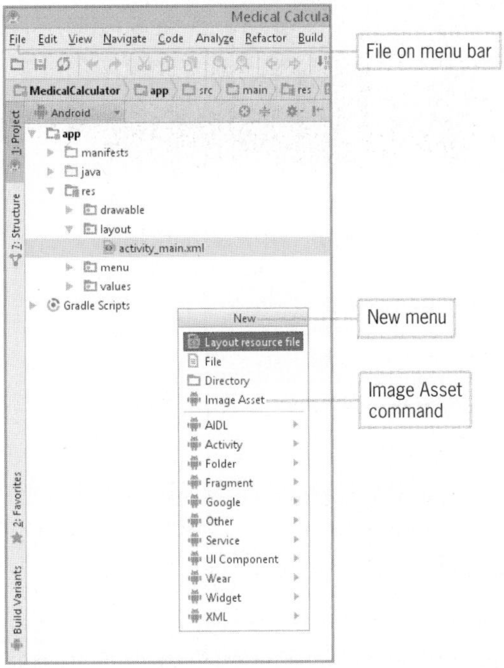

Figure 4-6 New menu

STEP 3

- Tap or click Image Asset on the New menu.

The Asset Studio dialog box opens to display the default launcher icons for the resolutions of various devices (Figure 4-7).

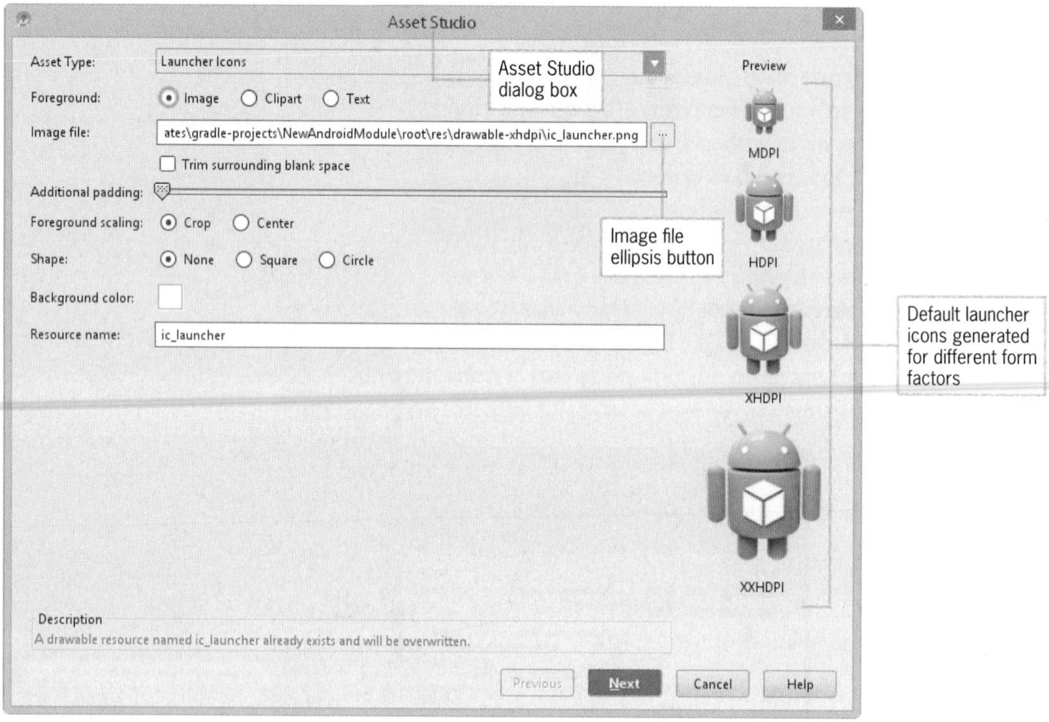

Figure 4-7 Default launcher icons

STEP 4

- Tap or click the ellipsis button to the right of the Image file text box.
- To add the custom launcher icon, copy the student files to your USB drive (if necessary). Open the USB folder containing the student files to locate and then select the file ic_launcher_weight.png.
- In the Select Path dialog box, navigate to the location of the ic_launcher_weight.png file, and then select the file.
- Tap or click the OK button to add the custom launcher icon.
- In the Shape category, tap or click the Circle radio button to trim the background from the icon launcher.

The custom launcher icon of a scale is displayed in different sizes in the Asset Studio dialog box with the icon's background removed (Figure 4-8). The Asset Studio replaces the present ic_launcher icon with the updated scale icon automatically.

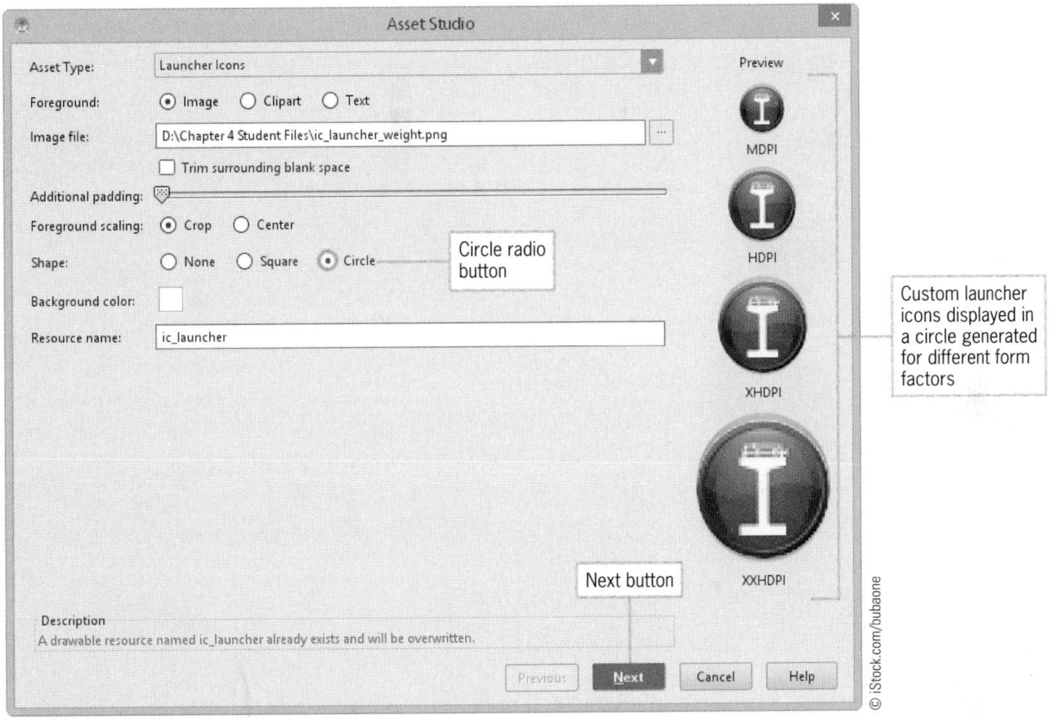

Figure 4-8 Custom launcher icons

STEP 5

- Tap or click the Next button.

The resized launcher icons are placed in the appropriate mipmap folders based on their size and resolution (Figure 4-9).

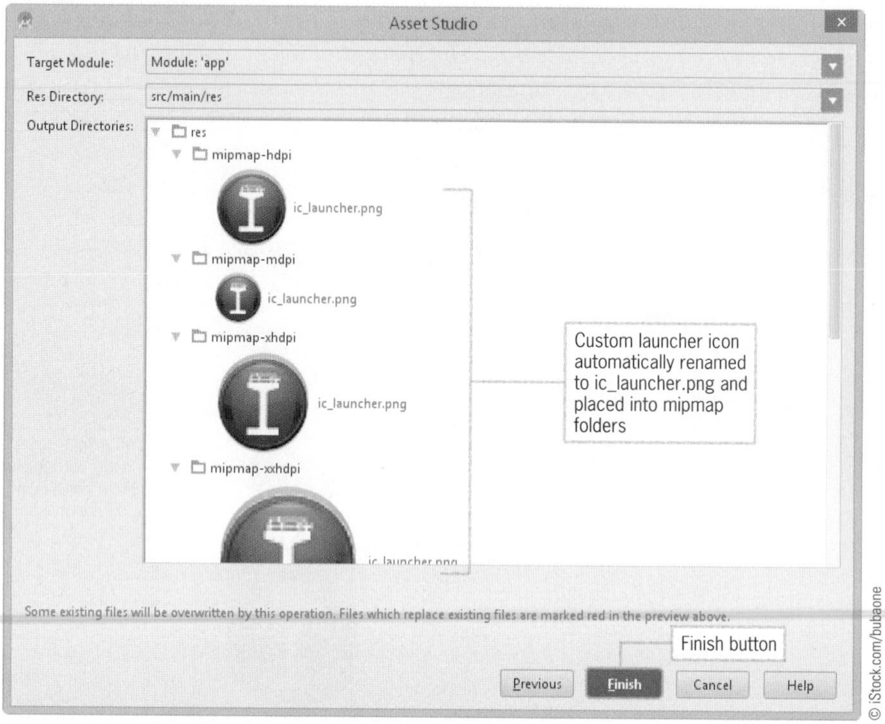

Figure 4-9 Custom icons displayed in res/mipmap folders

STEP 6

- Tap or click the Finish button. Notice that the default theme does not display the Action bar in the emulator displayed in the Design tab.
- In the activity_main.xml tab, tap or click the AppTheme button to change the default theme and open the Select Theme dialog box.
- Tap or click All on the left side of the Select Theme dialog box and scroll to find the Holo. Light theme.
- Tap or click Holo.Light on the right side of the Select Theme dialog box.

The Holo.Light theme is selected from the Select Theme dialog box (Figure 4-10).

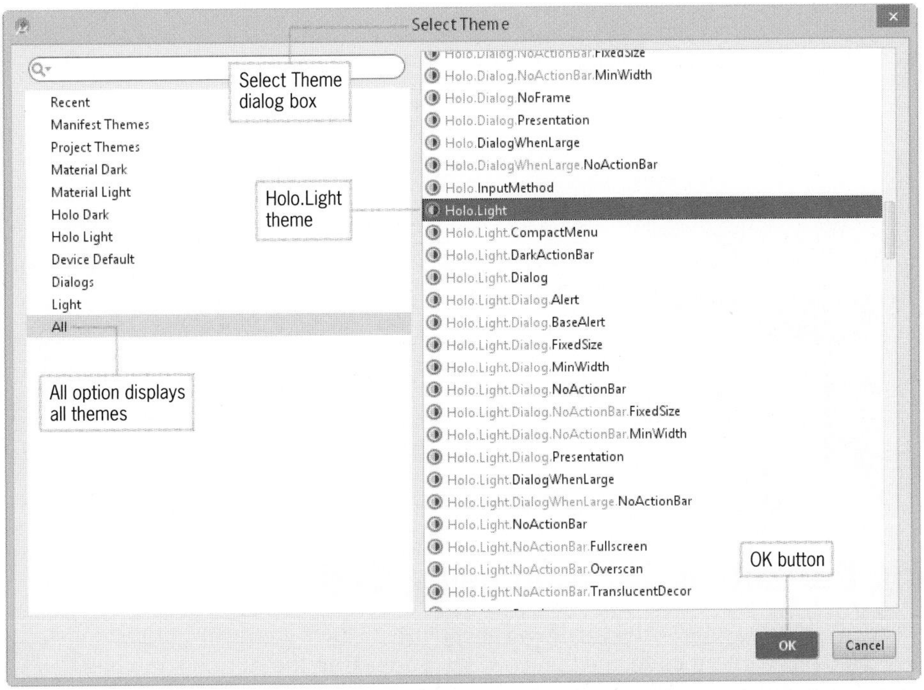

Figure 4-10 Selecting a theme for the application

STEP 7

- Tap or click the OK button.
- To update the theme in the finished app, in the Android project view, expand the values folder, and then double-tap or double-click styles.xml.
- Tap or click to the right of parent and change the parent theme to "Theme.AppCompat.Light."

The theme is updated in styles.xml to display a white background and a gray title bar when the application is executed (Figure 4-11). If you execute the app at this point, the icon launcher appears on the Home screen, but does not appear in the Action bar.

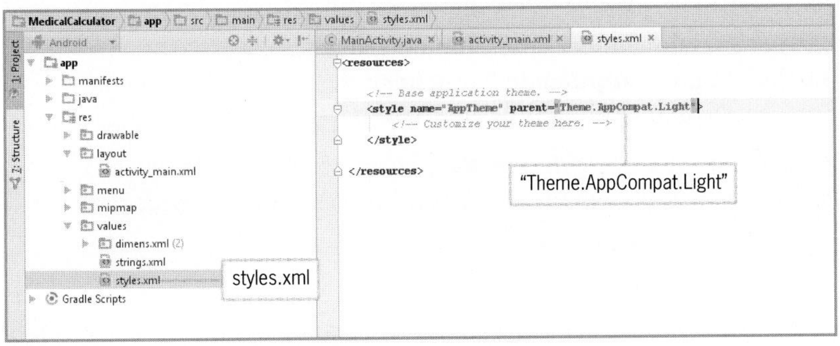

Figure 4-11 styles.xml with updated theme

STEP 8

- Close styles.xml and tap or click the Save All button.

The emulator displays the icon launcher in the Action bar of the Holo.Light theme in activity_main.xml (Figure 4-12).

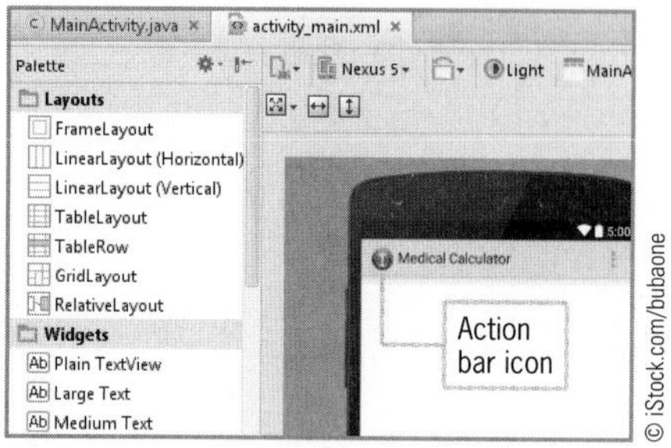

Figure 4-12 Action bar displays icon launcher in activity_main.xml

Displaying the Action Bar Icon using Code

The Medical Calculator app displays the medical scale image in the Action bar of the emulator in activity_main.xml, but without code, the image will not appear in the Action bar when you run the completed app. An Action bar icon as shown in Figure 4-12 is considered a **logo** that represents what the program's function is in a single glance; for example, the medical scale conveys the purpose and identity of the app. To display the Action bar logo in the completed app, follow these steps:

STEP 1

- In the Android project view, expand the java folder and the first net.androidbootcampmedicalcalculator folder, and then double-tap or double-click MainActivity to open the code window.
- Display the line numbers and delete Lines 18-38.
- Tap or click at the end of Line 14 (setContentView), press Enter, and type the following three statements to display the logo in the Action bar:

getSupportActionBar().setDisplayShowHomeEnabled(true);
getSupportActionBar().setLogo(R.mipmap.ic_launcher);
getSupportActionBar().setDisplayUseLogoEnabled(true);

MainActivity.java has three new statements to display the logo named ic_launcher that was placed in the mipmap folder (Figure 4-13). Line 16 displays the logo image of the scale near the line number.

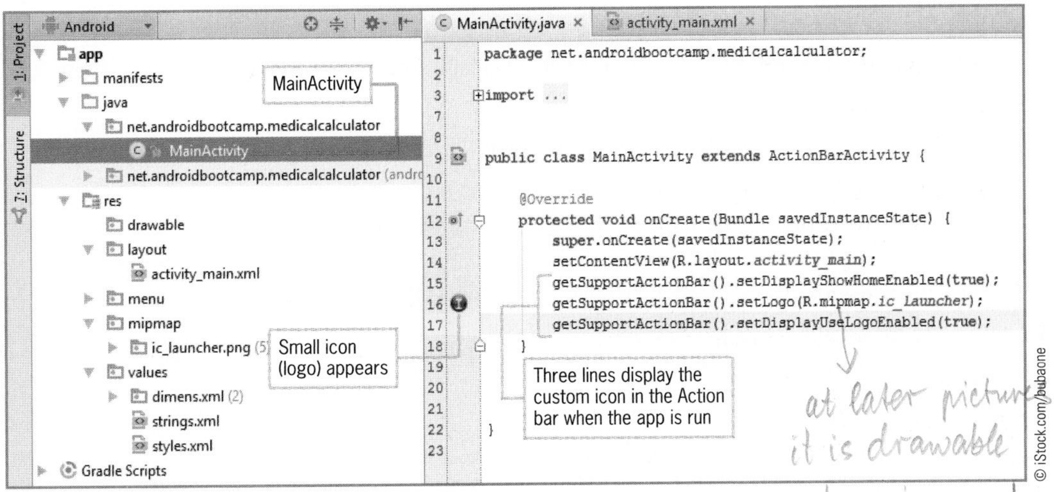

Figure 4-13 Code to display logo in finished app

GTK

Google provides an Android Asset Studio that allows you to generate your own custom launcher icons using Creative Commons images to include within your apps. The images are available at http://romannurik.github.io/AndroidAssetStudio.

String Table

In the Medical Calculator app, the String resources are stored within the /res/values/strings.xml file of the resource hierarchy for the text displayed in the TextView, RadioButton, EditText, and Button controls. Any strings you add to the strings.xml file are accessible within your application. In the following steps, you insert the string names and values shown in Table 4-2.

String Name	String Value
~~hint~~ txtWeight	Weight of Patient
radLbToKilo	Convert Pounds to Kilograms
radKiloToLb	Convert Kilograms to Pounds
btnConvert	Convert Weight

Table 4-2 String names and values to add

To begin the design of the Android user interface and create the String table, follow this step:

STEP 1

- In the Android project view, open the strings.xml file in the res\values folder.
- Tap or click the Open editor link.
- Tap or click the Add Key (plus sign) button in the Translations Editor.

- In the Key text box, type **txtTitle** to name the string for the TextView control.
- In the Default Value text box, type **Convert Patient Weight** to define the text to display, and then tap or click the OK button.
- Tap or click the Add Key button again and repeat the same process to add the remaining items listed in Table 4-2.

The strings.xml file is populated with the text used in the app (Figure 4-14).

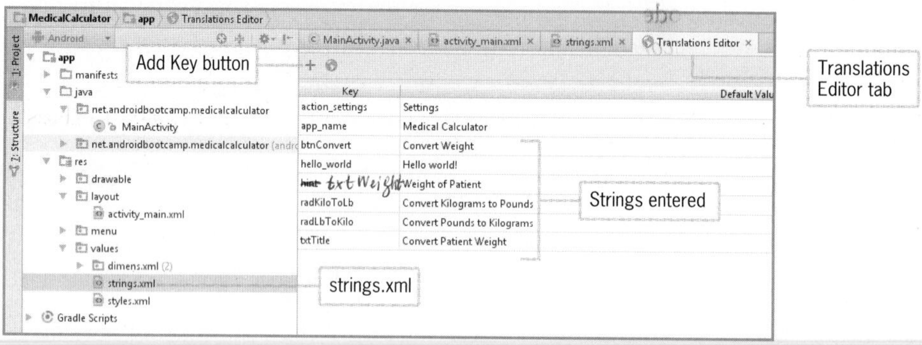

Figure 4-14 Translations Editor with new strings

RadioButton and RadioGroup Controls

RadioButton controls are used to select or deselect an option. In the chapter project, the user can select which mathematical conversion is needed. When a RadioButton is placed on the emulator, by default each control is arranged vertically. If you prefer the RadioButton controls to be listed horizontally, you can set the orientation property to horizontal. Each RadioButton control has a label defined by the Text property and a Checked property set to either true or false. RadioButton controls are typically used together in a **RadioGroup** container. Checking one radio button unchecks the other radio buttons within the group. In other words, within a RadioGroup control, only one RadioButton control can be selected at a time. When the RadioGroup container control is placed in the emulator window from the Container category in the Palette, three RadioButton controls are included in the group by default. If you need additional RadioButton controls, drag them from the Palette into the group. In the case of the Medical Calculator app, only two radio buttons are needed, so the third radio button is deleted.

To make the user's input as simple as possible, offer a default selection. For example, nurses more often convert weight from pounds to kilograms, so that RadioButton option should be checked initially. The Checked property of this RadioButton control is set to true to provide a default selection.

GTK

Like RadioButton controls, a CheckBox control allows a user to check or uncheck a listing. A user may select any number of check boxes, including zero, one, or several. In other words, each check box is independent of all other check boxes in the list, so checking one box does not uncheck the others. The shape of a radio button is circular and the check box is square.

Changing the Text Color of Android Controls

Thus far, each application in this text used the default color of black or white for the text color based on the theme for each Android control. The Android platform uses a color system called hexadecimal color codes to display different colors. A **hexadecimal color code** is a triplet of three colors. Colors are specified first by a ~~pound sign~~ followed by how much red (00 to FF), how much green (00 to FF), and how much blue (00 to FF) are in the final color. For example, the hexadecimal color of #FF0000 is a true red. The TextView and RadioGroup controls displayed in the chapter project have red text, which you designate by typing #FF0000 as the textColor property. To look up these color codes, search for hexadecimal color codes in a search engine or refer to *http://html-color-codes.com.* If you tap or click the ellipsis button on the textColor property, the Resources dialog box shown in Figure 4-15 appears. On the Color tab, you can select any color within the circle or enter RGB (Red, Green, Blue) or hexadecimal color values.

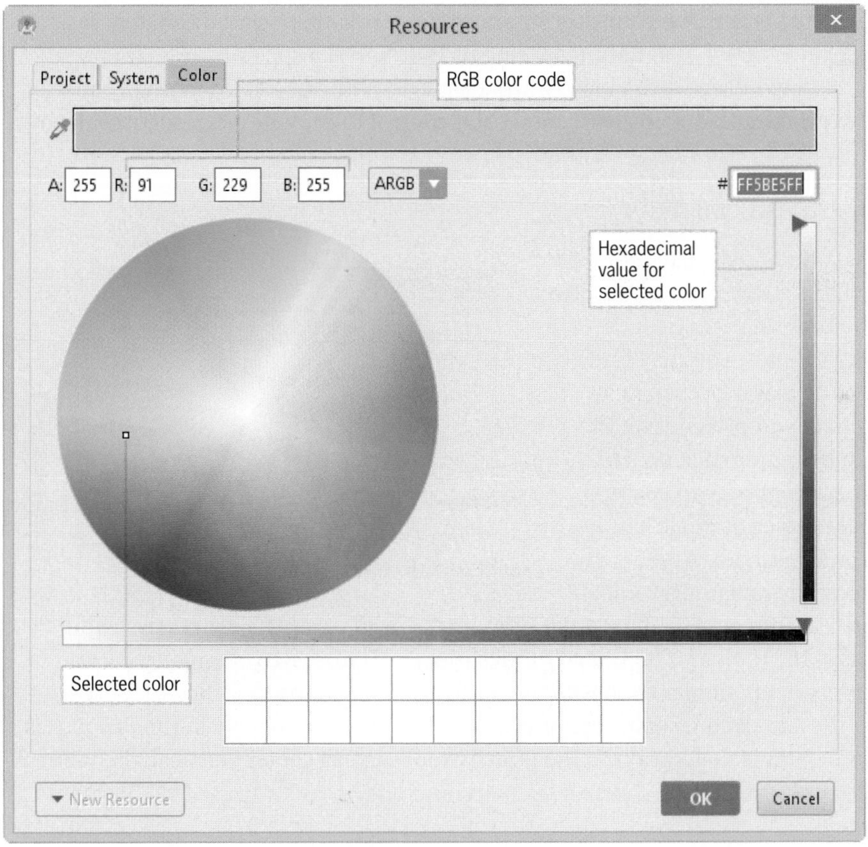

Figure 4-15 Color tab in the Resources dialog box

Critical Thinking

I noticed that the Color Resource dialog box has RBG text boxes. How do I locate a color using RGB coding?

A site such as rgbchart.com can provide a listing of all the possible color codes using RGB coding.

Changing the Margins

After placing a control on the user interface, you can change the alignment by adjusting the gravity of the control. For more flexibility in controlling your layout, use the **layout:margin** property to change the spacing around each object by changing all the margins equally, or the left, top, right, or bottom margin individually. Each control in the Medical Calculator app can use margins to add a certain amount of blank space measured in density independent pixels (dp) on each of its four sides. Instead of "eyeballing" the controls on the user interface for alignment, the layout:margin property creates equal spacing around controls. Using the layout:margin property helps make your user interface more organized and ultimately easier to use. For example, in Figure 4-1, a margin spacing of 15dp (pixels) specifies 15 extra pixels on the top side of the selected Plain Text View control displaying the title. As you design the user interface, use the same specified margins around each control to provide a symmetrical layout.

Changing the Layout Gravity

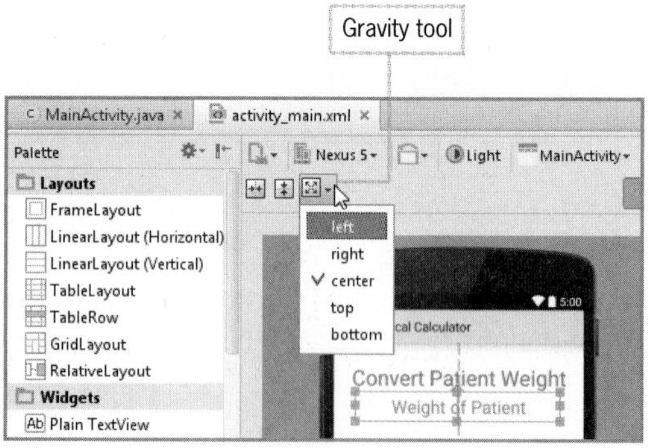

Figure 4-16 Gravity tool options

The Medical Calculator app displays controls from the Palette with Relative Layout. Relative Layout is the default layout setting on the Android emulator. At times, you may find the emulator might display a control in a different location than you placed it on the screen. Layout can be set for each control using a property named gravity to center a control horizontally as well as positioning it at other places on the screen. After each control is placed on the emulator, a toolbar appears above the emulator screen. The gravity can be changed using the Properties pane or with a shortcut on the toolbar. The **Gravity** tool shown in Figure 4-16 changes the linear alignment. Layout gravity is similar to the alignment feature in Microsoft Office that allows a control to snap to the left, center, right, top, or bottom. The gravity property in the Properties pane provides more options in addition to the Gravity tool such as center_vertical, fill_vertical, fill_horizontal, fill, clip_vertical, clip_horizontal, start, and end.

Adding the RadioButton Group

Earlier, you created a strings.xml file to hold the text used within the app. The app uses the text in the String table to assign the TextView title, hint property of the EditText control, the text on both RadioButton controls, and the Button control text. After creating the strings.xml file, you can add controls to the user interface. The Medical Calculator app displays a TextView control, Number Text Field, and RadioGroup control, all centered horizontally. The TextView and RadioGroup controls use the text color of gray. To name a RadioButton control, use the id property in the Properties pane to enter a name that begins with the prefix rad, which represents a radio button in the code. To add a TextView, EditText, and RadioGroup controls to the Medical Calculator app, follow these steps:

STEP 1

- Tap or click the Save All button on the toolbar.
- Close the Translations Editor tab and the strings.xml tab.
- With activity_main.xml open and displaying the emulator screen, drag and drop the Plain TextView control onto the top part of the emulator.
- To center the TextView control, drag the control to the center of the screen until a green dashed vertical line identifying the screen's center is displayed.
- Double-tap or double-click the Plain TextView control, and then type **txtTitle** in the id property.
- Tap or click the ellipsis button (three dots) in the text property, scroll down to tap or click txtTitle in the Resource dialog box to select the assigned string, and then tap or click the OK button.
- Change the textSize property to **30sp**.
- Tap or click the textColor property, type **#FF0000**, and then press Enter to change the text color to red to match the launcher icon.
- Expand the layout:margin property by tapping or clicking the arrow preceding the property.
- In the top property, enter **15dp** and press the Enter key to place 15 pixels of space above the control.

The layout:margin top property is displayed with 15dp entered. The Plain TextView control is added to the form with the text, size, and text color changed (Figure 4-17).

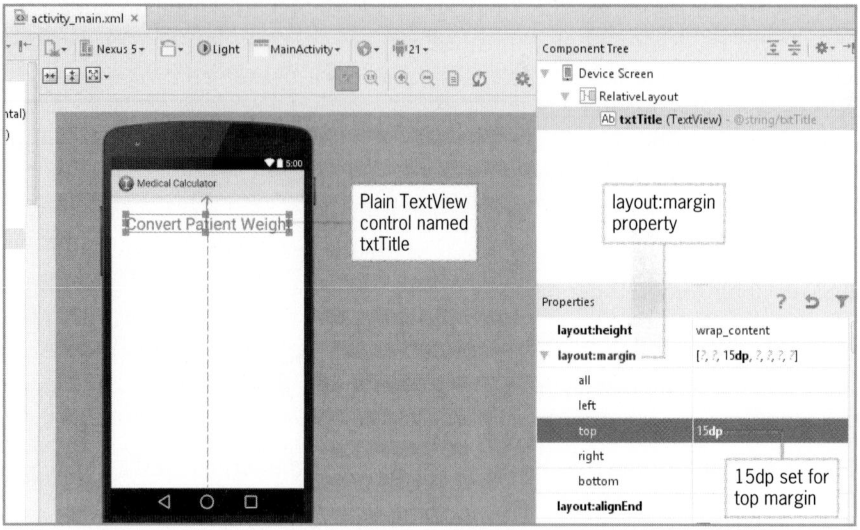

Figure 4-17 Plain TextView control and layout:margin property

STEP 2

- To add the Number Text Field, scroll down to the Text Fields category in the Palette.
- Drag and drop the Number Text Field control onto the emulator below the TextView control in the center.
- Double-tap or double-click the Number Text Field control, and then type **txtWeight** in the id property.
- Tap or click the ellipsis button in the hint property of the Properties pane.
- Tap or click hint in the Resources dialog box to select the assigned string, and then tap or click the OK button.
- Change the textSize property to **25sp**.
- Expand the gravity property and then select center_horizontal to center the hint within the control.
- In the layout:margin property, tap or click to the right of the top property, enter **15dp**, and press Enter to place 15 pixels of space between the Plain TextView and the Number Text Field control.

A Number Text Field control is placed on the emulator with the id, text size, text hint, gravity, and margins changed (Figure 4-18).

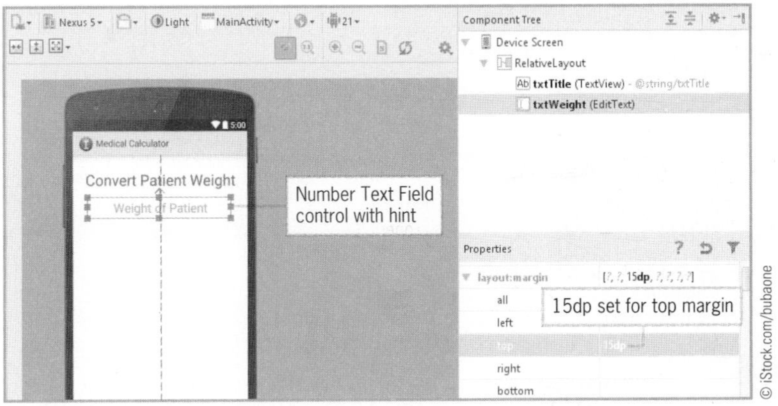

Figure 4-18 Number Text Field control

STEP 3

- In the Palette, scroll down to view the Containers category, select the Container named RadioGroup, and then drag and drop the RadioGroup control onto the user interface below the Number Text Field.
- Two radio buttons are needed for this app, so scroll up to the Widgets category, tap or click the RadioButton control, drag and drop two radio buttons inside the RadioGroup control, and center them using the green dashed line.
- Double-tap or double-click the first RadioButton control, and then change the id property of the RadioButton control to **radLbToKilo**.
- Tap or click the checked property indicating that the first radio button is the default selection.
- Tap or click the ellipsis button in the text property, tap or click radLbToKilo in the Resources dialog box to select the assigned string, and then tap or click the OK button.
- Change the textSize property to **20sp**.
- If necessary, expand the layout:margin property; in the left property, type **10dp** and in the top property, type **15dp**.
- Double-tap or double-click the second RadioButton control and change the id property to **radKiloToLb**.
- Tap or click the ellipsis button in the text property, and then tap or click radKiloToLb in the Resources dialog box to select the assigned string. Tap or click the OK button.
- Change the textSize property to **20sp**.
- If necessary, expand the layout:margins property, type **10dp** in the left property and type **5dp** in the top property to keep the RadioButtons close to one another within the group.

The RadioGroup object is placed on the emulator with the id, text, size, and margin properties changed (Figure 4-19).

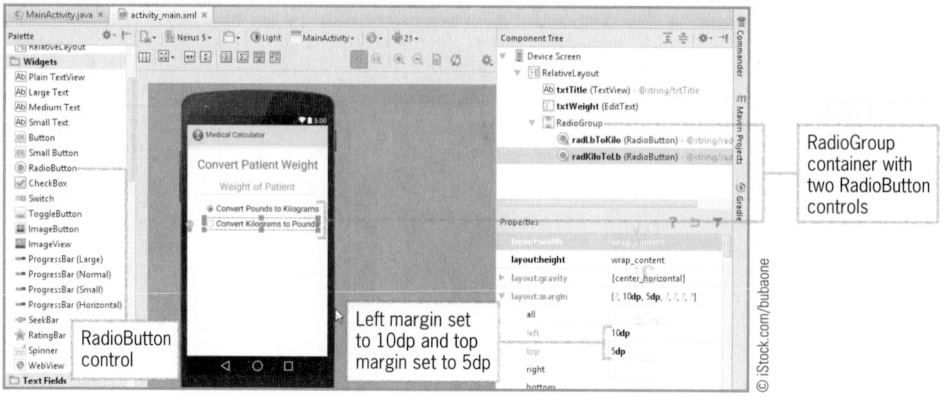

Figure 4-19 RadioGroup control with two RadioButton controls

Critical Thinking

Does the EditText controls have a property that displays the hint in a different text color?

Yes. The textHintColor property in the EditText control Properties pane allows you to change the hint color.

Completing the User Interface

As you design the Android interface, it is important to have a clean layout and use the entire screen effectively. To complete the user interface by adding a Button and TextView control and code the Button and TextView controls, follow these steps:

STEP 1

- In the activity_main.xml tab, drag the Button control from the Palette to the emulator below the RadioGroup.
- Double-tap or double-click the Button and change the id property of the Button control to **btnConvert**.
- Tap or click the ellipsis button in the text property, and then select btnConvert to change the text display. Tap or click the OK button in the Resources dialog box.
- Change the textSize property to **25sp**.
- In the gravity property, tap or click center_horizontal to center the control.
- In the top property of the layout:margin property, type **15dp** to place 15 pixels of space above the control.

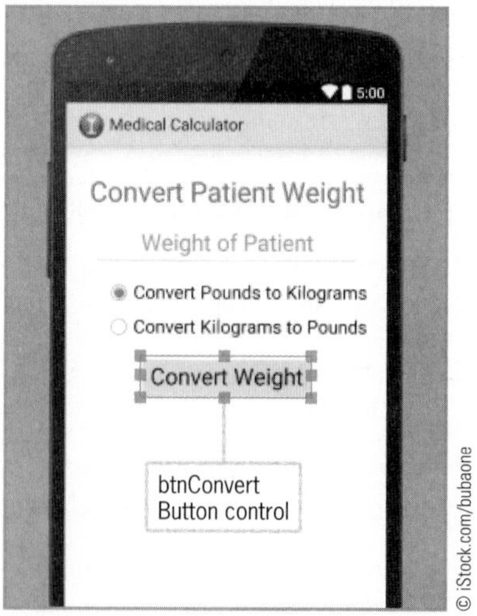

Figure 4-20 Button control

The Button control named btnConvert displays the text Convert Weight and its id, text size, gravity, and margins are changed (Figure 4-20).

STEP 2

- Drag another Plain TextView control to the emulator below the Button.
- Change the id property of the TextView control to **txtResult**.
- Delete the text in the text property.
- Change the textSize property to **25sp**.
- For the textColor property, enter **#FF0000** (red).
- In the top property of the layout:margin property, enter **25dp** to place 25 pixels of space above the control.
- Tap or click the Save All button on the Standard toolbar.

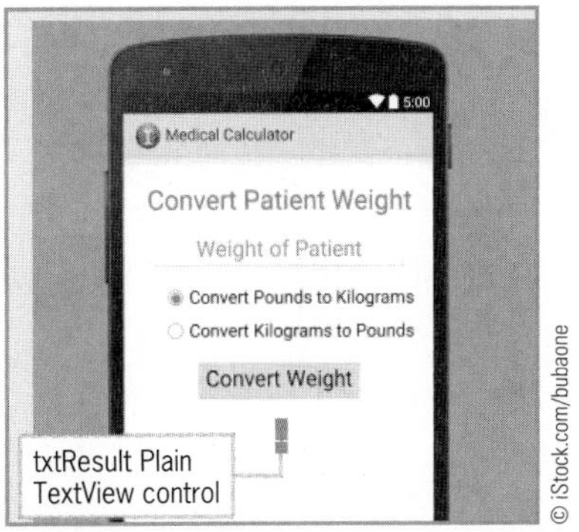

Figure 4-21 Plain TextView control to display the results

The TextView control is placed on the emulator with an empty text property (Figure 4-21).

Coding a RadioButton Control

Each of the RadioButton controls placed on the emulator need to be referenced by using the findViewByld Java command. In the following code syntax, lbsToKilo and kiloToLbs reference the two RadioButton controls in the Medical Calculator application:

Code Syntax

```
final RadioButton lbsToKilo = (RadioButton) findViewById(R.id.radLbToKilo);
final RadioButton kiloToLbs = (RadioButton) findViewById(R.id.radKiloToLb);
```

The keyword, **final** represents that the variable can be assigned only once. This variable can only be referenced within this class. After the RadioButton controls have been referenced, the next priority is to determine which of the two radio buttons the user selected. If the user selected the Convert Pounds to Kilograms radio button, the weight entered is divided by 2.2, but if the user selected the Convert Kilograms to Pounds radio button, the weight is multiplied by 2.2. A variable named conversionRate is assigned the decimal value 2.2. The variables weightEntered and convertedWeight contain the patient weight and converted weight result, respectively.

To create the Java code to declare the variables used in the application and to assign variables to reference the controls, follow these steps:

STEP 1

- Display the MainActivity.java tab.
- Tap or click in the blank line (Line 10) inside the MainActivity class, and then press Tab to indent the line.

- To initialize the conversion rate value of 2.2, type **double conversionRate = 2.2;** and press the Enter key.
- To initialize the weightEntered variable, type **double weightEntered;** and press the Enter key.

- To initialize the variable that will hold the converted weight, type **double convertedWeight;** and press the Enter key.

Three variables are declared in the Java code (Figure 4-22).

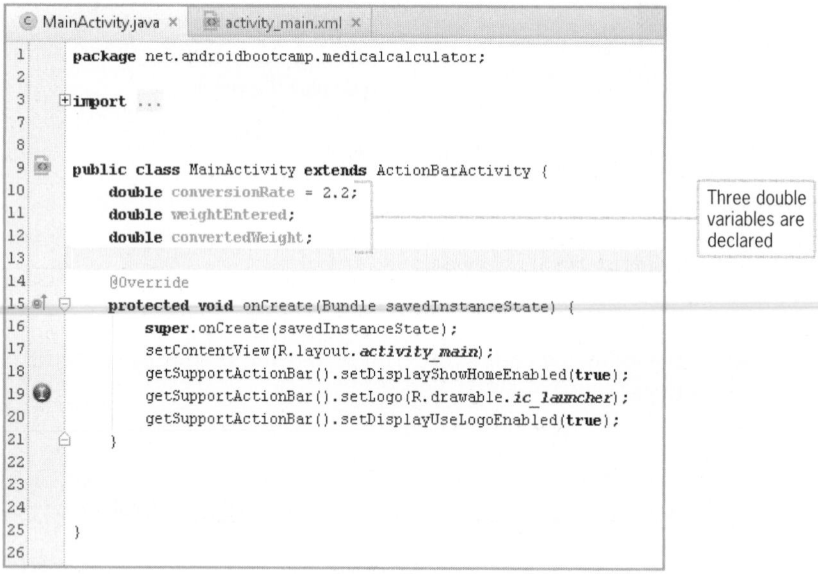

Figure 4-22 Variables declared

STEP 2

- Tap or click at the end of the Line 20, getSupportActionBar().setDisplayUseLogoEnabled(true);. Press the Enter key.
- To instantiate and reference the EditText class with the id name of txtWeight, type **final EditText weight = (EditText) findViewById(R.id.txtWeight);**.
- Tap or click EditText (displayed in red), press Alt+Enter, and then import the EditText class. After the closing semicolon, press the Enter key.
- To instantiate and reference the RadioButton class with the id name of radLbToKilo, type **final RadioButton lbToKilo = (RadioButton) findViewById(R.id.radLbToKilo);**.
- If necessary, tap or click the red text RadioButton and press Alt+Enter to import the RadioButton class. After the closing semicolon, press the Enter key.

- To instantiate and reference the RadioButton class for the second radio button with the Id name of radKiloToLb, type **final RadioButton kiloToLb = (RadioButton) findViewById(R.id.radKiloToLb);**.
- Save your work.

The EditText class extracts the value from the user's input for the patient weight and the RadioButton class extracts the checked value from the radio buttons (Figure 4-23).

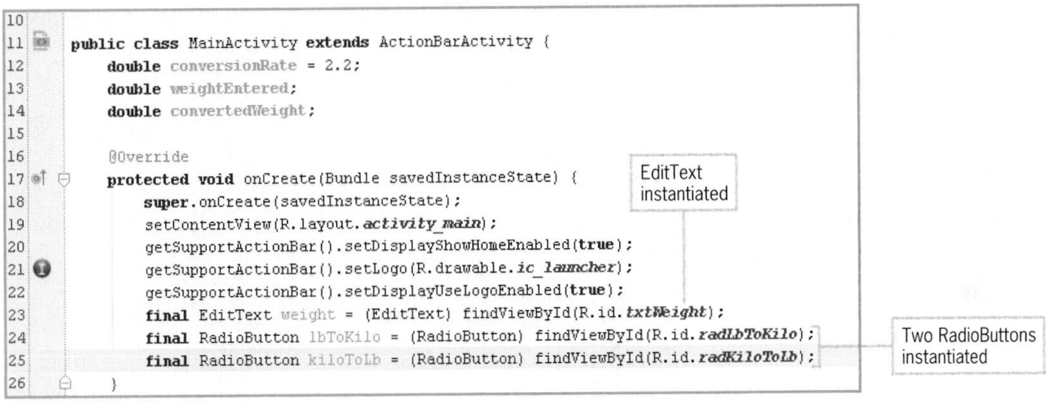

Figure 4-23 EditText and RadioButtons referenced

Coding the Button Control

The Button control detects user interaction using an event listener. The following steps instantiate the second TextView control, the Button control, and the OnClickListener.

STEP 1

- After the two lines of code referring to the RadioButton controls, type a new line with the code **final TextView result = (TextView) findViewById(R.id.txtResult);**.
- Import the TextView class.

The TextView control is instantiated to the variable result (Figure 4-24).

```
public class MainActivity extends ActionBarActivity {
    double conversionRate = 2.2;
    double weightEntered;
    double convertedWeight;

    @Override
    protected void onCreate(Bundle savedInstanceState) {
        super.onCreate(savedInstanceState);
        setContentView(R.layout.activity_main);
        getSupportActionBar().setDisplayShowHomeEnabled(true);
        getSupportActionBar().setLogo(R.drawable.ic_launcher);
        getSupportActionBar().setDisplayUseLogoEnabled(true);
        final EditText weight = (EditText) findViewById(R.id.txtWeight);
        final RadioButton lbToKilo = (RadioButton) findViewById(R.id.radLbToKilo);
        final RadioButton kiloToLb = (RadioButton) findViewById(R.id.radKiloToLb);
        final TextView result = (TextView) findViewById(R.id.txtResult);
    }
```

TextView instantiated and assigned to the variable result

Figure 4-24 TextView control referenced

STEP 2

- After the closing semicolon, press the Enter key.
- To code the button, type **Button convert = (Button) findViewById(R.id.btnConvert);**.
- Tap or click the Button code and import the Button class.
- After the closing semicolon, press the Enter key two times to separate the variables from the rest of the code.
- To code the Button listener, type **convert.setOn** and then if necessary, press Ctrl+spacebar to display an auto-complete code listing.
- Double-tap or double-click the setOnClickListener displayed in the auto-complete listing.
- Inside the parentheses, type **new On** and double-tap or double-click the first choice, which lists an OnClickListener with an Anonymous Inner Type event handler.

The btnConvert Button control and OnClickListener are coded (Figure 4-25).

Figure 4-25 OnClickListener for the Button control

Making Decisions with Conditional Statements

In the Medical Calculator chapter project, which converts the weight entered to either pounds or kilograms, the user selects one of two radio buttons. Then, based on the choice, the application either divides by 2.2 or multiplies by 2.2.

Java uses decision structures to deal with the different conditions that occur based on the values entered into an application. A **decision structure** is a fundamental control structure used in computer programming. A statement that tests the radio button is called a conditional statement and the condition checked is whether the first or second radio button is selected. If the first radio button is selected, the weight is divided by 2.2. When a condition is tested in a Java program, it is either true or false. Conditional statements allow the user to make a decision and to follow a path after the decision is made. To execute a conditional statement and the statements that are executed when a condition is true, Java uses the If statement and its variety of formats.

Using an If Statement

In the chapter program, an **If statement** is used to determine which RadioButton control is selected. The simplest form of the If statement is shown in the following code:

Code Syntax

```
if (condition) {
     //Statements completed if true
}
```

The statement(s) between the opening and closing braces are executed if the condition is true. If the condition is not true, no statements between the braces are executed, and program execution continues with the statement(s) that follows the closing brace.

Using If Else Statements

In many applications, the logic requires one set of instructions to be executed if a condition is true and another set of instructions to be executed if a condition is false. For example, a program requirement may specify that if a student's test score is 60 or greater, a message stating "You passed the examination" is displayed, but if the test score is less than 60, a message stating "You failed the examination" is displayed.

To execute one set of instructions if a condition is true, and another set of instructions if the condition is false, you can use the **If Else statement**, as shown in the following code:

Code Syntax

```
if (condition) {
     //Statements completed if condition is true
} else {
     //Statements completed if condition is false
}
```

GTK
Java automatically indents statements to be executed when a condition is true or not true to indicate that the lines of code are within the conditional If structure.

Relational Operators

In the syntax of the condition portion of the If statement, a condition is tested to determine if it is true or false. The conditions that can be tested are:

- Is one value equal to another value?
- Is one value not equal to another value?
- Is one value greater than another value?
- Is one value less than another value?
- Is one value greater than or equal to another value?
- Is one value less than or equal to another value?

To test these conditions, Java provides relational operators that are used within the conditional statement to express the relationship between the numbers being tested. Table 4-3 shows these relational operators.

Relational Operator	Meaning	Example	Resulting Condition
= =	Equal to	6 = = 6	True
! =	Not equal to	4! = 7	False
>	Greater than	3 > 2	True
<	Less than	8 < 1	False
>=	Greater than or equal to	5 >= 5	True
<=	Less than or equal to	9 <= 6	False

Table 4-3 Relational operators

In the chapter project, an If Else statement determines if the entered weight is valid. If the nurse is converting pounds to kilograms, the weight entered must be less than or equal to 500 to be considered within a valid range of acceptable entries. If the entered weight is valid, the weight is converted by dividing it by the conversion rate of 2.2, as shown in the following code:

Code Syntax

```
if (weightEntered <= 500) {
     convertedWeight = weightEntered / conversionRate;
} else {
     //Statements completed if condition is false
}
```

GTK

The most common mistake made with an If statement is the use of a single equal sign to compare equality. A single equal sign (=) is used for assigning a value to a variable, not for comparison.

In addition to numbers, strings can also be compared in a conditional statement. A string value comparison compares each character in two strings, starting with the first character in each string. All characters found in strings, including letters, numbers, and special characters, are ranked in a sequence from low to high based on how the characters are coded internally on the computer. The relational operators in Table 4-3 cannot be used with string comparisons. If you are comparing equality, string characters cannot be compared with the = = operator. Java strings are compared with the **equals method** of the String class.

If you are comparing whether a string is alphabetically before another string, use the compareTo method to determine the order of strings. Do not use the less-than or greater-than symbols as shown in Table 4-3 to compare string data types. The compareTo method returns a negative integer if the first string precedes the second string. It returns zero if the two strings being compared are equal. It returns a positive integer if the first string follows the second string. Examples of the equals and compareTo methods are shown in Table 4-4 using the following initialized variables:


```
String name1 = "Sara";
String name2 = "Shawna";
String name3 = "Ryan";
```

If Statement	Comparison	Resulting Condition
if (name1.equals(name2))	Strings are not equal	False
if (name1.compareTo(name1) = = 0)	Strings are equal	True
if (name1.compareTo(name3) = = 0)	Strings are not equal	False
if (name1.compareTo(name2) > 0)	The first string precedes the second string; returns a negative number	False
if (name1.compareTo(name3) < 0)	The first string follows the third string; returns a negative number	True
If (name3.compareTo(name2) > 0)	The first string follows the second string; returns a positive number	True
If (name3.compareTo(name2) > 0)	The first string follows the second string; returns a positive number	True

Table 4-4 Examples of the equals and compareTo methods

Logical Operators

An If statement can test more than one condition within a single statement. In many cases, more than one condition must be true or one of several conditions must be true in order for the statements within the braces to be executed. When more than one condition is included in an If statement, the conditions are called a **compound condition**. For example, consider the following business traveling rule: "If the flight costs less than $400.00 and the hotel is less than $120.00 per night, the business trip is approved." In this case, both conditions (flight less than $400.00 and hotel less than $120.00 per night) must be true for the trip to be approved. If either condition is not true, then the business trip is not approved.

To create an If statement that processes the business traveling rule, you must use a logical operator. The most common set of logical operators is listed in Table 4-5.

<table>
<tr><th>Logical Operator</th><th>Meaning</th><th>Example</th></tr>
<tr><td>&&</td><td>And—all conditions must be true</td><td>if (flight < 400 && hotel < 120)</td></tr>
<tr><td>||</td><td>Or—at least one condition must be true</td><td>if (stamp < 0.49 || rate = = 2)</td></tr>
<tr><td>!</td><td>Not—reverses the meaning of a condition</td><td>if (! (grade > 70))</td></tr>
</table>

Table 4-5 Common logical operators

Data Validation

In the chapter project, it is important to confirm that the number entered by the user is not a typo or other type of mistake. If a value greater than 500 is entered for the conversion from pounds to kilograms or greater than 225 for the conversion from kilograms to pounds, the user should be notified and asked for a valid entry. To alert the user that an incorrect value was entered, a message called a toast notification (or toast message) can appear on the screen temporarily.

Toast Notification

A **toast notification** communicates messages to the user. These messages pop up as an overlay on the user's current screen, often displaying a validation warning message. For example, a weather application may display a toast notification if a town is under a tornado warning. An instant messaging app might display a toast notification stating that a text message has been sent. In the chapter project, a toast notification displays a message warning the user that an invalid number was entered. A toast message only fills the amount of space required for the message to be displayed while the user's current activity remains visible and interactive. The notification automatically fades in and out on the screen.

The toast notification code uses a Toast object and the MakeText( ) method with three parameters: the context (displays the activity name), the text message, and the duration of the interval that the toast is displayed (LENGTH_SHORT or LENGTH_LONG). To display the toast notification, a show( ) method displays the Toast object.

Code Syntax

```
Toast toast = Toast.makeText(context, text, duration).show( );
```

The toast message is best used for short messages. If the user enters an invalid number into the Medical Calculator, a warning toast notification fades in and then out on the screen. Notice in the following syntax that the text notification message displays *Pounds must be less than 500.*

Code Syntax

```
Toast.makeText(MainActivity.this,"Pounds must be less than 500",
Toast.LENGTH_LONG).show( );
```

GTK

An ex-Microsoft employee of Google is credited with coining the term *toast*, which is a small notification window that slides upward into view, like toast popping out of a toaster.

Using the isChecked( ) Method of RadioButton Controls

You will recall that the RadioButton controls in the Medical Calculator Android application allow the user to select one conversion option. When the user selects the second radio button, a shaded small circle is displayed in that radio button. When a RadioButton is selected, the Checked property of the second RadioButton control changes from False (unselected) to True (selected). The Java code must check each RadioButton to determine if that RadioButton has been selected by the user. This checked property can be tested in an If statement using the **isChecked( ) method** to determine if the RadioButton object has been selected.

Code Syntax

```
if (lbToKilo.isChecked) {
     //Statements completed if condition is true
} else {
     //Statements completed if condition is false
}
```

If the user selects the lbToKilo RadioButton control, the statements within the If portion between the braces are completed. If the user selects the kiloToLb RadioButton control, the statements within the Else portion are completed.

Using Nested If Statements

At times, more than one decision must be made to determine what processing must occur. For example, if one condition is true, a second condition might need to be tested before the correct code is executed. To test a second condition only after determining that a first condition is true (or false), you must place an If statement within another If statement. When you do this, the inner If statement is said to be **nested** within the outer If statement. In the chapter Android app, if the user checks the first radio button to convert pounds to kilograms and if the entered weight is equal to 500 pounds or less, then the weight can be converted. If the weight is above 500 pounds, a toast notification appears with a warning. A second nested If statement evaluates whether the second radio button is checked and if the user entered 225 kilograms or less as part of the final code.

Code Syntax

```
if (lbToKilo.isChecked( )) {
   if (weightEntered <= 500) {
      convertedWeight = weightEntered / conversionRate;
   } else {
   Toast.makeText(MainActivity.this, "Pounds must be less than 500",
Toast.LENGTH_LONG).show( );
   }
}
```

Coding the Button Event

After the user enters the weight and selects the desired RadioButton, the Button control is tapped or clicked. The OnClickListener event is triggered and the conversion of the weight entered occurs. Within the onClick method, the weight entered must be converted to Double data. The syntax **Double.parseDouble** converts input to a Double data type and Integer.parseInt converts input to an Integer data type. A DecimalFormat layout is necessary to format the result to one place past the decimal point ("#.#"). If you would like to display two places past the decimal point, use the format ("#.##"). To convert the weight to a Double data type and establish the format for the output, follow these steps:

STEP 1

- On Line 35 inside the OnClick method stub of the MainActivity.java code, type **weightEntered=Double.parseDouble(weight.getText( ).toString( ));** to convert the weight entered to a Double data type.

The weight entered by the user is converted to a Double data type (Figure 4-26).

MainActivity.java × activity_main.xml ×

```
1   package net.androidbootcamp.medicalcalculator;
2
3   import ...
12
13
14  public class MainActivity extends ActionBarActivity {
15      double conversionRate = 2.2;
16      double weightEntered;
17      double convertedWeight;
18
19      @Override
20      protected void onCreate(Bundle savedInstanceState) {
21          super.onCreate(savedInstanceState);
22          setContentView(R.layout.activity_main);
23          getSupportActionBar().setDisplayShowHomeEnabled(true);
24          getSupportActionBar().setLogo(R.drawable.ic_launcher);
25          getSupportActionBar().setDisplayUseLogoEnabled(true);
26          final EditText weight = (EditText) findViewById(R.id.txtWeight);
27          final RadioButton lbToKilo = (RadioButton) findViewById(R.id.radLbToKilo);
28          final RadioButton kiloToLb = (RadioButton) findViewById(R.id.radKiloToLb);
29          final TextView result = (TextView) findViewById(R.id.txtResult);
30          Button convert = (Button) findViewById(R.id.btnConvert);
31
32          convert.setOnClickListener(new View.OnClickListener() {
33              @Override
34              public void onClick(View v) {
35                  weightEntered=Double.parseDouble(weight.getText( ).toString( ));
36              }
37          });
38      }
39
```

Converts the text assigned to weight to a double data type

Figure 4-26 Weight converted to a double data type

STEP 2

- After the closing semicolon, press the Enter key.
- To create a decimal layout that changes the weight to a decimal rounded to the nearest tenth for use in the result later in the code, type **DecimalFormat tenth = new DecimalFormat("#.#");**.
- Tap or click DecimalFormat, press Alt+Enter, and then import the DecimalFormat class.

The DecimalFormat code rounds off to the nearest tenth (Figure 4-27).

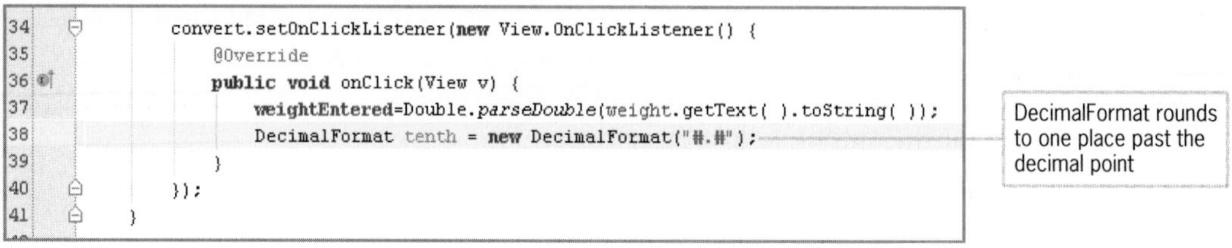

Figure 4-27 DecimalFormat—Rounding to one decimal place

Coding the Nested If Statements

After the weight entered is converted to Double data and a format is set, the next set of code determines which RadioButton was selected by using the isChecked property. Within each RadioButton If statement, the weight entered is converted to the appropriate weight unit and displayed, only if that weight is within the valid weight ranges (500 pounds or 225 kilograms). If the weight is not within the valid range, a toast notification appears warning the user to enter a value within the acceptable range. To code a nested If statement to display the result, follow these steps:

STEP 1

- After the DecimalFormat line of code, to determine if the first RadioButton control is selected, insert a new line, type **if(lbToKilo.isChecked( )) {** and press Enter. Java automatically adds the closing brace.

An If statement determines if the lbToKilo RadioButton control is checked (Figure 4-28).

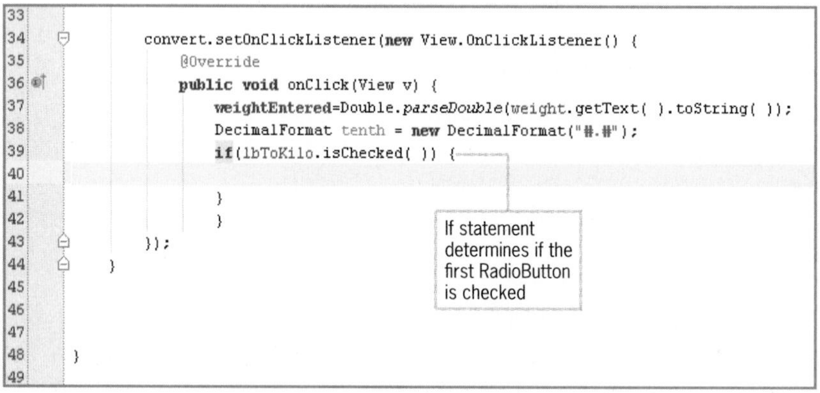

Figure 4-28 If statement to test if the first radio button is checked

STEP 2

- Within the first If statement, braces create a nested If Else statement that determines if the weight entered for pounds is less than or equal to 500. Type **if (weightEntered <=500) {** and press Enter. Java automatically adds the closing brace.
- On Line 42, after the closing brace, type **else** { and press Enter. Java automatically adds the closing brace.

A nested If Else statement determines if the number of pounds entered is valid (Figure 4-29).

```
22     protected void onCreate(Bundle savedInstanceState) {
23         super.onCreate(savedInstanceState);
24         setContentView(R.layout.activity_main);
25         getSupportActionBar().setDisplayShowHomeEnabled(true);
26         getSupportActionBar().setLogo(R.drawable.ic_launcher);
27         getSupportActionBar().setDisplayUseLogoEnabled(true);
28         final EditText weight = (EditText) findViewById(R.id.txtWeight);
29         final RadioButton lbToKilo = (RadioButton) findViewById(R.id.radLbToKilo);
30         final RadioButton kiloToLb = (RadioButton) findViewById(R.id.radKiloToLb);
31         final TextView result = (TextView) findViewById(R.id.txtResult);
32         Button convert = (Button) findViewById(R.id.btnConvert);
33
34         convert.setOnClickListener(new View.OnClickListener() {
35             @Override
36             public void onClick(View v) {
37                 weightEntered=Double.parseDouble(weight.getText( ).toString( ));
38                 DecimalFormat tenth = new DecimalFormat("#.#");
39                 if(lbToKilo.isChecked( )) {
40                     if (weightEntered <=500) {
41
42                     } else {
43
44                     }
45                 }
46             }
47         });
48     }
49
50
51
52 }
```

Nested If Else statement determines if weight is valid

Figure 4-29 Nested If Else statement

STEP 3

- After the pounds variable is validated, the weight must be converted. To divide the weight by the conversion rate of 2.2, inside the nested If statement (Line 41) after the weightEntered <= 500) { line, type **convertedWeight = weightEntered / conversionRate;** and press the Enter key.
- To display the result of the equation rounded to one place past the decimal point, type **result.setText(tenth.format(convertedWeight) + " kilograms");**.

The number of pounds is converted to kilograms and displayed in the result Plain TextView control (Figure 4-30).

```
        convert.setOnClickListener(new View.OnClickListener() {
            @Override
            public void onClick(View v) {
                weightEntered=Double.parseDouble(weight.getText( ).toString( ));
                DecimalFormat tenth = new DecimalFormat("#.#");
                if(lbToKilo.isChecked( )) {
                    if (weightEntered <=500) {
                        convertedWeight = weightEntered / conversionRate;
                        result.setText(tenth.format(convertedWeight) + " kilograms");
                    } else {

                    }
                    }
                }
        });
    }

}
```

Equation to convert pounds to kilograms

Converted weight displayed

Figure 4-30 Equation for weight conversion and displayed results

STEP 4

- If the weight is not within the valid range, a toast message requesting that the user enter a valid weight is displayed briefly. Tap or click the line after the Else statement and type **Toast.makeText(MainActivity.this,"Pounds must be less than 500", Toast.LENGTH_LONG).show( );**.
- Tap or click Toast and import the Toast class.

A toast message displays a reminder to enter a valid weight (Figure 4-31).

```
        convert.setOnClickListener(new View.OnClickListener() {
            @Override
            public void onClick(View v) {
                weightEntered=Double.parseDouble(weight.getText( ).toString( ));
                DecimalFormat tenth = new DecimalFormat("#.#");
                if(lbToKilo.isChecked( )) {
                    if (weightEntered <=500) {
                        convertedWeight = weightEntered / conversionRate;
                        result.setText(tenth.format(convertedWeight) + " kilograms");
                    } else {
                        Toast.makeText(MainActivity.this,"Pounds must be less than 500", Toast.LENGTH_LONG).show( );
                    }
                    }
                }
        });
    }

}
```

Toast message

Figure 4-31 Toast message

STEP 5

- For when the user selects the Convert the Kilograms to Pounds RadioButton control, type the following lines of code starting after the closing brace in Line 47 and press Enter after each line, as shown in Figure 4-32:

```
if(kiloToLb.isChecked( )) {
        if (weightEntered <= 225) {
              convertedWeight = weightEntered * conversionRate;
              result.setText(tenth.format(convertedWeight) + " pounds");
        } else {
         Toast.makeText(MainActivity.this, "Kilos must be less than 225",
Toast.LENGTH_LONG).show( );
```

The nested If statement is executed if the second RadioButton control is selected (Figure 4-32).

```
MainActivity.java ×    activity_main.xml ×
1     package net.androidbootcamp.medicalcalculator;
2
3    +import ...
15
16
17    public class MainActivity extends ActionBarActivity {
18        double conversionRate = 2.2;
19        double weightEntered;
20        double convertedWeight;
21
22        @Override
23        protected void onCreate(Bundle savedInstanceState) {
24            super.onCreate(savedInstanceState);
25            setContentView(R.layout.activity_main);
26            getSupportActionBar().setDisplayShowHomeEnabled(true);
27            getSupportActionBar().setLogo(R.drawable.ic_launcher);
28            getSupportActionBar().setDisplayUseLogoEnabled(true);
29            final EditText weight = (EditText) findViewById(R.id.txtWeight);
30            final RadioButton lbToKilo = (RadioButton) findViewById(R.id.radLbToKilo);
31            final RadioButton kiloToLb = (RadioButton) findViewById(R.id.radKiloToLb);
32            final TextView result = (TextView) findViewById(R.id.txtResult);
33            Button convert = (Button) findViewById(R.id.btnConvert);
34
35            convert.setOnClickListener(new View.OnClickListener() {
36                @Override
37                public void onClick(View v) {
38                    weightEntered = Double.parseDouble(weight.getText().toString());
39                    DecimalFormat tenth = new DecimalFormat("#.#");
40                    if (lbToKilo.isChecked()) {
41                        if (weightEntered <= 500) {
42                            convertedWeight = weightEntered / conversionRate;
43                            result.setText(tenth.format(convertedWeight) + " kilograms");
44                        } else {
```

Figure 4-32 Completed code *(continues)*

(continued)

```
                    Toast.makeText(MainActivity.this, "Pounds must be less than 500", Toast.LENGTH_LONG).show();
                }
            }
            if (kiloToLb.isChecked()) {
                if (weightEntered <= 225) {
                    convertedWeight = weightEntered * conversionRate;
                    result.setText(tenth.format(convertedWeight) + " pounds");
                } else {
                    Toast.makeText(MainActivity.this, "Kilos must be less than 225", Toast.LENGTH_LONG).show();
                }
            }
        }
    });
}



}

```

Figure 4-32 Completed code

Running and Testing the App

An app can be run and tested on an actual Android device or the emulator. It is best to leave the emulator running and run the app to test your code each time you make a change. To run your app, follow this step.

STEP 1

- To view the finished application, tap or click Run 'app' on the Standard toolbar, and then select an emulator to open the emulator. Unlock the emulator. Run the app again to send the code to the emulator and test the application in the emulator.
- The application opens in the emulator where you enter a weight and select a radio button.
- To view the results, tap or click the Convert Weight button.

The Medical Calculator Android app is executed (see Figures 4-1 and 4-2).

Wrap It Up—Chapter Summary

Beginning with a customized icon, this chapter has completed the steps to create the graphical user interface including a RadioGroup control for the Medical Calculator program. The decision structure including a nested If Else statement determines different outcomes based on user input. If necessary, a toast message reminds the user of the expected input. You have learned to customize feedback and make decisions based on any user's input.

- To display a custom launcher icon instead of the default icon on the home screen of an Android device, tap or click Image Asset on the New menu to open the Asset Studio dialog box.

- Include RadioButton controls to allow users to select or deselect an option. Each RadioButton control has a label defined by the Text property and a Checked property set to either true or false. In a RadioGroup control, only one RadioButton control can be selected at a time.
- Android apps can use hexadecimal color codes to set the color displayed in controls.
- For more flexibility in controlling your layout, use the layout:margin property to change the spacing between objects. Use the gravity property to position a control precisely on the screen. You can change this property using the Properties pane or the Gravity tool on the toolbar.
- A decision structure includes a conditional statement that checks whether the condition is true or false. To execute a conditional statement and the statements that are executed when a condition is true, Java uses the If statement and its variety of formats, including the If Else statement. An If statement executes one set of instructions if a specified condition is true and takes no action if the condition is not true. An If Else statement executes one set of instructions if a specified condition is true and another set of instructions if the condition is false.
- To test the conditions in a conditional statement such as an If statement, Java provides relational operators that are used within the conditional statement to express the relationship between the numbers being tested. For example, you can use a relational operator to test whether one value is greater than another.
- If more than one condition is tested in a conditional statement, the conditions are called a compound condition. To create an If statement that processes a compound condition, you must use a logical operator such as && (And).
- After including code that validates data, you can code a toast notification (also called a toast message) to display a brief message indicating that an incorrect value was entered.
- To test a second condition only after determining that a first condition is true or false, you nest one If statement within another If statement.

Key Terms

Action bar icon—An icon that appears in the top-left corner on the Action bar of an Activity.

compound condition—More than one condition included in an If statement.

decision structure—A fundamental control structure used in computer programming that deals with the different conditions that occur based on the values entered into an application.

equals method—A method of the String class that Java uses to compare strings.

Gravity—A tool that changes the linear alignment of a control, so that it is aligned to the left, center, right, top, or bottom of an object or the screen.

hexadecimal color code—A triplet of three colors using hexadecimal numbers, where colors are specified first by a pound sign followed by how much red (00 to FF), how much green (00 to FF), and how much blue (00 to FF) are in the final color.

If Else statement—A statement that executes one set of instructions if a specified condition is true and another set of instructions if the condition is false.

If statement—A statement that executes one set of instructions if a specified condition is true and takes no action if the condition is not true.

isChecked( ) method—A method that tests a checked property to determine if a RadioButton object has been selected.

launcher icon—An icon that appears on the home screen to represent the application.

margin—Blank space that offsets a control by a certain amount of density independent pixels (dp) on each of its four sides.

nest—To place one statement, such as an If statement, within another statement.

RadioGroup—A group of RadioButton controls; only one RadioButton control can be selected at a time.

toast notification—A message that appears as an overlay on a user's screen, often displaying a validation warning.

Developer FAQs

1. What is the name of the icon on the Android home screen of your device that opens an app?
2. What is the name of the icon that appears at the top-left of the opening bar across the opening screen (Activity) of the app?
3. What is the preferred prefix for a filename and file extension of the icon described in question 1?
4. To display a custom icon, what wizard can you use in Android Studio?
5. Which Plain TextView property is changed to identify the color of the control?
6. Which primary color is represented by the hexadecimal code of #00FF00?
7. What is the name of the property used to center an EditText control hint property horizontally?
8. Using the layout:margin property, in which text box would you type 18dp to move a control 18 density pixels down from the upper edge of the emulator?
9. When a RadioGroup control is placed on the emulator, the first RadioButton control is selected by default. Which property is set as true by default?

10. Write an If statement that tests if the value in the variable age is between 18 and 21 years of age, inclusive, with empty braces.
11. Write an If statement that tests if the radio button named *gender* is selected with empty braces.
12. Rewrite the following line of code without a Not logical operator but keeping the same logical processing: if (! (height <= 60) {
13. Write an If statement to compare if a string variable named *company* is equal to *AT&T* with empty braces.
14. Fix this statement: if (hours < 2 | | > 8) {
15. How many radio buttons can be selected at one time in a RadioGroup control?
16. Write an If statement that compares if wage is equal to 7.25 with empty braces.
17. If you compare two strings and the result is a positive number, what is the order of the two strings?
18. Using a relational operator, write an If statement that evaluates if a variable named *tipPercent* is not equal to .15 with empty braces.
19. Write a warning message that would display the comment "The maximum credits allowed is 18" with a long interval.
20. Write a quick reminder message that would display the comment "File saved" with a short interval.

Beyond the Book

Search the web for answers to the following questions to further your Android knowledge.

1. You have developed an application on music downloads. Search using Google Images to locate an appropriate icon and resize the icon using a paint-type program for use as a tablet app launcher icon (xhdpi).
2. Search the Google Play site for a popular app that has a Sudoku puzzle. Take a screen shot of one Sudoku puzzle's launcher icon and another screen shot of the larger graphic used for the description of the app.
3. An Android toast message can also be coded to appear at an exact location on the screen. Explain how this works and give an example of the code that would do this.
4. Research the average price of an individual paid app. Write 75-100 words on the average selling prices of Android and iPhone apps.

Case Programming Projects

Complete one or more of the following case programming projects. Use the same steps and techniques taught within the chapter. Submit the program you create to your instructor. The level of difficulty is indicated for each case programming project.

Easiest: ★

Intermediate: ★★

Challenging: ★★★

Case Project 4–1: Phone Photo Prints App ★

Requirements Document

Application title:	Phone Photo Prints App
Purpose:	The app determines the cost of printing photos from your phone. The pictures are delivered directly to your home.
Algorithms:	1. The opening screen requests the number of photos to print from a user's phone (Figure 4-33). 2. The user selects a radio button labeled 4 × 6 prints (19 cents each) or 5 × 7 prints (49 cents each) and 8 × 10 prints (79 cents each) then selects the ORDER PRINTS button. 3. The cost is displayed for the number of prints (Figure 4-34).
Conditions:	1. The result is rounded to the nearest penny. 2. Do not enter more than 50 prints. 3. Use a theme that displays an Action bar with the custom Action bar icon in the finished layout. 4. Use a custom launcher icon named ic_launcher_photo.png.

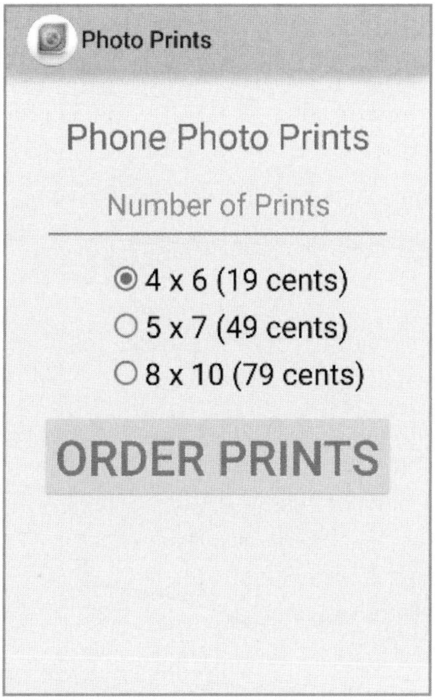

Figure 4-33 Phone Photo Prints opening screen

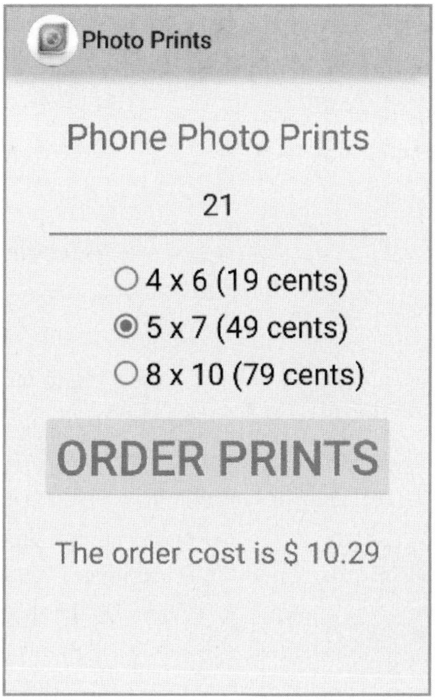

Figure 4-34 Number of prints and cost

Case Project 4–2: Car Wash App ★

Requirements Document

Application title:	Car Wash App
Purpose:	Large cities provide car wash apps where you can purchase packages for your vehicle.
Algorithms:	1. The opening screen requests the type of car wash package you would like to purchase (Figure 4-35). 2. The user selects which type of car wash – exterior only or exterior with interior vacuum services. The Car Wash app charges $8.99 for an exterior wash and $12.99 for an exterior wash with an interior vacuum for a package of 12 or more car washes. If you select less than 12 washes, the charge is $10.99 for an exterior wash or $15.99 for an exterior with interior vacuum. 3. When the CALCULATE PACKAGE button is selected, the total price is displayed for the number of car washes purchased (Figure 4-36).
Conditions:	1. Use a customized launcher icon (ic_launcher_carwash.png) and display the same icon in the Action bar using the Theme.AppCompat.Light theme. 2. Display an ImageView control (carwash.png). 3. Only one RadioButton control can be selected. 4. A toast message should pop up when the user enters less than 12 watches that they must buy 12 washes to receive a discount.

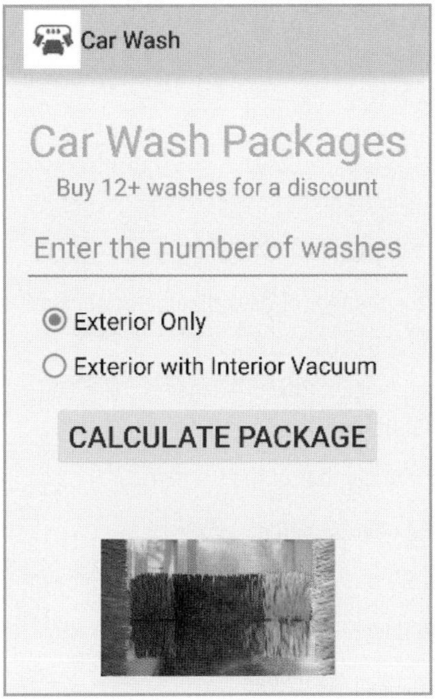

Figure 4-35 Car Wash Packages opening screen

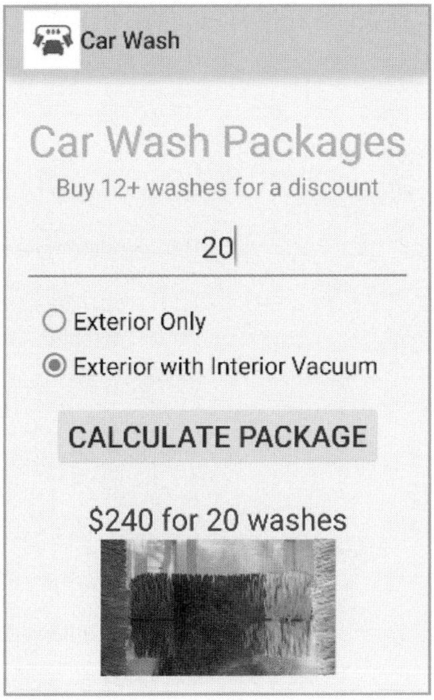

Figure 4-36 Number of washes and cost

Case Project 4–3: Power Tool Rental App ★★

Requirements Document

Application title: Power Tool Rental App

Purpose: The app determines the cost of a power washer or tiller.

Algorithms:

1. The opening screen requests the number of days that the power tool will be rented.
2. The user selects a radio button labeled Power Washer or Tiller and then selects the Compute Cost button.
3. The final cost is displayed for the number of days rented.

Conditions:

1. The result is rounded off to the nearest penny.
2. The power washer costs $55.99 a day and the tiller $68.99 a day.
3. Do not enter more than seven days.
4. Locate an image online and resize it for use as a custom launcher icon and Action bar icon.

Case Project 4–4: Floor Tiling App ★★

Requirements Document

Application title: Floor Tiling App

Purpose: The tiling app allows you to calculate how many tiles you need to cover a rectangular area.

Algorithms:

1. The opening screen requests the length and the width of a room in whole feet.
2. The user selects whether the tiles are 12 inches by 12 inches or 18 inches by 18 inches.
3. The number of tiles needed to cover the area in square feet is displayed.

Case Project 4–5: Currency Conversion App ★★★

Requirements Document

Application title:	Currency Conversion App
Purpose:	The Currency Conversion app converts U.S. dollars into euros, Mexican pesos, or Canadian dollars.
Algorithms:	1. The opening screen requests the amount of U.S. dollars to be converted. 2. The user selects euros, Mexican pesos, or Canadian dollars. 3. The conversion of U.S. dollars to the selected currency is displayed.
Conditions:	1. Use *http://xe.com* to locate current conversion rates. 2. The program only converts values below $100,000 U.S. dollars. 3. Use a customized launcher icon.

Case Project 4–6: Average Income Tax by Country App ★★★

Requirements Document

Application title:	Average Income Tax by Country App
Purpose:	The Average Income Tax by Country app allows the user to enter the amount of taxable income earned in the past year. The user selects his or her country of residence and the yearly income tax is displayed.
Algorithms:	1. The opening screen requests two integer values. 2. The user can select addition, subtraction, or multiplication. 3. The entire math problem is displayed with the result.
Conditions:	The following table displays the annual income tax percentages.

Country	**Average Income Tax**
China	25%
Germany	32%
Sweden	34%
USA	18%

CHAPTER 5

Investigate! Android Lists, Arrays, and Web Browsers

In this chapter, you learn to:

- Create an Android project using a list
- Develop a user interface that uses a ListView
- Extend the ListActivity class
- Use an array to create a list
- Code a setListAdapter to display an array
- Design a custom ListView layout with XML code
- Display an image with the ListView control
- Change the default title bar text
- Code a custom setListAdapter for a custom layout
- Call the onListItemClick method when a list item is selected
- Write code using the Switch decision structure
- Call an intent to work with an outside app
- Open an Android web browser
- Launch a website with a URI using an Android browser
- Test an application with multiple decisions

Displaying a list is one of the most common design patterns used in mobile applications. This morning you likely read the news designed as a listing of articles on a phone or tablet. You scrolled down the list of news articles and selected one by tapping the screen to display a full story with text, images, and hyperlinks. As you walked to class today, you probably scrolled a list of songs on a mobile device and listened to your favorite tunes.

From a list, you can open an article, play a song, open a website, or even launch a video. A list created with a ListView control may be one of the most important Android design elements because it is used so frequently. To select a list item, a design structure is necessary to route your request to the intended content. In Chapter 4, you learned about the decision structure called an If statement, one of the major control structures used in computer programming. In this chapter, you learn about another decision structure called the Switch statement.

To demonstrate the process of using a list to navigate to different content, you design a travel guide for Chicago, Illinois, highlighting the best attractions the city has to offer. The City Guide application shown in Figure 5-1 provides a list of city attractions. A guide for a large city can provide easy access to all its sights, activities, and restaurants in one handy place on your phone.

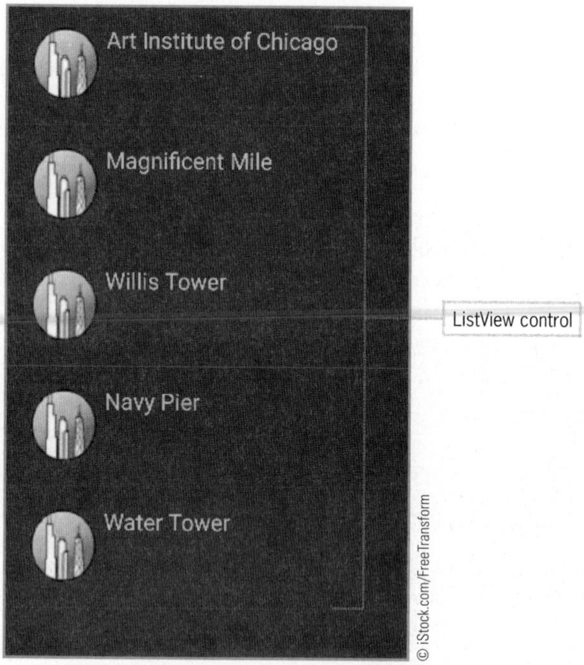

Figure 5-1 The City Guide Android app

The Android app in Figure 5-1 could be part of a larger app that displays city maps, detailed site information, and restaurant recommendations. This mobile app provides information about popular places tourists visit in Chicago. The City Guide app displays five Chicago attractions. When the user taps one of the attractions, a second window opens displaying either an image or a website providing more information about the site or activity. The first two items on the list link to websites, as shown in Figure 5-2. A browser opens to display a website for the Art Institute of Chicago or the Magnificent Mile. If the user selects Willis Tower, Navy Pier, or Water Tower, an image appears on a second screen, as shown in Figure 5-3. By pressing the left Hardware Button on the emulator, you can return to the list of the attractions.

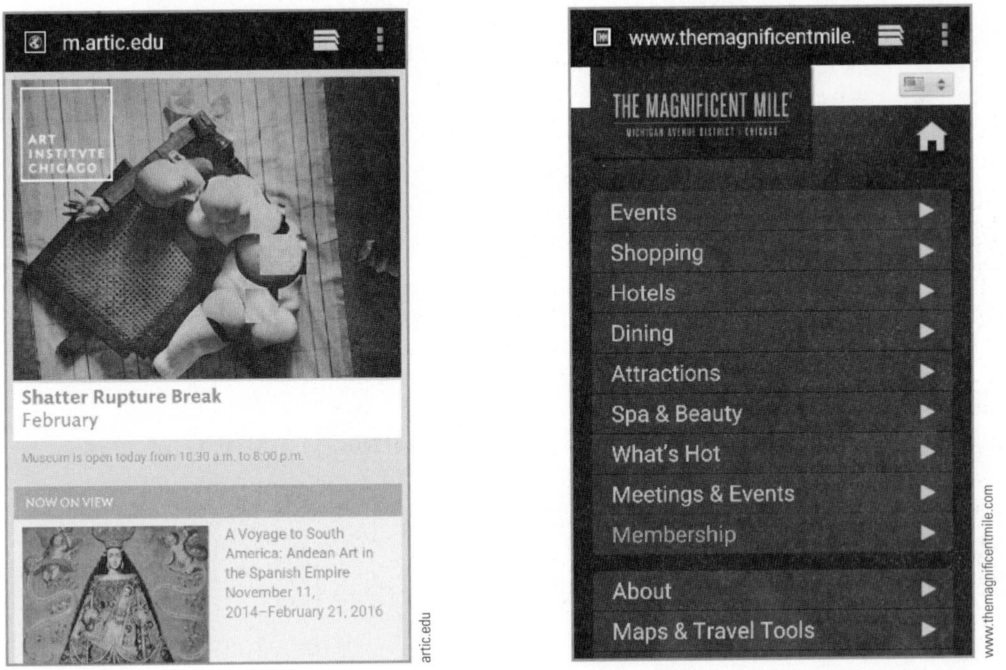

Figure 5-2 Art Institute of Chicago and Magnificent Mile websites

Figure 5-3 Chicago attractions

IN THE TRENCHES

To see a professional city guide app in action, download a free app created by Trip Advisor or Triposo.

To create this application, the developer must understand how to perform the following processes, among others:

1. Create a list using a ListView control.
2. Define an array to establish the items in the list.
3. Add the images used in the project.
4. Define an XML file to design the custom list with a leading image.
5. Code a Switch decision structure to handle the selection of items.
6. Open an Android web browser to display a specified Uniform Resource Identifier (URI).
7. Create multiple classes and XML layout files to display pictures of attractions.

Creating a List

The Chicago City Guide app begins with a vertical list of attractions on the opening screen, as shown in Figure 5-1. The Java View class creates the list and makes it scrollable if it exceeds the length of the screen. Lists can be used to display to-do items, your personal contacts, recipe names, shopping items, weekly weather, Twitter messages, and Facebook postings, for example. You use a ListView control to contain the list items. Android also has a TableLayout view that looks similar to a ListView, but a ListView allows you to select each row in the list for further action. Selecting an item opens a web browser to a related webpage or displays an image of the attraction. You can directly use the ListView control in the Composite category of the Palette in the layout of the emulator (Figure 5-4) as you can with any other user interface component, but coding the list in Java is the preferred method and is used in the chapter project.

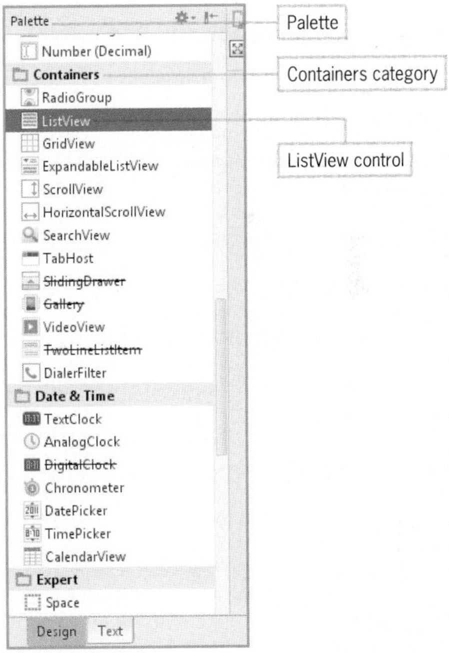

Figure 5-4 ListView control on the Palette

Extending a ListActivity

You begin creating a list by opening MainActivity.java and changing the type of Activity in the code. In the previous chapters, each opening class statement (public class Main extends Activity) extended the basic Activity class. If the primary purpose of a class is to display a ListView control, use a class named **ListActivity** instead, which makes it simple to display a list of items within the app. To add a custom icon launcher and extend the ListActivity class of MainActivity.java of the City Guide app, follow these steps to begin the application:

STEP 1

- Open the Android Studio program.
- On the Welcome to Android Studio page of the Android Studio dialog box, tap or click the Start a new Android Studio project selection in the Quick Start category.
- In the Create New Project dialog box, enter **City Guide** in the Application name text box.
- In the Company Domain text box, type **androidbootcamp.net**, if necessary.
- In the Project location text box, type **D:\Workspace\CityGuide** (if necessary, enter a different drive letter that identifies the USB drive) to select a workspace, and then tap or click the OK button.
- Tap or click the Next button on the Configure your new project page of the Create New Project dialog box.
- If necessary, tap or click the Phone and Tablet check box to select the form factor for your app.
- If necessary, select API 15: Android 4.0.3 (IceCreamSandwich) for the Minimum SDK.
- Tap or click the Next button on the Select the form factors your app will run on page.
- If necessary, tap or click Blank Activity to add an Activity to the new project.
- Tap or click the Next button on the Add an activity to Mobile page.
- Tap or click the Finish button on the Choose options for your new file page.
- Tap or click the Hello world! TextView widget (displayed by default) in the emulator and press the Delete key.
- Tap or click 'the virtual device to render the layout with' button (emulator) directly to the right of the Palette on the activity_main.xml tab, and then click Nexus 5 (5.0", 1080 × 1920, xxhdpi).

The new City Guide project has a MainActivity and activity_main.xml (Figure 5-5).

Figure 5-5 Application information for the new Android project

STEP 2

- Open MainActivity.java, show line numbers, and delete Lines 18–38.
- Tap or click File on the menu bar and then tap or click New to open the New menu.
- Tap or click Image Asset on the New menu.
- To add the custom launcher icon, copy the student files to your USB drive (if necessary). Tap or click the Image file ellipsis button, and then navigate to the USB folder containing the student files to locate and then select the file ic_launcher_chicago.png.
- Tap or click the OK button to add the custom launcher icon.
- In the Shape category, tap or click the Circle radio button to trim the background from the icon launcher.

The custom launcher icon of the Chicago skyline is displayed in different sizes (Figure 5-6).

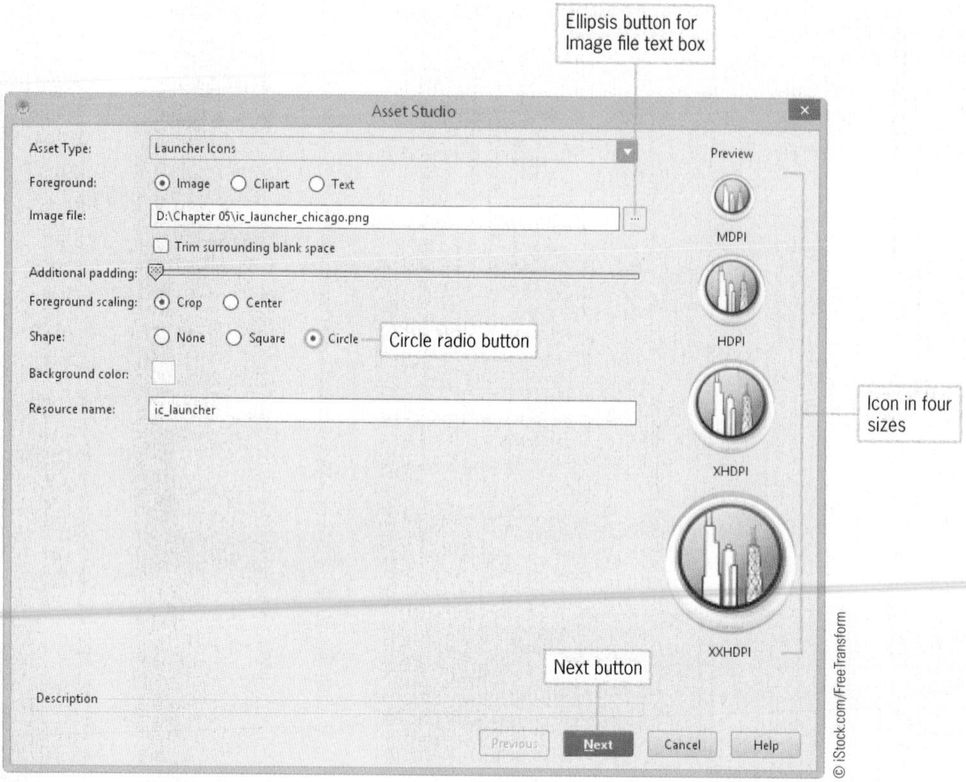

Figure 5-6 Asset Studio dialog box

STEP 3

- Tap or click the Next button to view the output directories and then tap or click the Finish button to update the launcher icon.
- Tap or click to the left of *Activity* in the public class MainActivity extends ActionBarActivity { line, and then change ActionBarActivity to **ListActivity**.
- Tap or click the red ListActivity text and then press Alt+Enter to import ListActivity.
- Delete the line setContentView(R.layout.activity_main); because the layout will be custom coded later in the XML code window.

Main extends ListActivity, which contains predefined methods for the use of lists (Figure 5-7).

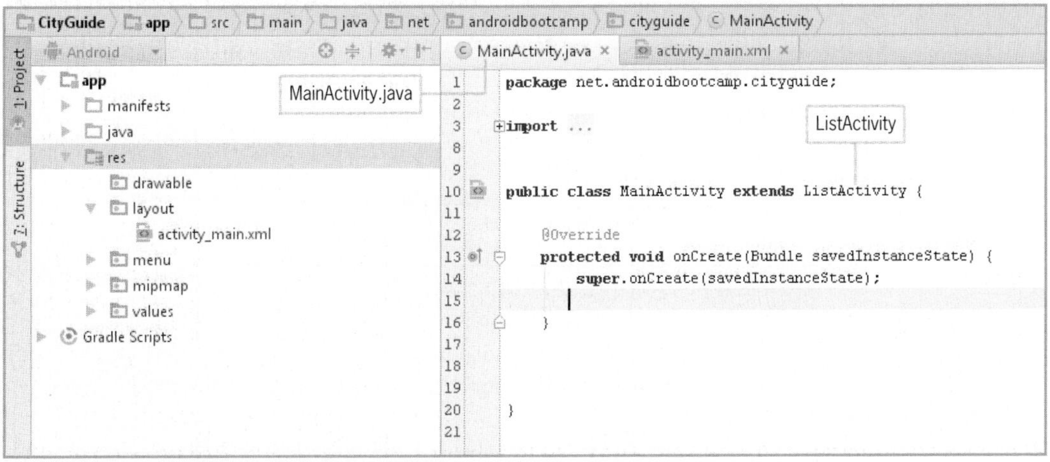

Figure 5-7 MainActivity extends ListActivity

IN THE TRENCHES

Another type of a ListView control is the ExpandableListView, which provides a two-level list. For example, if you were renting a car, a list of all the compact cars would be listed in one category on the top half of your phone and the economy cars in a separate category at the bottom. ExpandableListView provides two separate listings.

Creating an Array

Before the list of attractions can be displayed, the string of attraction names must be declared. By using an **array variable**, which can store more than one value, you can avoid assigning a separate variable for each item in the list. Every application developed thus far involved a limited number of variables. Professional programming applications commonly require much larger sets of data using multiple variables. You learned that data type variables can store only one value at a time. If you changed a variable's value, the previous value would be deleted because a typical variable can store only one value at a time. Each individual item in an array that contains a value is called an **element**.

Arrays provide access to data by using a numeric index, or subscript, to identify each element in the array. Using an array, you can store a collection of values of similar data types. For example, you can store five string values without having to declare five different variables. Instead, each value is stored in an individual element of the array, and you refer to each element by its index within the array. The index used to reference a value in the first element within an array is zero. Each subsequent element is referenced by an increasing index value, as shown in Table 5-1.

Element	Value
Attraction[0]	Art Institute of Chicago
Attraction[1]	Magnificent Mile
Attraction[2]	Willis Tower
Attraction[3]	Navy Pier
Attraction[4]	Water Tower

Table 5-1 Attraction array with index values

In Table 5-1, an array named attraction holds five attractions. Each attraction is stored in an array element, and each element is assigned a unique index. The first string is stored in the element with the index of 0. The element is identified by the term Attraction[0], pronounced "attraction sub zero."

Declaring an Array

Like declarations for variables of other types, an array declaration has two components: the array's data type and the array's name. An array is a container object that holds a fixed number of values of a single type. You can declare an array containing numeric values as in the following coding examples:

```
int[] age={18,21,38,88};
double[] weather={72.3, 65.0, 25.7, 99.5};
char[] initials={'P','N','D'};
```

Declare a String array containing the text values used in the chapter project with the following code:

Code Syntax

```
String[] attraction={"Art Institute of Chicago", "Magnificent Mile",
"Willis Tower", "Navy Pier", "Water Tower"};
```

The attraction list initialized in the array can easily be expanded to include more items at any time. To assign the listing of attractions to the String data type in an array named attraction, follow these steps:

STEP 1

- After the super.onCreate(savedInstanceState); statement in MainActivity.java, insert a new line.
- Type **String[ ] attraction={"Art Institute of Chicago", "Magnificent Mile", "Willis Tower", "Navy Pier", "Water Tower"}**;.

The String array named attraction is assigned the five attractions (Figure 5-8).

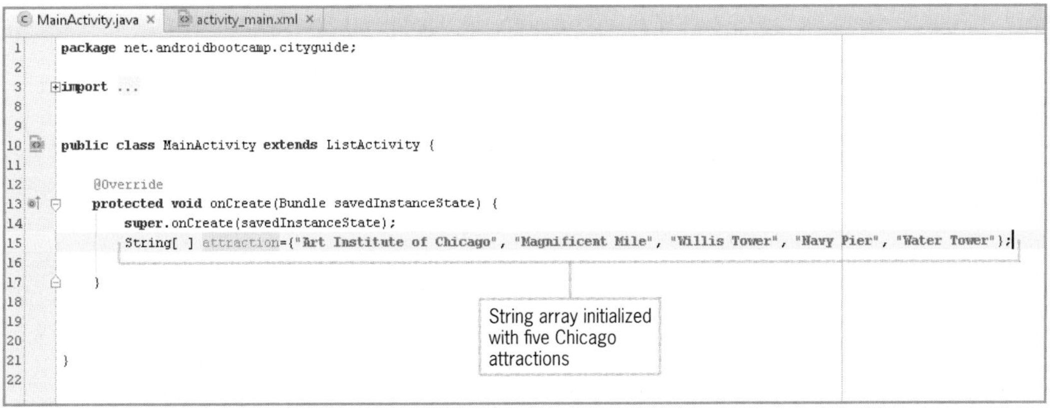

Figure 5-8 String array initialized with attractions

STEP 2

- Save your work.

GTK

To declare an array without assigning actual values, allocate the size of the array in the brackets to reserve the room needed in memory, as in int[ ] ages = new int[100];. The first number assigned to the ages array is placed in ages [0]. This array holds 101 elements in the array, one more than the maximum index. The actual values can be assigned later as input values.

Using a setListAdapter and Array Adapter

In the City Guide application, once the array is assigned, you can display an array listing using adapters. An **adapter** provides a data model for the layout of the list and for converting the data from the array into list items. The ListView and adapter work together to display a list. For example, if you want to share an iPad screen with a group, you need an adapter to connect to a projector to display the image on a large screen. Similarly, a **setListAdapter** projects your data to the on-screen list on your device by connecting the ListActivity's ListView object to the array data. A setListAdapter contains the information to connect the onscreen list with the attraction array in the chapter project. Calling a setListAdapter in the Java code binds the elements of the array to a ListView layout. In the next portion of the statement, a ListAdapter called an **ArrayAdapter<String>** supplies the String array data to the ListView. The three parameters that follow ArrayAdapter refer to the *this* class, a generic layout called simple_list_item_l, and the array named attraction. The following code syntax shows the complete statement:

Code Syntax

```
setListAdapter(new ArrayAdapter<String>(this,
    android.R.layout.simple_list_item_1, attraction));
```

Later in the chapter, instead of using the generic layout called simple_list_item_1, you design an XML layout to customize the layout to include the City Guide's logo. You can change the setListAdapter statement to reference the custom layout when you finish designing it. Follow these steps to add the setListAdapter that displays the array as a list and to change the theme style to a dark background:

STEP 1

- After the line of code initializing the String array, press Enter.
- Type **setListAdapter(new ArrayAdapter<String>(this, android.R.layout.simple_list_item_1, attraction));** and press Enter.
- Tap or click the red ArrayAdapter text and import ArrayAdapter by pressing Alt+Enter.

The setListAdapter displays the attraction array in a generic ListView layout (Figure 5-9).

```
public class MainActivity extends ListActivity {

    @Override
    protected void onCreate(Bundle savedInstanceState) {
        super.onCreate(savedInstanceState);
        String[ ] attraction={"Art Institute of Chicago", "Magnificent Mile", "Willis Tower", "Navy Pier", "Water Tower"};
        setListAdapter(new ArrayAdapter<String>(this, android.R.layout.simple_list_item_1, attraction));

    }

```

setListAdapter command

Generic built-in layout named simple_list_item_1

Figure 5-9 setListAdapter displays an array

STEP 2

- To display the attraction list in the generic ListView layout, tap or click Run 'app' on the toolbar, and then select the emulator. Tap or click the OK button.
- Unlock the emulator when the app starts and run the app again to display the ListView menu in the emulator.

The application opens in the emulator window displaying the ListView control with the five attractions in Chicago (Figure 5-10).

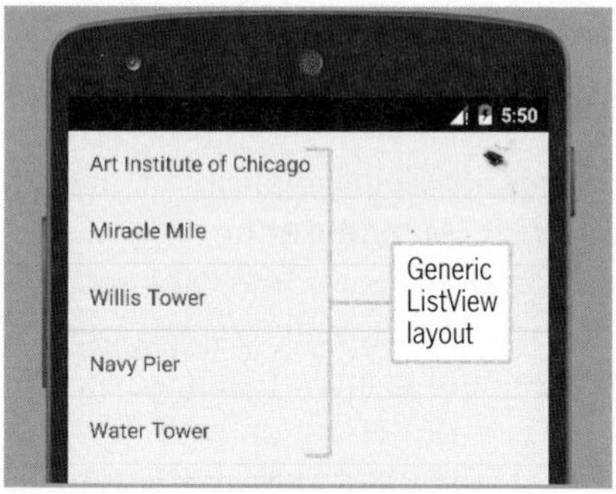

Figure 5-10 ListView built-in layout

STEP 3

- Close the emulated application window.
- To change the theme to a dark background in the finished app, expand the res\values folder in the Android project view, and then double-tap or double-click styles.xml.
- Tap or click to the right of parent= and change the parent theme to "Theme.AppCompat".

The theme is updated in styles.xml to display a dark gray background and a black title bar when the application is executed (Figure 5-11).

Figure 5-11 styles.xml with theme changed

STEP 4

- Close styles.xml and tap or click the Save All button.

GTK
Other generic layouts that display different layouts of the ListView object that you might want to try include simple_list_item_2, simple_list_item_checked (displays check boxes), and simple_list_item_multiple_choice.

Adding the Images to the Resources Folder

The City Guide application uses several images throughout the app. An icon logo called ic_launcher_chicago.png displays the skyline of Chicago and is used multiple times on the opening screen. Images of the Willis Tower, Navy Pier, and the Water Tower appear when the user selects those items from the opening list. To place a copy of the images from the USB drive into the res/drawable folder, follow these steps:

STEP 1

- If necessary, copy the student files to your USB drive. Open the USB folder containing the student files.
- To add the four image files to the drawable resource folder, select the four image files ic_launcher_chicago.png, pier.png, water.png, and willis.png on the USB drive, then press Ctrl+C.
- To paste the image files to the drawable folder, press and hold or right-click the drawable folder in the Android project view pane.
- Release the mouse button. Tap or click the OK button in the Copy dialog box, and then expand the drawable folder, if necessary.

Copies of the four files appear in the drawable folder (Figure 5-12).

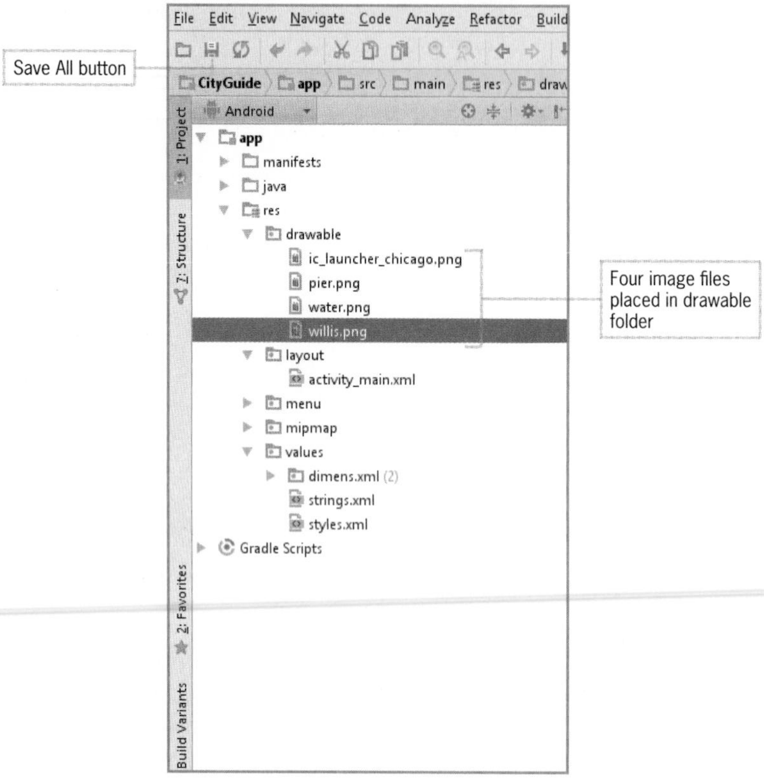

Figure 5-12 Images copied

STEP 2

- Tap or click the Save All button on the Standard toolbar to save your work.

IN THE TRENCHES

When publishing apps, you must follow copyright laws relative to copyrighted images used within your Android apps. Copyright is the legal protection extended to the authors or owners of original published and unpublished artistic and intellectual works, and you must seek copyright permissions. A copyright holder can also seek monetary or statutory damages for the violation of copyright. However, if the image is accompanied by the statement "This work is dedicated to the public domain," the image is available for fair use in your app.

Adding the String Table

To add three strings for the three ImageView control descriptions, follow these steps:

STEP 1

- In the res\values folder, double-tap or double-click the strings.xml file.
- Tap or click the Open editor link in strings.xml.

- Tap or click the Add Key button (plus sign), type **willis** in the Key text box, and then type **Willis Tower Image** in the Default Value text box. Tap or click the OK button.
- Tap or click the Add Key button again, type **pier** in the Key text box, and then type **Navy Pier Image** in the Default Value text box. Tap or click the OK button.
- Tap or click the Add Key button again, type **water** in the Key text box, and then type **Water Tower Image** in the Default Value text box. Tap or click the OK button.

The image description keys are entered in the Translations Editor (Figure 5-13).

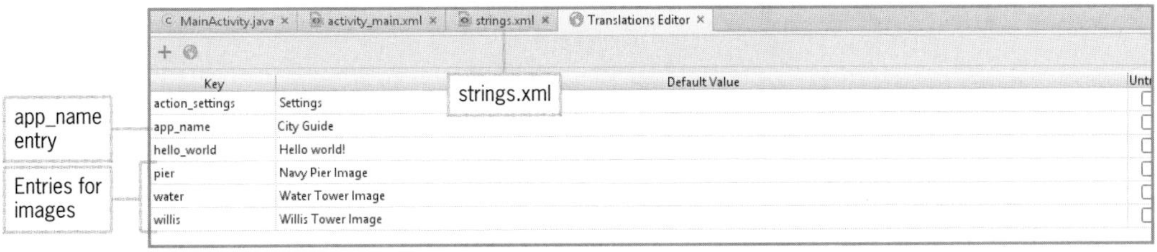

Figure 5-13 String table

STEP 2

- Save your work and close the Translations Editor and strings.xml tabs.

Creating a Custom XML Layout for a ListView

You can design a layout by using the emulator window on the Text tab and then drag and drop controls from the Palette, or you can code the activity_main.xml file using XML code. The XML code uses an auto-complete feature that assists you as you type XML code. As soon as you start typing an XML command or phrase, the XML code editor shows a list containing the probable words or phrases that you want to enter without requiring you to type it completely. This feature makes the application easier to use and improves the user experience.

It is often easier to use the Palette for a simple layout, but understanding how to manipulate XML code can assist you greatly in app design. Android Studio provides a live layout editing mode that lets you preview the XML code changes directly to the right of the XML code window in an emulator. The opening screen for the City Guide chapter project shown in Figure 5-1 requires a custom layout for the list that includes a Chicago City Guide logo and unique size and spacing of the attraction names. In the XML code, you must add a TextView control with the id name of travel. The text property of android:text="@+id/travel" is used in the setListAdapter in the Java code (MainActivity.java) and the actual items in the array named attraction display instead of the text object named travel. Next the layout is identified, and the textSize property is set to 20sp. To display the ic_launcher_chicago image file in front of the city attractions TextView object, the location source of the file is entered. The android:drawableLeft command directs that the drawable image be drawn to the left of the text. Other commands such as drawableTop would place the image above the text. To create a custom XML layout for activity_main.xml, follow these steps:

STEP 1

- Tap or click the activity_main.xml tab.
- Tap or click the Text tab at the bottom of the window to display the XML code and show line numbers. By default, a RelativeLayout is already set.
- Tap or click Line 7 above the closing statement </RelativeLayout>, and then press Enter.
- Type **<TextView** and press Enter.

The TextView control is added by typing XML code instead of dragging the TextView control to the emulator from the Palette (Figure 5-14).

Figure 5-14 TextView XML code in activity_main.xml

STEP 2

- Type the following code using auto-completion as much as possible:

```
android:layout_width="fill_parent"
android:layout_height="wrap_content"
android:id="@+id/travel"
android:textSize="20sp"
android:text="@+id/travel"
android:drawableLeft="@drawable/ic_launcher_chicago" />
```

- Press Enter after the closing angle bracket and save your work.

The TextView control is customized in the activity_main.xml file to display an image to the left of the attractions text from the array (Figure 5-14). Notice on the right side of the window, the live layout emulator displays the path of the activity_main.xml. Code is still needed to set the icon in the ListAdapter to display the icon before the attraction names.

Critical Thinking

Can an image be placed to the right of the text on each line in the ListView display?

Yes. Replace the android:drawableLeft XML statement in the last series of steps with android:drawableRight.

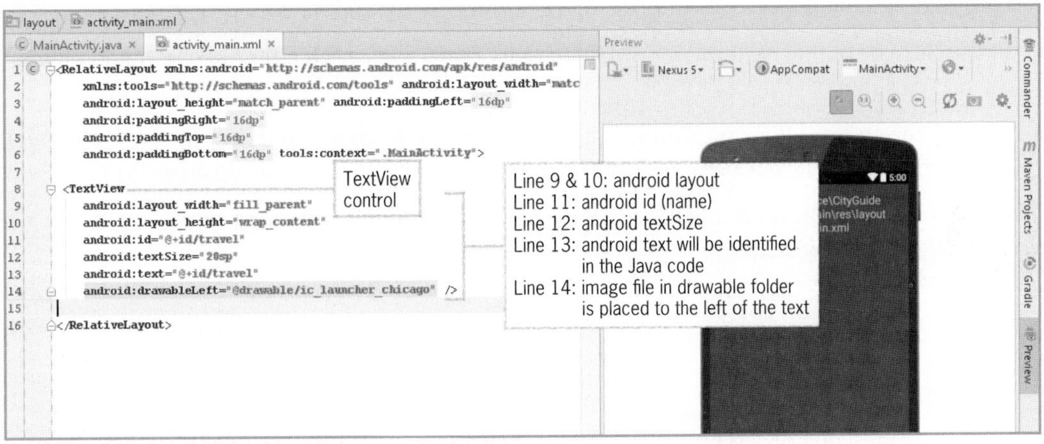

Figure 5-15 TextView XML code

Coding a setListAdapter with a Custom XML Layout

When the setListAdapter was coded earlier and executed as shown in Figure 5-10, the attractions list was displayed within a built-in layout called simple_list_item_1 in the following statement:

```
setListAdapter(new ArrayAdapter<String>(this,
android.R.layout.simple_list_item_1, attraction));
```

Instead of using a standard layout in the setListAdapter, the custom XML layout you designed in activity_main.xml in Figure 5-15 adds the Chicago City Guide icon and updates the TextView properties. The syntax changes from the default in two significant ways:

1. The second parameter in the default statement (android.R.layout.*simple_list_item_1*) is changed to R.layout.*activity_main*. The android reference is removed because the Android library default layout is not being used. Instead R.layout.*activity_main* references the activity_main.xml custom layout design for the TextView control.
2. A third parameter is added before the attraction array name to reference the variable travel, which identifies the TextView control created in the activity_main.xml file. The variable is substituted for the actual attraction names initialized in the attraction array.

The following code syntax shows the code for a custom XML layout:

Code Syntax

```
setListAdapter(new ArrayAdapter<String>(this,
  R.layout.activity_main, R.id.travel, attraction));
```

To edit the setListAdapter to use the custom XML layout, follow these steps:

STEP 1

- Close the activity_main.xml window.
- In the setListAdapter statement of MainActivity.java, tap or click after the comma following the *this* command.
- Change the android.R.layout.simple_list_item_1, text to **R.layout.activity_main, R.id.travel,** to add the custom layout named activity_main.xml before the comma and attraction.

The default setListAdapter is edited to include the custom layout referenced in activity_main.xml (Figure 5-16).

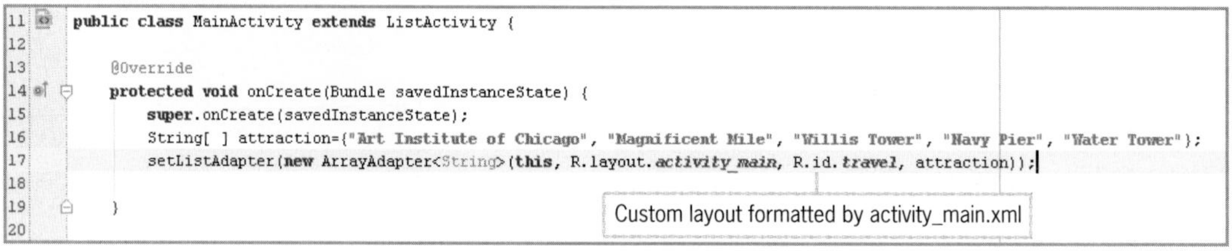

Figure 5-16 setListAdapter with custom layout for list

STEP 2

- Save and run the application to view the custom layout of the ListView.

The emulator displays the opening screen with a custom ListView (Figure 5-17).

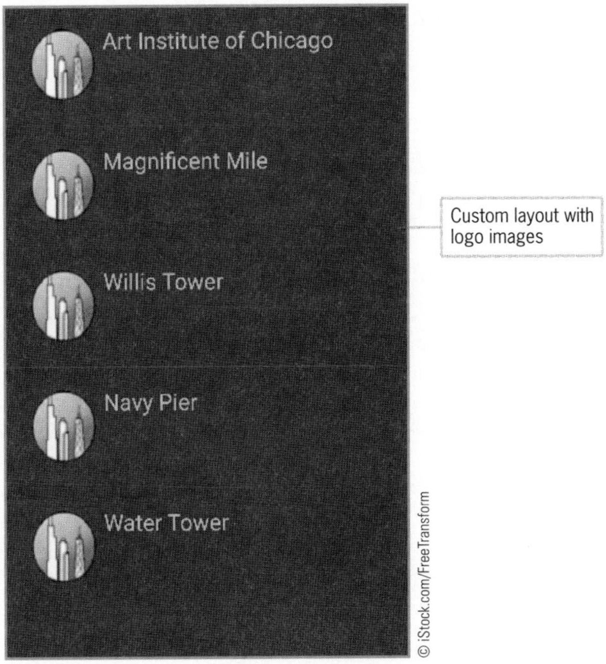

Figure 5-17 ListView custom layout in emulator

STEP 3

- Close the emulated application window.

Using the onListItemClick Method

The City Guide opening screen has a custom list shown in Figure 5-17. Each of the attractions displayed in the list can be selected by tapping the attraction name on the mobile device. The method **onListItemClick( )** is called when an item in the list is selected. The onListItemClick method is similar to the Button OnClickListener, which awaits user interaction. When an attraction in the list is selected, the **position** of the item is passed from onListItemClick and evaluated with a decision structure, as shown in the following code syntax. If the user selects the first attraction (Art Institute of Chicago), the position parameter is assigned an integer value of 0. The second item is assigned the position of 1, and so forth. The first position or index of an array is always zero.

Code Syntax

```
protected void onListItemClick(ListView l, View v, int position, long id){
  }
```

In the code syntax of the onListItemClick, the int position argument represents the position number of the selected attraction. To code the onListItemClick method to respond to the event of the user's selection, follow these steps:

STEP 1

- In MainActivity.java, tap or click after the closing brace of the onCreate method in Line 20 to add a new line.
- To respond to the user's selection, type **protected void onListItemClick(ListView l, View v, int position, long id)** to create an onListItemClick method to await the user's selection from the ListView items. (Be sure to type a lowercase letter l after ListView, not the number 1.)
- Type an opening brace { after the statement and press Enter. A closing brace is automatically placed in the code.
- After the code is entered to reference the ListView and View, tap or click the red ListView text, press Alt+Enter, and Import Class, if necessary.
- Tap or click the red View text and import View.

The onListItemClick method detects the selection's position (Figure 5-18).

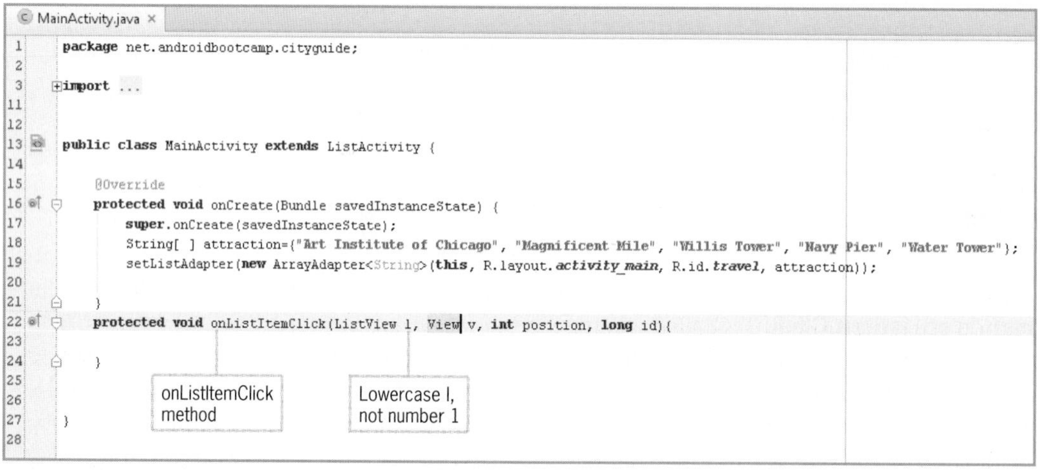

Figure 5-18 onListItemClick method

STEP 2

- Save your work.

Decision Structure—Switch Statement

Each item in the list produces a different result when selected, such as opening a web browser or displaying a picture of the attraction on a second screen. In Chapter 4, If statements evaluated the user's selection and the decision structure determined the results. You can use another decision structure called a Switch statement with a list or menu. The **Switch** statement allows you to choose from many statements based on an integer or char (single character) input. The switch keyword is followed by an integer expression in parentheses, which is followed by the cases, all enclosed in braces, as shown in the following code syntax:

Code Syntax

```
switch(position){
  case 0:
    //statements that are executed if position == 0
  break;
  case 1:
    //statements that are executed if position == 1
  break;
  default:
    //statements that are executed if position != any of the cases
}
```

The integer named *position* is evaluated in the Switch statement and executes the corresponding case. The **case** keyword is followed by a value and a colon. Typically the statement within a case ends with a **break** statement, which exits the Switch decision structure and continues with the next statement. Be careful not to omit the break statement or the subsequent case statement will be executed as well. If there is no matching case value, the default option is executed. A default statement is optional. In the chapter project, a default statement is not necessary because the user must select one of the items in the list for an action to occur.

Critical Thinking

When should I use an If statement versus a Switch statement decision structure?

Technically these statements are interchangeable, but a Switch statement is best when you would otherwise be using a list of If statements that all compare the value of the same variable.

In the City Guide app, five attractions make up the list, so the following positions are possible for the Switch statement: case 0, case 1, case 2, case 3, and case 4. To code the Switch decision structure, follow these steps:

STEP 1

- On Line 23, within the braces of the onListItemClick method, type **switch(position){** and press Enter for the closing brace to appear.

The Switch decision structure is coded within the onListItemClick method to determine which attraction was selected (Figure 5-19).

```
public class MainActivity extends ListActivity {

    @Override
    protected void onCreate(Bundle savedInstanceState) {
        super.onCreate(savedInstanceState);
        String[ ] attraction={"Art Institute of Chicago", "Magnificent Mile", "Willis Tower", "Navy Pier", "Water Tower"};
        setListAdapter(new ArrayAdapter<String>(this, R.layout.activity_main, R.id.travel, attraction));

    }
    protected void onListItemClick(ListView l, View v, int position, long id){
        switch(position){

        }
    }


}
```

Beginning of switch statement decision structure

Figure 5-19 Switch statement

STEP 2

- Within the braces of the switch statement, add the case integer options. Type the following code, inserting a blank line after each case statement:

```
case 0:
     break;

case 1:
     break;

case 2:
     break;

case 3:
     break;

case 4:
     break;
```

The case statements for the five selections from the attractions list each are coded (Figure 5-20).

```
@Override
protected void onCreate(Bundle savedInstanceState) {
    super.onCreate(savedInstanceState);
    String[ ] attraction={"Art Institute of Chicago", "Magnificent Mile", "Willis Tower", "Navy Pier", "Water Tower"};
    setListAdapter(new ArrayAdapter<String>(this, R.layout.activity_main, R.id.travel, attraction));

}
protected void onListItemClick(ListView l, View v, int position, long id){
    switch(position){
        case 0:

            break;
        case 1:

            break;
        case 2:

            break;
        case 3:

            break;
        case 4:

            break;
    }
}



}
```

case statements each conclude with break statement

Figure 5-20 Case statements

Critical Thinking

Is the last break statement necessary after case 4 considering the switch statement ends after case 4?

Technically the last break is not required, but it is recommended so that modifying the code is less error prone. For example, if another attraction is added to the Chicago City Guide app, case 5 would be placed after the last break statement.

GTK

Switch statements do not allow ranges such as 10–50. Use If statements when evaluating a range of number or specific strings.

Android Intents

When the user selects one of the first two list items in the project, Art Institute of Chicago or Magnificent Mile, a built-in Android browser launches a website about each attraction. A browser is launched with Android code using an intent. Android intents send and receive activities and services that include opening a webpage in a browser, calling a phone number, locating a GPS position on a map, posting your notes to a note-taking program such as Evernote, opening your contacts list, sending a photo, or even posting to your social network. Additional Android intents are explored throughout the rest of this book. Android intents are powerful features that allow apps to talk to each other in a very simple way.

To better understand an intent, imagine a student sitting in a classroom. To ask a question or make a request, the student raises a hand. The teacher is alerted to the hand and responds to the student. An intent works the same way. Your app raises its hand and the other apps state that they are ready to handle your request. When the chapter project sends an intent, the browser app handles the request and opens the website.

IN THE TRENCHES

Android platform devices have many options for supported browsers. Popular Android browsers include Chrome, Dolphin, Opera, Mozilla Firefox Mobile, and UC Browser.

Launching the Browser from an Android Device

Android phones have a built-in browser with an intent filter that accepts intent requests from other apps. The intent sends the browser a **URI** (Uniform Resource Identifier), a string that identifies the web resources. You might already be familiar with the term **URL** (Uniform Resource Locator), which means a website address. A URI is a URL with additional information necessary for gaining access to the resources required for posting the page.

Depending on the browsers installed on an Android device, Android selects a suitable browser (usually a user-set preferred browser), which accepts the action called ACTION_VIEW (must be in caps) and displays the site. **ACTION_VIEW** is the most common action performed on data. It is a generic action you can use to send any request to get the most reasonable action to occur. As shown in the following code syntax, a startActivity statement informs the present Activity that a new Activity is being started and the browser opens the website, in this case the Art Institute of Chicago site:

Code Syntax

```
startActivity(new Intent(Intent.ACTION_VIEW,
     Uri.parse("http://artic.edu")));
```

When the user selects the Art Institute of Chicago item from the attractions list, the Switch statement sends a zero integer value to the case statements. The case 0: statement is true, so the program executes the startActivity statement, which sends the browser a parsed string containing the URI web address. The browser application then launches the Art Institute of Chicago website. When you tap or click the Back button in some browser windows or the left arrow to the right of the menu button on the right side of the emulator, the previous Activity opens. In the chapter project, the attractions list ListView activity is displayed again. To code the startActivity that launches a website in an Android browser, follow these steps:

STEP 1

- In MainActivity.java, tap or click the blank line after the line containing case 0: inside the Switch decision structure.
- Type **startActivity(new Intent(Intent.ACTION_VIEW, Uri.parse ("*http://artic.edu* "));**.

- Tap or click Intent and press Alt+Enter, if necessary.
- Tap or click Uri and then press Alt+Enter.

The startActivity code launches the Art Institute of Chicago website when the user selects the first list item (Figure 5-21). Some websites are especially designed for mobile devices such as this one, which displays m.artic.edu. The letter m represents a mobile site that was launched automatically due to the platform of a mobile device.

```
    }
    protected void onListItemClick(ListView l, View v, int position, long id){
        switch(position){
            case 0:
                startActivity(new Intent(Intent.ACTION_VIEW, Uri.parse("http://artic.edu ")));
                break;
            case 1:

                break;
```

Opens web browser to display Art Institute of Chicago site

Figure 5-21 Code for launching the Art Institute of Chicago website

STEP 2

- In MainActivity.java, tap or click the blank line after the line containing case 1:.
- Type **startActivity(new Intent(Intent.ACTION_VIEW, Uri.parse ("*http://themagnificentmile.com*")));**.

The startActivity code launches the Magnificent Mile website when the user selects the second list item (Figure 5-22).

```
    }
    protected void onListItemClick(ListView l, View v, int position, long id){
        switch(position){
            case 0:
                startActivity(new Intent(Intent.ACTION_VIEW, Uri.parse("http://artic.edu ")));
                break;
            case 1:
                startActivity(new Intent(Intent.ACTION_VIEW, Uri.parse ("http://themagnificentmile.com" )));
                break;
            case 2:

                break;
```

Opens web browser to display Magnificent Mile site

Figure 5-22 Code for launching the Magnificent Mile website

STEP 3

- To display the Art Institute of Chicago website in the browser, tap or click Run on the menu bar, and then select Run.
- If necessary, select Android Application and tap or click the OK button.

- Save all the files in the next dialog box, if necessary, and unlock the emulator.
- Select the Art Institute of Chicago list item.

The first item is selected from the list in the emulator and the Android browser displays the Art Institute of Chicago website. The site loads slowly in the emulator (Figure 5-23).

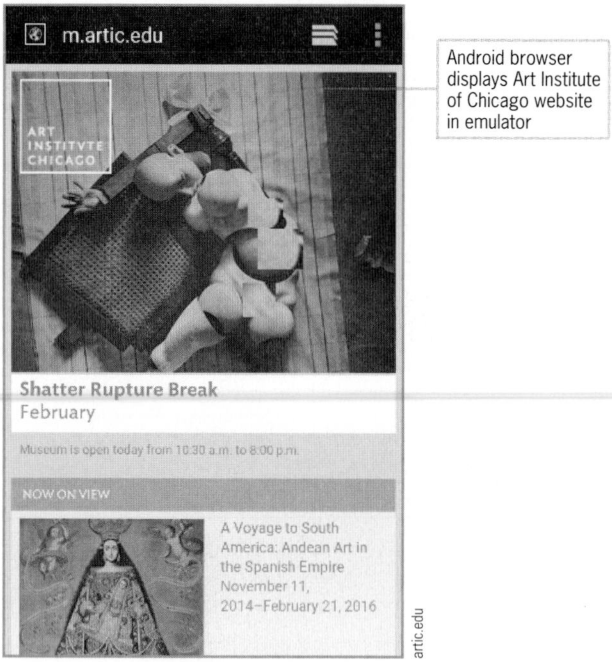

Figure 5-23 Browser opens in the emulator

STEP 4

- Close the emulated application window.

IN THE TRENCHES
Be sure to test any links within your Android apps often. If you have hundreds of links, verifying Web links can be simple in concept but very time consuming in practice. A good place to start is with the World Wide Web Consortium's free Web Site Validation Service (http://validator.w3.org).

Adding Multiple Class Files

Multiple classes are needed to display images on the screen when the user selects Willis Tower, Navy Pier, or Water Tower on the opening ListView control. An onCreate method requests that the user interface opens to display an image of the attraction. Remember, each time you add a class to an application, the class must begin with a capital letter and a coordinating XML layout file with the same name with a lowercase letter is automatically created. To create three class files and the coordinating XML layout files, follow these steps:

STEP 1

- In the Android project view, to create a second class, expand the java folder and press and hold or right-click the first net.androidbootcamp.cityguide folder, point to New on the shortcut menu, and then tap or click Activity. Next, tap or click Blank Activity.
- Type **Willis** in the Activity Name text box to create a second class that will define the Willis Activity and a layout associated with the class named activity_willis.
- Type **Willis Tower** in the Title text box, which is displayed on the Action bar on the top of the Activity.

A new class named Willis that creates activity_willis.xml appears in New Android Activity dialog box with the title Willis Tower (Figure 5-24).

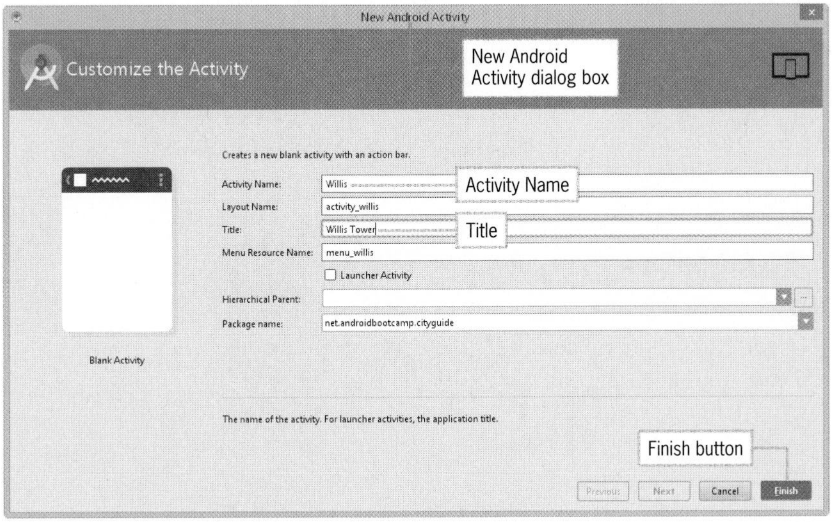

Figure 5-24 Creating the Willis.java class file

STEP 2

- Tap or click the Finish button. Notice the Activity includes an onCreate method to launch activity_willis.
- Close the Willis.java file tab.
- To create a third class, press and hold or right-click the first net.androidbootcamp.cityguide folder, point to New on the shortcut menu, and then tap or click Activity. Next, tap or click Blank Activity.

- Type **Pier** in the Activity Name text box to create a third class that will define the Pier Activity.
- Type **Navy Pier** in the Title text box.
- Tap or click the Finish button.
- Close the Pier.java file tab.
- To create a fourth class, press and hold or right-click the net.androidbootcamp.cityguide folder, point to New on the shortcut menu, and tap or click Activity. Next, tap or click Blank Activity.
- Type **Water** in the Activity Name text box to create a fourth class that will define the Water Activity.
- Type **Water Tower** in the Title text box.
- Tap or click the Finish button and save your work.
- Close the Water.java tab.

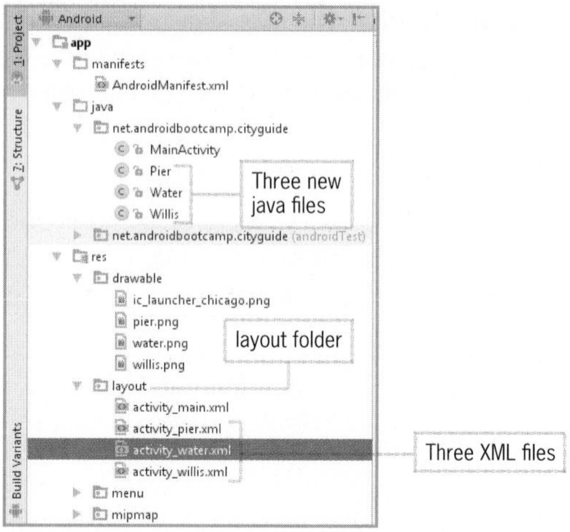

Figure 5-25 Three new activity XML files displayed

Three new Activity java files are created with three XML layout files in Android project view (Figure 5-25).

Designing XML Layout Files

The last three case statements open a second screen that displays a picture of the selected attraction. Three XML layout files must be designed to display an ImageView control with an image source file. To add an ImageView control in the three XML layout files, follow these steps:

STEP 1

- Open the activity_willis.xml tab and if necessary, tap or click the Design tab at the bottom.
- Delete the Hello World! TextView control from the emulator.
- In the Widgets category in the Palette, drag the ImageView control to the top of the emulator.
- Double-tap or double-click the placeholder from the ImageView control to open the src and id editing panel.
- Type **imgWillis** in the id text box to name the ImageView control.
- Tap or click the ellipsis button (three dots) to the right of the src text box.
- Scroll down the Resources listing on the Projects tab to locate willis and then tap or click willis.

- Tap or click the OK button to close the Resources dialog box.
- Tap or click to the right of the contentDescription property in the Properties pane and then tap or click the ellipsis button.
- Select willis within the Resources dialog box and then tap or click the OK button.

The willis XML file is designed with an image of the Willis Tower with the accessibility text set in the contentDescription property (Figure 5-26).

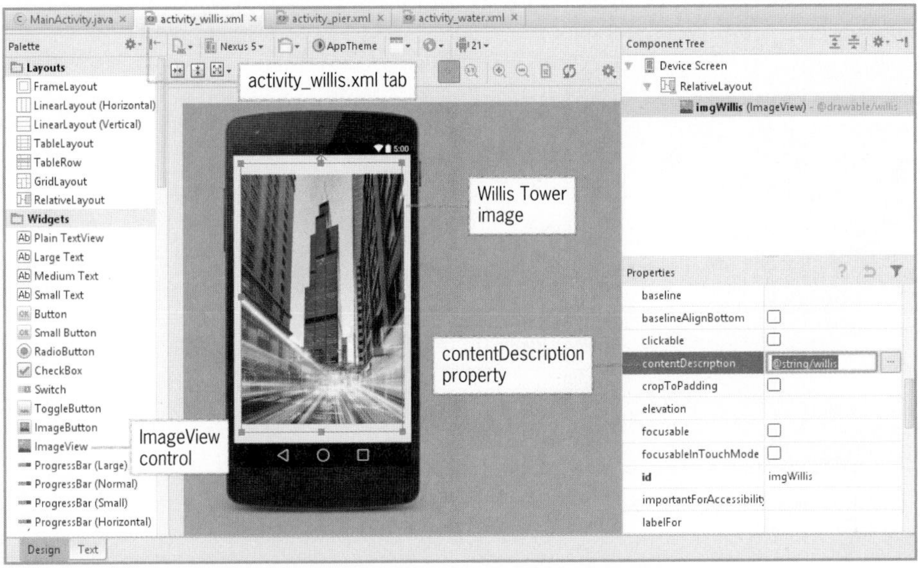

Figure 5-26 activity_willis.xml layout file

STEP 2

- Close the activity_willis.xml file tab and save your work.
- Tap or click the activity_pier.xml tab and if necessary, tap or click the Design tab to open the emulator window.
- Delete the Hello World! TextView control from the emulator.
- In the Widgets category in the Palette, drag the ImageView control to the top of the emulator.
- Double-tap or double-click the placeholder from the ImageView control to open the src and id editing panel.
- Type **imgPier** in the id text box to name the Navy Pier ImageView control.
- Tap or click the ellipsis button (three dots) to the right of the src text box.
- Scroll down the Resources listing on the Projects tab to locate pier and then tap or click pier.

- Tap or click the OK button to close the Resources dialog box.
- Tap or click to the right of the contentDescription property in the Properties pane and then tap or click the ellipsis button.
- Select pier within the Resources dialog box and then tap or click the OK button.

The activity_pier XML file is designed with an image of the Navy Pier in Chicago (Figure 5-27).

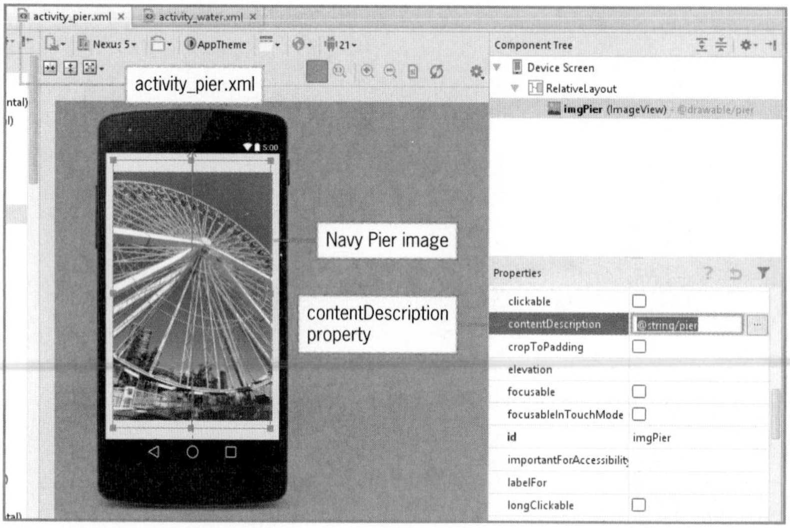

Figure 5-27 activity_pier.xml designed

STEP 3

- Close the activity_pier.xml file tab and save your work.
- Tap or click the activity_water.xml tab and if necessary, tap or click the Design tab to open the emulator window.
- Delete the Hello World! TextView control from the emulator.
- In the Widgets category in the Palette, drag the ImageView control to the top of the emulator.
- Double-tap or double-click the placeholder from the ImageView control to open the src and id editing panel.
- Type **imgWater** in the id text box to name the Water Tower ImageView control.
- Tap or click the ellipsis button (three dots) to the right of the src text box.
- Scroll down the Resources listing on the Projects tab to locate the water image and then tap or click water.
- Tap or click the OK button to close the Resources dialog box.

- Tap or click to the right of the contentDescription property in the Properties pane and then tap or click the ellipsis button.
- Select water within the Resources dialog box and then tap or click the OK button.

The water XML file is designed with an image of the Chicago Water Tower (Figure 5-28).

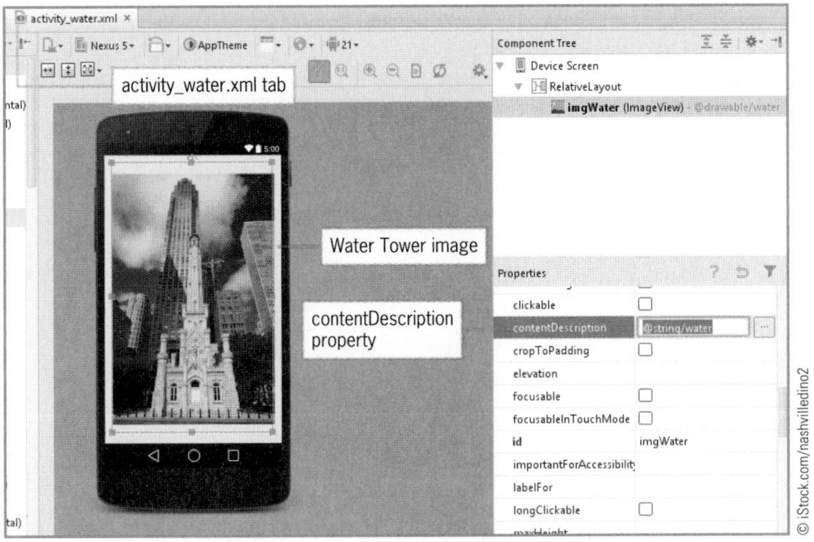

Figure 5-28 activity_water.xml designed

Opening the Class Files

The last step in the development of the Chicago City Guide app is to launch the class files when the user selects Willis Tower (case 2), Navy Pier (case 3), or Water Tower (case 4) from the ListView control. A startActivity method opens the next Activity, which in turn launches the appropriate XML layout displaying an image of the attraction. To code the remaining case statement within the Switch decision structure that starts each of the Activities, follow these steps:

STEP 1

- Close the activity_water.xml tab.
- In MainActivity.java, tap or click the blank line below the statement containing case 2: and type **startActivity(new Intent(MainActivity.this, Willis.class));**.
- Tap or click the blank line below the one containing case 3: and type **startActivity(new Intent(MainActivity.this, Pier.class));**.
- Tap or click the blank line below the one containing case 4: and type **startActivity(new Intent(MainActivity.this, Water.class));**.

The case statements 2 through 4 are coded with a startActivity that executes the appropriate class (Figure 5-29).

MainActivity.java

```java

public class MainActivity extends ListActivity {

    @Override
    protected void onCreate(Bundle savedInstanceState) {
        super.onCreate(savedInstanceState);
        String[ ] attraction={"Art Institute of Chicago", "Magnificent Mile", "Willis Tower", "Navy Pier", "Water Tower"};
        setListAdapter(new ArrayAdapter<String>(this, R.layout.activity_main, R.id.travel, attraction));

    }
    protected void onListItemClick(ListView l, View v, int position, long id){
        switch(position){
            case 0:
                startActivity(new Intent(Intent.ACTION_VIEW, Uri.parse("http://artic.edu ")));
                break;
            case 1:
                startActivity(new Intent(Intent.ACTION_VIEW, Uri.parse ("http://themagnificentmile.com" )));
                break;
            case 2:
                startActivity(new Intent(MainActivity.this, Willis.class));
                break;
            case 3:
                startActivity(new Intent(MainActivity.this, Pier.class));
                break;
            case 4:
                startActivity(new Intent(MainActivity.this, Water.class));
                break;
        }
    }



}
```

startActivity statements launch the three classes

Figure 5-29 Complete code for MainActivity.java class

STEP 2

- Compare your code to Figure 5-29, make changes as necessary to match the code in the figure, and then save your work.

Running and Testing the Application

As you save and run the Chicago City Guide application, be sure you test every option of this app. Before publishing to Google Play, it is critical to make sure all the fields can gracefully handle any tap or click or any value entered in any Android app. Tap or click Run on the menu bar, and then select Run to save and test the application in the emulator. A dialog box requesting how you would like to run the application opens the first time the application is executed. Select Android Application and tap or click the OK button. Save all the files in the next dialog box, if necessary, and unlock the emulator. The application opens in the emulator window where you can test each list item in the Chicago City Guide app, as shown in Figures 5-1, 5-2, and 5-3.

IN THE TRENCHES

Testing an Android app is called usability testing. In addition to the traditional navigation and ease of use, Section 508 compliance is a third component to be tested. The 1998 Amendment to Section 508 of the Rehabilitation Act spells out accessibility requirements for individuals with certain disabilities. For more details, refer to *www.section508.gov*.

Wrap It Up—Chapter Summary

This chapter described the steps to create a list with items users select to launch websites and XML layouts through the use of a Switch decision structure in the City Guide program. The introduction of intents to outside services such as a web browser begins our adventure of many other intent options used throughout the rest of this book.

- The Java View class creates a list and makes it scrollable if it exceeds the length of the screen. To contain the list items, use a ListView control, which allows you to select each row in the list for further action, such as displaying an image or webpage.
- Instead of extending the basic Activity class in MainActivity.java by using the public class Main extends Activity opening class statement, when you want to display a ListView control, extend the ListActivity class in MainActivity.java with the statement public class Main extends ListActivity.
- Before you can specify the items in a list, declare the item names using an array variable, which can store more than one value of similar data types. For example, you can store five string values in an array without having to declare five variables.
- Arrays provide access to data by using a numeric index to identify each element in the array. Each value is stored in an element of the array, which you refer to by its index. The index for the first element in an array is zero. For example, Attraction[0] is the first element in the Attraction array.
- To declare an array, specify the array's data type and name followed by the values in braces, as in String[ ] attraction={"Art Institute of Chicago", "Magnificent Mile", "Willis Tower", "Navy Pier ", "Water Tower"};.
- You can display the values in an array using an adapter, which provides a data model for the layout of the list and for converting the array data into list items. A ListView control is the container for the list items, and an adapter such as the setListAdapter command connects the array data to the ListView control so the items are displayed on the device screen. In other words, calling a setListAdapter in the Java code binds the elements of an array to a ListView layout.
- To design a simple layout, you drag controls from the Palette to the emulator on the Text tab. To design a custom layout, you add code to the main XML file for the application, such as activity_main.xml.
- A setListAdapter statement has three parameters: One refers to the *this* class, the second refers to the layout used to display the list, and the third refers to the array containing the list values to display. For the second parameter, setListAdapter can use a standard layout, as in android.R.layout.*simple_list_item_1,* which specifies the built-in simple_list_item_1 layout to display the list. To use a custom layout instead, replace the name of the standard layout

with the name of the custom layout, as in R.layout.*activity_main,* which references a custom layout named activity_main.xml. You also remove the *android* reference because you are no longer using an Android library default layout.

- To have an app take action when a user selects an item in a list, you code the onListItemClick method to respond to the event of the user's selection.
- You can use the Switch decision structure with a list or menu. In a Switch statement, an integer or character variable is evaluated and the corresponding case is executed. Each case is specified using the *case* keyword followed by a value and a colon. For example, if a list contains five items, the Switch statement will have five cases, such as case 0, case 1, case 2, case 3, and case 4. End each case with a break statement to exit the Switch decision structure and continue with the next statement.
- Android intents send and receive activities and services, including opening a Web page in a browser. An intent can use the ACTION_VIEW action to send a URI to a built-in Android browser and display the specified website.
- As you develop an application, you must test every option and possible user action, including incorrect values and selections. Thoroughly test an Android app before publishing to Google Play.

Key Terms

ACTION_VIEW—A generic action you can use to send any request to get the most reasonable action to occur.

adapter—Provides a data model for the layout of a list and for converting the data from the array into list items.

array variable—A variable that can store more than one value.

ArrayAdapter<String>—A ListAdapter that supplies string array data to a ListView object.

break—A statement that ends a case within a Switch statement and continues with the statement following the Switch decision structure.

case—A keyword used in a Switch statement to indicate a condition. In a Switch statement, the case keyword is followed by a value and a colon.

element—A single individual item that contains a value in an array.

ListActivity—A class that displays a list of items within an app.

onListItemClick( )—A method called when an item in a list is selected.

position—The placement of an item in a list. When an item in a list is selected, the position of the item is passed from the onListItemClick method and evaluated with a decision structure. The first item is assigned the position of 0, the second item is assigned the position of 1, and so forth.

setListAdapter—A command that projects your data to the onscreen list on your device by connecting the ListActivity's ListView object to array data.

Switch—A type of decision statement that allows you to choose from many statements based on an integer or a char input.

URI—An acronym for Uniform Resource Identifier, a URI is a string that identifies the resources of the web. Similar to a URL, a URI includes additional information necessary for gaining access to the resources required for posting the page.

URL—An acronym for Uniform Resource Locator; a URL is a website address.

Developer FAQs

1. Typically in a MainActivity.java file, the class extends ActionBarActivity. When the primary purpose of the class is to display a list, what is the opening MainActivity class statement?
2. Which Android control displays a vertical listing of items?
3. When does a scroll bar appear in a list?
4. Initialize an array named temps with the integers 22, 56, 38, 30, and 57.
5. Answer the following questions about the following initialized array:

   ```
   String[]pizzaToppings = new String[10];
   ```

   a. What is the statement to assign mushrooms to the first array location?
   b. What is the statement to assign green peppers to the fourth location in the array?
   c. How many toppings can this array hold?
   d. Rewrite this statement to initially be assigned the following four toppings only: extra cheese, black olives, mushrooms, and bacon.
6. Write a line of code that assigns the values Samsung, HTC, Sony, Motorola, and Asus to the elements in the array phoneBrands.
7. Fix this array statement:

   ```
   doubles { } driveSize = ["32.0", "64.0", "128.0"]
   ```

8. Write two lines of code that assign an array named coding with the items Java, C#, Python, Visual Basic, and Ruby and display this array as a generic list.
9. Which type of pictures can be used for free fair use without copyright?
10. What does URI stand for?
11. Write a statement that opens the Android Help Site: *http://developer.android.com*
12. Write a single line of XML code that changes the size of the text of a TextView control to 39 scaled-independent pixels.

13. Write a line of XML code that displays the text 'Win Instantly' in a control
14. Write a Switch decision structure that tests the user's age in an integer variable named teenAge and assigns the variable schoolYear as in Table 5-2.

Age	High School Year
14	Freshman
15	Sophomore
16	Junior
17	Senior
Any other age	Not in High School

Table 5-2 Data for Switch decision structure

15. Change the following If decision structure to a Switch decision structure:

```
if (count == 3) {
     result = "Password incorrect";
} else {
     result = "Request password";
}
```

16. What is the purpose of a default statement in a decision structure?
17. Name two decision structures.
18. What happens when a webpage opens in the emulator and the Back button is tapped or clicked in the chapter project?
19. What does the "R" in R.id.travel stand for?
20. Write a startActivity statement that launches a class named Studio.

Beyond the Book

Search the Web for answers to the following questions to further your Android knowledge.

1. Create a five-item list array program of your own favorite hobby and test three types of built-in Android list formats. Take a screenshot comparing the three layouts identified by the layout format.
2. Compare four different Android browsers. Write a paragraph about each browser.
3. Research the 508 standards for Android app design. Create a list of 10 standards that should be met while designing Android applications.
4. Besides the 508 standards, research the topic of Android usability testing. Write one page on testing guidelines that assist in the design and testing process.

Case Programming Projects

Complete one or more of the following case programming projects. Use the same steps and techniques taught within the chapter. Submit the program you create to your instructor. The level of difficulty is indicated for each case programming project.

Easiest: ★

Intermediate: ★★

Challenging: ★★★

Case Project 5–1: Beach and Mountain Bike Rentals App ★

Requirements Document

Application title:	Beach and Mountain Bike Rental App
Purpose:	A bike rental shop would like an app that displays information about their beach and mountain bike rental services. As each bike is selected, a rental bike is displayed.
Algorithms:	1. The opening screen displays a list of bikes for rent: beach bikes, mountain bikes, and full bike rental shop website (Figure 5-30). 2. When the user selects an item from the list, a full-screen image of the item is displayed for the first two bike rentals (Figure 5-31). The third option opens the website http://www.campusbikeshopcom.
Conditions:	1. The pictures of the two types of bikes are provided with your student files (beach.png and mountain.png). 2. Use the built-in layout simple_list_item_1. 3. Use the Switch decision structure. 4. Use a String table for image descriptions.

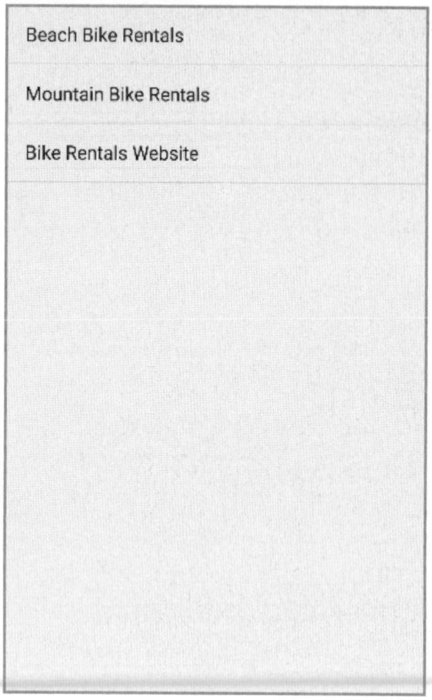

Figure 5-30 Bike and Mountain Bike Rental Apps Opening Screen

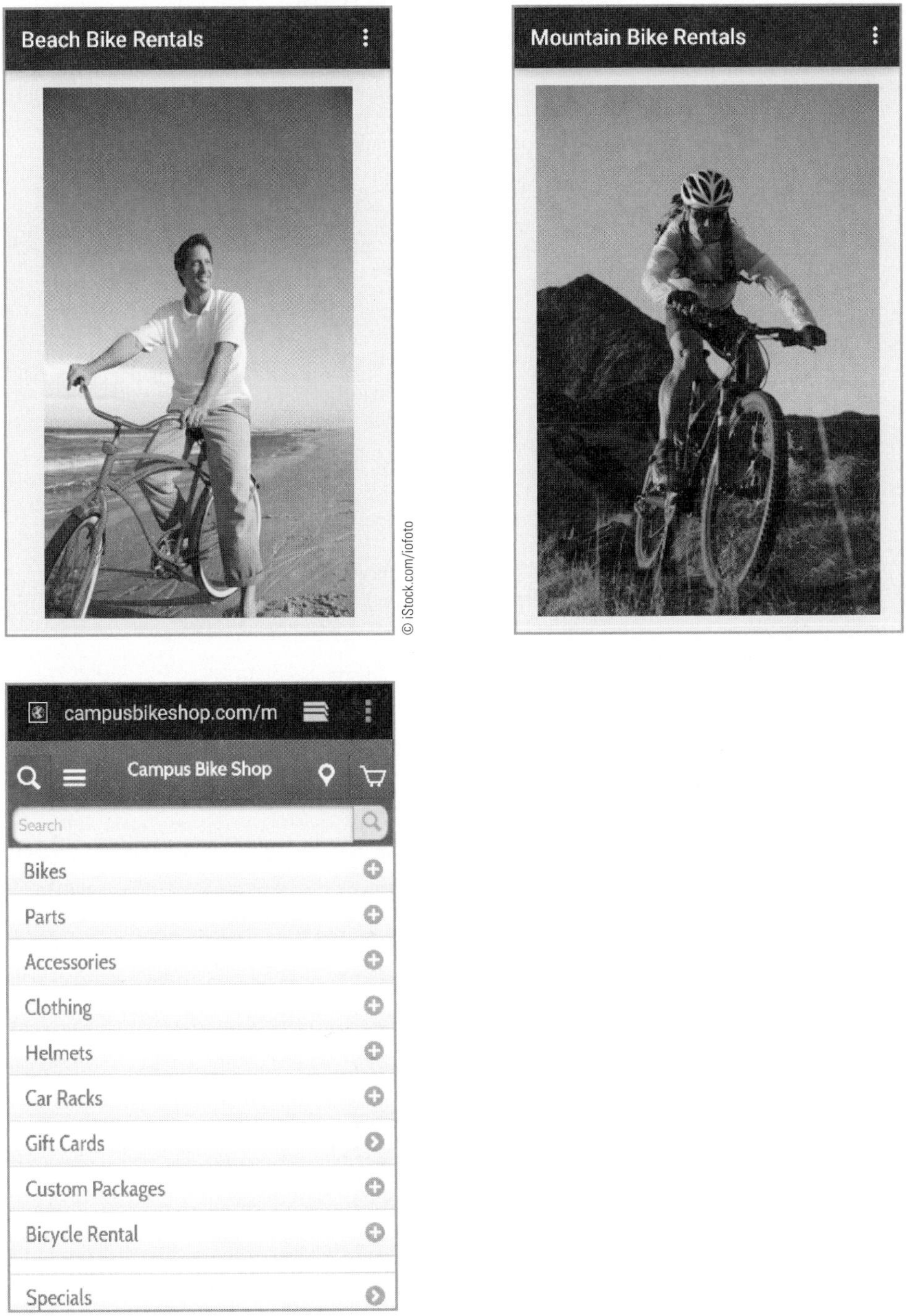

© iStock.com/iofoto

© iStock.com/Gorfer

Figure 5-31

Case Project 5–2: Chocolate Cafe App ★

Requirements Document

Application title:	Chocolate Cafe App
Purpose:	A café specializing in chocolate desserts is named Chocolat and would like an app that lists the specials of the day. As each dessert special is selected, an image is displayed.
Algorithms:	1. The opening screen lists the three dessert specials of the day and displays the restaurant's full website with a custom icon (Figure 5-32). 2. When the user selects one of the three specials (chocolate mousse, chocolate cake, or chocolate macarons), an image of the special is displayed. If the full website is requested, http://www.chocolatharlem.com opens.
Conditions:	1. The dessert icon is provided with your student files and is named ic_launcher_dessert.png. The three images for the specials are named mousse.png, cake.png, and macaron.png. 2. Design a custom layout similar to Figure 5-33. 3. Use the Switch decision structure. 4. Use a String table.

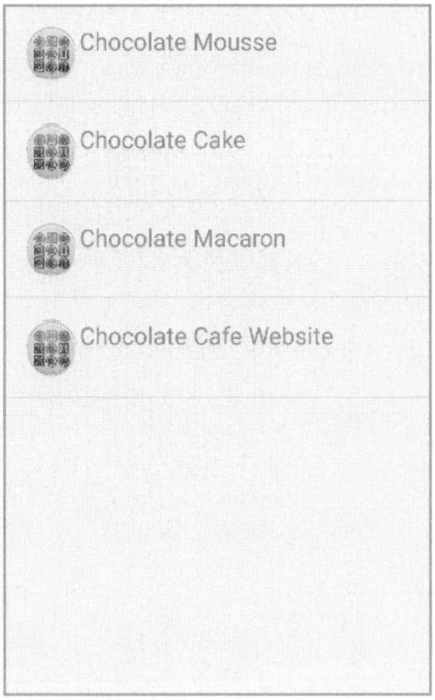

© iStock.com/kathykonkle

Figure 5-32

© iStock.com/MarkSkalny

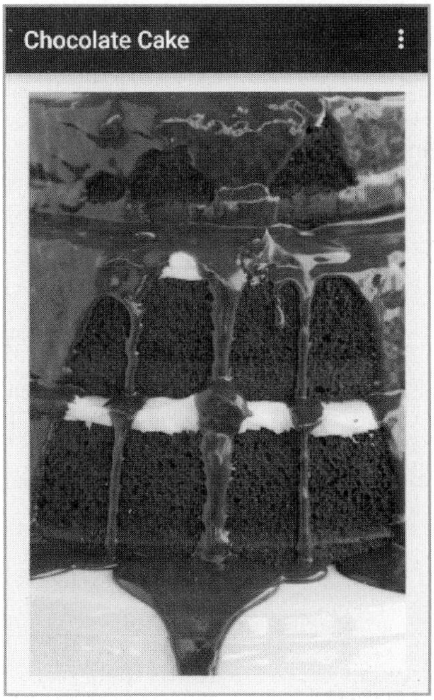

© iStock.com/Karcich

Figure 5-33 *(continues)*

(continued)

Figure 5-33

Case Project 5–3: Rent a Car App ★★

Requirements Document

Application title:	Rent a Car App
Purpose:	A rental car app provides a listing of six nationally known car rental companies. By selecting a car company, a car rental site opens.
Algorithms:	1. An opening screen displays an image of a car and a button. 2. The second screen displays a listing of six car rental companies. This screen also contains a custom icon and layout. 3. Each car rental agency can be selected to view a website of the corresponding company.
Conditions:	1. Select your own images. 2. Create a custom layout for the list.

Case Project 5–4: Coffee Finder App ★★

Requirements Document

Application title:	Coffee Finder App
Purpose:	This Coffee Finder App locates four places in your town or city to get a great cup of joe.
Algorithms:	1. The opening screen displays the names of four coffee shops. 2. When the user selects a coffee shop, a second screen displays the name and address of the selected coffee shop with a picture or logo for the coffee shop.
Conditions:	1. Select your own images. 2. Create a custom layout for the list.

Case Project 5–5: Tech Gadgets App ★★★

Requirements Document

Application title:	Tech Gadgets App
Purpose:	The Tech Gadgets app shows the top five technology gifts on your wish list.
Algorithms:	1. The opening screen displays names of five technology gadgets of your own choosing. 2. If the user selects any of the gadgets, a second screen opens that has an image and a button. If the user clicks the button, a webpage opens that displays more information about the tech gadget.
Conditions:	1. Select your own images. 2. Create a custom layout for the list.

Case Project 5–6: Create Your Own App ★★★

Requirements Document

Application title:	Create Your Own App
Purpose:	Get creative! Create an app with five to eight list items with a custom layout and a custom icon that links to webpages and other XML layout screens.
Algorithms:	1. Create an app on a topic of your own choice. Create a list. 2. Display XML layout pages as well as webpages on different list items.
Conditions:	1. Select your own images. 2. Use a custom layout and icon.

CHAPTER 6

Jam! Implementing Audio in Android Apps

In this chapter, you learn to:

- Create an Android project using a splash screen
- Design a TextView control with a background image
- Pause the execution of an Activity with a timer
- Understand the Activity life cycle
- Open an Activity with onCreate( )
- End an Activity with finish( )
- Assign class variables
- Create a raw folder for music files
- Play music with a MediaPlayer method
- Start and resume music playback using the start( ) and pause( ) methods
- Change the Text property of a control
- Change the visibility of a control

Playing music on a smartphone is one of the primary uses of a mobile device, especially as MP3 players are losing popularity. The most common phone activities include texting, talking, gaming, and playing music. Talking and texting continue to be mainstream communication channels, but a growing proportion of users take advantage of apps, games, and multimedia on their phones. The principal specification when purchasing a smartphone is typically the amount of memory it has. Consumers often purchase a phone with more memory so they can store music.

To demonstrate how to play music through an Android built-in media player, the Chapter 6 project is named Aloha Music and opens with an image and the text "Sounds of Hawaii." This opening screen (Figure 6-1), also called a splash screen, is displayed for approximately five seconds, and then the program automatically opens the second window. The Aloha Music application (Figure 6-2) plays two songs that feature different instruments: Ukulele, a small guitar that originated in Hawaii; and Drums. If the user selects the first button, the Ukulele song plays until the user selects the first button again to pause the Ukulele song. If the user selects the second button, the Drums song plays until the user selects the second button again. The emulator plays the music through your computer's speakers.

Figure 6-1 Aloha Music Android app

Figure 6-2 Music played in the Android app

IN THE TRENCHES

Android music apps can play music on the memory card, download music available for purchase or free from music-sharing sites, tune into Internet-based streaming radio stations, or connect to music saved in a cloud service.

To create this application, the developer must understand how to perform the following processes, among others:

1. Create a splash screen with a timer.
2. Design a TextView control with a background image.
3. Initialize a TimerTask and a timer.
4. Launch a second Activity.
5. Design a second XML layout.
6. Add music files to the raw folder.
7. Initialize the MediaPlayer class.
8. Play and pause music with a Button control.

Creating a Splash Screen

The Aloha Music app opens with a window that is displayed for approximately five seconds before automatically launching the next window. Unlike the project in Chapter 2 (Healthy Recipes), which required a button to be tapped to begin a click event that opened a second screen, this program does not require user interaction to open the second Activity class. Many Android applications on the market show splash screens that often include the name of the program, display a brand logo for the application, or identify the author. A splash screen opens as you launch your app, providing time for Android to initialize its resources. Extending the length of time that your splash screen is displayed enables your app to load necessary files.

Critical Thinking

What kind of Android resources are loaded during a splash screen?

Background processes like loading a mobile database to view a listing of inventory or images, or making a call over a network, can consume multiple seconds when an app is initiated.

In the Aloha Music app, instead of using Main as the name of the initial Activity, the opening Activity shown in Figure 6-4 is named SplashActivity. A second .java file named MainActivity.java is added later in the chapter. The MainActivity class is responsible for playing the two songs. To start the Aloha Music application with a splash screen, complete the following steps:

STEP 1

- Open the Android Studio program.
- On the Welcome to Android Studio page of the Android Studio dialog box, tap or click Start a new Android Studio project in the Quick Start category.

- In the Create New Project dialog box, enter the Application name **Aloha Music**.
- If necessary, in the Company Domain text box, type the name **androidbootcamp.net**, and in the Project location text box, type **D:\Workspace\AlohaMusic**.
- A new application named Aloha Music is configured to save on the USB drive (Figure 6-3).

The new Android Aloha Music project has an application name (Figure 6-3).

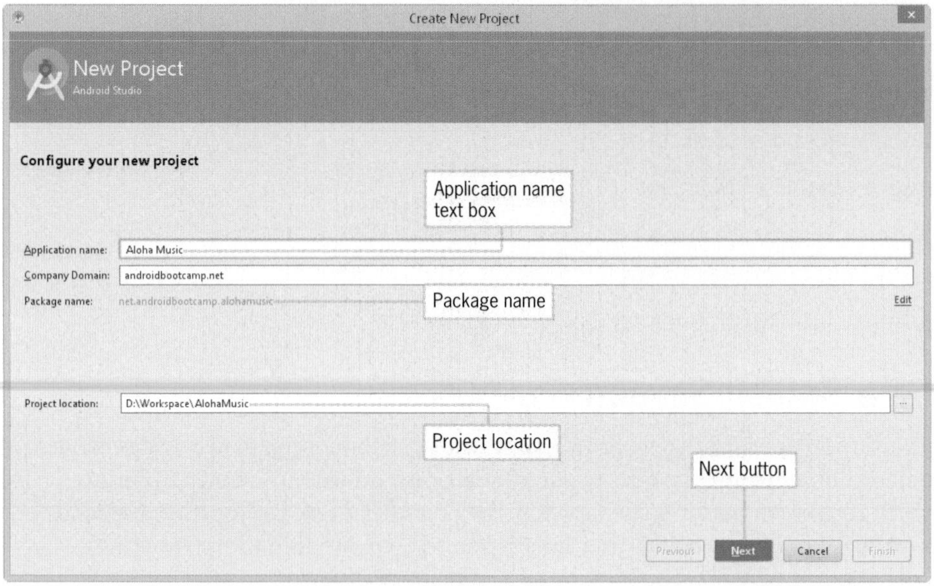

Figure 6-3 Setting up the Aloha Music project

STEP 2

- Tap or click the Next button on the Configure your new project page of the Create New Project dialog box.
- If necessary, tap or click the Phone and Tablet check box to select the form factor for your app.
- If necessary, select API 15: Android 4.0.3 (IceCreamSandwich) for the Minimum SDK.
- Tap or click the Next button on the Select the form factors your app will run on page.
- If necessary, tap or click Blank Activity to add an Activity to the new project.
- Tap or click the Next button on the Add an activity to Mobile page.
- Replace MainActivity with the text **SplashActivity** in the Activity Name text box.
- Replace the title with the text **Aloha Music** in the Title text box.

The new Android Aloha Music project has an initial opening class named SplashActivity and a title of Aloha Music (Figure 6-4).

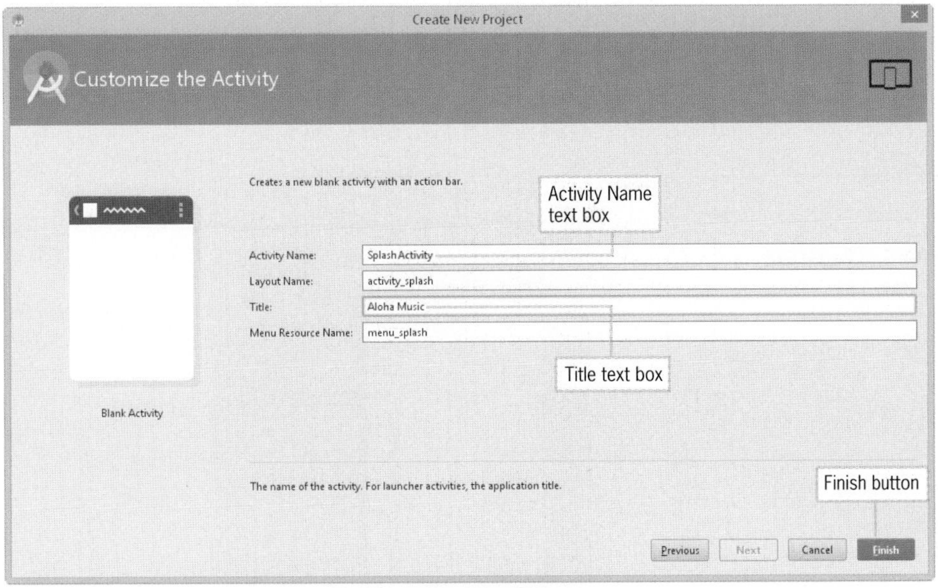

Figure 6-4 Setting up the Splash Activity (splash screen)

STEP 3

- Tap or click the Finish button to display the Android project view of the Aloha Music app.

Adding a Background Image to a TextView Widget

On the splash screen in Figure 6-1, an image with the text "Sounds of Hawaii" is displayed. The text for the TextView image as well as the image descriptions for the two ImageView controls and button text are stored in the strings.xml file. The opening image is not an ImageView control, but instead a TextView control with a background image. You use a TextView property named background to specify the image. The image is first placed in the drawable folder and then referenced in the TextView background. The TextView background can display an image or a solid-color fill such as the hexadecimal color #964B00 for brown. The margins and gravity properties are used to place the text in the location of your choice. To add the images for this project and an activity_splash.xml file with a TextView widget that contains a background image, follow these steps:

STEP 1

- Open the USB folder that contains the student files.
- To add the three image files to the drawable resource folder, tap or click hawaii.png, ukulele.png, and drums.png, then press Ctrl+C.
- To paste the image files to the drawable folder, press and hold or right-click the drawable folder in the Android project view pane.

- Tap or click Paste on the shortcut menu.
- Tap or click the OK button in the Copy dialog box.

Copies of the three image files appear in the drawable folder (Figure 6-5).

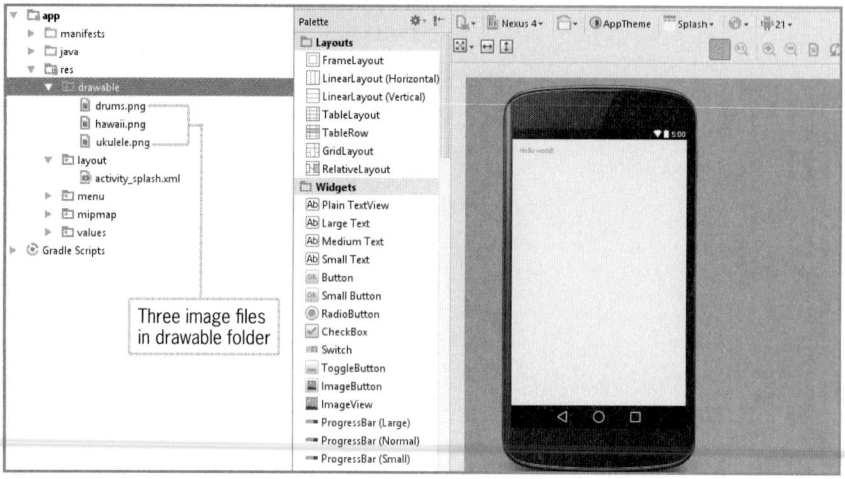

Figure 6-5 Image files in the drawable folder

STEP 2

- Expand the res\values folder and then double-tap or double-click the strings.xml file.
- Tap or click the Open editor link.
- Tap or click the Add Key (plus sign) button in the Translations Editor.
- In the Key text box, type **txtSplash** to name the string for the Plain TextView control.
- In the Default Value text box, type **Sounds of Hawaii** to define the text to display.
- Using the techniques taught in this step, add the strings in Table 6-1 to the String table in the Translations Editor.

Key	Default Value
ukulele	Ukulele Image
drums	Drums Image
btnUkulele	Play Ukulele Song
btnDrums	Play Drums Song

Table 6-1 Strings for the Aloha Music app

The Translations Editor contains the String values necessary in this app (Figure 6-6).

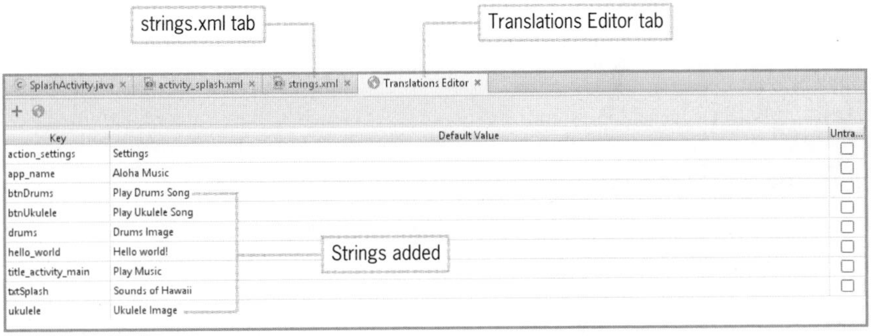

Figure 6-6 Translations Editor

STEP 3

- Save your work and close the Translations Editor and strings.xml tabs.
- If necessary, open the activity_splash.xml layout file, and then delete the Hello world! placeholder.
- Change the virtual device to Nexus 5.
- In the Widgets category in the Palette, drag the Plain TextView control to the top left of the emulator.
- Double-tap or double-click the TextView control on the emulator to display the text and id editing panel and type **txtTitle** in the id text box.
- Tap or click the ellipsis button and scroll down the Resources listing on the Projects tab to locate txtSplash, and then tap or click txtSplash.
- Type **#964B00** for the textColor property to create a brown font color.
- Set the textSize property to **38sp**.
- Expand the textStyle property, and then tap or click the bold check box.
- Expand the gravity property, then select the bottom check box and the center check box to place the text in the bottom center of the screen.
- In the background property, tap or click the ellipsis button.
- In the Resources dialog box, tap or click hawaii. Tap or click the OK button.

A Plain TextView control with an image background is displayed in the activity_splash.xml file (Figure 6-7).

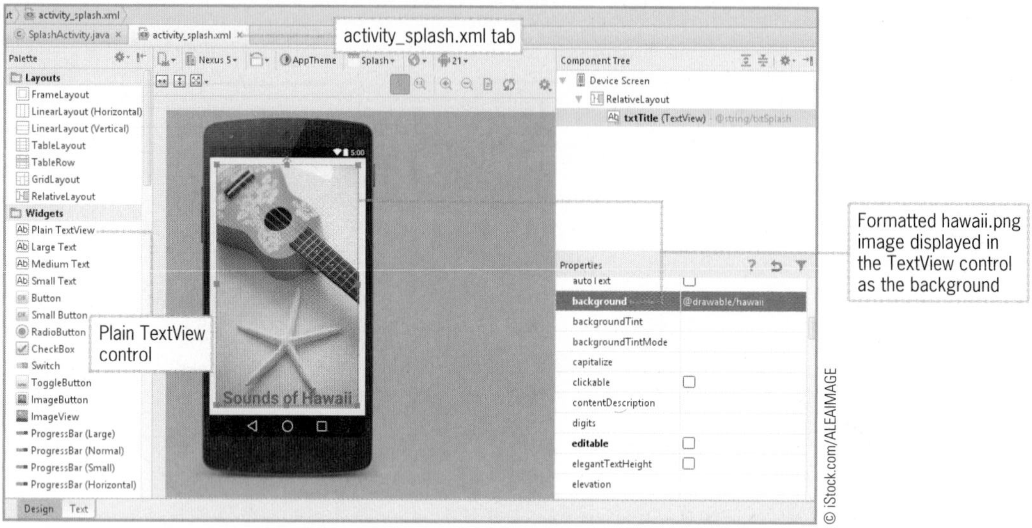

Figure 6-7 activity_splash.xml displays a TextView control with a background image

STEP 4

- Close the activity_splash.xml tab and save your work.

Creating a Timer

When most Android apps open, a splash screen is displayed for a few seconds, often preloading database files and information behind the scenes in large-scale applications. In the Aloha Music app, a timer is necessary to display the splash.xml file for approximately five seconds before the Main Activity intent is called. A **timer** in Java executes a one-time task such as displaying an opening splash screen, or it performs a continuous process, such as a morning wake-up call set to run at regular intervals.

Timers can be used to pause an action temporarily or for time-dependent or repeated activities such as animation in a cartoon application. The timer object uses milliseconds as the unit of time. On an Android device, 1,000 milliseconds is equivalent to about one second. This fixed period of time is supported by two Java classes, namely **TimerTask** and **Timer**. To create a timer, the first step is to create a TimerTask object, as shown in the following syntax:

Code Syntax

```
TimerTask task = new TimerTask( ) {
}
```

GTK

Each time a timer runs its tasks, it executes within a single thread. A **thread** is a single sequential flow of control within a program. Java allows an application to have multiple threads of execution running concurrently. You can assign multiple threads so they occur simultaneously, completing several tasks at the same time. For example, a program could display a splash screen, download files needed for the application, and even play an opening sound at the same time.

A TimerTask invokes a scheduled timer. A timer may remind you of a childhood game called hide-and-seek. Do you remember covering your eyes and counting to 50 while your friends found a hiding spot before you began searching for everyone? A timer might only count to five seconds (5,000 milliseconds), but in a similar fashion, the application pauses while the timer counts to the established time limit. After the timed interval is completed, the program resumes and continues with the next task.

After entering the TimerTask code, tap or click the red error line under the TimerTask( ) to add the run( ) method, an auto-generated method stub, as shown in the following code syntax. Any statements within the braces of the run( ) method are executed after the TimerTask class is invoked.

Code Syntax

```
TimerTask task = new TimerTask( ) {
     @Override
     public void run() {
     // TODO Auto-generated method stub
}
```

The TimerTask must implement a run( ) method that is called by the timer when the task is scheduled for execution. To add a TimerTask class to the SplashActivity, follow these steps:

STEP 1

- In the Android project view, expand the java folder, expand the first net.androidbootcamp.alohamusic, and then double-tap or double-click SplashActivity.java to open the code window.
- Display the line numbers and delete Lines 17–38.
- After the setContentView(R.layout.activity_splash); statement, press the Enter key to insert a new line, type **TimerTask task = new TimerTask( ) {** to add the TimerTask, and then press the Enter key.
- Tap or click the red text TimerTask( ) and press Alt+Enter to import the TimerTask.

The TimerTask class is initiated and a red curly line appears below TimerTask (Figure 6-8).

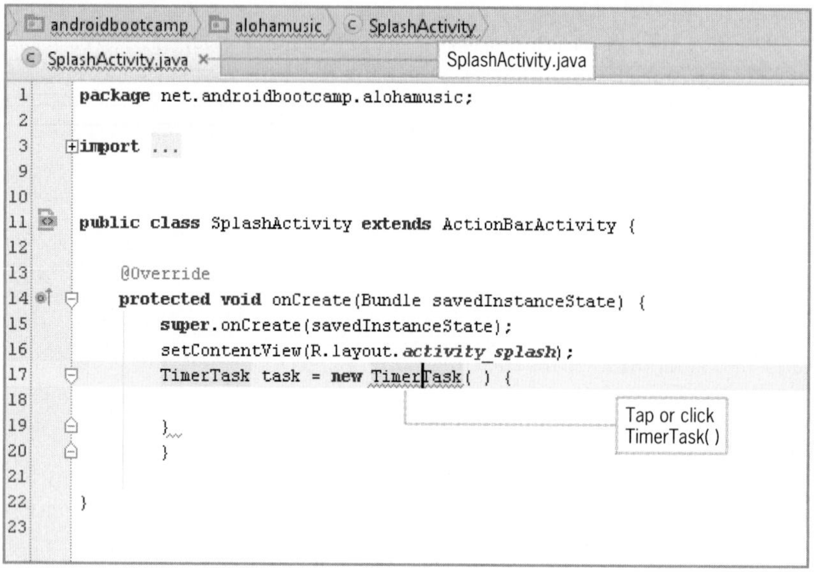

Figure 6-8 setContentView and TimerTask statements

STEP 2

- Tap or click the red curly line below TimerTask( ) and press Alt+Enter to view the quick fix suggestion.
- Tap or click Implement Methods and tap or click the OK button in the Select Methods to implement dialog box to add the auto-generated method stub for the run( ) method.
- To complete the stub, tap or click to the right of } in Line 23 at the end of the stub, and then type a semicolon to close the class.

The auto-generated stub for the run( ) method is created automatically for the TimerTask (Figure 6-9).

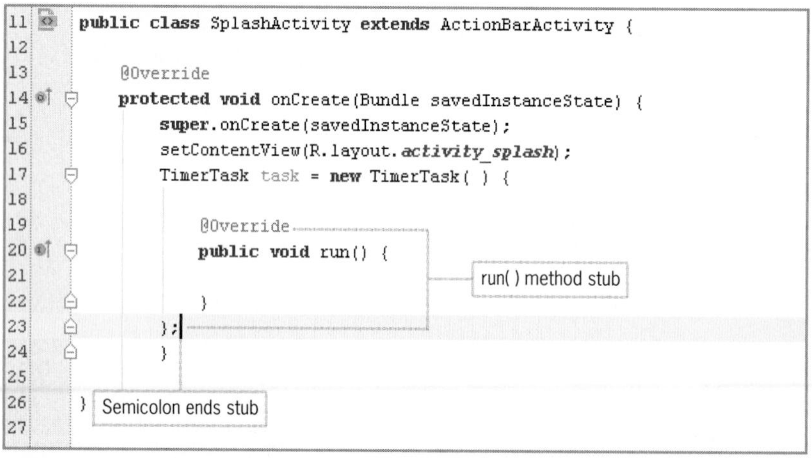

Figure 6-9 run( ) method

IN THE TRENCHES

Timers can also be used to display updates of how long an installation is taking by displaying a countdown, monitor what a user is doing, or execute other routines while an Activity is running.

Scheduling a Timer

After including a reference to the TimerTask class, a timer must be scheduled for the amount of time that the splash screen is displayed. The Timer class shown in the following code syntax creates a timed event when the schedule method is called. A delay timer is scheduled in milliseconds using the Timer class. Delay schedules simply prompt an event to occur once at a specified time.

Code Syntax

```
Timer opening = new Timer();
opening.schedule(task,5000);
```

In the first line of the code syntax, the object named opening initializes a new instance of the Timer class. When the schedule method of the Timer class is called in the second line, two arguments are required. The first parameter (task) is the name of the variable that was initialized for the Timer class. The second parameter represents the number of milliseconds (5,000 milliseconds = about 5 seconds). Follow these steps to add the scheduled timer:

STEP 1

- In the code on the SplashActivity.java tab, after the closing braces for the TimerTask class and the semicolon (Line 24), insert a new line.
- Type **Timer opening = new Timer( );**.
- Tap or click Timer and press Alt+Enter. Tap or click Import Class.

An instance of the Timer class is created (Figure 6-10).

```java

    @Override
    protected void onCreate(Bundle savedInstanceState) {
        super.onCreate(savedInstanceState);
        setContentView(R.layout.activity_splash);
        TimerTask task = new TimerTask( ) {

            @Override
            public void run() {

            }
        };
        Timer opening = new Timer( );
        }

}

```

Instance of Timer

Figure 6-10 Timer class

STEP 2

- To schedule a timer to pause for five seconds using the schedule method from the Timer class, press the Enter key at the end of the line.
- Type **opening.schedule(task,5000);**.

The timer named opening, which lasts five seconds, is scheduled (Figure 6-11).

```java
    @Override
    protected void onCreate(Bundle savedInstanceState) {
        super.onCreate(savedInstanceState);
        setContentView(R.layout.activity_splash);
        TimerTask task = new TimerTask( ) {

            @Override
            public void run() {

            }
        };
        Timer opening = new Timer( );
        opening.schedule(task,5000);
        }

}

```

Timer scheduled for 5 seconds

Figure 6-11 Timer scheduled for 5 seconds

IN THE TRENCHES

Be careful not to code excessively long timers that waste the time of the user. A user-friendly program runs smoothly without long delays.

Life and Death of an Activity

In Line 15 of the Aloha Music app, as shown in Figure 6-11, the SplashActivity begins its life in the Activity life cycle with the onCreate( ) method. Each Activity has a **life cycle**, which is the series of actions from the beginning of an Activity to its end. Actions that occur during the life cycle provide ways to manage how users interact with your app. Each Activity in this book begins with an onCreate( ) method. The onCreate( ) method initializes the user interface with an XML layout; the life of the Activity is started. As in any life cycle, the opposite of birth is death. In this case, an **onDestroy( ) method** is the end of the Activity. The onCreate( ) method sets up all the resources required to perform the Activity, and onDestroy( ) releases those same resources to free up memory on your mobile device. The life cycle of the SplashActivity also begins with onCreate( ) and ends with onDestroy( ). Other actions can take place during the life of the Activity. For example, when the scheduled timer starts (Line 26 in Figure 6-11), the SplashActivity is paused. If you open multiple apps on a smartphone and receive a phone call, you must either pause or terminate the other apps to secure enough available memory to respond to the incoming call. To handle the life cycle actions between onCreate( ) and onDestroy( ), you use methods such as onRestart( ), onStart( ), onResume( ), onPause( ), and onStop( ). Each of these methods changes the state of the Activity. The four **states** of an Activity determine whether the activity is active, paused, stopped, or dead. The life cycle of an application affects how an app works and how the different parts are being orchestrated. Table 6-2 shows the development of an Activity throughout its life cycle.

Method	Description
onCreate( )	The onCreate( ) method begins each Activity. This method also provides a Bundle containing the Activity's previously frozen state, if it had one.
onRestart( )	If the Activity is stopped, onRestart( ) begins the Activity again. If this method is called, it indicates your Activity is being redisplayed to the user from a stopped state. The onRestart( ) method is always followed by onStart( ).
onStart( )	If the Activity is hidden, onStart( ) makes the Activity visible.
onResume( )	The onResume( ) method is called when the user begins interacting with the Activity. The onResume( ) method is always followed by onPause( ).
onPause( )	This method is called when an Activity is about to resume.
onStop( )	This method hides the Activity.
onDestroy( )	This method destroys the Activity. Typically, the finish( ) method (part of the onDestroy( ) method) is used to declare that the Activity is finished; when the next Activity is called, it releases all the resources from the first Activity.

Table 6-2 Methods used in the life cycle of an Activity

When an Activity is launched using onCreate( ), the app performs the actions in the Activity. In other words, the Activity becomes the top sheet of paper on a stack of papers. When the methods shown in Table 6-2 are used between the onCreate( ) and onDestroy( ) methods, they shuffle the order of the papers in that stack. When onDestroy( ) is called, imagine that the pile of papers is thrown away. The finish( ) method is part of the onDestroy( ) method and is called when the Activity is completed and should be closed. Typically, the finish( ) method occurs directly before another Activity is launched. As an Android developer, you should be well acquainted with the life cycle of Activities because an app that you publish in the Android market must "play" well with all the other apps on a mobile device. For example, your Android app must pause when a text message, phone call, or other event occurs.

The diagram in Figure 6-12 shows the life cycle of an Activity. The rectangles represent the methods you can implement to perform operations when the Activity moves between states. The colored ovals are the possible major states of the Activity.

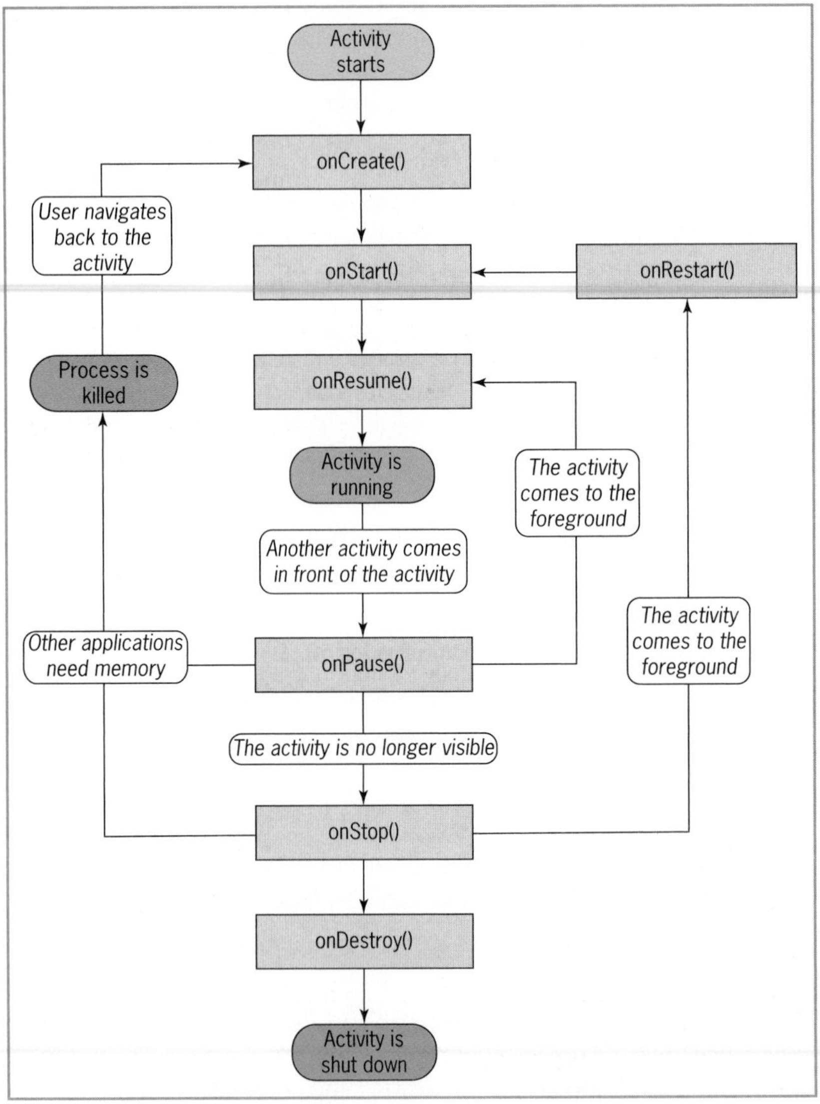

Courtesy of developer.android.com

Figure 6-12 Android life cycle

As an example of the Activity life cycle, the native Android application designed for taking a picture using the built-in camera transitions through each stage in the life cycle. When the user launches the camera app, the camera Activity executes the onCreate( ) method to display the opening screen and the image captured through the camera lens. The user taps a Button control to take a picture. The onStop( ) method is called to hide the live image displayed after the picture is taken. The onRestart( ) method is called after the picture is taken to restart the rest of the app. The onStart( ) method is called to display the picture that was just taken. If the user taps the screen to upload the image to Facebook, the onPause( ) method is called to pause operations of the camera app while the image is uploaded. The onResume( ) method is launched after the picture is uploaded to reactivate the camera. The user can choose to take another image, which repeats the process, or to exit the camera app. If the user selects the exit option, onDestroy( ) or finish( ) frees the saved resources from the temporary memory of the device and closes the camera application.

In the Aloha Music application, after the timer pauses the program temporarily, the SplashActivity should be destroyed with onDestroy( ) before launching the second Activity. The app should call the onDestroy( ) method from within the run( ) method of the timer task that was invoked by TimerTask. Doing so guarantees that the ongoing task execution is the last task this timer performs. To close the SplashActivity, follow these steps:

STEP 1

- In SplashActivity.java, tap or click inside the run( ) auto-generated method stub in Line 22.
- Type **finish**( );.

The finish( ) statement releases the resources that were created for the SplashActivity and closes the Activity (Figure 6-13).

```
13
14      @Override
15      protected void onCreate(Bundle savedInstanceState) {
16          super.onCreate(savedInstanceState);
17          setContentView(R.layout.activity_splash);
18          TimerTask task = new TimerTask( ) {
19
20              @Override
21              public void run() {
22                  finish();           finish( ) method
23              }
24          };
25          Timer opening = new Timer( );
26          opening.schedule(task,5000);
27          }
28
29  }
30
```

Figure 6-13 finish( ) method called

STEP 2

- Save your work.

Launching the Next Activity

After the Activity for the splash screen is destroyed, an intent must request that the next Activity is launched. An XML layout named main.xml already exists as the default layout. A second class named Main must be created before the code can launch this Java class. You must update the Android Manifest file to include the Main Activity. The Main Activity is responsible for playing music. To create a second class and launch the Main Activity, follow these steps:

STEP 1

- In the Android project view, press and hold or right-click the first net.androidbootcamp.alohamusic folder, tap or click New on the shortcut menu, and then tap or click Activity. Next, tap or click Blank Activity.
- The Activity Name text box is set to MainActivity by default with the class named activity_main.
- Type **Play Music** in the Title text box. This text is displayed on the Action bar at the top of the Activity.

A second class named MainActivity and activity_main.xml are created (Figure 6-14).

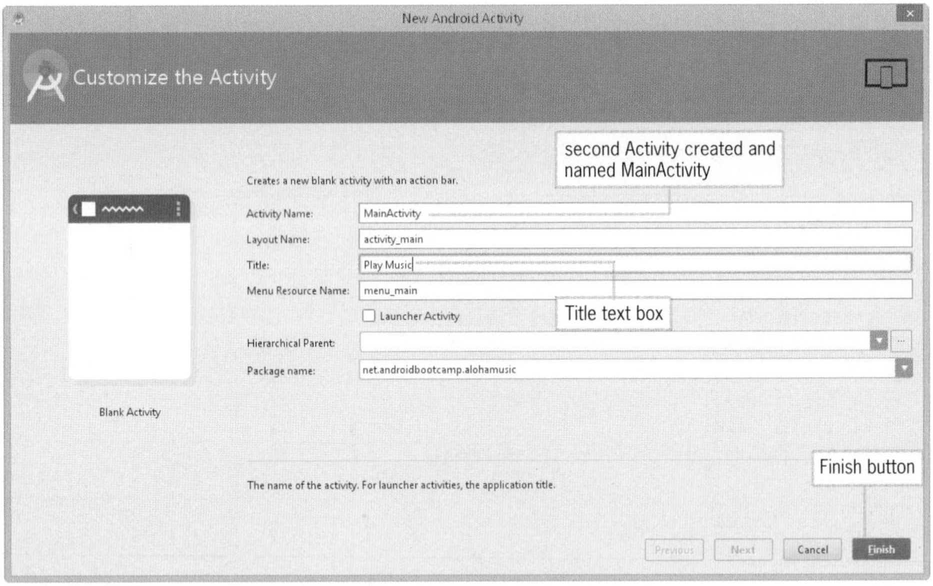

Figure 6-14 Second Activity, which is called MainActivity

STEP 2

- Tap or click the Finish button to finish creating the MainActivity class.
- To launch the MainActivity class from the splash screen, open the SplashActivity.java tab.
- Insert a new line in the run( ) auto-generated method stub after the finish( ); statement.

- Type **startActivity(new Intent(SplashActivity.this, MainActivity.class));** to launch the second Activity.
- If necessary, tap or click the red text Intent and press Alt+Enter to import the Intent statement. Save your work.

The second Activity named MainActivity is launched with an Intent statement (Figure 6-15).

Figure 6-15 Launching MainActivity after the Splash screen is displayed for 5 seconds

Designing the activity_main.xml File

In the Aloha Music app, after the first Activity displaying the splash screen finishes and the second Activity named MainActivity is launched, a second XML layout file is displayed when the onCreate( ) method is called within the MainActivity.java file. The MainActivity.java file uses the default Relative layout with two ImageView and Button controls. To create and design the XML layout for activity_main.xml, follow these steps:

STEP 1

- Close the SplashActivity.java tab.
- Open the activity_main.xml tab.
- Delete the Hello World! TextView control.
- Drag an ImageView control from the Widgets category of the Palette to the emulator window and center the placeholder in the upper third of the emulator.
- Double-tap or double-click the placeholder from the ImageView control to open the src and id editing panel.
- Type **imgUkulele** in the id text box to name the ImageView control.

- Tap or click the ellipsis button (three dots) to the right of the src text box.
- Scroll down the Resources listing on the Projects tab to locate ukulele and then tap or click ukulele.
- Tap or click the OK button to close the Resources dialog box.
- Tap or click to the right of the contentDescription property in the Properties pane and then tap or click the ellipsis button.
- Select ukulele within the Resources dialog box and then tap or click the OK button.
- Change the layout:height property to **150dp** and the layout:width to **320dp**.
- Expand the layout:margin property, and type **20dp** in the top text box.

The image for the first song named Ukulele is placed in activity_main.xml (Figure 6-16).

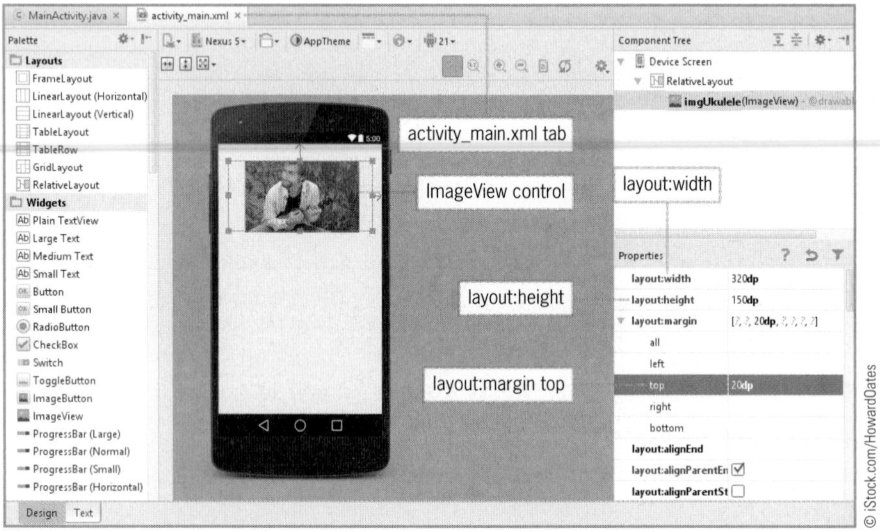

Figure 6-16 Second XML layout

STEP 2

- Drag a Button from the Widgets category of the Palette and center it below the image.
- Double-tap or double-click the button and type **btnUkulele** to the right of the id property.
- Tap or click the ellipsis button for the text property, select btnUkulele, and then tap or click the OK button.
- Set the textSize property to **22sp**.
- If necessary, expand the layout:margin property, and type **10dp** in the top and bottom text box.

The button to select the first song named Ukulele is placed on the emulator (Figure 6-17).

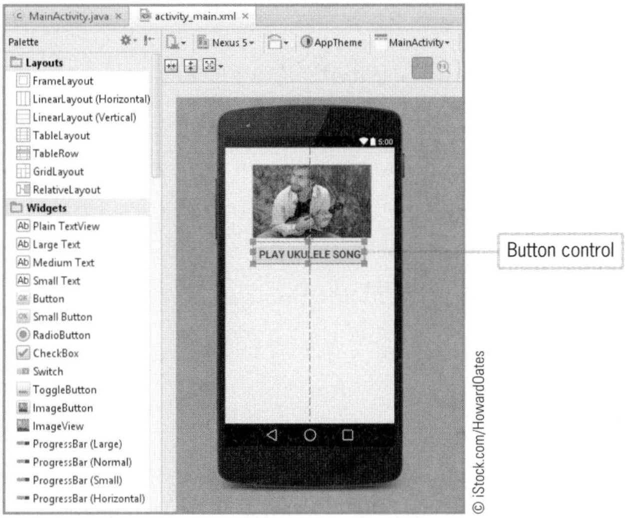

Figure 6-17 Second XML layout, continued

STEP 3

- Drag another ImageView control to the emulator and center it below the Button control.
- Double-tap or double-click the image placeholder and type **imgDrums** in the id text box to name the ImageView control.
- Tap or click the ellipsis button to the right of the src text box and then tap or click drums.
- Tap or click the OK button to close the Resources dialog box.
- Tap or click to the right of the contentDescription property in the Properties pane and then tap or click the ellipsis button.
- Select drums within the Resources dialog box and then tap or click the OK button.
- Change the layout:height property to **150dp** and the layout:width to **320dp**.
- If necessary, expand the layout:margin property and type **20dp** in the top text box.
- Drag another Button to the emulator and center it below the drums image.
- Double-tap or double-click the button and type **btnDrums** to the right of the id property.
- Tap or click the ellipsis button for the text property, select btnDrums, and then tap or click the OK button.
- Set the textSize property to **22sp**.
- In the layout:margin property, type **10dp** in the top and bottom text box.

The image and button to select the second song named Drums are designed in activity_main.xml (Figure 6-18).

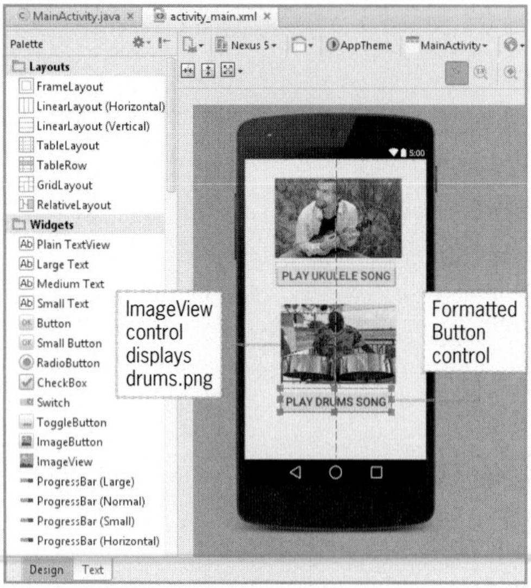

Figure 6-18 activity_main.xml layout complete

Class Variables

In the coding examples used thus far in this book, variables have been local variables. **Local variables** are declared by variable declaration statements within a method, such as a primitive integer variable within an onCreate( ) method. The local variable effectively ceases to exist when the execution of the method is complete. The **scope** of a variable refers to the variable's visibility within a class. Variables that are accessible only to a restricted portion of a program, such as a single method, are said to have local scope. Variables that are accessible from anywhere in a class, however, are said to have global scope. If a variable is needed in multiple methods within a class, the global variable is assigned at the beginning of a class, not within a method. This global scope variable is called a **class variable** in Java and can be accessed by multiple methods throughout the program. In the chapter project, the Button, MediaPlayer (necessary for playing sound), and an integer variable named playing are needed in the onCreate( ) method and within both onClick( ) methods for each Button control. To keep the value of these variables throughout multiple classes, the variables are defined as class variables that cease to exist when their class or activity is unloaded.

After class variables are defined in MainActivity.java, the onCreate( ) method opens the activity_main.xml layout and defines the two Button controls. The Activity waits for the user to select one of the two buttons, each of which plays a song. If a button is clicked twice, the music pauses. Each button must have a setOnClickListener that awaits the user's tap or click. After the user taps a button, the setOnClickListener method implements the Button.

OnClickListener, creating an instance of the OnClickListener and calling the onClick method. The onClick method responds to the user's action. For example, in the chapter project, the response is to play a song. The onClick method is where you place the code to handle playing the song. To code the class variables, display the activity_main.xml layout, reference the two Button controls, and set an OnClickListener, follow these steps:

STEP 1

- Close the activity_main.xml window and save your work.
- Open MainActivity.java and show line numbers. After the public class Main extends ActionBarActivity statement, type **Button button1, button2;** to create a class variable that refers to the two Button controls. When you finish, press Enter.
- Tap or click the red text Button and press Alt+Enter to import the Button class.
- On the next line, type **MediaPlayer mpUkulele, mpDrums;** to create a class variable reference for the media player.
- Tap or click MediaPlayer and press Alt+Enter to import the MediaPlayer class.
- Insert a new line and then type **int playing;** to create a primitive class variable named playing, which keeps track of whether a song is playing. When you finish, press the Enter key.

Class variables that can be accessed by the rest of the program are initialized (Figure 6-19).

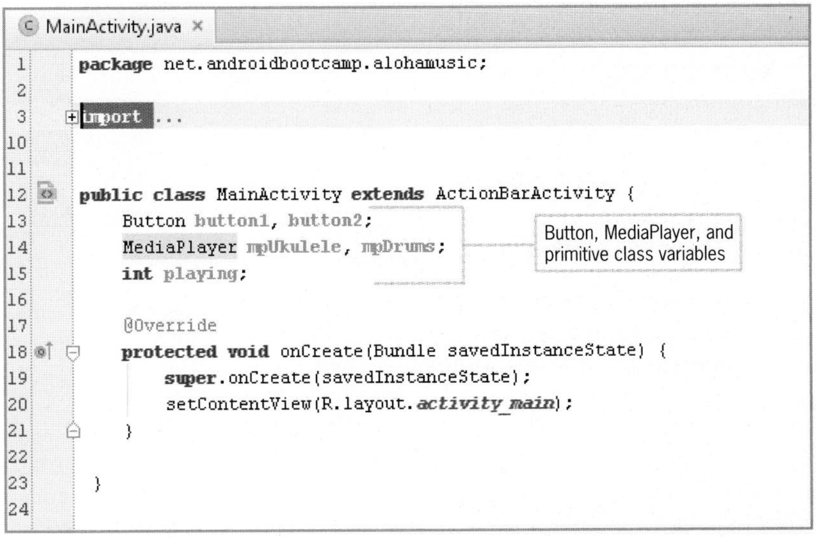

Figure 6-19 Class variables

STEP 2

- Both Button references were made as class variables. To create an instance of each Button control, press the Enter key after Line 20 (the setContentView statement) and type **button1 = (Button)findViewById(R.id.btnUkulele);**.
- Press the Enter key and then type **button2 = (Button)findViewById(R.id.btnDrums);**.

The Button controls named button1 and button2 are referenced in MainActivity.java (Figure 6-20).

MainActivity.java ×

```
1   package net.androidbootcamp.alohamusic;
2
3   +import ...
10
11
12  public class MainActivity extends ActionBarActivity {
13      Button button1, button2;
14      MediaPlayer mpUkulele, mpDrums;
15      int playing;
16
17      @Override
18      protected void onCreate(Bundle savedInstanceState) {
19          super.onCreate(savedInstanceState);
20          setContentView(R.layout.activity_main);
21          button1 = (Button) findViewById(R.id.btnUkulele);
22          button2 = (Button) findViewById(R.id.btnDrums);
23      }
24
25  }
26
```

Button controls instantiated

Figure 6-20 Adding Button controls

STEP 3

- To create a setOnClickListener method so the first Button (button1) waits for the user's tap, press the Enter key and type **button1.setOnClickListener(bUkulele);**.
- To create an instance of the Button OnClickListener, tap or click between the two ending braces (Line 26), type **Button.OnClickListener bUkulele = new Button.OnClickListener(){**, and then press the Enter key.
- Place a semicolon after the new closing brace on Line 30.
- This OnClickListener is designed for a class variable for a Button. Tap or click the red curly error line below Button.OnClickListener, press Alt+Enter, select Implement method to add the quick fix, and then tap or click the OK button.

An OnClickListener auto-generated stub appears in the code for the first button (Figure 6-21).

Figure 6-21 Inserting the first Button OnClickListener stub

STEP 4

- To create a setOnClickListener method so the second Button (button2) for the Drums song waits for the user's tap or click, tap or click after the button1.setOnClickListener(bUkulele); statement and then press the Enter key.
- Type **button2.setOnClickListener(bDrums);**.
- To create an instance of the button2 OnClickListener, tap or click after the brace with the semicolon at the end of the code in Line 31 and then press the Enter key.
- Type **Button.OnClickListener bDrums = new Button.OnClickListener**( ) { and then press the Enter key to create the closing brace.
- Place a semicolon after the new closing brace.
- Tap or click the red error line below Button.OnClickListener, press Alt+Enter, select Implement Methods to add the quick fix, and then tap or click the OK button. Save your work.

An OnClickListener auto-generated stub appears in the code for the second button (Figure 6-22).

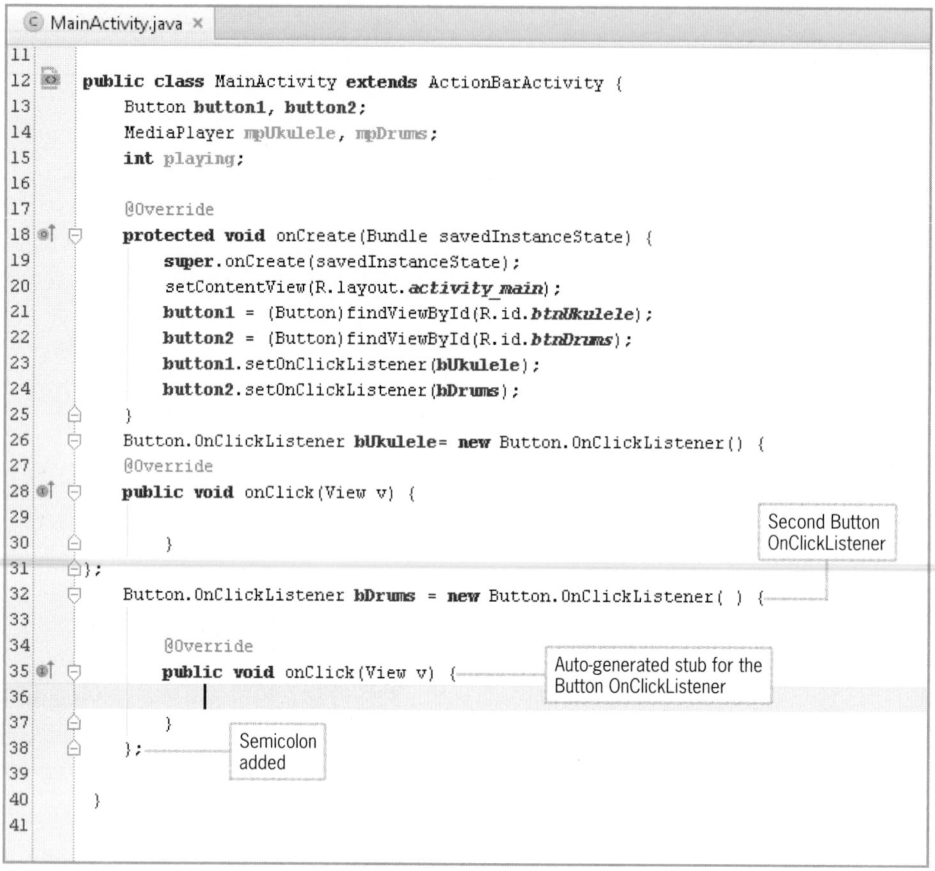

Figure 6-22 Inserting the second Button OnClickListener stub

Playing Music

Every Android phone and tablet includes a built-in music player where you can store your favorite music. You can also write your own applications that offer music playback capabilities. To enable the Aloha Music chapter project to play two songs, Android includes a MediaPlayer class that can play both audio and music files. Android lets you play audio and video from several types of data sources. You can play audio or video from media files stored in the application's resources (a folder named raw), from stand-alone files in the Android file system of the device, from an SD (Secure Digital) memory card in the phone itself, or from a data stream provided through an Internet connection. The most common file type of media supported for audio playback with the MediaPlayer class is .mp3, but other audio file types such as .wav, .ogg, and .midi are typically supported by most Android hardware. The Android device platform supports a wide variety of media types based on the codecs included in the device by the manufacturer. A **codec** is a computer technology used to compress and decompress audio and video files.

IN THE TRENCHES

The Android platform provides a class to record audio and video, where supported by the mobile device hardware. To record audio or video, use the MediaRecorder class. The emulator does not provide the capability to capture audio or video, but an actual mobile device can record media input, accessible through the MediaRecorder class.

Critical Thinking

What types of video file formats can be played on an Android device?

Android currently supports the following video formats: MPEG-4, H.263, H.264, and VP8.

Creating a Raw Folder for Music Files

In an Android project, music files are typically stored in a new resource directory called raw, which is a subfolder created in the res folder. The raw resource directory must be created before music files can be placed in that folder. The two .mp3 files played in the Aloha Music app are named ukulele.mp3 and drums.mp3, and they should be placed in the raw folder. To create a raw folder that contains music files, follow these steps:

STEP 1

- In the Android project view, press and hold or right-click the res folder.
- Tap or click New on the shortcut menu and then tap or click Android resource directory. The New Resource Directory dialog box opens.
- Tap or click the arrow to the right of the Resource type and select raw from the drop-down entries.

A resource directory named raw is created using the New Resource Directory dialog box (Figure 6-23).

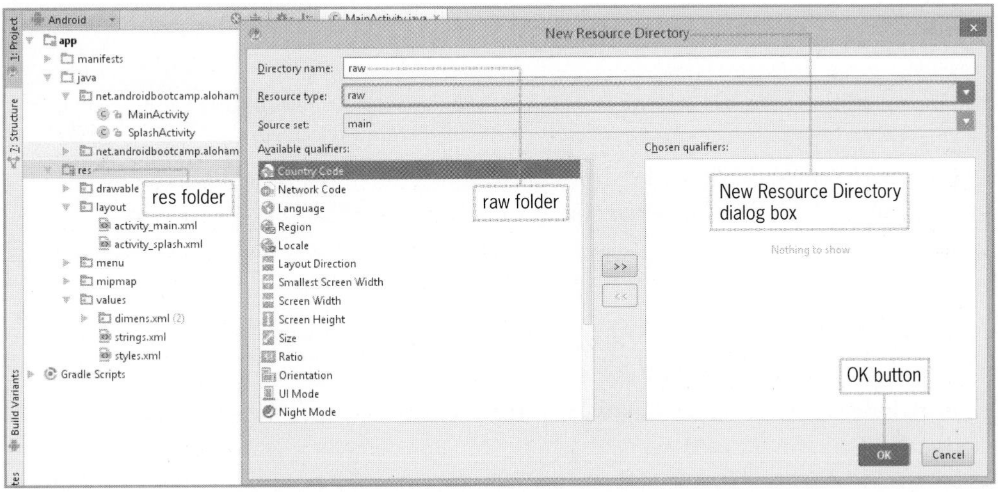

Figure 6-23 The raw folder added for sound files

STEP 2

- Tap or click the OK button.
- To add the project music files to the raw folder, open the USB folder that contains your student files.
- To add the two music files to the raw resource folder, copy ukulele.mp3 and drums.mp3 by pressing Ctrl+C, and then press and hold or right-click the raw folder and tap or click Paste.
- Tap or click the OK button in the Copy dialog box.

Copies of the music files appear in the raw folder (Figure 6-24).

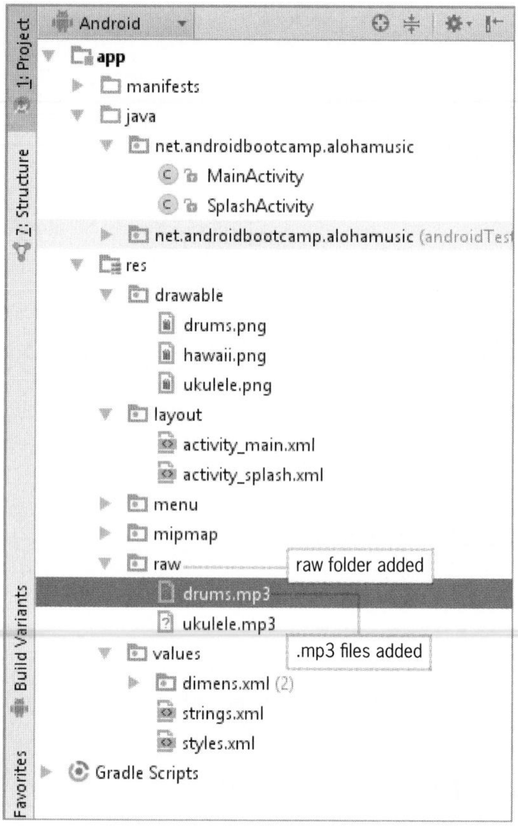

Figure 6-24 MP3 files added to raw folder

Using the MediaPlayer Class

The **MediaPlayer class** provides the methods to control audio playback on an Android device. At the beginning of the MainActivity.java code, two MediaPlayer class variables are declared. After the variables are declared, an instance of the MediaPlayer class is assigned to each variable. In the following code syntax, mpUkulele is assigned to an instance of the MediaPlayer class that accesses the ukulele music file in the raw folder.

Code Syntax

```
MediaPlayer mpUkulele = MediaPlayer.create(this, R.raw.ukulele);
```

The class variables mpUkulele and mpDrums are assigned the music files from the raw folder. To declare an instance of the MediaPlayer class, follow this step:

STEP 1

- In MainActivity.java, press the Enter key after the button2.setOnClickListener(bDrums); statement (Line 24) to create a new line.
- Type **mpUkulele = new MediaPlayer();** to create a new instance of MediaPlayer.

When we create the raw folder it does not appear in the res folder. We have to go into Window Explorer the AlohaMusic directory then

app/src/main/res/raw

and paste the .mp3 file in this way there.

Then the raw folder will appear in the Project Window in Android Studio

This is not a problem in Android 2.1.3 (on my computer), the raw folder does appear when created. It is a problem on the laptop as I have an older version of Android there.

- Insert a new line and type **mpUkulele = MediaPlayer.create(this, R.raw.ukulele);** to assign the first song to mpUkulele. Press the Enter key after the closing semicolon.
- Type **mpDrums = new MediaPlayer();** to add an instance for the second MediaPlayer variable.
- Insert a new line and type **mpDrums = MediaPlayer.create(this, R.raw.drums);** to assign the second song to mpDrums.

The two class variables are assigned an instance of the MediaPlayer class (Figure 6-25).

MainActivity.java

```
public class MainActivity extends ActionBarActivity {
    Button button1, button2;
    MediaPlayer mpUkulele, mpDrums;
    int playing;

    @Override
    protected void onCreate(Bundle savedInstanceState) {
        super.onCreate(savedInstanceState);
        setContentView(R.layout.activity_main);
        button1 = (Button)findViewById(R.id.btnUkulele);
        button2 = (Button)findViewById(R.id.btnDrums);
        button1.setOnClickListener(bUkulele);
        button2.setOnClickListener(bDrums);
        mpUkulele = new MediaPlayer();
        mpUkulele = MediaPlayer.create(this, R.raw.ukulele);
        mpDrums = new MediaPlayer();
        mpDrums = MediaPlayer.create(this, R.raw.drums);
    }
    Button.OnClickListener bUkulele= new Button.OnClickListener() {
    @Override
    public void onClick(View v) {

    }
};
```

MediaPlayer statements for both songs

Figure 6-25 MediaPlayer instance statements

GTK

Music can be used in many ways throughout Android apps. Music can provide sound effects to inform the user of a recent email or to praise you when you reach the winning level on your favorite game. Background music is often used as a soundtrack to create a theme in an adventure game.

The MediaPlayer State

Android uses the MediaPlayer class to control the playing of the audio file. What determines whether the music file is playing is called the state of the MediaPlayer. The three common states of the audio file are when the music starts, when the music pauses, and when the music stops. The state of the music is established by the MediaPlayer's temporary behavior. Table 6-3 provides an example of the most common MediaPlayer states.

Method	Purpose
start( )	Starts media playback
pause( )	Pauses media playback
stop( )	Stops media playback

Table 6-3 Common MediaPlayer states

In the Aloha Music project, the user first taps a button to start playing the music. The start( ) method is used to begin the playback of the selected music file. When the user taps the same button again, the app temporarily pauses the music file by calling the pause( ) method. To restart the song, the start( ) method must be called again. To determine the state of the MediaPlayer, the code must assess whether this is the first time the user is tapping the button to start the song or if the user is tapping the same button twice to pause the song. The user can tap the button a third time to start the song again. This cycle continues until the user exits the project. In the chapter project, an integer variable named playing is initially set to zero. Each time the user taps the button, the playing variable changes value. The first time the user taps the button, the variable is changed to the value of 1 to assist the program in determining the state of the MediaPlayer. If the user taps the same button again to pause the song, the variable changes to the value of 0. Android does not have a method for determining the present state of the MediaPlayer, but by using this simple primitive variable, you can keep track of the state of the music. A Switch decision structure uses the variable named playing to change the state of the music. The onClick( ) method is called every time the user selects a button. To initiate the variable used to determine the state of the MediaPlayer and to code a Switch decision structure to determine the state, follow these steps:

STEP 1

- In MainActivity.java, press the Enter key after the mpDrums = MediaPlayer.create(this, R.raw.drums); statement (Line 28) to create a new line.
- Type **playing = 0;** to initialize the variable named playing as the value 0. When the user clicks a button, the Switch statement follows the path of case 0, which begins the audio playback of one of the songs.

The variable named playing is initialized as the value 0 (Figure 6-26).

MainActivity.java ×

```
12  public class MainActivity extends ActionBarActivity {
13      Button button1, button2;
14      MediaPlayer mpUkulele, mpDrums;
15      int playing;
16
17      @Override
18      protected void onCreate(Bundle savedInstanceState) {
19          super.onCreate(savedInstanceState);
20          setContentView(R.layout.activity_main);
21          button1 = (Button)findViewById(R.id.btnUkulele);
22          button2 = (Button)findViewById(R.id.btnDrums);
23          button1.setOnClickListener(bUkulele);
24          button2.setOnClickListener(bDrums);
25          mpUkulele = new MediaPlayer();
26          mpUkulele = MediaPlayer.create(this, R.raw.ukulele);
27          mpDrums = new MediaPlayer();
28          mpDrums = MediaPlayer.create(this, R.raw.drums);
29          playing = 0;
30      }
31      Button.OnClickListener bUkulele= new Button.OnClickListener() {
32      @Override
33      public void onClick(View v) {
34
35      }
36  };
```

Variable that changes as state of the music changes

Figure 6-26 Variable named "playing" is set to 0

STEP 2

- Inside the braces of the first onClick method, tap or click the blank Line 34 and then type the following Switch decision structure, which is used to determine the state of the music:

```
switch(playing) {
    case 0:
        mpUkulele.start();
        playing = 1;
        break;
    case 1:
        mpUkulele.pause();
        playing = 0;
        break;
}
```

The Switch decision structure that determines the state of the music is coded for the first onClick method (Figure 6-27).

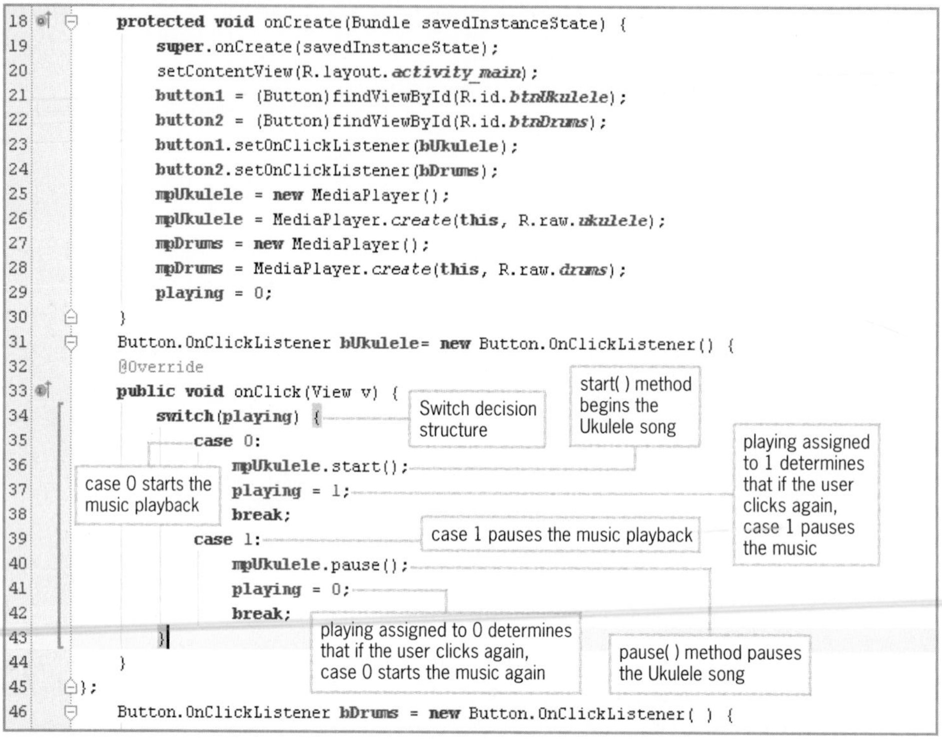

Figure 6-27 Switch statements for first onClick method

IN THE TRENCHES

Music playback control may fail due to various reasons, such as an unsupported audio/video format, poorly interleaved audio/video, a file size that overwhelms memory capabilities, or a streaming timeout on the Internet.

Changing the Text Property Using Code

To play the first song in the chapter project, the user taps the Button control with the text "Play Ukulele Song." To pause the song, the user must tap the same button, but the text should be changed to a more fitting action, such as "Pause Ukulele Song." A property can initially be entered in the XML layout or coded in Java. In Chapter 4, the setText( ) method displays text in the TextView control. To change the Text property for a Button control using Java code, the control name and the setText( ) method are separated by a period that precedes a string of text within parentheses, as shown in the following code syntax:

Code Syntax

```
btnUkulele.setText("Pause Ukulele Song");
```

The btnUkulele Button control displays the text "Pause Ukulele Song." If the user wants to restart the song, a second setText( ) method changes the text back to "Play Ukulele Song." To change the text on the Button control for the first button, follow these steps:

STEP 1

- In MainActivity.java, in the first onClick( ) method, press the Enter key after the statement playing = 1; in case 0 (Line 37).
- Type **button1.setText("Pause Ukulele Song");** to change the text displayed on the Button control.
- To change the text back to the original text if the user restarts the music, go to case 1 of the Switch decision structure and press the Enter key after the statement playing = 0; (Line 42).
- Type **button1.setText("Play Ukulele Song");** to change the text displayed on the Button control.

The first button changes text while the music is paused or restarted (Figure 6-28).

```
31  Button.OnClickListener bUkulele= new Button.OnClickListener() {
32      @Override
33      public void onClick(View v) {
34          switch(playing) {
35              case 0:
36                  mpUkulele.start();
37                  playing = 1;
38                  button1.setText("Pause Ukulele Song");
39                  break;
40              case 1:
41                  mpUkulele.pause();
42                  playing = 0;
43                  button1.setText("Play Ukulele Song");
44                  break;
45          }
46      }
47  };
```

setText ( ) changes the Button text

Figure 6-28 The setText( ) method changes the button control in both case statements

STEP 2

- To test the music and text on the first Button control, save and run the program. The second Button control has not been coded yet.

When you tap the first Button control, the Ukulele song plays and the Button text is changed. You can restart or pause the music by pressing the button again (Figure 6-29).

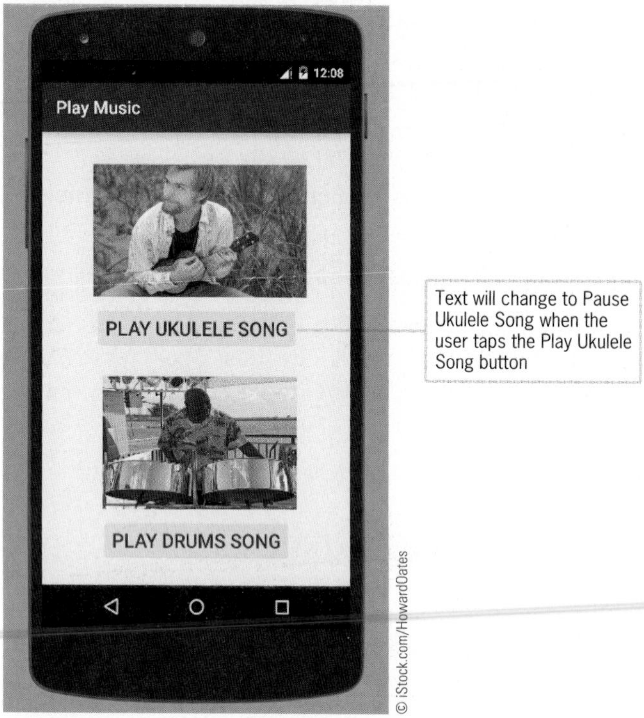

Figure 6-29 Coding the button

Changing the Visibility Property Using Code

When the program is complete, the user can select the button that plays the Ukulele song or the Drums song. One problem is that a user can tap the Ukulele song button and then tap the Drums button, playing both songs at once. To resolve this problem when the user has already selected one of the songs, the button to the other song can be coded to disappear until the user has paused the current song from playing. The Java property that determines whether a control is displayed on the emulator is the **Visibility property**. By default, the Visibility property is set to display any control you place on the emulator when the program runs. To cause the control not to appear, you must code the setVisibility property to change the view to invisible. To change the visibility of the button to reappear, the setVisibility property is changed to visible, as shown in the following code syntax:

Code Syntax

To hide the control: `btnUkulele.setVisibility(View.INVISIBLE);`
To display the control: `btnUkulele.setVisibility(View.VISIBLE);`

To set the setVisibility property for the Ukulele button control to change the view to invisible and to copy and paste the first onClick code to create a Switch decision structure for the second button, you can complete the following steps:

STEP 1

- In MainActivity.java, in the first onClick( ) method in the case 0 option, press the Enter key after the statement button1.setText("Pause Ukulele Song");.
- Type **button2.setVisibility(View.INVISIBLE);** to hide the Drums button when the Ukulele song is playing. When the music is paused, the Drums button should be visible again.
- In the case 1 option, press the Enter key after the statement button1.setText("Play Ukulele Song");.
- Type **button2.setVisibility(View.VISIBLE);** to change the visibility of the Drums button.

The Drums button is hidden when the music plays and displayed when the music stops (Figure 6-30).

```
31    Button.OnClickListener bUkulele= new Button.OnClickListener() {
32    @Override
33    public void onClick(View v) {
34        switch(playing) {
35            case 0:
36                mpUkulele.start();
37                playing = 1;
38                button1.setText("Pause Ukulele Song");
39                button2.setVisibility(View.INVISIBLE);
40                break;
41            case 1:
42                mpUkulele.pause();
43                playing = 0;
44                button1.setText("Play Ukulele Song");
45                button2.setVisibility(View.VISIBLE);
46                break;
47        }
48    }
49 };
50    Button.OnClickListener bDrums = new Button.OnClickListener( ) {
51
52        @Override
53        public void onClick(View v) {
54
```

setVisibility( ) method hides Drums button

setVisibility( ) method displays Drums button

Figure 6-30 The setVisibility( ) method changes the visibility of the Button control

STEP 2

- To code the second onClick( ) method for the Drums button, select and copy Lines 34–47 in Figure 6-30 by clicking Edit on the menu bar and then clicking Copy. Tap or click Line 54 inside the second onClick() method, tap or click Edit on the menu bar, and then tap or click Paste. Change every reference of mpUkulele to **mpDrums**. Change every reference of button1 to **button2** or vice versa.
- Change the setText messages to **Pause Drums Song** and **Play Drums Song**. You might need to add }; as the second-to-last line of code. Compare your code with the complete code, making changes as necessary.

The second onClick( ) method is coded using a Switch decision structure (Figure 6-31). The code for MainActivity.java is complete.

MainActivity.java ×

```java
package net.androidbootcamp.alohamusic;

import ...


public class MainActivity extends ActionBarActivity {
    Button button1, button2;
    MediaPlayer mpUkulele, mpDrums;
    int playing;

    @Override
    protected void onCreate(Bundle savedInstanceState) {
        super.onCreate(savedInstanceState);
        setContentView(R.layout.activity_main);
        button1 = (Button)findViewById(R.id.btnUkulele);
        button2 = (Button)findViewById(R.id.btnDrums);
        button1.setOnClickListener(bUkulele);
        button2.setOnClickListener(bDrums);
        mpUkulele = new MediaPlayer();
        mpUkulele = MediaPlayer.create(this, R.raw.ukulele);
        mpDrums = new MediaPlayer();
        mpDrums = MediaPlayer.create(this, R.raw.drums);
        playing = 0;
    }
    Button.OnClickListener bUkulele= new Button.OnClickListener() {
    @Override
    public void onClick(View v) {
        switch(playing) {
            case 0:
                mpUkulele.start();
                playing = 1;
                button1.setText("Pause Ukulele Song");
                button2.setVisibility(View.INVISIBLE);
                break;
            case 1:
                mpUkulele.pause();
                playing = 0;
                button1.setText("Play Ukulele Song");
                button2.setVisibility(View.VISIBLE);
                break;
        }
    }
};
    Button.OnClickListener bDrums = new Button.OnClickListener( ) {

        @Override
        public void onClick(View v) {
            switch (playing) {
                case 0:
                    mpDrums.start();
                    playing = 1;
                    button2.setText("Pause Drums Song");
                    button1.setVisibility(View.INVISIBLE);
                    break;
                case 1:
                    mpDrums.pause();
                    playing = 0;
                    button2.setText("Play Drums Song");
                    button1.setVisibility(View.VISIBLE);
                    break;

            }
        }

    };
}
```

Figure 6-31 Complete code for MainActivity.java

Critical Thinking
What would have happened if the second button was visible while the first song was playing and both buttons were pressed?
Both songs would play at the same time.

Running and Testing the Application

Your first experience with media in an Android application is complete. Tap or click Run on the menu bar and then select Run to save and test the application in the emulator. If necessary, select Android Application and tap or click the OK button. Save all the files in the next dialog box, if necessary, and unlock the emulator. The application opens in the emulator window, as shown in Figures 6-1 and 6-2. The splash screen opens for five seconds. The activity_main layout screen opens next, requesting your button selection to play each of the songs. Test both buttons and make sure your speakers are on so you can hear the music play.

Wrap It Up—Chapter Summary

In this chapter, the Android platform created a memorable multimedia experience with the sounds of Hawaiian music. A splash screen provided time to load extra files if needed and displayed an initial logo for brand recognition. Methods such as setText( ) and setVisibility( ) helped to create an easy-to-use Android application that was clear to the user. The app used the start( ) and pause( ) methods of the MediaPlayer to fill your classroom or home with music.

- An Android application can show a splash screen that displays the name of the program, a brand logo for the application, or the name of the author. The splash screen opens as you launch your app, providing time for Android to initialize its resources.
- A TextView widget can display a background color or image stored in one of the project's drawable folders.
- A timer in Java executes a one-time task such as displaying an opening splash screen, or it performs a continuous process, such as a wake-up call that rings each morning at the same time. Timers can be used to pause an action temporarily or for time-dependent or repeated activities. The timer object uses milliseconds as the unit of time.
- After including a reference to the TimerTask class in your code, schedule a timer for the amount of time that an event occurs, such as a splash screen being displayed.
- Each Activity has a life cycle, which is the series of actions from the beginning of an Activity to its end. An Activity usually starts with the onCreate( ) method, which sets up all the resources required to perform the Activity. An Activity usually ends with the onDestroy( ) method, which releases those same resources to free up memory on the mobile device. Other actions can take place during the life of the Activity, including onRestart( ), onStart( ), onResume( ), onPause( ), and onStop( ).

- Local variables are declared by variable declaration statements within a method. The local variable effectively ceases to exist when the execution of the method is complete.
- The scope of a variable refers to the variable's visibility within a class. Variables that are accessible only to a restricted portion of a program, such as a single method, have local scope. Variables that are accessible from anywhere in a class, however, have global scope. If a variable is needed in multiple methods within a class, the global variable is assigned at the beginning of a class, not within a method. This global scope variable is called a class variable in Java and can be accessed by multiple methods throughout the program.
- Every Android phone and tablet includes a built-in music player where you can store music. You can also write applications that offer music playback capabilities. The media types an Android device platform supports are determined by the codecs the manufacturer included in the device. A codec is a computer technology used to compress and decompress audio and video files.
- In an Android project, music files are typically stored in the res\raw subfolder. In newer versions of Android, you must create the raw subfolder before storing music files.
- The MediaPlayer class provides the methods to control audio playback on an Android device. First declare the MediaPlayer class variables and then assign an instance of the MediaPlayer class to each variable. Whether the music file is playing is called the state of the MediaPlayer. The three common states of the audio file are when the music starts, when the music pauses, and when the music stops.
- The Java property that determines whether a control is displayed on the emulator is the Visibility property. By default, the Visibility property is set to display any control you place on the emulator when the program runs. To cause the control not to appear, you must code the setVisibility property in Java to change the view to invisible. To change the visibility of the button to reappear, change the setVisibility property to visible.

Key Terms

class variable—A variable with global scope; it can be accessed by multiple methods throughout the program.

codec—A computer technology used to compress and decompress audio and video files.

life cycle—The series of actions from the beginning, or birth, of an Activity to its end, or destruction.

local variable—A variable declared by a variable declaration statement within a method.

MediaPlayer class—The Java class that provides the methods to control audio playback on an Android device.

onDestroy( ) method—A method used to end an Activity. Whereas the onCreate( ) method sets up required resources, the onDestroy( ) method releases those same resources to free up memory.

scope—A reference to a variable's visibility within a class.

state—A stage in an Activity's life cycle that determines whether the Activity is active, paused, stopped, or dead.

thread—A single sequential flow of control within a program.

Timer—A Java class that creates a timed event when the schedule method is called.

timer—A tool that performs a one-time task such as displaying an opening splash screen, or that performs a continuous process, such as a morning wake-up call set to run at regular intervals.

TimerTask—A Java class that invokes a scheduled timer.

Visibility property—The Java property that determines whether a control is displayed on the emulator.

Developer FAQs

1. What is the name of the initial window that typically displays a company logo for a few seconds?
2. Which property of TextView displays a solid color behind the text?
3. Which property of TextView displays an image as a backdrop behind the text?
4. Write a line of code that creates an instance of the TimerTask class with the object named welcome.
5. Write a line of code that creates an instance of the Timer class with the object named stopwatch.
6. Write a line of code that would hold the initial opening screen for four seconds. The Timer object is named stopwatch and the TimerTask object is named welcome.
7. How long (identify units) does this statement schedule a pause in the execution?

   ```
   logo.schedule(task, 3000);
   ```
8. Write a line of code that closes the resources of the existing Activity.
9. Typically, which method begins an Activity?
10. Typically, which method releases the resources used within an Activity and ends the Activity?
11. What are the four states of an Activity?
12. Which method follows an onPause( ) method?
13. Write two statements that initialize the media player to create an instance of a file named blues stored in your raw folder. Name the variable mpJazz.

14. Write a statement that is needed to begin playing the song from question 13.
15. Write a statement that is needed to pause the song from question 14.
16. Write a statement that is needed to change the text on a button named btnJazz to the text "Pause Unforgettable."

17. Write a statement that hides the button in question 16.
18. What is the name of the folder that typically holds media files in the Android project?
19. Why are class variables sometimes used instead of local variables?
20. What is the most common extension for a song played on an Android device?

Beyond the Book

Search the Web for answers to the following questions to further your Android knowledge.

1. Research the four most common music file types played on an Android device. Write a paragraph about each music file type. Compare the file size, music quality, and usage of each file type.
2. Using a typical weather app as an example, describe the Android life cycle using each of the methods and a process that happens within the weather app. (*Hint:* See the example using the camera app in this chapter.)
3. In Google Play, research five music apps. Write a paragraph that includes the name, features, and purpose of each app.
4. The MediaPlayer class has a method named seekTo( ). Research the purpose of this method.

Case Programming Projects

Complete one or more of the following case programming projects. Use the same steps and techniques taught within the chapter. Submit the program you create to your instructor. The level of difficulty is indicated for each case programming project.

Easiest: ★

Intermediate: ★★

Challenging: ★★★

Case Project 6–1: Celtic Songs App ★

Requirements Document

Application title:	Celtic Songs App
Purpose:	A music app compares the different types of Celtic music.
Algorithms:	1. A splash screen opens and displays the celtic.png image with the title "Celtic Sounds" for four seconds (Figure 6-32). 2. Two types of Celtic music are available in this app. An Irish jig named jig.mp3 can be played while displaying an image of Irish dancers (jig.png). A second selection of bagpipe music plays bagpipes.mp3 while displaying an image of a man playing bagpipes (Figure 6-33).
Conditions:	1. The pictures of the two types of music (jig and bagpipe) and the two music files are provided with your student files. 2. The music should be played and paused by a button control. 3. When a song is playing, the other button should not be displayed.

© iStock.com/darkbird77

Figure 6-32 Celtic Songs splash screen

© iStock.com/stu99, © iStock.com/RiccardoTravani

Figure 6-33 Two types of Celtic songs

Case Project 6–2: Animal Voices Children's App ★★

Requirements Document

Application title:	Animal Voices Children's App
Purpose:	The Animal Voices app plays sounds of cows and pigs in the barnyard.
Algorithms:	1. The opening screen displays an image of a farm and the title "Animal Voices" for six seconds (Figure 6-34). 2. The second screen displays two buttons with two images that allow the user to select cow sounds or pig sounds (Figure 6-35).
Conditions:	1. The cows.png and pigs.png images are available in the student files and the sound effects are named cows.mp3 and pigs.mp3. 2. When a sound effect is playing, the other button should not be displayed. Each sound effect can play and pause on the user's selection.

Figure 6-34 Animal Voices splash screen

Figure 6-35 Two types of animal sounds

Case Project 6–3: Serenity Sounds App ★★

Requirements Document

Application title: Serenity Sounds App

Purpose: A relaxation app provides songs to allow you to breathe deeply and meditate.

Algorithms:
1. An opening screen displays an image of a relaxing location.
2. The second screen displays two song names with a description of each song. A button is available that plays each song or pauses each song.

Conditions:
1. Choose your own image for the splash screen from images available on the Web.
2. Choose your own songs from songs available at free sites online. Listen to each song and create your own description of each song.
3. When a song is playing, the other button should not be displayed. Each song can play and pause on the user's selection.

Case Project 6–4: Guitar Solo App ★★

Requirements Document

Application title: Guitar Solo App

Purpose: A new guitar performance artist needs an Android app to demo her talent.

Algorithms:
1. The opening screen displays the text "Solo Guitar Demo" and an image of a guitar.
2. A second screen displays the guitar image and a button. When the user selects the Play Guitar Solo button, a guitar solo plays.

Conditions:
1. The opening screen is displayed for three seconds.
2. The song can be paused by the user and restarted.
3. Locate images and music files on free sites online.

Case Project 6–5: Ring Tones App ★★★

Requirements Document

Application title: Ring Tones App

Purpose: The Ring Tones app allows you to listen to three different ring tones using RadioButton controls for selection.

Algorithms:
1. Create an app that opens with a picture of a mobile phone and a title for three seconds.
2. The second screen shows three RadioButton controls that display different ring tone titles and a description of each ring tone.

Conditions:
1. Select your own images and free ring tones available by searching the Web.
2. When a ring tone is playing, the other buttons should not be displayed. Each ring tone can play and pause on the user's selection.

Case Project 6–6: Your Personal Playlist App ★★★

Requirements Document

Application title: Your Personal Playlist App

Purpose: Get creative! Play your favorite three songs on your own personal playlist app.

Algorithms:
1. Create an app that opens with your own picture and a title for six seconds.
2. The second screen shows three buttons that display different song titles and an image of the artist or group.

Conditions:
1. Select your own images and music files.
2. When a song is playing, the other buttons should not be displayed. Each song can play and pause on the user's selection.

CHAPTER 7

Reveal! Displaying Pictures in a GridView

In this chapter, you learn to:

- Create an Android project using a GridView control
- Add a GridView to display a two-dimensional grid of images
- Reference images through an array
- Create an ImageAdapter class
- Code an OnItemClickListener
- Display a custom toast message
- Define a Context resource
- Understand the use of constructors
- Return a value from a method
- Determine the length of an array
- Assign an ImageView control using setImageResource
- Change the scale and layout size of the GridView

Using multimedia within an Android program brings personality and imagery to your app. Images are a powerful marketing tool and add visual appeal to any Android application, but it is essential to create a clean, professional effect with those images. To meet this goal, Android provides a layout tool called a GridView, which shows items in a two-dimensional scrolling grid.

To demonstrate the visual appeal of a GridView control, you will design a grid displaying animals on the endangered species list. The Endangered Species application shown in Figure 7-1 allows users to select the animal they want to symbolically adopt and contribute funds for support groups that work to protect these iconic animals. Users can then scroll the image grid by flicking their fingers across a horizontal listing of thumbnail-sized pictures of the endangered animals. To view a larger image, users can tap a thumbnail to display a full-size image below the grid.

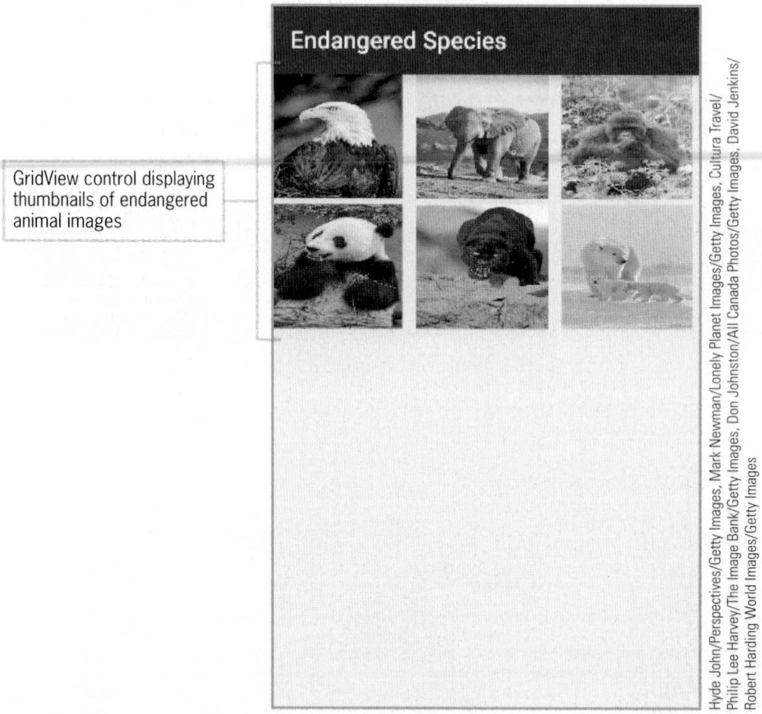

Figure 7-1 Endangered Species Android app

The Android app in Figure 7-1 is more visually appealing than one that simply displays images of the six endangered species in a tiled layout or grid view. The Endangered Species app also provides an easy way for a donor to select an animal to symbolically adopt. The app displays six different animals on the endangered species list, or animals at risk of becoming extinct. The images include an American eagle, Asian elephant, mountain gorilla, giant panda, panther, and polar bear. When a user selects the panda bear in the GridView control, for example, a larger image is displayed with a toast message stating "Selected Species 4," as shown in Figure 7-2. A different image is displayed each time the user selects another thumbnail in the grid.

Hyde John/Perspectives/Getty Images, Mark Newman/Lonely Planet Images/Getty Images, Cultura Travel/Philip Lee Harvey/The Image Bank/Getty Images, Don Johnston/All Canada Photos/Getty Images, David Jenkins/Robert Harding World Images/Getty Images

Figure 7-2 Panda image selected in the grid

GTK

A GridView control of images is typically used to select a wallpaper image for the background of an Android device.

To create this application, the developer must understand how to perform the following processes, among others:

1. Add a GridView control and an ImageView control to the emulator.
2. Update the XML code for an ImageView control not linked to a particular image.

3. Place six images in a drawable folder.
4. Define an array to hold the image files.
5. Instantiate the GridView and ImageView controls.
6. Create an ImageAdapter class.
7. Display a custom toast message.
8. Display the selected image.
9. Customize the ImageAdapter class.
10. Define the layout using the getView( ) method.

Adding a GridView Control

The Endangered Species app opens with a horizontal scrolling list of animal pictures in a View container called a GridView, as shown in Figure 7-1. A **View** container is a rectangular area of the screen that displays an image or text object. A View container can include layouts such as GridView, RadioGroup, ScrollView, TabHost, and ListView. In Chapter 5, you used the ListView layout to create a vertical list of Chicago attractions. In the Endangered Species project, the **GridView** container displays a horizontal list of objects with the center item displaying the current image. A GridView is mainly useful when you want to show data in a grid layout to display images or icons, for example. This layout can be used to build applications such as image viewers and audio or video players to show elements in a table or grid. If you have more images than can be displayed on the screen, you can move through the grid by scrolling the page. The photos in a grid can be sized as small as thumbnail images or as large as full-screen images. The photos can be stored in the drawable folders, in your phone's storage (SD card), or even on a website such as Picasa.

The GridView control is a widget in the Composite category of the Palette. Each GridView control can be customized with the attributes shown in Table 7-1.

GridView Attribute Name	Description
android:columnWidth	Specifies the fixed width for each column of the grid
android:numColumns	Defines the number of columns in the grid
android:horizontalSpacing	Defines the default horizontal spacing between columns in the grid
android:verticalSpacing	Defines the default vertical spacing between rows in the grid

Table 7-1 GridView control attributes

To add a GridView control to activity_main.xml, follow these steps to begin the application:

STEP 1

- Open the Android Studio program.
- Tap or click the Start a new Android Studio project selection in the Quick Start category.
- In the Create New Project dialog box, type **Endangered Species** in the Application name text box.
- If necessary, in the Company Domain text box, type **androidbootcamp.net** and in the Project location text box, type **D:\Workspace\EndangeredSpecies**.

The new Endangered Species project has an application name (Figure 7-3).

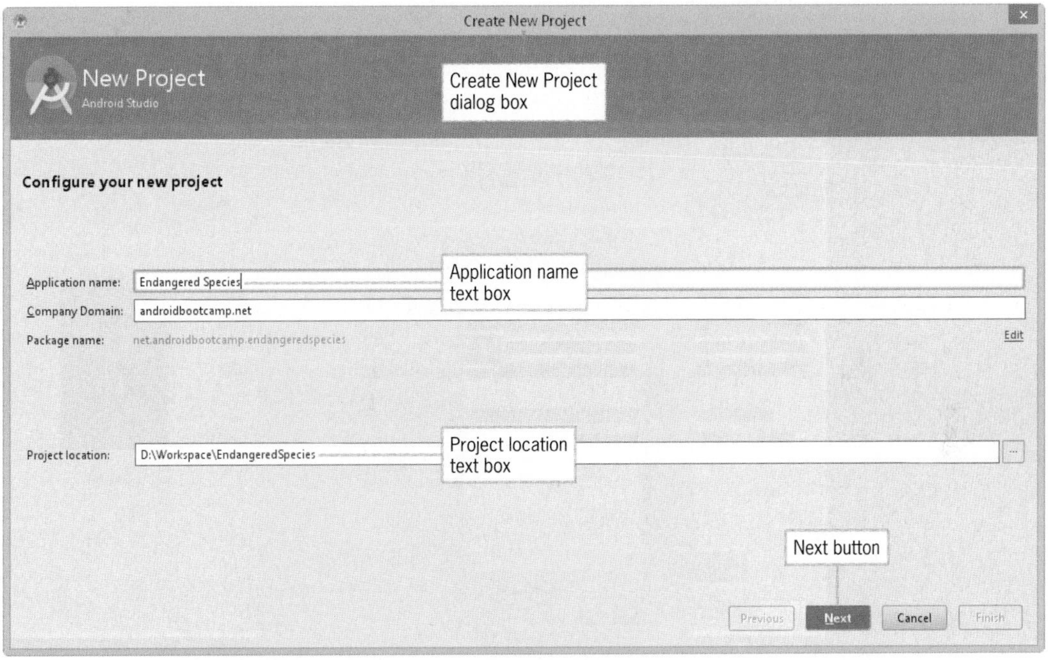

Figure 7-3 Application information for the Endangered Species project

STEP 2

- Tap or click the Next button on the Configure your new project page of the Create New Project dialog box.
- If necessary, tap or click the Phone and Tablet check box to select the form factor for your app.
- If necessary, select API 15: Android 4.0.3 (IceCreamSandwich) for the Minimum SDK.

- Tap or click the Next button on the Select the form factors your app will run on page.
- If necessary, tap or click Blank Activity to add an Activity to the new project.
- Tap or click the Next button on the Add an activity to Mobile page.
- Tap or click the Finish button on the Choose options for your new file page.
- Tap or click the Hello world! TextView widget (displayed by default) in the emulator and press the Delete key.
- Tap or click 'the virtual device to render the layout with' button (emulator) directly to the right of the Palette on the activity_main.xml tab, and then tap or click Nexus 5.
- In the Containers category of the Palette, drag the GridView control to the upper-center part of the emulator on the activity_main.xml tab.

The activity_main.xml is displayed in the emulator with the GridView control (Figure 7-4).

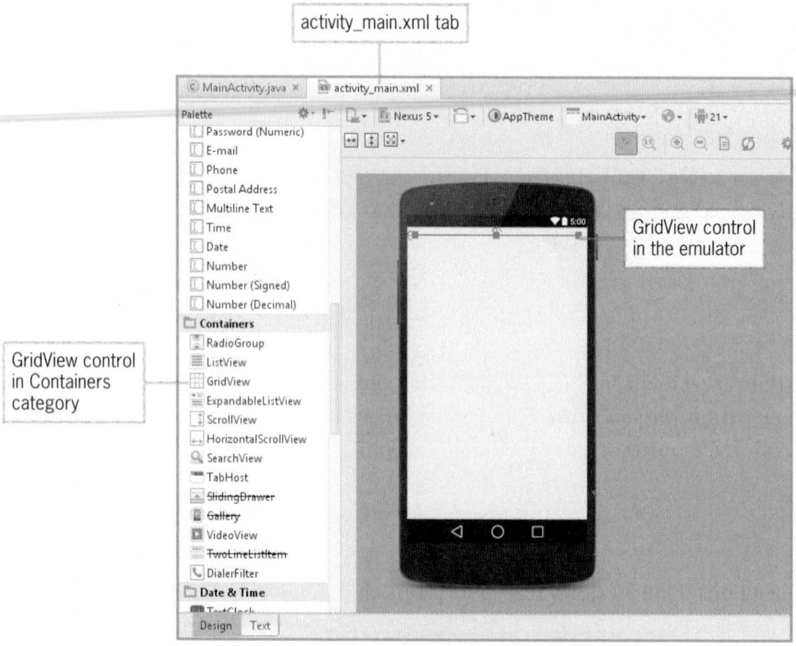

Figure 7-4 GridView control in the emulator for the Endangered Species project

STEP 3

- Tap or click the Text tab at the bottom of activity_main.xml to display the XML code and then display the line numbers.
- To customize the layout, change the first and last line of code from RelativeLayout to **LinearLayout**. When you add the ImageView control later, this layout aligns the ImageView control vertically with the GridView control.

- Delete the padding XML codes from the end of Line 3 through Line 6 (paddingLeft, paddingRight, paddingTop, and paddingBottom).
- On Line 4, type **android:orientation="vertical"** > to display controls vertically down the page.

The activity_main.xml is displayed in the emulator with the GridView control (Figure 7-5). The GridView control is displayed in a single vertical column.

Figure 7-5 Displaying the LinearLayout XML code

STEP 4

- To customize the GridView control, change the layout_height in Line 8 from "wrap_content" to **"200dp"**.
- Delete the additional layout commands in Line 10 through Line 12.

- Beginning on Line 10, type the following XML code before the closing GridView tag:

```
android:numColumns="3"
android:columnWidth="160dp"
android:horizontalSpacing="5dp"
android:verticalSpacing="5dp" />
```

The GridView control is customized with three columns, each 160dp wide, with the horizontal and vertical spacing set to 5dp between the individual grid items (Figure 7-6).

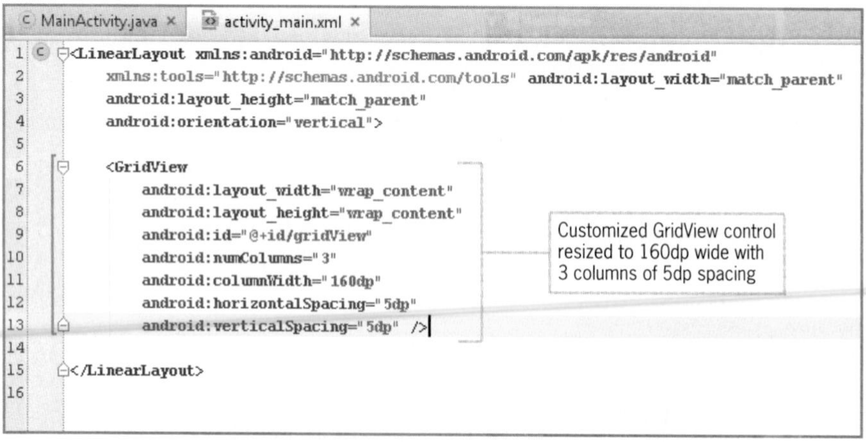

Figure 7-6 Custom GridView XML code

Adding the ImageView Control and Image Files

In the Endangered Species chapter project, the GridView control displays a grid containing two rows with three columns of six thumbnail-sized animal photos stored in the drawable folder. When the user taps one of these images, a full-size image appears in an ImageView control below the GridView control, as shown in Figure 7-2. Typically, you add an ImageView control by dragging the control onto the emulator. A dialog box automatically opens requesting which image file in the drawable folder should be displayed. In the case of the chapter project, an image appears in the ImageView only if the user taps the thumbnail image in the grid. Otherwise, no image should appear in the ImageView control. To prevent an image from being assigned to (and displayed in) the ImageView control, you must enter the XML code for the ImageView control in the activity_main.xml file. The ImageView source will be displayed in the control when the user selects a particular animal. The source display will be coded in the

MainActivity.java file. To add the XML code for the ImageView control named imgLarge, add the String table, and add the six image files to the drawable folder, follow these steps:

STEP 1

- On the line below the closing GridView XML code, press the Enter key twice to insert two blank lines, and then type the following custom ImageView XML code on Line 15 using auto-completion as much as possible:

```
<ImageView
        android:id="@+id/imgLarge"
        android:layout_marginTop="10dp"
        android:layout_width="270dp"
        android:layout_height="300dp"
        android:layout_gravity="center_horizontal"
        android:contentDescription="@string/imgLarge" />
```

The ImageView control is coded in the activity_main.xml file (Figure 7-7). The ImageView control includes a top margin of 10 dp, has a size of 270 by 300 pixels, and is centered below the GridView layout.

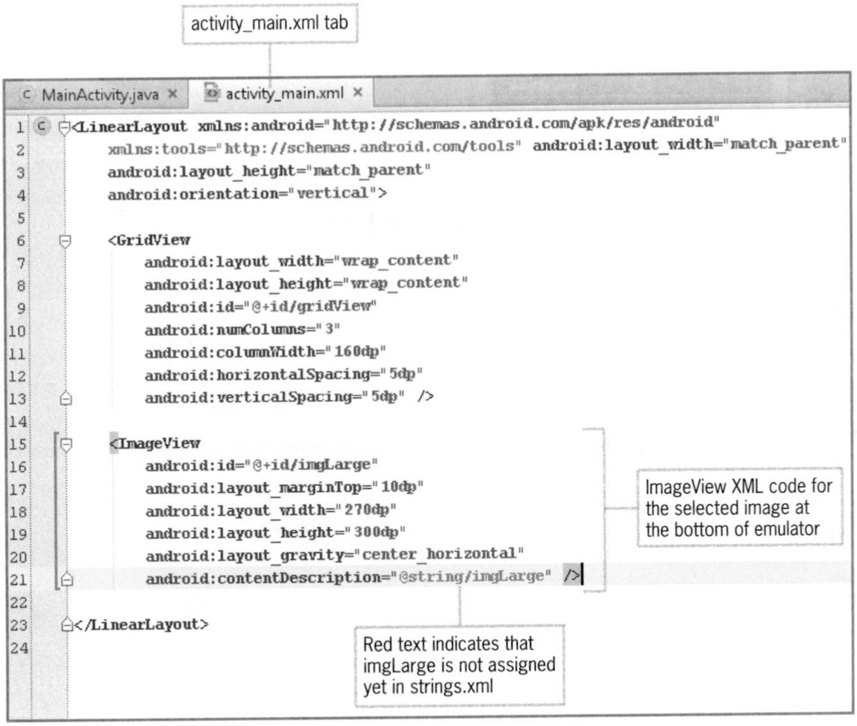

Figure 7-7 ImageView XML code

STEP 2

- Close and save the activity_main.xml tab.
- To add the content description to the String table, in the values folder in the Android project view, open strings.xml.
- Tap or click the Open editor link.
- Tap or click the Add Key button in the Translations Editor, and then type **imgLarge** in the Key text box and type **Endangered Species Images** in the Default Value text box.

The strings.xml file contains the String value necessary in this app (Figure 7-8).

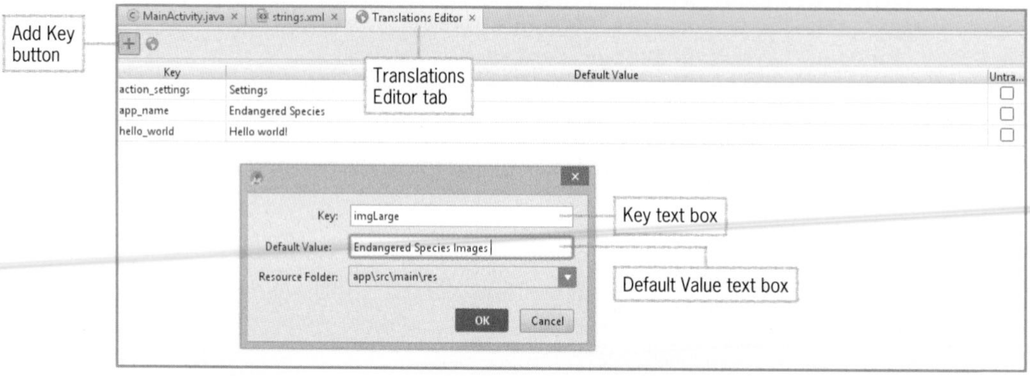

Figure 7-8 String table

STEP 3

- Tap or click the OK button and then close the Translations Editor and strings.xml tabs.
- To add the six image files to the drawable folder, if necessary, copy the student files to your USB drive.
- Open the USB folder containing the student files. Select the files and press Ctrl+C to copy the images.
- To add the six image files to the drawable resource folder, press and hold or right-click the drawable folder and then tap or click Paste.
- Tap or click the OK button in the Copy dialog box.

Copies of the six files appear in the drawable folder (Figure 7-9).

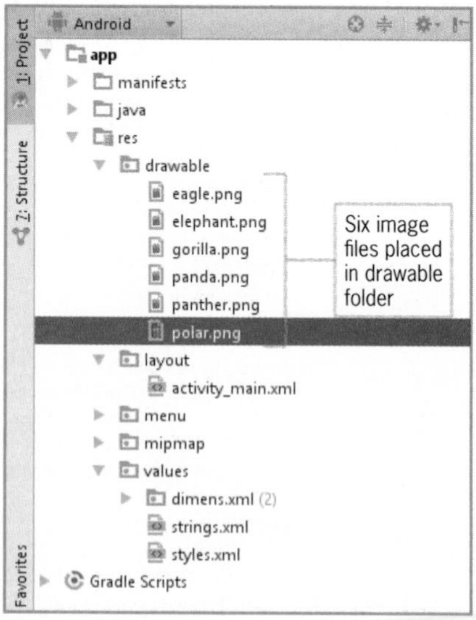

Figure 7-9 Images copied

Creating an Array for the Images

Before the images can be displayed in the GridView control, the images in the drawable folder must be referenced in the code and assigned to an array. By using an array variable, which can store more than one value, you can avoid assigning a separate variable for each image in the folder. You could add tens of images to be displayed in the GridView control based on the need of your app. For example, an app can display three rows of four images each in a grid to represent the top 12 selling Android phones on the market, and then users can scroll over the grid to select an image of their favorite phone. If more phone images are added to the grid, the GridView control automatically becomes scrollable, allowing users to view every image in the grid.

Arrays provide access to data by using a numeric index, or subscript, to identify each element in the array. In the chapter project, the images are assigned to an integer array named Animals and each image is associated with an integer value. For example, the first image of the eagle is assigned to the subscript of 0, as shown in Table 7-2. Typically an array is used to assign values to a GridView control that has multiple items.

Element of Array	Image File
Animals[0]	eagle.png
Animals[1]	elephant.png
Animals[2]	gorilla.png
Animals[3]	panda.png
Animals[4]	panther.png
Animals[5]	polar.png

Table 7-2 Animals array

In MainActivity.java, the Animals array and ImageView control are declared as class-level variables because they are referenced in multiple methods throughout the application. Recall that class-level variables are accessed from anywhere within a Java class. The array is available throughout the entire Activity. To declare the Animals array and ImageView control in MainActivity.java, follow these steps:

STEP 1

- If necessary, open the MainActivity.java tab to open its code window and then display line numbers.
- Delete Lines 16-38.
- Tap or click at the end of the public class MainActivity extends ActionBarActivity { line, press the Enter key, and then use auto-completion as much as possible to type the following code as a class variable to create the Animals array which can be used by multiple methods. Press Enter after typing **R.drawable.gorilla**, to have your code match the figures.

```
Integer[] Animals = {R.drawable.eagle, R.drawable.elephant,
R.drawable.gorilla, R.drawable.panda, R.drawable.panther,
R.drawable.polar};
```

The Animals array references the images stored in the drawable folder (Figure 7-10).

MainActivity.java

```
package net.androidbootcamp.endangeredspecies;

import ...

public class MainActivity extends ActionBarActivity {
    Integer[] Animals = {R.drawable.eagle, R.drawable.elephant, R.drawable.gorilla,
            R.drawable.panda, R.drawable.panther, R.drawable.polar};
    @Override
    protected void onCreate(Bundle savedInstanceState) {
        super.onCreate(savedInstanceState);
        setContentView(R.layout.activity_main);
    }

}
```

Animals array

Figure 7-10 Animals array declared

STEP 2

- Press the Enter key.
- To declare ImageView as a class variable, type **ImageView pic;**.
- Tap or click ImageView (red text) and then press Alt+Enter to import the ImageView control.

ImageView is referenced as a class variable (Figure 7-11).

MainActivity.java

```
package net.androidbootcamp.endangeredspecies;

import ...


public class MainActivity extends ActionBarActivity {
    Integer[] Animals = {R.drawable.eagle, R.drawable.elephant, R.drawable.gorilla,
            R.drawable.panda, R.drawable.panther, R.drawable.polar};
    ImageView pic;
    @Override
    protected void onCreate(Bundle savedInstanceState) {
        super.onCreate(savedInstanceState);
        setContentView(R.layout.activity_main);
    }

}
```

ImageView initialized

Figure 7-11 ImageView referenced

Instantiating the GridView and ImageView Controls

The GridView and ImageView controls in activity_main.xml must be instantiated in the onCreate( ) method of MainActivity.java. The first GridView control in a project is named gridView1 by default. The code to instantiate the GridView assigns the control created in activity_main.xml the name gridView1, as shown in the following code syntax:

Code Syntax

```
GridView grid = (GridView)findViewById(R.id.gridView);
```

To instantiate the GridView and ImageView controls, follow these steps:

STEP 1

- To instantiate the GridView, in the onCreate( ) method of MainActivity.java, tap or click at the end of the setContentView(R.layout.*activity_main*); line, and then press the Enter key.
- Type **GridView grid = (GridView)findViewById(R.id.gridView);**.
- If necessary, tap or click GridView, press Alt+Enter, and then tap or click Import Class.

The GridView control is instantiated (Figure 7-12).

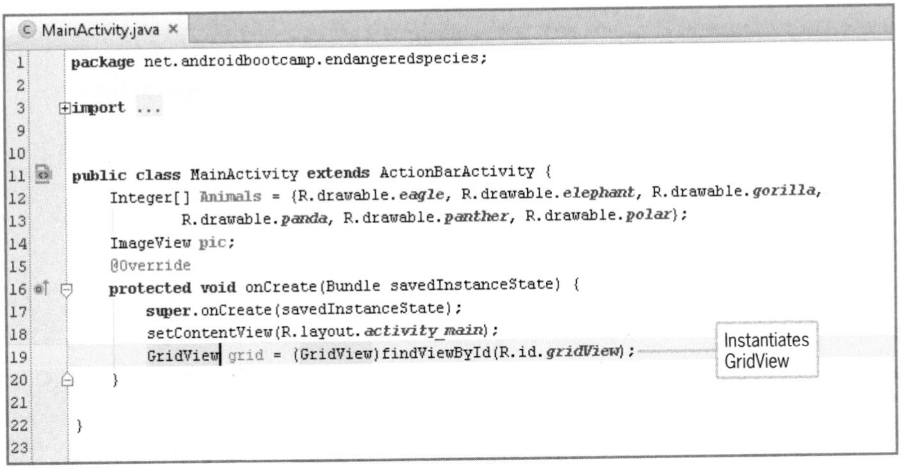

Figure 7-12 GridView control is instantiated

STEP 2

- Insert a new line. To instantiate the ImageView that is assigned as a class variable, type **final ImageView pic = (ImageView)findViewById(R.id.imgLarge);**.

The ImageView control is instantiated (Figure 7-13).

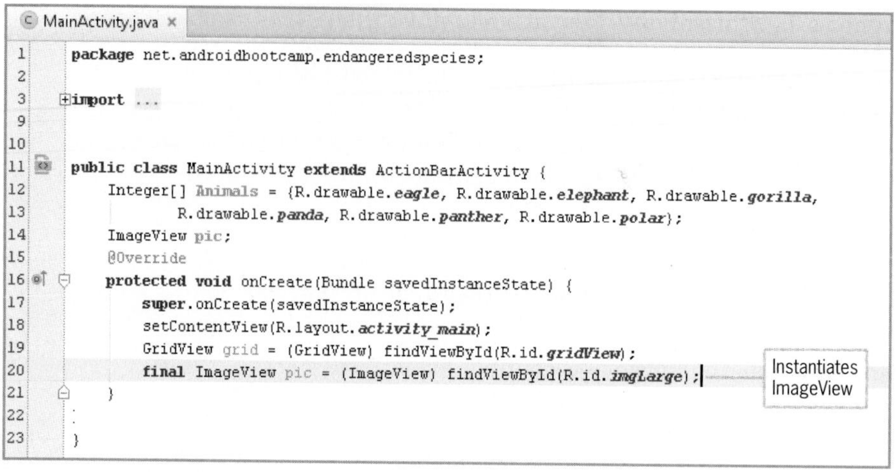

Figure 7-13 ImageView control is instantiated

Critical Thinking

What does it mean by making the ImageView variable pic to final?

The keyword final designates that the referenced variable cannot be changed. If you assign a new value to this variable later in code, a compilation error will occur.

Using a setAdapter with an ImageAdapter

In Chapter 5, an adapter was used to display a ListView control. Similarly, a **setAdapter** provides a data model for the GridView layout. The GridView data model functions as a photo GridView in touch mode. The following code syntax shows how to instantiate a custom BaseAdapter class called ImageAdapter and apply it to the GridView using setAdapter( ):

Code Syntax

```
grid.setAdapter(new ImageAdapter(this));
```

After the ImageAdapter is instantiated, the Android Java ImageAdapter class must be added to extend the custom BaseAdapter class. Using controls such as the GridView, ListView, and Spinner, the adapter binds specific types of data and displays that data in a particular layout. To instantiate the ImageAdapter class for the GridView control, follow these steps:

STEP 1

- Press the Enter key and type **grid.setAdapter(new ImageAdapter(this));**.
- Notice the red ImageAdapter text. Instead of automatically creating the class, a custom ImageAdapter class is added in the next step, so do not import the class now.

The ImageAdapter is coded for the GridView control. ImageAdapter appears in red text (Figure 7-14).

MainActivity.java ×

```
1   package net.androidbootcamp.endangeredspecies;
2
3   import ...
9
10
11  public class MainActivity extends ActionBarActivity {
12      Integer[] Animals = {R.drawable.eagle, R.drawable.elephant, R.drawable.gorilla,
13              R.drawable.panda, R.drawable.panther, R.drawable.polar};
14      ImageView pic;
15      @Override
16      protected void onCreate(Bundle savedInstanceState) {
17          super.onCreate(savedInstanceState);
18          setContentView(R.layout.activity_main);
19          GridView grid = (GridView)findViewById(R.id.gridView);
20          final ImageView pic= (ImageView)findViewById(R.id.imgLarge);
21          grid.setAdapter(new ImageAdapter(this));
22      }
23
24  }
25
```

ImageAdapter class displays images in the grid

Figure 7-14 Instance of the ImageAdapter class

STEP 2

- To add an ImageAdapter class that extends the BaseAdapter custom class, tap or click after the first closing brace at the end of Line 22.
- Press the Enter key and type **public class ImageAdapter extends BaseAdapter** {.
- Press the Enter key to display a closing brace.
- If necessary, tap or click the red BaseAdapter text, tap or click Alt+Enter, and then tap or click Import Class.
- Tap or click ImageAdapter in the same line with a red curly underline, press Alt+Enter, and then tap or click Implement Methods. Tap or click the OK button on the Select Methods to Implement dialog box.
- Tap or click the red curly underline in the grid.setAdapter(new ImageAdapter (this)); line and then press Alt+Enter. Select Create Constructor.

The ImageAdapter class is coded to handle the image display (Figure 7-15). The methods within the ImageAdapter are auto-generated.

Press Alt+Enter and choose Create inner class 'ImageAdapter' from the menu
select

MainActivity.java

```
        setContentView(R.layout.activity_main);
        GridView grid = (GridView)findViewById(R.id.gridView);
        final ImageView pic= (ImageView)findViewById(R.id.imgLarge);
        grid.setAdapter(new ImageAdapter(this));
    }
    public class ImageAdapter extends BaseAdapter {

        public ImageAdapter(MainActivity mainActivity) {
        }

        @Override
        public int getCount() {
            return 0;
        }

        @Override
        public Object getItem(int position) {
            return null;
        }

        @Override
        public long getItemId(int position) {
            return 0;
        }

        @Override
        public View getView(int position, View convertView, ViewGroup parent) {
            return null;
        }
    }

}
```

ImageAdapter class added

Auto-generated methods

Figure 7-15 ImageAdapter class

Coding the OnItemClickListener

Like the OnClickListener used for a Button control in previous chapter projects, the OnItemClickListener awaits user interaction within the GridView control. When the user touches the GridView display layout, the OnItemClickListener processes an event called onItemClick.

The **onItemClick** method defined by OnItemClickListener provides a number of arguments, which are listed in the parentheses included in the line of code. The two controls—ListView and GridView—enable the Android device to monitor for tap or click events using the OnItemClickListener and onItemClick commands. The following code syntax shows how to use onItemClick in the chapter project.

Code Syntax

```
grid.setOnItemClickListener(new OnItemClickListener( ) {
  @Override
  public void onItemClick(AdapterView<?> arg0,
    View arg1, int arg2, long arg3) {
  }
}};
}
```

In this code syntax example, the grid variable is the instance of the GridView control. The OnItemClickListener executes the onItemClick method as soon as the user touches any image within the GridView control. The onItemClick method has four arguments. Table 7-3 describes the role of the four arguments in the onItemClick method.

Argument	Purpose
AdapterView<?> parent	The AdapterView records "where" the user actually touched the screen in the argument variable parent. In other words, if the app has more than one View control, the AdapterView determines if the user touched this GridView control or another control in the application.
View view	The View parameter is the specific View within the item that the user touched. This is the View provided by the adapter.
int position	This is one of the most important portions of this statement in the chapter project. The position argument is an integer value that holds the position of the View in the adapter. For example, if the user taps the elephant picture, the integer value of 1 is stored in position because the elephant picture is the second image in the Animals array.
long id	The GridView control is displayed across multiple rows of the Android device. The argument id determines the row id of the item that was selected by the user. This is especially useful for a GridView control that has multiple rows in the layout.

Table 7-3 Arguments in the onItemClick method

Users can change their minds more than once when selecting picture images in the GridView. The onItemClick method responds an unlimited number of times throughout the life of the class based on the user's interaction with the GridView control. To code the OnItemClickListener and onItemClick method, follow these steps:

STEP 1

- In MainActivity.java, press the Enter key after the grid.setAdapter command line.
- To set up the OnItemClickListener, type **grid.setOnItemClickListener(new OnItemClickListener( ) {**.

- Press the Enter key to display a closing brace.

  A red error line appears under OnItemClickListener. Tap or click OnItemClickListener, press Alt+Enter, and then select Import Class. Tap or click android.widget.AdapterView.OnItemClickListener.

- After the closing brace on Line 28, type a closing parenthesis and a semicolon to complete the statement.

The GridView OnItemClickListener awaits user interaction. A red error line appears below AdapterView.OnItemClickListener (Figure 7-16).

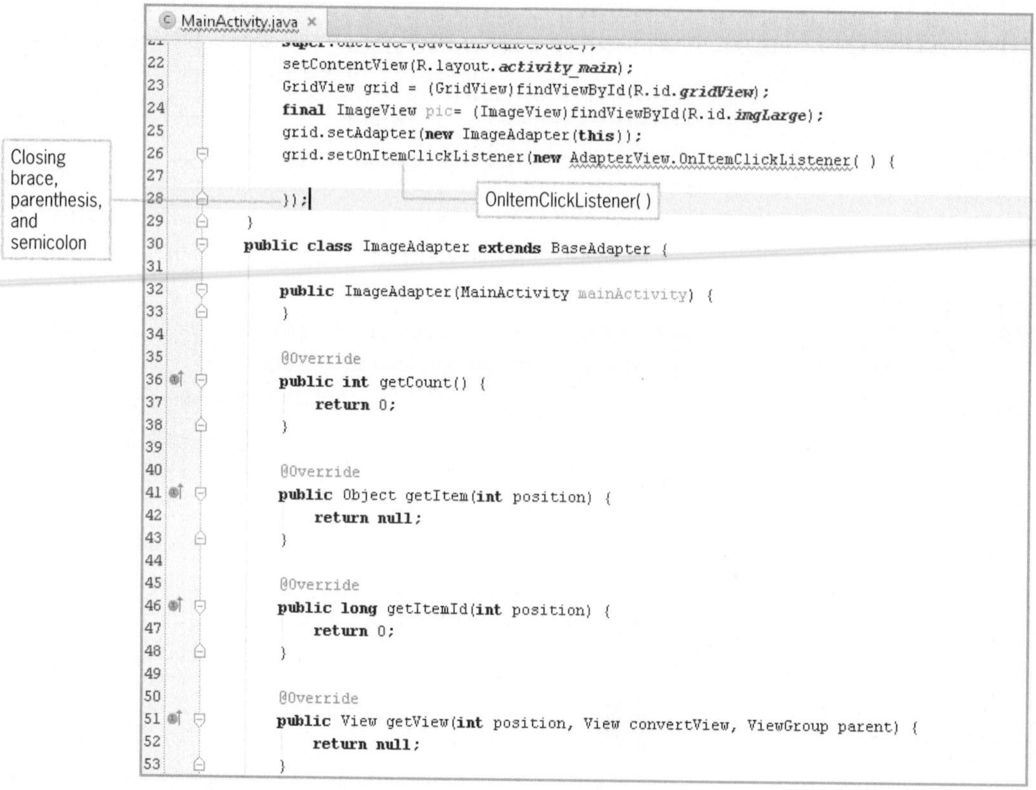

Figure 7-16 GridView OnItemClickListener

STEP 2

- To add the onItemClick method within the OnItemClickListener, tap or click the red error line under the AdapterView.OnItemClickListener, press Alt+Enter, and select Implement Methods. Tap or click the OK button and save your work.

The onItemClick method stub appears automatically (Figure 7-17).

- Additional step here (see my comments on the figure!)

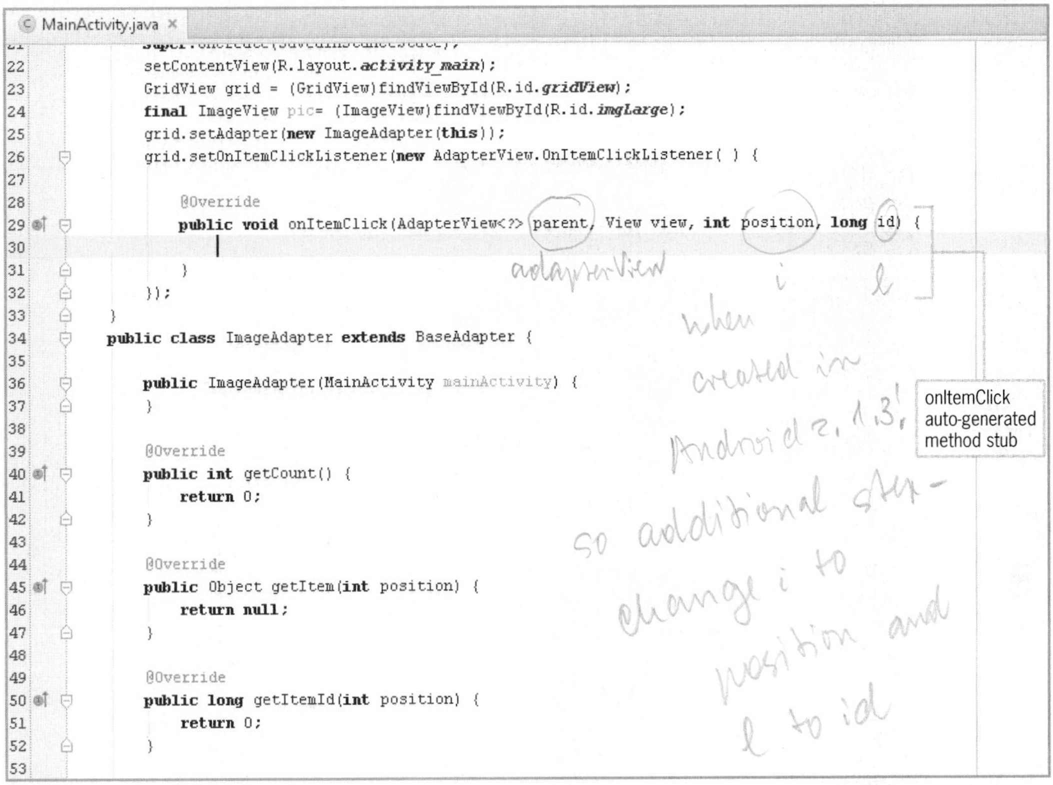

Figure 7-17 onItemClick method

Coding a Custom Toast Notification

A toast notification in the Endangered Species program provides feedback as to which animal image is selected. When the toast message is shown to the user, it floats over the application so it will never receive focus. In earlier chapters, you entered a toast notification displaying a temporary message in this form:

```
Toast.makeText(MainActivity.this, "Typical Toast Message",
Toast.LENGTH_SHORT).show();
```

In the Endangered Species project, the toast notification message is different in two ways. First, the toast message in the GridView control appears in the onItemClick method that is executed only when the user makes a selection. Because the toast notification is not used directly in the MainActivity, the reference to MainActivity.this in the toast statement creates an error. To use a toast message within an onItemClick method, considered an AlertDialog class, you must replace MainActivity.this with a Context class called getBaseContext( ). In Android programs, you can place the **getBaseContext( )** method in another method (such as onItemClick) that is triggered only when the user touches the GridView control. If you do, the getBaseContext( ) method obtains a Context instance.

A second difference is that the toast message includes a variable. The variable indicates which image number is selected in the Animals array. Figure 7-18 shows the message when the user selects the panther.

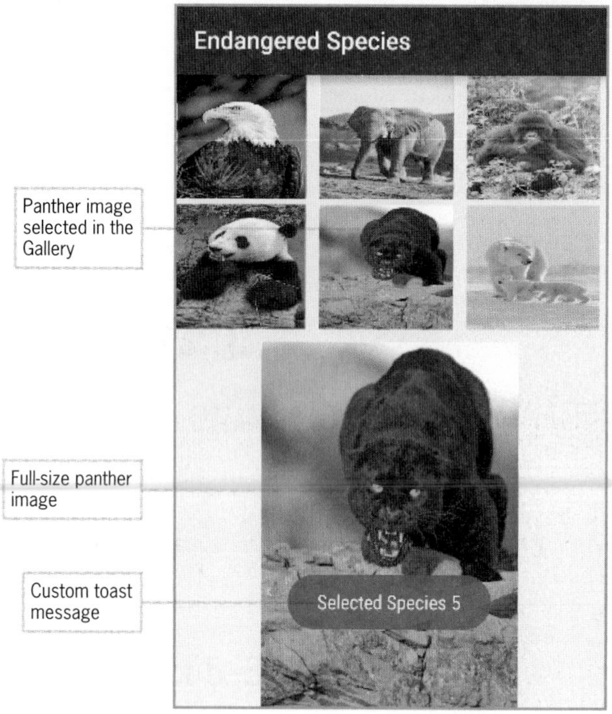

Figure 7-18 Toast message displayed when user selects the panther image

Notice that even though the panther is in position Animals[4] in Table 7-2, the custom toast message states "Selected Species 5". Array position 4 is really the fifth image because the array values begin with 0. The value of 1 is added in the toast message shown in the following code syntax to the integer position value. The position argument is an integer value that holds the position number of the View in the adapter that was an argument of the onItemClick( ) method. The position identifies the image placement in the array.

Code Syntax

```
Toast.makeText(getBaseContext(), "Selected Species" + (position + 1),
Toast.LENGTH_SHORT).show();
```

To code the custom toast message that includes a getBaseContext( ) method and variables, follow this step:

STEP 1

- In MainActivity.java, tap or click the blank line after the onItemClick statement in Line 30 to add the custom toast message.
- Use auto-completion to type **Toast.makeText(getBaseContext( ), "Selected Species " + (position + 1), Toast.LENGTH_SHORT).show( );**.
- If necessary, tap or click Toast and press Alt+Enter. Tap or click Import Class.

The custom toast message provides feedback to the user of his or her picture selection from the GridView (Figure 7-19).

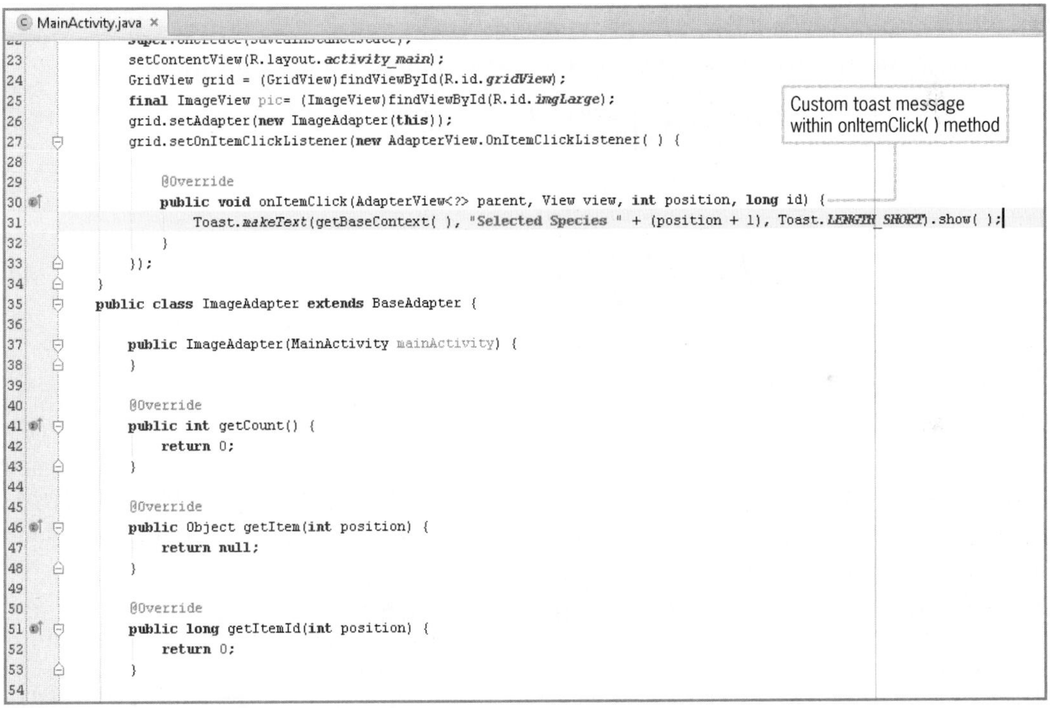

Figure 7-19 Custom toast message

Displaying the Selected Image

When the user touches an animal picture in the GridView, a toast message appears with an ImageView control displaying the selected image. The ImageView control was previously coded in activity_main. xml, though a specific image was not selected in the code. Instead, the full-sized picture in the ImageView control should be displayed dynamically to the user.

An ImageView control is defined either by the android:src attribute in the XML element or by the setImageResource(int) method. The setImageResource method indicates which image is selected, as shown in the following code syntax:

Code Syntax

```
pic.setImageResource(Animals[position]);
```

Animals is the name of the array and position represents the index of the array. The argument position is defined as the position of the selected image in the GridView. To assign a picture to the ImageView control, follow this step:

STEP 1

- In MainActivity.java, tap or click at the end of the Toast statement, if necessary, and press the Enter key.
- To display the selected image, type **pic.setImageResource(Animals[position]);**.

The selected image in the GridView control is displayed in the ImageView control with the use of setImageResource (Figure 7-20).

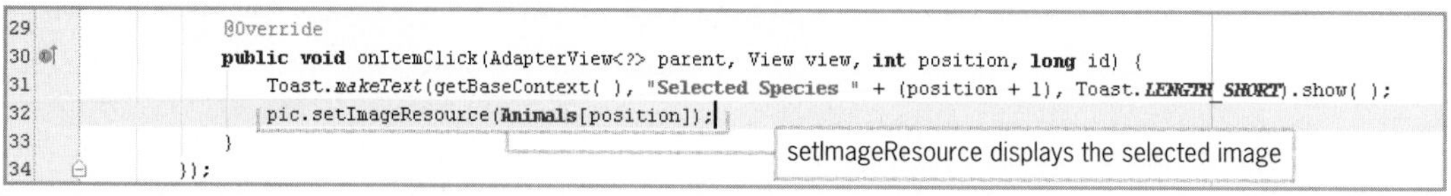

Figure 7-20 ImageView control displays selected GridView picture

IN THE TRENCHES

An image can also be placed on the surface of a Button control by the android:src attribute in the XML code or by the setImageResource(int) method of a button.

Customizing the ImageAdapter Class

At this point in the chapter project code, the GridView and ImageView are initialized, the onClickListener awaits interaction, the toast message and ImageView are prepared for display, but the ImageAdapter class is simply a set of auto-generated method stubs. The ImageAdapter class was called with this line of code: gr.setAdapter(new ImageAdapter (this));. Recall that the ImageAdapter class determines the layout of the GridView. The context and images of the GridView need to be referenced within the ImageAdapter class. The tasks to complete inside the ImageAdapter class are to manage the layout of the GridView and connect the data sources from the array for display within the GridView control.

Defining the Context of the ImageAdapter Class

The ImageAdapter class must provide the information to set up the GridView with data and specifications necessary for the display. A Context variable is used to load and access resources for the application. In the following code syntax, the class variable named context is initialized so it can hold each image in the GridView temporarily before it is displayed. The ImageAdapter constructor is changed from the MainActivity to handle the Context resources necessary for the GridView. **Constructors** are used to initialize the instance variables of an object. Constructors enable the programmer to set default values, limit instantiation, and write code that is flexible and easy to read. This command is called a constructor because it constructs the values of data members of the class.

Code Syntax

```
private Context context;
public ImageAdapter(Context c){
  context=c;
}
```

This ImageAdapter class constructor is where the Context for an ImageAdapter instance is defined. To define the Context for the ImageAdapter, follow these steps:

STEP 1

- Save your work. Tap or click the blank line after the public class ImageAdapter extends BaseAdapter { line.
- Initialize the Context variable by typing **private Context context;**.
- Tap or click Context, press Alt+Enter, and select Import Class.

The Context variable named context is initialized (Figure 7-21).

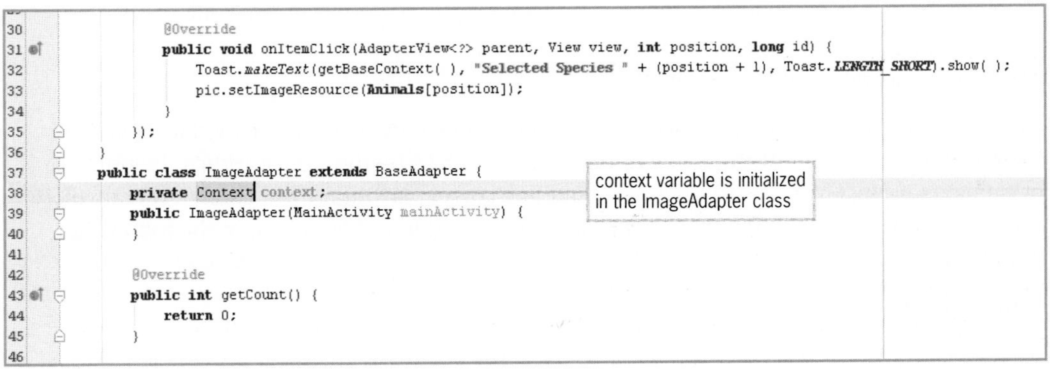

Figure 7-21 Context variable

STEP 2

- To change the ImageAdapter constructor to define the Context in the next statement, change public ImageAdapter(MainActivity mainActivity) { on the next line to **public ImageAdapter (Context c) {**.

- Press the Enter key to insert a blank line. Type **context=c;**.

The ImageAdapter constructor for the ImageAdapter class holds the Context (Figure 7-22).

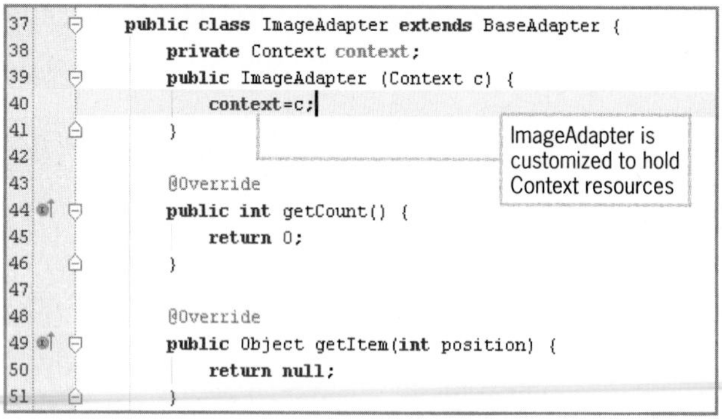

Figure 7-22 ImageAdapter constructor

Calculating the Length of an Array

The next method in the ImageAdapter class is the getCount( ) method. When the ImageAdapter class is called, the getCount( ) method determines how many pictures should be displayed in the GridView control. It does so by finding the length of the Animals array, which references the pictures of the endangered species. To determine the length of an array, Java provides a method named length( ) that returns an integer value of any given string or array. For example, if a variable named phone is assigned the text Android, the integer phoneLength is assigned the integer value of 7, representing the length of the word "Android".

```
String phone = "Android";
int phoneLength = phone.length();
```

The length of an array is determined by the number of elements in the array. The length of the Animals array is an integer value of 6. The getCount( ) method must return the number of elements in the GridView in order to create the correct layout for the GridView control. To do so, include in the getCount( ) method a return statement as shown in the following code syntax:

Code Syntax

```
return Animals.length;
```

A Java **method** is a series of statements that perform some repeated task. In the case of the chapter project, the method is called within the ImageAdapter class. The purpose of the getCount( ) method is to return the number of elements in the array. You declare a method's return type in its method declaration. In the following syntax, the declaration statement public int getCount( ) includes int. The data type int indicates that the return data type is an integer. Within the body of the method, you use the return statement to return the value. Any method declared void does not return a value because it returns to the method normally. Therefore, no return statement is necessary. Any method that is not declared void must contain a return statement with a corresponding return value such as the length of an array.

Code Syntax

```
public int getCount() {
  return Animals.length;
}
```

To return the length of an array from the getCount( ) method, follow this step:

STEP 1

- In the return statement for public int getCount( ) in Line 45, change the return type from return 0; to **return Animals.length;**.

The getCount( ) method returns the length of the Animals array (Figure 7-23).

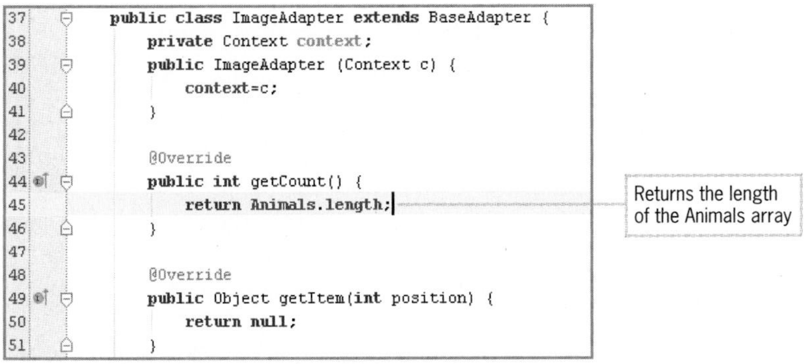

Figure 7-23 Length of the Animals array

Critical Thinking

If I add more animal images to the Animals array, would the Animals.length command return the additional number of images?

Yes. Write your programs to be easily scalable to function well as it handles more information in order to meet the user's needs.

GTK

The length of an array is one more than the maximum subscript number.

Coding the getView Method

The most powerful method in the ImageAdapter class is the getView( ) method. The getView( ) method uses Context to create a new ImageView instance that temporarily holds each image displayed in the GridView. In addition, the ImageView is scaled to fit the GridView control and sized according to a custom height and width. The following code syntax shows how the chapter project uses the getView( ) method:

Code Syntax

```
public View getView(int position, View convertView, ViewGroup parent){
     pic = new ImageView(context);
     pic.setImageResource(Animals[position]);
     pic.setScaleType(ImageView.ScaleType.FIT_XY);
     pic.setLayoutParams(new GridView.LayoutParams(330,300));
     return pic;
  }
```

In the getView( ) method, notice that a return type of View is expected (in the View convertView argument). Recall that a View occupies a rectangular area on the screen and is responsible for drawing the GridView component. When pic is returned at the end of the method, it includes a scaled, resized image, ready to display in the GridView control.

In the getView( ) method, an instance of an ImageView control named pic is established in the pic = new ImageView(context); Java code. On the next line, pic is given an image to display in the GridView as defined by a position in the Animals array. As each position is passed to the getView( ) method, the ImageView control changes to hold each of the images referenced in the Animals array. The setImageResource method assigns an image from the drawable folder to the ImageView control. After an animal picture is assigned to pic, the layout of the ImageView control needs to be established. In the next statement, setScaleType scales the image to the bounds of the ImageView. Scaling keeps or changes the aspect ratio of the image within the ImageView control. When an image is scaled, the aspect ratio is changed; for example, the picture may be stretched horizontally, but not vertically. Notice that the ScaleType is set to the option FIT_XY. Several ScaleType options are available, but the most popular options are listed in Table 7-4.

ScaleType Option	Meaning
ImageView.ScaleType.CENTER	This option centers the image within the View type, but does not change the aspect ratio (no scaling).
ImageView.ScaleType.CENTER_CROP	This option centers the image within the View type and scales the image uniformly, maintaining the same aspect ratio.
ImageView.ScaleType.FIT_XY	This option scales the image to fit the View type. The aspect ratio is changed to fit within the control.

Table 7-4 Popular ScaleType options

After the image is scaled, the GridView images are resized to fit the custom layout. The design of the Endangered Species app calls for small thumbnail-sized images, so the setLayoutParams are set to the GridView.LayoutParams(330,300). The first value, 330, represents the number of pixels across the width of the image. The second value, 300, determines a height of 300 pixels. If you want to display a large GridView, the setLayoutParams can be changed to larger dimensions. The last statement in the getView( ) method (return pic;) must return the instance of the ImageView control named pic to display in the GridView control. To code the getView( ) method, follow these steps:

STEP 1

- Scroll down to the statement beginning with public View getView. Tap or click at the end of the statement, after the opening brace, and press the Enter key to insert a blank line.
- To create an ImageView control that holds the images displayed in the GridView, type **pic = new ImageView(context);**.

An instance of ImageView named pic is created (Figure 7-24).

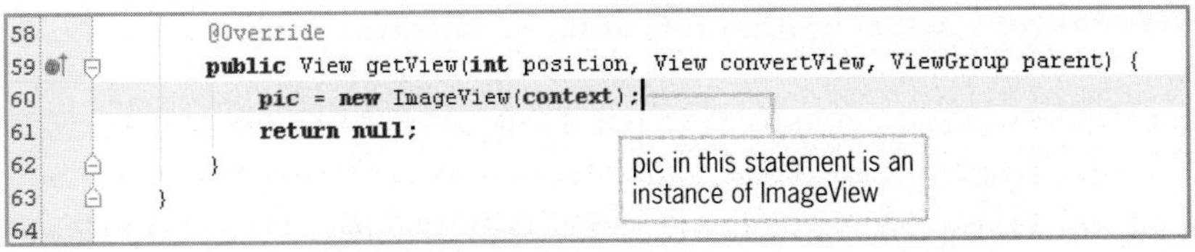

Figure 7-24 Code for the ImageView control

STEP 2

- Press the Enter key.
- To assign each of the images and their positions referenced in the Animals array, type **pic.setImageResource(Animals[position]);**.

The instance of pic holds each of the images within the array (Figure 7-25).

```
        @Override
        public View getView(int position, View convertView, ViewGroup parent) {
            pic = new ImageView(context);
            pic.setImageResource(Animals[position]);
            return null;
        }
    }

}
```

Each image referenced in the Animals array is displayed in pic

Figure 7-25 Assigning images in the Animals array to the pic ImageView control

STEP 3

- Press the Enter key.
- To set the scale type of the ImageView control, type **pic.setScaleType(ImageView.ScaleType.FIT_XY);**.

The scale type for the ImageView pic is set to FIT_XY (Figure 7-26).

```
        public View getView(int position, View convertView, ViewGroup parent) {
            pic = new ImageView(context);
            pic.setImageResource(Animals[position]);
            pic.setScaleType(ImageView.ScaleType.FIT_XY);
            return null;
        }
    }
```

ImageView control is scaled to fit

Figure 7-26 Setting the scale type for the ImageView control

STEP 4

- Press the Enter key.
- To resize the images displayed in the GridView control to 330 pixels wide and 300 pixels tall, type **pic.setLayoutParams(new GridView.LayoutParams(330,300));**.

The size of the images displayed in the GridView is set to 330 pixels wide by 300 pixels tall (Figure 7-27).

```
        @Override
        public View getView(int position, View convertView, ViewGroup parent) {
            pic = new ImageView(context);
            pic.setImageResource(Animals[position]);
            pic.setScaleType(ImageView.ScaleType.FIT_XY);
            pic.setLayoutParams(new GridView.LayoutParams(330,300));
            return null;
        }
    }
```

GridView images are resized

Figure 7-27 Resizing the GridView images

STEP 5

- To return pic to the MainActivity, change the return null; statement to **return pic;**.

The pic instance is returned to the MainActivity (Figure 7-28).

MainActivity.java

```
package net.androidbootcamp.endangeredspecies;

import ...


public class MainActivity extends ActionBarActivity {
    Integer[] Animals = {R.drawable.eagle, R.drawable.elephant, R.drawable.gorilla,
            R.drawable.panda, R.drawable.panther, R.drawable.polar};
    ImageView pic;
    @Override
    protected void onCreate(Bundle savedInstanceState) {
        super.onCreate(savedInstanceState);
        setContentView(R.layout.activity_main);
        GridView grid = (GridView)findViewById(R.id.gridView);
        final ImageView pic= (ImageView)findViewById(R.id.imgLarge);
        grid.setAdapter(new ImageAdapter(this));
        grid.setOnItemClickListener(new AdapterView.OnItemClickListener( ) {

            @Override
            public void onItemClick(AdapterView<?> parent, View view, int position, long id) {
                Toast.makeText(getBaseContext( ), "Selected Species " + (position + 1), Toast.LENGTH_SHORT).show( );
                pic.setImageResource(Animals[position]);
            }
        });
    }
    public class ImageAdapter extends BaseAdapter {
        private Context context;
        public ImageAdapter (Context c) { context=c; }

        @Override
        public int getCount() { return Animals.length; }

        @Override
        public Object getItem(int position) {
            return null;
        }

        @Override
        public long getItemId(int position) {
            return 0;
        }

        @Override
        public View getView(int position, View convertView, ViewGroup parent) {
            pic = new ImageView(context);
            pic.setImageResource(Animals[position]);
            pic.setScaleType(ImageView.ScaleType.FIT_XY);
            pic.setLayoutParams(new GridView.LayoutParams(330,300));
            return pic;
        }
    }
```

Return variable pic

Figure 7-28 Complete code of MainActivity.java

GTK

Aspect ratio is the fractional relation of the width of an image compared with its height. The two most common aspect ratios are 4:3 and 16:9 in HDTV. Keeping the aspect ratio means that an image is not distorted from its original ratio of width to height.

Running and Testing the Application

It is time to see your finished product. Tap or click Run app on the menu bar, and then select an emulator, and test the application in the emulator. Save all the files in the next dialog box, if necessary, and unlock the emulator. The application opens in the emulator window where you can touch the GridView to view the images and select an image, as shown in Figures 7-1 and 7-2.

Wrap It Up—Chapter Summary

Many Android applications display a GridView to easily accommodate viewing a large amount of pictures. Creating a GridView in this chapter to dynamically display images from an array provided experience with using a second class, a custom toast message, methods with return variables, and the length of an array. Creating a second class called the ImageAdapter class provided the customization for the GridView layout.

- A View container is a rectangular area of the screen that displays an image or text object. It can include various layouts, including a GridView layout, which displays a grid of objects such as images, songs, or text. Users can scroll the GridView list to select an object such as a photo and display it in another control such as an ImageView control.
- To display an image in an ImageView control only if the user selects the image in the GridView, you must enter XML code for the ImageView control in activity_main.xml.
- An array variable can store more than one value. Arrays provide access to data by using a numeric index, or subscript, to identify each element in the array. For example, the first element in the array is assigned to the subscript of 0. An array can assign more than one image to a GridView control to eventually display only one image.
- A setAdapter provides a data model for the GridView layout. With the GridView control, the adapter binds certain types of data and displays that data in a specified layout.
- Like the OnClickListener used for a Button control, the OnItemClickListener waits for user interaction in a GridView control. When the user selects an item in the GridView, the OnItemClickListener processes an onItemClick event, which includes four arguments. The position argument is an integer value that contains the position of the View in the adapter. For example, if the user taps the second image in the GridView, the integer value of 2 is stored in position.
- By including a toast notification in the onItemClick method, you can display a message indicating which image is selected in a GridView control. The message can include a variable

to display the number of the image selected in the GridView. The toast message can float over the other controls so it never receives focus.

- Because the toast notification is not used directly in the Main Activity, you must replace Main.this in the onItemClick method with a Context class called getBaseContext( ). In Android programs, you use the getBaseContext( ) method to obtain a Context instance. This Context instance is triggered only when the user touches the GridView control.
- To display in an ImageView control the image selected in the GridView, you use the setImageResource( ) method with an int argument. The setImageResource command inserts an ImageView control and the int argument specifies which image is selected for display. If you are using an array to identify the images, you can use position as the int argument because it represents the position of the selected image in the GridView.
- The ImageAdapter class must provide information to set up the GridView so it can display the appropriate images. You use the Context class to load and access resources for the application. A class variable can hold each image in the GridView temporarily before it is displayed. To handle the Context resources necessary for the GridView, you use the ImageAdapter constructor. A constructor can initialize the instance variables of an object. In other words, it constructs the values of data members of the class. You define the Context for an ImageAdapter instance in the ImageAdapter class constructor.
- The chapter project uses the getCount( ) method to determine how many pictures to display in the GridView control. It does so by referencing the array specifying the images for the GridView. To determine the length of an array, Java provides a method named length( ) that returns an integer type value of any given string or array. The length of an array is determined by the number of its elements. The getCount( ) method uses length( ) to return the number of elements in the GridView.
- The declaration statement public int getCount( ) indicates that the return data type (int) is an integer. Because the getCount( ) method is not declared void, it must contain a return statement with a corresponding return value such as the length of an array.
- In the chapter project, the getView( ) method uses Context to create a new ImageView instance to temporarily hold each image displayed in the GridView. The getView( ) method also contains statements that scale the ImageView to fit the GridView control and a specified height and width.

Key Terms

constructor—A part of the Java code used to initialize the instance variables of an object.

GridView—A View container that displays a grid of objects with rows and columns.

getBaseContext()—A Context class method used in Android programs to obtain a Context instance. Use getBaseContext( ) in a method that is triggered only when the user touches the GridView control.

method—In Java, a series of statements that perform some repeated task.

onItemClick—An event the OnItemClickListener processes when the user touches the GridView display layout. The onItemClick method is defined by OnItemClickListener and sends a number of arguments in the parentheses included within the line of code.

setAdapter—A command that provides a data model for the GridView layout, similar to an adapter, which displays a ListView control.

View—A rectangular container that displays a drawing or text object.

Developer FAQs

1. Which Android control displays a two-dimensional grid of images?
2. In which category on the Palette is the control mentioned in question #1 located?
3. Name three locations where photos that are used in the Android environment can be stored.
4. Why was the ImageView control coded in the XML code in the chapter project instead of dragging the ImageView control onto the emulator?
5. Name five View containers.
6. Write a line of code that uses an instance of a GridView control named gridLayout in a new ImageAdapter class using setAdapter( ).
7. Write a line of code that creates a reference array named Games for the images named legendofzelda, candycrush, halo, and titanfall.
8. What are the array names and indexes of halo in question 7?
9. What is the array length of the Games array in question 7?
10. Write a line of code that determines the length of the Games array from question 7 and assigns the value to an int variable named numberOfGames.
11. Write a line of code that assigns dentalLength to the length of a string named dental.
12. What is the purpose of the argument position in the chapter project?
13. In the chapter project, if the user selects panda, what is the value of position?
14. Write a custom toast message that resides within an onItemClick( ) method and states *You have selected picture 4 of the political photos* when position is 4.
15. What do the numbers in the following statement represent?

    ```
    pic.setLayoutParams(new GridView.LayoutParams(300,325));
    ```
16. What does the aspect ratio 3:2 mean?

17. In the following method, what does int (integer) represent?

```
public int getCount( ) {
  return Soccer.length;
}
```

18. What would be returned in the method in question 17 if the Soccer array has the maximum index of 25?
19. What term does the following define? Constructs the values of data members of the class.
20. Write a statement that sets the scale type to CENTER for an ImageView instance named tower.

Beyond the Book

Search the Web for answers to the following questions to further your Android knowledge.

1. Find GridView images from three websites that display a GridView with images and provide a URL and screenshot of each website.
2. Name five types of apps not discussed in this chapter and how they would each use a GridView control.
3. An excellent website that provides up-to-date information about the Android world can be found at *http://android.alltop.com.* Read an article that interests you and write a summary of that article of at least 100 words.
4. One of the major issues in the Android world is the multiple operating systems currently running on Android devices. Write a one-page report about the issue of upgrading Android devices to the newest OS available.

Case Programming Projects

Complete one or more of the following case programming projects. Use the same steps and techniques taught within the chapter. Submit the program you create to your instructor. The level of difficulty is indicated for each case programming project.

Easiest: ★

Intermediate: ★★

Challenging: ★★★

Case Project 7–1: Quick Healthy Snack Ideas App ★

Requirements Document

Application title:	Quick Healthy Snack Ideas App
Purpose:	Stocking your fridge with quick and healthy snacks helps you resist eating diet-damaging foods. The Snack apps displays five healthy snack options.
Algorithms:	1. The screen displays five snacks with three on each row in a GridView control (Figure 7-29). 2. When the user selects a thumbnail image of a healthy snack, a larger image appears below the GridView (Figure 7-30).
Conditions:	1. The pictures of the five healthy snacks are provided with your student files with the names snack1 through snack5. 2. Display each image in the GridView using a layout height of 400dp, two columns, 2dp for horizontal and vertical spacing, and a column width of 150dp.

Edyta Anna Grabowska/E+/Getty Images, whitewish/E+/Getty Images, Aleksandar Zoric/E+/Getty Images, Chris Cheadle/All Canada Photos/Getty Images

Figure 7-29 Healthy Snack Ideas app

Edyta Anna Grabowska/E+/Getty Images, whitewish/E+/Getty Images, Aleksandar Zoric/E+/Getty Images, Chris Cheadle/All Canada Photos/Getty Images

Figure 7-30 Healthy Snack Ideas app with snack selected

Case Project 7–2: New Seven Wonders of the World App ★

Requirements Document

Application title:	New Seven Wonders of the World (Monuments)
Purpose:	Wikipedia would like you to build an app to showcase the new seven wonders of the world and allow users to select any monument to see a large picture.
Algorithms:	1. The opening screen should display in a grid the seven images representing the new seven wonders of the world—Great Wall of China, Petra, The Redeemer, Machu Picchu, Chichen Itza, Colosseum, and Taj Mahal (Figure 7-31). 2. When the user selects a monument image in the GridView control, a larger version of the image appears below the GridView. A toast message states which monument image the user selected by number (Figure 7-32).
Conditions:	1. The pictures of the seven wonders of the world are provided with your student files with the names wonder1 through wonder7. 2. Display each image in the GridView control with four images across each row, and use a column width of 60dp, horizontal spacing of 3dp, and vertical spacing of 3dp.

best-photo/E+/Getty Images, HUGHES HervÃ/hemis.fr/Getty Images, Stuart Dee/Photolibrary/Getty Images, Jeffrey Bosdet/All Canada Photos/Getty Images, Images Etc Ltd/Getty Images, xenotar/E+/Getty Images, Feverstockphoto/E+/Getty Images

Figure 7-31 Seven Wonders app

best-photo/E+/Getty Images, HUGHES HervÃ/hemis.fr/Getty Images, Stuart Dee/Photolibrary/Getty Images, Jeffrey Bosdet/All Canada Photos/Getty Images, Images Etc Ltd/Getty Images, xenotar/E+/Getty Images, Feverstockphoto/E+/Getty Images

Figure 7-32 Seven Wonders app with a monument selected

Case Project 7–3: S.P.C.A. Rescue Shelter App ★

Requirements Document

Application title:	S.P.C.A. Rescue Shelter App
Purpose:	Your local S.P.C.A. needs an app to display pictures of dogs in need of a home.
Algorithms:	1. The screen displays six dogs from the shelter in a large GridView control. 2. When the user selects a thumbnail image of a dog, a full-size image appears below the GridView.
Conditions:	1. Online, find six pictures of the dogs eligible for adoption. 2. Display each image in the GridView with the size 300, 250.

Case Project 7–4: Car Rental App ★★

Requirements Document

Application title:	Car Rental App
Purpose:	A car rental company would like to display its car rental choices in a GridView.
Algorithms:	1. The opening screen displays images of six rental car models in a GridView control. 2. When the user selects a car thumbnail image, a full-size image appears below the GridView. Using an If statement, a toast message states the type of car and cost of each rental car.
Conditions:	1. Locate six rental car images on the Internet. 2. Create a custom layout using the CENTER scale type.

Case Project 7–5: Anthology Wedding Photography App ★★★

Requirements Document

Application title:	Anthology Wedding Photography App
Purpose:	Anthology Wedding Photography would like to display a sample of its work with 10 wedding images in a GridView.
Algorithms:	1. Create a GridView that displays 10 wedding photos. 2. When the user selects a specific wedding image in the GridView, a large image appears with a custom toast message that displays *Anthology Wedding Photo* and the image number. 3. A text line appears at the bottom of the screen: *Contact us at anthology@wed.com.*
Conditions:	1. Select wedding images from the Internet. 2. Use a layout of your choice.

Case Project 7–6: Personal Photo App ★★★

Requirements Document

Application title:	Personal Photo App
Purpose:	Create your own photo app with eight images of your family and friends in a GridView control.
Algorithms:	1. Create a GridView that displays eight images of your friends and family. 2. When the user selects a specific thumbnail image in the GridView, a large image appears with a custom toast message that states the first name of the pictured person.
Conditions:	1. Select your own images. 2. Use a layout of your choice.

CHAPTER 8

Design! Using a DatePicker on a Tablet

In this chapter, you learn to:

- Create an Android project on a tablet
- Understand tablet specifications
- Follow design principles for the Android tablet
- Add a second Android Virtual Device
- Add a custom launcher and tablet theme
- Understand the Calendar class
- Use date, time, and clock controls
- Determine the system date
- Display a DatePicker control
- Launch a dialog box containing a DatePicker control
- Code an onDateSetListener method to await user interaction
- Determine the date entered on a calendar control
- Test an application on a tablet emulator

The explosion of the Android market is not limited to the phone platform. Android tablet sales are successfully competing with the Apple iPad as well, proving that consumers are ready for a tablet environment. Now more than ever, mobile designers are being asked to create experiences for a variety of tablet devices. In today's post-PC world, the tablet market provides the mobility and simplicity users demand for connecting to the Internet, playing games, using Facebook, checking email, and more. Lower price points and a large app marketplace are driving growth in the Android tablet market. Android tablets come in various sizes, often ranging from 7.3 inches to 10.1 inches, comparable to the iPad Mini and the full-size iPad. To understand the process of designing an application on the Android tablet, in this chapter you design a calendar program on a 10.1-inch tablet that books a reservation on a deep sea fishing boat in Hawaii called Sailing Adventures. The Sailing Adventures application shown in Figure 8-1 provides information about one of its fishing adventures located in Kona, Hawaii. This single-screen experience could be part of a larger app featuring fishing trips throughout the world.

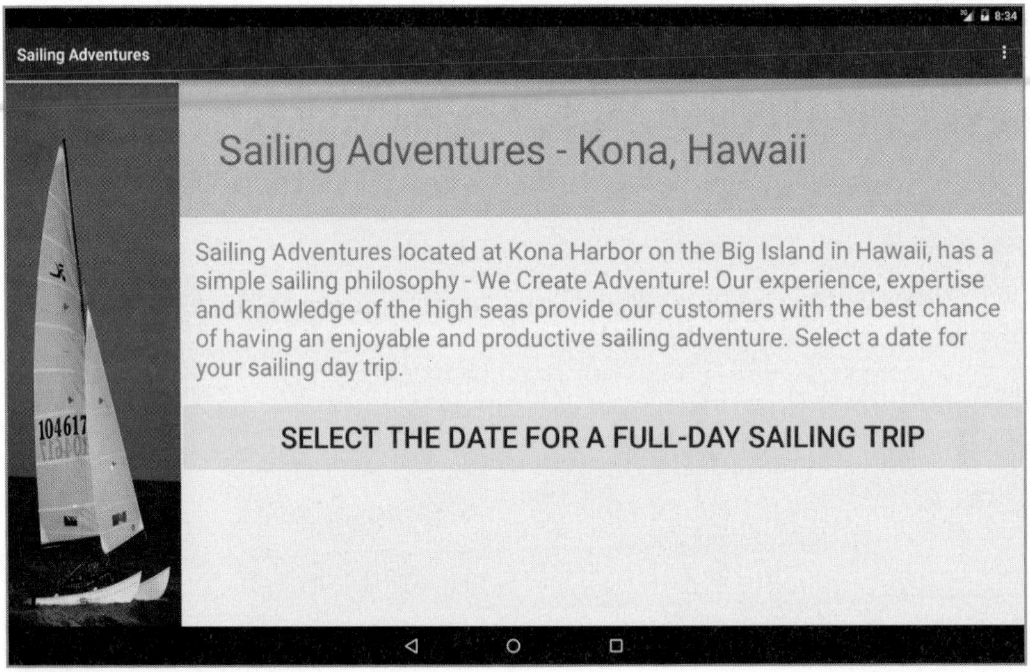

Richard I'Anson/Lonely Planet Images/Getty Images

Figure 8-1 Sailing Adventures Android tablet app

The Android tablet app in Figure 8-1 appears on a 10.1-inch Nexus 10 display. When the user makes a reservation by touching the button control, a floating dialog box opens with a DatePicker calendar control, as shown in Figure 8-2. When the date is set by the user, a TextView control confirms the reservation for the deep sea fishing day trip, as shown in Figure 8-3.

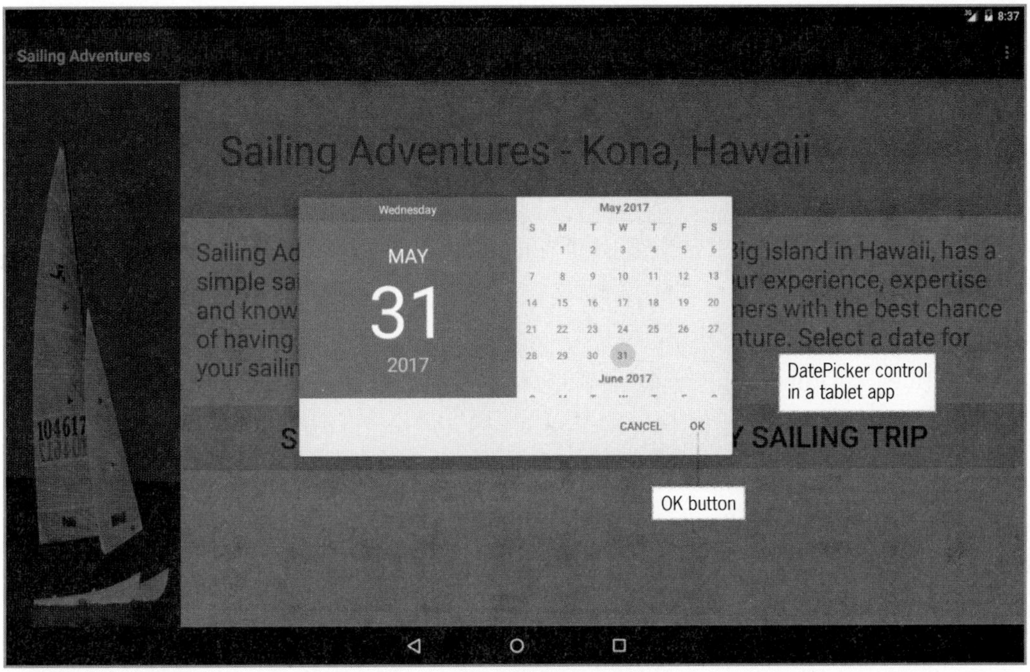

Richard I'Anson/Lonely Planet Images/Getty Images

Figure 8-2 DatePicker calendar control in a dialog box

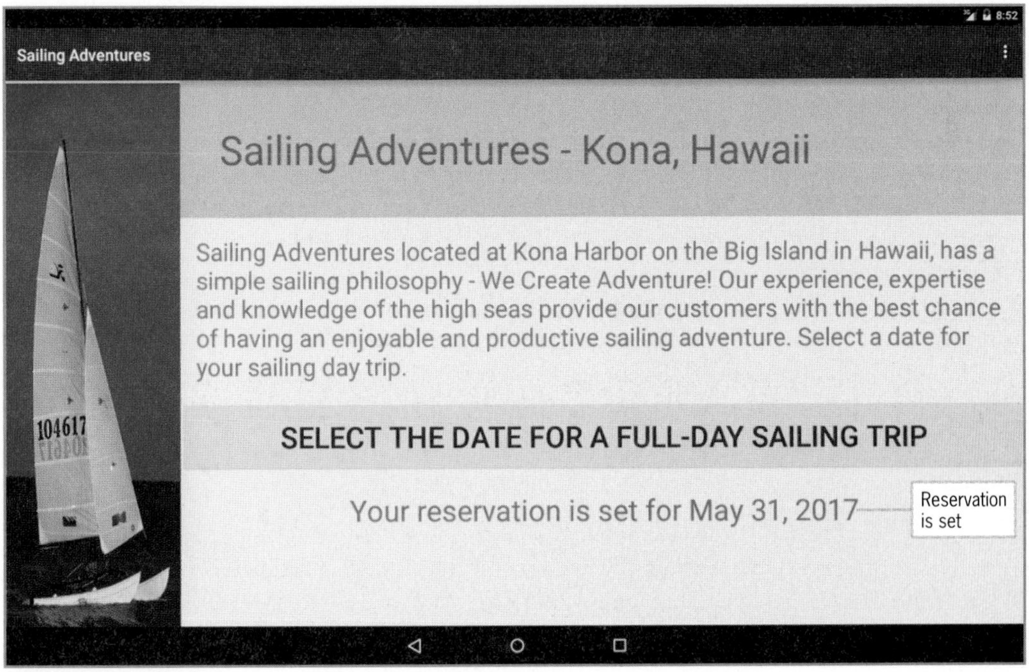

Richard I'Anson/Lonely Planet Images/Getty Images

Figure 8-3 TextView control displays reservation

IN THE TRENCHES
The Android platform has been ported to many kinds of devices beyond phones and tablets, such as toasters, televisions, microwaves, and laptops.

To create this application, the developer must understand how to perform the following processes, among others:

1. Add an Android Virtual Device specifically designed for tablets.
2. Add the images used in this project.
3. Change the theme and icon for the tablet display.
4. Create a custom XML file with a Table layout.
5. Add and initialize the TextView controls and the Button control.
6. Initialize a DatePickerDialog with the present date and listen for the user to select a date.
7. Return the selected date.
8. Display the selected reservation date in the TextView control.

Designing a Tablet Application

The Android market initially only included mobile phone devices, but the recent popularity of the tablet device provides a new platform for Android app programming. The growth of the Android tablet market goes hand in hand with dedicated applications designed especially for the tablet, not just enlarged versions of a phone app. **Native applications** are programs locally installed on a specific platform such as a phone or tablet. A native application is typically designed for a specific platform such as a phone on a 5-inch screen or a tablet on a 10.1-inch screen. In contrast, an **emulated application** is converted in real time to run on a variety of platforms such as a webpage, which can be displayed on various screen sizes through a browser. A native Android tablet app creates an optimal user experience based on the most common tablet screen sizes between approximately 7.3 and 10.1 inches, a 2560 × 1600 pixel resolution, and a 16:10 screen ratio, as shown in Figure 8-4. In comparison, an Apple iPad Air has a 9.7-inch screen, a 2048 × 1536 pixel resolution, and a screen ratio of 4:3. If you plan to create apps on multiple platforms, the different screen specifications will affect your design.

Figure 8-4 Android tablet

As you consider creating an Android tablet application, remember that tablets are not simply huge smartphones. Even the primary use of each device is different. A smartphone is most likely used on the go in a truly mobile fashion to quickly check email, update your Facebook status, or send a text message between classes or as you run errands. Tablets are typically used for longer periods of time. This prolonged interaction on tablets is more involved, with users sitting down at a table in Starbucks, riding a train, or relaxing with the tablet positioned in their laps while watching a movie. Whereas phone app design relies on simplicity, a tablet can handle the complexity of more graphics, more text, and more interaction during longer sessions.

IN THE TRENCHES

To gain some inspiration for your tablet design best practices, download the YouTube, CNN, CNBC, Pulse, WeatherBug, and Kindle apps.

Design Best Practices for Tablets

As you begin designing an Android app, first consider how the user most likely will interact with your app. Will the tablet be in his or her lap, held with two hands (games often require this), or in a tablet stand? Will the user spend seconds, minutes, or hours using your app?

What is the optimal way to deliver the content? As you consider the answers to each of these questions, also keep these design guidelines in mind:

- Keep screens uncluttered and ensure touch controls such as buttons and radio buttons are of sufficient size for user interaction. Larger controls are easier to find and enable simpler interaction for the user.

- Focus apps on the task at hand. Keep the design simple. Do not force the user to spend undue time figuring out how to use the application.
- Resist filling the large screen with "cool" interactions that distract the user without adding to the quality of the program.
- Use flexible dimension values such as dp and sp instead of px or pt.
- Provide higher resolution resources for screen densities (DPI) to ensure that your app looks great on any screen size.
- Create a unique experience for both the phone and tablet designs.
- Use larger fonts than with a phone app. Consider printing your user interface design to see how it looks. Do not make users double-tap or pinch your content to read it clearly. Instead, increase the font size to at least 16dp.

IN THE TRENCHES

Consumers of all ages are spending more time playing games on tablets. This trend affects the retail market sales of console-based video games and traditional children's toys. This shift leaves retailers out of the sales streams because most digital content is distributed within the different phone platform markets.

Adding an Android Virtual Device for the Tablet

To make sure your Android tablet app deploys to any device in the Android platform starting with Android Honeycomb 3.2 operating system (API 13), which is the first generation of API's dedicated to tablet applications, you can add multiple Android Virtual Devices (AVDs) in Android Studio for your intended device and platform. Honeycomb was initially designed for the Xoom, the first Android tablet introduced, but newer SDKs support the full range of new Android tablet devices on the market. When you create an Android tablet app, the minimum required SDK should be set to API 13: Android 3.2 (Honeycomb) to cover the first generation of Android tablets and the target API is automatically set to cover the most recent versions of Android tablets covered. Each Android device configuration is stored in AVD. This same technique can be used to cover earlier models of smartphone app development.

Creating a Tablet App

To create an Android tablet application for the Sailing Adventures app, follow these steps to begin the application and change the emulator:

STEP 1

- Open the Android Studio program.
- On the Welcome to Android Studio page of the Android Studio dialog box, tap or click Start a new Android Studio project in the Quick Start category.

- In the Create New Project dialog box, enter **Sailing Adventures** in the Application name text box.
- If necessary, in the Company Domain text box, type **androidbootcamp.net** and in the Project location text box, type **D:\Workspace\SailingAdventures**.
- Tap or click the Next button on the Configure your new project page of the Create New Project dialog box.
- If necessary, tap or click the Phone and Tablet check box to select the form factor for your app.
- Select API 13: Android 3.2 (Honeycomb) for the Minimum SDK to display on older Android tablets as well as newer devices.

The new Android Sailing Adventures project has an application name, a package name, and a minimum SDK of API 13, which supports tablet design (Figure 8-5).

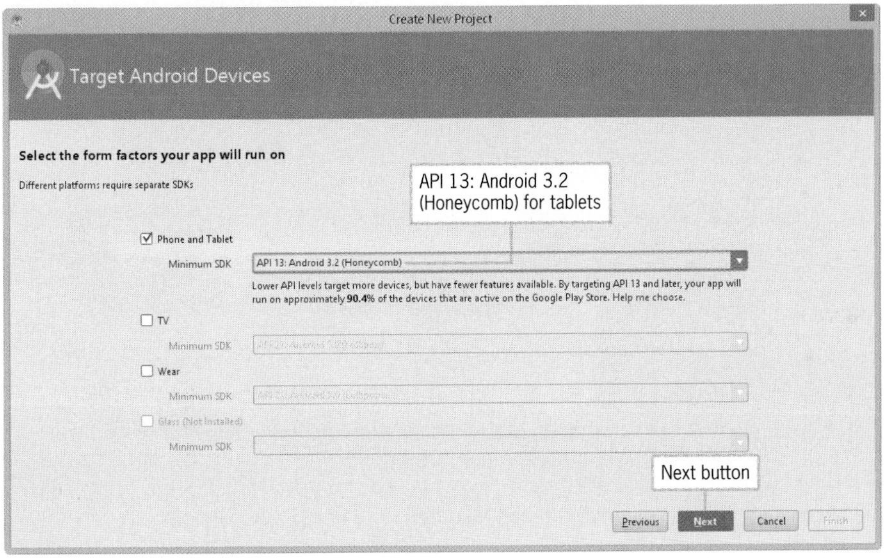

Figure 8-5 Create New Project dialog box

STEP 2

- Tap or click the Next button on the Select the form factors your app will run on page.
- If necessary, tap or click Blank Activity to add an Activity to the new project.
- Tap or click the Next button on the Add an activity to Mobile page.
- Tap or click the Finish button.

- On the activity_main.xml Design tab, tap or click the Hello world! TextView (displayed by default) in the emulator and press the Delete key.
- To change the emulator display for activity_main.xml, tap or click 'the virtual device to render the layout with' button (emulator) and select Nexus 10 (10.1", 2560 × 1600).

The activity_main.xml file is displayed in landscape orientation as a Nexus 10 tablet on the Design tab and the Hello world! TextView widget is deleted (Figure 8-6).

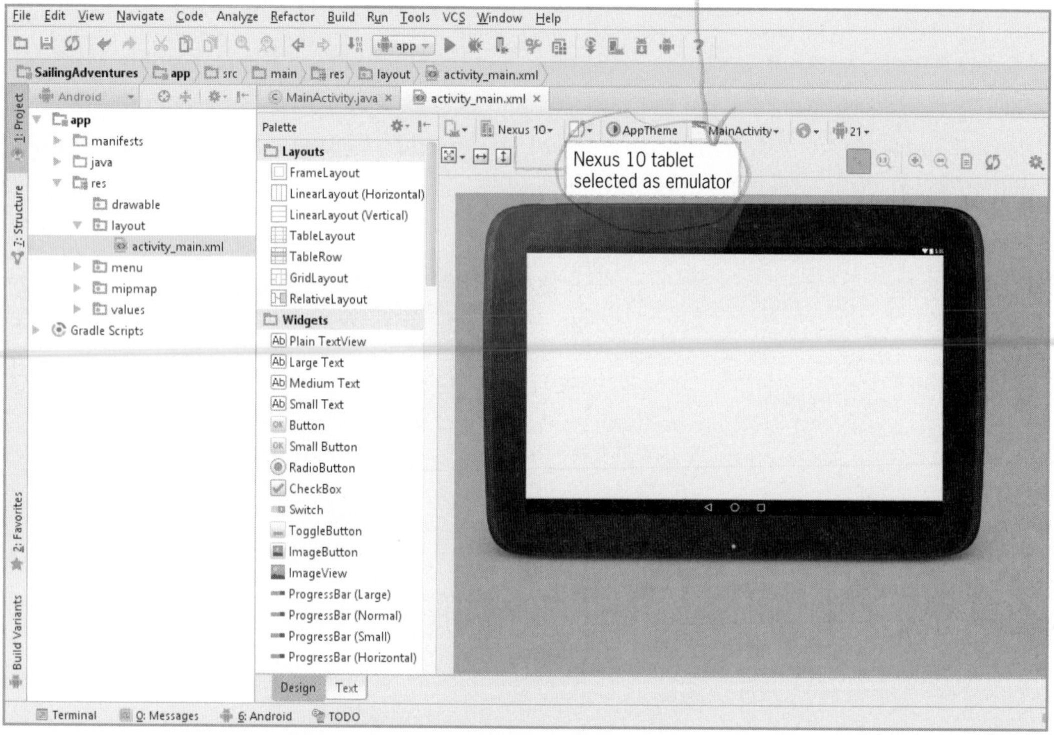

Figure 8-6 activity_main.xml is displayed as a tablet layout

To use the most recent tablet emulator, you first add the appropriate AVD configuration. The Nexus 10 works well on newer computers with high resolution, but if you are testing your project on an older computer, please select the WXGA 10.1" tablet with landscape orientation in the following steps. To select the Android Development Tools for the Nexus 10 emulator, follow these steps:

STEP 1

- Tap or click the Run 'app' button to open the Choose Device dialog box.
- Tap or click the ellipsis button to the right of Android virtual device to add a tablet emulator.

The Android Virtual Device Manager dialog box opens (Figure 8-7).

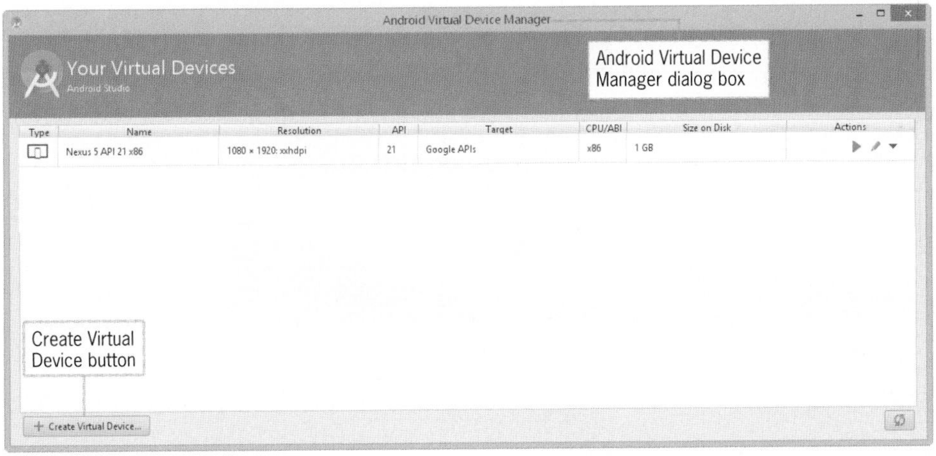

Figure 8-7 Adding a tablet emulator

STEP 2

- Tap or click the Create Virtual Device button to add a tablet emulator.
- In the Virtual Device Configuration dialog box, tap or click Tablet in the Category column.
- Tap or click Nexus 10 in the second column to select the hardware emulator. (If you are testing your project on an older computer, select the 10.1" WXGA tablet with landscape orientation.) → does not have landscape orientation in my laptop!

The Nexus 10 tablet is selected in the Virtual Device Configuration dialog box (Figure 8-8).

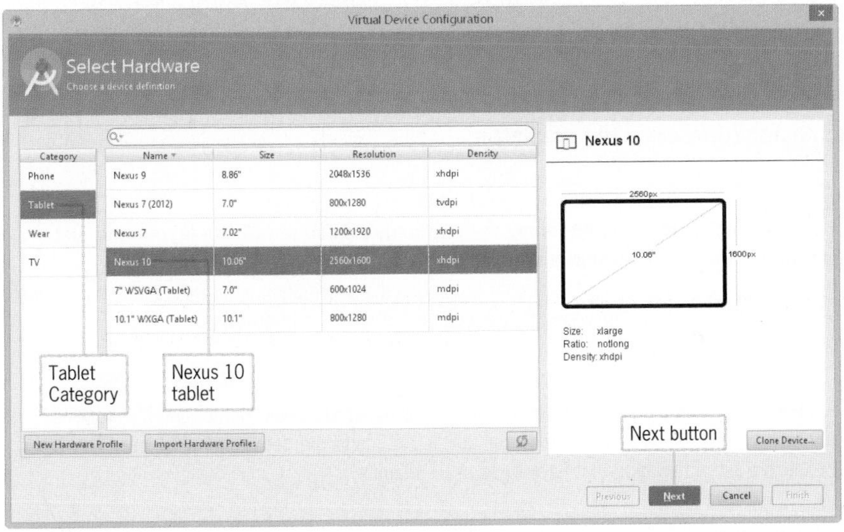

Figure 8-8 Selecting a virtual device

STEP 3

- Tap or click the Next button to open the System Image window.
- If necessary, select Lollipop in the Release Name column and then tap or click the Next button.

The Virtual Device Configuration dialog box displays the AVD settings (Figure 8-9).

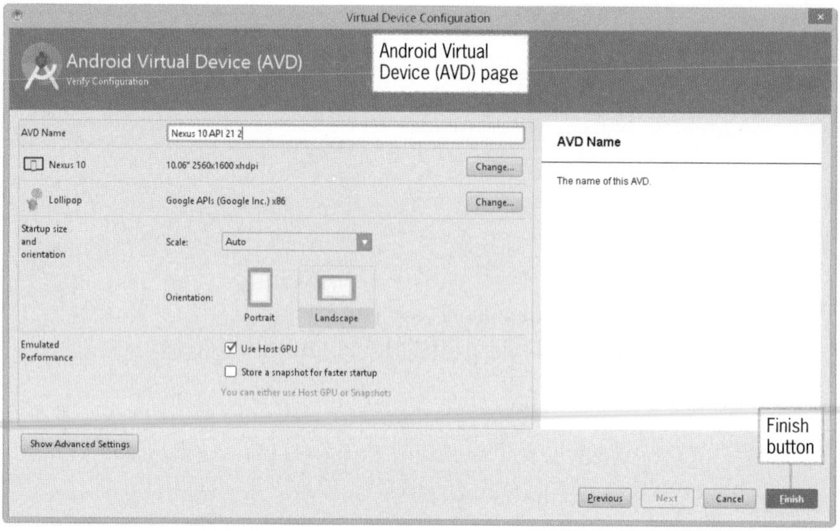

Figure 8-9 Android Virtual Device settings

STEP 4

- Tap or click the Finish button to add the Nexus 10 tablet to your virtual devices (emulators).
- Close the Android Virtual Device Manager dialog box.
- Tap or click the OK button to launch the tablet emulator.
- After the tablet emulator runs, close the emulator.

Critical Thinking

When designing a tablet native app, should I copy the company's existing website layout and just reduce the size of the elements to fit within a smaller screen?

You should start from scratch, deciding how a tablet user might use the information differently. Make the design an integrated experience with an impression similar to the existing website and phone app.

GTK

The three navigation buttons centered on the bottom of the Android tablet are Back, Home, and Multitasking. The Back button returns to the previous action. The Home button returns to the default home screen. The Multitasking button opens a list of the apps that have been used recently.

Creating the String Table

The chapter project app contains four text strings—the content description for the image as shown in Figure 8-1, the text title in the first TextView object, the description about the sailing trip, and the Button control text. To add the image to the drawable folder and text values to strings.xml, follow these steps.

STEP 1

- In the Android Project view, expand the values folder within the res folder.
- Double-tap or double-click the strings.xml file to display its contents.
- Tap or click the Open editor link.
- Tap or click the Add Key (plus) button.
- In the Key text box, type **imgSail** to name the String.
- In the Default Value text box, type **Sailing Image** to define the text that will be displayed as a content description for the ImageView control.
- Tap or click the OK button.
- Tap or click the Add Key (plus) button.
- In the Key text box, type **txtTitle** to name the String.
- In the Default Value text box, type **Sailing Adventures - Kona, Hawaii** to define the text that will be displayed in the first TextView control.
- Tap or click the OK button.
- Tap or click the Add Key (plus) button.
- In the Key text box, type **txtDescription** to name the String.
- In the Default Value text box, type the following text: **Sailing Adventures located at Kona Harbor on the Big Island in Hawaii, has a simple sailing philosophy - We Create Adventure! Our experience, expertise and knowledge of the high seas provide our customers with the best chance of having an enjoyable and productive sailing adventure. Select a date for your sailing day trip.**
- Tap or click the OK button.
- Tap or click the Add Key (plus) button.
- In the Key text box, type **btnDate** to name the String.
- In the Value text box, type **Select the Date for a Full-Day Sailing Trip** to define the text.
- Tap or click the OK button and save your work.

The Keys and Default Values of the ImageView, TextView, and Button controls are entered into the strings.xml file (Figure 8-10).

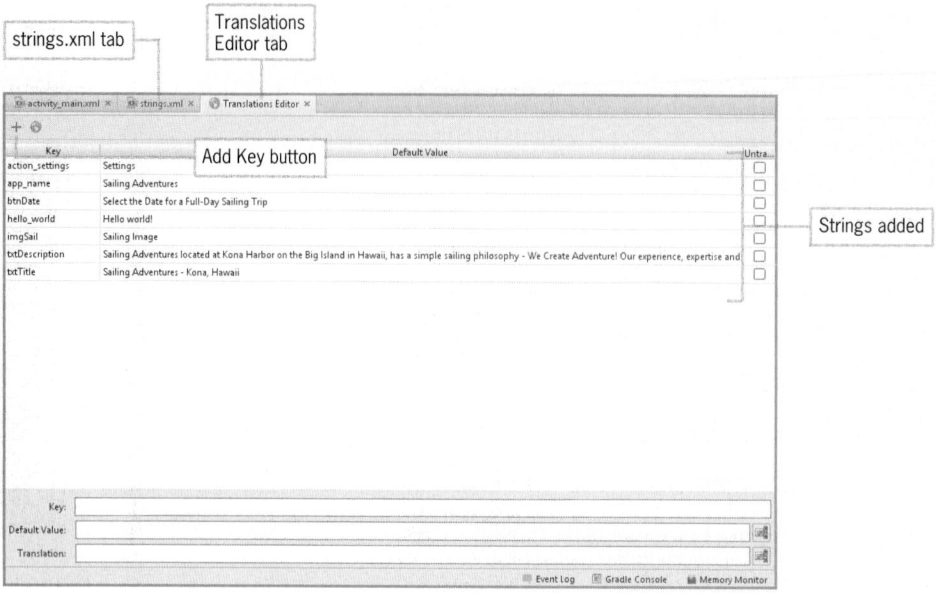

Figure 8-10 Strings added for the Sailing Adventures app

STEP 2

- Close the Translations Editor and strings.xml tabs.
- Open the USB folder containing the student files.
- Copy the sail.png file from the USB folder containing the student files and paste it in the drawable folder.
- Tap or click the OK button in the Copy dialog box.

The sail.png image is placed in the drawable folder (Figure 8-11).

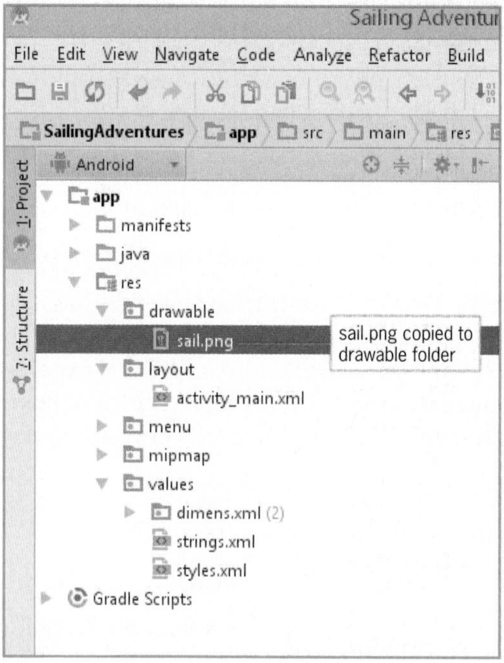

Figure 8-11 sail.png added to the drawable folder

Go to the folder where your project is stored and choose app\src\main\res\drawable

it is easier to do it directly in Android Studio – go to the drawable in \res and do Paste

GTK

Google created an Android Design website (http://developer.android.com/design) to assist in best practices and to set a uniform look and feel across the various Android platforms.

Designing a Tablet Table Layout

In the Sailing Adventures application, two layouts are combined in activity_main.xml to organize the tablet user interface controls. The Linear layout and the Table layout create a simple, clean interface on the tablet containing both rows and columns. The left column described in Table 8-1 uses the Linear layout to display the sail.png image. On the right side of Table 8-1, four rows are inserted in a Table layout to display the title, description, button, and reservation result. (Figure 8-3 shows this layout with all the design elements.)

sail.png	Title
	Day trip description
	Reservation button
	Display reservation date after selection

Table 8-1 Table for Linear layout

A user interface design layout named **TableLayout** is composed of TableRow controls—one for each row in your table in activity_main.xml. In Table 8-1, the layout consists of four rows and one column. The contents of each TableRow are the view controls that will go in each cell of the table grid. The TableLayout shown in the following code has four TableRow controls with either a TextView or Button control within each row within a LinearLayout:

Code Syntax

```
<?xml version="1.0" encoding="utf-8"?>
<LinearLayout xmlns:android="http://schemas.android.com/apk/res/android"
  <ImageView />
  <TableLayout
     <TableRow>
        <TextView />
     </TableRow>
     <TableRow>
        <TextView />
     </TableRow>
     <TableRow>
        <Button />
     </TableRow>
     <TableRow>
        <TextView />
     </TableRow>
  </TableLayout>
  </LinearLayout>
```

To create additional columns, you add a view to a row. Adding a view in a row forms a cell, and the width of the largest view determines the width of the column.

Within the XML layout file, an Android property named padding is used to spread out the content displayed on the tablet. The **padding property** can be used to offset the content of the control by a specific number of pixels. For example, if you set a padding of 20 pixels, the content of a control is distanced from other controls by 20 pixels. Another Android property named **typeface** sets the style of the text to font families that include monospace, sans_serif, and serif.

The Sailing Adventures app displays the table within a horizontal LinearLayout. By default, the Android layout is set to RelativeLayout, which allows you to place controls anywhere on the emulator. Follow these steps to change the layout of activity_main.xml for the tablet to a LinearLayout.

STEP 1

- Drag the LinearLayout (Horizontal) widget from the Layouts category of the Palette to the emulator.

The LinearLayout (Horizontal) appears in the emulator (Figure 8-12).

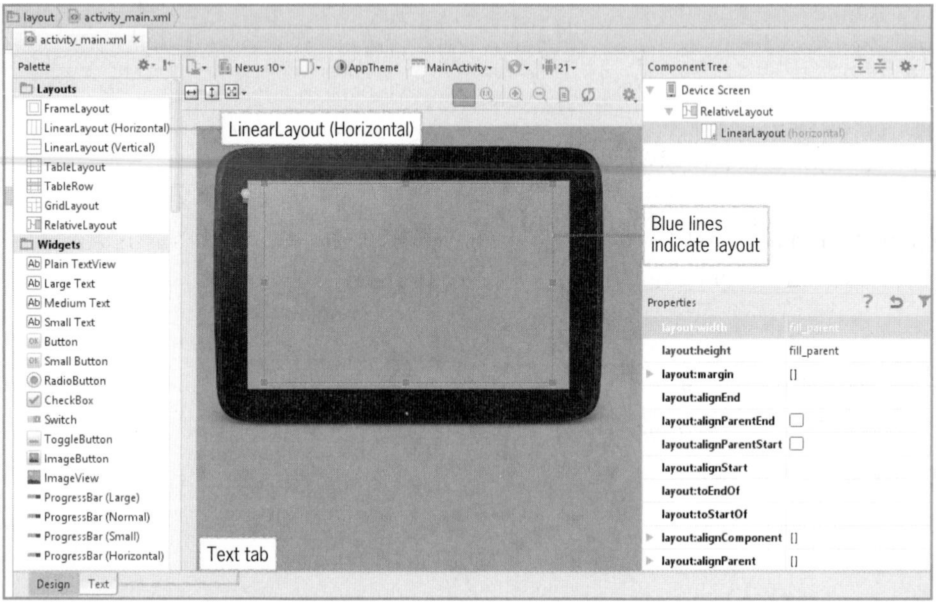

Figure 8-12 LinearLayout (Horizontal) in the emulator

STEP 2

- Tap or click the Text tab at the bottom of window.
- Show line numbers.
- Delete the padding property settings in Lines 3–6, which define the Relative layout.

The activity_main.xml displays the LinearLayout code, which will horizontally align the elements on the emulator and the padding properties are deleted (Figure 8-13).

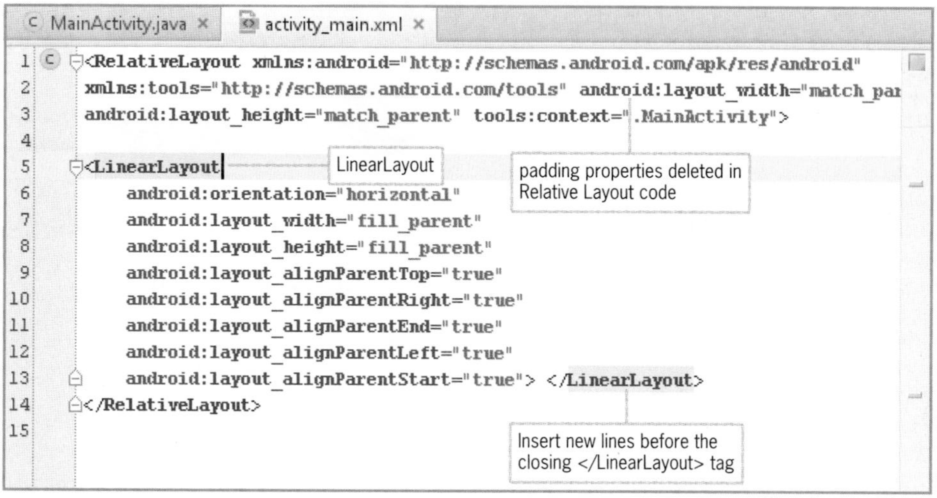

Figure 8-13 LinearLayout in Text XML code

After the layout is set, the ImageView control and the table can be coded with four rows within the activity_main.xml file by following these steps.

STEP 1

- To the left of the < bracket in </LinearLayout> in Line 13, press the Enter key twice to insert a blank line and then type **<ImageView** in the blank line.
- Press the Enter key.
- Type the following code to add the ImageView control using auto-completion as much as possible:

```
android:id="@+id/imgSail"
android:layout_width="220dp"
android:layout_height="727dp"
android:contentDescription="@string/imgSail"
android:src="@drawable/sail" />
```

The ImageView control is coded in activity_main.xml (Figure 8-14).

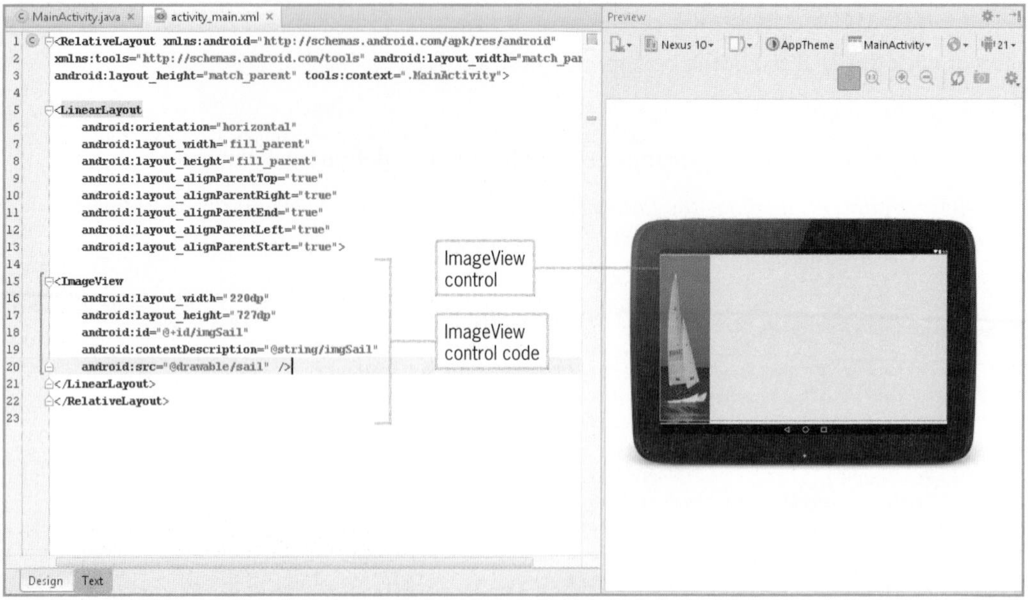

Richard I'Anson/Lonely Planet Images/Getty Images

Figure 8-14 ImageView control

STEP 2

- To code the TableLayout for the first two table rows to display the title and description TextView controls, press the Enter key.
- Type the following code using auto-completion as much as possible:

```
<TableLayout
   android:layout_width="fill_parent"
   android:layout_height="wrap_content" >
<TableRow android:layout_width="wrap_content">
<View android:layout_height="60dp" />
<TextView
   android:id="@+id/txtTitle"
   android:layout_width="wrap_content"
   android:background="#B0C4DE"
   android:gravity="fill_horizontal"
   android:padding="50dp"
   android:text="@string/txtTitle"
   android:textSize="50sp"
   android:typeface="serif" />
</TableRow>
<TableRow>
<View android:layout_height="60dp" />
<TextView
   android:id="@+id/txtDescription"
   android:layout_width="wrap_content"
   android:layout_gravity="left"
```

40

reduced the text sizes and manage to make it work in Nexus 9 but not 10 (see p. 354, Critical Thinking for the sizes of table columns)

```
    android:padding="20dp"
    android:text="@string/txtDescription"
    android:textSize="30sp" />
</TableRow>
</TableLayout>
```

The first two rows of the table display the title and description of Sailing Adventures (Figure 8-15).

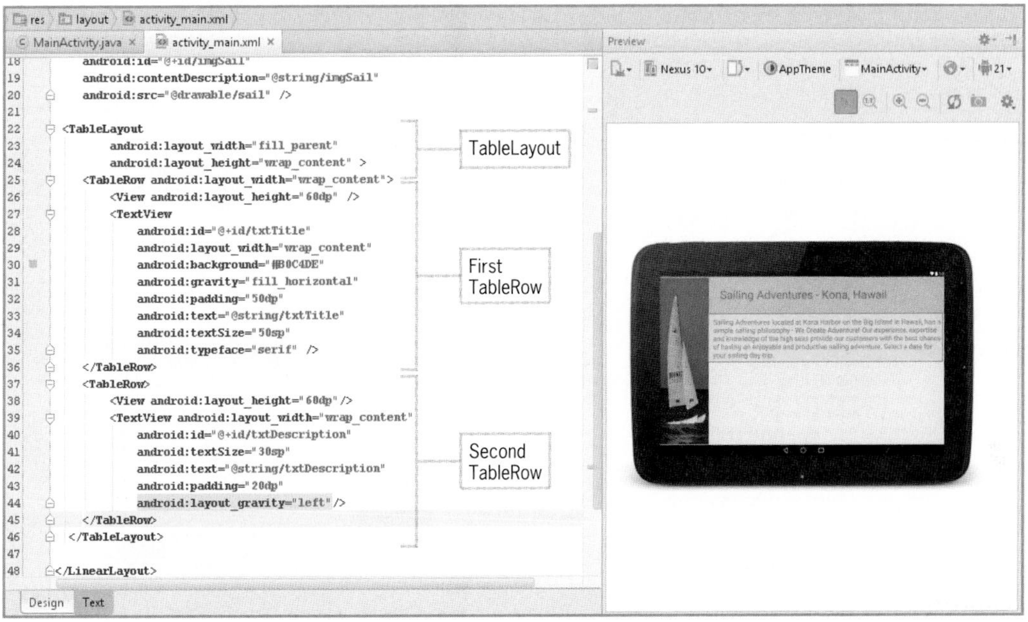

Figure 8-15 TableLayout XML code for first two TableRows

STEP 3

- Next, write the XML code for the third and fourth table rows, which display a Button and TextView control. Press the Enter key after the closing </TableRow> tag, and then type the following code using auto-completion as much as possible:

```
<TableRow>
<View android:layout_height="50dp" />
<Button
    android:id="@+id/btnDate"
    android:layout_width="wrap_content"
    android:gravity="center_horizontal"
    android:padding="20dp"
    android:text="@string/btnDate"
    android:textSize="36sp" />
</TableRow>
```

```
<TableRow>
<View android:layout_height="60dp" />
<TextView
   android:id="@+id/txtReservation"
   android:layout_gravity="center"
   android:padding="20dp"
   android:textSize="36sp" />
</TableRow>
```

The last two rows of the table display the button and reservation date of Sailing Adventures (Figure 8-16). To view the finished design, tap or click the Design tab at the bottom of the window (Figure 8-17).

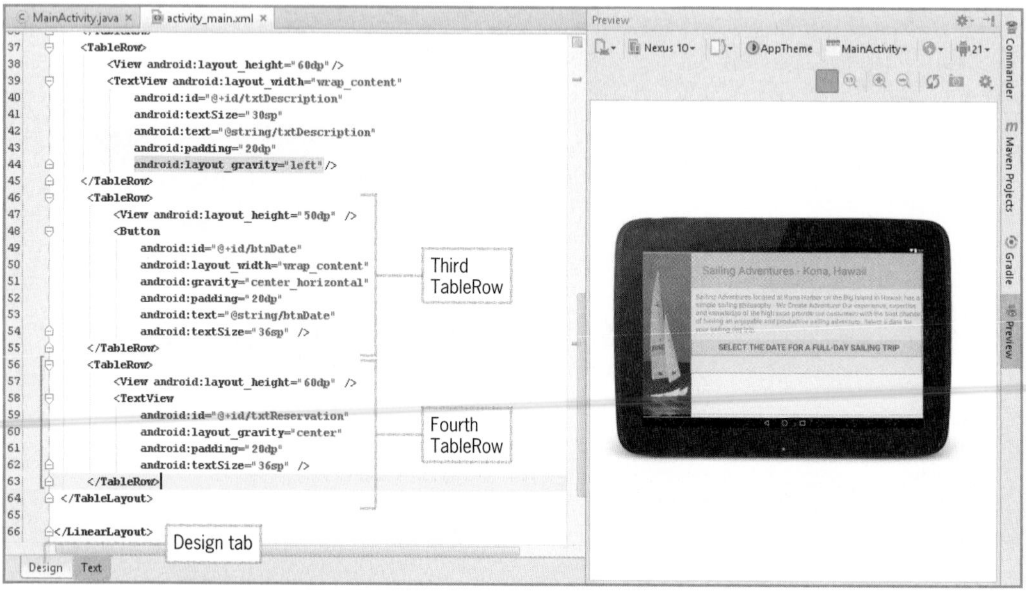

Figure 8-16 TableLayout XML code for last two TableRows

Richard I'Anson/Lonely Planet Images/Getty Images

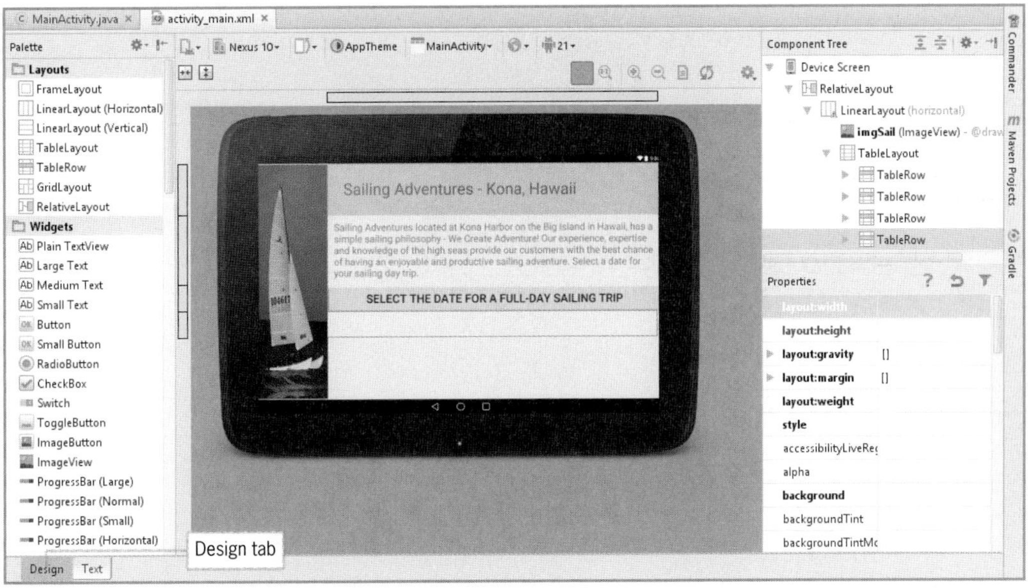

Richard I'Anson/Lonely Planet Images/Getty Images

Figure 8-17 Tablet layout in activity_main.xml

IN THE TRENCHES

After an app is published, it is the developer's responsibility to monitor comments and reviews for the app at Google Play. Consider conducting user surveys and doing further usability testing to update new versions to create a popular application.

Date, Time, and Clocks

A common Android application topic is managing calendars and time. Whether you are a student or a businessperson, a solid scheduling app can assist in personal organization to remind you about that upcoming test or to pay that bill, and an alarm clock app can help you wake up each morning. Android provides controls for the user to pick a time or a date as ready-to-use controls or to code using Java called dialogs. In the chapter project, a calendar tool called a DatePicker control is displayed in a dialog box to determine the user's preferred date for a full-day fishing trip. In the Time & Date category in the Palette, many calendar controls are available: TimePicker, DatePicker, CalendarView, Chronometer, and AnalogClock, as shown in Figure 8-18. Each picker provides controls for selecting each part of the time (hour, minute, AM/PM) or date (month, day, year).

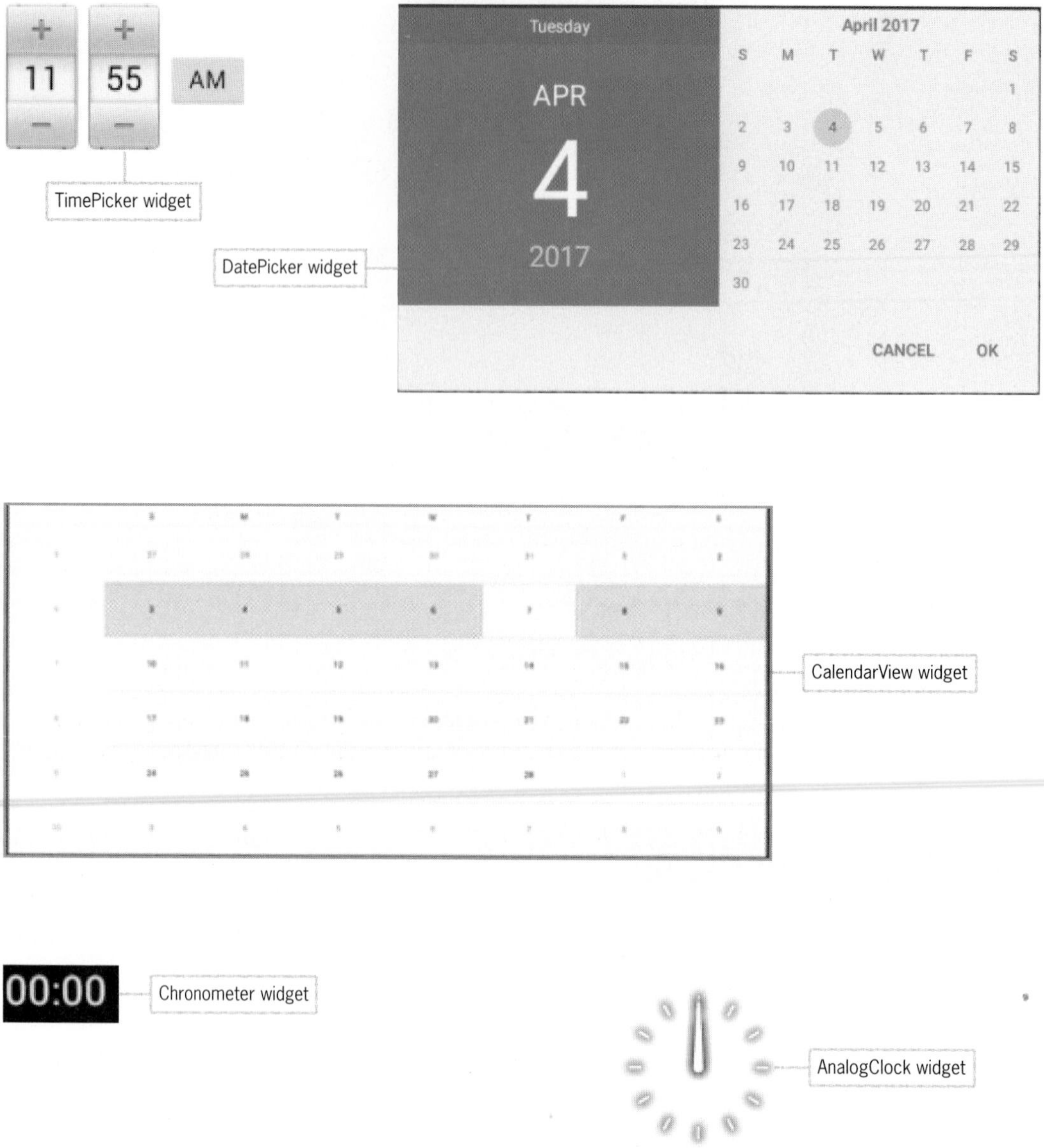

Figure 8-18 TimePicker, DatePicker, CalendarView, Chronometer, and AnalogClock widgets

All Android devices keep a numeric representation of the system's current date and time. These numbers can be displayed in multiple formats based on the cultural preferences of the user's location. For example, in the United States, the format of dates looks like this: March 17th, 2016, or 03/17/ 2016. In Canada and Europe, the day value normally precedes the month, like this: 17 March 2016 or 17/03/2016. Similarly, some countries use the concept of AM and PM with a 12-hour clock, whereas others commonly use a 24-hour clock. Developers often program these cultural differences based on user preference and location.

Creating a control to enter the date is crucial because requiring users to type the date in a text box can lead to multiple errors, including incorrect format or typos. Websites primarily rely on some type of calendar control for input in the same way that the Sailing Adventures app requests the reservation in a DatePicker control to streamline the process. Initially, the Sailing Adventures app does not display a DatePicker widget. The user taps or clicks the button to launch a dialog box that includes a coded DatePicker widget displaying today's date. Date and time controls are often launched in dialog boxes to keep the user interface uncluttered.

Instantiating the Objects

In the Sailing Adventures app, the activity_main layout opens, displaying the btnDate button. When the user interacts with the app and taps the btnDate button, a DatePickerDialog box opens and displays today's date in the calendar. After the user selects the date of the desired sailing date using the calendar and taps the OK button at the bottom of the calendar, the reservation date is displayed within the txtReservation TextView control. The txtReservation TextView control is referenced in multiple methods, so this instantiation must be declared as a class variable. To instantiate the TextView control, Button control, and the Button OnClickListener, follow these steps.

STEP 1

- Save your work and then close the activity_main.xml tab.
- In the Android Project view, expand the java folder, expand net.androidbootcamp.sailingadventures, and then double-tap or double-click MainActivity to open it.
- In MainActivity, tap or click after the public class MainActivity extends Activity { statement and press the Enter key to insert a blank line.
- To initialize the class variable, type **private TextView reservation;**.
- Tap or click TextView, press Alt+Enter, and then import the class.

A class variable that can be accessed by the rest of the program is initialized (Figure 8-19).

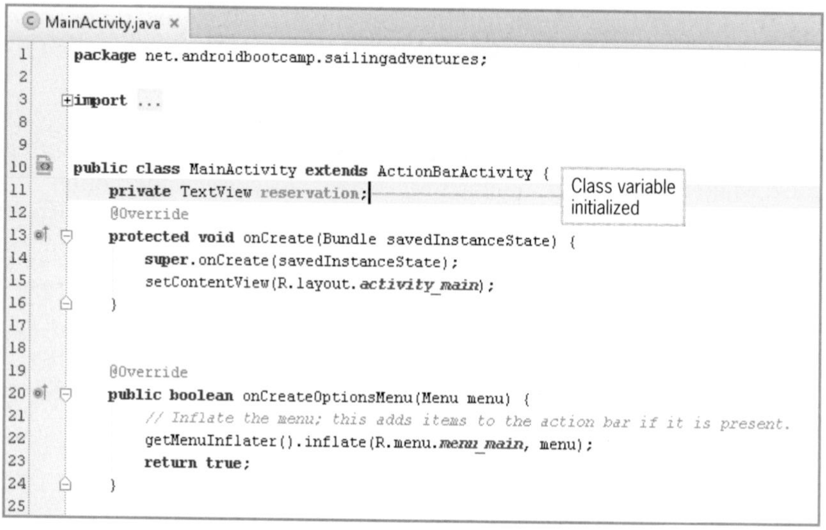

Figure 8-19 Date class variable

STEP 2

- In the onCreate( ) method, tap or click at the end of the setContentView(*R.layout.activity_main*); line and press the Enter key to insert a blank line.
- To reference the txtReservation id, type **reservation = (TextView) findViewById(R.id.txtReservation);** and then press the Enter key.
- To create an instance of the Button control from the XML layout, type **Button btDate = (Button) findViewById(R.id.btnDate);** and then press the Enter key.
- Tap or click Button, press Alt+Enter, and then import the class.

The Button and TextView controls named btnDate and txtReservation are referenced in MainActivity.java (Figure 8-20).

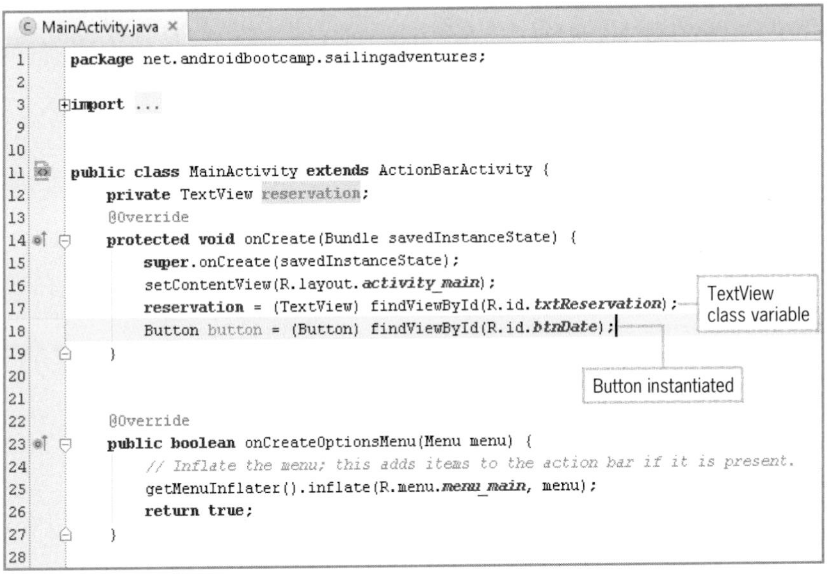

Figure 8-20 Class variables for Button and TextView controls

STEP 3

- To create the btDate button setOnClickListener method necessary to wait for the user to tap or click the button, type **btDate.setOnClickListener(new View.OnClickListener( ) {** and then press the Enter key to insert the closing brace.
- This onClickListener is designed for a Button control's variable. Tap or click View, press Alt+Enter, and then import the class.
- Tap or click the red error line below View.OnClickListener, press Alt+Enter, select Implement Methods, and then tap or click the OK button to add the quick fix.
- At the end of Line 26, type a right parenthesis and semicolon to complete the statement.

An onClick auto-generated stub appears in the code for the button (Figure 8-21).

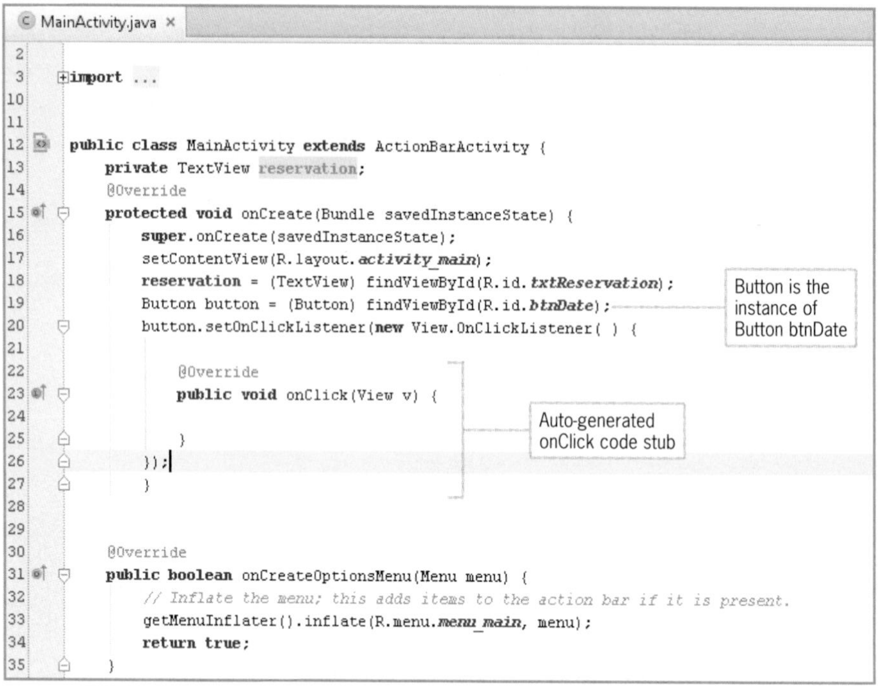

Figure 8-21 OnClickListener( ) method for the button

Using the Calendar Class

The Android system date can be accessed by using the Java **Calendar class**, which is responsible for converting between a Date object and a set of integer fields such as YEAR, MONTH, and DAY_OF_MONTH. Typically, an Android mobile device connects to a cell phone tower or wireless network, which automatically updates the time zone and date. When using the Calendar class, a method of this class called **getInstance** returns a calendar date or time based on the system settings. The date constants in this class are **YEAR**, **MONTH**, and **DAY_OF_MONTH**; they retrieve an integer value of the system's current year, month, and day, respectively. Another Calendar constant includes **DAY_OF_YEAR**, which displays the day number of the current year, as shown in the following code. For example, February 1 would be identified as the value 32 for the 32nd day of the year.

To request the local date from your computer, the following syntax creates an instance of the Calendar class named c. The Calendar class is part of the java.util.Calendar class.

Code Syntax

```
Calendar c = Calendar.getInstance( ) ;
```

Date Format

The DateFormat class in Java, as the name suggests, formats the date into a String value and is part of the java.text.DateFormat class. By default, the DateFormat class sets the date to the default long style for your default country format with a full representation of the date such as March 17, 2017, in the United States. If you were in France, the default format and the country format for the same date would be 17 March 2017 because most countries list the day before the month.

Code Syntax

```
DateFormat fmtDate = DateFormat.getDateInstance();
```

DatePickerDialog Input

The Android platform has multiple dialog boxes that allow different types of user input. Each input dialog box has a specialized purpose, for example, the DatePickerDialog allows you to select a date from a DatePicker View, the TimePickerDialog allows you to select a time from the TimePicker View, and ProgressDialog displays a progress bar below a message text box to inform you of how long a time-consuming operation is taking. In the Sailing Adventures app, a DatePickerDialog box opens when the user taps the Button object. The DatePickerDialog is launched in the onClick method, and must be passed the values for the present year, month, and day. The values for the present date must be set for the DatePicker to display today's date. When the DatePickerDialog opens, an OnDateSetListener is necessary to await the user's selection of the desired reservation date.

In the code syntax discussed earlier, notice that c is an instance of the Calendar class. The statement c.set(Calendar.YEAR, year) represents the device system's year, c.set(Calendar.MONTH, monthOfYear) represents the system's month, and c.set(Calendar.DAY_OF_MONTH, dayOfMonth) represents which day of the month is set on the system calendar. The field manipulation method called **get** accesses the system date or time, and **set** changes the current date or time.

Code Syntax

```
public void onClick(View v) {
// TODO Auto-generated method stub
   new DatePickerDialog(MainActivity.this, d,
      c.get(Calendar.YEAR), c.get(Calendar.MONTH),
      c.get(Calendar.DAY_OF_MONTH)).show();
}
```

The variable d in the code syntax is assigned later in the code to the date selected by the user for the sailing reservation, when the OnDateSetListener is established. Just like the button listener that awaits user interaction, a second listener is necessary to "listen" for the user to select a date after the dialog box displays a DatePicker control. To get an instance to the Calendar and DateFormat class, and get the current date from the system calendar within the onClick method, follow these steps:

STEP 1

- In MainActivity.java, tap or click to the right of the closing brace of the onCreate method and press the Enter key.
- To create an instance of the Calendar class, type **Calendar c = Calendar.getInstance( );**.
- Tap or click Calendar, press Alt+Enter, and then import the class.

An instance of the Calendar class named c is created (Figure 8-22).

no need to do that, the environment does it automatically

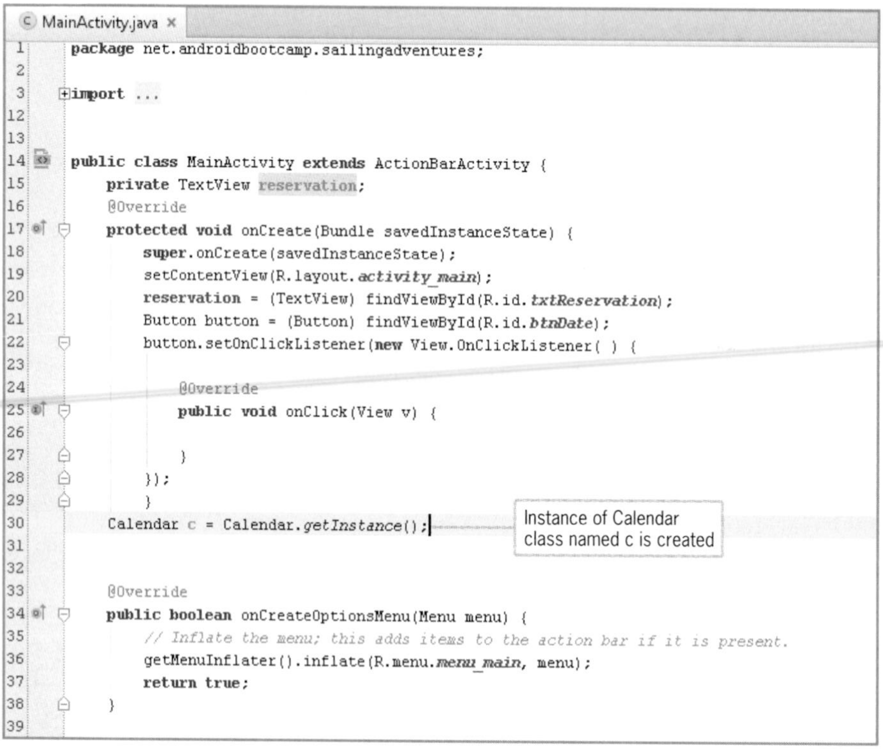

Figure 8-22 Instance of Calendar class

STEP 2

- Press the Enter key and type **DateFormat fmtDate = DateFormat.getDateInstance();** to set the default format of the date.
- Tap or click DateFormat, press Alt+Enter, and then import the java.text.DateFormat class. *Note*: Do not import android.text.format.DateFormat.

An instance of the DateFormat class named fmtDate is created (Figure 8-23).

```
15   public class MainActivity extends ActionBarActivity {
16       private TextView reservation;
17       @Override
18       protected void onCreate(Bundle savedInstanceState) {
19           super.onCreate(savedInstanceState);
20           setContentView(R.layout.activity_main);
21           reservation = (TextView) findViewById(R.id.txtReservation);
22           Button button = (Button) findViewById(R.id.btnDate);
23           button.setOnClickListener(new View.OnClickListener( ) {
24
25               @Override
26               public void onClick(View v) {
27
28               }
29           });
30       }
31       Calendar c = Calendar.getInstance();
32       DateFormat fmtDate = DateFormat.getDateInstance();
33
34
```

Instance of DateFormat class named fmtDate is created

Figure 8-23 Format set with DateFormat

STEP 3

- To display the DatePicker dialog box after the user selects the Button object, tap or click at the end of the onClick(View v) method (Line 26 in Figure 8-23; your line number may vary).
- Press the Enter key.
- To show the device's system year, month, and day of the month in the DatePicker, type **new DatePickerDialog(MainActivity.this, d, c.get(Calendar.YEAR), c.get(Calendar.MONTH), c.get(Calendar.DAY_OF_MONTH)).show();**
- Import the DatePickerDialog class.

The calendar instance named c is assigned the current system date. The variable d is red. It will be assigned the date that the user selects for the sailing reservation in the next steps (Figure 8-24).

```
24           button.setOnClickListener(new View.OnClickListener( ) {
25
26               @Override
27               public void onClick(View v) {
28                   new DatePickerDialog(MainActivity.this, d, c.get(Calendar.YEAR), c.get(Calendar.MONTH), c.get(Calendar.DAY_OF_MONTH)).show();
29               }
30           });
31       }
32       Calendar c = Calendar.getInstance();
33       DateFormat fmtDate = DateFormat.getDateInstance();
34
35
```

DatePickerDialog displays the current date of the device

Figure 8-24 DatePickerDialog launched within the onClick method

Selecting the Date from the DatePickerDialog

When the app launches the DatePickerDialog control after tapping the Button control, the Android system date is initially displayed, making it easier for the user to select a future date without having to move forward in a calendar from a date decades ago. To access the system date, the variables are initialized and displayed for the present YEAR, MONTH, and

DAY_OF_MONTH. Next, the DatePickerDialog control must await user interaction by coding an OnDateSetListener named d, which listens for a callback, indicating the user is done filling in the reservation date.

Code Syntax

```
DatePickerDialog.OnDateSetListener d = new
DatePickerDialog.OnDateSetListener() {
}
```

Adding the onDateSet( ) Method

When the user selects a date from the DatePickerDialog, the **onDateSet( ) method** automatically obtains the date selected by the user. Three portions of the date must be set for the YEAR, MONTH, and DAY_OF_MONTH of the new reservation. The Sailing Adventures application calls the onDateSet( ) method in reaction to the user tapping the OK button at the bottom of the DatePickerDialog. Notice earlier in the code, the statement get was used to display the current system date and the statement, and set is now used to hold the selected date.

Code Syntax

```
public void onDateSet(DatePicker view, int year,
      int monthOfYear, int dayOfMonth) {
   c.set(Calendar.YEAR, year);
   c.set(Calendar.MONTH, monthOfYear);
   c.set(Calendar.DAY_OF_MONTH, dayOfMonth);
}
```

The next set of steps code the onDateSetListener and onDateSet methods that respond to the user's selected date.

STEP 1

- Save your work.
- At the end of the DateFormat statement (Line 33 in Figure 8-24), press the Enter key and type the following code on a new line:

  DatePickerDialog.OnDateSetListener d = new
  DatePickerDialog.OnDateSetListener() {
- Press the Enter key to display a closing brace.
- Type a semicolon after the closing brace to complete the statement.
- Tap or click OnDateSetListener( ), press Alt+Enter, and implement methods.

The auto-generated stub for onDateSet( ) method is displayed (Figure 8-25).

```
protected void onCreate(Bundle savedInstanceState) {
    super.onCreate(savedInstanceState);
    setContentView(R.layout.activity_main);
    reservation = (TextView) findViewById(R.id.txtReservation);
    Button button = (Button) findViewById(R.id.btnDate);
    button.setOnClickListener(new View.OnClickListener( ) {

        @Override
        public void onClick(View v) {
            new DatePickerDialog(MainActivity.this, d, c.get(Calendar.YEAR), c.get(Calendar.MONTH), c.get(Calendar.DAY_OF_MONTH)).show();
        }
    });
}
Calendar c = Calendar.getInstance();
DateFormat fmtDate = DateFormat.getDateInstance();
DatePickerDialog.OnDateSetListener d = new DatePickerDialog.OnDateSetListener() {

    @Override
    public void onDateSet(DatePicker view, int year, int monthOfYear, int dayOfMonth) {

    }
};
```

OnDateSetListener( ) statement

Auto-generated method stub

Semicolon added

Figure 8-25 OnDateSetListener awaits the user to select reservation date

STEP 2

- Tap or click the blank line within the onDateSet method stub, indent the line, and then type the following statements to set the desired date for the sailing reservation:

```
c.set(Calendar.YEAR, year);
c.set(Calendar.MONTH, monthOfYear);
c.set(Calendar.DAY_OF_MONTH, dayOfMonth);
```

The calendar holds the selected reservation date consisting of the YEAR, MONTH, and DAY_OF_MONTH (Figure 8-26).

```
    }
    Calendar c = Calendar.getInstance();
    DateFormat fmtDate = DateFormat.getDateInstance();
    DatePickerDialog.OnDateSetListener d = new DatePickerDialog.OnDateSetListener() {

        @Override
        public void onDateSet(DatePicker view, int year, int monthOfYear, int dayOfMonth) {
            c.set(Calendar.YEAR, year);
            c.set(Calendar.MONTH, monthOfYear);
            c.set(Calendar.DAY_OF_MONTH, dayOfMonth);
        }
    };
```

Selected year, month, and day are set

Figure 8-26 Setting the desired date for the sailing reservation

Displaying the Date Using the getTime( ) Method

After the user has selected the sailing date reservation, the final step is to display the reservation date in the TextView object named txtReservation, with the instance name of reservation. The reservation variable displays the sailing trip date in the default format named fmtDate. The **getTime( ) method** returns the time value in the Date object. The Sailing Adventures application at this point is one of many bookings that might be part of a larger application. Typically, the application would either email the reserved date to the owners or verify the date in a connected database. The final step is to display the selected date in the TextView object.

STEP 1

- Press Enter and type **reservation.setText("Your reservation is set for " + fmtDate.format(c.getTime()));** to display the date in the default local country of the device.
- Save your work.

The reservation is displayed in the TextView object (Figure 8-27).

MainActivity.java ×

```java
package net.androidbootcamp.sailingadventures;

import ...


public class MainActivity extends ActionBarActivity {
    private TextView reservation;
    @Override
    protected void onCreate(Bundle savedInstanceState) {
        super.onCreate(savedInstanceState);
        setContentView(R.layout.activity_main);
        reservation = (TextView) findViewById(R.id.txtReservation);
        Button button = (Button) findViewById(R.id.btnDate);
        button.setOnClickListener(new View.OnClickListener( ) {

            @Override
            public void onClick(View v) {
                new DatePickerDialog(MainActivity.this, d, c.get(Calendar.YEAR), c.get(Calendar.MONTH), c.get(Calendar.DAY_OF_MONTH)).show();
            }
        });
    }
    Calendar c = Calendar.getInstance();
    DateFormat fmtDate = DateFormat.getDateInstance();
    DatePickerDialog.OnDateSetListener d = new DatePickerDialog.OnDateSetListener() {

        @Override
        public void onDateSet(DatePicker view, int year, int monthOfYear, int dayOfMonth) {
            c.set(Calendar.YEAR, year);
            c.set(Calendar.MONTH, monthOfYear);
            c.set(Calendar.DAY_OF_MONTH, dayOfMonth);
            reservation.setText("Your reservation is set for " + fmtDate.format(c.getTime()));
        }
    };

    @Override
    public boolean onCreateOptionsMenu(Menu menu) {
        // Inflate the menu; this adds items to the action bar if it is present.
        getMenuInflater().inflate(R.menu.menu_main, menu);
        return true;
    }

    @Override
    public boolean onOptionsItemSelected(MenuItem item) {
        // Handle action bar item clicks here. The action bar will
        // automatically handle clicks on the Home/Up button, so long
        // as you specify a parent activity in AndroidManifest.xml.
        int id = item.getItemId();

        //noinspection SimplifiableIfStatement
        if (id == R.id.action_settings) {
            return true;
        }

        return super.onOptionsItemSelected(item);
    }
}
```

getTime( ) displays the selected reservation date in the TextView control

Figure 8-27 Complete code

GTK
This same program would function with a TimePicker control, Calendar.HOUR_OF_DAY, Calendar.MINUTE, and TimePickerDialog method.

Running and Testing the Application

It's time to make your day trip reservation using the Sailing Adventures apps. Tap or click Run on the menu bar, and then select Run to save and test the application in the tablet emulator. Choose the tablet AVD you set up earlier, wait for the app to load, and unlock the tablet emulator. If the app doesn't load, run it again. If necessary, tap or click the Apps icon and then tap or click Sailing Adventures. The application opens in the tablet 10.1-inch emulator window, where you can test the Button and DatePicker controls in the Sailing Adventures app, as shown in Figure 8-1 and Figure 8-2.

IN THE TRENCHES
On the Windows and Mac computer platforms, the newest operating systems are quickly replacing installed programs launched by icons with an app platform that allows full use of download markets such as the Windows Store and the Apple App Store. Sales of desktop tower cases are declining. Most computer devices now are mobile and app driven.

Wrap It Up—Chapter Summary

This chapter described the steps to create a tablet application on a much larger screen. Creating a calendar control is a common specification on many Android applications. This same DatePicker application would work with a smaller Android phone window with a different design, but the code would work the same. Just like a well-made tool, your Android app, whether it is displayed on a phone or tablet, should strive to combine beauty, simplicity, and purpose to create a magical experience that is effortless to the end user.

- When designing apps for an Android tablet, keep your users' objectives and the size of the device in mind.
- To use an Android emulator designed for tablets, you first add an AVD configuration appropriate for a tablet.
- You can combine the Linear layout and the Table layout to create a simple, clean layout that takes advantage of a tablet's width. The TableLayout contains TableRow controls—one for each row in your table in activity_main.xml. In each TableRow, you can insert a view control such as a Button or TextView.
- You can display a calendar tool called a DatePicker control in a dialog box so users can select a date from the control. The Time & Date category in the Palette contains many calendar controls, including TimePicker, DatePicker, CalendarView, Chronometer, AnalogClock, and DigitalClock. In the chapter project, the user taps or clicks the button to launch a dialog box that includes a coded DatePicker widget displaying today's date.

- To display the current system date when the DatePicker control opens, you use the YEAR, MONTH, and DAY_OF_MONTH class variables to access the system date.
- To create a DatePickerDialog instance, you must create OnDateSetListener( ) method to await user interaction. If you include a control, such as a Button, that users tap to display a calendar, use the setOnClickListener method to implement the Button. The onClick method responds to the user's action, so you place the code to launch the DatePicker dialog box in the onClick method.
- When a dialog box containing a DatePicker appears, users can select a date and tap a Button control. Tapping the Button invokes an onDateSetListener in DatePickerDialog, which passes integers representing the year, month, and day from the DatePicker into onDateSet. The selected date can then be displayed in a TextView control using setText using the getTime( ) method.

Key Terms

Calendar class—A class you can use to access the Android system date. The Calendar class also is responsible for converting between a Date object and a set of integer fields such as YEAR, MONTH, and DAY_OF_MONTH.

DAY_OF_MONTH—A date constant of the Calendar class that retrieves an integer value of the system's current day.

DAY_OF_YEAR—A date constant of the Calendar class that retrieves the day of the current year as an integer. For example, February 1 is day 32 of the year.

emulated application—An application that is converted in real time to run on a variety of platforms such as a webpage, which can be displayed on various screen sizes through a browser.

get—The field manipulation method that accesses the system date or time.

getInstance—A method of the Calendar class that returns a calendar date or time based on the system settings.

getTime( ) method—A method of the Calendar class that returns the time value in the Date object.

MONTH—A date constant of the Calendar class that retrieves an integer value of the system's current month.

native application—A program locally installed on a specific platform such as a phone or tablet.

onDateSet( ) method—A method that automatically obtains the date selected by the user.

padding property—A property that you can use to offset the content of a control by a specific number of pixels.

set—The field manipulation method that changes the system date or time.

TableLayout—A user interface design layout that includes TableRow controls to form a grid.

typeface—A property that you can use to set the style of control text to font families, including monospace, sans_serif, and serif.

YEAR—A date constant of the Calendar class that retrieves an integer value of the system's current year.

Developer FAQs

1. Explain the difference between a native app and a webpage.
2. What is the range of the diagonal measurement of Android tablet screens?
3. What is the diagonal size of the iPad screen?
4. Describe the three most common activities mentioned in the chapter used with an Android phone.
5. How do the activities in question 4 differ from how you would typically use a tablet?
6. Which Android AVD was first designed specifically for tablets? Identify the name and version. It is used for the minimum required SDK.
7. What is the purpose of the three buttons on the bottom of the tablet?
8. Inside of an XML Table layout, what is the XML code name of each row?
9. True or False? A LinearLayout and TableLayout cannot be used in the same XML layout file.
10. Write the single line of XML code to set the padding to 32 density independent pixels.
11. Write the single line of XML code to set the text to the font family of sans serif.
12. Name six calendar widgets.
13. If a date is displayed as 9/30/2017 in the United States, how would that same date be displayed in Europe?
14. Why is it best to use a dialog box for a DatePicker control?
15. Which method retrieves the selected date of the DatePicker?
16. Name three purposes of a dialog box.
17. Write a line of code that, for the calendar instance named cal, assigns dueDay to the day of the month.
18. Write the New Year's Eve date of the year 2017 in the default layout of your locale.
19. Write a line of code that, for the calendar instance named c, assigns currentHour to the hour of the day.
20. Write a line of code that, for the calendar instance named c, assigns currentMinute to the minute within an hour.

Beyond the Book

Search the Web for answers to the following questions to further your Android knowledge.

1. Research Android tablet design. Find five design tips not mentioned in the chapter and describe them using complete sentences.
2. Research five popular Android calendar apps available in Google Play. Write a paragraph about the purpose of each one.
3. In the Information Technology (IT) field, Gartner, Inc., is considered one of the world's leading IT research and advisory companies. Research Gartner's opinion on the growth of the tablet. Locate a recent article by Gartner and write a summary of at least 150 words of the tablet trend.
4. The Android style guide online at *http://developer.android.com/design* provides a foundation in Android best practices. Create a bulleted list of 15 best practices from this site.

Case Programming Projects

Complete one or more of the following case programming projects. Use the same steps and techniques taught within the chapter. Submit the program you create to your instructor. The level of difficulty is indicated for each case programming project.

Easiest: ★

Intermediate: ★★

Challenging: ★★★

Case Project 8–1: Appalachian Trail Festival Tablet App ★

Requirements Document

Application title:	Appalachian Trail Festival Tablet App
Purpose:	The Appalachian Trail Festival would like an Android tablet app that displays a title and event description. When the user taps a button, a calendar for reserving a ticket for the festival appears. The date is then shown as available for a reservation.
Algorithms:	1. The opening tablet screen displays an image, a title, an event description, and a button to create a reservation for a day at the festival (Figure 8-28). 2. When the user taps a button, a DatePicker is displayed in a dialog box (Figure 8-29). The dialog box allows the user to select the date to attend the year-long festival.
Conditions:	1. The picture named hike.png is provided with your student files. 2. Write your own description of the festival. 3. Research the hexadecimal color for red. 4. Use the Theme.Black theme. 5. Use a Table layout with four rows within a Linear layout.

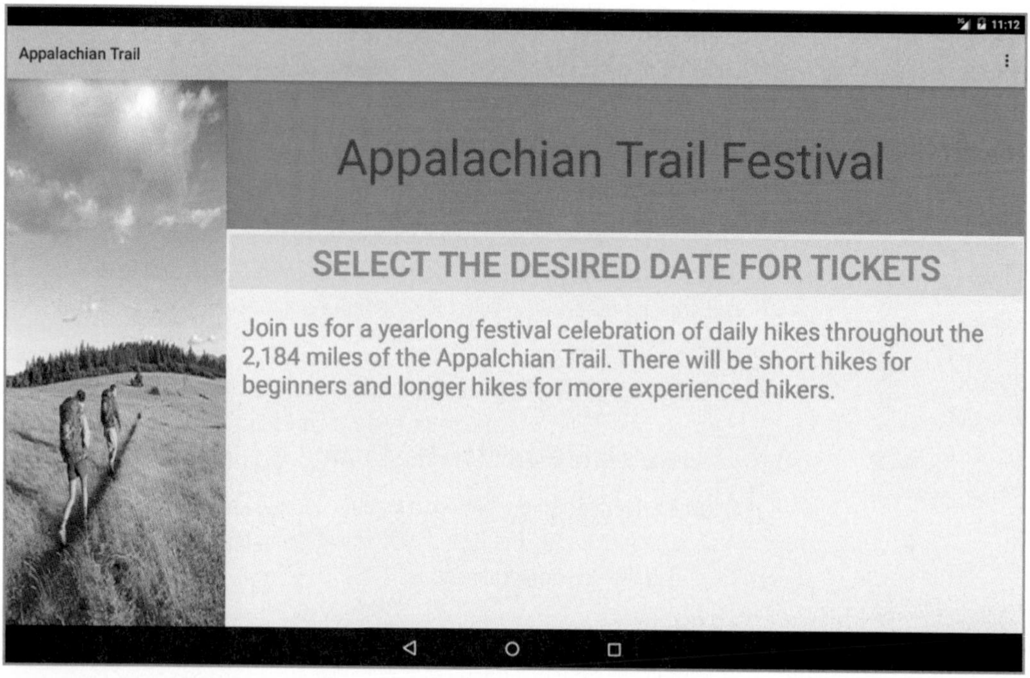

Jordan Siemens/Digital Vision/Getty Images

Figure 8-28 Appalachian Trail Festival tablet app

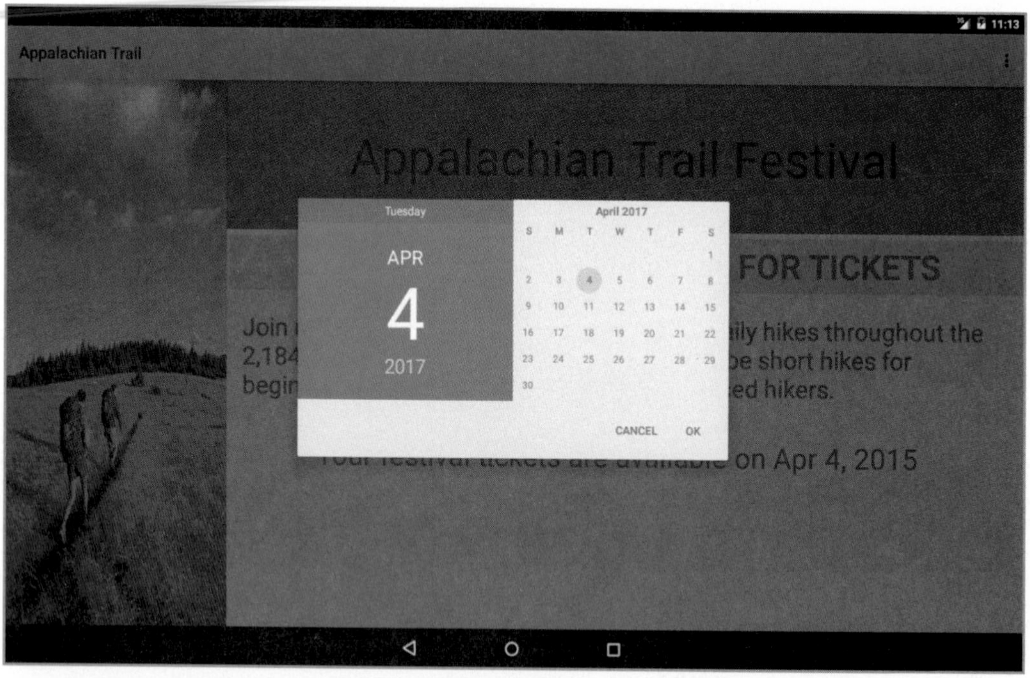

Jordan Siemens/Digital Vision/Getty Images

Figure 8-29 Calendar for reserving a festival ticket

Case Project 8–2: The Dog Sledding Experience Tablet App ★

Requirements Document

Application title: The Dog Sledding Experience Tablet App

Purpose: The Dog Sledding Experience tablet app provides a reservation button to select a date to sign up for the full immersion experience of a full-day dog sledding trip in Alaska.

Algorithms:

1. The opening screen displays an image, a tour description, and a button that launches a DatePicker dialog box (Figure 8-30).
2. When the user taps the button, a DatePicker control is displayed in a dialog box (Figure 8-31). The dialog box confirms the date of the reservation.

Conditions:

1. A picture of the dog sledding experience named sled.png is provided with your student files.
2. Write your own description of the sledding experience.
3. Select your own colors and font.
4. Use a Table layout.

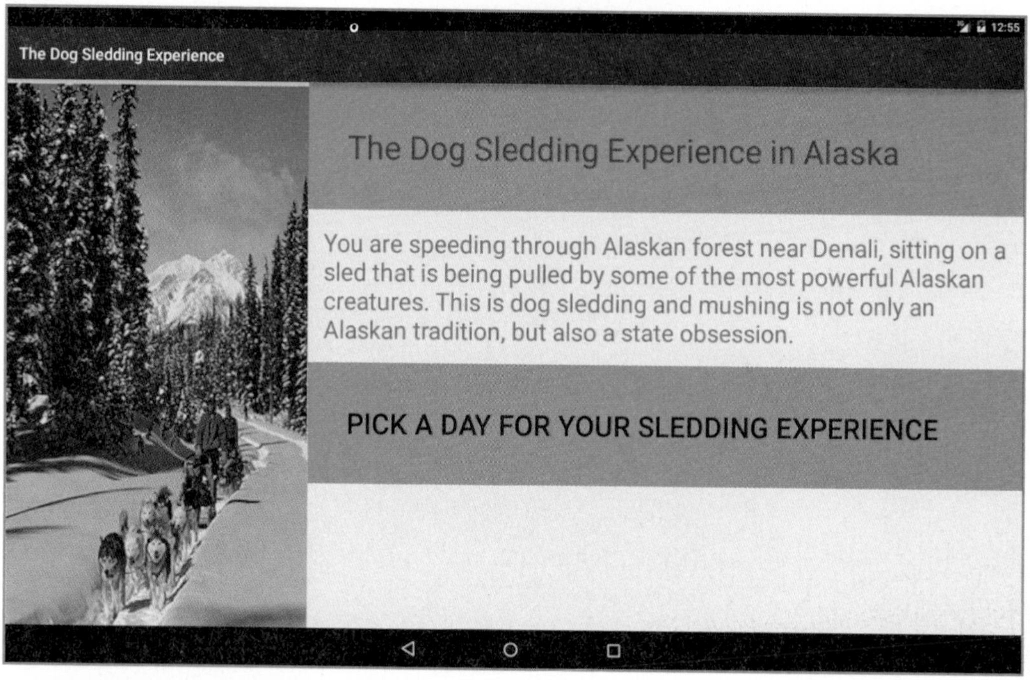

Figure 8-30 The Dog Sledding Experience tablet app

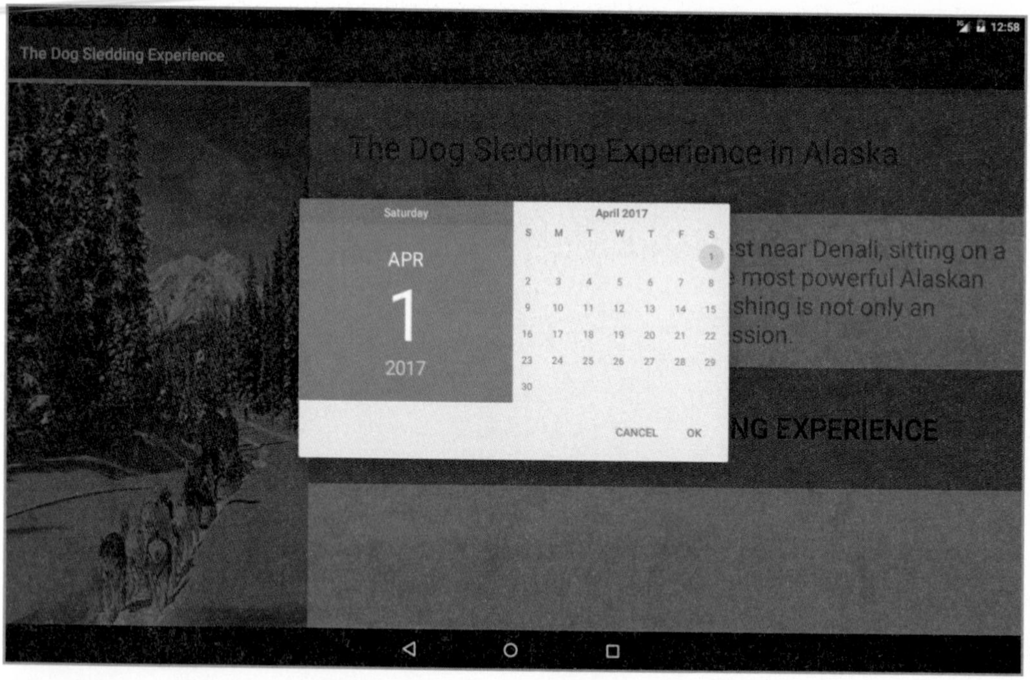

Figure 8-31 Calendar confirms the date of the reservation

Case Project 8–3: Country Cabin Rental Tablet App ★★

Requirements Document

Application title:	Country Cabin Rental Tablet App
Purpose:	The Country Cabin Rental realty agency provides cabins for rental. Two cabins are available for a minimum three-night stay.
Algorithms:	1. The opening screen displays an image, cabin descriptions, two radio button controls with different cabin names, and a button that launches a DatePicker dialog box. 2. When the user taps the button, a DatePicker control is displayed in a dialog box. The user selects the first night of a three-night reservation. The dialog box displays the date range of the three-night reservation with the name of the selected cabin.
Conditions:	1. Find an appropriate picture on the Web. 2. Write your own descriptions of the cabins. 3. Do not use the default theme. 4. Only one radio button can be selected at a time. 5. Use a Table layout.

Case Project 8–4: Final Touch Auto Detailing Tablet App ★★

Requirements Document

Application title:	Final Touch Auto Detailing Tablet App
Purpose:	The Final Touch Auto Detailing business provides a variety of detailing services. The company wants an app to list each service and its price and display a calendar for making a service reservation.
Algorithms:	1. The opening screen displays an image, service descriptions, four check boxes offering different detailing services each with different prices, and a button that launches a DatePicker dialog box to make a reservation for the all-day auto-detailing services. 2. When the user taps the button, a DatePicker control is displayed in a dialog box. The user selects the date for the reservation. The dialog box displays the date and final cost of the detailing services.
Conditions:	1. Select your own image(s) 2. Write your own descriptions about the car detailing services. 3. Do not use the default theme. 4. More than one check box can be checked at once. 5. Use a Table layout.

Case Project 8–5: Wild Ginger Dinner Delivery Tablet App ★★★

Requirements Document

Application title: Wild Ginger Dinner Delivery Tablet App with TimePicker

Purpose: Wild Ginger Dinner Delivery service delivers dinners in the evening. The business wants an app that customers can use to select a dinner and reserve a delivery time.

Algorithms:

1. The opening screen displays an image, a Wild Ginger food description, and a button that launches a TimePicker dialog box to make a reservation for delivery tonight.
2. When the user taps the button, a TimePicker control is displayed in a dialog box. The user selects the time for delivery, and the app confirms the delivery time, which is available only from 5 pm to 11 pm.

Conditions:

1. Select your own image(s).
2. Write your own description of the great food offered at Wild Ginger.
3. Do not use the default theme.
4. Use a Table layout.

Case Project 8–6: Create Your Own Tablet App ★★★

Requirements Document

Application title: Create Your Own Tablet App

Purpose: Create an app with a DatePicker and a TimePicker to create a reservation.

Algorithms:

1. Create an app on a topic of your own choice.
2. Use two buttons. The first button allows the user to select the date and the second button allows the user to select the time.

Conditions:

1. Select your own image(s).
2. Use a custom layout and icon.

CHAPTER 9

Customize! Navigating with a Master/Detail Flow Activity on a Tablet

In this chapter, you learn to:

- Understand responsive design for Android apps
- Create an Android tablet project using an application template
- Understand the Master/Detail Flow template
- Modify the Master/Detail Flow template
- Add a WebView control
- Display a Web browser within a tablet app
- Add an Internet permission to the Android Manifest
- Customize the content of the sample template file
- Display a custom layout in the details pane

Creating an attractive user interface that provides simple navigation can be challenging when programming an Android app for a tablet, phone, and other mobile devices. Fortunately, the Android platform provides a flexible way to simplify layout and navigation using built-in Android templates. To construct apps that automatically fit the device, you need design elements such as fluid grids and flexible images that can adapt to various screen sizes. Instead of creating a number of rigid XML layouts heavily optimized to a number of predefined screen sizes, built-in templates are available using the best presentation mode based on the size of the device. Like multiple windows, multipane layouts can be used to show different topics within a single window in an intuitive interface.

In this chapter, you use a template to create a multipane interface in an Android application designed for providing information about a European bike and barge cruise vacation. Bike and barge cruises combine two popular ways of exploring Europe—cycling and river cruising. On a bike and barge experience, you spend your days cycling through historic European sites and your nights cruising down scenic rivers through cities such as Amsterdam and Budapest. The Bike and Barge application shown in Figure 9-1 features a three-item list containing Photos, Tour, and Web site items. When the app first opens, the item list is displayed in the left pane and the right pane is blank.

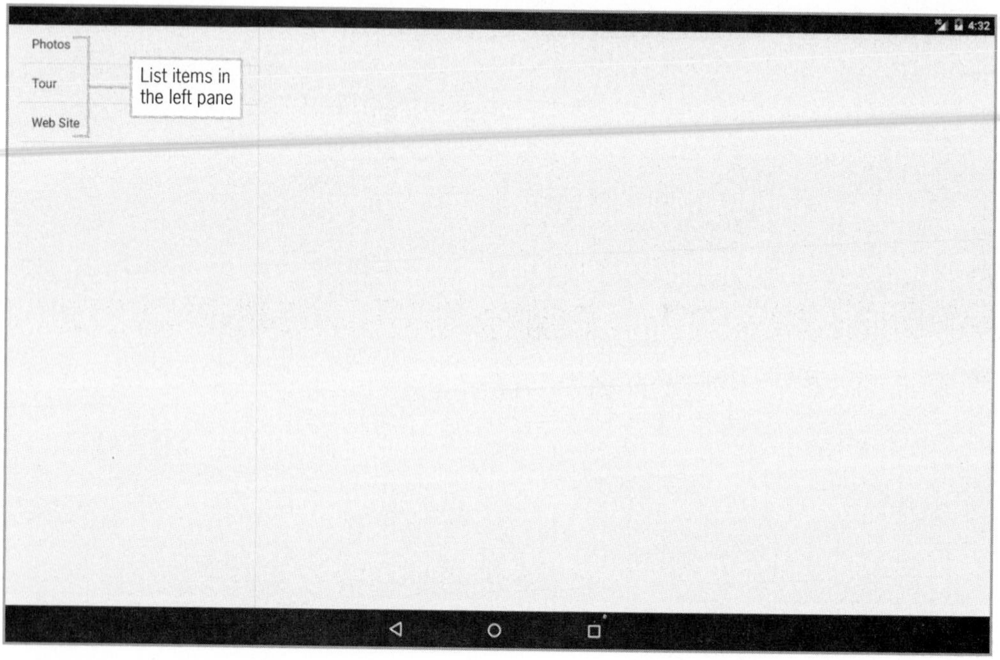

Figure 9-1 Opening screen of the Bike and Barge tablet app

This Android tablet app provides images, text, and a link that opens a webpage within the Android browser. If the user selects Photos, which is the first item in the left pane, a TableLayout displays three images with text descriptions in the right pane as shown in Figure 9-2. When the user taps Tour, the second list item on the left, the item details in the right pane change to display tour information, as shown in Figure 9-3. Web Site, the third list item, links to a browser that displays the full Bike and Barge website, including tour company contact information, as shown in Figure 9-4. The intuitive list items eliminate the need for additional instructions for navigation.

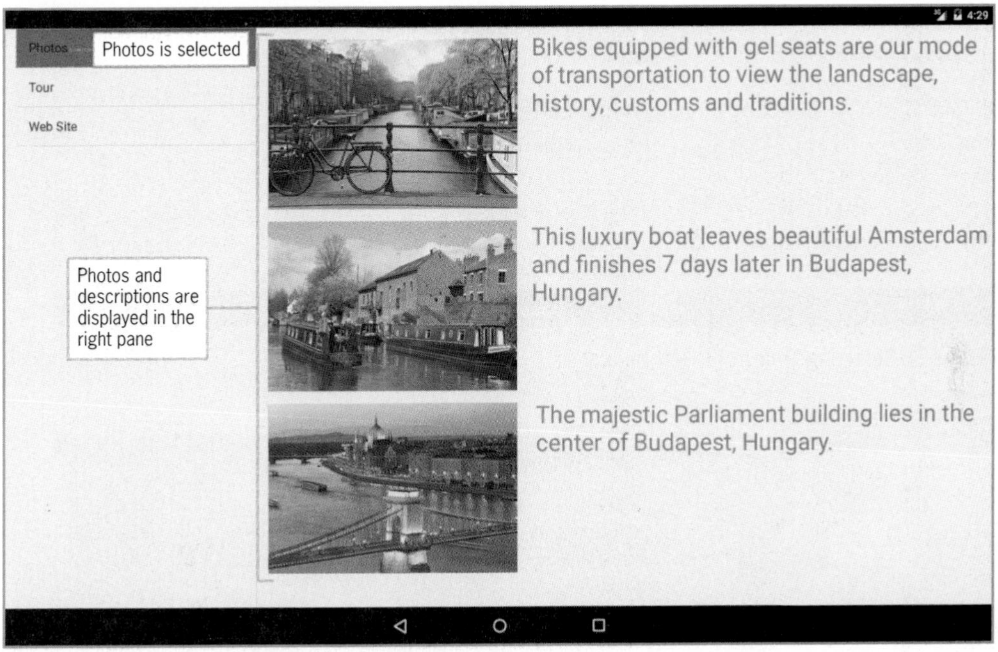

Figure 9-2 Selecting Photos in the left pane

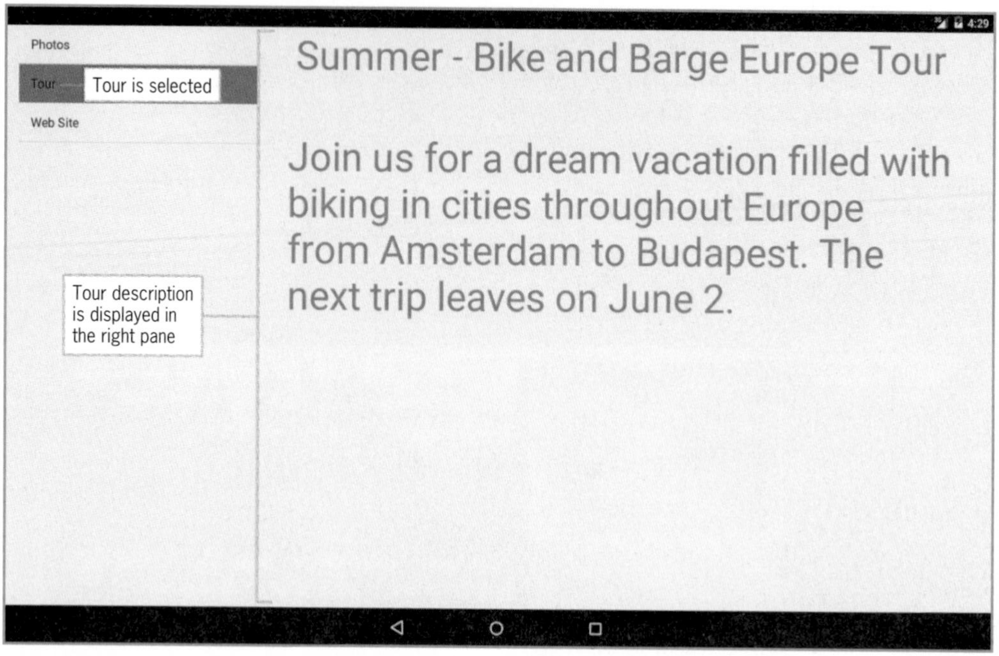

Figure 9-3 Selecting Tour in the left pane

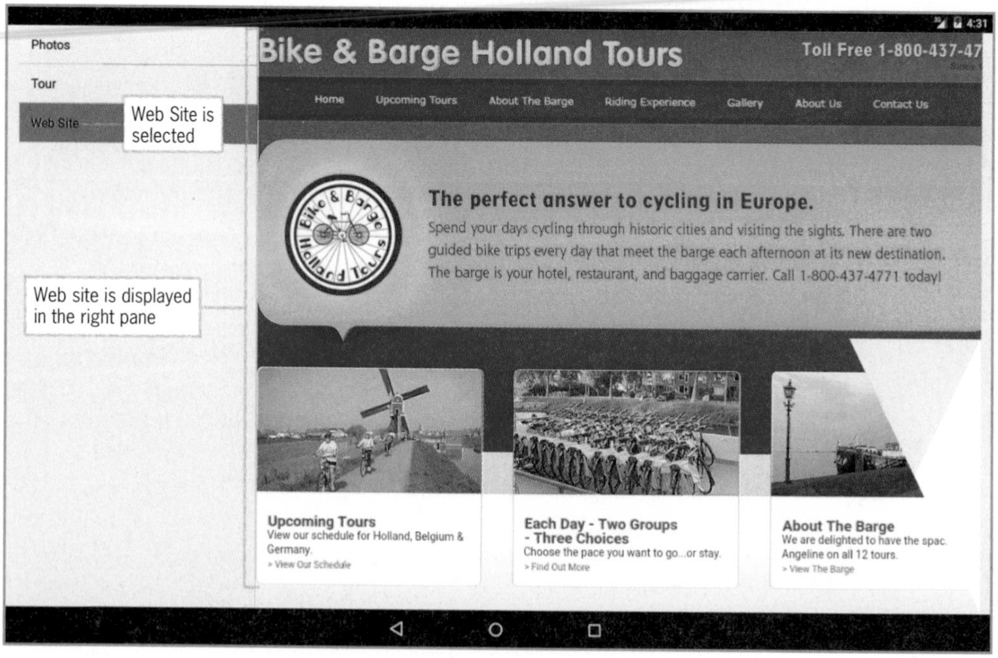

Source: bikebarge.com

Figure 9-4 Selecting Web Site in the left pane

IN THE TRENCHES
Cycling apps already in Google Play include GPS-based biking routes, personal cycling logs, mountain biking trails, bike repair, distance tracking, and cycling fitness to use on your trip. In addition, these apps can often be used on Android watches.

To create this application, the developer must understand how to perform the following processes, among others:

1. Create a Master/Detail Flow template app.
2. Add the images to the drawable folder.
3. Add text to the String table.
4. Create the photos.xml TableLayout XML file for the details pane of the first list item.
5. Create the tour.xml file for the details pane of the second list item.
6. Change the default TextView widget to a WebView widget.
7. Update the Android Manifest file to include an Internet permission.
8. Customize the DummyContent class to display the item list.
9. Customize the DummyContent class to connect to the website.
10. Modify the ItemDetailFragment.java class to:
    a. Display the photos.xml in the details pane.
    b. Display the tour.xml in the details pane.
    c. Display a website in a browser.

GTK
Watch out for that stretched-out look! On tablets, single-pane layouts lead to awkward white space and excessive line lengths. Use padding to reduce the width of UI elements and consider using multipane layouts.

Understanding Responsive Design

When mobile devices first were developed, the apps displayed simple text content designed for small screens, but the tablet and smartphone landscape can now handle complicated processes and full web access. This design approach is especially true for the Android platform. Instead of developers creating apps for multiple sizes of Android devices, apps and webpages should be developed once for a wide range of displays. **Responsive design** is an approach to designing apps and websites that provide an optimal viewing experience across as many devices as possible. Similarities between webpages and Android apps do not end with screen sizes. When building for the web, designers also have to take into account multiple browsers and multiple versions of each one. Earlier in this book, you learned to use scalable pixels to change the size of text or margins as appropriate for the device resolution, but more tools are necessary for a complete approach to designing for all device sizes. To assist with responsive design in recent Android API versions, Android Studio has responsive design templates, which allow you to build the app once, but display it on multiple devices. You can run the Bike and Barge app on a smartphone emulator as shown in Figure 9-5 without any change in code. The first screen shows the list of items. If you select Web Site, a separate Activity is displayed on the smartphone showing the Bike and Barge website.

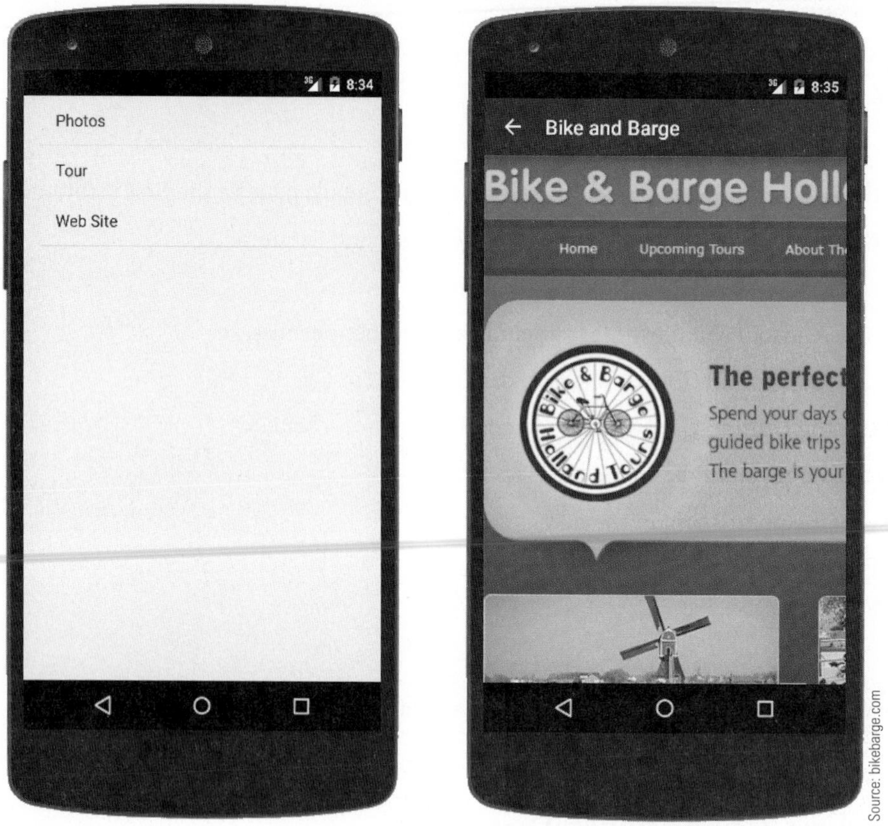

Opening screen

Screen after selecting Web Site

Figure 9-5 Bike and Barge app runs as two Activities on a smartphone

GTK
Adobe Dreamweaver Creative Cloud is the most popular tool to build responsive design websites.

Using Application Templates

The Android Studio software development kit provides tools for quickly creating Android apps that follow the Android design and development guidelines and include code that can be customized to the exact needs of your app. These tools are called **application templates**; you use them to create basic Android applications that you can immediately run and test on an Android device of any size. Android templates are available when you create a new Android project, as shown in Figure 9-6. Throughout this text, you selected the Blank Activity, but in this chapter's project app, you use the Master/Detail Flow application template.

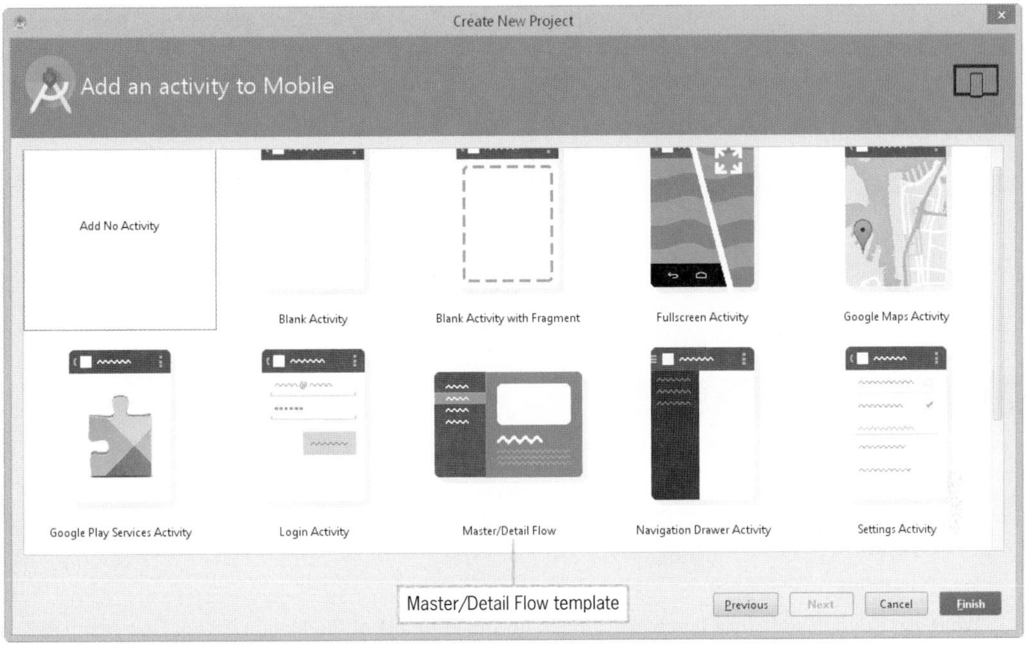

Figure 9-6 Android application templates

Master/Detail Flow Template

The Bike and Barge tablet app features an opening screen with three list items on the left, as shown in Figure 9-1. List items function as they do in a framed browser window. A menu of list items on the left of a browser window displays webpage content using intuitive navigation on the right side of the page. You can switch between items on the list to display new content without opening more browser windows. The **Master/Detail Flow template** creates an adaptive, responsive layout for a set of list items and associated detail content. The Master list appears in a narrow vertical pane along the left edge of the screen. Without any customization, the Master/Detail Flow template as shown in Figure 9-7 can be displayed on a tablet or on a smartphone. On a tablet, the master item appears in a narrow vertical pane along the left edge of the screen. The item details are displayed on the right side of the tablet screen in the wider detail pane. This arrangement is referred to as a two-pane layout. The Master/Detail Flow template is considered a responsive screen design. On a smaller device, the list and details are displayed on separate screens when you select a list item.

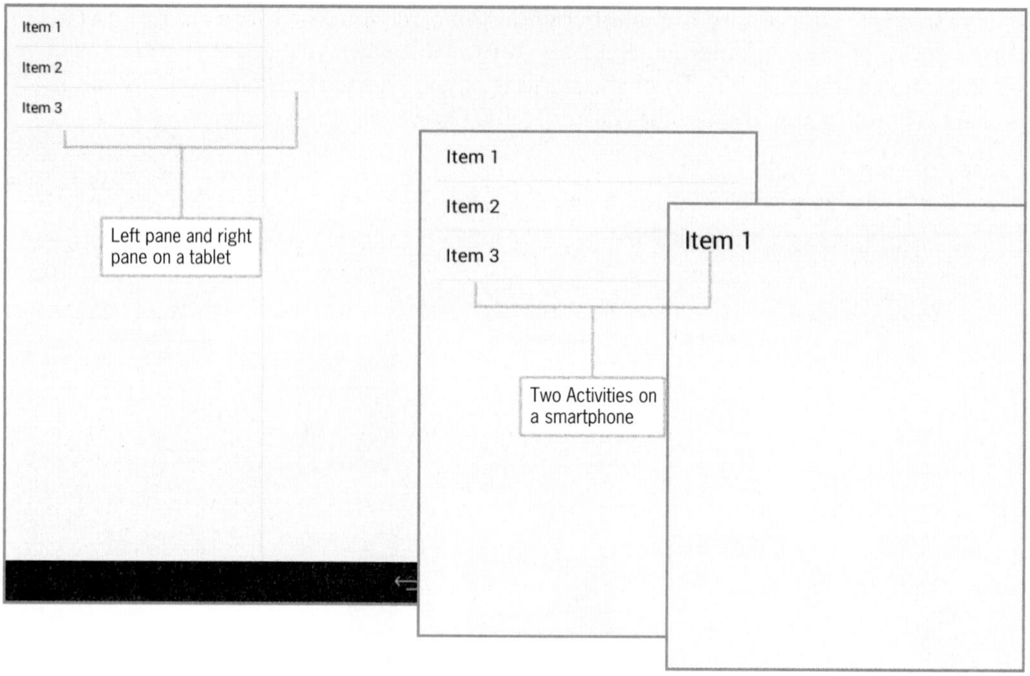

Figure 9-7 Master/Detail Flow template on a tablet and a smartphone

Critical Thinking

What are examples of other types of list items for the left pane of the Master/Detail Flow template?

A list can include items such as news stories, songs, movies, pets, or homes for sale. When the list item is selected, the details for the specific item is displayed in the right pane.

To begin the application using the Master/Detail Flow template on the tablet, follow these steps.

STEP 1

- Open the Android Studio program.
- Tap or click the Start a new Android Studio project selection in the Quick Start category.
- In the Create New Project dialog box, type **Bike and Barge** in the Application name text box.
- If necessary, in the Company Domain text box, type **androidbootcamp.net** and in the Project location text box, type **D:\Workspace\BikeandBarge**.
- Tap or click the Next button on the Configure your new project page of the Create New Project dialog box.
- If necessary, tap or click the Phone and Tablet check box to select the form factor for your app.
- Change the Minimum SDK to API 13: Android 3.2 (Honeycomb), the first API generation that includes tablet designs.

The new Bike and Barge project has an application name and a package name (Figure 9-8).

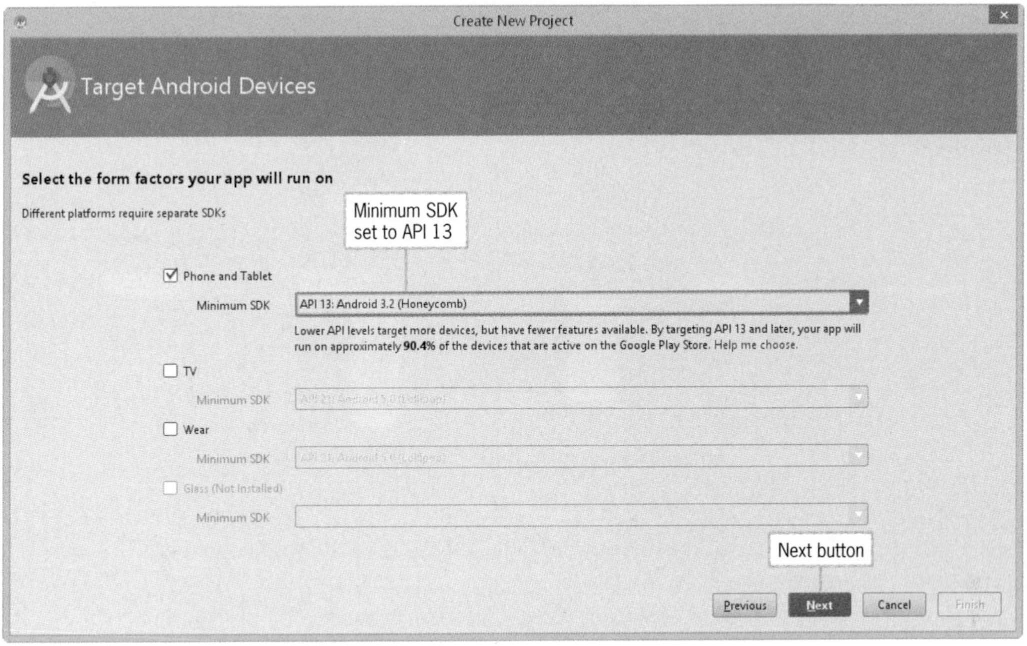

Figure 9-8 Creating the Bike and Barge Android app

STEP 2

- Tap or click the Next button.
- Select the Master/Detail Flow template in the list of Activities.

The Master/Detail Flow template is selected (Figure 9-9).

Figure 9-9 Selecting the Master/Detail Flow template

STEP 3

- Tap or click the Next button. By default, the Object Kind and Title are set to Item and the Object Kind Plural is set to Items.

The Master/Detail Flow template automatically enters the Item as the Object Kind and Title settings and Items as the Object Kind Plural setting (Figure 9-10).

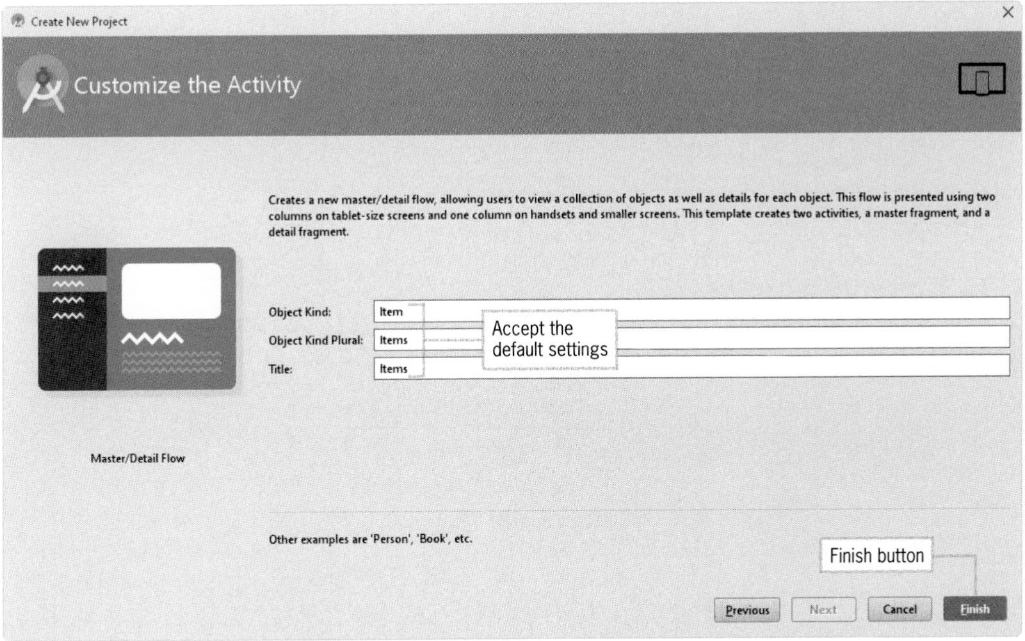

Figure 9-10 Entering the object settings

STEP 4

- Tap or click the Finish button to create the new application based on the Master/Detail Flow template.
- Tap or click the screen size arrow button and then select Nexus 10 (10.1", 2560 × 1600: xhdpi).

Understanding the Structure of the Master/Detail Flow Template

When the Bike and Barge app is created as shown in Figure 9-11, Android Studio adds a number of Java and XML layout resource files automatically.

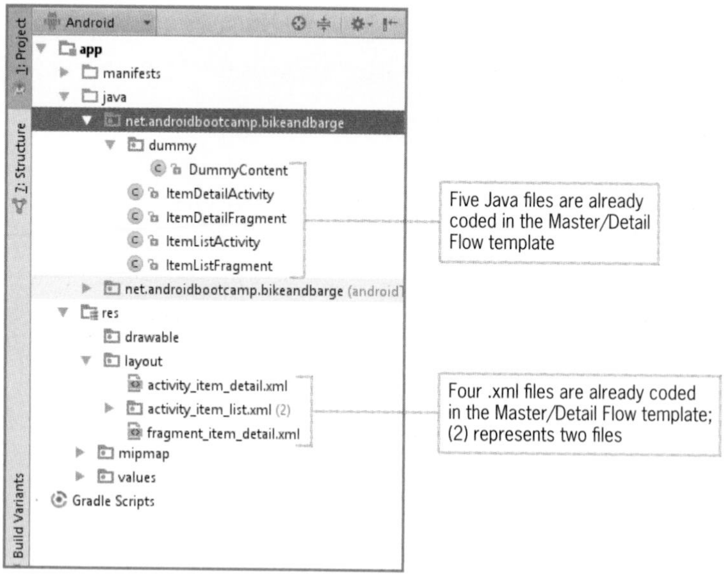

Figure 9-11 Template code files in the java folder

Each of the Java and layout files in the Master/Detail Flow template has a specific purpose, as described in the following lists. Most of these files will not be altered in the development of the Bike and Barge app.

Java Files

- *ItemDetailActivity.java*: The purpose of this class is to display the activity_item_detail.xml layout file if a smartphone is detected.
- *ItemDetailFragment.java*: The purpose of this class is to display the fragment_item_detail.xml layout file. This class can be customized to determine which detailed items to display.
- *ItemListActivity.java*: The purpose of this initial Activity is to display the master list in a two-pane mode if a tablet device is detected or to launch a second Activity to display the detail items if a smaller device is detected.
- *ItemListFragment.java*: The purpose of this class is to display the activity_item_list.xml layout file.
- *DummyContent.java*: The purpose of this Java file is to provide sample code you customize to suit your specific app content.

Layout Files

- *activity_item_detail.xml*: When a smartphone is detected, the app uses this layout to display the FrameLayout instance.
- activity_item_list.xml(2): Contains two files:
  - *activity_item_list.xml* is displayed when a smartphone is detected; the app uses this layout to display the master list fragment.
  - *activity_item_list.xml* (sw600dp) is displayed when a tablet is detected; the app is displayed in a two-pane layout containing both the master item list fragment and the item detail container.
- *fragment_item_detail.xml*: When a smartphone or a tablet is detected, this layout file displays the detail pane using the onCreateView( ) method.

Adding Images to the Drawable Folder

Before designing the XML layouts, first place three images in the drawable folder and then reference them in the photos.xml layout. To add the images for this project, follow this step:

STEP 1

- Open the USB folder containing the student files.
- To add the three image files to the drawable resource folder, select the bike.png, barge.png, and budapest.png files and then press Ctrl+C to copy the files.
- To add the three image files to the drawable resource folder, press and hold or right-click the drawable folder and then tap or click Paste.
- Tap or click the OK button in the Copy dialog box.

Copies of the three files appear in the drawable folder (Figure 9-12).

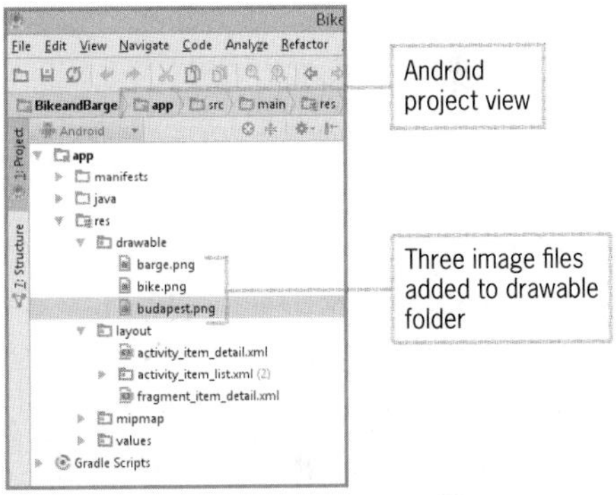

Figure 9-12 Image files for the Bike and Barge app

Designing an XML TableLayout

When the user selects the first list item in the Bike and Barge app, three images are displayed in a table: a bike in Amsterdam, a barge passenger boat on the Danube River, and the Parliament building in Budapest. Each image has a text description in an XML TableLayout as shown in Figure 9-2. In Android Studio, a TableLayout can be used to arrange images and text in rows and columns just like a table in Microsoft Word. Each row within a TableLayout is associated with a TableRow instance, which is divided into cells. In the chapter project, you create this layout in a new layout resource file named photos.xml.

Critical Thinking

How can I create a wider TableRow within a TableLayout?

The size of each TableRow is determined by the size of the text or image placed within the TableRow. If you want the TableRow to be wider, change the size of the text or image.

The String table, responsible for the text displayed in the app, has two initial strings in the template. The first string is named appName and is displayed in the title bar of the tablet. By default, it is set to Bike and Barge, the application name. The second string is named title_item_detail and is displayed in the title bar of a smaller device such as a smartphone. By default, it is set to Item Detail. This text should be changed to Bike and Barge to create a consistent experience whether someone is using a tablet or smartphone. An image description appears for each of the three images in the app. To create a String table for the text descriptions necessary throughout the app and to code the XML layout for photos.xml, follow these steps:

STEP 1

- In the Android Project view, expand the values folder within the res folder.
- Double-tap or double-click the strings.xml file to display its contents.
- Tap or click the Open editor link.
- Tap or click title_item_detail in the String table and change the text in the Value text box to **Bike and Barge**.
- Tap or click the Add Key button.
- In the Key text box, type **txtBike** to name the string.
- In the Default Value text box, type **Bikes equipped with gel seats are our mode of transportation to view the landscape, history, customs and traditions.**
- Tap or click the OK button, and then tap or click the Add Key button.
- In the Key text box, type **txtBarge** to name the string.
- In the Default Value text box, type **This luxury boat leaves beautiful Amsterdam and finishes 7 days later in Budapest, Hungary.**
- Tap or click the OK button, and then tap or click the Add Key button.

- In the Key text box, type **txtBudapest** to name the string.
- In the Default Value text box, type **The majestic Parliament building lies in the center of Budapest, Hungary.**
- Tap or click the OK button, and then tap or click the Add Key button.
- In the Key text box, type **txtTitle** to name the string.
- In the Default Value text box, type **Summer - Bike and Barge Europe Tour**.
- Tap or click the OK button, and then tap or click the Add Key button.
- In the Key text box, type **txtInfo** to name the string.
- In the Default Value text box, type **Join us for a dream vacation filled with biking in cities throughout Europe from Amsterdam to Budapest. The next trip leaves on June 2.**
- Tap or click the OK button, and then tap or click the Add Key button.
- In the Key text box, type **txtDescription** to name the string.
- In the DefaultValue text box, type **Bike and Barge Image**.
- Tap or click the OK button and then save your work.

The Keys and Default Values of the TextView controls are entered into the Translations Editor (Figure 9-13).

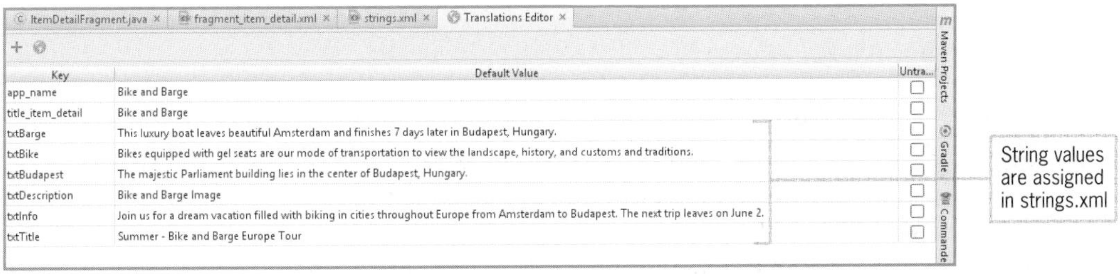

Figure 9-13 String table for the Bike and Barge app

STEP 2

- Close the Translations Editor and the strings.xml tabs.
- In the Android project view, collapse the drawable and values subfolders.
- Press and hold or right-click the layout folder, tap or click New on the shortcut menu, and then tap or click Layout resource file to open the New Resource File dialog box.
- In the File name text box, type **photos.xml** to name the layout file.
- In the Root element text box, type **TableLayout**.
- Tap or click the OK button to create an XML layout file named photos.xml.

- Tap or click the Go to next state button on the Standard toolbar and then select Switch to Landscape to display the emulated tablet in landscape mode.
- Tap or click the Text tab of photos.xml at the bottom of the window.

The XML file is named photos.xml and the layout is set to TableLayout. The photos.xml code is displayed (Figure 9-14).

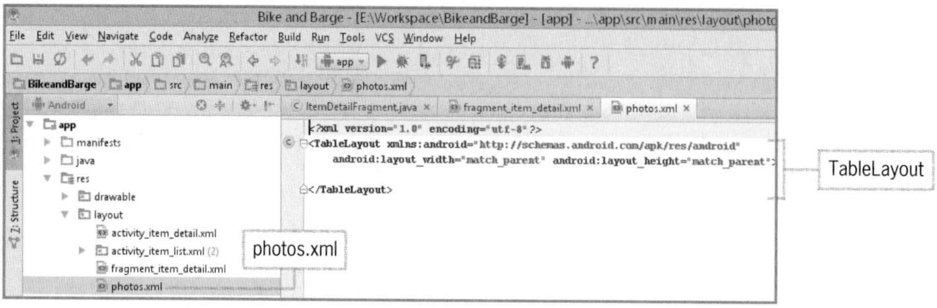

Figure 9-14 photos.xml created

STEP 3

- Display line numbers and starting on Line 4 of photos.xml, type the following code to add a table row that displays an image and text:

```
<TableRow>
  <ImageView
    android:id="@+id/imgBike"
    android:contentDescription="@string/txtDescription"
    android:layout_width="wrap_content"
    android:layout_height="wrap_content"
    android:src="@drawable/bike"
    android:padding="15sp" />
  <TextView
    android:layout_width="600dp"
    android:layout_height="wrap_content"
    android:text="@string/txtBike"
    android:textSize="30sp"/>
</TableRow>
```

A table row displays an ImageView and TextView control in the TableLayout (Figure 9-15).

Go to next state button ↑ Standard Toolbar

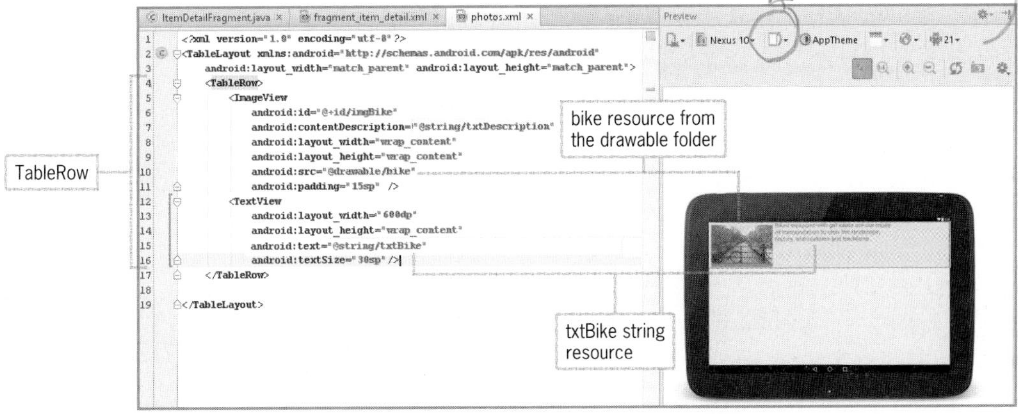

Waltraud Ingerl/E+/Getty Images

Figure 9-15 First row of the TableLayout

STEP 4

- Copy the TableRow commands from Step 3, paste them two times in the photos.xml code, and then customize the new commands to match the following code:

```
<TableRow>
  <ImageView
    android:id="@+id/imgBarge"
    android:contentDescription="@string/txtDescription"
    android:layout_width="wrap_content"
    android:layout_height="wrap_content"
    android:src="@drawable/barge"
    android:padding="15sp" />
  <TextView
    android:layout_width="600dp"
    android:layout_height="wrap_content"
    android:text="@string/txtBarge"
    android:textSize="30sp"/>
</TableRow>
<TableRow>
  <ImageView
    android:id="@+id/imgBudapest"
    android:contentDescription="@string/txtDescription"
    android:layout_width="wrap_content"
    android:layout_height="wrap_content"
    android:src="@drawable/budapest"
    android:padding="15sp" />
  <TextView
    android:layout_width="600dp"
    android:layout_height="wrap_content"
    android:text="@string/txtBudapest"
    android:textSize="30sp"/>
</TableRow>
```

reducing in TextView the layout_width to 400 instead of 600 and the textSize to 20sp instead of 30sp makes the full length of text to display correctly

padding to 10sp instead of 15 (if it is 15, the third images dislays smaller)

The second and third table rows display more ImageView and TextView controls in the TableLayout (Figure 9-16).

Figure 9-16 Second and third rows of the TableLayout

STEP 5

- Tap or click the Design tab at the bottom of the window.
- Tap or click the Save All button on the Standard toolbar.

The TableLayout is displayed in the emulator for photos.xml (Figure 9-17).

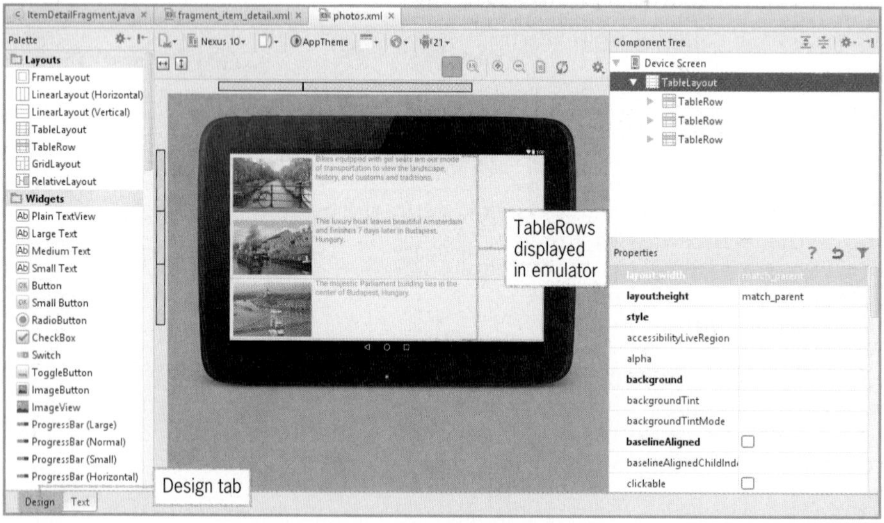

Figure 9-17 Completed TableLayout in photos.xml

Creating a TextView XML Layout for the Second List Item

For the second list item of the Bike and Barge app, two TextView controls display the tour details within the LinearLayout. To create an XML layout file that displays two TextView controls, follow these steps:

STEP 1

- Close the photos.xml tab.
- In the Android project view, press and hold or right-click the layout folder, tap or click New on the shortcut menu, and then tap or click Android resource file to open the New Resource File dialog box.
- In the File name text box, type **tour.xml** to name the layout file.
- Tap or click the OK button to create an XML layout with a default LinearLayout and open the emulator window.
- Tap or click the Go to next state button on the Standard toolbar, and then select Switch to Landscape to display the tablet interface in landscape mode.
- Tap or click Text tab at the bottom of the window and then show line numbers.
- Starting on Line 5, type the following XML code for the first TextView control using auto-completion as much as possible:

```
<TextView
  android:id="@+id/txtTitle"
  android:layout_width="wrap_content"
  android:layout_height="wrap_content"
  android:text="@string/txtTitle"
  android:textSize="50sp"
  android:paddingLeft="50sp"
  android:paddingBottom="60sp" />
```

The first TextView control is coded in tour.xml with a LinearLayout (Figure 9-18).

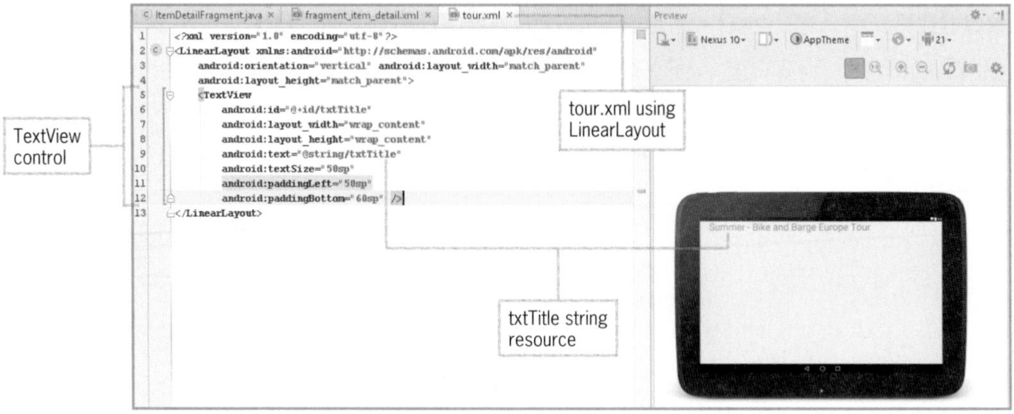

Figure 9-18 LinearLayout for tour.xml

STEP 2

- Press the Enter key, and then type the following XML code for the second TextView control using auto-completion as much as possible:

```
<TextView
  android:id="@+id/txtInfo"
  android:layout_width="wrap_content"
  android:layout_height="wrap_content"
  android:text="@string/txtInfo"
  android:textSize="50sp"
  android:paddingLeft="40sp"
  android:paddingRight="40sp" />
```

- Save your work.

The second TextView control is coded in tour.xml (Figure 9-19).

Figure 9-19 Second TextView control in tour.xml

Creating a WebView XML Layout for the Third List Item

Initially the Master/Detail Flow template displays each list item using the TextView object displayed in the fragment_item_detail.xml layout file. In the Bike and Barge app, if the user selects the first list item, the photos.xml layout is displayed, and if the user selects the second list item, the tour.xml layout is shown. The third list item in the Bike and Barge app uses the default fragment_item_detail.xml layout, but its TextView object cannot display a webpage. Instead, the TextView control must be changed to a **WebView** object, a View widget that displays webpages. The WebView object allows you to place a web browser or simply display some online content within your Activity. The WebView object uses a built-in rendering engine to display webpages.

After placing the WebView object in the XML layout of the app, you must add Internet permissions to the Android Manifest file in order for your Activity to access the Internet and load webpages. A **permission** is a restriction limiting access to a part of the code or to data on the device. The permission protects critical data and code that could be misused to cause issues for your app and others. Permissions can be set in the Android Manifest file within an Android app to allow certain actions such as to set the background wallpaper, check the device's power levels, read your contacts, write events to your calendar, and display a webpage. Every Android application must have an AndroidManifest.xml file in its app directory. The Android Manifest file presents essential information about an app to the Android system, information the system must have before it can run the code of the application. The AndroidManifest.xml file declares the theme, each Activity run within the application, and permissions necessary for the application to interact with other applications. Without the proper permission, attempts to access the Internet or complete similar actions will fail. The general structure of the AndroidManifest.xml is as follows:

```
<?xml version="1.0" encoding="utf-8"?>
<manifest>
    <uses-permission />
    <permission />
       <application>
          icon
           label
           theme
        <activity>
            <intent-filter>
                <action />
                <category />
                <data />
            </intent-filter>
            <meta-data />
        </activity>
    </application>
</manifest>
```

Code Syntax

Following is the code syntax for requesting permission to connect to the Internet within the AndroidManifest.xml file:

```
<uses-permission android:name="android.permission.INTERNET" />
```

To change the TextView control to a WebView control in the fragment_item_detail.xml layout file and to add permission for the WebView widget to use the Internet within the app, follow these steps:

STEP 1

- Close the tour.xml tab.
- If necessary, expand the layout folder and double-tap or double-click the fragment_item_detail.xml layout file to open it.
- Tap or click the Text tab to display the default TextView control code.
- Show line numbers.
- In Line 1, change TextView to **WebView**.

The WebView control replaces the TextView control, enabling the fragment_item_detail.xml layout to display a webpage (Figure 9-20).

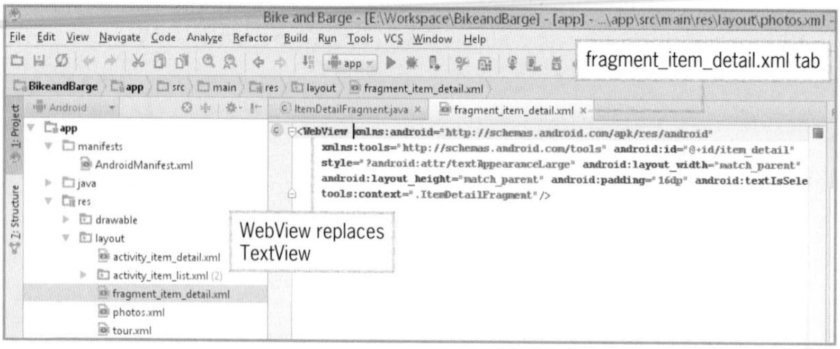

Figure 9-20 TextView control is changed to a WebView control

STEP 2

- Save your work and close the fragment_item_detail.xml tab.
- To set the permissions for the webpage to open in the app, expand the manifests folder in the Android project view.
- Double-tap or double-click the AndroidManifest.xml file and show line numbers.
- Tap or click Line 4 and then type **<uses-permission android:name="android.permission.INTERNET"** /> to add permission to connect the WebView control to the Internet.

The permission to connect to the Internet is set within the AndroidManifest.xml file before the application code begins (Figure 9-21).

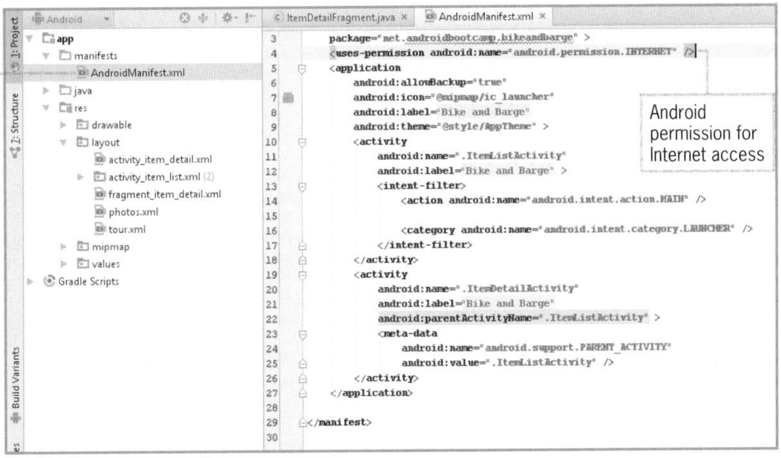

Figure 9-21 Setting permission for WebView control to connect to the Internet

GTK

If you run the app without the Internet permission, the error "The webpage at the site could not be loaded because: net::ERR_CACHE_MISS" appears when you tap or click the website list item.

Customizing the Item List

The Master/Detail Flow template provides a folder named dummy in the net.androidbootcamp.bikeandbarge folder that contains a Java class file named DummyContent.java. The purpose of this class is to provide sample content to display in the user interface of the template. This class can be customized or replaced by classes that are fully created from scratch. In Lines 27–30 of the DummyContent.java, three items are added in the following sample code:

Code Syntax

```
// Add 3 sample items.
       addItem(new DummyItem("1", "Item 1"));
       addItem(new DummyItem("2", "Item 2"));
       addItem(new DummyItem("3", "Item 3"));
```

The command addItem displays list items in the left pane of the tablet display or in the first Activity display of a smartphone. You can add more addItem commands if your app has more than three list items. In the Bike and Barge app, the list items should display the text Photos (Item 1), Tour (Item 2), and Web Site (Item 3). The third item is different from the first two items because selecting it displays the bikebarge.com site in the right pane of the tablet screen.

Because it displays the website within the app in the detail pane, the Bike and Barge app is different from the Chicago City Guide app designed in Chapter 5, which launched the phone's built-in browser to display the city websites.

The DummyContent.java file by default is displayed in a two-pane layout on a tablet with a TextView control displayed in the detail pane. Because the TextView control cannot display a website, you specify the WebView control in the fragment_item_detail.xml page, which can display webpages. To specify the home page of the Bike and Barge website as the content to display in the WebView control, you add code to the addItem statement in the DummyContent.java file. Originally the addItem statement contains two strings: the id number to identify the user's selection and the string Item1, which is displayed in the item list in the left pane of the tablet. When the website is added to the third item, you must modify the code to contain three String objects: the id, the item list string, and the website URL. The original DummyItem class, which is coded to handle two String objects shown below, must be updated to handle three String objects.

Original DummyItem Class Syntax

```
public static class DummyItem {
        public String id;
        public String content;
        public DummyItem(String id, String content) {
              this.id = id;
              this.content = content;
        }
}
```

Modified DummyItem Class Syntax Including a New Constructor to Handle the Website URL

```
public static class DummyItem {
      public String id;
      public String content;
      public String item_name;
      public String item_url;
      public DummyItem(String id, String content) {
        this.id = id;
        this.content = content;
      }
public DummyItem(String id, String item_name, String item_url) {
      {
            this.id = id;
            this.item_name = item_name;
            this.item_url = item_url;
            content=item_name;
        }
  }
}
```

The auto-generated construct stub is created when you add the constructor. Constructors are used to initialize the instance variables of an object. The id is the string value assigned to the user's selection in the item list. The item_name is the string value displayed in the list item in the left pane of the tablet. The item_url variable is assigned to the website displayed in the detail pane. To customize the display of the list items in the DummyContent.java file within the template, follow these steps:

STEP 1

- Save your work and close the AndroidManifest.xml tab.
- If necessary, expand the java folder and the first net.androidbootcamp.bikeandbarge folder in the Android Project view.
- Expand the dummy folder.
- Double-tap or double-click the DummyContent.java class and then show line numbers.
- On Line 28, replace Item 1 with the text **Photos**.
- On the next line, replace Item 2 with the text **Tour**.
- On the next line, replace the existing code with the statement: **addItem(new DummyItem("3", "Web Site", "http://bikebarge.com"));**

The DummyContent.java file is customized with the item list in the left pane of the tablet (Figure 9-22). A red line appears below the code for the third list item.

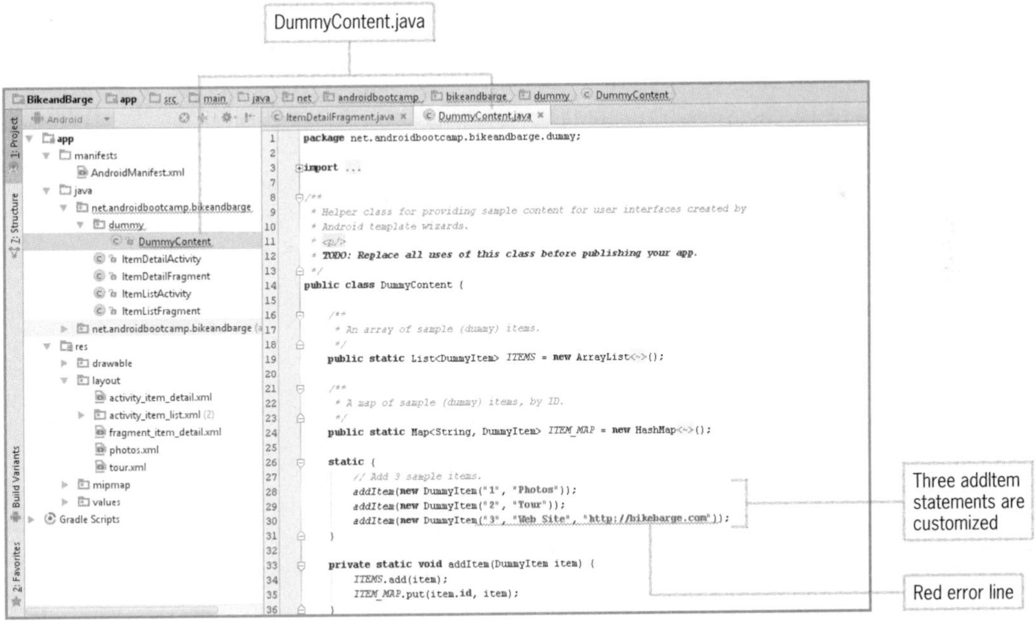

Figure 9-22 DummyContent.java content file

STEP 2

- To handle the three string addItem statements, which display the three strings, and to modify the DummyItem class, tap or click the third list item code with a red wavy line to view a light bulb at the beginning of the line.
- Tap or click the light bulb and select Create Constructor to add a constructor named public DummyItem as an auto-generated constructor stub.
- In the auto-generated constructor stub in Line 50, modify the statement public DummyItem (String string, String string2, String string3) { to:

```
public DummyItem(String id, String item_name, String item_url) {
```

The DummyItem constructor is added to handle the third list item (Figure 9-23).

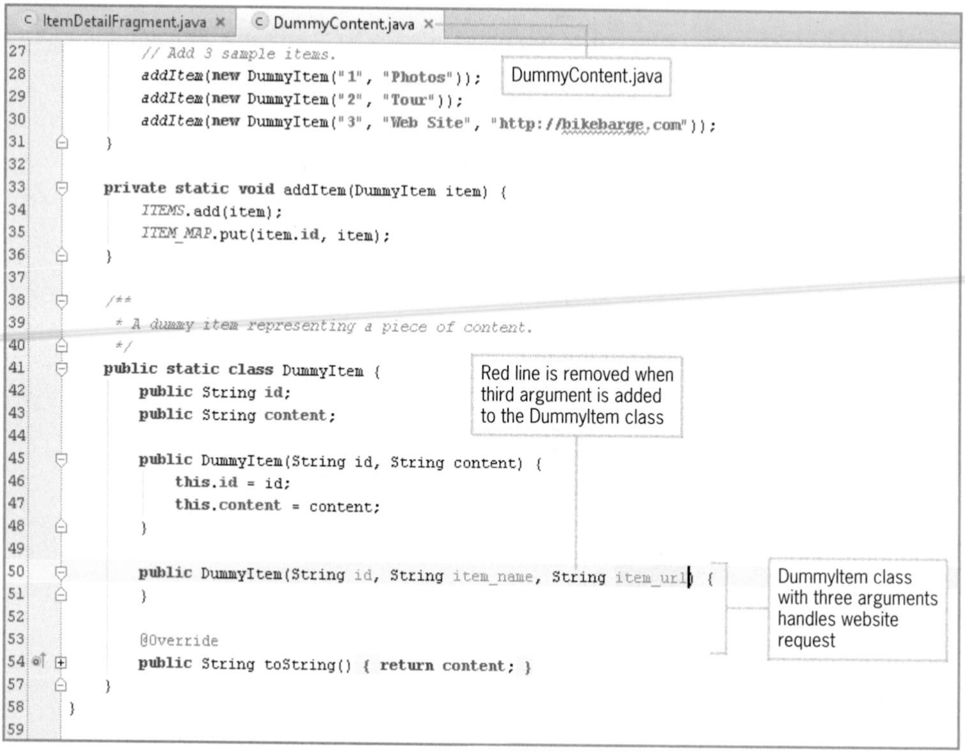

Figure 9-23 Customizing the DummyItem class

STEP 3

- To declare the item_name and item_url variables in the DummyItem class, add the two declaration statements below the public String content statement starting on Line 44:

```
public String item_name;
public String item_url;
```

- Tap or click at the end of Line 52 and then press Enter.
- Starting on Line 53 in the DummyItem auto-generated constructor stub, assign the following variables for the id, item_name, and item_url:

```
this.id = id;
this.item_name = item_name;
this.item_url = item_url;
content = item_name;
```

The DummyContent class is coded to handle the website request for the third list item (Figure 9-24).

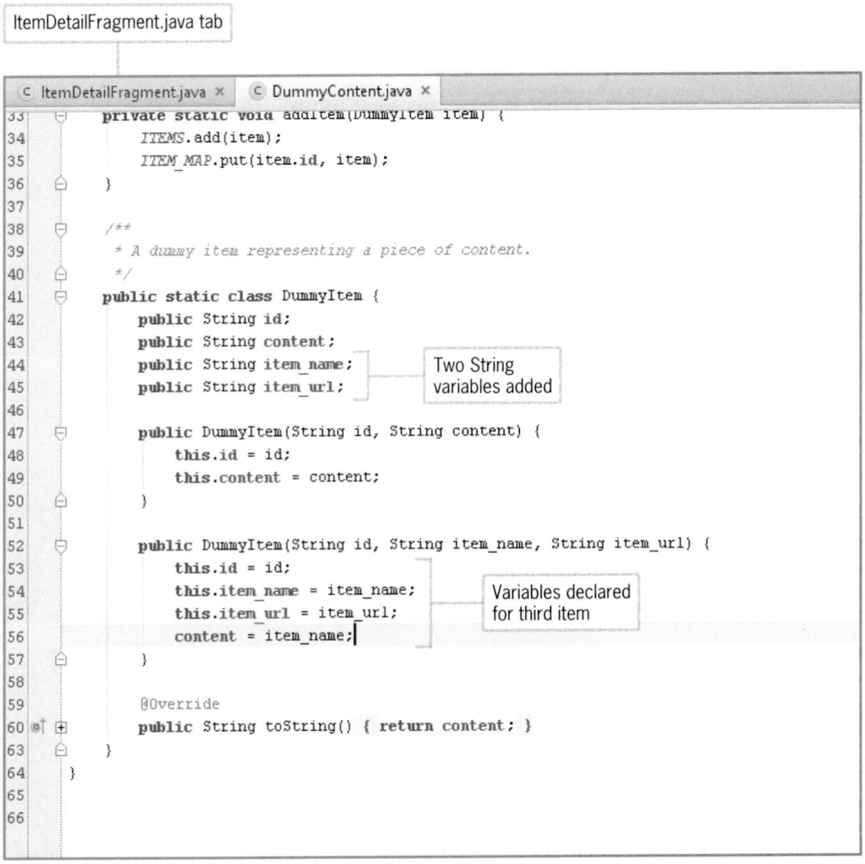

Figure 9-24 DummyContent class handles the third item to display a website

Displaying the Custom Layout in the Detail Pane

According to the design of the Bike and Barge app, if the user selects the first item, the photos.xml layout is displayed in the detail pane. If the user selects the second item, the tour.xml layout is displayed in the detail pane. If the user selects the third item, the WebView in the template fragment_item_detail.xml file displays the home page of the Bike and Barge website. To display the correct details in the right pane, the ItemDetailFragment.java file works with a **fragment**, which is a piece of an application's user interface or behavior that can be placed in an Activity. A fragment is essentially a sub-Activity hosted inside another Activity. By dividing components of the user interface and displaying them in fragments, it is easier for developers to reuse these components across various Activities. For example, in the chapter project, a fragment is displayed in the right pane, while the left pane remains unchanged. Android introduced fragments in Android 3.2, API level 13, primarily to support more dynamic and flexible user interface designs on large screens.

Three conditional if statements are necessary in the ItemDetailFragment.java file. In the DummyContent.java file, the variable id was set to the string value of the user's selection of the three list items. To determine if two String objects match exactly, you should use the **.equals method**, not the == operator. The == operator compares two objects to determine whether they are exactly the same object. Two strings may be different objects, but have the same exact characters. The .equals() method is used to compare strings for equality. When you compare the value of a string, the following syntax is necessary in Java:

Code Syntax

```
if (mItem.id.equals("1")) {
    }
```

Within the ItemDetailFragment.java file, the following code displays a custom XML layout file named photos.xml in the details pane:

Code Syntax

```
View rootView = inflater.inflate(R.layout.photos, container, false);
```

The inflate method has three arguments: The first part displays the XML layout, the second part applies the layout parameters to the container, and the third part is false, a Boolean type declaring that that layout was already passed to the container.

To display the webpage URL with the variable named item_url within the WebView widget, the following syntax is necessary:

Code Syntax

```
((WebView)
rootView.findViewById(R.id.item_detail)).loadUrl(mItem.item_url);
```

To code the three conditional if statements to display the XML layout and the webpage within the detail pane, complete the following steps:

STEP 1

- Save your work and close the DummyContent.java tab.
- If necessary, open the ItemDetailFragment.java file, which displays the layout files for the detail list in the right pane of the tablet, and then show line numbers.
- Scroll down and delete Lines 56–58, which originally displayed the detail list in a TextView widget.
- Starting on Line 56, and type the following code to display the XML layout if the first list item is selected:

```
if (mItem.id.equals("1")) {
        rootView = inflater.inflate(R.layout.photos, container, false);
}
```

- Starting on the next line, type the following code to display the XML layout if the second list item is selected:

```
if (mItem.id.equals("2")) {
        rootView = inflater.inflate(R.layout.tour, container, false);
}
```

The first and second list items are displayed in the detail pane with their corresponding XML layout (Figure 9-25).

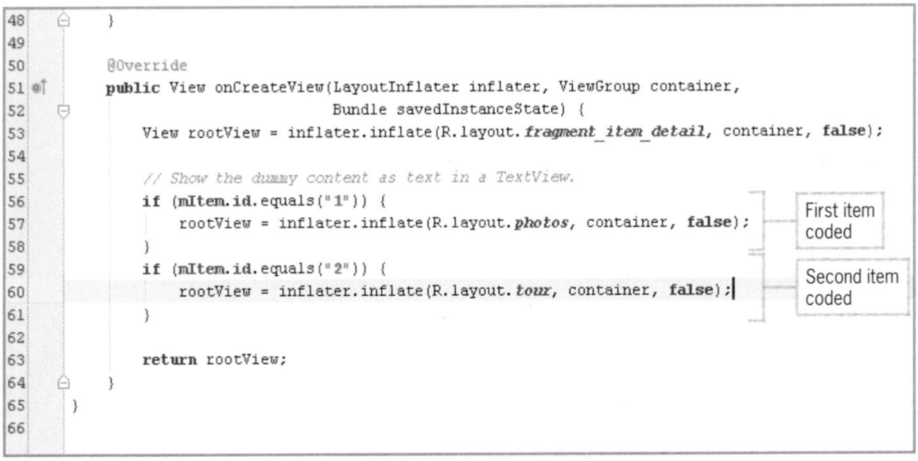

Figure 9-25 ItemDetailFragment.java class customized for the first and second items

STEP 2

- On the next line, type the following code to display the Bike and Barge home page if the third list item is selected:

```
if (mItem.id.equals("3")) {
      ((WebView)rootView.findViewById(R.id.item_detail)).loadUrl(mItem.
      item_url);
}
```

- Tap or click WebView and press Alt+Enter to import the class.

The third list item displays the Bike and Barge URL in a WebView widget (Figure 9-26).

```
    @Override
    public View onCreateView(LayoutInflater inflater, ViewGroup container,
                             Bundle savedInstanceState) {
        View rootView = inflater.inflate(R.layout.fragment_item_detail, container, false);

        // Show the dummy content as text in a TextView.
        if (mItem.id.equals("1")) {
            rootView = inflater.inflate(R.layout.photos, container, false);
        }
        if (mItem.id.equals("2")) {
            rootView = inflater.inflate(R.layout.tour, container, false);
        }
        if (mItem.id.equals("3")) {
            ((WebView)rootView.findViewById(R.id.item_detail)).loadUrl(mItem.item_url);
        }
        return rootView;
    }
}
```

Third detail pane displays Bike and Barge website

Figure 9-26 ItemDetailFragment.java class customized for the third item

STEP 3

- Scroll to the top of ItemDetailFragment.java and expand the import list by tapping or clicking the expand icon (plus sign) in Line 3.
- Delete the import android.widget.TextView statement because the TextView library is not necessary.
- Save your work.

Critical Thinking
How would this app differ if all the list items in the left pane of the tablet opened a website within the right pane?
Each list item would use code similar to the code of list item 3 in this chapter project.

Running and Testing the Application

The Android Master/Detail Flow template provides an easy-to-use navigation to display multiple windows within the tablet interface or two separate Activities on a smartphone device. To test the Bike and Barge Android app, tap or click the Run 'app' button on the Standard toolbar, select the Nexus 10 emulator to test the application in the emulator, and then tap or click the OK button. Unlock the emulator, and then run the application again to open it in the tablet emulator window where you can test list items in the Bike and Barge app, as shown in Figures 9-1, 9-2, 9-3, and 9-4. You must have Internet connectivity to open the webpage and enough memory available to handle the app connection to the web. If you have trouble using the Nexus 10 emulator on an older computer with low resolution, add the 10.1" WXGA tablet emulator to use instead.

GTK

Because a tablet's screen is much larger than that of a smartphone, it provides more room to combine and interchange user interface components.

Wrap It Up—Chapter Summary

Using responsive design helps to meet the challenges of creating apps for the wide range of Android devices. The wide screen of a tablet allows for easy navigation using list items in the left pane and displaying details in the right pane. The chapter provided steps to use a custom Master/Detail Flow template that created a simple structure to display three screens of content. The WebView control was introduced for opening Internet content directly within an app using AndroidManifest Internet permissions.

- Responsive design is an approach to designing apps and websites that provide an optimal viewing experience across as many devices as possible.
- Android templates are available when you create a new Android project. You use them to create basic Android applications that you can run and test on an Android device of any size.
- A tablet app created with the Master/Detail Flow template displays a master list of items in a narrow vertical pane along the left side of the screen. When the user selects an item in the list, associated content appears in the detail pane on the right. On a smaller device, such as a smartphone, the master list and detail content are displayed on separate screens.
- To display the detail content for the first list item in the Bike and Barge app, you provide images and text descriptions in an XML TableLayout. Each row in the TableLayout displays an ImageView and TextView control.
- To display the detail content for the second list item, you code two TextView controls in a Linear layout that include the tour details.

- To display the detail content for the third list item, you customize the default fragment_item_detail.xml layout to use a WebView object instead of a TextView object. A WebView object allows you to place a web browser or simply display online content within your Activity, and uses a built-in rendering engine to display webpages.
- After including a WebView object in the XML layout of an app, you must add the Internet permissions to the Android Manifest file so the app can access the Internet and load webpages.
- To associate the content displayed in the detail pane with each list item in the left pane, you customize the DummyContent.java class file by adding code to the addItem statements so they reference three String objects: the id, the item list string, and the website URL.
- To handle the responses to user selections, you add conditional statements to the ItemDetailFragment.java file.

Key Terms

.equals method—A method used to compare strings for equality.

Application template—A design you can use to create basic Android applications and then customize them.

fragment—A piece of an application's user interface or behavior that can be placed in an Activity.

Master/Detail Flow template—A template Android Studio provides for creating an Android app with an adaptive, responsive layout; it displays a set of list items on the left and the associated details on the right.

permission—A restriction limiting access to a part of the code or to data on the device.

responsive design—An approach to designing apps and websites that provide an optimal viewing experience across as many devices as possible.

WebView—A View widget that displays webpages.

Developer FAQs

1. In the chapter project, the Master/Detail Flow template was selected when creating the app. Which Activity has been used in the first eight chapters of this book?
2. Which template XML layout file displays the item list fragment and the item detail container for a tablet?
3. How many list items are in the Master/Detail Flow template by default?
4. What is the name of the sample Java file that contains content in the Master/Detail Flow template?
5. True or false? Each list item launches a full-screen separate Activity on a smartphone.

6. Which layout was used in the photos.xml file?
7. Write a line of code starting with addItem to display the first list item named Hotel Location.
8. Write a line of code starting with addItem to display the second list item named View News Site connecting to the site cnn.com.
9. In which file would the lines in questions 7 and 8 be written?
10. When a smartphone is detected, the app uses which XML layout to display the FrameLayout instance?
11. Which XML code creates rows within a TableLayout?
12. True or false? You cannot add more list items to the Master/Detail Flow template.
13. Does the WebView widget open a full-screen browser on the tablet?
14. Which XML file in the chapter project was switched from a TextView widget to a WebView widget?
15. Give four examples of Android device permissions mentioned in this chapter.
16. What type of permission is necessary when using the WebView widget?
17. In which file are permissions set?
18. What do fragments make it easier for developers to code?
19. Write an If structure to compare if mItem is equal to 4. The value 4 has been assigned to an Integer value.
20. Write an If structure to compare if mItem is equal to 5. The value 5 has been assigned to a String value.

Beyond the Book

Search the Web for answers to the following questions to further your Android knowledge.

1. Research three Android tablet devices. Write a paragraph about the cost, usage, dimensions, and posted reviews of each of these three tablets.
2. Using cnet.com (a popular review site), compare the newest Android, iPad, and Windows tablets and summarize their recommendations in a one-page paper.
3. Using developer.android.com, research the topic of permissions. After writing many Android projects, the Android help files should be easier to understand now. Explain the use of permissions in your own words (at least 100 words).
4. A common user complaint is that it is difficult to use an onscreen keyboard to type long documents. Discuss three alternatives beyond using the traditional onscreen keyboard layout for input. Write a paragraph about each.

Case Programming Projects

Complete one or more of the following case programming projects. Use the same steps and techniques taught within the chapter. Submit the program you create to your instructor. The level of difficulty is indicated for each case programming project.

Easiest: ★

Intermediate: ★★

Challenging: ★★★

Case Project 9–1: Oasis Spa Tablet App ★

Requirements Document

Application title:	Oasis Spa Tablet App
Purpose:	This tablet app describes the services of a full-service spa named Oasis Spa.
Algorithms:	1. The opening screen displays three list items titled Spa Services, Spa Address, and Full Web Site. The first list item displays two table rows within a table layout with an image in each row (spa1.png and spa2.png) with the text shown in Figure 9-27. 2. The second item displays the address and phone number of Oasis Spa at 1268 Andrew Lane, Pond, OK 43277, 555-332-3366. 3. The third list item opens http://www.theoasisspa.net/ in a browser (Figure 9-28).
Conditions:	1. The pictures are provided with your student files. 2. Use the Master/Detail Flow template.

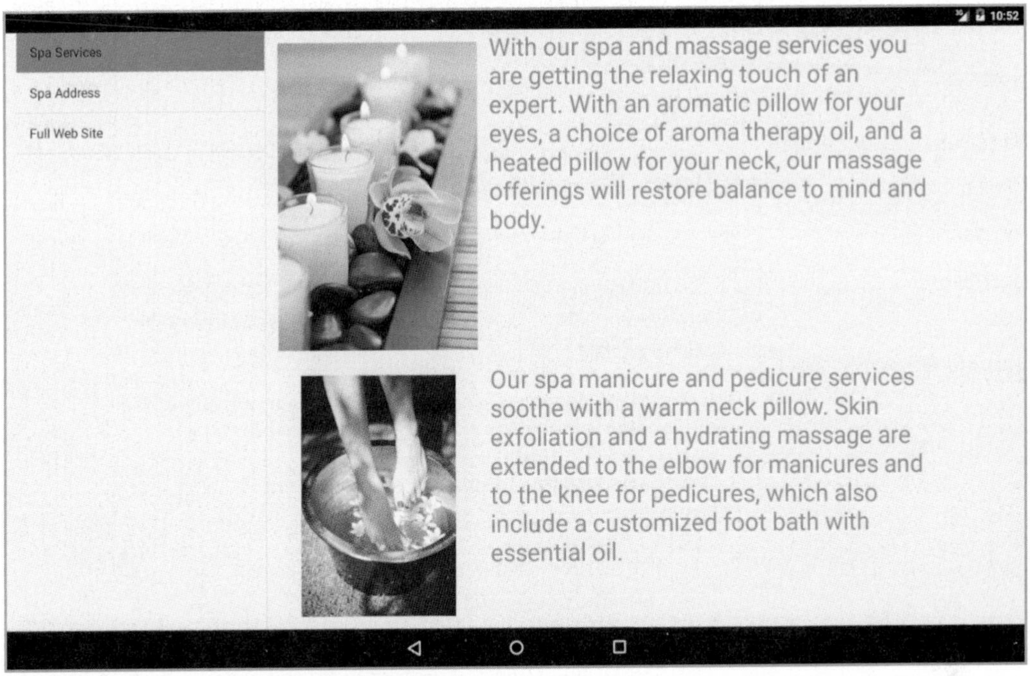

Paul Barbera/Photographer's Choice/Getty Images; Vstock/Getty Images

Figure 9-27 Opening screen of the Oasis Spa tablet app

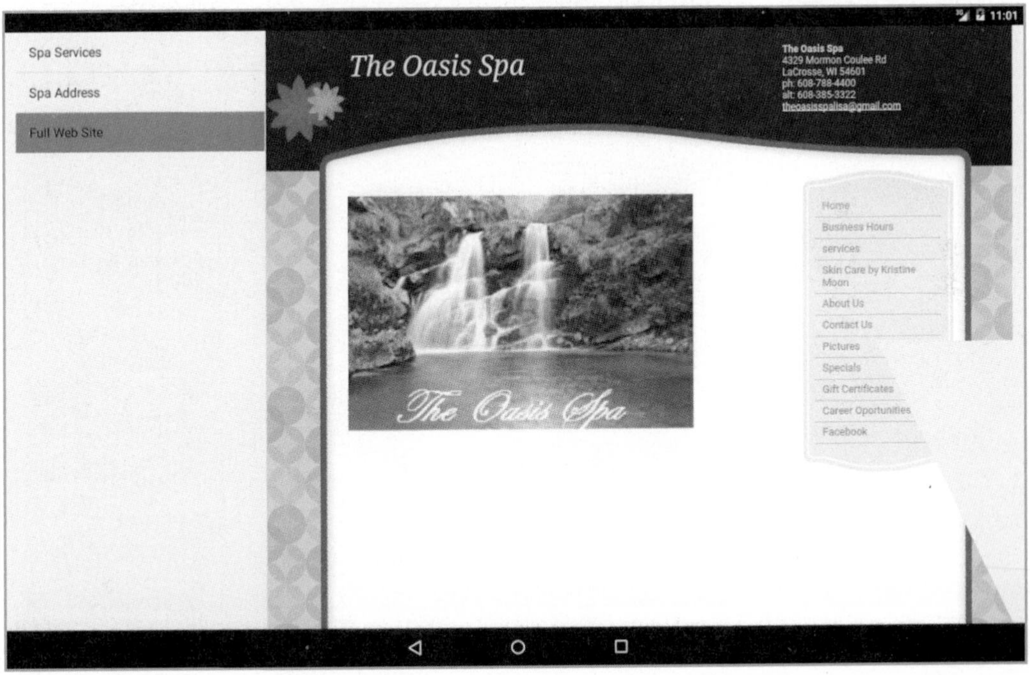

Source: www.theoasisspa.net/

Figure 9-28 Selecting the third list item in the left pane

Case Project 9–2: Modern Art Museums ★

Requirements Document

Application title: Modern Art Museums Tablet App

Purpose: The app shows three of the world's famous art museum websites.

Algorithms:

1. The opening screen displays three list items: Barnes Museum (www.barnesfoundation.org), Tate Modern (www.tate.org.uk), and Van Gogh Museum (www.vangoghmuseum.nl/en) (Figure 9-29).
2. The first list item displays the Barnes Museum website in the detail pane.
3. The second list item displays the Tate Modern Museum website in the detail pane.
4. The third list item displays the Van Gogh Museum website in the detail pane.

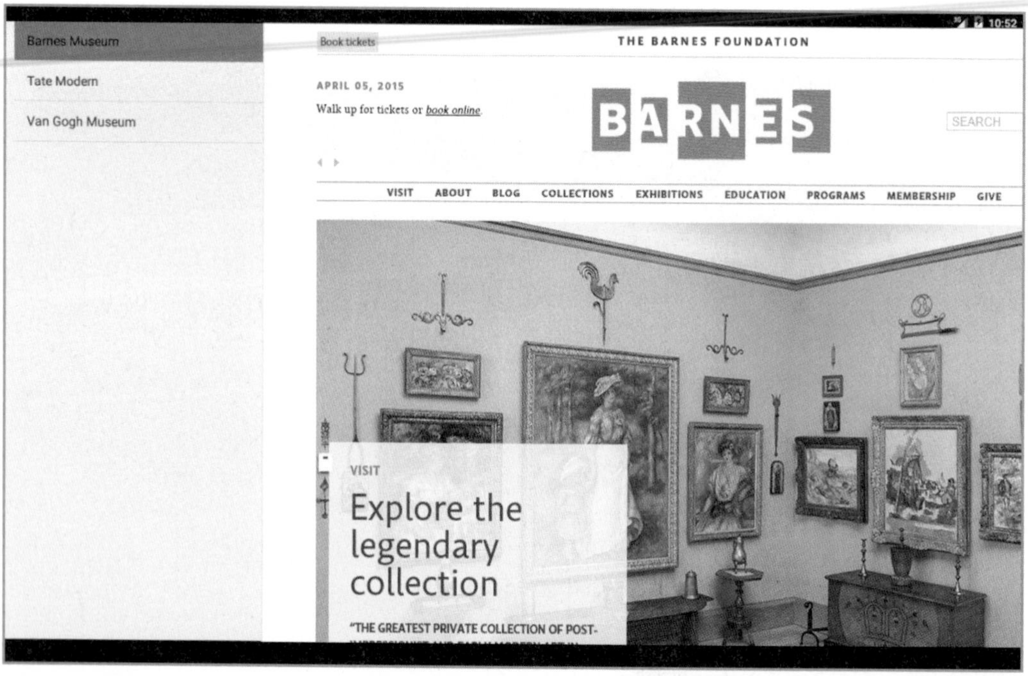

Source: barnesfoundation.org

Figure 9-29 Opening screen of the Modern Art Museums tablet app

Case Project 9–3: Famous Athlete Tablet App ★★

Requirements Document

Application title: Famous Athlete Tablet App

Purpose: Create one tablet screen of a large app that features information about the famous athletes of the world. You can select your favorite athlete to feature.

Algorithms:

1. The first list item uses a TableLayout to display the name of the athlete. The second row should have an image of the athlete and text about the athlete.
2. The second list item displays the athlete's birth date, his or her hometown, and stats. Research the information needed.
3. The third list opens a link about the featured athlete.

Case Project 9–4: Snap Fitness Tablet App ★★

Requirements Document

Application title: Snap Fitness Tablet App

Purpose: The local fitness gym in your area wants an app that provides information about the activities and memberships at the gym.

Algorithms:

1. The list items display the text Site, Info, and Photos. The first list item links to the website of a local gym.
2. The second list item displays the costs for the gym:

   Youth (ages 14–17): $25

   Adult (18 and over): $50

   Family/Household: $75

   Active Senior: $50
3. The third list item displays four photos in four rows with information about the gym next to each one.

Case Project 9–5: Top Tablet Apps ★★★

Requirements Document

Application title:	Top Tablet Apps
Purpose:	The app displays six of your favorite web technology sites.
Algorithms:	1. An opening screen displays the names of six top technology sites. 2. Each list item opens the corresponding tech site.

Case Project 9–6: Pick Your Topic Tablet App ★★★

Requirements Document

Application title:	Pick Your Topic Tablet App
Purpose:	Get creative! Create an app with four list items on a topic of your choice.
Algorithms:	1. Create four list items on the opening screen. 2. The four list items should link to a TableLayout with three rows, one TextView layout, one large ImageView layout, and a webpage.
Conditions:	Select your own images.

CHAPTER 10

Move! Creating Animation

In this chapter, you learn to:

- Create an Android application with Frame and Tween animation
- Understand Frame animation
- Understand Tween animation
- Add an animation-list XML file
- Code the AnimationDrawable object
- Set the background Drawable resource
- Launch the start( ) and stop( ) methods
- Add Tween animation to the application
- Create a Tween XML file that rotates an image
- Determine the rotation pivot, duration, and repeat count of a Tween animation
- Load the startActivity Tween animation in a second Activity
- Change the orientation of the emulator

Computer animation is widely used by television, the video game industry (as on Xbox, Vita, and Wii), and gaming applications on mobile devices. Animation displays many images in rapid succession or displays many changes to one image to create an illusion of movement. Animation is an integral part of many of the most popular Android apps on Google Play, including *Words with Friends, Angry Birds, Cut the Rope,* and *Candy Crush.* Android developers see the value in using 3D graphics to create more graphical apps and in-demand games.

Using Android animation, the chapter project named Northern Lights Animation displays multiple photos of the Iceland Aurora Borealis, also called the Northern Lights, during a single night in Iceland. The app includes a Start Frame Animation button that reveals the animated images frame by frame. When the user taps the Stop Frame Animation button, the frame-by-frame animation stops and the last image of the lights rotates several times using Tween animation. A **motion tween** specifies a start state of an object, and then animates the object using a uniform transition type such as rotating a predetermined number of times or an infinite number of times. The Northern Lights Animation Android smartphone app shown in Figure 10-1 allows the user to start and stop the animated images of the Iceland Northern Lights at different moments in a frame-by-frame sequence and then launches a second Activity that plays a rotation of the last image of the Northern Lights spiraling through the sky six times.

Figure 10-1 Northern Lights Animation Android app using Frame animation

The animation in the Android app in Figure 10-1 displays frame-by-frame animation where the time between each photo is measured in 100-millisecond intervals. Tapping or clicking the Start Frame Animation button begins displaying the Northern Lights images, and tapping or clicking the Start Tween Animation button stops the continuous Frame animation and begins the Tween animation of rotating the last Northern Lights image, as shown in Figure 10-2. The Tween animation rotates the image six times in a perfect circle. The orientation of the emulator is changed to landscape in Figure 10-2.

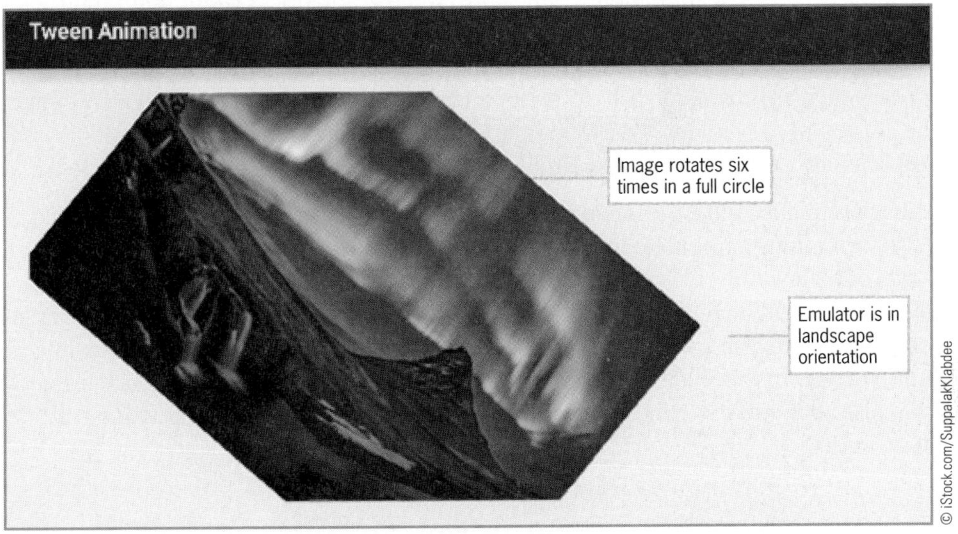

Figure 10-2 Northern Lights Animation Android app using Tween animation

GTK

Professional Android animation can be created by using complex programs such as Maya or Cinema 4D. A freeware program named Blender develops 3D animated content in the gaming environment.

To create this application, the developer must understand how to perform the following processes:

1. Add the four images to the drawable folder.
2. Add a Frame animation XML file to the project.
3. Add the layout for the image and button objects in activity_main.xml.
4. Set the duration between frames in the frame-by-frame animation.
5. Declare and instantiate the ImageView, Button, and AnimationDrawable controls.
6. Code the OnClickListeners for the Button controls.
7. Run the Frame animation application.

8. Add a Tween animation XML file to rotate the last image.
9. Create a second Activity named Tween.java to launch the rotation Tween animation with an XML layout.
10. When the application executes, change the orientation of the emulator.

Android Animation

Android provides two types of animation: Frame and Tween animation. **Frame animation**, also called frame-by-frame animation, assigns a sequence of photos to play as in a slide show with a predefined interval between images. Frame-by-frame animation is typically created to show steps in a process such as how to fly-fish or to play a fast-paced sequence such as in a cartoon. To create the illusion of movement, a cartoon image can be displayed on the screen and repeatedly replaced by a new image that is similar, but slightly advanced in the time sequence.

Instead of using a sequence of images, **Tween animation** creates an animation by performing a series of transformations on a single image such as position, size, rotation, and transparency on the contents of a View object. Text can fly across the screen, an image of an engine can be rotated to display different angles, or the transparency of an image can change from transparent to solid. A sequence of animation instructions defines the Tween animation using either XML or Android code. In this chapter project, the application first displays a frame-by-frame animation. Code is added to the same application to display a second type of animation called a Tween rotation effect.

Adding the Layout for the Frame Image and Button Controls

The layout specifications for the chapter project reside within the activity_main.xml file in a RelativeLayout. The single ImageView control named imgLights displays the Northern Lights images in a frame-by-frame animation. The two Button controls named btnStart and btnStop start and stop the Frame animation, respectively. In the Relative layout, an ImageView control displays the animation images. Insert this control and its properties in the activity_main.xml file to specify precise settings for the control. Below the ImageView control, two Button controls are added and centered in the emulator. Later in the chapter, a Tween animation is added to the application and launched when the Frame animation ends. This application is coded to display a modern smartphone platform such as Lollipop, Kit Kat, Jelly Bean, or Ice Cream Sandwich. As shown in Figure 10-3, as you create an app, a link named Help me choose is available when you select a form factor to show the distribution of active devices running each version of Android, based on the number of devices that visit the Google Play Store. The versions with high APIs have more features but fewer users than versions with low APIs. You want to balance features and users. Generally, it is best to support about 90 percent of the active devices in the present market. To begin the application, view the distribution of devices, set up the String table, and code the activity_main.xml layout, follow these steps:

STEP 1

- Open the Android Studio program.
- On the Welcome to Android Studio page of the Android Studio dialog box, tap or click Start a new Android Studio project in the Quick Start category.
- In the Create New Project dialog box, enter the Application name **Northern Lights Animation**.
- If necessary, in the Company Domain text box, type **androidbootcamp.net**, and in the Project location text box, type **D:\Workspace\NorthernLightsAnimation**.
- Tap or click the Next button on the Configure your new project page of the Create New Project dialog box.
- If necessary, tap or click the Phone and Tablet check box to select the form factor for your app.
- Select API 15: Android 4.0.3 (IceCreamSandwich) for the Minimum SDK.
- Tap or click the Help me choose link to open the API version distribution list and note the cumulative distribution for API 15.

The new Android Northern Lights Animation project has an application name and the Android Platform/API Version Distribution dialog box opens (Figure 10-3).

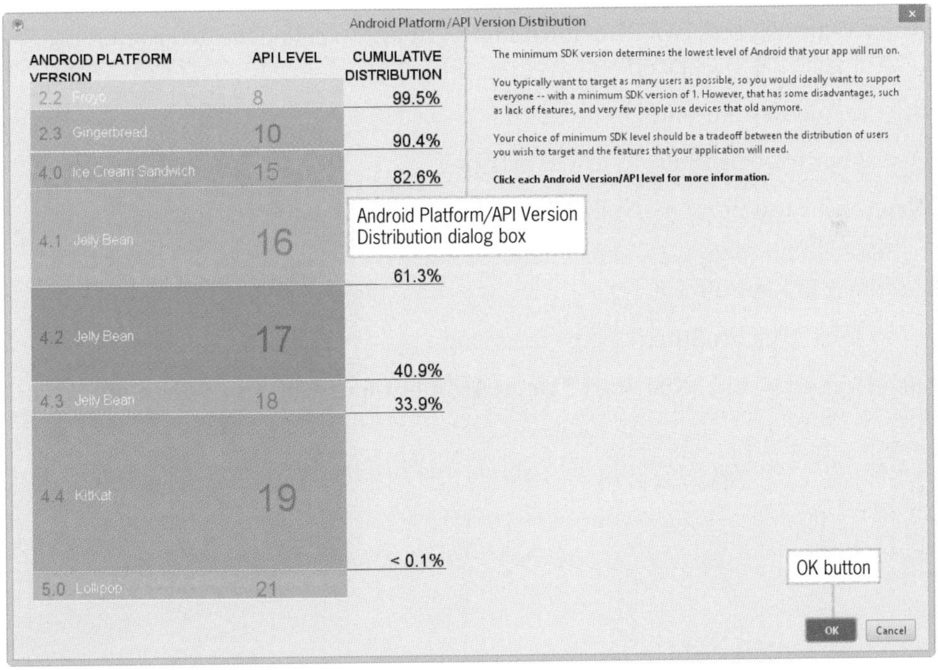

Figure 10-3 Targeting Android users

Critical Thinking

What is the benefit of only targeting an app to the most recent Android platform?

When a new platform of Android arrives, few devices initially upgrade, but if you are building an app based on a brand new feature, then you must target the latest platform.

STEP 2

- Tap or click the OK button to close the API distribution list dialog box.
- Tap or click the Next button on the Select the form factors your app will run on page.
- If necessary, tap or click Blank Activity to add an Activity to the new project.
- Tap or click the Next button on the Add an activity to Mobile page.
- Tap or click the Finish button.
- Delete the Hello world! TextView object in the emulator.
- Change the virtual device to Nexus 5.
- In the Android project view, expand the res\values folder, and then double-tap or double-click the strings.xml file to display its contents.
- Tap or click the Open editor link.
- Tap or click the Add Key (plus sign) button in the Translations Editor.
- In the Key text box, type **imgDescription** to name the string.
- In the Default Value text box, type **Northern Lights Image** to define the description text and then tap or click the OK button.
- Tap or click the Add Key button.
- In the Key text box, type **btnStart** to name the string.
- In the Default Value text box, type **Start Frame Animation** to define the text and then tap or click the OK button.
- Tap or click the Add Key button.
- In the Key text box, type **btnStop** to name the string.
- In the Default Value text box, type **Start Tween Animation** to define the text and then tap or click the OK button.

The Translations Editor includes an image description and two Button control text strings (Figure 10-4).

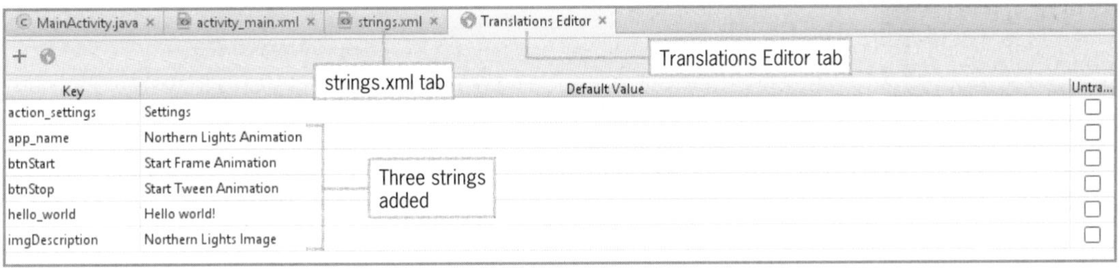

Figure 10-4 Translations Editor

STEP 3

- Save your work. Close the Translations Editor and the strings.xml tabs.
- In the res/layout folder, double-tap or double-click activity_main.xml to display the graphical layout.
- If necessary, tap or click the Text tab at the bottom of the window. By default, a RelativeLayout is set.
- Show line numbers.
- Tap or click Line 7, press the Enter key, and then add the ImageView control within the RelativeLayout by typing the following custom XML code using auto-completion as much as possible:

```
<ImageView
    android:id="@+id/imgLights"
    android:layout_width="300dp"
    android:layout_height="300dp"
    android:layout_alignParentTop="true"
    android:layout_centerHorizontal="true"
    android:contentDescription="@string/imgDescription" />
```

The ImageView control is coded in activity_main.xml (Figure 10-5).

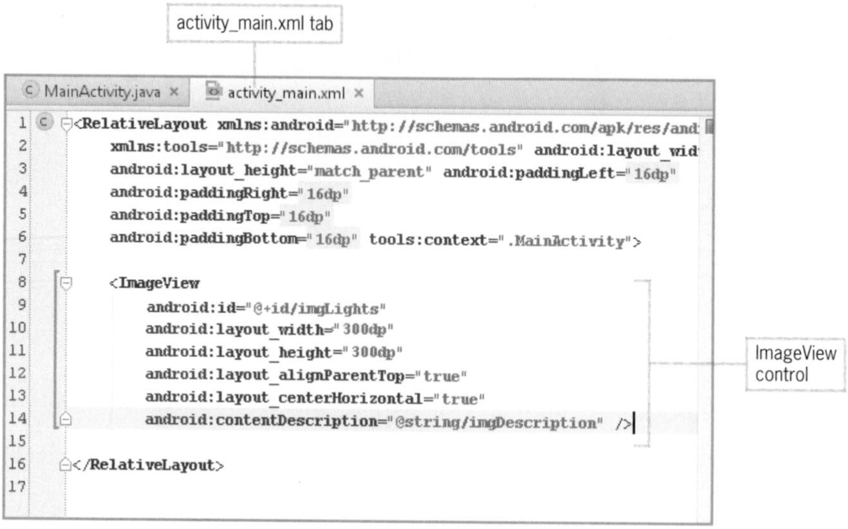

Figure 10-5 ImageView XML code

STEP 4

- Press the Enter key, and then add the two Button controls to place the buttons on the same line by typing the following custom XML code, using auto-completion as much as possible:

```
<Button
   android:id="@+id/btnStart"
   android:layout_width="wrap_content"
   android:layout_height="wrap_content"
   android:layout_centerHorizontal="true"
   android:layout_below="@+id/imgLights"
   android:layout_marginTop="10dp"
   android:text="@string/btnStart"
   android:textSize="25sp" />
 <Button
   android:id="@+id/btnStop"
   android:layout_width="wrap_content"
   android:layout_height="wrap_content"
   android:text="@string/btnStop"
   android:textSize="25sp"
   android:layout_below="@+id/btnStart"
   android:layout_alignParentLeft="true"
   android:layout_alignParentStart="true"
   android:layout_marginTop="10dp" />
```

The two Button controls are coded in activity_main.xml (Figure 10-6).

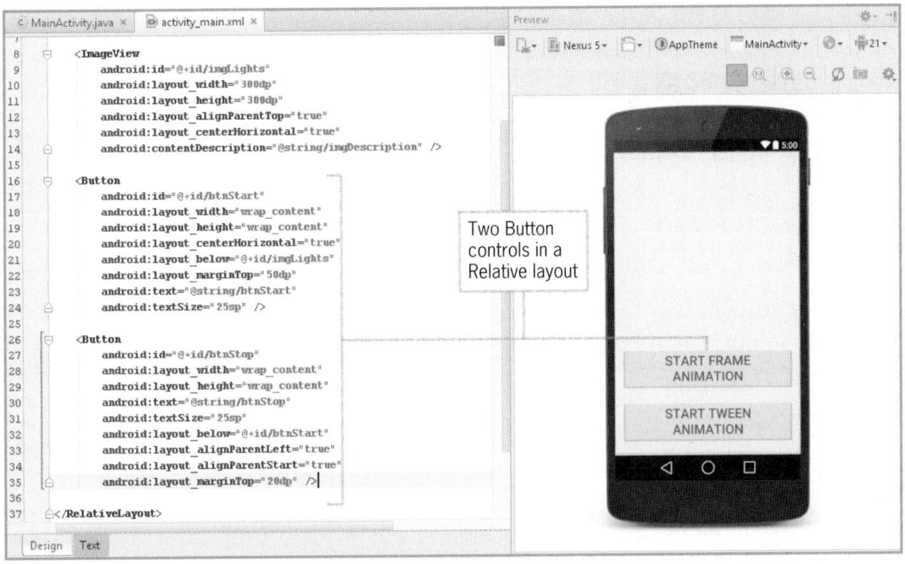

Figure 10-6 Two Button controls in the XML code

Creating Frame-by-Frame Animation

In the Northern Lights Animation app, the frame-by-frame animation loads and displays a sequence of Northern Lights images from the drawable folder. A single XML file named frame.xml lists the frames that constitute the Northern Lights animation. You create animation.xml in the res\drawable folder. Frame-by-frame animations are also known as drawable animations. In the XML code, an **animation-list** root element references four Northern Lights images stored in the drawable folder. Each item in the animation-list specifies how many milliseconds to display each image. In the chapter project, each image is displayed for 1/10 of a second. The animation-list code includes the oneshot property, which is set to true by default. By setting the **android:oneshot** attribute of the animation-list to false, as shown in the following code, the animation plays repeatedly like a film until the Start Tween Animation button is tapped. If the oneshot attribute is set to true, the animation plays once and then stops and displays the last frame. Note that you add the oneshot attribute to the code in the opening animation-list tag.

Code Syntax for animation.xml

```
<?xml version="1.0" encoding="utf-8"?>
<animation-list xmlns:android="http://schemas.android.com/apk/res/
android" android:oneshot="false" >
<item android:drawable="@drawable/lights1" android:duration= "100"/>
<item android:drawable="@drawable/lights2" android:duration= "100"/>
<item android:drawable="@drawable/lights3" android:duration= "100"/>
<item android:drawable="@drawable/lights4" android:duration= "100"/>
</animation-list>
```

When the XML file is added to the Android project, the Android resource type is selected and animation-list is specified as the root element of the XML code. An animation-list displays a listing of the images in the preferred order. Store the animations.xml file in the drawable folder. To copy the images into the drawable folder and code the animation-list XML code for the frame-by-frame animation, follow these steps:

STEP 1

- Save and close the activity_main.xml file.
- If necessary, copy the student files to your USB drive. Open the USB folder containing the student files.
- To add the four image files to the drawable resource folder, copy the lights1.png, lights2.png, lights3.png, and lights4.png files (press Ctrl+C) and then paste the files in the drawable folder.
- Tap or click the OK button in the Copy dialog box.

Copies of the four files appear in the drawable folder (Figure 10-7).

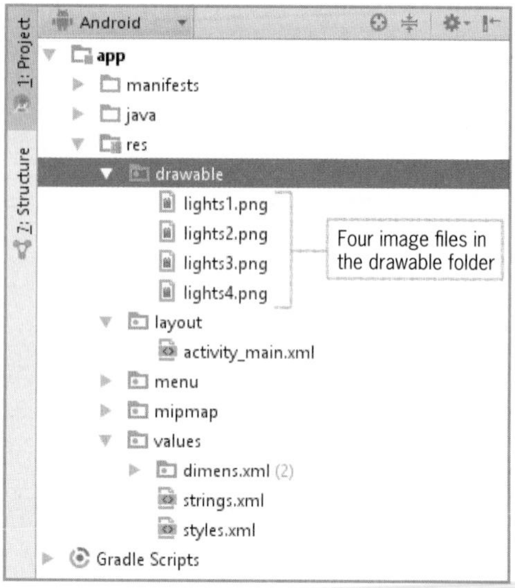

Figure 10-7 Copied images in the drawable folder

STEP 2

- Press and hold or right-click the res folder.

  Note: For animations, you cannot select the drawable folder, because the full set of resources are not available at the subfolder level.
- Tap or click New on the shortcut menu, and then tap or click Android resource file to open the New Resource file dialog box.
- In the File name text box, type **animation**.
- In the Resource type list box, select Animator
- In the Root element text box, type **animation-list** as the type of element to add to the XML file.
- In the Directory name text box, type **drawable** as the name of the folder for storing animation.xml.

An XML file named animation is created in a folder named drawable with the root element animation-list and a resource type of Animator (Figure 10-8).

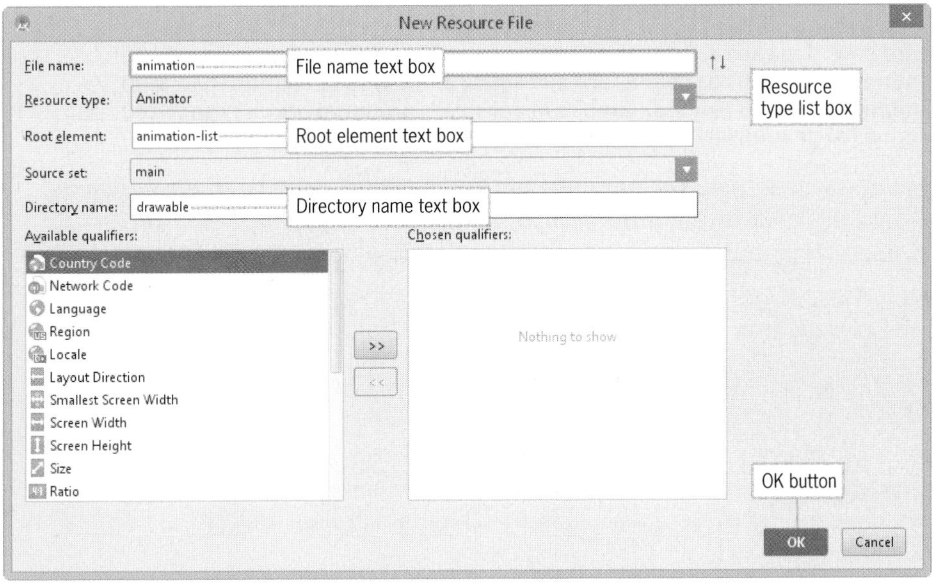

Figure 10-8 Creating the animation.xml file

STEP 3

- Tap or click the OK button. When the animation.xml file opens with the animation-list element already coded, show line numbers.
- Tap or click the animation-list source tag, tap or click before the closing tag (>) in Line 2, and then press the spacebar to insert a space.
- To add the oneshot attribute to create a continuous loop of animation, type **android:oneshot="false"**.

In animation.xml, the oneshot attribute is set to false in the animation-list code to animate the frames continuously (Figure 10-9).

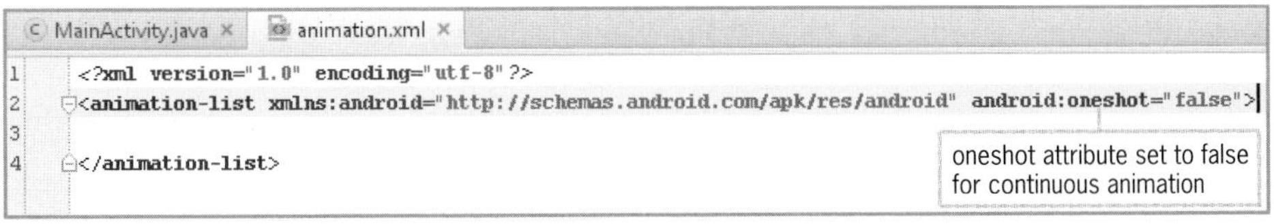

Figure 10-9 Setting the oneshot attribute

STEP 4

- Tap or click Line 3 within the animation-list element to add the four list items that are displayed within the frame-by-frame animation. Type the following four lines to reference the images and millisecond durations:

```
<item android:drawable="@drawable/lights1" android:duration="100"/>
<item android:drawable="@drawable/lights2" android:duration="100"/>
<item android:drawable="@drawable/lights3" android:duration="100"/>
<item android:drawable="@drawable/lights4" android:duration="100"/>
```

In animation.xml, the four frames of the animation are entered as items in the animation-list element and the time in milliseconds that each frame should be displayed (Figure 10-10).

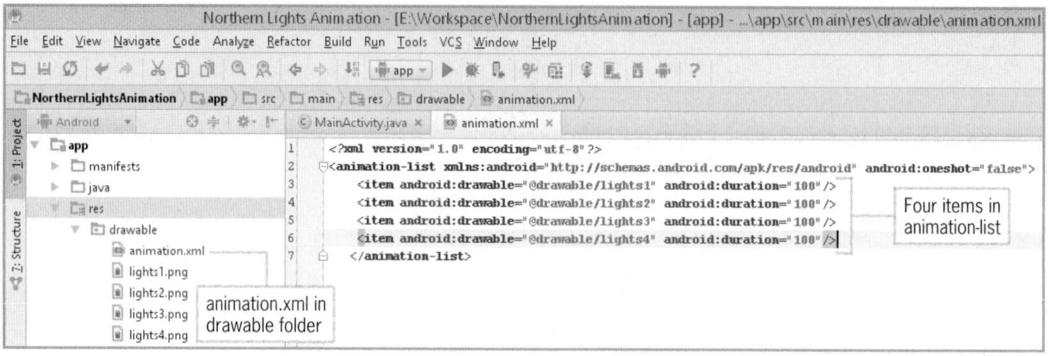

Figure 10-10 Entering the animation-list items with image names and duration

GTK

Android includes support for high-performance 2D and 3D graphics with the Open Graphics Library named OpenGL. OpenGL is a cross-platform graphics API that specifies a standard software interface for 3D graphics processing hardware and uses a coordinate system to map the image to the screen.

Coding the AnimationDrawable Object

The **AnimationDrawable class** provides the methods for drawable animations to create a sequence of frame-by-frame images. In Android development, frame-based animations and image transitions are defined as drawables. The instance of AnimationDrawable is instantiated as a class variable because it is used in multiple methods within the MainActivity class. To instantiate the AnimationDrawable object in MainActivity.java as a class variable, follow this step:

STEP 1

- Save your work and then close the animation.xml tab.
- If necessary, open the MainActivity.java tab and display the line numbers.

- Delete Lines 17-39.
- On Line 10 within the MainActivity class, type **AnimationDrawable lightsAnimation;** to instantiate the object.
- Tap or click AnimationDrawable and press Alt+Enter to import AnimationDrawable, which moves the new code to Line 11.

The AnimationDrawable instance named lightsAnimation is coded within MainActivity.java (Figure 10-11).

Figure 10-11 Instantiating the AnimationDrawable class variable

Setting the Background Resource

The ImageView control named imgLights that was coded in activity_main.xml must be coded in MainActivity.java to bind the drawable resource files to the Background property. The Background property of an image can be set to any full Drawable resource such as a .png file, a 9-patch image file, or a solid color designated with hexadecimal code such as #FF0000 for red. A special image, called a **9-patch image**, has predefined "stretching" areas that maintain the same look on different screen sizes. These 9-patch graphics are named for their nine areas, called patches, that scale separately. For example, a button may change sizes when it is stretched across different form factors.

The images used in the Northern Lights Animation application are .png files, referenced in animation.xml as items in the animation-list. In the following code, a new instance of ImageView named imgFrame is assigned to the ImageView control named imgLights, which was defined in the activity_main.xml layout. The list of drawable images in the animation-list is connected to the imgFrame instance by the imgFrame.setBackgroundResource method. The **setBackgroundResource** method shown in the following code places the four Northern Lights images in the frame-by-frame slide type display. Each frame points to one of the Northern Lights images that were assembled in the XML resource file. The imgFrame instance is the image that you want to animate and is set to the animation drawable as its background.

Code Syntax

```
ImageView imgFrame=(ImageView)findViewById(R.id.imgLights );
imgFrame.setBackgroundResource(R.drawable.animation);
lightsAnimation=(AnimationDrawable) imgFrame.getBackground( );
```

In the third line of the code syntax, the instance of AnimationDrawable called lightsAnimation is assigned as the background of the four images to display in the animation. Android constructs an AnimationDrawable Java object before setting it as the background. At this point, the animation is ready to display the four images, but must wait for you to code the start( ) method, which actually begins the movement in the Frame animation. To instantiate the ImageView control and assign the four images to the Background property, follow these steps:

STEP 1

- Tap or click at the end of the setContentView(R.layout.*activity_main*); line, press the Enter key, and then instantiate the ImageView that accesses imgLights in the XML layout file by typing **ImageView imgFrame=(ImageView)findViewById(R.id.imgLights);**.
- Tap or click ImageView and press Alt+Enter to Import the ImageView control.

The ImageView control that displays the frame animation is instantiated (Figure 10-12).

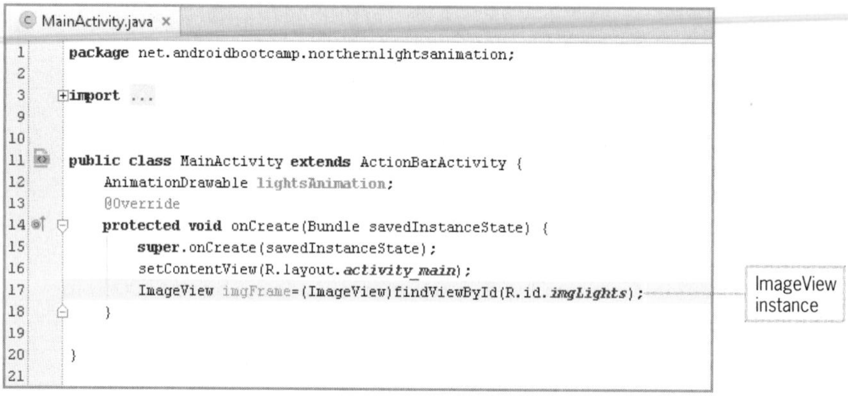

Figure 10-12 Instantiating the ImageView control

STEP 2

- Press the Enter key to insert a blank line, and then set the background resource image (the instance of the ImageView control) for the animation-list in animation.xml by typing **imgFrame.setBackgroundResource(R.drawable.animation);**.

The animation-list within animation.xml is set as the Background property of the imgFrame ImageView (Figure 10-13).

MainActivity.java ×

```java
package net.androidbootcamp.northernlightsanimation;

import ...


public class MainActivity extends ActionBarActivity {
    AnimationDrawable lightsAnimation;
    @Override
    protected void onCreate(Bundle savedInstanceState) {
        super.onCreate(savedInstanceState);
        setContentView(R.layout.activity_main);
        ImageView imgFrame=(ImageView)findViewById(R.id.imgLights);
        imgFrame.setBackgroundResource(R.drawable.animation);
    }

}
```

setBackgroundResource method

Figure 10-13 Setting setBackgroundResource for the ImageView control

STEP 4 3

- Next, access the AnimationDrawable object by "getting" the view object. Press the Enter key, and then type **lightsAnimation=(AnimationDrawable)imgFrame.getBackground();**.

The AnimationDrawable is ready to display the four images (Figure 10-14).

MainActivity.java ×

```java
package net.androidbootcamp.northernlightsanimation;

import ...


public class MainActivity extends ActionBarActivity {
    AnimationDrawable lightsAnimation;
    @Override
    protected void onCreate(Bundle savedInstanceState) {
        super.onCreate(savedInstanceState);
        setContentView(R.layout.activity_main);
        ImageView imgFrame=(ImageView)findViewById(R.id.imgLights);
        imgFrame.setBackgroundResource(R.drawable.animation);
        lightsAnimation=(AnimationDrawable)imgFrame.getBackground();
    }

}
```

getBackground method

Figure 10-14 getBackground prepares the Animation drawable

IN THE TRENCHES

Common frame-by-frame animations include rotating timers, email symbols, activity icons, page-loading animations, cartoons, sequenced timelines, and other useful user interface elements.

Adding Two Button Controls

The Button controls in the Northern Lights Animation project turn the frame-by-frame animation on and off. Both buttons use a setOnClickListener to await user interaction. To instantiate the two Button controls and add the setOnClickListener, follow these steps:

STEP 1

- To code the first button, press the Enter key and then type **Button button1 = (Button) findViewById(R.id.btnStart);**.
- Tap or click Button, import the Button object, and then tap or click at the end of the line.

The first Button control that begins the animation is instantiated (Figure 10-15).

MainActivity.java

```
package net.androidbootcamp.northernlightsanimation;

import ...


public class MainActivity extends ActionBarActivity {
    AnimationDrawable lightsAnimation;
    @Override
    protected void onCreate(Bundle savedInstanceState) {
        super.onCreate(savedInstanceState);
        setContentView(R.layout.activity_main);
        ImageView imgFrame=(ImageView)findViewById(R.id.imgLights);
        imgFrame.setBackgroundResource(R.drawable.animation);
        lightsAnimation=(AnimationDrawable)imgFrame.getBackground();
        Button button1=(Button) findViewById(R.id.btnStart);
    }

}
```

First instance of the Button control

Figure 10-15 Coding the button for the Frame animation

STEP 2

- To code the second button, press the Enter key and type **Button button2 = (Button) findViewById(R.id.btnStop);**.

The second Button control that stops the animation and begins the Tween animation is instantiated (Figure 10-16).

MainActivity.java

```
1  package net.androidbootcamp.northernlightsanimation;
2
3  import ...
10
11
12 public class MainActivity extends ActionBarActivity {
13     AnimationDrawable lightsAnimation;
14     @Override
15     protected void onCreate(Bundle savedInstanceState) {
16         super.onCreate(savedInstanceState);
17         setContentView(R.layout.activity_main);
18         ImageView imgFrame=(ImageView)findViewById(R.id.imgLights);
19         imgFrame.setBackgroundResource(R.drawable.animation);
20         lightsAnimation=(AnimationDrawable)imgFrame.getBackground();
21         Button button1=(Button) findViewById(R.id.btnStart);
22         Button button2=(Button) findViewById(R.id.btnStop);
23     }
24
25 }
26
```

Second instance of the Button control

Figure 10-16 Coding the button to start the Tween animation

STEP 3

- To code the first Button listener, press the Enter key and type **button1** followed by a period (.) to open a code listing.
- Double-tap or double-click the first setOnClickListener displayed in the auto-completion list.
- Inside the parenthesis, type **new On** and then press the Ctrl+spacebar keys to display the auto-completion list.
- Double-tap or double-click the first choice, which is a View.OnClickListener.
- If necessary, insert a right parenthesis and a semicolon after the closing brace on Line 29 or 30 for the auto-generated onClick stub (the button1.setOnClickListener statement).

The first button OnClickListener awaits user interaction for button1 (Figure 10-17).

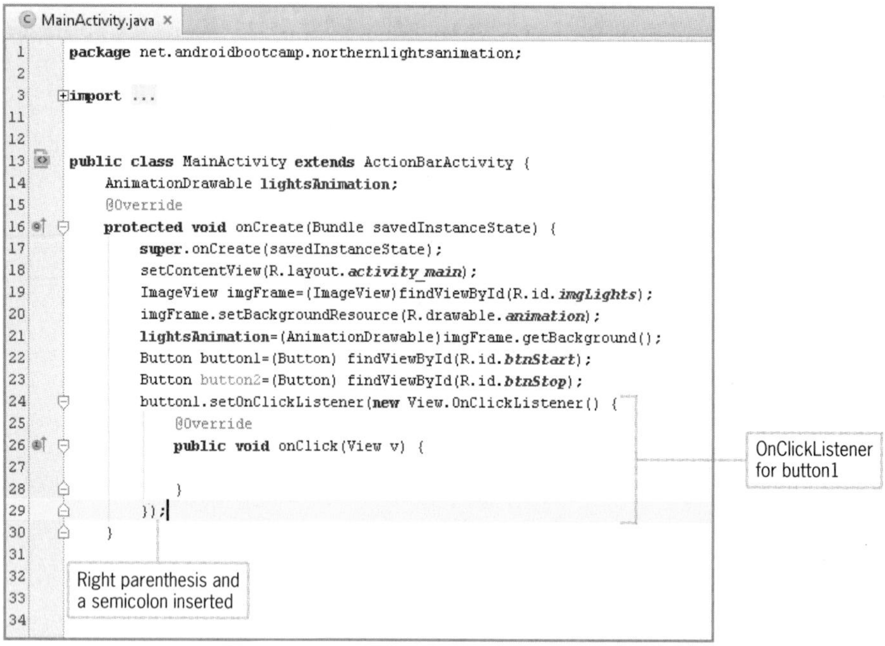

Figure 10-17 OnClickListener for the first button

STEP 4

- Press the Enter key after the semicolon to code the second Button listener.
- Type **button2** followed by a period (.) to open a code listing.
- Double-tap or double-click the first setOnClickListener displayed in the auto-completion list.
- Inside the parenthesis, type **new On** and then press the Ctrl+spacebar keys to display the auto-completion list.
- Scroll down and double-tap or double-click the first choice, which is a View.OnClickListener with an Anonymous Inner Type event handler.

The second button OnClickListener awaits user interaction for button2 (Figure 10-18).

MainActivity.java

```java
package net.androidbootcamp.northernlightsanimation;

import ...


public class MainActivity extends ActionBarActivity {
    AnimationDrawable lightsAnimation;
    @Override
    protected void onCreate(Bundle savedInstanceState) {
        super.onCreate(savedInstanceState);
        setContentView(R.layout.activity_main);
        ImageView imgFrame=(ImageView)findViewById(R.id.imgLights);
        imgFrame.setBackgroundResource(R.drawable.animation);
        lightsAnimation=(AnimationDrawable)imgFrame.getBackground();
        Button button1=(Button) findViewById(R.id.btnStart);
        Button button2=(Button) findViewById(R.id.btnStop);
        button1.setOnClickListener(new View.OnClickListener() {
            @Override
            public void onClick(View v) {

            }
        });
        button2.setOnClickListener(new View.OnClickListener() {
            @Override
            public void onClick(View v) {

            }
        });
    }

}
```

OnClickListener for button2

Figure 10-18 OnClickListener for the second button

Using the Start and Stop Methods

After associating AnimationDrawable with the animation images and coding the buttons, you can use the start( ) and stop( ) methods of the drawable objects to control the Frame animation. When the user taps the Start Frame Animation button, the start( ) method begins the Frame animation continuously because oneshot is set to false. The Frame animation stops only when the user taps the Start Tween Animation button, which launches the stop( ) method and then initiates the startActivity, launching the second Activity named Tween.java. In the following code, the start( ) method is placed within the onClick( ) method for the Start Frame Animation button and the stop( ) method is placed within the onClick( ) method for the Start Tween Animation button:

Code Syntax

```java
lightsAnimation.start( );
lightsAnimation.stop( );
```

The start( ) method launches the lightsAnimation.xml file displaying the animation-list items, and the stop( ) method ends the display of the animation-list. To add the start( ) and stop() methods, follow these steps:

STEP 1

- Tap or click the blank line within the first onClick method for the first button, and then type **lightsAnimation.start( );**.

The Start Frame Animation button is coded to start lightsAnimation.xml (Figure 10-19).

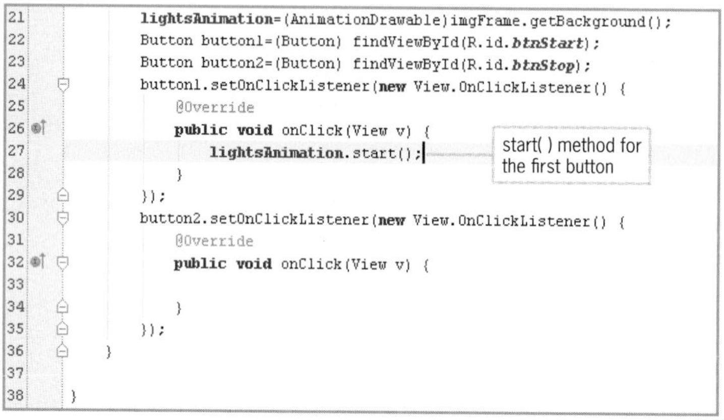

Figure 10-19 Entering the start( ) method

STEP 2

- Tap or click the blank line within the second onClick method for the second button and then type **lightsAnimation.stop( );**.

The Start Tween Animation button is coded to stop the Frame animation within lightsAnimation.xml and then begin the tween animation (Figure 10-20).

MainActivity.java

```
package net.androidbootcamp.northernlightsanimation;

import ...


public class MainActivity extends ActionBarActivity {
    AnimationDrawable lightsAnimation;
    @Override
    protected void onCreate(Bundle savedInstanceState) {
        super.onCreate(savedInstanceState);
        setContentView(R.layout.activity_main);
        ImageView imgFrame=(ImageView)findViewById(R.id.imgLights);
        imgFrame.setBackgroundResource(R.drawable.animation);
        lightsAnimation=(AnimationDrawable)imgFrame.getBackground();
        Button button1=(Button) findViewById(R.id.btnStart);
        Button button2=(Button) findViewById(R.id.btnStop);
        button1.setOnClickListener(new View.OnClickListener() {
            @Override
            public void onClick(View v) {
                lightsAnimation.start();
            }
        });
        button2.setOnClickListener(new View.OnClickListener() {
            @Override
            public void onClick(View v) {
                lightsAnimation.stop();
            }
        });
    }

}
```

stop( ) method for the second button

Figure 10-20 Entering the stop( ) method

STEP 3

- To test the Frame animation, tap or click the Run 'app' button on the Standard toolbar, and then select the Nexus 5 emulator to launch the emulator. Unlock the emulator and then run the application.
- Tap or click the START FRAME ANIMATION button to view the Northern Lights animation.

The emulator displays the frame-by-frame animation (Figure 10-21).

Figure 10-21 Frame-by-frame animation displayed in the emulator

Critical Thinking

To make an object move across the screen, I can either use Frame animation to redraw the object or use Tween animation to move the object. Which is easier?

Using Tween animations to move an object's position, change the size of the object, or make opacity changes are less labor intensive than manually redrawing the image over and over again like a cartoon to show movement.

Creating Tween Animation

Instead of rendering several images in a sequence in Frame animation, Tween animation manipulates a drawable image by adding tween effects. Defined in an XML file, **tween effects** are transitions that change objects from one state to another. An ImageView or TextView object can move, rotate, grow, or shrink. As shown in Table 10-1, Tween animations include a built-in library of tween effects. These effects are saved within an animation XML file that belongs in the res/anim/ folder of your Android project. With Tween animation, an Android game could show the avatar hero moving toward the treasure, change the opacity of a treasure chest so you can see inside, and spin the clock to indicate the passing of time.

Tween effect	Purpose
Alpha	Transitions an object from one level of transparency to another where 0.0 is transparent and 1.0 is opaque
Rotate	Spins an object from one angular position to another. To rotate an object completely around, start at 0 degrees and rotate to 359 degrees (a full circle). A pivotX and pivotY percentage shows the amount of pivot based on the object's left edge
Scale	Transitions the size of an object (grow or shrink) on an X/Y scale
Translate	Moves the object vertically or horizontally a percentage relative to the element width (e.g., deltaX="100%" would move the image one image width away)

Table 10-1 Tween animation effects

The four Tween animation effects in Table 10-1 can be coded in an XML file and individually configured or nested together to animate an object in any possible direction or size.

GTK

Android requires that your animated image stay within the original bounds of the View object. Rotations, movement, and scaling transformations that extend beyond the original boundaries clip the image.

Creating a Second Activity and XML Layout to Launch the Tween Animation

When the user taps the Start Tween Animation button in the Northern Lights Animation app, two actions are triggered within the second onClick( ) method. The Frame animation is concluded with the stop( ) method and a startActivity intent launches a second Activity named Tween.java. To code a second Activity and launch the startActivity, follow these steps:

STEP 1

- Minimize the emulator.
- To create a second class and XML layout file, press and hold or right-click the first net.androidbootcamp.northernlightsanimation folder in the java folder, tap or click New on the shortcut menu, tap or click Activity, and then tap or click Blank Activity.
- Type **Tween** in the Activity Name text box in the New Android Activity dialog box to create a second class that defines the Tween Activity.
- Type **Tween Animation** in the Title text box.

A new class named Tween.java and a second XML layout file named activity_tween is created (Figure 10-22).

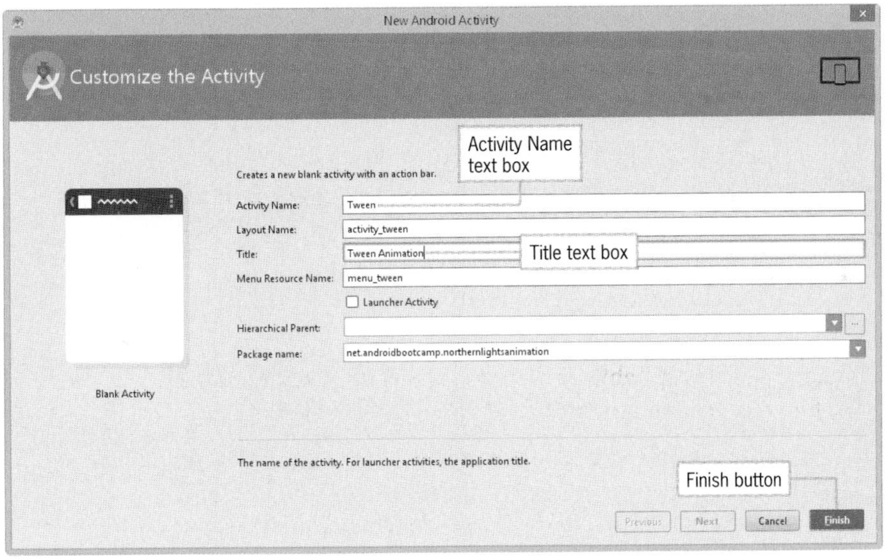

Figure 10-22 Creating the Tween.java class and activity_tween layout

STEP 2

- Tap or click the Finish button to finish creating the Tween class and the associated XML layout file.
- To launch the Tween Activity class from the MainActivity.java class, open MainActivity.java. Display the line numbers. if necessary.
- Scroll down to the statement lightsAnimation.stop( ).
- Tap or click at the end of the statement and press the Enter key.
- To launch an intent that starts the second Activity, type **startActivity (new Intent (MainActivity.this, Tween.class));**.
- Tap or click the red text Intent and then press Alt+Enter to import the Intent to launch the second class.

A startActivity launches the Tween.java class (Figure 10-23).

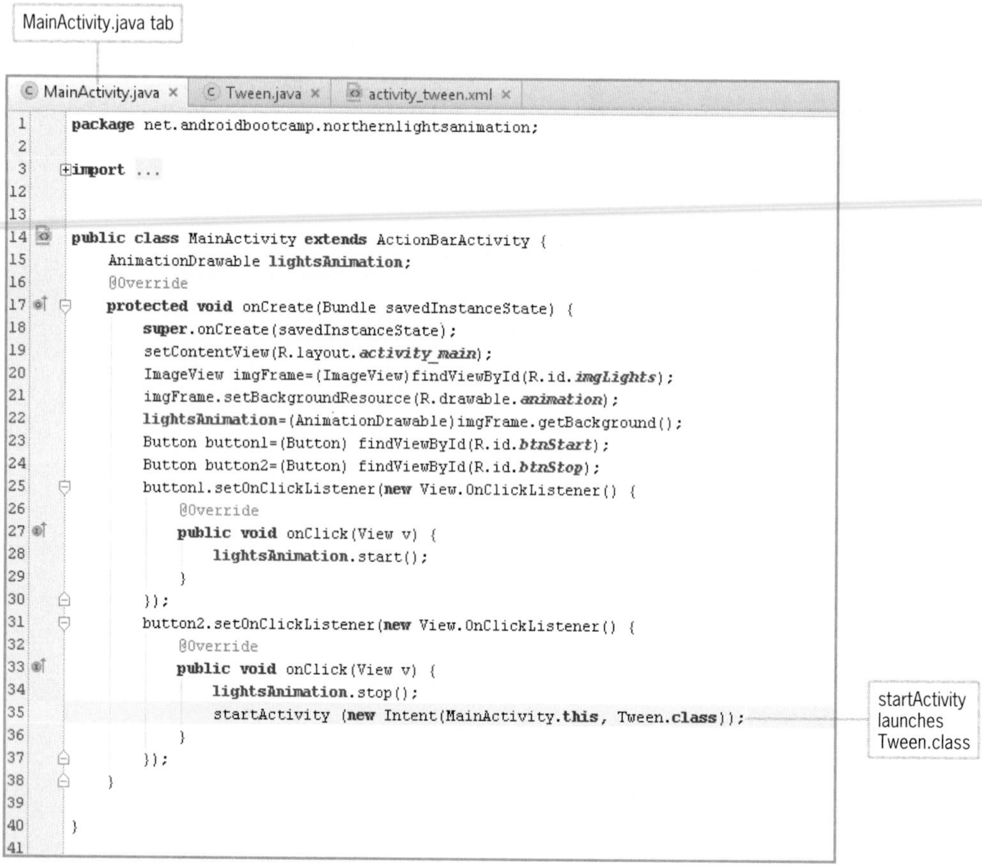

Figure 10-23 startActivity launches the Tween class

Adding the Layout for the Tween Image

After the user taps the START TWEEN ANIMATION button, the Frame animation ends and a second Activity is launched. This second Activity is named Tween.java, and it defines a second layout named activity_tween.xml with a single ImageView control identified as imgTween, referencing the fourth image named lights4 that will be rotated with Tween animation. To code the activity_tween.xml file layout to display an ImageView control, follow this step:

STEP 1

- Open the activity_tween.xml tab. Tap or click the Design tab at the bottom of the window, if necessary, and then delete the Hello World! TextView object.
- Tap or click the Text tab at the bottom of the activity_tween.xml tab. Display the line numbers.
- Tap or click Line 8 and press the Enter key to insert a new blank line.
- Add the ImageView control by typing the following custom XML code beginning on Line 9, using auto-completion as much as possible:

```
<ImageView
  android:id="@+id/imgTween"
  android:layout_width="wrap_content"
  android:layout_height="wrap_content"
  android:layout_gravity="center"
  android:contentDescription="@string/imgDescription"
  android:src="@drawable/lights4" />
```

A second XML layout named activity_tween.xml displays an ImageView control (Figure 10-24).

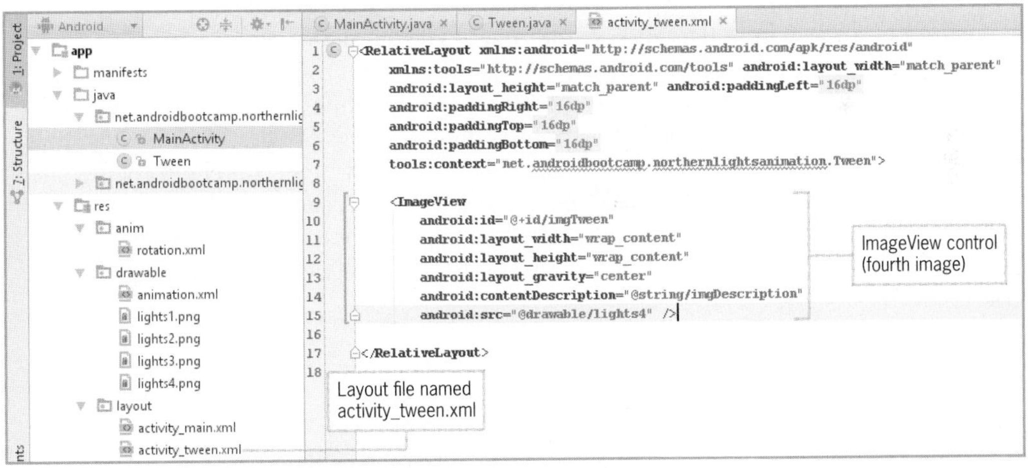

Figure 10-24 ImageView control coded in activity_tween.xml

Coding a Tween Rotation XML File

In the Northern Lights Animation application, the last image (lights4.png) is rotated when the user taps or clicks the START TWEEN ANIMATION button. Android uses an XML file-creator utility that supports 10 different resource types. The default resource type is Layout, but in the chapter project, you select Tween animation. After entering the XML filename as rotation.xml, tap or click the root element of rotate to store the rotation.xml code for a Tween animation in the /res/anim folder. Recall that the XML file for a Frame animation is stored in the /res/drawable folder. The rotation.xml statements are shown in the following code:

Code Syntax

```
<?xml version="1.0" encoding="utf-8"?>
<rotate
xmlns:android="http://schemas.android.com/apk/res/android"
android:fromDegrees="0"
android:toDegrees="359"
android:pivotX="50%"
android:pivotY="50%"
android:duration="2000"
android:repeatCount="5"
```

The rotation.xml code defines the attributes of the Tween animation. Notice the tween effect is set to rotate in the second line. The fromDegrees and toDegrees rotate attributes spin the object from 0 to 359 degrees, which equals 360 degrees for a full circle. The image in the chapter project completes several clockwise rotations. The pivotX and pivotY attributes pivot an object from its center by setting the pivot point, which can be a fixed coordinate or a percentage. By default, the object pivots around the (0,0) coordinate, or the upper-left corner of the object. Notice pivotX and pivotY are set to 50% in the code example, which determines that the pivot location is from the center of the object. The duration for each rotation is set for 2,000 milliseconds. The repeatCount represents how many times the object rotates after the initial rotation. You can set repeatCount to an integer or to "infinite" if you do not want the rotation to stop. Remember that the number of rotations is always one greater than the repeat value, so if you set the repeatCount to the integer 5, the object rotates six times. It rotates once initially and then repeats the rotation four more times. By creating an XML file, it is easier to make simple changes to fine-tune the animation. You might want to try different values in the rotation.xml file to see how the animation changes. To code the Tween animation to rotate an image, follow these steps:

STEP 1

- Save and close the activity_tween.xml layout file.
- To create a new rotation XML file, press and hold or right-click the res folder.
- Tap or click New on the shortcut menu, and then tap or click Android resource file. The New Resource File dialog box opens.

- In the File name text box, type the XML filename **rotation**.
- In the Resource type list box, select Animator.
- In the Root element text box, type **rotate** as the type of element that is added to the XML file.
- In the Directory name text box, type **anim** as the name of the folder in which the tween animation file is stored.

The New Android XML File dialog box opens and the File name, Resource type, Root element, and Directory name settings are specified (Figure 10-25).

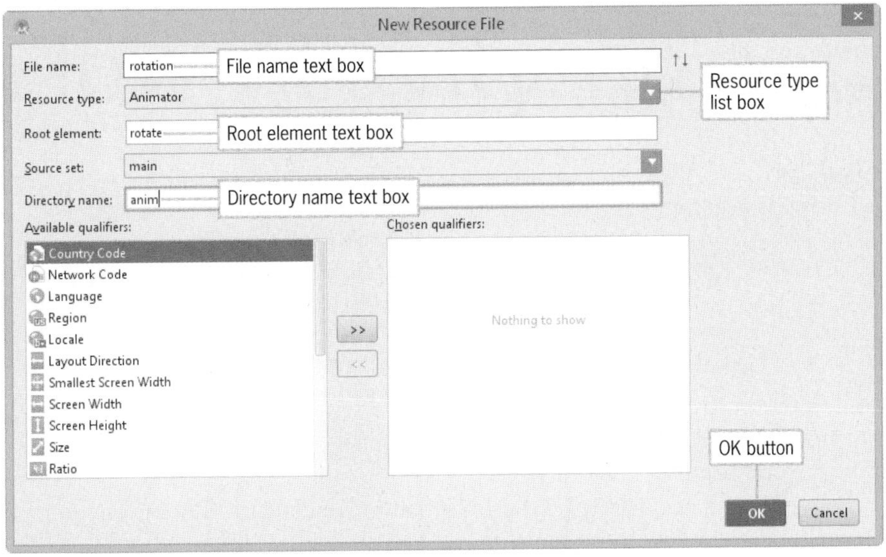

Figure 10-25 New Android XML dialog box

STEP 2

- Tap or click the OK button. → If this does not appear, you have to collapse and expand again the res folder
- Expand the anim folder in the Android project view. The rotation.xml file opens with the rotate element already coded. Display line numbers.
- Delete the closing rotate code on Line 4 and the right angle bracket (>) on Line 2.
- Tap or click Line 3 and type the following code after the opening rotate root element:

```
android:fromDegrees="0"
android:toDegrees="359"
android:pivotX="50%"
android:pivotY="50%"
android:duration="2000"
android:repeatCount="5" />
```

In rotation.xml, the Tween animation attributes are coded to rotate the image (Figure 10-26).

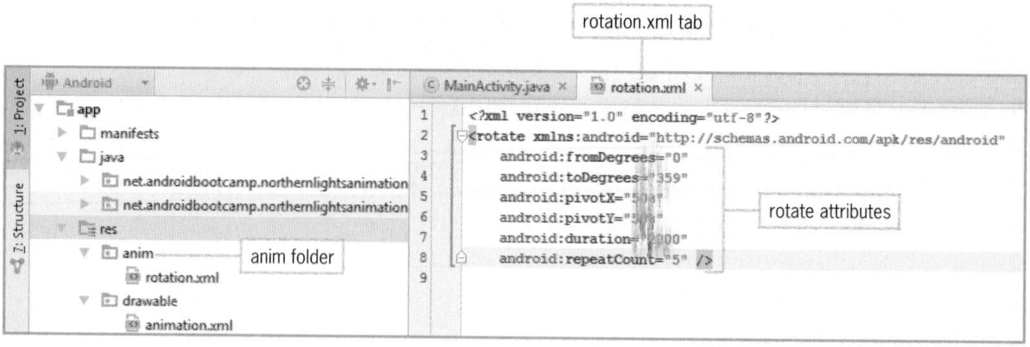

Figure 10-26 rotate attributes in rotation.xml in the anim folder

IN THE TRENCHES

To change an image from transparent to opaque, code an alpha statement in an XML file such as <alpha xmlns:android = *http://schemas.android.com/apk/res/android* android:fromAlpha="0.0" android:toAlpha = "1.0" android:duration="100">.

Coding a StartAnimation

Now that the layout, rotation XML file, and second Activity are ready, the Tween animation can be launched using the StartAnimation method. Applying the Tween rotation animation, the **StartAnimation** method begins animating a View object by calling the AnimationUtils class utilities to access the resources necessary to load the animation. To code the StartAnimation method to launch the rotation, follow these steps:

STEP 1

- Save and close rotation.xml.
- Open Tween.java from the first java\netandroidbootcamp.northernlightsanimation folder and display the line numbers.
- Delete Lines 17-39. Make sure the code ends with two closing curly braces on separate lines.
- Tap or click at the end of Line 14 and press Enter. To instantiate the ImageView control named imgTween, type **ImageView imgRotate = (ImageView) findViewById(R.id.imgTween);**.
- Tap or click ImageView, press Alt+Enter to import the control in this class, and then tap or click at the end of the line.

An instance of the ImageView control named imgRotate is instantiated (Figure 10-27).

Figure 10-27 Instantiating the ImageView

STEP 2

- To begin the Tween rotation animation, press the Enter key and type **imgRotate.startAnimation(AnimationUtils.loadAnimation(this, R.anim.rotation));**.
- Tap or click AnimationUtils and then press Alt+Enter to import the animation utilities into the app.

The Tween animation is started. The fourth image rotates six times and stops (Figure 10-28).

Figure 10-28 Image rotates using Tween animation (complete code for Tween.java)

Critical Thinking

What is the purpose of using AnimationUtils?

The AnimationUtils class launches the animation file from the anim folder by using the loadAnimation method to begin the rotation.

Changing the Emulator to Landscape Orientation

Most Android phones and tablets automatically rotate the display from portrait to landscape orientation when the user turns the device 90 degrees. In most chapters, the emulator has been shown in a portrait orientation because when you first install the Android emulator, the default screen orientation layout is vertical. To switch the emulator to a landscape orientation on a PC, press the Fn+left Ctrl+F12 keys simultaneously (or press the 7 key on the keypad when Num Lock is turned off) when the emulator is displayed during execution, as shown in Figure 10-2. To rotate the phone emulator back to the initial portrait position, press the Fn+left Ctrl+F12 keys again. Mac users can also press the Fn+Ctrl+F12 keys to change the orientation.

Running and Testing the Application

With all this exciting animation, it is time to see both types of animation running in the Android emulator. Tap or click the Run 'app' button on the Standard toolbar and display the app in the Nexus 5 emulator. Tap or click the START FRAME ANIMATION button to begin the Frame animation of the four Northern Lights images, as shown in Figure 10-1. To end the Frame animation and begin the rotation shown in Figure 10-2, tap or click the START TWEEN ANIMATION button. The Tween animation rotates the image six times in a complete circle and ends. Practice changing the orientation of your emulator.

Wrap It Up—Chapter Summary

Android supports two types of animations: frame-by-frame and Tween animations, as shown in the Northern Lights Animation application in this chapter. Frame-by-frame animation shows different drawable images in a View in the opening window. The second Activity displays a Tween animation that rotates an image. Using the animation methods provided in the Android environment, developers can explore the user interface layouts that provide more usability and interest.

- Frame animation assigns a sequence of images to play as in a slide show with a specified interval between images. Tween animation performs a series of transformations on a single image, such as to change its position, size, rotation, and transparency.
- To create a Frame animation, you write code in an XML file to load a sequence of images from the drawable folder. In the XML code, an animation-list root element references these images. Each item in the animation-list specifies how many milliseconds to display the image.

- In the animation-list code, you can include the oneshot property to determine how many times to play the animation. The oneshot property is set to true by default, meaning the animation plays once and then stops. Set the oneshot property to false to have the animation repeatedly play through to the end and then play again from the beginning.
- When you add the XML file with the animation-list code to the Android project, select Drawable as the resource type and select animation-list as the root element so that Android stores the XML file in the res/drawable folder.
- The AnimationDrawable class provides the methods for drawable animations to create a sequence of frame-by-frame images. In Android development, frame-based animations and image transitions are defined as drawables.
- You can set the Background property of an image to any full Drawable resource such as a .png file. In MainActivity.java, you must specify the ImageView control that contains the animation images so you can bind the Drawable resource files to the Background property. Assign a new instance of ImageView to the ImageView control that was originally defined in the activity_main.xml layout. Use the setBackgroundResource method to connect the images in the animation-list to the instance of ImageView.
- In MainActivity.java, also include an instance of AnimationDrawable and assign it as the background of the animation images. Android constructs an AnimationDrawable Java object before setting it as the background. The animation is now ready to display the images, though it does not actually start playing them until the start( ) method is triggered.
- You can use the start( ) and stop( ) methods of the drawable objects to control a Frame animation. When the user taps one button, the start( ) method begins playing the animation continuously if the oneshot property is set to false. The animation stops only when the user taps another button to execute the stop( ) method. The code can then initiate a startActivity that launches another Activity.
- A Tween animation manipulates a Drawable image by adding tween effects, which are predefined transitions that change an object from one state to another. Save a tween effect within an animation XML file. Specify the Resource type of this XML file as Tween animation so that Android stores the file in the res/anim/ folder of your Android project.
- The XML file for a Tween animation defines rotate attributes such as the number of degrees to spin, the pivot location, the rotation duration, and the number of times to repeat the rotation.
- To launch a Tween animation, use the startAnimation method, which begins animating a View object by calling the AnimationUtils class utilities to access the resources it needs to play the animation.
- To switch the emulator to use a landscape orientation on a PC, press the Fn+left Ctrl+F12 keys. To rotate the emulator to the original portrait position, press the Fn+left Ctrl+F12 keys again. Mac users can press the Fn+Ctrl+F12 keys to change the orientation.

Key Terms

9-patch image—A special image with predefined stretching areas that maintain the same look on different screen sizes.

android:oneshot—An attribute of the animation-list that determines whether an animation plays once and then stops or continues to play until the Stop Animation button is tapped.

AnimationDrawable class—A class that provides the methods for Drawable animations to create a sequence of frame-by-frame images.

animation-list—An XML root element that references images stored in the drawable folders and used in an animation.

Frame animation—A type of animation, also called frame-by-frame animation, that plays a sequence of images, as in a slide show, with a specified interval between images.

motion tween—A type of animation that specifies the start state of an object, and then animates the object a predetermined number of times or an infinite number of times using a transition.

setBackgroundResource—A method that places images in the frame-by-frame display for an animation, with each frame pointing to an image referenced in the XML resource file.

startAnimation—A method that begins the animation process of a View object by calling the AnimationUtils class utilities to access the resources necessary to load the animation.

Tween animation—A type of animation that, instead of using a sequence of images, creates an animation by performing a series of transformations on a single image, such as position, size, rotation, and transparency, on the contents of a View object.

tween effect—A transition that changes objects from one state to another, such as by moving, rotating, growing, or shrinking.

Developer FAQs

1. What are the two types of built-in Android animation?
2. Which type of animation displays a slide show type of presentation?
3. Which type of animation is applied to a single image?
4. What is the root element of a Frame animation within the XML file?
5. Write the code that sets an attribute to play a Frame animation until the app ends.
6. Write the code that sets an attribute to play a Frame animation for three seconds.
7. Would the oneshot property be set to true or false in question 6?
8. Which type of drawable image stretches across different screen sizes?
9. Name three types of drawable objects that can be set as a Background drawable.

10. Which method launches a Frame animation?
11. Which method ends a Frame animation?
12. Name four tween effects.
13. Which tween effect shrinks an image?
14. Which tween effect changes the transparency of the image?
15. When you create a Tween XML file, which folder is the file automatically saved in?
16. If you wanted to turn an image one-quarter of a circle starting at 0 degrees, write two lines of the code necessary to make that rotation.
17. Write the attribute for a rotation that repeats 10 times.
18. When an emulator launches, which orientation type is displayed?
19. Which keys change the orientation of the emulator on a PC?
20. What happens to the image if you animate an object past the edges of the View object?

Beyond the Book

Search the web for answers to the following questions to further your Android knowledge.

1. Research how smartphone animation games have changed the sales of console games in the gaming industry. Write at least 200 words on this topic.
2. Research OpenGL graphic development. Write at least 150 words on this topic.
3. A relatively new player to the mobile platform is the Windows 8 smartphone. Research why this phone might or might not be successful in the long term. Write at least 150 words on this topic.
4. On the Google Play site, determine the top four grossing apps. Write a paragraph about each.

Case Programming Projects

Complete one or more of the following case programming projects. Use the same steps and techniques taught within the chapter. Submit the program you create to your instructor. The level of difficulty is indicated for each case programming project.

Easiest: ★

Intermediate: ★★

Challenging: ★★★

Case Project 10–1: Facial Expressions App ★

Requirements Document

Application title:	Facial Expressions App
Purpose:	A series of images uses Frame animation to demonstrate seven facial expressions of an actor.
Algorithms:	1. The opening screen displays the first image of a man with a happy facial expression (Figure 10-29). 2. When the user taps the SEE THE ACTOR button, the seven facial expressions are each displayed for two seconds. After each image is shown once, the animation ends.
Conditions:	1. The pictures of the seven facial expressions of the actor are provided with your student files with the names face1 through face7.

Figure 10-29 Facial Expressions app

Case Project 10–2: Improve Your Golf Stroke App ★

Requirements Document

Application title:	Improve Your Golf Stroke App
Purpose:	A series of images uses Frame animation to demonstrate the proper positions of the perfect golf swing.
Algorithms:	1. The screen displays six images, each showing the proper position during the process of making a golf swing. Display the images in a Frame animation with 0.5 seconds between each image. Each image should only be displayed once when the user taps the ~~ROTATE~~ PERFECT YOUR SWING button (Figure 10-30). 2. When the user taps the ROTATE YOUR SWING button, rotate the fifth image around 270 degrees nine times with an interval of three seconds.
Conditions:	1. Six pictures of a golfer at different moments in a golf stroke are provided with your student files with the names golf1 through golf6. 2. Display each image with the size 700, 1000.

Figure 10-30 Improve Your Golf Stroke app

Case Project 10–3: Android Rotation App ★★

Requirements Document

Application title: Android Rotation App

Purpose: As an advertisement at the end of a television commercial, an Android phone rotates in a perfect circle four times.

Algorithms:

1. The opening screen displays an Android phone in the center and automatically begins rotating the image four times in a perfect circle with an interval of 1.5 seconds.

Conditions:

1. Find a picture online of an Android phone.
2. Display the image with the size 100, 170.
3. Code a theme with no title bar.

Case Project 10–4: Cartoon Animation App ★★

Requirements Document

Application title: Cartoon Animation App

Purpose: A sequence of cartoon images is displayed to create the sense of motion.

Algorithms:

1. The opening screen displays one of four cartoon images of a man with an idea. When the user taps the START CARTOON button, each image is displayed for 0.15 seconds.
2. When the user taps the STOP CARTOON button, the current image rotates once and then stops.

Conditions:

1. Find cartoons online to create a moving animation.
2. Display each image with the size 300, 400.

Case Project 10–5: Flags of the World App ★★★

Requirements Document

Application title: Flags of the World App

Purpose: A sequence of flag images appears when the app starts.

Algorithms:

1. The opening screen displays images of seven world flags. When the user taps a START FLAGS button, a Frame animation displays each flag for 0.75 seconds until the app ends.
2. When the user taps the STOP FLAGS button, the Frame animation stops. The last flag image fades away for 10 seconds until it is no longer visible.

Conditions:

1. Find pictures of the seven world flags online.
2. Display each image with the size 170, 100.
3. Code a theme with no title bar.

Case Project 10–6: Frame and Tween Animation Game App ★★★

Requirements Document

Application title: Frame and Tween Animation Game App

Purpose: Display images of your favorite game in action.

Algorithms:

1. Locate at least four images of your favorite game character (such as one in Angry Birds) and create a custom Frame animation of your choice.
2. Create a Tween animation with one of the images that uses at least two of the tween effects.

Conditions:

1. Select your own images.
2. Use a layout of your choice.

CHAPTER 11

Discover! Persistent Data

In this chapter, you learn to:

- Create an Android project using persistent data
- Understand different types of persistent data
- Understand SharedPreferences persistent data
- Understand internal storage
- Understand external storage
- Understand saving data using a network connection
- Understand saving to a database connection
- Write data using a SharedPreferences object
- Instantiate a SharedPreferences object
- Write data using getString( ) method
- Retrieve data from a SharedPreferences object
- Read data using a putString( ) method
- Display an ImageView control using code

An Android app typically requests data and then modifies that data to produce a result throughout multiple activities. To demonstrate the use of storing that data across classes, this chapter's Electric Car Financing project requests the numbers of years for the loan, the cost of the electric car, and interest rate. A government program provides lower subsidized electric car loans starting at an interest rate of 1.9% if you are approved for a three, four, or five year auto loan. The opening screen (Figure 11-1a) provides three EditText controls to accept the number of years for the loan (3, 4, or 5), the cost of the electric car, and the interest rate. The three variables are stored in a local variable on the computer (Figure 11-1b). These values will persist throughout the life of the app and after the program stops execution. After the user taps the button on the opening screen, a second Activity (Figure 11-2) opens and the monthly payment for the loan is calculated for a four-year loan, entered in the first Activity. A unique image is displayed in an ImageView control based on whether the user selected a three, four, or five-year loan.

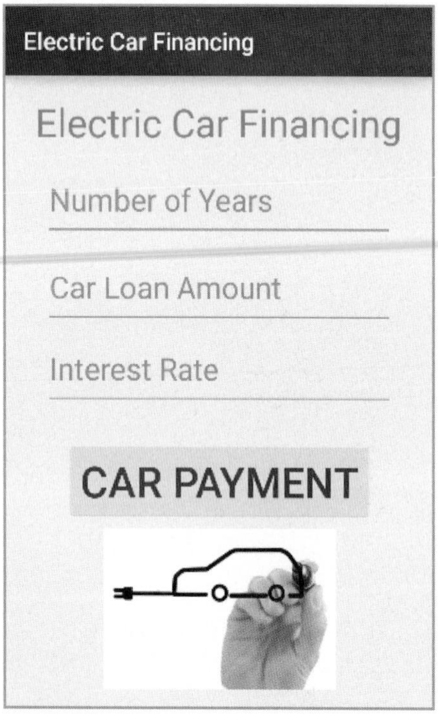

© iStock.com/Gajus

(a) Opening screen

© iStock.com/Gajus

(b) Persistent data entered

Figure 11-1 Electric Car Financing Android app

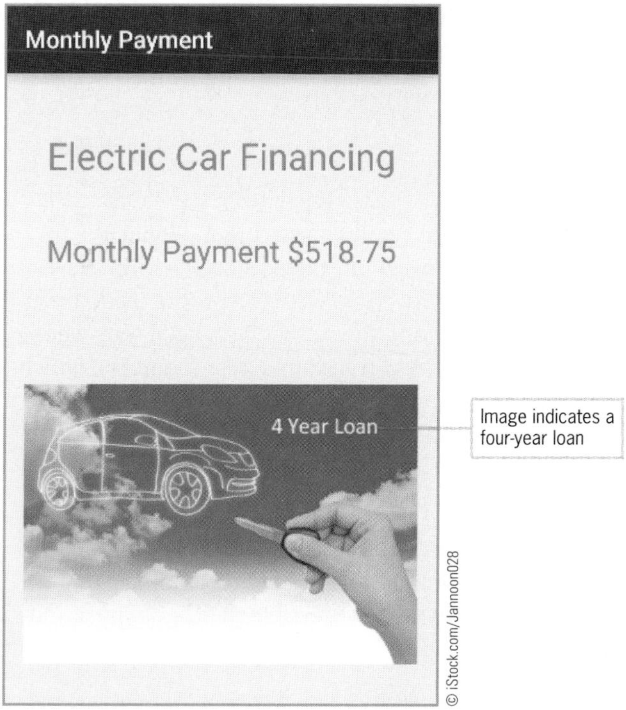

Figure 11-2 Car payment computed using persistent data on second Activity

IN THE TRENCHES

The persistent data structure is available in some form in every programming language.

To create this application, the developer must understand how to perform the following processes, among others:

1. Add strings to the String table.
2. Add images to the drawable folder.
3. Design two XML layouts for the first and second Activity.
4. Instantiate the XML controls in the first Activity.
5. Establish a SharedPreferences object to store the data entered.
6. Write data to the SharedPreferences object.
7. Launch a second Activity.
8. Initialize the XML controls on the second Activity.
9. Retrieve the data from the SharedPreferences object.

10. Calculate the monthly payment and display the appropriate image for the number of loan years using an If structure.
11. Display the monthly payment on the second Activity.

Understanding Persistent Data

The Electric Car Financing app opens with a window that requests user input. Unlike the project in Chapter 2 (Healthy Recipes), this program allows input that is stored within the device. That data survives to be used in the second Activity class. With the programs that you have written so far, the values entered did not persist beyond the Activity in which they were created. The data was lost because the data is stored in RAM (random access memory), which is cleared when the app (or the device) stops running. Android applications can save data on the device's drive or other storage media such as a memory card or cloud service so that the data be retrieved later within the app or after the termination of the program. **Persistent data** stores values permanently by placing the information in a file.

Android provides several options for you to save persistent application data. Persistent data can be saved within a variable or within a database, based on the specific need of the app. Some apps may require private storage, while others should be accessible to other applications. Persistent data can be stored in five different ways in Android applications:

- Shared preferences—Stores private data in key–value pairs
- Internal storage—Stores private data in the memory of the device
- External storage—Stores data, which can be available to other apps on shared external storage
- SQLite database—Stores structured data in a private database
- Network connection—Stores data on a web server

Using Shared Preferences

The SharedPreferences class provides one of the easiest ways to save and load primitive data, whether you are looking to save the user's name or settings such as the font size the user prefers. In the Electric Car Financing app, the SharedPreferences object is used to store user data even if the user closes the application. Shared preferences can save any data including user preferences, such as what wallpaper a user has chosen or individual values entered by the user in an EditText control.

Shared preferences can be used to save any primitive data: Booleans, floats, ints, longs, and strings. In the chapter project app this includes, the number of years for the loan (int), the amount of the loan (float), and the interest rate (float) for the electric car loan. In the first Activity, these values are saved using shared preferences, and in the second Activity, they are retrieved to determine which of the three images that display the numbers of years in the loan should be used. Shared preferences are best when your app needs to save small chunks of data such as a name–value pair.

The two-part pair specifies a name for the data you want to save and the actual value. The pair is saved to an XML file that can be retrieved later in the app or after the app closes. To save data in a SharedPreferences file, the following steps must be completed when writing persistent data:

- Obtain an instance of the SharedPreferences file.
- Create a SharedPreferences.Editor object.
- Assign values into SharedPreferences objects using the putString( ) method.
- Save the values to the preferences file using the commit( ) method.

Using Internal Storage

Another option when saving persistent data is to store the information directly on the device's internal drive. The saved files on the device are available only to the app that created the files. Other applications cannot access files saved with the internal storage method. Use caution when storing internal files, because low internal storage space can drastically affect the speed of an Android device and battery life.

Using External Storage

Android apps can save persistent data to external storage, for example, the device's SD (Secure Digital) card. All applications can read and write files placed on the external storage and the Android smartphone or tablet owner can remove them. To use external storage, the following permissions are necessary in the Android Manifest file:

```
<uses-permission android:name="android.permission.WRITE_EXTERNAL_STORAGE"/>
<uses-permission android:name="android.permission.READ_EXTERNAL_STORAGE"/>
```

Using SQLite Databases

If you have a large amount of data to store as persistent data, a database is the perfect choice. The default database engine for Android is SQLite. **SQLite** (SQL stands for Structured Query Language) is a lightweight, preloaded mobile database engine, which has been available since the Cupcake 1.5 version of Android and occupies a small amount of disk memory. The data is stored within the SQLite database so that it persists even after the app is terminated. In contrast to a traditional database, SQLite is embedded into the user's program or browser. Using a SQLite database, Android apps model data items in tables and columns, with optional relationships between the entities within the database. The tables can be queried using SQL statements.

Critical Thinking

Does Android SQLite store the information in a managed interface on the smartphone?

No. Android SQLite is created within the app by creating a class that handles all the operations required to deal with the database such as creating the database, adding tables, and updating records.

Using a Network Connection

If your device is connected to the Internet, persistent data can be stored and retrieved on a web service. Before an app attempts to connect to a network connection, it should check to see whether an Internet connection is available. The device may be out of range of a 3G/4G network or the user may have disabled both Wi-Fi and mobile data access. If a connection is not available, the user cannot save or retrieve the persistent data.

Creating XML Layout Files

The Electric Car Financing app begins with the activity_main.xml layout, which displays a title, three Number EditText controls, and a Button control. A second XML layout named payment.xml displays an ImageView control with the appropriate image of the number of years in the loan and a TextView control to display the monthly payment. To start the Electric Car Financing application by adding images, a String table, and the first XML layout file, complete the following steps:

STEP 1

- Open the Android Studio program.
- Tap or click the Start a new Android Studio project selection in the Quick Start category.
- In the Create New Project dialog box, type **Electric Car Financing** in the Application name text box.
- If necessary, in the Company Domain text box, type **androidbootcamp.net** and in the Project location text box, type **D:\Workspace\ElectricCarFinancing**.

The new Android Electric Car Financing project has an application name (Figure 11-3).

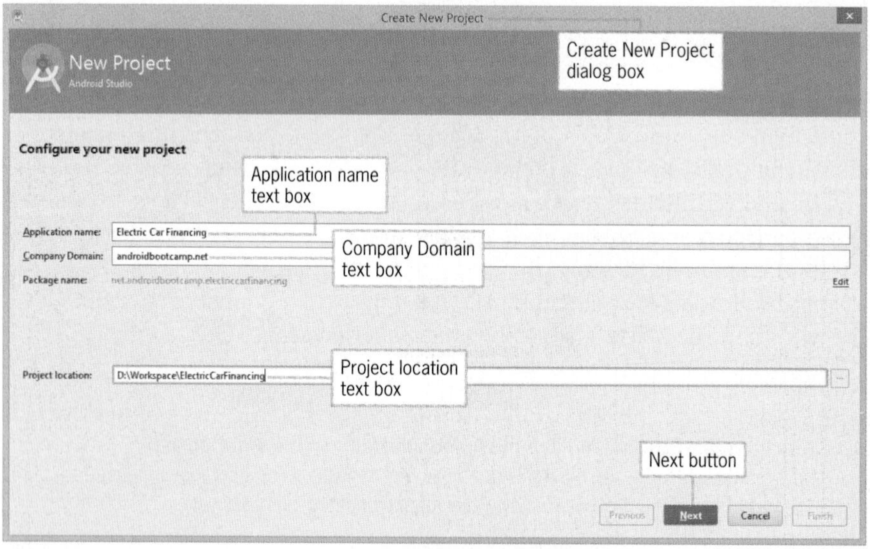

Figure 11-3 Setting up the Electric Car Financing project

STEP 2

- Tap or click the Next button on the Configure your new project page of the Create New Project dialog box.
- If necessary, tap or click the Phone and Tablet check box to select the form factor for your app.
- If necessary, select API 15: Android 4.0.3 (IceCreamSandwich) for the Minimum SDK.
- Tap or click the Next button on the Select the form factors your app will run on page.
- If necessary, tap or click Blank Activity to add an Activity to the new project.
- Tap or click the Next button on the Add an activity to Mobile page.
- Tap or click the Finish button on the Choose options for your new file page.
- Tap or click the Hello world! TextView widget (displayed by default) in the emulator and press the Delete key.
- Tap or click 'the virtual device to render the layout with' button (emulator) directly to the right of the Palette on the activity_main.xml tab, and then tap or click Nexus 5.
- To add the four image files to the drawable resource folder, copy opening.png, three.png, four.png, and five.png from the student folder on the USB drive and paste the files in the drawable folder.
- Tap or click the OK button in the Copy dialog box.

Copies of the four image files appear in the drawable folder (Figure 11-4).

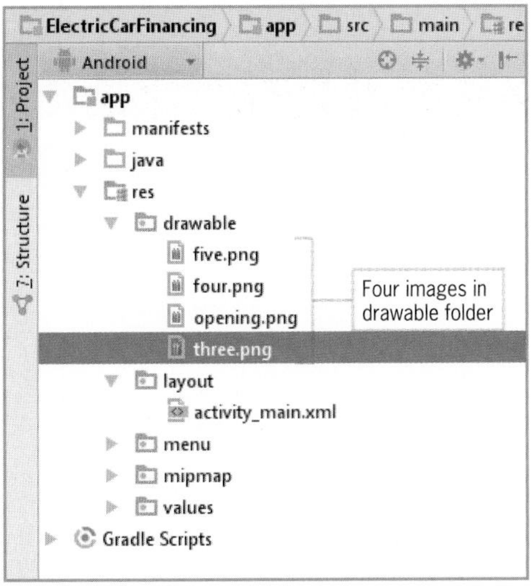

Figure 11-4 Image files in the drawable folder

STEP 3

- Expand the res\values folder and then double-tap or double-click the strings.xml file.
- Tap or click the Open editor link and then tap or click the Add Key button.
- Type **txtTitle** in the Key text box and type **Electric Car Financing** in the Default Value text box.
- Repeat the process of adding the following strings shown in Table 11-1 to the Translations Editor:

Key	Default Value
hint1	Number of Years
hint2	Car Loan Amount
hint3	Interest Rate
btnPayment	Car Payment
imgDescription	Number of Years Image
txtPayment	Monthly Payment

Table 11-1 String table

- Save your work.

The strings.xml file contains the string values necessary in this app (Figure 11-5).

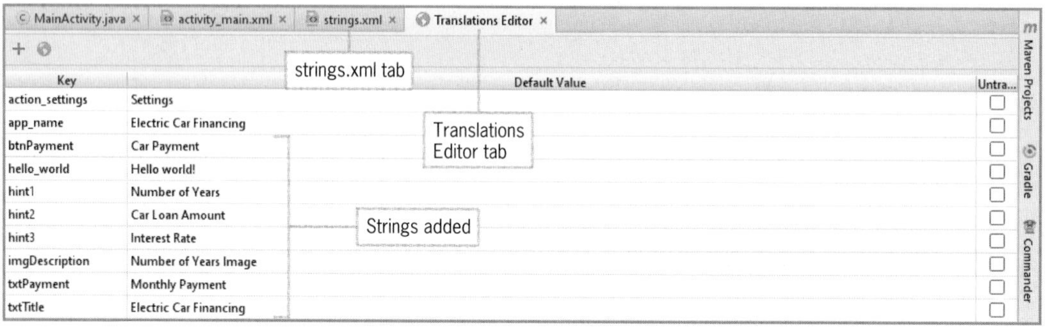

Figure 11-5 String values for the app

STEP 4

- Close the Translations Editor and strings.xml tab.
- If necessary, open the activity_main.xml layout file.
- Drag a Plain TextView control to the top center part of the emulator.
- Drag a Number control for the number of years of the loan from the Text Fields category of the Palette, and then center the Number control below the Plain TextView control.
- Drag another Number EditView control for the loan amount to the emulator, and then center it below the first Number EditView control.
- Drag a Number (Decimal) EditView control for the interest rate to the emulator, and then center it below the second Number EditView control.
- Drag Button control from the Form Widgets category, and then center it below the third EditText control.
- Drag an ImageView control from the Widgets category, and then center it below the Button control.
- Double-tap or double-click the image placeholder, tap or click the src ellipsis button, and then select opening from the Resource Chooser dialog box.
- Tap or click the OK button.
- Tap or click the Text tab at the bottom of the window to view the XML code.
- Alter the XML code to match the following customized code:

```
<TextView
     android:layout_width="wrap_content"
     android:layout_height="wrap_content"
     android:text="@string/txtTitle"
     android:id="@+id/txtTitle"
     android:layout_alignParentTop="true"
     android:layout_centerHorizontal="true"
     android:textSize="32sp" />

    <EditText
     android:layout_width="wrap_content"
     android:layout_height="wrap_content"
     android:inputType="number"
     android:ems="10"
     android:id="@+id/txtYears"
     android:layout_below="@+id/txtTitle"
     android:layout_centerHorizontal="true"
     android:layout_marginTop="20dp"
     android:textSize="25sp"
     android:hint="@string/hint1" />
```

```
<EditText
 android:layout_width="wrap_content"
 android:layout_height="wrap_content"
 android:inputType="number"
 android:ems="10"
 android:id="@+id/txtLoan"
 android:layout_below="@+id/txtYears"
 android:layout_centerHorizontal="true"
 android:layout_marginTop="20dp"
 android:textSize="25sp"
 android:hint="@string/hint2"/>

<EditText
 android:layout_width="wrap_content"
 android:layout_height="wrap_content"
 android:inputType="numberDecimal"
 android:ems="10"
 android:id="@+id/txtInterest"
 android:layout_below="@+id/txtLoan"
 android:layout_centerHorizontal="true"
 android:layout_marginTop="15dp"
 android:textSize="25sp"
 android:hint="@string/hint3"/>

<Button
 android:layout_width="wrap_content"
 android:layout_height="wrap_content"
 android:text="@string/btnPayment"
 android:id="@+id/btnPayment"
 android:layout_below="@+id/txtInterest"
 android:layout_centerHorizontal="true"
 android:layout_marginTop="28dp"
 android:textSize="35sp" />

<ImageView
 android:layout_width="wrap_content"
 android:layout_height="wrap_content"
 android:id="@+id/imgOpening"
 android:layout_below="@+id/btnPayment"
 android:layout_centerHorizontal="true"
 android:contentDescription="@string/imgDescription"
 android:src="@drawable/opening"
 android:layout_marginTop="5dp"  />
```

The activity_main.xml file contains TextView, EditText, Button, and ImageView controls (Figure 11-6).

activity_main.xml

```
<RelativeLayout xmlns:android="http://schemas.android.com/apk/res/android"
    xmlns:tools="http://schemas.android.com/tools" android:layout_width="match_parent"
    android:layout_height="match_parent" android:paddingLeft="@dimen/activity_horizontal_margin"
    android:paddingRight="@dimen/activity_horizontal_margin"
    android:paddingTop="@dimen/activity_vertical_margin"
    android:paddingBottom="@dimen/activity_vertical_margin" tools:context=".MainActivity">

    <TextView
        android:layout_width="wrap_content"
        android:layout_height="wrap_content"
        android:text="@string/txtTitle"
        android:id="@+id/txtTitle"
        android:layout_alignParentTop="true"
        android:layout_centerHorizontal="true"
        android:textSize="32sp" />

    <EditText
        android:layout_width="wrap_content"
        android:layout_height="wrap_content"
        android:inputType="number"
        android:ems="10"
        android:id="@+id/txtYears"
        android:layout_below="@+id/txtTitle"
        android:layout_centerHorizontal="true"
        android:layout_marginTop="20dp"
        android:textSize="25sp"
        android:hint="@string/hint1" />

    <EditText
        android:layout_width="wrap_content"
        android:layout_height="wrap_content"
        android:inputType="number"
        android:ems="10"
        android:id="@+id/txtLoan"
        android:layout_below="@+id/txtYears"
        android:layout_centerHorizontal="true"
        android:layout_marginTop="20dp"
        android:textSize="25sp"
        android:hint="@string/hint2"/>

    <EditText
        android:layout_width="wrap_content"
        android:layout_height="wrap_content"
        android:inputType="numberDecimal"
        android:ems="10"
        android:id="@+id/txtInterest"
        android:layout_below="@+id/txtLoan"
        android:layout_centerHorizontal="true"
        android:layout_marginTop="15dp"
        android:textSize="25sp"
        android:hint="@string/hint3"/>

    <Button
        android:layout_width="wrap_content"
        android:layout_height="wrap_content"
        android:text="@string/btnPayment"
        android:id="@+id/button"
        android:layout_below="@+id/txtInterest"
        android:layout_centerHorizontal="true"
        android:layout_marginTop="28dp"
        android:textSize="35sp" />

    <ImageView
        android:layout_width="wrap_content"
        android:layout_height="wrap_content"
        android:id="@+id/imgOpening"
        android:layout_below="@+id/button"
        android:layout_centerHorizontal="true"
        android:contentDescription="@string/imgDescription"
        android:src="@drawable/opening"
        android:layout_marginTop="5dp"  />

</RelativeLayout>
```

activity_main.xml tab

TextView control

First EditText control

Second EditText control

Third EditText control

Button control

ImageView control

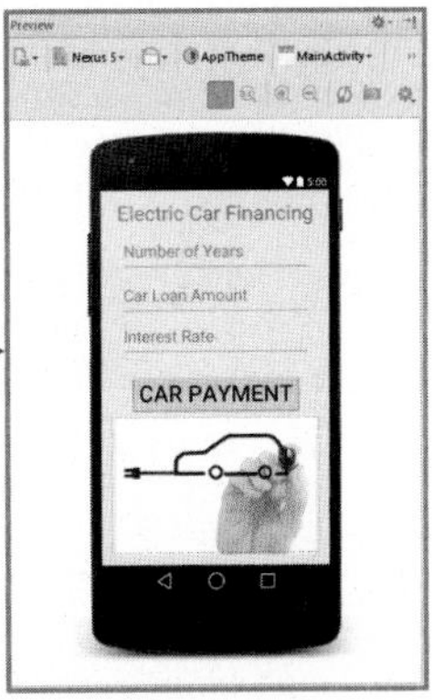

© iStock.com/Gajus

Figure 11-6 First XML layout

STEP 5

- Close the activity_main.xml tab and save your work.

Creating a Second Activity and XML Layout

When the user taps the CAR PAYMENT button in the Electric Car Financing application, a startActivity intent launches a second Activity named Payment.java which opens a second XML layout named activity_payment.xml to display the monthly car payment and an appropriate image that displays whether the loan is a 2-year, 3-year, or 4-year loan. To create a second class and a second XML layout and then to design the second layout, follow these steps:

STEP 1

- Save and close the activity_main.xml tab.
- To create a second class and XML layout file, press and hold or right-click the first java/net.androidbootcamp.electriccarfinancing folder, tap or click New on the shortcut menu, tap or click Activity, and then tap or click Blank Activity.
- Type **Payment** in the Activity name text box in the New Android Activity dialog box to create a second class that defines the Payment Activity.
- Type **Monthly Payment** in the Title text box.

A new class named Payment.java and a second XML layout file named activity_payment is created (Figure 11-7).

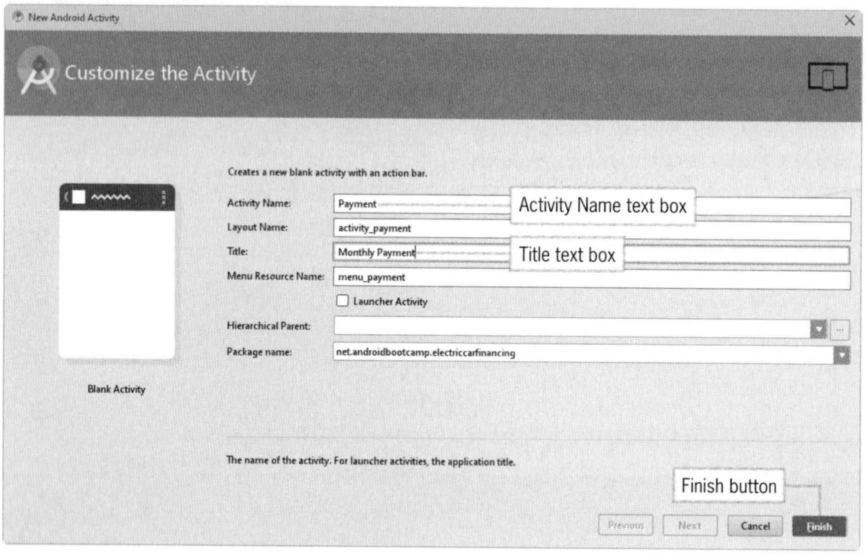

Figure 11-7 Create a second class named Payment and a second XML layout named activity_payment

STEP 2

- Tap or click the Finish button to finish creating the Payment class and the associated XML layout file.
- Tap or click the Design tab on the activity_payment.xml.
- Delete the Hello World! TextView control.
- Drag a Plain TextView control from the Palette to the top center part of the activity_payment emulator.
- Drag a second Plain TextView to the emulator, and then center it below the first one.
- Drag an ImageView control below the two TextView controls, and then center it horizontally.
- Tap or click the Text tab at the bottom of the window to display the XML code for this layout.
- Alter the XML code to match the following customized code, and then save your work:

```
<TextView
 android:layout_width="wrap_content"
 android:layout_height="wrap_content"
 android:text="@string/txtTitle"
 android:id="@+id/txtTitle2"
 android:layout_alignParentTop="true"
 android:layout_centerHorizontal="true"
 android:layout_marginTop="30dp"
 android:textSize="30sp"/>

<TextView
 android:layout_width="wrap_content"
 android:layout_height="wrap_content"
 android:id="@+id/txtMonthlyPayment"
 android:layout_below="@+id/txtTitle2"
 android:layout_centerHorizontal="true"
 android:layout_marginTop="40dp"
 android:textSize="25sp"/>

<ImageView
 android:id="@+id/imgYears"
 android:layout_width="350dp"
 android:layout_height="250dp"
 android:layout_alignParentBottom="true"
 android:layout_centerHorizontal="true"
 android:layout_marginBottom="5dp"
 android:contentDescription="@string/imgDescription" />
```

The activity_payment.xml file contains two TextView controls and an ImageView control (Figure 11-8).

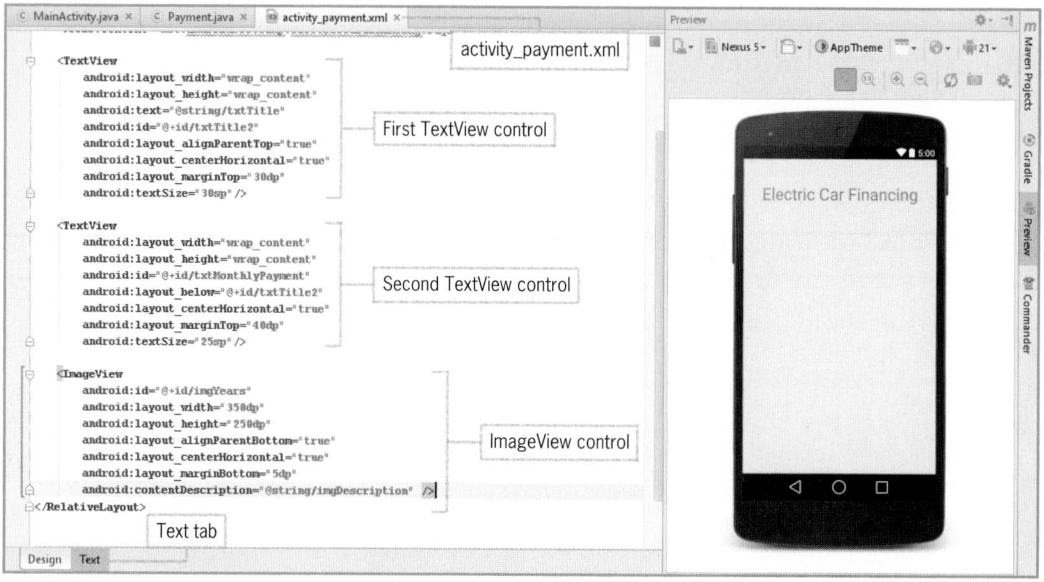

Figure 11-8 TextView and ImageView controls for activity_payment.xml

Instantiating the XML Controls

When the Electric Car Financing app starts, the activity_main.xml layout opens, displaying the TextView control title, and requests the user to enter the number of years for financing the loan, the loan amount, and the interest rate as a decimal value. When the user taps the Button control, the values are assigned to the variables within the MainActivity class. To instantiate the XML controls from the first Activity, follow these steps:

STEP 1

- Close the activity_payment.xml tab.
- Open the MainActivity.java code window.
- Show the line numbers and delete Lines 16-38.
- Press the Enter key to insert a new line after Line 14, type **final EditText years = (EditText) findViewById(R.id.txtYears);** to instantiate the first EditText control, and then press the Enter key.
- Tap or click EditText and import the class by pressing Alt+Enter.
- Type **final EditText loan = (EditText)findViewById(R.id.txtLoan);** to instantiate the second EditText control, and then press the Enter key.
- Type **final EditText interest = (EditText)findViewById(R.id.txtInterest);** to instantiate the third EditText control, and then press the Enter key.

The three EditText controls are instantiated (Figure 11-9).

Figure 11-9 EditText controls instantiated

STEP 2

- Type **Button button = (Button)findViewById(R.id.btnPayment);** to instantiate the Button control, and then press the Enter key twice.
- Tap or click the red Button text and press Alt+Enter to import the Button library.
- Tap or click the next line (Line 21). To create a setOnClickListener method so the Button control waits for the user's tap or click, type **button.setOn** and wait for the auto-complete listing to appear.
- Double-tap or double-click setOnClickListener to select it from the auto-complete listing.
- In the parentheses, type **new On** and wait for the auto-complete listing to appear.
- Double-tap or double-click the first choice, which lists a View.OnClickListener.

An OnClickListener auto-generated stub appears in the code (Figure 11-10).

MainActivity.java × | Payment.java ×

```
1  package net.androidbootcamp.electriccarfinancing;
2
3  import ...
10
11
12 public class MainActivity extends ActionBarActivity {
13
14     @Override
15     protected void onCreate(Bundle savedInstanceState) {
16         super.onCreate(savedInstanceState);
17         setContentView(R.layout.activity_main);
18         final EditText years=(EditText) findViewById(R.id.txtYears);
19         final EditText loan=(EditText)findViewById(R.id.txtLoan);
20         final EditText interest=(EditText)findViewById(R.id.txtInterest);
21         Button button= (Button)findViewById(R.id.btnPayment);
22
23         button.setOnClickListener(new View.OnClickListener() {
24             @Override
25             public void onClick(View v) {
26
27             }
28         });
29     }
30
31 }
32
```

Button control instantiated

OnClickListener( ) stub

Figure 11-10 Button OnClickListener stub

STEP 3

- On Line 13, initialize the variables by typing **int intYears;** and then press Enter.
- On the next line type **int intLoan;** and then press Enter.
- On the next line type **float decInterest;** and press Enter.
- Tap or click within the onClick method on Line 29 and assign the number of years for the life of the loan to strName by typing **intYears = Integer.parseInt(years.getText().toString());** and then press Enter.
- On the next line, assign the amount of the requested loan to an integer value by typing **intLoan = Integer.parseInt(loan.getText().toString());** and then press Enter.
- On the next line, assign the amount of the requested loan to an integer value by typing **decInterest = Float.parseFloat(interest.getText().toString());**.

The variables intYears, intLoan, and intInterest are assigned to the entered number of years, the loan amount, and the decimal interest rate (Figure 11-11).

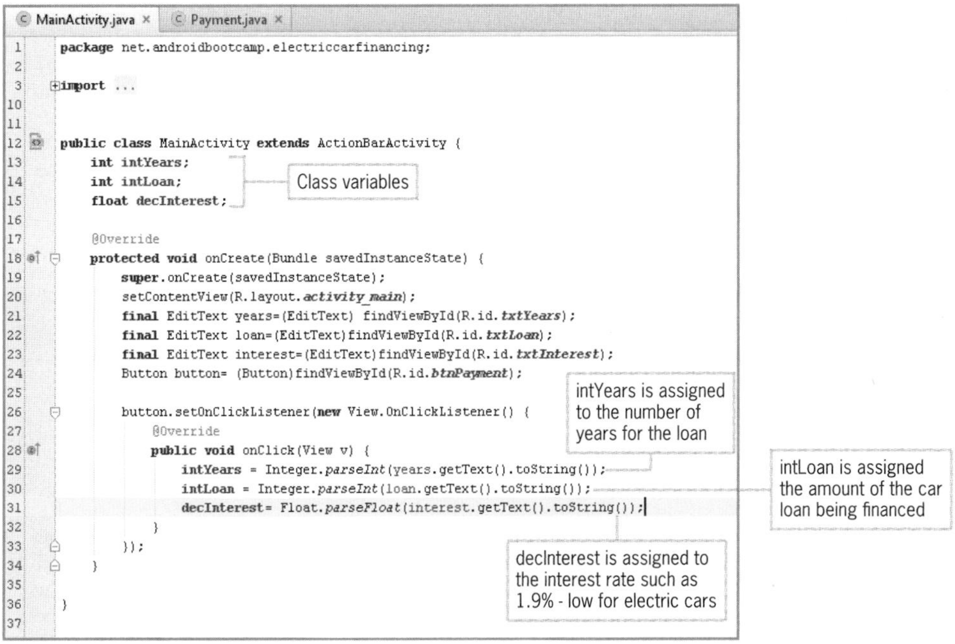

Figure 11-11 Variables intYears, intLoan, and decInterest assigned

IN THE TRENCHES

When you write data using SharedPreferences, you can make changes to the data by using the SharedPreferences Editor.

Writing Persistent Data with SharedPreferences

One of the most effective ways to save simple application data to an Android device is by using the SharedPreferences object. The data is saved to an XML file as a key–value pair. The **key** is a string such as "key1" that uniquely identifies the preference, and the **value** is the data represented as a string, int, long, float, or Boolean. Android SharedPreferences can store data that can be used in different Activities of your application or by another application. A common example of using SharedPreferences may be in a game like Angry Birds. The Angry Birds app needs to save the high score from game to game, the user name, and current level achieved. Preferences can be stored at the Activity or application level.

In the chapter project app, the first data to be stored is the number of years for the life of the loan. The SharedPreference for this name data is a set of data values: key1 uniquely identifies the preference and intYears represents the actual value of the integer. A preference can be any of a number of different data types. The following data types are supported by the SharedPreferences class:

- putString( )—Stores string values
- putInt( )—Stores integer values

- putLong( )—Stores long values
- putFloat( )—Stores float values
- putBoolean( )—Stores Boolean values

To create an instance of the SharedPreferences object from an Activity, you use the following code syntax:

Code Syntax

```
final SharedPreferences sharedPref = PreferenceManager.
getDefaultSharedPreferences(this);
SharedPreferences.Editor editor = sharedPref.edit();
editor.putInt("key1", intYears);
editor.putInt("key2", intLoan);
editor.putFloat("key3", decInterest);
editor.commit();
```

In the first line, a valid SharedPreferences object is instantiated. Next, a SharedPreferences. Editor provides a method to add, modify, or delete preference content. Within the editor, you can also remove a specific preference by name using the remove( ) method, or remove all preferences within the set using the clear( ) method. The two putInt and one putFloat methods are not called immediately. The commit( ) method must be called to actually write the values to the XML file. Save values as persistent data using SharedPreferences by following these steps:

STEP 1

- In the code on the MainActivity.java tab, after the Button is instantiated (Line 25), type **final SharedPreferences sharedPref = PreferenceManager.getDefaultSharedPreferences(this);**.
- Tap or click SharedPreferences and press Alt+Enter to import SharedPreferences.
- Tap or click PreferenceManager and press Alt+Enter to import the library.

An instance of the SharedPreferences class is created named sharedPref in the MainActivity class (Figure 11-12).

MainActivity.java × Payment.java ×

```
1  package net.androidbootcamp.electriccarfinancing;
2
3  import ...
12
13
14 public class MainActivity extends ActionBarActivity {
15     int intYears;
16     int intLoan;
17     float decInterest;
18
19     @Override
20     protected void onCreate(Bundle savedInstanceState) {
21         super.onCreate(savedInstanceState);
22         setContentView(R.layout.activity_main);
23         final EditText years=(EditText) findViewById(R.id.txtYears);
24         final EditText loan=(EditText)findViewById(R.id.txtLoan);
25         final EditText interest=(EditText)findViewById(R.id.txtInterest);
26         Button button= (Button)findViewById(R.id.btnPayment);
27         final SharedPreferences sharedPref = PreferenceManager.getDefaultSharedPreferences(this);
28         button.setOnClickListener(new View.OnClickListener() {
29             @Override
30             public void onClick(View v) {
31                 intYears = Integer.parseInt(years.getText().toString());
32                 intLoan = Integer.parseInt(loan.getText().toString());
33                 decInterest= Float.parseFloat(interest.getText().toString());
34             }
35         });
36     }
37
38 }
39
```

Instantiate the SharedPreferences object

Figure 11-12 SharedPreferences class

STEP 2

- Tap or click at the end of Line 33 (assignment of decInterest) and then press Enter to add a new line within the OnClick method.
- To store data using the editor, type **SharedPreferences.Editor editor = sharedPref.edit();** and then press Enter.
- On the next line, assign the first key–value pair by typing **editor.putInt("key1", intYears);** and then press Enter.
- On the next line, assign the second key–value pair by typing **editor.putInt("key2", intLoan);** and then press Enter.
- On the next line, assign the third key–value pair by typing **editor.putFloat("key3", decInterest);** and then press Enter.
- To write the values to the XML data file, on the next line type **editor.commit();**.

Three values are saved to the SharedPreferences XML data file (Figure 11-13).

MainActivity.java × Payment.java ×

```
import ...

public class MainActivity extends ActionBarActivity {
    int intYears;
    int intLoan;
    float decInterest;

    @Override
    protected void onCreate(Bundle savedInstanceState) {
        super.onCreate(savedInstanceState);
        setContentView(R.layout.activity_main);
        final EditText years=(EditText) findViewById(R.id.txtYears);
        final EditText loan=(EditText)findViewById(R.id.txtLoan);
        final EditText interest=(EditText)findViewById(R.id.txtInterest);
        Button button= (Button)findViewById(R.id.btnPayment);
        final SharedPreferences sharedPref = PreferenceManager.getDefaultSharedPreferences(this);
        button.setOnClickListener(new View.OnClickListener() {
            @Override
            public void onClick(View v) {
                intYears = Integer.parseInt(years.getText().toString());
                intLoan = Integer.parseInt(loan.getText().toString());
                decInterest= Float.parseFloat(interest.getText().toString());
                SharedPreferences.Editor editor = sharedPref.edit();
                editor.putInt("key1", intYears);
                editor.putInt("key2", intLoan);
                editor.putFloat("key3", decInterest);
                editor.commit();
            }
        });
    }
```

Persistent data written to the SharedPreferences object

Figure 11-13 Three values (persistent data) written in an XML data file

IN THE TRENCHES

There is no limit to the number of different shared preferences you can create.

Launching the Second Activity

After the persistent data is saved to a local XML file, MainActivity starts a second Activity named Payment.java. The second Activity is responsible for retrieving the persistent data, which is tested using a conditional If statement to determine the payment amount based on the number of years for the loan. To launch the second class, follow these steps:

STEP 1

- To launch the Payment class from the first Activity, insert a new line in the onClick(View v) auto-generated method stub after the editor.commit(); statement.
- Type **startActivity(new Intent(MainActivity.this, Payment.class));** to launch the second Activity.
- Tap or click Intent, and then press Alt+Enter. Save your work.

The second Activity named Payment is launched with an Intent statement (Figure 11-14).

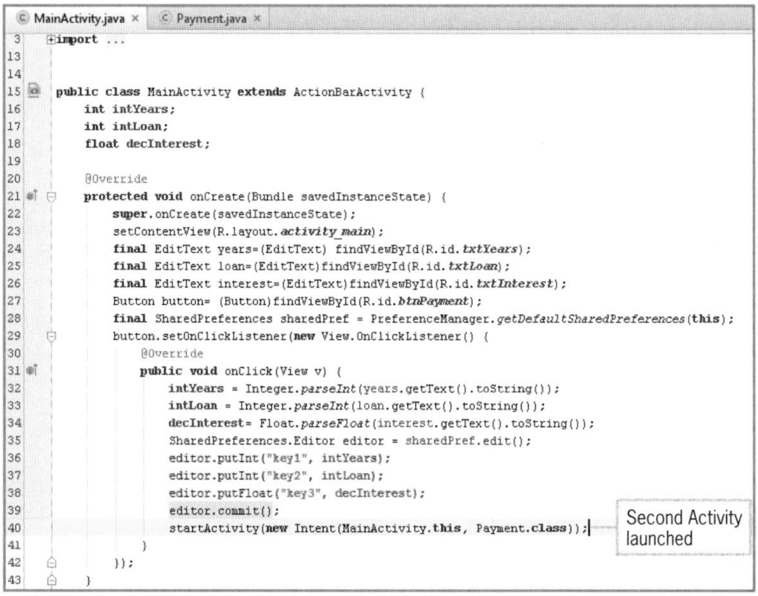


```java
import ...

public class MainActivity extends ActionBarActivity {
    int intYears;
    int intLoan;
    float decInterest;

    @Override
    protected void onCreate(Bundle savedInstanceState) {
        super.onCreate(savedInstanceState);
        setContentView(R.layout.activity_main);
        final EditText years=(EditText) findViewById(R.id.txtYears);
        final EditText loan=(EditText)findViewById(R.id.txtLoan);
        final EditText interest=(EditText)findViewById(R.id.txtInterest);
        Button button= (Button)findViewById(R.id.btnPayment);
        final SharedPreferences sharedPref = PreferenceManager.getDefaultSharedPreferences(this);
        button.setOnClickListener(new View.OnClickListener() {
            @Override
            public void onClick(View v) {
                intYears = Integer.parseInt(years.getText().toString());
                intLoan = Integer.parseInt(loan.getText().toString());
                decInterest= Float.parseFloat(interest.getText().toString());
                SharedPreferences.Editor editor = sharedPref.edit();
                editor.putInt("key1", intYears);
                editor.putInt("key2", intLoan);
                editor.putFloat("key3", decInterest);
                editor.commit();
                startActivity(new Intent(MainActivity.this, Payment.class));
            }
        });
    }
```

Figure 11-14 startActivity Intent launches Payment class (complete code)

Instantiating the Second Activity Controls

As soon as the second Activity launches, the activity_payment.xml layout file is displayed. Next, the Payment class must instantiate the TextView control that displays the monthly payments for the car loan and an ImageView control displaying the appropriate image denoting the number of years for the loan. To set the layout and instantiate the TextView and ImageView controls in the second Activity, follow these steps:

STEP 1

- Close the MainActivity.java tab, show the line numbers on the Payment.java tab, and delete Lines 16–39.
- Tap or click at the end of Line 14 and press Enter.
- To create an instance of the TextView control, type **TextView monthlyPayment = (TextView)findViewById(R.id.txtMonthlyPayment);** and press Enter.
- Tap or click TextView and press Alt+Enter to import the class.
- To create an instance of the ImageView control, on the next line type **ImageView image = (ImageView)findViewById(R.id.imgYears);**. Import the ImageView class.

The TextView and ImageView controls named monthlyPayment and image are referenced in Payment.java (Figure 11-15).

Figure 11-15 Instantiating the TextView and ImageView controls in Payment.java

Retrieving Preferences

Retrieving Android data is just as easy as saving it when you are working with SharedPreferences. Loading data saved in the SharedPreferences XML file begins in the second Activity by instantiating the SharedPreferences object. You do not need an editor to read the saved data in the SharedPreferences. Instead, retrieve the SharedPreferences object and use the appropriate method to retrieve a key's value by name:

- getString( )—Retrieves string values
- getInt( )—Retrieves integer values
- getLong( )—Retrieves long values
- getFloat( )—Retrieves float values
- getBoolean( )—Retrieves Boolean values

Each of these methods has two parameters: the preference key string and a default value to return if the preference is undefined. If a string value is undefined, it is set to a null value, represented by empty quotes. If a numeric value is undefined, the variable is assigned the value of zero. If the key is not found, the default value is given in response. To create an instance of the SharedPreferences object and to load the data from the persistent data XML file, use the following code syntax:

Code Syntax

```
SharedPreferences sharedPref =
PreferenceManager.getDefaultSharedPreferences(this);
int intYears = sharedPref.getInt("key1", 0);
int intLoan = sharedPref.getInt("key2", 0);
float decInterest = sharedPref.getFloat("key3", 0);
```

In this code, intYears is assigned the number of years for the life of the loan and the value for the loan amount is assigned to intLoan stored in the XML persistent data file. The variable decInterest is assigned the float value of the interest rate of the loan. To retrieve the data from the SharedPreferences object, follow these steps:

STEP 1

- In Payment.java, press Enter at the end of Line 18 to insert a new line.
- On the new line, to create an instance within the Status class of the SharedPreferences object, type **SharedPreferences sharedPref = PreferenceManager.getDefaultSharedPreferences(this);** and then press Enter key.
- Tap or click SharedPreferences and press Alt+Enter and then tap or click PreferenceManager and press Alt+Enter again to import both libraries.

An instance of the SharedPreferences class is created named sharedPref in the Payment class (Figure 11-16).

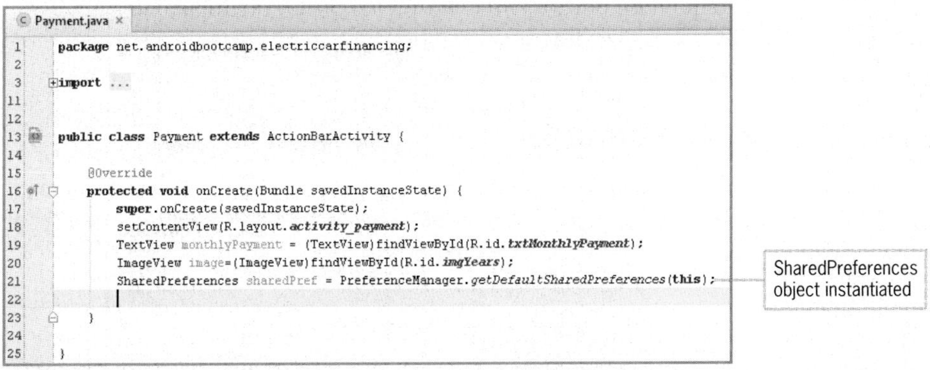

Figure 11-16 SharedPreferences instance in the Payment class

STEP 2

- To read the first value written in the XML file and assign the integer value to intYears, type **int intYears = sharedPref.getInt ("key1", 0);** and press Enter.
- On the next line, to read the second value saved as persistent data and assign the integer value to intLoan, type **int intLoan = sharedPref.getInt("key2", 0);** and press Enter.
- On the next line, to read the third value retrieved from the SharedPreferences object and assign the float value to **float decInterest = sharedPref.getFloat("key3", 0);**.
- Save your work.

The three values are retrieved from the SharedPreferences object from the first Activity (Figure 11-17).

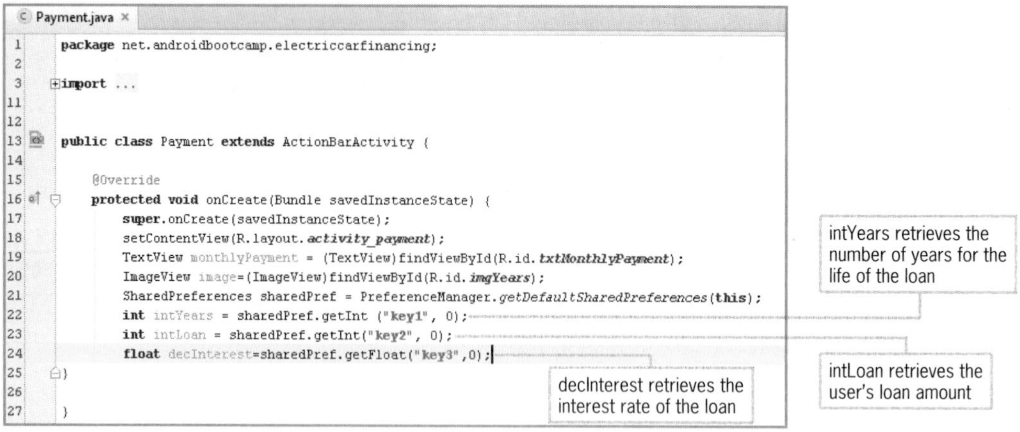

Figure 11-17 SharedPreferences values are retrieved

IN THE TRENCHES

You can assign literal text to the SharedPreferences object by coding:

```
editor.putString("key", "literal text");
```

Coding an ImageView Control

In an Android project, an ImageView control can display an image by assigning a source path (android:src="drawable/filename") in the XML layout file or by dynamically assigning the image within the Java code.

Code Syntax

```
image.setImageResource(R.drawable.three);
```

In the Electric Car Financing app, the image displayed in Payment.java depends on the number of years for the loan: three, four, or five years. The three values retrieved from the SharedPreferences object stored in memory are used in an equation that calculates the monthly payments and are assigned to the variable named decMonthlyPayment. The formula to calculate the monthly payment is:

```
decMonthlyPayment = (intLoan * (1 + (decInterest * intYears)))/ (12 * intYears)
```

After the monthly payment is computed, the number of years is compared in the nested If structure. If the car loan is paid over three years, the three.png image is displayed. If the loan is paid over four years, the four.png file is shown, and if the loan is paid over five years, the five.png file image is shown. A nested If decision structure is used to determine which image is displayed. If the user does not enter three, four, or five years for the loan, then no image is displayed and a text response appears stating that the user has not selected an appropriate number of years for this type of loan. To code the nested Else If decision structure and display the TextView result and ImageView controls, follow these steps:

STEP 1

- At the end of Line 24, press Enter to insert a new line. To declare the variable assigned the monthly payment, type **float decMonthlyPayment;**.
- Press Enter two times to skip a line.
- To compute the monthly payments for the car loan, type **decMonthlyPayment = (intLoan * (1 + (decInterest * intYears))) / (12 * intYears);** and press Enter.
- To format the monthly payment as currency and two places past the decimal place, type **DecimalFormat currency = new DecimalFormat("$###,###.##");**.
- Tap or click DecimalFormat and press Alt+Enter to import DecimalFormat.

The monthly payment is computed based on the values entered in the first Activity and formatted as currency (Figure 11-18).

Payment.java

```
1   package net.androidbootcamp.electriccarfinancing;
2
3   import ...
13
14
15  public class Payment extends ActionBarActivity {
16
17      @Override
18      protected void onCreate(Bundle savedInstanceState) {
19          super.onCreate(savedInstanceState);
20          setContentView(R.layout.activity_payment);
21          TextView monthlyPayment = (TextView)findViewById(R.id.txtMonthlyPayment);
22          ImageView image=(ImageView)findViewById(R.id.imgYears);
23          SharedPreferences sharedPref = PreferenceManager.getDefaultSharedPreferences(this);
24          int intYears = sharedPref.getInt ("key1", 0);
25          int intLoan = sharedPref.getInt("key2", 0);
26          float decInterest=sharedPref.getFloat("key3",0);
27          float decMonthlyPayment;
28
29          decMonthlyPayment= (intLoan * (1+ (decInterest * intYears)))/ (12 * intYears);
30          DecimalFormat currency = new DecimalFormat("$###,###.##");
31  }
32
33  }
34
```

Equation for computing the monthly payments for the loan

DecimalFormat adds dollar sign, comma if needed, and two places past the decimal point

Figure 11-18 Computing the monthly payments of the loan and formatting the result

STEP 2

- At the end of Line 30, press Enter to insert a new line. To display the monthly payment amount, type **monthlyPayment.setText("Monthly Payment " + currency.format(decMonthlyPayment));** and press Enter.

The monthly payment text is displayed (Figure 11-19).

```
28
29            decMonthlyPayment= (intLoan * (1+ (decInterest * intYears)))/ (12 * intYears);
30            DecimalFormat currency = new DecimalFormat("$###,###.##");
31            monthlyPayment.setText("Monthly Payment " + currency.format(decMonthlyPayment));
32    }
33
34 }
```

Display the monthly payment result

Figure 11-19 The monthly payment is displayed on the second Activity

STEP 2

- To determine if the car loan is paid over 3, 4, or 5 years and display the associated image, type the following If structure:

  if (intYears == 3) {
  image.setImageResource(R.drawable.three);
  }

> **GTK**
> In Java, two equal signs are used to compare the references of the objects and not to assign a value to a variable.

- To display the appropriate four-year image, after the closing curly brace on Line 34, type **else if (intYears == 4) {** and press the Enter key to insert the closing brace for the Else If statement.
- To display the four.png image type:

  image.setImageResource(R.drawable.four);

- To display the five-year image, after the closing curly brace on Line 36, type **else if (intYears == 5) {** and press the Enter key to insert the closing brace for the Else If statement.
- To display the five.png image type:

  image.setImageResource(R.drawable.five);

The appropriate image appears for the corresponding loan years (Figure 11-20).

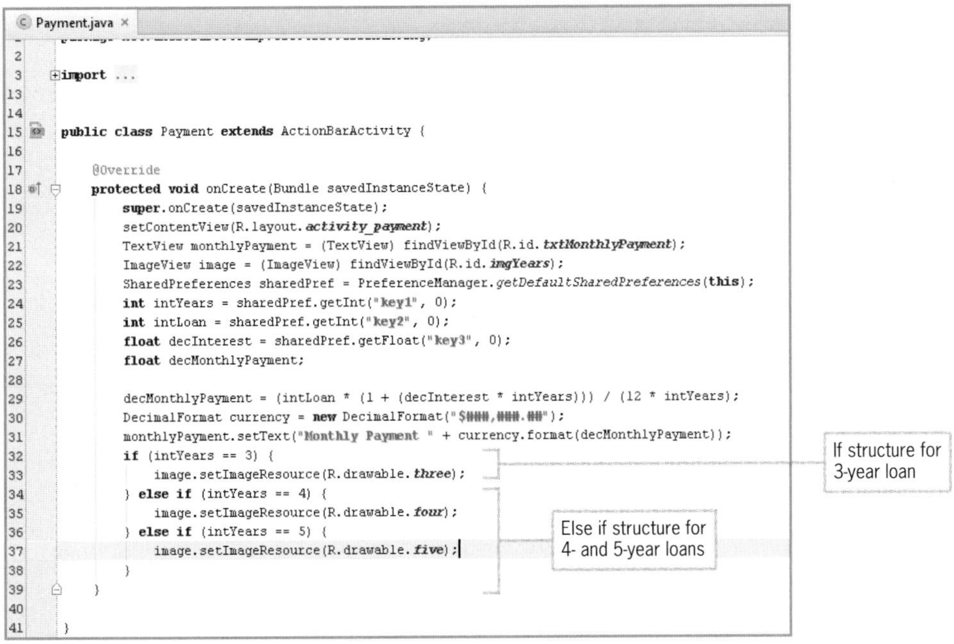

Figure 11-20 Else If structure for four-year and five-year loans

STEP 3

- If the number of years for the loan is not valid based on the three-, four-, or five-year loans that are available, display a message by typing the following code after the closing curly brace on Line 38:

```
else {
        monthlyPayment.setText("Enter 3, 4, or 5 years");
}
```

A closing else statement displays a message if the user has not entered an appropriate number of years (Figure 11-21).

Payment.java

```
public class Payment extends ActionBarActivity {

    @Override
    protected void onCreate(Bundle savedInstanceState) {
        super.onCreate(savedInstanceState);
        setContentView(R.layout.activity_payment);
        TextView monthlyPayment = (TextView) findViewById(R.id.txtMonthlyPayment);
        ImageView image = (ImageView) findViewById(R.id.imgYears);
        SharedPreferences sharedPref = PreferenceManager.getDefaultSharedPreferences(this);
        int intYears = sharedPref.getInt("key1", 0);
        int intLoan = sharedPref.getInt("key2", 0);
        float decInterest = sharedPref.getFloat("key3", 0);
        float decMonthlyPayment;

        decMonthlyPayment = (intLoan * (1 + (decInterest * intYears))) / (12 * intYears);
        DecimalFormat currency = new DecimalFormat("$###,###.##");
        monthlyPayment.setText("Monthly Payment " + currency.format(decMonthlyPayment));
        if (intYears == 3) {
            image.setImageResource(R.drawable.three);
        } else if (intYears == 4) {
            image.setImageResource(R.drawable.four);
        } else if (intYears == 5) {
            image.setImageResource(R.drawable.five);
        } else {
            monthlyPayment.setText("Enter 3, 4, or 5 years");
        }

    }

}
```

Closing else statement for users that did not enter 3, 4, or 5 years

Figure 11-21 Closing else statement

Running and Testing the Application

Your first experience with persistent saved data in an Android application is complete. Tap or click the Run 'app' button on the Standard toolbar, and then select the Nexus 5 emulator. The application opens in the emulator window, as shown in Figure 11-1a, Figure 11-1b, and Figure 11-2. The first Activity requests the number of years, the loan amount, and the interest rate which is saved to an XML file by use of the SharedPreferences object. The second Activity launches the Payment.java file, which retrieves your stored data and calculates the monthly payment for the car loan. The monthly payment is shown, and then a decision structure determines which image should be displayed.

Wrap It Up—Chapter Summary

In this chapter, the Android SharedPreferences object was used to easily store application persistent data. Application preferences are stored as key–value pairs and can be many different data types, including numbers, strings, and Boolean values. Different sets of preferences can be stored in named preference sets. Use shared preferences to store simple application primitive data in a persistent manner such as the user's name or numeric information.

- When data users enter in an Android app is stored in RAM, it is lost when the app or the device stops running. Persistent data, on the other hand, is stored on the device's drive or other storage medium such as a memory card or cloud service so that the data can be retrieved later within the app or after the termination of the program.

- Persistent data can be stored using shared preferences, internal storage, external storage, a SQLite database, or a network connection. Use the SharedPreferences object to save any primitive data: Booleans, floats, ints, longs, and strings.
- When you save application data using the SharedPreferences object, the data is saved to an XML file as a key-value pair. The key is a string such as "key1" that uniquely identifies the preference, and the value is the data represented as a string, int, long, float, or Boolean.
- You can use the key-value pairs stored in SharedPreferences in different Activities of your application or in another application.
- Use a put*DataType*( ) method to store the data in a SharedPreferences object, and use a get*DataType*( ) method to retrieve the data.

Key Terms

key—The string part of a key-value pair that uniquely identifies a preference.

persistent data—The type of data that stores values permanently by placing the information in a file.

SQLite—A lightweight, preloaded mobile database engine, which has been available since the Cupcake 1.5 version of Android and occupies a small amount of disk memory.

value—The data part of a key-value pair that represents a string, int, long, float, or Boolean value.

Developer FAQs

1. What is the general name of the type of data that is saved after the app is executed?
2. Name five ways to store data in an app.
3. When is it best to use SharedPreferences to save persistent data?
4. What does each part of the SharedPreferences data pair represent? Explain each part of the pair.
5. True or false. When you save persistent data with internal storage, other apps cannot access and use the data.
6. Why should an app not store massive amounts of data using internal storage?
7. You can save data using external storage to your SD card. What does SD stand for?
8. What does SQL stand for?
9. If you decide to use a network connection to save an app's persistent data, what is the limitation?

10. What kind of file is persistent data saved in when using the SharedPreferences object?
11. Which method stores a String value using the SharedPreferences object?
12. Write a statement that assigns the variable floatShoeSize with the key of key1 to the SharedPreferences object.
13. The preference values are not saved until which method is executed?
14. What is the maximum number of preferences saved to a SharedPreferences object?
15. Write a line of Java code that displays an image named airplane.
16. Which method retrieves an integer value?
17. If a float value is retrieved from the SharedPreferences object and the value does not exist, which value is retrieved?
18. Write a line of Java code to retrieve an integer value that is referenced by the key, key1, and saves the value to intAudienceCount.
19. Write a line of Java code to retrieve a string value that is referenced by the key, key3, and saves the value to strPolitician.
20. In a single line of Java code, assign a string value of "App Developer" to a SharedPreferences object with a key value named key5.

Beyond the Book

Search the web for answers to the following questions to further your Android knowledge.

1. Research the SD cards that are available for Android devices. Write 100 words about your findings.
2. Find five apps in the Google Play store that use mobile databases to save the data used in the app. Name and describe the reason the database connection is necessary.
3. Google Maps now require a paid account to access map features as an Android developer. Write a summary of at least 100 words describing some of the latest Google mapping features.
4. Research more information about saving to an SQLite database. Write a 200-word paragraph and show sample code of saving information to a local mobile database.

Case Programming Projects

Complete one or more of the following case programming projects. Use the same steps and techniques taught within the chapter. Submit the program you create to your instructor. The level of difficulty is indicated for each case programming project.

Easiest: ★

Intermediate: ★★

Challenging: ★★★

Case Project 11–1: BMI Calculator App ★

Requirements Document

Application title:	Body Mass Index (BMI) Calculator App
Purpose:	A body mass index calculator app computes your BMI using a formula.
Algorithms:	1. The first Activity opens displaying the bmi1.png image with the title "BMI Calculator". 2. The first screen requests your weight in pounds to the nearest whole pound and your height in inches to the nearest whole inch (Figure 11-22). These values are saved in persistent data using SharedPreferences. 3. The second Activity opens and retrieves the saved values. 4. The BMI formula needed is: $\frac{\text{Weight in pounds} * 703}{\text{height in inches}^2}$ 5. The body mass index is displayed to one-tenth of a decimal place and the image bmi2.png is displayed (Figure 11-23).
Conditions:	1. The two image files are provided with your student files.

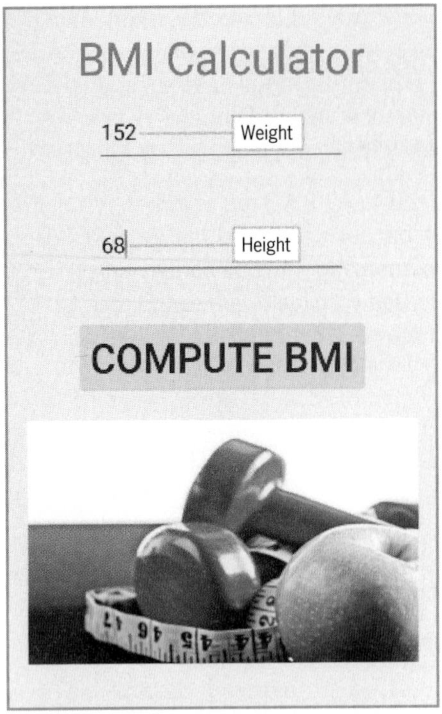

Figure 11-22 First Activity of BMI Calculator app

Figure 11-23 Second Activity of BMI Calculator app

Case Project 11–2: Home Mortgage Interest App ★

Requirements Document

Application title:	Home Mortgage Interest App
Purpose:	The Home Mortgage Interest App computes the total interest paid for the life of a home mortgage loan.
Algorithms:	1. The opening screen displays an image (mortgage.png) and the title Mortgage Loan Interest. 2. The user enters the amount of their monthly mortgage payment, number of years (10, 20, or 30) which must be converted to months, and the initial principal of the loan. Save these values using the SharedPreferences object (Figure 11-24). 3. In the second Activity, retrieve the three values and compute the total interest paid over the life of the loan with this formula: **`Total Interest = (Monthly Payment * Number of Months) - Initial Principal`** 4. The second screen displays the result of interest paid with an appropriate image (ten.png, twenty.png, or thirty.png) for a 10-, 20-, or 30-year loan (Figure 11-25).
Conditions:	1. The four images are provided with your student files. 2. The result should appear in currency format.

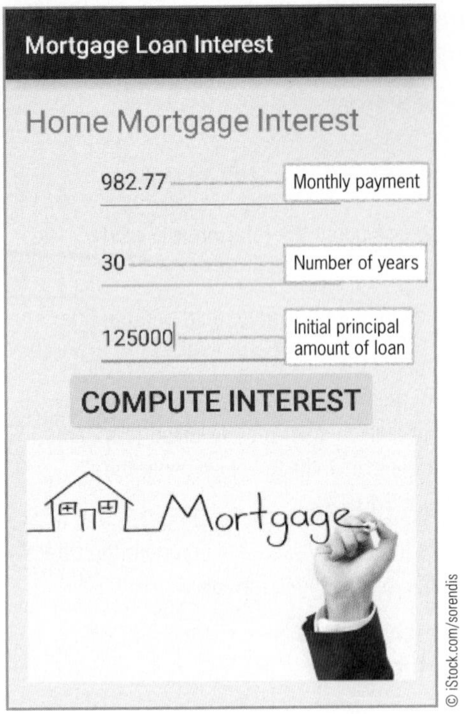

Figure 11-24 First Activity of Home Mortgage Interest app

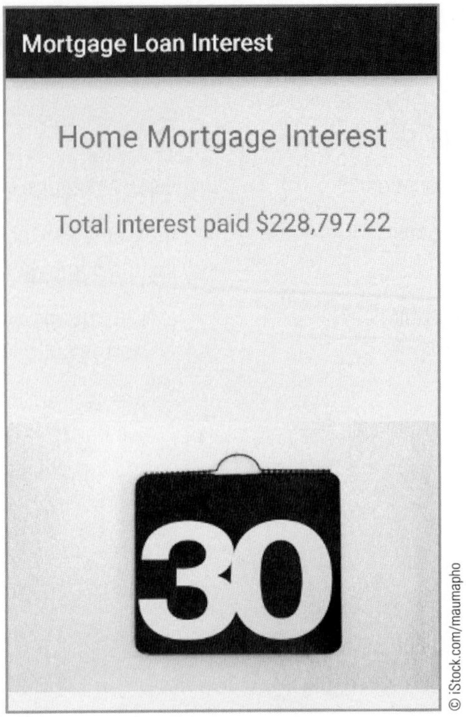

Figure 11-25 Second Activity of Home Mortgage Interest app

Case Project 11–3: Relocation Moving Truck Rental App ★★

Requirements Document

Application title:	Relocation Moving Truck Rental App
Purpose:	A relocation moving truck app provides the costs of renting a truck.
Algorithms:	1. An opening screen displays an image of a moving truck and a title. 2. The first Activity requests whether you are renting a 10-foot truck ($19.95), 17-foot truck ($29.95), or a 26-foot truck ($39.95) for a one-day rental. The number of miles is also requested (99 cents per mile). This data is saved to the SharedPreferences object. 3. The second screen displays a picture of a rental truck the same size that you are renting and the full cost of the rental for one day with the cost of mileage included.
Conditions:	1. Locate images for this app online. 2. The moving costs should be displayed as currency.

Case Project 11–4: Marathon Race App ★★

Requirements Document

Application title:	Marathon Race App
Purpose:	Your city is planning a full 26-mile marathon race. Your time is ranked in the top, middle, or bottom third of runners.
Algorithms:	1. The opening screen displays the text "Marathon Race" and an image of a marathon. 2. Your total time to run the entire race is requested in two TextView controls, which save the hour and the minutes (for example, 3 hours and 27 minutes). 3. A second screen displays the average time that it took to run one mile. 4. If your average time to run each mile is under 11 minutes, display a top one-third gold medal image. 5. If your average time to run each mile is under 15 minutes, display a middle-third silver medal image. 6. If your average time to run each mile is equal to or more than 15 minutes, display a completion bronze medal image.
Conditions:	1. The completion time for the marathon cannot be more than 10 hours. 2. The number of minutes entered cannot be more than 59 minutes. 3. Locate images for this app online.

Case Project 11–5: Amtrak Train App ★★★

Requirements Document

Application title:	Amtrak Train App
Purpose:	The Amtrak Train app determines your arrival time after you enter the boarding time and length of trip.
Algorithms:	1. Create an app that opens with a picture of the Amtrak logo and a title. This activity should request: a. The boarding time with separate input for hour and minutes on a 24-hour clock. b. The length of the entire train trip in minutes only. c. The three values are saved using SharedPreferences. 2. The second screen shows the arrival time of the train by hour and minutes of a 24-hour clock. 3. If the arrival is past midnight, display the message "Red-Eye Arrival" in addition to an appropriate image.
Conditions:	1. Locate images for this app online. 2. The maximum hour entered for the boarding time is 23 and the minutes is 59. 3. The maximum number of minutes for length of travel entered is 1500 minutes.

Case Project 11–6: Your Personal Limerick App ★★★

Requirements Document

Application title:	Your Personal Limerick App
Purpose:	Get creative! Request a city, an occupation, a number, and an action verb and create a happy limerick with the text entered.
Algorithms:	1. Create an app that opens with an image and title and requests a city, occupation, number, and action verb. Save these four items to an XML file using SharedPreferences. 2. The second screen should display a limerick with the four requested items in a poem-like fashion with an image.
Conditions:	1. Select your own images and limerick wording.

CHAPTER 12

Finale! Publishing Your Android App

In this chapter, you learn to:

- Understand Google Play
- Target various device configurations and languages
- Prepare your app for publishing
- Create an APK package by exporting an app
- Prepare promotional materials
- Publish your app on Google Play

After all the work of designing your Android app, the time to publish it has arrived. Similar to the many Android devices available, an Android app can be published to a variety of application distribution networks. As an Android developer, you can publish your app to Google Play, as well as many other online Android app stores, such as Amazon Appstore, AppBrain, and SlideME. Because Google Play is the largest marketplace, this chapter targets the publication of apps on this Android network. The process to publish an app consists of preparing your app for publication, and then registering, configuring, uploading, and finally publishing it.

Before publishing an application, the developer must understand how to perform the following processes, among others:

1. Test your app.
2. Prepare the app for publication.
3. Create an APK package and digitally sign your application.
4. Prepare promotional materials.
5. Publish your app to Google Play.

Understanding Google Play

Google Play (https://play.google.com) is a digital repository that serves as the storefront for Android devices and apps. It includes an online store for paid and free Android apps as well as music, movies, books, and games. Android phones, tablets, and Google television can all access the Google Play services. The Google Play website, shown in Figure 12-1, includes the features and services of Android apps, Google Music, and Google e-books. In addition, Google Play provides free cloud storage services, which saves space on an Android device. Google Play is entirely cloud based, so you can store all your music, movies, books, and apps online and have them always available to you. Over 130 countries around the world presently use Google Play. Competing companies such as the Apple App Store and Windows Store also market their applications within a similar structure. When you select an app on Google Play, the app installs directly to your Android device. Google Play is part of the default setup on new Android devices.

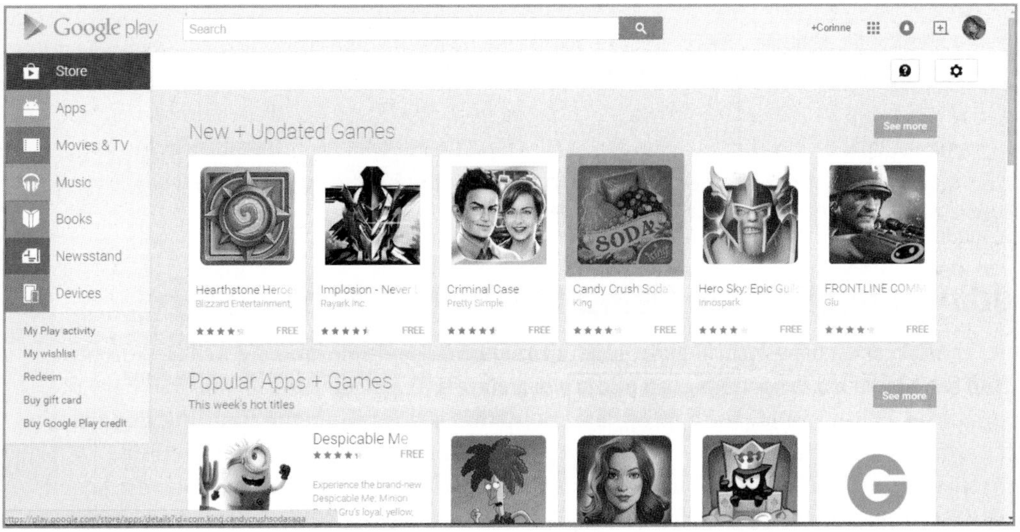

Source: Google

Figure 12-1 Google Play

GTK

With Google Play, you can store up to 20,000 songs for free using the cloud services.

Targeting Device Configurations and Languages

To reach a larger audience within the Google Play market, consider targeting multiple Android devices and translating your app into multiple languages. The Android platform runs on a variety of devices that offer different screen sizes and pixel densities. With over 100 Android handheld devices, using flexible design layouts that work on many screen sizes and resolutions ensures that your app works on a wider range of Android phones and tablets. Creating a custom experience for different screen sizes, pixel densities, orientations, and resolutions guarantees that each user feels that the app was designed specifically for his or her phone or tablet.

Android users live in every corner of the world and speak hundreds of different languages. As you design an Android app, you can provide alternate resources such as app text translated into multiple languages that change depending on the default locale detected on the device. For example, if your home country is Spain, most likely your phone's locale for the dialect selection is set to Spanish (Spain). If you want your application to support both English and Spanish text, you can create two resource directories in the strings directory (the strings.xml file) using the Translations Editor. By customizing the strings resource files, you can write one application that recognizes many local languages. When creating your app in English, remember that the majority of the world does not speak English and consider extending your app's reach to a worldwide pool of Android users.

GTK
To translate the languages used in your app, you can use Google Translate (http://translate.google.com), a free translation service that provides instant translations among 70 languages.

GTK
Only 5.3 percent of the world's population speaks English as their first language. Research shows that to reach 90 percent of Internet users, app developers need to support 21 languages.

Adding Localization Using the Translations Editor

The Translations Editor within Android Studio supports multiple languages. Based on the default language of a device, you can add translated text as you develop an app and have the Translations Editor display the appropriate translation strings when the app runs. **Localization** is the process of adapting an app or webpage to a language while considering cultural differences such as whether the language is read left-to-right or right-to-left, calendar layout, measurements, currency, number formats such as date and time, and traditions of your target audience. For example, the language and the date formats of Spain are different from those of the United States. If an app promises to deliver goods on 8/10/2017, Spanish users expect this to be October 8, 2017, while American users read the delivery date as August 10, 2017. Within the Translations Editor, the globe-shaped Add Locale localization icon provides access to a listing of locales around the world. To add localization for another country, follow these steps:

STEP 1

- Create an Android Project named Locale in Android Studio with a Blank Activity.
- Expand the values folder in the Android Project view, open strings.xml, and then tap or click the Open editor link.
- Tap or click the Add Locale button in the Translations Editor.

A list of countries is displayed to add app localization (Figure 12-2).

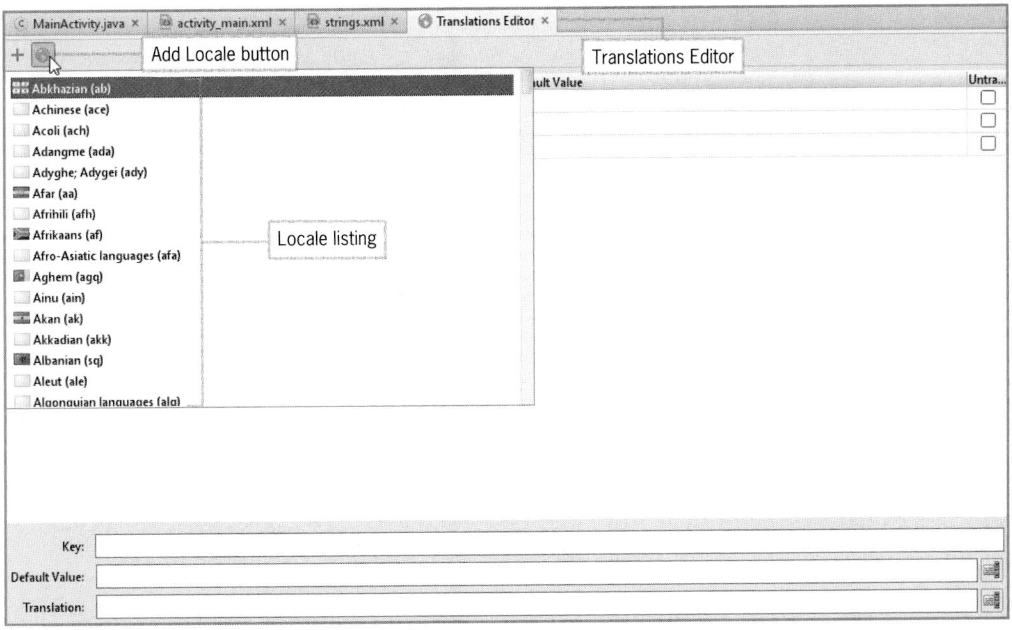

Figure 12-2 Locale listing in the Translations Editor

STEP 2

- Scroll down and tap or click Spanish (es).

A new column appears in the Translations Editor for the Spanish (es) locale (Figure 12-3).

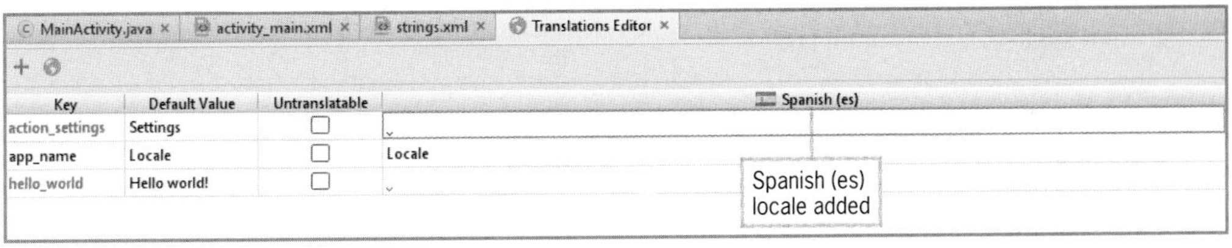

Figure 12-3 Spanish (es) added as another locale

STEP 3

- Tap or click the hello_world row in the Spanish (es) column.
- At the bottom of the Translations Editor window, tap or click the Translation text box.
- Type **Hola mundo!** (the Spanish translation for Hello world! from translate.google.com).

The translation for Hello world! is entered into the Translation text box (Figure 12-4). If the app is run on a device with the Spanish locale setting, Hola mundo! is displayed instead of Hello world!

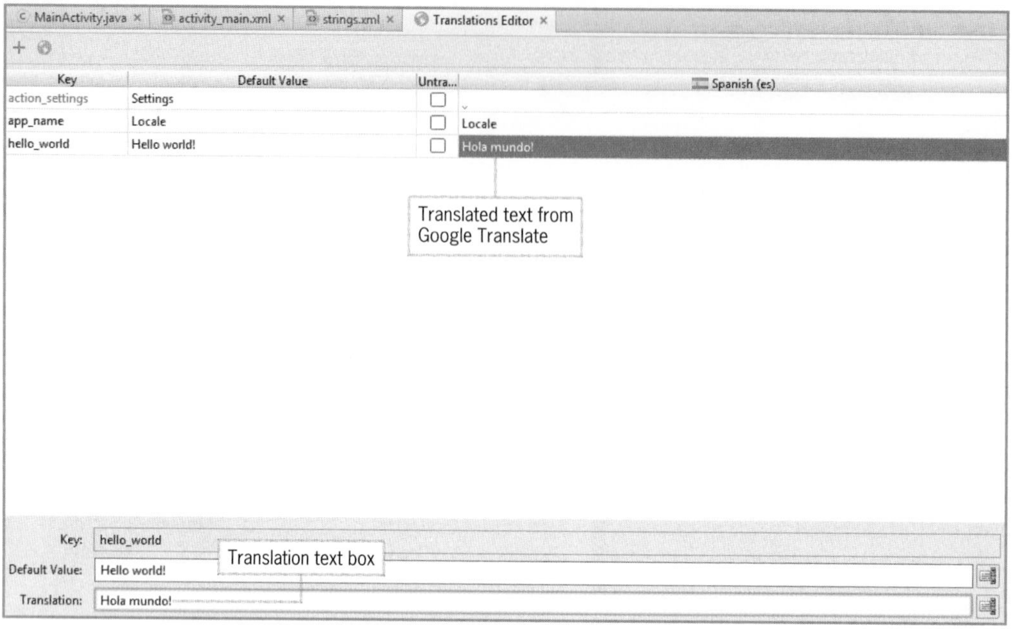

Figure 12-4 Spanish translation of Locale app text

GTK

If your app includes proper nouns such as first and last names, check Untranslatable in the Translations Editor to display the word "as is" in other languages.

Critical Thinking

Can I add multiple locales to an app?

Yes. Repeat the steps shown in Figure 12-2 to add as many locales as you need to target.

GTK

Sites such as Google Translate are helpful, but before you publish your app to Google Play, have a natural speaker of the target language check the translation for correctness, formality, cultural cues, and grammar.

Testing Your App on an Android Device

After completing and adding locales to your Android app, you must test the app on various devices before publication. Using the built-in emulators in Android Studio, you can test the design and functionality of your app on a wide range of devices. You can also see how your development application will perform in a real-world environment by using Android Studio to install and test it directly on an Android phone. With an Android-powered device, you can develop and debug your Android applications just as you would on the emulator. After you change the settings on your Android phone or tablet, you can use a versatile tool called the **Android Debug Bridge (ADB)** to communicate with a connected Android device. To set up a device for testing your app, follow these steps:

STEP 1

- On the home screen of an Android device, tap the Settings app to display the device settings.
- If your device is running Android 3.2 or older, select Applications, and then select Development.

  If your device is running Android 4.0 or newer, select Developer options. The Developer options command is hidden by default. To make it available, select Settings, select About device (or About phone) in the System category, and then tap Build number seven times. A message appears that you are now a developer.
- Go back to Settings and tap Developer's options. Check the USB debugging option and then tap the OK button.

The Android device changes the settings to enable USB debugging.

STEP 2

- To set up your computer to detect your Android device, first install a USB driver for Android Debug Bridge on a Windows computer following the steps at http://developer.android.com/sdk/oem-usb.html.
- Each Android phone brand, such as Motorola and Samsung, has its own drivers that must be downloaded and installed on your Windows computer. Be sure to install the drivers for the appropriate device brand. If you are using a Mac, you do not need to install a driver.

The USB drivers are installed on a Windows computer.

STEP 3

- Attach an Android device to a USB cable.
- Run your application from Android Studio as usual (i.e., using the Run 'app' button).
- When the Choose Device dialog box opens, listing the available emulator(s) and connected device(s), select the running device upon which you want to install and run the application, and then tap or click the OK button.

The Android application is tested on your Android device.

Creating an APK Package

After testing and refining your Android application, you must create a release-ready package that users can install and run on their Android phones and tablets. The release-ready package is called an **.apk file (application package file)**, which is a compressed archive similar to a .zip file that contains the application, the manifest file, and all associated resources, such as image files, music, and other required content. Google created the .apk file format. Using the Android Studio Build menu, you can build a release-ready .apk file that is signed with your private key and optimized for publication. A private key digitally signs your application with information from your local system. All Android applications must be digitally signed with a certificate before the system can create an .apk package of your app for distribution in the Google Play store as shown in Figure 12-5. The Android system uses the certificate as a means of identifying the author of an application and establishing trust relationships between applications.

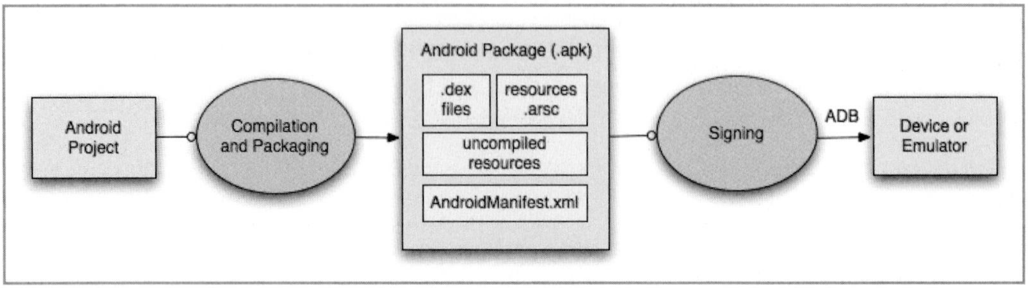

Source: Google

Figure 12-5 Process of publishing an Android project

To create an .apk package that generates a private key for your local system, follow these steps:

STEP 1

- Open a completed project in Android Studio that has been tested and runs properly.
- To create a signed .apk package, tap or click Build on the menu bar and then tap or click Generate Signed APK.

The Generate Signed APK Wizard dialog box opens (Figure 12-6).

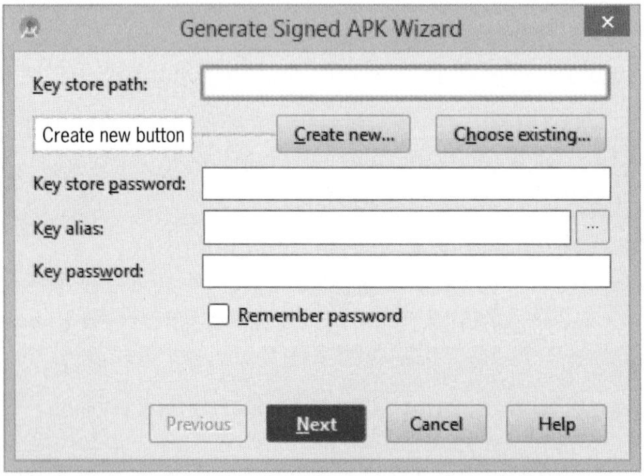

Figure 12-6 Generate Signed APK Wizard dialog box

STEP 2

- Tap or click the Create new button to create a new signed key.
- A signed key file can be placed in any location on your computer or USB drive. Type a path similar to the one shown in Figure 12-7 or ask your instructor for a specified path for the Key store path text box.
- Enter a password of your own choosing in the Password text box.
- Type the same password again in the Confirm text box.
- In the Alias text box, enter **MyAndroidKey**.
- In the Password and Confirm text boxes, enter your password again.
- In the Validity (years) text box, enter a valid number of years from 25 to 1,000 years. Fill in the rest of the requested text boxes. You can leave the Organization text box blank if you do not belong to an organization.

The information needed to create a new key is entered in the New Key Store dialog box (Figure 12-7).

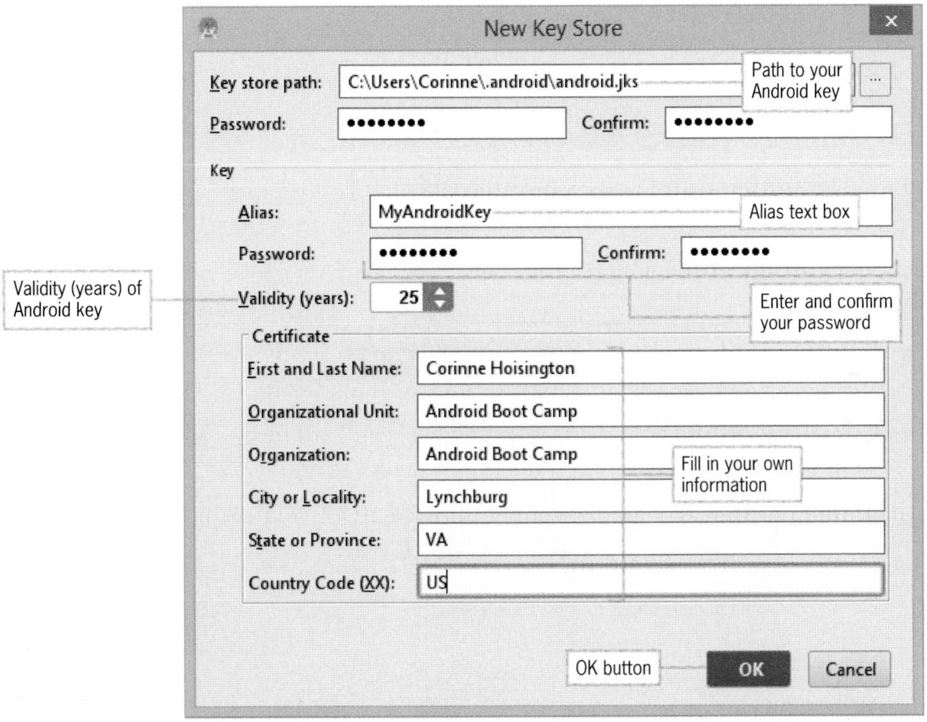

Figure 12-7 New Key Store dialog box

STEP 3

- Tap or click the OK button.

The Generate Signed APK Wizard displays the information needed to create a signed key (Figure 12-8).

Figure 12-8 Creating a signed key

STEP 4

- Tap or click the Next button to open the Master Password dialog box.
- If necessary, type your password again in the New Password and Confirm New Password text boxes.

Your password is entered twice in the Master Password dialog box (Figure 12-9).

Figure 12-9 Setting the Master Password

STEP 5

- Tap or click the Set Password button.

The Generate Signed APK Wizard dialog box displays the APK destination folder (Figure 12-10). Your folder path will be different.

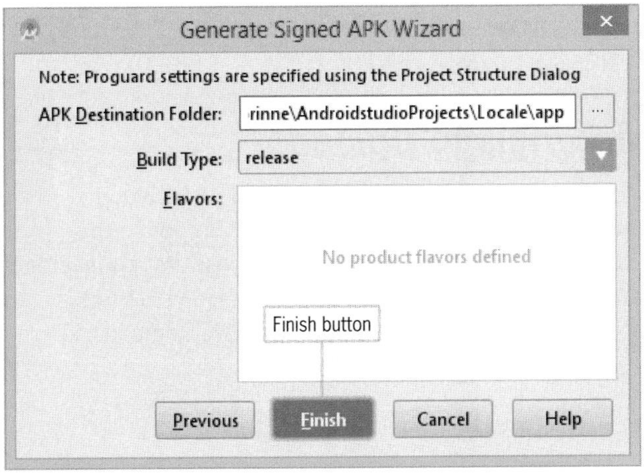

Figure 12-10 Generate Signed APK Wizard dialog box

STEP 6

- Tap or click the Finish button to generate a signed APK file.

The signed APK file is saved locally on your computer or USB drive (Figure 12-11). To view the saved location of your APK file, tap or click the Show in Explorer button to view the file location.

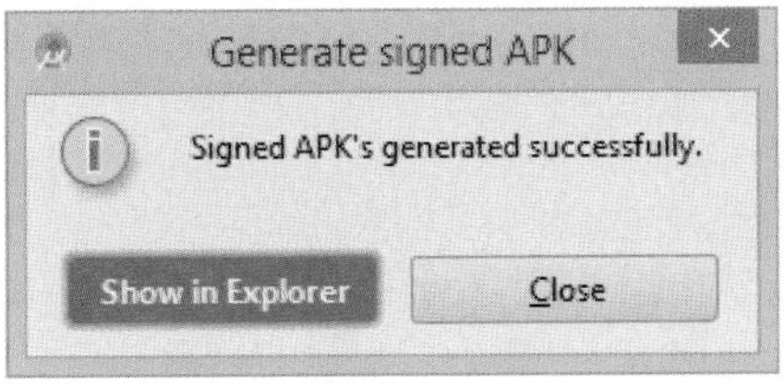

Figure 12-11 Signed APK generated

STEP 7

- Tap or click the Close button.

The Android app is now signed and ready to be saved to Google Play.

GTK
Android .apk files can be installed and run directly on an Android device. You can email the .apk files to others so that they can install the file attachment directly onto their device.

IN THE TRENCHES
The key creates your private key for Android deployment. It is best to back up your key in a safe file location. If you lose your key file, you will not be able to upgrade your Android Google Play app.

Preparing Promotional Materials to Upload

When you publish your app in Google Play, you are required to post several images that accompany your app to assist with marketing. With hundreds of thousands of apps in the store, you must publicize your app so it stands out and is noticed by casual visitors. To leverage your app in the Google Play store, you can upload your app with screenshots, a video link, promotional graphics, and descriptive text, as in the Angry Birds Rio page at Google Play, which is shown in Figure 12-12.

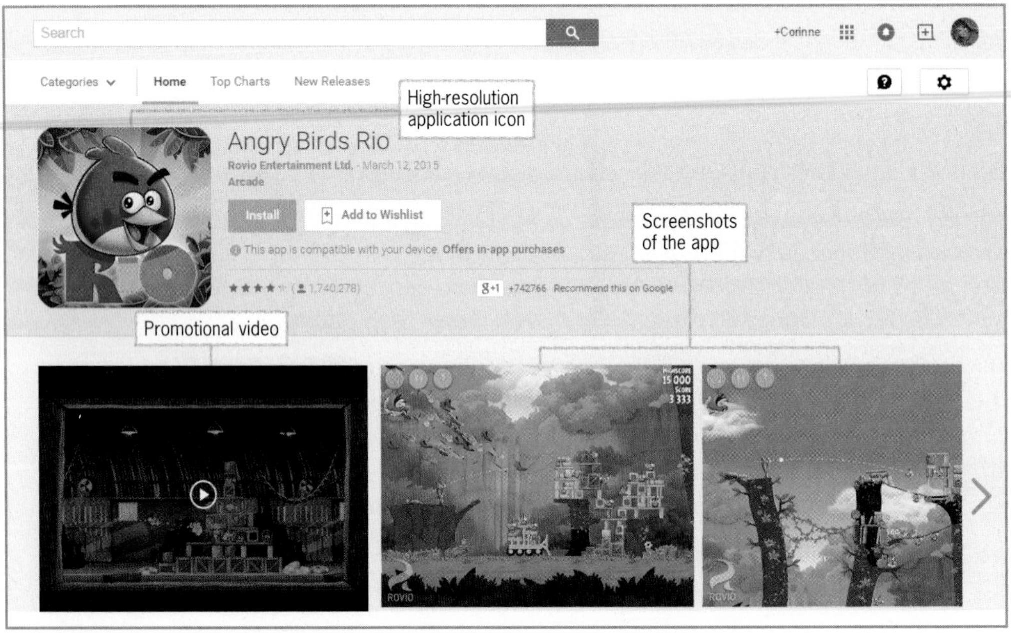

Figure 12-12 Angry Birds Rio Android app from Google Play

Providing Images

In the Angry Birds Rio Android app, a high-resolution application icon is displayed near the top of the page. The application icon does not replace your launcher icon, but serves to identify and brand your app. The size of the application icon should be 512 × 512 pixels and stored in a PNG file. In addition, Google Play requires a minimum of two screenshots of the app to display in the Details section of your app page on the Google Play site. Large images (typically in the PNG format), such as those of the Angry Birds Rio game (Figure 12-12) are displayed in any of the following dimensions: 480 × 320, 800 × 480, or 854 × 480 pixels. You can upload up to eight screenshots for the app page. The screenshots appear before a written description. You can also display a video to demo your app, though Google Play does not require one. As an alternative, you can upload with your app a video link to your demo video on YouTube.com. The short video should highlight the top features of your app and last between 30 seconds and 2 minutes. Remember that these visual elements are the first impression potential users have of your app. Quality media helps improve an app's marketability.

GTK
Google Play has over 1.5 million published apps and over 100 billion downloads.

Providing a Description

In addition to the promotional media items, an app description provides a quick overview of the purpose of the app and what it does. To intrigue your readers, you can include some of the features your application provides and describe why your app is unique in comparison with other competitors without mentioning their names. The description needs to sell your app to the widest audience possible. The description of the Angry Birds Rio app in Figure 12-13 appeals to a gaming audience searching for a new Angry Birds experience. Notice that the Angry Birds Rio description highlights the features and benefits of the app using direct and concise language. A good description is written to motivate users to download the app. Revise the description with each update of your app, adding information such as new features and user reviews. In Figure 12-13, notice the Review section and the ratings. If you scroll down the site, you can also display the date of last update, current version, Android platform requirement, category, size, price, and content rating. Users search for the most popular apps as measured by their ratings. Prospective app buyers read user reviews to determine if your app is worth their time and money. When a visitor writes a good review about your application, you can quote the review within your description. Customers value good reviews and are more likely to download your app if it has many of them.

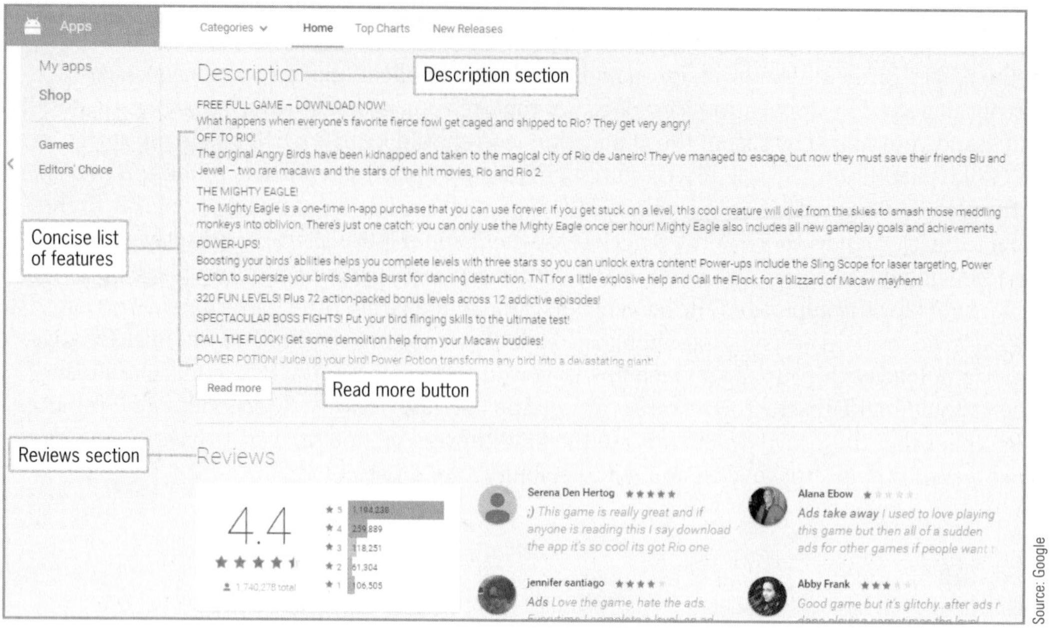

Figure 12-13 Angry Birds Rio Android app Description page

The Angry Birds Rio game on Google Play is free, but has optional in-app purchases. So how do the developers make money? At the bottom of the Google Play Angry Birds page is a list of other products created by this developer. Upon mastering the free game, users are often motivated to buy the full version of a product or buy additional features including in-app purchases such as extra lives or more levels. As you price your app, consider that some users will never want to pay for an app, but many will pay for a great app. Consider also adding Facebook, Twitter, and other social networking links on your app's page at Google Play so users can also market your app within their friend networks.

When you upload your app into Google Play, you select one of the application categories shown in Table 12-1. If your app fits into more than one category, be sure to include each category to attract visitors in each category searched.

Category	Example Types of Apps
Comics	Comic players, comic titles
Communications	Messaging, chat/IM, dialers, address books, browsers, and call management
Finance	Banking, payment, ATM finders, financial news, insurance, taxes, portfolio/trading, and tip calculators
Health & Fitness	Personal fitness, workout tracking, diet and nutritional tips, and health and safety
Medical	Drug and clinical references, calculators, handbooks for healthcare providers, and medical journals and news
Lifestyle	Recipes and style guides
Media & Video	Subscription movie services, remote controls, and media/video players
Music & Audio	Music services, radios, and music players
Photography	Cameras, photo-editing tools, and photo management and sharing
News & Magazines	Newspapers, news aggregators, magazines, and blogging
Weather	Weather reports
Productivity	Notepad, to-do list, keyboard, printing, calendar, backup, calculator, and conversion
Business	Document editor/reader, package tracking, remote desktop, email management, and job search
Books & Reference	Book readers, reference books, text books, dictionaries, thesaurus, and wikis
Education	Exam preparations, study-aids, vocabulary, educational games, and language learning
Shopping	Online shopping, auctions, coupons, price comparison, grocery lists, and product reviews
Social	Social networking, check-in, and blogging
Sports	Sports news and commentary, score tracking, fantasy team management, and game coverage
Personalization	Wallpapers, live wallpapers, home screen, lock screen, and ring tones
Tools	System utility tools
Travel & Local	City guides, local business information, and trip management tools
Libraries & Demo	Software libraries

Table 12-1 Category types

Including Social Networks

On the Angry Birds Rio page, a Read more button within the Description provides links to social networks. You can become a fan of Angry Birds on Facebook or follow Angry Birds on Twitter (Figure 12-14). By creating a social networking presence for your app, you can build a social relationship among your customers who share common interests, backgrounds, or hobbies. By creating a Facebook and Twitter page, you have the advantage of communicating with your fans in a more entertaining manner. Customers might suggest additions for future versions of the app.

Figure 12-14 Angry Birds Twitter page

Critical Thinking
How much does it cost to create a fan page for my app on Facebook or Twitter?
You can create a fan page on Facebook or Twitter for free.

Registering for a Google Play Account

Google Play is a publishing platform that helps you distribute your Android apps to users around the world. Before you can publish apps through Google Play, you must register as a developer using your Gmail account username and password at http://play.google.com/apps/publish. Registering at Google Play requires a one-time-only payment of $25, which registers you as an Android application developer and enrolls you in a Google Merchant account. Google charges the one-time fee to encourage higher quality products on Google Play. To receive payment for the purchased apps, you must first specify a bank account. Bank account information is not added or updated within your Google Checkout account, but rather in the

Google Wallet Merchant Center. You can allow an unlimited number of people to access your Google Play developer's account. You will remain the owner of the account and will be the only person who can grant or revoke access to other users.

The registration process requires you to have a Google account, agree to the legal terms, and pay the fee via your Google Merchant account. If you charge for your app, Google Merchant disperses revenue for application sales. If you register to sell applications, you must also be registered as a Google Merchant with your Google Wallet. As a developer, you have access to your app ratings, comments, and number of downloads. If you charge for your application, you will receive 70 percent of the application price, with the remaining 30 percent distributed among the phone carriers. The profit after your first sale arrives in your Google Merchant account 24 hours later. After a purchaser buys and installs an app, his or her credit card is charged 24 hours later. If the user uninstalls the app before the 24-hour time period, Google issues a full refund of the purchase price. To register as a Google Play Android developer, follow these steps:

STEP 1

- To register at Google Play, open a browser and go to the site http://play.google.com/apps/publish.
- If necessary, enter your Gmail account information. Enter the password for your Gmail account.

Your Gmail account username and password are entered in the Google Play Developer Console (Figure 12-15).

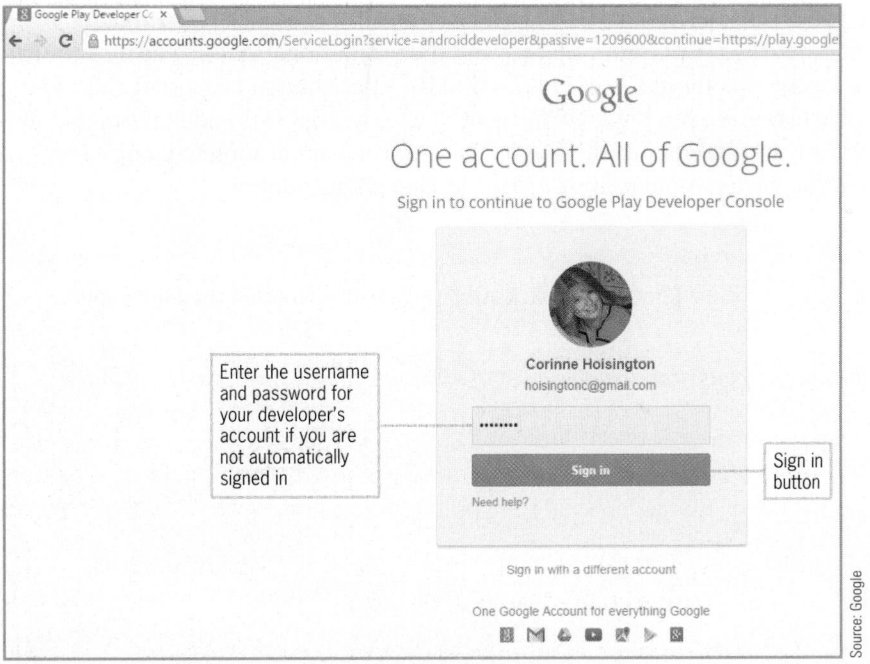

Figure 12-15 Signing into a Google developer's account

STEP 2

- Tap or click the Sign in button to sign in with your Google account information.
- Tap or click the check box acknowledging that you read the Google Play Developer distribution agreement, and then tap or click the Continue to payment button.
- Complete the payment process.
- To complete your account details and register for a developer's Google Play account, in the Developer name text box, type your name. The email address is already added based on your Google account.
- In the Phone Number text box, type your phone number. Follow the steps to complete your registration.

On the Developer Console page in the Google Play Developer Console, the developer's name and details are entered.

IN THE TRENCHES

After creating your account in Google Play, it may take up to 48 hours for your account to be approved for publishing Android apps.

Uploading an App to Google Play

As you upload your app to Google Play, you will be prompted to enter information about your application. Once you create an account, the Developer Console pages take you through the steps to upload your unlocked application .apk file and the promotional assets. The maximum supported file size for the .apk file at Google Play is 50 MB. After your app is posted and rises in popularity, Google Play gives you higher placement in weekly "top" lists and in promotional slots in collections such as Top Free Apps. To upload an Android application to Google Play, follow these steps if you have created a Google Play Developer's account:

STEP 1

- To upload your app to Google Play, tap or click All Applications to open the Developer's Console.

The All Applications page opens and displays a list of any apps (if any) previously uploaded (Figure 12-16).

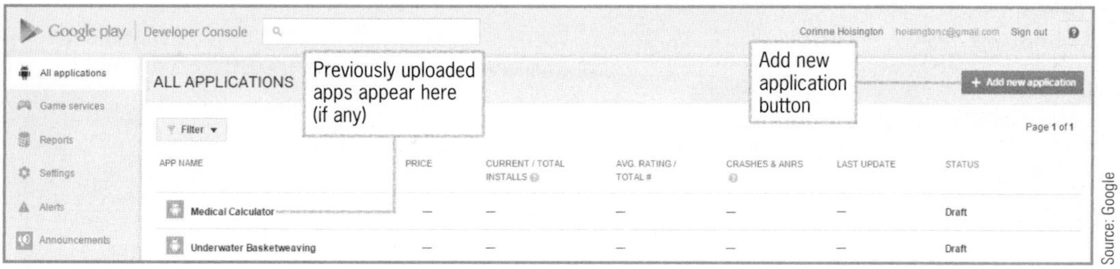

Figure 12-16 Entering account details

STEP 2

- Tap or click the Add new application button to upload the .apk file.

The Add New Application dialog box opens (Figure 12-17).

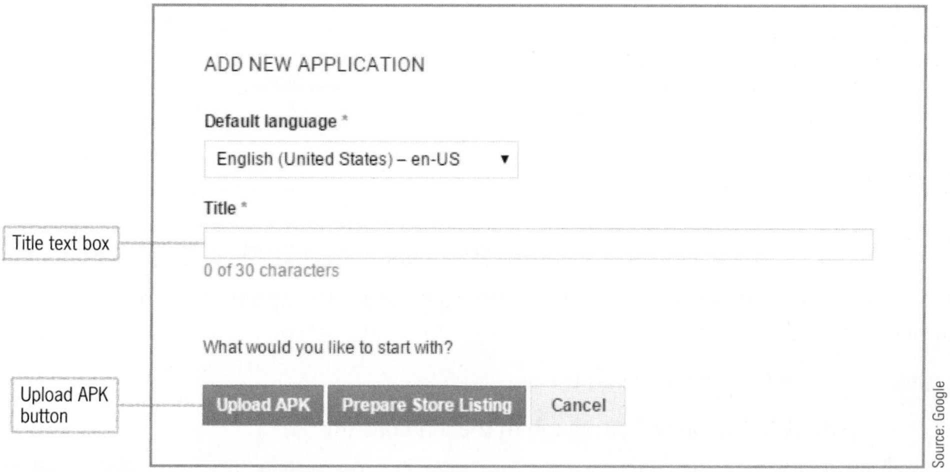

Figure 12-17 Add New Application dialog box

STEP 3

- Type the name of the app in the Title text box.
- Tap or click the Upload APK button.

The APK tab on the left side of the window opens within the browser (Figure 12-18).

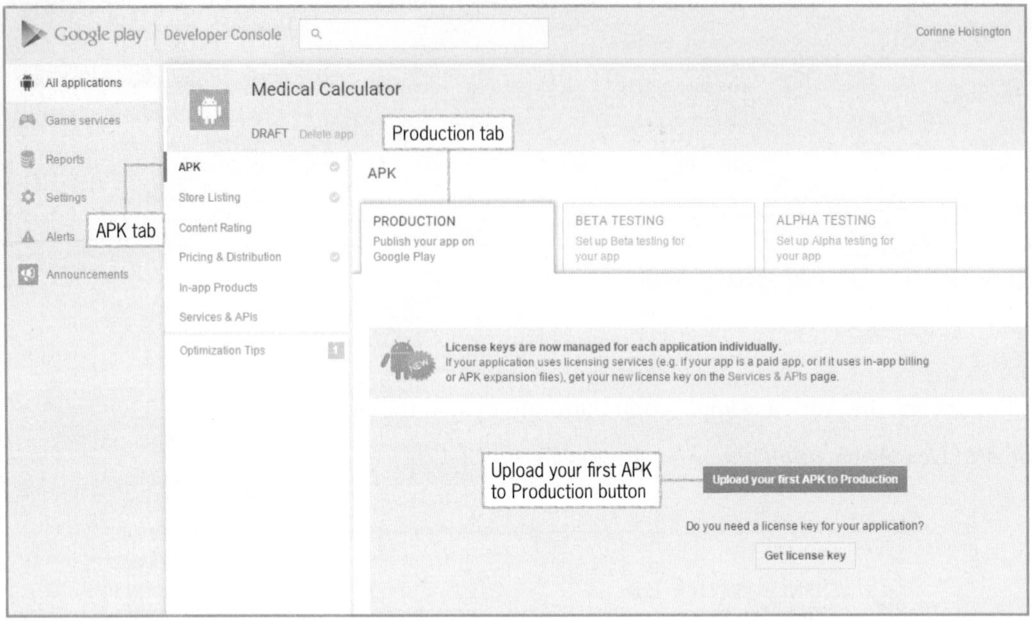

Source: Google

Figure 12-18 Displaying previously uploaded applications

STEP 4

- To upload your .apk file, tap or click the Upload your first APK to Production button.
- Tap or click the Browse files button and locate the .apk file for the app that you are publishing.
- Tap or click the Open button to upload the app.
- If necessary, tap or click the Store Listing tab in the left column.

The app uploads to the Google Play store and the Store Listing Product Details page is opened (Figure 12-19).

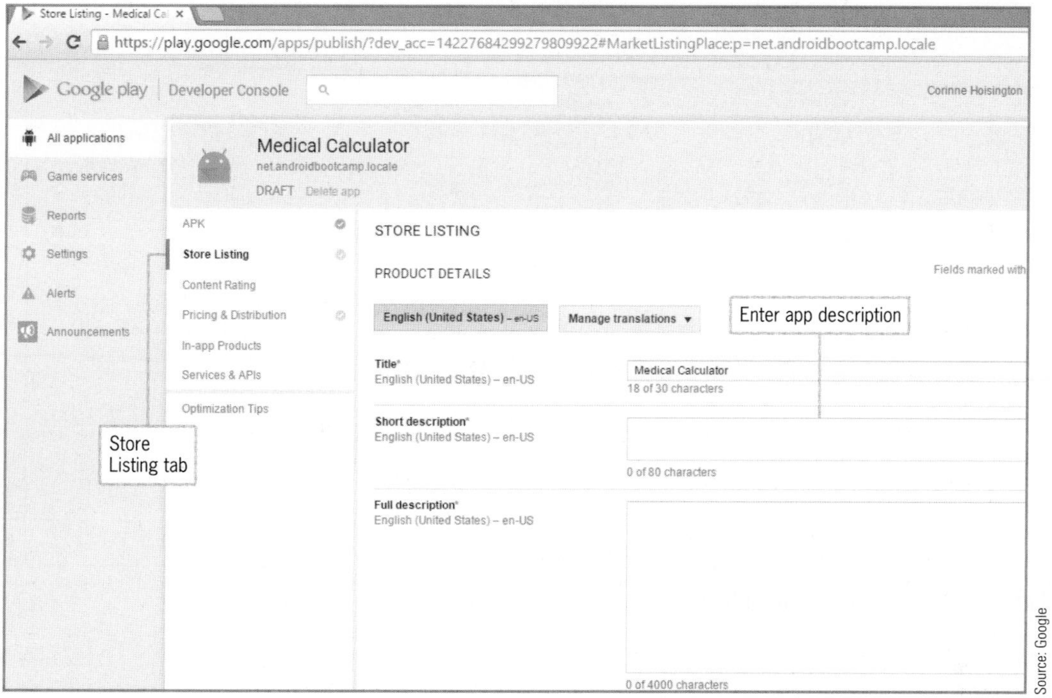

Figure 12-19 Store Listing Product Details page

STEP 5

- In the Store Listing Product Details page, you can enter a Description, Promo text, and Recent changes, upload screenshots of a phone, 7-inch tablet, 10-inch tablet, High-res icon, Feature Graphic, Promo Graphic, and TV Banner, and provide a Promo Video URL link.
- Scroll down the page to display additional details.

After scrolling down the page, the Categorization, Contact rating, Contact Details, and Privacy Policy settings for the app are displayed (Figure 12-20).

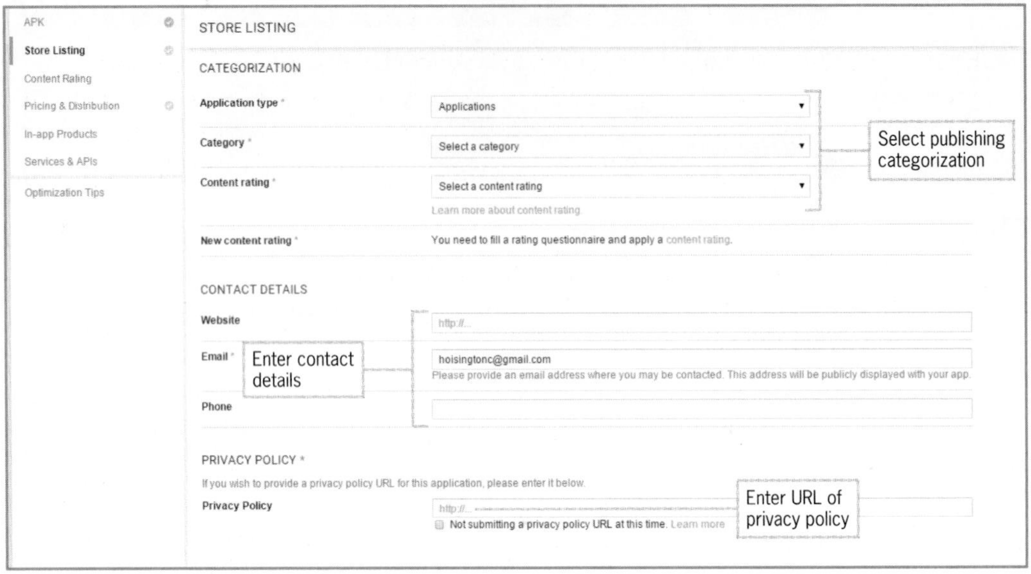

Source: Google

Figure 12-20 Publishing options

STEP 6

- In the Store Listing Product Details page, enter the information requested in the Categorization, Contact Details, and the Privacy Policy sections.
- Tap or click the Pricing & Distribution tab in the left column.

The Pricing & Distribution page is displayed for the app (Figure 12-21).

Source: Google

Figure 12-21 Pricing & Distribution page

STEP 7

- In the Pricing & Distribution page, enter whether the application is Free or Paid, select appropriate countries in the Distribute in These Countries list, enter whether the app can be run on Android Wear, Android TV, Android Auto, Designed for Families, Google Play for Education, Consent for Marketing opt-out, Content guidelines, and US export laws sections.

Critical Thinking

Can I upload separate apps for the form factors of different devices?

Yes. If you cannot support all devices with a single APK file, you can upload multiple APKs using the same app listing to target different device configurations, each with a maximum size of 50 MB.

Wrap It Up—Chapter Summary

Before you can publish your application on Google Play, the app should be localized with multiple languages, fully tested in the emulator and on multiple Android devices. To prepare your app for publishing, an APK package is exported using Android Studio. Successful app marketing requires paying attention to promotional materials that appear on Google Play, such as images, videos, and clear descriptions of the app. Publishing your app involves uploading the promotional materials that accompany the .apk file.

- Google Play is the storefront for Android devices and apps, and provides access to Android apps, Google Music, and Google e-books. It includes an online store for paid and free Android apps, music, movies, books, and games. Android phones, tablets, and Google television can access the Google Play services.
- To reach a larger audience within the Google Play market, you should target multiple Android devices and translate your app into multiple languages using the Translations Editor and Locale features. Create a custom experience for devices with different screen sizes, pixel densities, orientations, and resolutions so that each user feels that the app was designed specifically for his or her phone or tablet.
- As you design an Android app, you can provide alternate resources such as strings of text translated into multiple languages that change depending on the default locale detected on the device.
- Before publishing an Android app, test it on various devices. Using different built-in emulators in Android Studio, you can test the design and functionality of your application on a wide range of devices and see how your development application performs in a real-world environment. Using the Android Debug Bridge (ADB) tool in Android Studio, you can develop and debug an Android application on an Android device.
- After testing an Android app, you must create an .apk file (application package file), which is a release-ready package that users can install and run on their Android phones and tablets. An .apk file is a compressed archive that contains the application, the manifest file, and

all associated resources, such as image files, music, and other required content. Using the Android Studio Generate Signed APK Wizard, you can build a release-ready .apk file that is signed with your private key and optimized for publication.

- When you publish your app in Google Play, you must post several images, including an application icon and screenshots. You can also post an optional video or link to a video that demonstrates your app. You must also provide a description that provides an overview of the purpose and features of the app. Finally, include app information such as ratings, Android platform requirement, category, and price.
- To publish apps through Google Play, you must register as a developer using your Gmail account username and password at https://play.google.com/apps/publish. The registration process requires you to have a Google account, agree to the legal terms, and pay a $25 fee via your Google Checkout account.
- After creating a Google Play account, the Developer Console pages at the Google Play website step you through uploading your unlocked application .apk file and its promotional assets.

Key Terms

.apk file (application package file)—A release-ready package of an Android app stored in a compressed archive similar to a Zip file that contains the application, the manifest file, and all associated resources, such as image files, music, and other required content.

Android Debug Bridge (ADB)—An Android tool you use to communicate with a connected Android device.

Google Play—A digital repository that serves the Android Market and includes an online store for paid and free Android apps, as well as music, movies, books, and games.

Developer FAQs

1. What is the URL of Google Play?
2. Approximately how many countries use Google Play?
3. Name four services of Google Play.
4. What is the name of the two largest competitors to Google Play?
5. To increase your target audience in Google Play, what two considerations should you make?
6. How do you change your app to multiple languages?
7. What is the address of the Google website that assists with language translation?
8. What does ADB stand for?

9. What does APK stand for?
10. Can you deploy your app to your Android phone?
11. Do you have to install ADB drivers on a Mac computer?
12. Name four promotional assets that you can upload with your app at Google Play.
13. What is the maximum number of screenshots of your app in action that you can post in Google Play?
14. Where must you post your promotional video?
15. What are the minimum length and maximum length of the promotional video?
16. In which two social networking sites should you create a marketing presence?
17. Which category would you select on Google Play for a calendar app?
18. Which category would you select for a recipe app?
19. How much is the registration fee to publish Android apps on Google Play?
20. What is the maximum size of an .apk file on Google Play?

Beyond the Book

To answer the following questions, create an idea for an app that you think would sell well on Google Play.

1. Write about 200 words describing your Google Play app idea, beginning with a catchy title for the app.
2. Locate an image link that could work as your application icon for your Android app idea. (If you plan to use the icon, you would of course need to properly obtain this image following copyright guidelines.)
3. Consider the price for selling your app. Write at least 150 words explaining why you selected this price after researching the Internet for price points for Android apps.
4. Create a short YouTube video to market your app idea, and provide the link to your instructor.

Glossary

.apk file (application package file) A release-ready package of an Android app stored in a compressed archive similar to a zip file that contains the application, the manifest file, and all associated resources, such as image files, music, and other required content.

.equals method A method used to compare strings for equality.

9-patch image A special image with predefined stretching areas that maintain the same look on different screen sizes.

A

Action bar icon An icon that appears in the upper-left corner of the Action bar for an Activity.

ACTION_VIEW A generic action you can use to send any request to have the most reasonable action to occur.

Activity An Android component that represents a single screen with a user interface.

adapter A component that provides a data model for the layout of a list and for converting the data from the array into list items.

Android Debug Bridge (ADB) An Android tool you use to communicate with a connected Android device.

Android Manifest A file with the filename AndroidManifest.xml that is required in every Android application. This file provides essential information to the Android device, such as the name of the Java application and a listing of each Activity.

Android project view A pane on the left side of the Android Studio program window that contains the folders for the current project.

Android Studio The recommended IDE for writing Java programs and for building and integrating application development tools and open-source projects for Android.

Android Virtual Device (AVD) An Android Studio feature that displays an emulator configuration for design and layout purposes.

android:oneshot An attribute of the animation-list that determines whether an animation plays once and then stops or continues to play until the user taps a specified button, such as the Stop Animation button.

AndroidManifest.xml *See* Android Manifest.

AnimationDrawable class A class that provides the methods for Drawable animations to create a sequence of frame-by-frame images.

animation-list An XML root element that references images stored in the drawable folder and used in an animation.

app A mobile application.

Application template A design you can use to create basic Android applications and then customize them.

array variable A variable that can store more than one value.

ArrayAdapter<String> i A ListAdapter that supplies string array data to a ListView object.

B

break A statement that ends a case within a Switch statement and continues with the statement following the Switch decision structure.

C

Calendar class A class you can use to access the Android system date. The Calendar class also is responsible for converting between a Date object and a set of integer fields such as YEAR, MONTH, and DAY_OF_MONTH.

case A keyword used in a Switch statement to indicate a condition. In a Switch statement, the case keyword is followed by a value and a colon.

class variable A variable with global scope; it can be accessed by multiple methods throughout the program.

class A group of objects that establishes an introduction to each object's properties.

codec A computer technology used to compress and decompress audio and video files.

Component Tree A pane in the Android Studio project window that displays the structure of the emulator layout.

compound condition More than one condition included in an If statement.

constructor A part of the Java code used to initialize the instance variables of an object.

D

DAY_OF_MONTH A date constant of the Calendar class that retrieves an integer value of the system's current day.

DAY_OF_YEAR A date constant of the Calendar class that retrieves the day of the current year as an integer. For example, February 1 is day 32 of the year.

DecimalFormat A class that provides patterns for formatting numbers in program output.

decision structure A fundamental control structure used in computer programming that deals with the different conditions that occur based on the values entered into an application.

E

element A single individual item that contains a value in an array.

emulated application An application that is converted in real time to run on a variety of platforms such as a webpage, which can be displayed on various screen sizes through a browser.

emulator Software that duplicates how an app looks and feels on a particular device.

entries A Spinner property that connects a string array to the Spinner control for display.

equals method A method of the String class that Java uses to compare strings.

event handler A part of a program coded to respond to a specific event.

F

final A type of variable that can only be initialized once; any attempt to reassign the value results in a compile error when the application is executed.

fragment A piece of an application's user interface or behavior that can be placed in an Activity.

Frame animation A type of animation, also called frame-by-frame animation, that plays a sequence of images, as in a slide show, with a specified interval between images.

G

get A field manipulation method that accesses the system date or time.

getBaseContext() A Context class method used in Android programs to obtain a Context instance. Use getBaseContext( ) in a method that is triggered only when the user touches the GridView control.

getInstance A method of the Calendar class that returns a calendar date or time based on the system settings.

GetSelectedItem( ) A method that returns the text of the selected Spinner item.

GetText( ) A method that reads text stored in an EditText control.

getTime( ) method A method of the Calendar class that returns the time value in the Date object.

Google Play A digital repository that serves the Android Market and includes an online store for paid and free Android apps, as well as music, movies, books, and games.

Gravity A tool that changes the linear alignment of a control, so that it is aligned to the left, center, right, top, or bottom of an object or the screen.

GridView A View container that displays a grid of objects with rows and columns.

H

hexadecimal color code A triplet of three color values using hexadecimal numbers, where colors are specified first by a pound sign followed by a value for red (00 to FF), a value for green (00 to FF), and a value for blue (00 to FF).

hint A short description of a field that appears as light text in a Text Field control.

I

If Else statement A statement that executes one set of instructions if a specified condition is true and another set of instructions if the condition is false.

If statement A statement that executes one set of instructions if a specified condition is true and takes no action if the condition is not true.

ImageView control A control that displays an icon or a graphic from a picture file.

import To make the classes from a particular Android package available throughout the application.

import statement A statement that makes more Java functions available to a program.

instantiate To create an object of a specific class.

intent Code in the Android Manifest file that allows an Android application with more than one Activity to navigate among Activities.

isChecked( ) method A method that tests a checked property to determine if a RadioButton object has been selected.

item In a Spinner control, a string of text that appears in a list for user selection.

J

Java An object-oriented programming language and a platform originated by Sun Microsystems.

java folder The folder that includes the Java code source files for the project.

K

key The string part of a key-value pair that uniquely identifies a preference.

L

launcher icon An icon that appears on the home screen to represent the application.

layout A container that can hold widgets and other graphical elements to help you design an interface for an application.

life cycle The series of actions from the beginning, or birth, of an Activity to its end, or destruction.

Linear layout A layout that arranges components in a vertical column or horizontal row.

ListActivity A class that displays a list of items within an app.

local variable A variable declared by a variable declaration statement within a method.

localization The use of the String table to change text based on the user's preferred language.

M

manifests folder The folder that includes the AndroidManifest.xml file, which contains all the information about the application that Android needs to run.

margin Blank space that offsets a control by a certain amount of density independent pixels (dp) on each of its four sides.

Master/Detail Flow template A template Android Studio provides for creating an Android app with an adaptive, responsive layout; it displays a set of list items on the left and the associated details on the right.

MediaPlayer class The Java class that provides the methods to control audio playback on an Android device.

method A set of Java statements that can be included inside a Java class to perform a repeated task.

method body The part of a method containing a collection of statements that defines what the method does.

MONTH A date constant of the Calendar class that retrieves an integer value of the system's current month.

motion tween A type of animation that specifies the start state of an object, and then animates the object a predetermined number of times or an infinite number of times using a transition.

N

native application A program locally installed on a specific platform such as a phone or tablet.

nest To place one statement, such as an If statement, within another statement.

O

object A specific, concrete instance of a class.

object-oriented programming language A type of programming language that allows good software engineering practices such as code reuse.

onDateSet( ) method A method that automatically obtains the date selected by the user.

onDestroy( ) method A method used to end an Activity. Whereas the onCreate( ) method sets up required resources, the onDestroy( ) method releases those same resources to free up memory.

onItemClick An event the OnItemClickListener processes when the user touches the GridView display layout. The onItemClick method is defined by OnItemClickListener and sends a number of arguments in the parentheses included within the line of code.

onListItemClick( ) A method called when an item in a list is selected.

Open Handset Alliance An open-source business alliance of organizations that develop open standards for mobile devices.

open-source operating system An operating system for which organizations and developers can extract, modify, and use the source code free of charge and copyright restrictions.

P

padding property A property that you can use to offset the content of a control by a specific number of pixels.

Parse A class that converts a string into a number data type.

Pascal case Text that begins with an uppercase letter and uses an uppercase letter to start each new word.

permission A restriction limiting access to a part of the code or to data on the device.

persistent data The type of data that stores values permanently by placing the information in a file.

position The placement of an item in a list. When an item in a list is selected, the position of the item is passed from the onListItemClick method and evaluated with a decision structure. The first item is assigned the position of 0, the second item is assigned the position of 1, and so forth.

prompt Text that displays instructions at the top of the Spinner control.

Properties pane The window that contains the properties and settings of the currently active project or object.

property A characteristic of a project or object that describes what it can do.

R

RadioGroup A group of RadioButton controls; only one RadioButton control can be selected at a time.

Relative layout A layout that arranges components in relation to each other. Relative layout is the default layout of the emulator.

res folder A project folder that contains all the resources, such as images, music, and video files, that an application may need.

responsive design An approach to designing apps and websites that provide an optimal viewing experience across as many devices as possible.

S

scope A reference to a variable's visibility within a class.

setAdapter A command that provides a data model for the GridView layout, similar to an adapter, which displays a ListView control.

setBackgroundResource A method that places images in the frame-by-frame display for an animation, with each frame pointing to an image referenced in the XML resource file.

setContentView The Java code necessary to display the content of a specific screen.

setListAdapter A command that projects your data to the onscreen list on your device by connecting the ListActivity's ListView object to array data.

set The field manipulation method that changes the system date or time.

soft keyboard An on-screen keyboard positioned over the lower part of an application's window.

Software Development Kit (SDK) A package containing development tools for creating applications.

sp A unit of measurement that stands for scaled-independent pixels.

Spinner control A widget similar to a drop-down list for selecting a single item from a fixed listing.

SQLite A lightweight, preloaded mobile database engine, which has been available since the Cupcake 1.5 version of Android and occupies a small amount of disk memory.

startAnimation A method that begins the animation process of a View object by calling the AnimationUtils class utilities to access the resources necessary to load the animation.

state A stage in an Activity's life cycle that determines whether the Activity is active, paused, stopped, or dead.

string A series of alphanumeric characters that can include spaces.

string array Two or more text strings.

strings.xml A default file that is part of every Android application and holds commonly used strings in an application.

stub A piece of code that serves as a placeholder to declare itself, containing just enough code to link to the rest of the program.

Switch A type of decision statement that allows you to choose from many statements based on an integer or a char input.

T

TableLayout A user interface design layout that includes TableRow controls to form a grid.

text property A property that references a string resource to display text within a control.

textSize property A property that sets the size of text in a control.

theme A style applied to an Activity or an entire application.

thread A single sequential flow of control within a program.

Timer A Java class that creates a timed event when the schedule method is called.

timer A tool that performs a one-time task such as displaying an opening splash screen, or that performs a continuous process, such as a morning wake-up call set to run at regular intervals.

TimerTask A Java class that invokes a scheduled timer.

toast notification A message that appears as an overlay on a user's screen, often displaying a validation warning.

Tween animation A type of animation that, instead of using a sequence of images, creates an animation by performing a series of transformations on a single image, such as position, size, rotation, and transparency, on the contents of a View object.

tween effect A transition that changes objects from one state to another, such as by moving, rotating, growing, or shrinking.

typeface A property that you can use to set the style of control text to font families, including monospace, sans_serif, and serif.

U

URI An acronym for Uniform Resource Identifier, a URI is a string that identifies the resources of the web. Similar to a URL, a URI includes additional information necessary for gaining access to the resources required for posting a webpage.

URL An acronym for Uniform Resource Locator; a URL is a website address.

V

value The data part of a key-value pair that represents a string, int, long, float, or Boolean value.

variable A name used in a Java program to contain data that changes during the execution of the program.

View A rectangular container that displays a drawing or text object.

Visibility property The Java property that determines whether a control is displayed on the emulator.

W

WebView A View widget that displays webpages.

widget A single element such as a TextView, Button, or CheckBox control, and is also called an object.

X

XML An acronym for Extensible Markup Language, a widely used system for defining data formats. XML assists in the layout of the Android emulator.

Y

YEAR A date constant of the Calendar class that retrieves an integer value of the system's current year.

Index

Note: Page numbers in **bold** indicate where keywords are defined.

B

C

F

G

H

I

P